Handbook of
Police
Administration

PUBLIC ADMINISTRATION AND PUBLIC POLICY

A Comprehensive Publication Program

EDITOR-IN-CHIEF

EVAN M. BERMAN

Huey McElveen Distinguished Professor
Louisiana State University
Public Administration Institute
Baton Rouge, Louisiana

Executive Editor

JACK RABIN

Professor of Public Administration and Public Policy
The Pennsylvania State University—Harrisburg
School of Public Affairs
Middletown, Pennsylvania

1. *Public Administration as a Developing Discipline,*
   Robert T. Golembiewski
2. *Comparative National Policies on Health Care,* Milton I. Roemer, M.D.
3. *Exclusionary Injustice: The Problem of Illegally Obtained Evidence,*
   Steven R. Schlesinger
5. *Organization Development in Public Administration,* edited by
   Robert T. Golembiewski and William B. Eddy
7. *Approaches to Planned Change,* Robert T. Golembiewski
8. *Program Evaluation at HEW,* edited by James G. Abert
9. *The States and the Metropolis,* Patricia S. Florestano
   and Vincent L. Marando
11. *Changing Bureaucracies: Understanding the Organization before
    Selecting the Approach,* William A. Medina
12. *Handbook on Public Budgeting and Financial Management,* edited by
    Jack Rabin and Thomas D. Lynch
15. *Handbook on Public Personnel Administration and Labor Relations,*
    edited by Jack Rabin, Thomas Vocino, W. Bartley Hildreth,
    and Gerald J. Miller
19. *Handbook of Organization Management,* edited by William B. Eddy
22. *Politics and Administration: Woodrow Wilson and American Public
    Administration,* edited by Jack Rabin and James S. Bowman
23. *Making and Managing Policy: Formulation, Analysis, Evaluation,*
    edited by G. Ronald Gilbert
25. *Decision Making in the Public Sector,* edited by Lloyd G. Nigro
26. *Managing Administration,* edited by Jack Rabin, Samuel Humes,
    and Brian S. Morgan
27. *Public Personnel Update,* edited by Michael Cohen
    and Robert T. Golembiewski

Available Electronically

Principles and Practices of Public Administration, edited by Jack Rabin, Robert F. Munzenrider, and Sherrie M. Bartell

PublicADMINISTRATION*netBASE*

Handbook
of Police
Administration

Edited by

Jim Ruiz
Pennsylvania State University–Harrisburg
Middletown, Pennsylvania, U.S.A.

Don Hummer
Pennsylvania State University–Harrisburg
Middletown, Pennsylvania, U.S.A.

Vincennes University
Shake Learning Resources Center
Vincennes, In 47591-9986

CRC Press
Taylor & Francis Group
Boca Raton London New York

CRC Press is an imprint of the
Taylor & Francis Group, an **informa** business

CRC Press
Taylor & Francis Group
6000 Broken Sound Parkway NW, Suite 300
Boca Raton, FL 33487-2742

© 2008 by Taylor & Francis Group, LLC
CRC Press is an imprint of Taylor & Francis Group, an Informa business

No claim to original U.S. Government works
Printed in the United States of America on acid-free paper
10 9 8 7 6 5 4 3 2 1

International Standard Book Number-13: 978-1-57444-559-6 (Hardcover)

Library of Congress Cataloging-in-Publication Data

Ruiz, Jim (James M.)
    Handbook of police administration / Jim Ruiz, Don Hummer.
        p. cm. -- (Public administration and public policy ; 133)
    Includes index.
    ISBN 1-57444-559-6 (alk. paper)
    1. Police administration--United States--Handbooks, manuals, etc.
2. Law enforcement--United States--Handbooks, manuals, etc. 3. Police
administration--Handbooks, manuals, etc. I. Hummer, Donald C. (Donald
Charles) II. Title. III. Series.

HV8141.R85 2008
363.2068--dc22   2007015538

Visit the Taylor & Francis Web site at
http://www.taylorandfrancis.com

and the CRC Press Web site at
http://www.crcpress.com

Contents

SECTION I   Leadership and Police Administration

SECTION II Legal Issues in Police Administration

SECTION III The Role of Empirical Research, Education and Training, and Technology in Police Administration

SECTION IV Special Topics in Police Organization, Management, and Administration

Foreword

This *Handbook of Police Administration*, co-edited by Jim Ruiz and Don Hummer, provides a smorgasbord of topics that are at the coalface of policing: the difficulties police encounter dealing with drug problems, traffic issues, race and ethnicity challenges, and street gang problems. Cross-cutting themes such as leadership in policing, use of force, and understanding how the law shapes (or fails to shape) police practice are relevant to students of police studies, practitioners, and scholars alike. There is something in here for everyone, which is a credit to the editors in accessing their network of colleagues in the field of policing and bringing them together in this one volume. Scholars will find original research articles. Practitioners will relate to the stories that abound in the text of many chapters. Police recruits will find the down-to-earth presentation of issues interesting and engaging. University and college students of policing will find the handbook to be an excellent reference book covering a wide scope of territory.

The handbook also dedicates an entire section to police administration issues in Australia. The inclusion of material from Australia adds an interesting dimension to the book and stemmed from some informal conversations with Professor John Kleinig (also a contributor to this work). John spends half the year at John Jay College in New York and the other half at Charles Sturt University and The Australian National University in Canberra, so he was instrumental in helping Jim and Don gather an excellent collection of chapter topics from the Australian authors. In doing so, the book straddles issues that are relevant across two western democratic countries that have both similarities and important differences. Students of police administration will be struck by the similarities in the issues that confront police agencies all over the world. For example Layton and Jennett, in their chapter about solving problems down under, raise a number of dilemmas and difficulties posed by police agencies in all corners of the world trying to implement problem-oriented policing.

Importantly, the handbook succeeds in raising a range of perspectives, different viewpoints, and controversies. The content of chapters is at the cutting edge of debate in the field of policing. The handbook will thus stimulate discussion and, as I am sure Jim and Don hope, invigorate students to ask questions, delve into the literature, conduct their own research, and find out more about the ever-changing world of policing.

Lorraine Mazerolle
Griffith University, Australia

Preface

July 22, 2006 — Defend the police department against criticism
regarding a homicide crisis unfolding in the city (Philadelphia ends
2006 with 406 homicides and nearly 2000 shooting victims).

January 4, 2007 — Attend 'town-meeting' in Manayunk section of
the city to hear citizen complaints pertaining to unruly bar and
nightclub patrons who are ruining 'the quality of life in our
neighborhoods' by shouting late at night and leaving litter behind.

Police leaders are asked to do many things and solve a multitude of problems. Consider the plight of Philadelphia Police Commissioner Sylvester Johnson and the portion of his schedule reproduced above. Putting aside for a moment the myriad of "normal" challenges and responsibilities associated with managing a large urban police department, Commissioner Johnson defended himself for months against those calling for his resignation as Philadelphia's homicide rate ballooned to a level not seen in more than a decade. At the same time, he was the figurehead of the department at a concerned neighbors' meeting where the major issues revolved around noise and trash. That policing is the most visible segment of the criminal justice system, with more citizen contact than any other CJ agency, is common knowledge. However, with the police supervisor being in the forefront as a figurehead for praise and, more often, criticism, it is more crucial than ever presently to recruit and retain capable leaders to guide law enforcement agencies at this pivotal time in history. Threats both global and local have resulted in challenges never before faced by police administrators, requiring flexibility, innovative thinking, and an ability to foster and maintain relationships with stakeholders in the community. Further, police leaders are now required to operate in a public realm where transparency is demanded and is created (intentionally or unintentionally) with technology. Citizens expect that police chiefs and commissioners will be responsive to their needs, accessible when problems arise, forthcoming with information that is pertinent, make wise decisions, and take decisive action.

From the drafting of a formal mission statement to motivating line staff to representing the agency's core values through leadership by example, the "health" of a department's culture is facilitated by the top administrator. Maintaining a positive organizational culture is most certainly a demanding task; however, reforming a "damaged" culture requires leadership skills that are, at present, in short supply. It is with these ideas in mind that proactive leadership will enable policing agencies to maintain a positive organizational culture that promotes cooperation with an increasingly diverse citizenry. The effective police administrator must continually foster relationships and work with the constituency regardless of the difficulties being faced, for the leader who loses the confidence of the public can expect a short tenure.

In all likelihood the reader of this text falls into one of three general categories: the policing scholar using information from the book as source reference material or as a text assigned to a college-level course; the law enforcement executive reading the book as part of his or her own professional development; or a student enrolled in a policing course at the college-level. Whatever category the reader falls under, the purpose of this book is to examine some of the key contemporary issues that must be considered by law enforcement professionals. Police leaders are required to possess the skills and traits of a politician, an accountant, an attorney, a field lieutenant, and a futurist. The volume contains 26 chapters divided into five thematic sections, examining a variety of contemporary issues surrounding police administration and management. It considers the legal aspects of overseeing a public sector organization as well as how research, technology, and training can assist modern police leaders in performing their duties more effectively and efficiently. Issues that have been problematic for some, such as officers accepting gratuities, undercover work, and the promotional criteria time are given fresh examination. The text concludes with a section on comparative administrative issues in Australia. A number of the chapters in this concluding section correspond with earlier chapters examining similar issues in the United States (i.e., Chapters 3 and 22, Chapters 11 and 26). The reader can get a sense of similarities and differences in how issues are addressed in both nations.

Without question the job of the police executive is more challenging than ever before and will likely become more so in coming years. While specific issues will emerge and subsequently diminish with time, what remains static is the need for police leaders who anticipate challenges and implement strategies for addressing the problem at hand with a rational approach. It is hoped that the readings selected for this book will help foster the kind of creative thinking necessary to lead in a dynamic environment.

Jim Ruiz
Don Hummer

Contributors

Michael L. Arter, Ph.D.
Pennsylvania State University
Altoona, Pennsylvania

Thomas Barker, Ph.D
Eastern Kentucky University
Richmond, Kentucky

William P. Bloss, Ph.D.
Department of Political Science and
   Criminal Justice
The Citadel
Charleston, South Carolina

Christine Bono
Westfield State College
Westfield, Massachusetts

Charles Burckhardt
Pennsylvania State University
York Haven, Pennsylvania

James M. Byrne
Department of Criminal Justice
College of Arts and Sciences
University of Massachusetts–Lowell
Lowell, Massachusetts

John Casey, Ph.D.
Australian Graduate School of Policing
Charles Sturt University
Sydney, New South Wales
Australia

Sutham Cheurprakobkit, Ph.D.
Department of Sociology, Geography,
   Anthropology & Criminal Justice
Kennesaw State University
Kennesaw, Georgia

Stephen Coleman
University of New South Wales and
   Centre for Applied Philosophy and
   Public Ethics
Canberra, Australia

Anna Corbo Crehan, Ph.D.
School of Policing Studies and Centre
   for Applied Philosophy and Public
   Ethics
Charles Sturt University
Goulburn, New South Wales
Australia

Doug Dailey
Department of Commerce
Texas A&M University
College Station, Texas

Venessa Garcia, Ph.D.
Kean University
Department of Criminal Justice
Union, New Jersey

Randy Garner, Ph.D.
College of Criminal Justice
Sam Houston State University
Huntsville, Texas

Albert J. Gorman
Department of Criminal Justice
Monmouth University
West Long Branch, New Jersey

Craig Hemmens, J.D., Ph.D.
Department of Criminal Justice
Boise State University
Boise, Idaho

Don Hummer
Pennsylvania State University
Middletown, Pennsylvania

Christine Jennett, Ph.D.
School of Social Sciences and Liberal
  Studies
Charles Sturt University
Bathurst, New South Wales
Australia

John Kleinig
Department of Law and Police
  Science
John Jay College of Criminal Justice
New York, New York
CAPPE
Charles Sturt University
Canberra, Australia

Catherine Layton, Ph.D.
School of Policing Studies
Charles Sturt University
Goulburn, New South Wales
Australia

Jeffery C. Lee
Department of Criminal Justice
Troy University
Troy, Alabama

Margaret Mitchell, Ph.D.
Sellenger Centre for Research in Law,
  Justice and Policing
Edith Cowan University
Perth, Australia

Erin Morrow
Pennsylvania State University
Ivyland, Pennsylvania

Lisa S. Nored
Department of Administration of
  Justice
The University of Southern Mississippi
Hattiesburg, Mississippi

Pamela Preston
Pennsylvania State University
Schuylkill Haven, Pennsylvania

Jim Ruiz
Pennsylvania State University
Middletown, Pennsylvania

Barbara Sims, Ph.D.
Pennsylvania State University
Middletown, Pennsylvania

R. Alan Thompson
Department of Administration of
  Justice
The University of Southern Mississippi
Hattiesburg, Mississippi

Thomas S. Whetstone
Cassandra Consulting Group, LLC
Louisville, Kentucky

Deborah G. Wilson
Department of Justice Administration
University of Louisville
Louisville, Kentucky

Barry O. Williams, Ph.D.
Pennsylvania State University
Middletown, Pennsylvania

Vicki S. Williams, Ph.D.
Pennsylvania State University
University Park, Pennsylvania

Section I

Leadership and Police Administration

1 Psychology for Police Leadership

Randy Garner

CONTENTS

INTRODUCTION

Many of the articles and texts that deal with the subject of psychology in policing often provide a discussion of general psychological terms and concerns that are more oriented toward mental health issues than a better understanding of matters that impact leadership and collective interactions. Although such a "clinical" orientation can be valuable, the focus here is more on the importance of understanding the social implications of human interactions. In other words, what psychological factors are involved in influencing our own behavior or the behavior of others? Additionally, what are some of the biases and heuristics that we all have a tendency to use when trying to interpret the actions of others or our own?

As a former police chief, having more than 25 years of law enforcement experience, I found the topic of social psychology to be of great interest during my doctoral education. In fact, on many an occasion I said to myself, "I wish I had known that back when ... ." The subject of social psychology is so interconnected to many of the leadership issues I faced as a police administrator; it has become a minor mission of mine to provide at least a sampling of the areas that have been examined by social psychologists and relate those to real-world events.

Roughly defined, social psychology is the way people think about, relate to, and interact with one another. If we consider this definition, it becomes clear that this is what we do in most of our daily interactions. We are constantly trying to figure out why someone may have acted as he or she did, or even wonder why *we* may have behaved in a particular way. These issues become all the more important considering the social interactions we have with others in the leadership environment.

The area of social psychology covers a great many topics; however, for the present purpose we will be examining some of the biases and heuristics that we all tend to employ when we try to make sense of the world and the people who operate within it. This has important implications for our relations with those we lead, those we follow, and the myriad of circumstances in which we find ourselves.

DO YOU HAVE AN ATTITUDE?

All of us have attitudes. An attitude—a term originally borrowed from the nautical world—is merely a psychological predisposition to evaluate someone or something in either a favorable or unfavorable light. The fact that we all possess attitudes about many different subjects is not particularly surprising. The way in which we come to form an attitude, however, can be very interesting, particularly when the attitude is formed through some potentially biased means. How do you form an evaluative reaction toward something or someone? Among other means, you may do so by personal experience, by information received through a variety of ways, or by accepting the statements or beliefs of others. In each case, the attitude-formation process can be fraught with potential errors. For example, what if your personal experience with an individual was on a particularly bad day—for either of you? Because of this potentially isolated situation, you may not evaluate that person very positively even though he or she might otherwise be a charming individual. What if the media source, for example, that you use to form your attitude has presented information in a biased or one-sided fashion? Not too far fetched given the media hype we see every day, not to mention the intentional attempts at persuasion that marketers' work so hard to have us believe. Or, what if the person in whose opinion you are confident, is personally in error or biased in his or her views? This merely results in transferring another's faulty opinion to yourself.

The point here is that there is a great deal of potential for bias and error when we are forming our opinions of others. Further, when it comes to recalling our attitudes, we seem to have a very short memory. In fact, research has shown that if we are unclear or unsure about our past attitude toward something, we usually indicate that the way we *currently* feel is the way we have always felt about the issue, topic, or person. I once conducted a study of police cadets going through the academy in which we measured their attitudes about a number of issues, including those related to their ability to impact society, influence the greater good, have a strong positive impact on crime, and various other topics related to the "truth, justice, and the American way" philosophy. We were able to sample most of these same individuals over a year later—long after graduating from the academy, completing their field training program, and having considerable real-world "street" experience. The results were as expected: The police officers reported significantly less robust confidence in their ability to deal with many of the societal issues than they once had. What was more interesting, however, was that most of the officers believed that their current feelings and reported attitudes reflected the way they had always felt. In fact, some believed this so strongly that we had to actually show them their original responses to demonstrate that change had indeed occurred.

In other studies (e.g., Holmberg and Holmes 1994; McFarland and Ross 1985), attitudes reported by married couples or even steady dating partners revealed similar results. As compared to attitudinal measures taken months earlier, those who were still together recalled having said that their significant other was even more caring and positive than they had earlier indicated; those who were now apart recalled having identified signs that their partner was exhibiting signals of selfishness, distance, etc.—qualities not revealed in the previous surveys. Again, we often tend to believe that the current attitude we now hold is much the same we have always had. A metaphorical example is that of the caterpillar that became a butterfly, only to maintain that in its youth it had always been a butterfly, just a bit smaller; thus, failing to recollect that it was ever a caterpillar. As leaders, we must recognize these phenomena, remain vigilant regarding our own potentially biased recollections, and be attentive to the misrememberings of others. The person who today finds offense with your actions or positions may not recall that he or she may have shared a similar view a year ago. When I was chief, I frequently had key supervisors, leaders, and even council members complete survey forms or required them to actually sign off on particular matters, such as changes in policy, requiring that they note any objections. This proved to be a very valuable exercise when changes later occurred with personnel or with the political environment. It was easy for me to remind certain individuals who had attempted to "sing another tune" that they themselves were previously favorably disposed to the issue.

In forming our attitudes, it is also important to recognize a number of potentially strong influences. For example, things that come first can have an impact on things that come later. If one is given—in advance—negative information about an individual, for example, one may form an attitude about this person even before there is an opportunity to meet him or her. Of course, the strength of this attitude is based on a number of factors, including the credibility of the speaker and the importance of the interaction. Additionally, the psychological principle of "belief perseverance" may come into play. Once we establish a belief or attitude, we tend to psychologically work to confirm our original assumptions rather than seek disconfirming information. Thus, if we are told that Officer Roberts is intelligent, industrious, impulsive, and critical, we might form a somewhat favorable impression. We might reason that those individuals who are intelligent are often industrious and a bit impulsive, too. They may also be more self-critical because of their intellectual proclivities. Alternatively, if we are told that Sergeant Nelson is a very critical, impulsive, and industrious individual who possesses intelligence, we may form a much different impression based on the order in which the information is received. Here, we start off learning that he is a critical and impulsive individual. That alone may cast a different hue on all the characteristics that follow. Of course, the descriptions are merely placed in reverse order; however, several studies have demonstrated that this seemingly minor manipulation can have a big impact on likeability ratings of the described individuals.

Another attitude-forming concern may relate to how you get your information when developing your attitudes. For example, many people defer to their friends or coworkers who may appear to be "in the know." Before you latch onto their belief structure, you might want to ask yourself, "Why is this person my friend?" Could it be that they are similar to you in several ways? Could it be that they think like you? If that is possible, you might consider that you are not really moving toward an independent assessment of your attitude. Numerous studies have demonstrated that oftentimes attitudes can be acquired from persons of influence whose views are readily absorbed by those around them (see Katz 1957). In particular, the media may play a much larger role than you might realize in determining how you think about a particular issue or topic. After all, how do you learn a great deal about what is going on in the world? Unless you have your own private sources, chances are you are getting your information from the media. Further, it is the decisions made by media managers about what to disseminate, how to present it, and what spin to give that could impact your understanding and your attitude.

Another source I often find interesting is the proliferation of information polls; whether it is regarding a candidate, a bond issue, or the credibility of a celebrity, these media-based polls are often presented as scientific fact. Without going into a discussion on sample size, population parameters, and biased selection issues it is simply important to recognize that the information you might receive from these so-called opinion polls may be little more than a report on a group of people who were conveniently available—not exactly the hallmark of methodological rigor. As an example, I recently heard a news radio talk show report that their news poll had indicated that there was a certain percentage of people in favor of the topic de jour (actually it related to gun control). The fact that it was identified as a "news" poll suggested a level of sophistication and credibility that was not warranted. If one were to actually examine the sample that made up this "news poll," one would learn that it comprised fewer than 40 people—in a metropolitan area of many millions. This is not even close to what a *bad* student of statistics would offer as a representative sample. Now, let us see the facts. First, this morning news radio station was primarily a commuter station, meaning that most listeners were in transit to their places of work or business. Second, there is a general tendency to *not* actually call in to such programs (according to the station's own information, the number of people who call in to such polls is miniscule, compared to their actual listenership). Third, considering that those engaged in the perils of driving do not routinely feel compelled to tempt fate by fumbling with a cell phone so they might be "heard" on another of a series of endless topics, this reduces our population pool even further. Of course, we have not even considered that many more people listen to more popular music radio stations during their drive time than to AM talk radio. As a result, we are left with very few individuals who have nothing better to do than call in to this station—most likely from their homes (who listens to talk radio at home?)—and *these* are the individuals who are potentially helping you form your opinion on a topic of possible importance. After all, it is a *news* poll, so it must be correct. Not surprisingly, you have probably not really given much thought to all of this, as we have a great psychological tendency to economize our thinking in such circumstances. "Distracted" by driving (in our example), we may only peripherally attend to the information and may not discount its accuracy, because we are not engaged in any form of careful analysis or argument (e.g., Petty and Cacioppo 1986; Petty and Wegener 1999).

Of course, we must all recognize that there are a great many ways in which our attitudes are formed, with many strong and weak influences. The important point is to *recognize* the potential pitfalls in the process. We must often rely on other people, other sources, and other means of information beyond our own experiences to develop our attitudes. However, understanding this process and the way such information may interact with our strongly held values and beliefs can help mitigate rampant errors. The antidote to misplaced attitudinal allegiance is understanding, recognition, and inquiry. Before you accept any information you are exposed to, ask yourself a series of critical questions. For example, in a reported opinion poll, you might want to ask the following: Who were asked the questions? How were these people selected? How were the questions worded? Who asked the questions and in what manner? The list could go on, but the general idea is to be an informed consumer of information, as that may influence your attitudes and beliefs.

DO YOUR ATTITUDES MATCH YOUR BEHAVIOR?

Frequently, attitudes do not match one's behavior. Although most people believe that another's expressed public opinion reflects his or her true attitude, research evidence often finds quite the contrary. Remember that an attitude is really a construct, it does not physically exist in nature. In fact, when you are asked about your attitude toward something, you may choose to offer a more socially desirable response than your true feelings. This is the difficulty encountered in surveys, questionnaires, interviews, and other forms of inquiry regarding attitudes. The attitude–behavior consistency correlation can be very weak and is dependent on a number of things. The point here, however, is to sound a caution: when people tell you what they think about something or someone, they may or may not be providing you their true feeling. There are a great number of social pressures that come to bear in such situations. Police administrators frequently complain about not getting correct information or a true read on a particular situation. In fact, I have known several police chiefs who felt they were almost always the last to know when something potentially bad was brewing. When you consider the psychology of social interaction, this is not all that surprising. Typically, people want to please their bosses and do not want to be the bearers of bad news. Imagine a police administrator calling each officer under his command into his or her office to get a feel about how things are going on his or her watch. Those persons being asked will not want to offer criticism or other information that could be associated with not being a team player or that could result in a less-than-favorable response by the administrator. The old saying "you go along to get along" sums up this issue rather well. As a result, something happens, and the officers may develop a poor attitude about the administrator, the agency, the supervision, or something else—but chances are that they will often refrain from expressing that opinion, offering a more generic "Things are going ok."

Again, the caution is to realize that what we say and what we may truly believe are not always synchronous. Keep in mind that public opinion polls often report that we do not like violence in the media; yet the most violent movies, television programs, and video games are the most popular. We report that we are changing our lifestyles, eating more healthy food, and exercising more; yet, as a nation, we are fatter than ever before in history. In fact, the obesity problem in America has been labeled by some as an epidemic. We say that we want political reform and change; yet fewer people even know who the candidates are, and fewer still manage to vote. We hold many attitudes—however, they may be formed with faulty information and reported inaccurately to make ourselves look or feel better. Just remember that the next time you ask about a topic or how things are going at work, the answer you hear may or may not be a true reflection of the opinions and attitudes held by others.

ATTRIBUTIONS: WHY I DO WHAT I DO AND WHY YOU DO WHAT YOU DO

Particularly important to leaders is the process of attributing the cause of another's actions or behavior to some identified explanation. This is what psychologists call the Attribution Theory. The problem, of course, is that this procedure is ripe for misinterpretation, misunderstanding, bias, and error. The way we tend to psychologically process information lends itself to making quick judgments and snap conclusions. We often tend to ignore useful information if it does not fit with our preconceived notions. We tend to suffer from several generalized biases when we try to attribute causes for why something happened or why someone behaved in a certain way. In general, (1) we fail to appreciate that our understanding of the world around us is an active process, subject to construal and interpretation; (2) we frequently do not appreciate how two people looking at the "same" situation or circumstance can form different interpretations; (3) we fail to appreciate that the past experiences and history of any individual may be unique and can guide his or her interpretation of events; (4) we have a strong psychological tendency to see other people's behavior as a product of who they are or their character, whereas we examine our own behavior as a result of the situation or environment; and finally (5) a central message of leadership psychology is our failure to appreciate the potent situational forces that influence our own and others behavior (Myers 2005).

A SAMPLING OF ERRORS OR BIASES IN ATTRIBUTIONS

There are several biases, errors, or heuristics that have been identified by social psychologists that impact the way we process information and make judgments. As police administrators, we must realize that in order to understand others, we must first know ourselves. An appreciation of certain psychological biases we all tend to have when making sense of the world can help us become better leaders. If we realize that such biases exist, we will better recognize them when we see them occurring in our own behavior or in the behavior of others. I have outlined some of the more common attributional errors that can influence our interpretations. Each one provides some insight into how we may make certain assumptions and how we are influenced by biases that we may not even know we have.

THE FUNDAMENTAL ATTRIBUTION ERROR

Although the fundamental attribution error is technically a bias, it is considered fundamental because we all tend to use it, whether intended or not (Ross 1977). Essentially, it is a bias whereby we somewhat unconsciously attribute the cause of another's behavior to their disposition, internal traits, or personality. We make this error because we often psychologically and interpretatively overestimate the extent to which a person's behavior, for example, represents his or her character, attitudes, or individual traits, whereas we significantly underestimate the influence of the situation or the environment in which the person finds himself or herself. The power of the situation is one of the most important lessons to be learned when studying leadership psychology. People do things as a result of the situation in which they find themselves—things that they would never do otherwise—if not for the situational influence. In the case of the fundamental attribution error, a minimization of these situational forces occurs because of something called the Actor–Observer Bias.

THE ACTOR–OBSERVER BIAS

The actor–observer bias occurs when we tend to explain our own behavior in terms of the situation, but interpret others' behavior in terms of their personality or disposition. In other word, we presume that others *are* the way that they act. If we see someone who is visibly angry, we tend to assume that he or she is a hothead. However, if *we* are angry, it is because of the situation—of course, we would never be a hothead. As one comedian once put it, when driving down the highway, everyone who goes slower than you is a moron, and everyone who goes faster than you is an idiot! We tend to view the world from our self-centered perspective. As a police officer, if I speed, I do so because I have a good reason (the situation); if you speed, it is because you are a reckless, child-endangering jerk. When teaching these topics at the police academy, it is important that cadets recognize that just because someone engages in a minor infraction, it does not mean this person is from the Land of Jerkdom. Unfortunately, interviews with traffic officers consistently find that their first impulse or impression on seeing a person speeding past their radar is something akin to "What a jerk." The perspective we hold is the key. If I trip on the sidewalk, most observers would immediately—and rather unconsciously—say to themselves, "Klutz!" In contrast, *I* would be considering the *situation* or the imperfection in the sidewalk that needs immediate attention.

As leaders, we must reflect on the danger of not properly considering the implications of the environment or the situation. Failing to do so ignores important information that may cause us to infer incorrect conclusions regarding the actions of others. I recall the story of a businessman who was on a late-night commuter train on his way home. Weary from a long day's work and crisis management, he started to become particularly annoyed by several young and overly rambunctious kids who were roaming the train car, obviously with no oversight or direction from their father, who was seated on the opposite side. The businessman became increasingly irritated and started to attribute all sorts of negative traits to the father. After all, who would have their kids out this late on a school night? Why would he allow them to roam the train car, bothering other passengers? What a terrible father and parent he must be. After some time, our businessman finally had it. He shouted at the father and expressed his displeasure over the children's behavior and his deficient skills as a parent. Slowly, the father looked up as if coming out of an unconscious stupor and apologized. He then related that they were only now coming back from the hospital where his wife and the mother of his children had just died. He admitted that he was not his normal self and immediately asked his children to calm down. As you read this, think about how the businessman must have felt. He had completely ignored the possibility of any situational influence and, instead, had focused only on the alleged characteristics of the father. This is a lesson from which we should all learn regarding the perils of the actor–observer bias.

Self-Serving Bias

The self-serving bias is a tendency that we have to protect our self-esteem and look good to others. We try to project our actions or ourselves in a positive light, regardless of the circumstances. It is not surprising that we want to look good to others. The psychological literature has hundreds of articles that deal with this topic, as well as the related issues of impression management, self-presentation theory, self-monitoring theory, and the like (see Myers 2005). People typically ascribe a high exam score, for example, to their superior intellect rather than to their luck. Keeping a positive and psychologically protected self-esteem can be a good thing. The problem comes, however, when people significantly depart from reasonableness. In other words, their self-serving tendency becomes an impediment by preventing people from dealing with the reality of the situation. It is OK to see something through rose-colored glasses, but make sure the tint is not so dark that it obscures the truth.

Self-Handicapping Strategy

Self-handicapping strategy is a process whereby an individual will protect his or her self-esteem by handily creating a real or imaginary excuse for failure. In other words, if people believe that there is a likelihood of failure in some task or event in which they are about to engage, they may create a reason in advance as to why such a failure might occur. Have you ever started making excuses as to why something might not go so well before you even began the task? In teaching at the university for many years, I have noticed two things: (1) an extraordinary correlation between the reported death of a grandparent and an exam day, and (2), more to the point for this discussion, students entering the classroom on exam days are often telling others all the reasons why they did not have time to prepare or study. Whether it was noisy neighbors, work, dealing with relationships, or other obligations, some students will begin the process of creating an excuse in advance for possible failure. What is all the more interesting is that many of these same students actually did study and, in fact, studied a great deal. However, should the questions in the exam not match their knowledge base, they have the ready excuse to use, rather than attribute the failure to their lack of acumen. Not a bad strategy to protect one's self-esteem. Of course, if by some stroke of luck the questions did match, you can bet the self-serving bias would be in full swing, and they would proudly announce their triumphant achievements *despite* all of the previously identified obstacles (providing even a greater ego boost). As a police chief, I once administered a promotional exam for the rank of sergeant. One particular individual, who was considered by many to be intellectually challenged, decided to create an actual excuse for his possible poor showing when taking the exam. The night before the exam, he decided to go out for a late night party and made sure that everyone knew of this event before he took the exam. Sure enough, the results were as expected and his explanation was as anticipated. In his eyes, he protected his self-esteem by attributing his poor showing to the night of partying rather than to his lack of knowledge.

BIASES IN ACCURACY, CAUSE, AND CONTROL

In addition to attributional errors, we also have problems in judgments regarding our social beliefs about many issues. Although there is something we call "ground truth," or objective reality, we have a propensity to view the world through the spectacles of our expectations, our attitudes, our beliefs, and our values. In fact, studies have repeatedly demonstrated that we readily deny real influences that act upon us in favor of explanations that may better match, not reality, but, our social beliefs. A few examples can be very instructive.

BELIEF PERSEVERANCE

Belief perseverance is often a subconscious process, whereby we tend to cling to our initial conceptions of an idea, issue, circumstance, or problem, even in the face of information that tends to discredit it. This is one reason that stereotypes are so enduring. Even if we know that they are not accurate, we tend to more likely notice examples that are consistent with our previously held attitudes, rather than those that are not. Psychologists relate this to our tendency to process information by way of our confirmation bias. Whether it is a nickname, a reputation, or a particular belief, once formed it is very difficult to overcome.

One study (Garner and Cioffi 1992) used an example of the trait of risk taking as it relates to being an effective police officer (similar to a study using risk taking and firefighters; see Anderson, Lepper, and Ross 1980). One group was told in great detail that because of the type of work required by the police, those who score high on a measure of risk-taking made better officers. This group was given several plausible explanations for this conclusion and was then asked to write a paragraph or two as to why they thought this might be true. In another room, a different group was told that those who score high in risk-taking made very poor police officers, and they were also given several plausible explanations and asked to write a paragraph or two as to why this might be true. In reality, there is no strong correlation between scoring high on a measure of risk-taking and later performance as a police officer. However, the seed had been planted, and each group, though receiving opposing information, created strong arguments as to why their position was the correct one. Having created this false belief, the groups where then told the truth that in reality, no such strong correlation had been found. What do you think happened? As predicted, each group continued to maintain that their position was probably still correct; even in the face of the disconfirming information, the belief persisted.

In my policing days, I once had an officer who did not do particularly well at report writing. His idea of an auto theft report was, "Arrived on scene, car gone." Needless to say, he developed quite a reputation for his poor communication and detail skills. As a result, we provided him with intensive training that significantly improved his overall communication abilities and his report writing, in particular. However, his reputation once firmly established was difficult to change. Assume that, in a given performance-review period, this officer completed 100 reports and had only 10 returned for correction or modification. This is a rate that is probably better than or rivaled most other officers. However, his reputation was firmly in the mind of his reviewing supervisor. Instead of highlighting the 90 reports that were correct, the supervisor reconfirmed his preexisting belief by focusing on the 10 that were subpar. After all, he *is* a bad report writer.

Overconfidence Phenomena

Overconfidence phenomena is another tendency we use, expressing more confidence than accuracy. In fact, studies have demonstrated that even in the area of eyewitness testimony, the level of confidence that is expressed by a witness is unrelated to its accuracy. In other words, a witness could express strong confidence in his or her identification but still be completely incorrect. In more general circumstances, we tend to be overconfident that others behave just as we do, that they would do the same sorts of things that we would agree to do, and would even watch the same TV stations that we watch. As leaders, we overestimate our own ability to hire quality personnel (Garner and Cioffi 1992). Although we may have made many good hiring decisions, we do not see the ones who were not selected, those who would have gone on to even greater success. There are plenty of anecdotal stories from the world of sports, business, and other areas that support this phenomenon.

False Consensus Effect

I am sure that we may all be able to picture a person in our minds eye who nicely fits this description: Have you ever known or worked with someone who believed that whatever his or her opinion was on a topic, it was the one shared by most others? This attitude can be particularly problematic with certain performance-challenged employees. They will often report to you their personal beliefs and relate that *everyone* feels the same way. Again, this is another strong reason to ensure that you do not accept such statements at face value.

Base-Rate Fallacy

Base-rate fallacy bias occurs when we tend to ignore the true rate of occurrence of some event and are instead influenced by some immediate or vivid example. In other words, we ignore the reality of how frequently something happens in favor of some less accurate but potentially more dramatic event. This was a particular pet peeve of mine as a police chief. On occasion, we would have an individual speak at a city council meeting about some particular topic. Of course, this would be dramatically expressed and, interweaving both the overconfidence and the false consensus effects, the speaker would provide an example of some event that would bear little resemblance to reality. Astonishingly, however, often the council members would be offering solutions, identifying strategies, assessing blame, and taking other such action without first even checking whether what they had just heard was merely a product or opinion of a single individual's concerns. In case after case, the city—and the police department—were inappropriately placed in the spotlight because the council chose to ignore the true base rate of the event and were instead influenced by the immediate presence of the speaker and his or her vivid description.

AVAILABILITY HEURISTIC

A heuristic is essentially a rule of thumb. Although such cognitive saving devices can be effective, they are also subject to fallibility. In this case, individuals tend to judge the occurrence or likelihood of some event in terms of its availability in memory. In other words, if instances come readily to mind, the event or circumstance may be presumed to be commonplace. If I were to ask you to complete a survey on community safety, you may immediately recall all of the newspaper articles dealing with crime. Now it may be that these articles were based on crime reports in another community, or that the true rate of crime in your community had significantly decreased. Nevertheless, because these articles come readily to mind, you would offer a low score on the community safety survey, even though more objective measures may demonstrate just the opposite.

ILLUSORY CORRELATION

In the case of illusory correlation, you have an illusion (like performances of a magician) that some things are correlated. In other words, it is an illusion that two or more things are actually related, despite strong evidence to the contrary. Here, individuals see relationships between events even when no such relationship exists, or even if it does exist, it is much weaker than believed. For example, I have heard of the relationship between a full moon and things going crazy for the police services for as long as I can remember. So, a full moon is correlated with an increase in police activity, right? Well, actual statistics do not bear this out. When one checks statistical records for things such as weekends—which are already busy—and other such artifacts, one sees no such strong correlation between a full moon and increased criminal activity.

Unfortunately, I can hear it now as you read this: you "know" that the moon correlation is true. Consider the possibility that you are engaging in belief perseverance and confirmation bias. After all, you have been told this was true, so you have developed a strong belief that may have little chance of being swayed by my assertions in this chapter. Further, consider our tendency to confirm rather than disconfirm information. Therefore, chances are that, when things might be going crazy on the night shift, we look up to see a full moon and say, "Ah, I told you so!" On the other hand, consider a time when things were going crazy and you looked up and found no full moon. As we are not predisposed to disconfirm our beliefs, we just attribute the increased activity to some other source and move on, without dismissing our confidence in the moon–crazy hypothesis. In fact, this belief is so engrained that when you notice things are relatively active and you lookup to the night sky for an explanation, your biases may tend to show you a full moon, even though it may not be "technically" true. After all, how full does full have to be? However, trust your local statistician; the phenomena is not strongly correlated, no matter how convincingly the belief perseveres.

GROUP INFLUENCES THAT BIAS

There are a number of influences that involve group dynamics, including issues of conformity, compliance, obedience, group polarization, and *groupthink* to name a few. For the present purposes, let us focus on the topic of groupthink, a term coined by Irving Janis (1971, 1989) to describe a mode of thinking engaged in by a confirmation-seeking group. When group influences become so predominant that realistic appraisals are overridden and alternate courses of actions not considered— all in the name of the group—disastrous consequences can ensue. One only has to look at the well-documented events that led to the Bay of Pig fiasco or the sequence of events that preceded the terrible space shuttle Challenger disaster, to see the dangers of a consensus-seeking, alternative-excluding, unrealistic-appraising group. Leaders are not immune to these influences and must take measures to avoid them. One such solution is the appointment of a Devil's advocate. The role of this committee member is to challenge and refute the ideas or positions of the group. This allows others to consider alternative points of view and break the group-conformity phenomenon.

CONCLUSIONS

I have only scratched the surface of the important topics of social and leadership psychology, and it is hoped that this information will help us, as leaders, to be more aware and become more informed consumers of information—understanding better the circumstances that influence us. The amount of information that we must address on a daily basis can be staggering. As a result, our mind places a premium on making efficient judgments regarding the actions of others and our own. Unfortunately, with this efficiency, comes the danger and vulnerability of error, bias, and misjudgments. As leaders, we must not only educate ourselves about such issues, but also help others to understand the cognitive biases that can cause us to inaccurately interpret events and the actions of others. We must reflect on our own biases and prejudices and consider how they might influence our interpretations. We must try to see others through our newly informed perspective and attempt to remove our preconceived notions and biased thinking. By addressing these challenges, we can see the complicated dynamics of the social world more clearly, allowing us to develop as stronger leaders. By better knowing ourselves, we will be more able to understand the complexities involved when working with others.

REFERENCES

Anderson, C., Lepper, M., & Ross, L. (1980). Perseverance of social theories: The role of explanation in the persistence of discredited information. *Journal of Personality and Social Psychology*, 39, 1037–1049.

Garner, R. & Cioffi, D. (1992). *Classic studies in social psychology revisited*. Houston, TX: University of Houston Press.

Holmberg, D. & Holmes, J. (1994). Reconstruction of relationship memories: A mental models approach. In N. Schwarz & S. Sudman (Eds.), *Autobiographical memory and the validity of retrospective reports*. New York: Springer-Verlag.

Janis, I. (1971, November). Groupthink. *Psychology Today*, pp. 43–46.

Janis, I. (1989). *Crucial decisions: Leadership in policymaking and crisis management*. New York: Free Press.

Katz, E. (1957). The two-step flow of communication: An up-to-date report on a hypothesis. *Public Opinion Quarterly,* 21, 61–78.

McFarland, C. & Ross, M. (1985). *The relation between current impressions and memories of self and dating partners*. University of Waterloo.

Myers, D. (2005). *Social psychology* (8th ed.). New York: McGraw Hill.

Petty, R. & Cacioppo, J. (1986). *Communication and persuasion: Central and peripheral routes to attitude change*. New York: Springer-Verlag.

Petty, R. & Wegener, D. (1999). The elaboration likelihood model: Current status and controversies. In S. Chaiken & Y. Trope (Eds.), *Dual-process theories in social psychology*. New York: Guilford.

Ross, L. (1977). The intuitive psychologist and his shortcomings: Distortions in the attribution process. In L. Berkowitz (Ed.), *Advances in experimental social psychology* (Vol. 10). New York: Academic Press.

2 The Importance and Incorporation of Community Policing Characteristics in Midsize and Large Police Departments: Police Chiefs' Views

Sutham Cheurprakobkit

CONTENTS

ABSTRACT

This nationwide study surveyed 225 city police chiefs from America's midsize and large cities regarding their attitudes about the current practice of community-oriented policing (COP). Using thirteen COP characteristics derived from G.W. Cordner's four definitive dimensions of COP (i.e., philosophical, strategic, tactical, and organizational) as a model, this study examined the disparities between the importance of COP characteristics viewed by these police chiefs, and the extent to which their departments incorporated such characteristics into their department policies and practices. The findings showed that although police chiefs viewed all COP characteristics as important, they did not believe each one was incorporated into their policies to that extent. Four COP characteristics (i.e., problem-solving strategies, use of information, leadership and management styles, and proactive and preventive orientation) were found to have the largest disparity between the importance and incorporation scales. Chiefs' attitudes toward external and internal support for COP were found to be directly related to attitudes toward incorporating COP characteristics into police policies. Policy implications were discussed.

Although community-oriented policing (COP) has become almost a household word among law enforcement agencies in recent years, there is no doubt that the term *community policing* has been defined differently and adopted in different ways (see Barlow 2000, 225; G.W. Cordner 1998; Rosenbaum and Lurigio 1994). Seagrave (1996) reviewed the literature and categorized COP into five categories (i.e., a meaningless rhetorical term, a philosophy aiming at the police and the community as co-producers to solve crime problems, a particular crime prevention program, a form of increased social control, and an imprecise notion that is impossible to define). One main reason for these various perspectives on COP may be the different levels and magnitudes of successes and failures in implementing community policing programs perceived by many. However, despite such contrasting views, COP has become very popular among academics, practitioners, and citizens.

One of the most comprehensive definitions of COP is that of G.W. Cordner's (1998). Modifying Manning's (1984) definition, Cordner (1998) characterized COP into four main dimensions (philosophical, strategic, tactical, and organizational). Cheurprakobkit (2001, 2002) argued that these four dimensions of COP are comprehensive enough to accommodate all the definitional differences of COP given by many. There are advantages in using a well-defined COP concept, in that it helps ease any potential confusion among law enforcement officials over what COP should really mean. Other significant benefits are that the study's results can be analyzed and interpreted more reliably.

A review of the COP literature revealed that, despite the importance of COP characteristics, no previous study examined police chiefs' attitudes toward COP using Cordner's (1998) model. Very few empirical studies examined Cordner's model. Cheurprakobkit (2002) conducted a qualitative study by asking police officers what they thought were key COP characteristics and found that overall the officers' responses reflected the tactical dimension the most, followed by the organizational, strategic, and philosophical dimensions, respectively. He concluded that COP involves many fundamental changes of policing; therefore, these four dimensions must be looked at as a whole in context, not as separate individual components. The purpose of this study was to examine the attitudes of police chiefs regarding the importance of COP characteristics and how much they believed that they have incorporated each of these characteristics into their police programs and practices using Cordner's (1998) COP definition as a theoretical model.

This study attempted to address several questions: (1) Do police chiefs receive training on COP? (2) Do they perceive each of the COP characteristics as important? (3) How much do police chiefs believe that they incorporate COP characteristics into their police policies and practices? and (4) Is there any perceived internal or external support for COP? Police chiefs were selected for the current study for two main reasons: First, attitudes of police leaders and police officers toward COP must be examined separately due to different organizational roles each group has, which would enhance the relevancy and accuracy in understanding how the COP concept is being operationalized (Seagrave 1996). Second, as leaders, police chiefs should fully understand its concept and be able to initiate and nurture the required changes COP needs (Glensor and Peak 1996).

THE IMPORTANCE OF COMMUNITY POLICING CHARACTERISTICS: CORDNER'S MODEL

In both theory and practice, COP requires new fundamental changes in the basic roles of the police. These changes include police day-to-day activities, interaction, officers' skills, problem solving, and even organizational and managerial adjustments, which are well beyond the traditional roles for which police are recruited, trained, and assessed (Buerger, A.J. Petrosino, and C. Petrosino 1999; Glensor and Peak, 1996; Wasserman and Moore 1988). COP is not replacing the traditional law enforcement model, but it helps the police in situations where traditional police work is irrelevant or maybe even counterproductive. Therefore, it is important that COP officers and its proponents understand the principles before adopting and practicing this philosophy.

Cordner (1998) identified four dimensions (i.e., philosophical, strategic, tactical, and organizational) that are of importance to the success of the COP implementation. First, the philosophical dimension includes the central ideas and beliefs underlying COP and is comprised of three elements (citizen input, broad police function, and personal service). As American society grows demographically, technologically, and ethnically, law enforcement has been pressured to restructure to handle increased workloads, with the majority of calls relating to service and order maintenance rather than criminal cases (Mastrofski 1983, 40), dealing with ethnically diverse groups of people, and solving more sophisticated criminal cases. The police roles as service providers and personalized officers are indubitably crucial for police effectiveness under this new police philosophy.

W. Lyons (2002) emphasized the importance of the COP philosophy in today's time of terror. Supporting COP wisdom that police ability to gather information is crucial to the success of COP implementation (Rosenbaum 1994), Lyons (2002) argued that local police forces must expand their resources to encourage information sharing, especially from those communities that are least likely to assist the police, including the Arab-American and Islamic-American communities. For members of these communities to share crime or terror-related information, law enforcement must police and protect them, or even exercise their discretion selectively in ways that respond to their concerns and needs as they understand and articulate them. Cordner (1998) calls this *personalized policing*. To fail to do so is to create an information gap as shown consistently in previous research's findings (Lamm-Weisel and Eck 1994; Skogan et al. 2000): COP implementation could not include some minority or neighborhood sections that need assistance the most from these programs, resulting in the lack of reciprocal and desired communications.

Second, the strategic dimension includes the key operational concepts that translate philosophy into action, and it is comprised of three elements: (1) reoriented operation, which emphasizes more face-to-face interaction between the police and the citizen, (2) geographic focus, which recommends patrol officers stay in the same geographical area for an extended period of time to gain more familiarity with the people, and (3) prevention emphasis, which suggests police be more proactive and preventive than reactive to community problems. The concept of police–citizen face-to-face interaction has been realized after the police reform era (1930–1970s), in which the adoption of technologies and vehicle patrol techniques had led to the isolation problem between the police from the public; therefore, more foot, bike, and mounted patrols have now been deployed whenever possible to generate more contacts with citizens. For the purpose of crime prevention, law enforcement has increasingly utilized information received from crime analysis and computer technology (i.e., the geographic information system [GIS]) in their planning and operation. For example, the GIS crime-mapping techniques have been used by many police departments to generate crime maps to track criminal activities in the neighborhood (Rich 2001, 1996).

Third, the tactical dimension translates philosophy, ideas, and strategies into programs that consist of three elements (positive interaction, partnerships, and problem solving). Police experience (i.e., positive police–citizen interaction) has been cited as an important factor that is directly correlated to attitudes toward the police (Cheurprakobkit 2000; G.E. Cordner and Jones 1995; Reno Police Department 1992, 10; Zevitz and Rettammel 1990). Positive interaction between the police and the public even helped neutralize or ameliorate the negative attitudes of citizens (Cheurprakobkit 2000; Cox and White 1988). In his police–citizen contact study, Cheurprakobkit (2000) emphasized the importance of positive police–citizen contact by concluding that police must learn to understand cultural differences and work with the Hispanic communities to achieve desired, reciprocal, and realistic goals.

Positive interaction can yield trust and respect that the police need from people to create good working relationships for crime prevention and problem solving. Without trust and respect, police–citizen cooperation and information sharing through partnerships are less likely to occur. In the COP context, partnerships include the collaboration between both the police and the community, and between the police and other city agencies as well (P. Lyons 1997). Effective partnerships also rely upon the problem-solving process (i.e., problem identification, analysis, implementing appropriate responses, and assessing partnership efforts), which has proved to be effective in solving crime problems (Eck and Spelman 1987; Green 1995; Kennedy 1997).

Fourth, the organizational dimension covers three elements: structure, management, and information. Goldstein (1987) stated that to incorporate COP into a police agency's philosophy, the organization must transcend its structural and operational constructs and rethink relationships, both internal and external. Organizational change is crucial in encompassing incident-driven policing, traditional police tactics, and strategies with the COP model that emphasizes the participation and promotion of all interested community stakeholders to come together to solve community problems. Several studies showed that the success of the COP implementation was hindered by police departments being unable to gain necessary internal changes such as lack of support from middle management (Sadd and Grinc 1994), department's organizational climate and police chief's management style not being conducive to the COP implementation (Cheurprakobkit 2001), and lack of training on COP and confusion as to what COP is (Zhao, Thurman and Lovich 1995).

Although little evidence showed that police agencies have changed their organizational structure as a consequence of implementing COP (Walker and Katz 2002, 210), a few studies conducted on this issue did reveal positive findings. Mastrofski et al. (1998) found that sergeants in Indianapolis believed that the supportive role of helping officers working through problems in their neighborhood was much more important than performing constraining activities like enforcing departmental policies. Wycoff and Skogan (1994) similarly found that a participatory management style implemented in the Madison, Wisconsin, police department made officers feel more satisfied with their work, think that their job was more important, and believe they had much more autonomy at work. However, one qualitative study did examine police leaders' attitudes toward the interpretations of COP (Seagrave 1996). The study revealed that all of the police leaders' responses fell only under the philosophical and tactical dimensions, not the strategic or organizational one. Seagrave's (1996) study's finding was supported by those of others (Buerger 1998; Cheurprakobkit 2002), which suggested training on COP is needed at all levels of the police organization to enhance the understanding of the COP principles.

Training on COP has been considered a major determinant that helps law enforcement understand and realize the importance of COP characteristics (Bradford and Pynes 1999). Improper COP training or lack thereof can create confusion over the meaning of COP among officers or result in overemphasis of certain COP characteristics over the others. Such a negative repercussion will have a greater impact if those who lack COP training are police executives whose decisions can determine the distribution of the already limited resources and the success of the COP implementation. Police executives who are proponents of COP should realize that all COP characteristics must be looked at as a whole in context instead of as individual components, because each characteristic/element can more or less affect the others, and also emphasizing certain elements can create the oversight of the others as well (Cheurprakobkit 2002).

However, although training on COP has become so important that it has been incorporated as part of the basic training curricula in many police academies across the United States, organizational structure and police leadership style may quickly dissipate police recruits' basic beliefs and attitudes toward the COP principles and practices they gained during basic academy training (Mastrofski and Ritti 1996). Haarr (2001) conducted a pretest/posttest longitudinal survey with 446 police recruits from the Phoenix Regional Police Training Academy (i.e., on the first day of the academy, during the 16-week academy, at the end of recruits' field training period, and after the completion of a 1 yr. probationary period), as well as surveyed 21 police chiefs/commanders regarding COP implementation and practice. The study's findings supported that of Mastrofski and Ritti's (1996): leadership, management style, organizational arrangements, and informal work groups within a police agency set the tone for COP regardless of the training on COP that the police recruits received (Haarr 2001). In other words, whether the recruits will be likely to continue to have attitudes and beliefs supportive of COP that they learned from the academy depends

greatly upon whether the leadership style of that agency, the organizational structure, and environment are conducive to the COP practice.

METHODOLOGY

The data for this study were part of the larger survey study that was sent to city
police chiefs regarding their attitudes toward the practice of COP (30 items), computer crime (20 items), and legal liability (25 items). As this study emphasized
COP practice, the analysis excluded the data on computer crime and legal liability. Targeting midsize and large cities, the self-administered survey was mailed
nationwide to police chiefs in city police departments that serve in cities with a
population of fifty thousand or more. Using the *1999 National Directory of Law
Enforcement Administrators* as a sampling frame, 545 police chiefs were selected
to participate in this study. The survey was first mailed out on June 7, 2001, to
each of the police chiefs including a cover letter stating the purpose of the study,
the right not to participate in it, an assurance of data confidentiality, and a postage-paid reply envelope. Follow-up surveys were sent on July 3, 2001. Of the 230
respondents who completed the survey, 224 were usable, which consisted of a
response rate of 41 percent.

SURVEY MEASUREMENT

Other than personal background information (see Table 2.1), two community policing characteristic variables were constructed to measure whether police chiefs
received COP training (via a question with a simple yes/no answer), and the extent of
perceived internal and external support for COP implementation. Support for COP
was measured by asking police chiefs if they believed their mid-management and
first-line officers, as well as the local politicians and people in the city, supported
them in COP efforts; the possible responses were 4 (extensively), 3 (moderately), 2
(slightly), or 1 (none).

The attitudes toward the importance of the COP characteristics and the extent to
which police chiefs incorporated COP into their police policies and practices were
measured using the four dimensions (which were broken down into thirteen COP
elements) derived from Cordner's (1998) COP model. The philosophical dimension
consisted of citizen input, broad police function, and personalized service elements;
the strategic dimension comprised the face-to-face interaction, geographical focus,
and crime prevention elements; the tactical dimension included the positive interaction, police–citizen partnerships, police partnering with other agencies, and problem-solving elements; and the organizational dimension consisted of the structure,
management, and information elements. The possible responses for the importance
scale were 4 (very important), 3 (important), 2 (somewhat important), and 1 (not
important). For the incorporation scale, the chosen responses were 4 (great extent), 3
(certain extent), 2 (somewhat), and 1 (not at all).

Internal consistency for both the importance and incorporation scales was calculated for each of the four COP dimensions. Analyses indicated low reliability coefficients (alpha) for each dimension in both scales, except for the tactical dimension

TABLE 2.1

Respondents' Demographic Information (N = 225)

Variable	Frequency	Percentage
Gender		
Male	218	98.6
Female	3	1.4
Age		
Under 35 years	7	3.2
35–40 years	15	6.8
41–45 years	89	40.6
46–50 years	108	49.4
51 years or older		
Race/ethnicity		
White/non-Hispanic	178	80.5
Black	23	10.4
Hispanic	14	6.3
Asian	5	2.3
Others	1	0.5
Education level		
High school	3	1.4
Some college hours	12	5.5
Associate's degree	7	3.2
Bachelor's degree	75	3.4
Master's or above graduate	121	55.5
How long have you served as police chief in your current department?		
Less than 3 years	95	43.4
3–6 years	66	30.1
7–10 years	32	14.6
11–14 years	20	9.2
More than 14 years	6	2.7
How long have you been in law enforcement?		
Less than 15 years	1	0.5
15–20 years	16	7.3
21–25 years	51	23.2
More than 25 years	152	69.0

TABLE 2.2

Participants' Responses Regarding Internal and External Support for the Implementation of COP Programs (N = 225)

	Extensively	Moderately	Slightly	None	Mean Score
Support from the midmanagement officers	108(48.9)	80(36.2)	29(13.1)	4(1.8)	3.32
Support from the first-line officers	53(23.9)	124(55.9)	41(18.5)	4(1.8)	3.02
Support from the local politicians	138(62.2)	69(31.1)	13(5.9)	2(.9)	3.55
Support from people in the city	134(60.4)	72(32.4)	15(6.8)	1(.5)	3.53

Note: Scale ranged from 1 to 4, with 1 meaning "none" and 4 meaning "extensively"; percentage of participants is given in parentheses.

of the incorporation scale (alpha = .78); therefore, each characteristic was compared individually (Table 2.5).

FINDINGS

The data showed that the overwhelming majority of police chiefs (96 percent) received COP training, whereas only 4 percent did not. Consistently, almost all the police chiefs surveyed reported that their department had been practicing COP three years or longer. However, when asked about the success of the COP implementation, 71 percent of police chiefs said that they either had a great success or only to a certain extent; 15 percent said that their COP programs were somewhat successful; and the other 14 percent reported no success at all. The data regarding police chiefs' training on COP indicated the police department's commitment and willingness to adopt and practice COP, and also helped answer one of the concerns raised in the conclusion of Cheurprakobkit's (2001) study. It stated that to be more successful in implementing COP, police executives should understand the principles of COP and undergo COP training, which is a good initial step toward the COP philosophy. However, the different levels of COP success implied that there were some obstacles hindering the progress of this endeavor and warranted further examination.

Table 2.2 revealed the perceptions of both external and internal support ($M >$ 3.00). Police chiefs perceived local politicians as most supportive ($M = 3.55$), followed by people in the city ($M = 3.53$), midmanagement officers ($M = 3.32$), and first-line officers ($M = 3.02$), in that order. These findings suggest internal support is less likely to be perceived than external support, especially from patrol officers. Given that these first-line officers are the ones who deliver COP programs for the police department, and whose discretionary actions may greatly affect the outcomes of the programs, police chiefs are in need of more support from these officers.

As to the importance of COP characteristics, Table 2.3 showed that each characteristic was perceived as important ($M \geq 3.14$), with the positive police–public interaction element being the highest ($M = 3.88$) and the face-to-face police–citizen interaction element being second ($M = 3.81$). The leadership and management ele-

TABLE 2.3

Respondents' Beliefs about the Importance of COP Characteristics (N = 225)

COP Characteristics	Very Important	Important	Somewhat Important	Not Important	Mean
Citizen input	154(70.3)	63(28.8)	1(.5)	1(.5)	3.69
Broader role of the police (crime control, order maintenance, service, etc.)	108(50.7)	91(42.7)	14(6.6)	—	3.44
Personalized service (tailored policing based on local norms and values)	94(43.1)	100(45.9)	24(11.0)	—	3.32
Face-to-face police–citizen interactions	175(81.8)	38(17.8)	1(0.5)	—	3.81
Geographic basis of assignment (24 h responsibility for smaller area)	105(48.2)	83(38.1)	30(13.8)	—	3.34
Proactive and preventive orientation	143(66.8)	68(31.8)	3(1.4)	—	3.65
Positive interaction between the police and the public	193(88.5)	23(10.6)	2(0.9)	—	3.88
Police–citizen partnerships	170(78.7)	44(20.4)	2(0.9)	—	3.78
Partnerships with other agencies	135(61.6)	73(33.3)	11(5.0)	—	3.57
Problem-solving strategies	150(68.8)	66(30.3)	2(0.9)	—	3.68
Restructuring the organization to facilitate COP	109(49.8)	81(37.0)	26(11.9)	3(1.4)	3.35
Leadership and management styles that place more emphasis on organizational culture and values, and less on written rules and formal discipline	76(34.9)	100(45.9)	38(17.4)	4(1.8)	3.14
The importance of quality (results, outcomes) rather than quantity (numbers of arrests made and tickets issued) of policing	112(51.4)	91(41.7)	15(6.9)	—	3.45

Note: Scale ranged from 1 to 4, with 1 meaning "not important" and 4 meaning "very important"; percentage of respondents is given is parentheses.

ment was viewed as least important ($M = 3.14$). For the incorporation of COP characteristics shown in Table 2.4, the overall mean scores were relatively high, which indicated that police chiefs felt they incorporated each one into their police policies at least to a certain extent. However, when one compared each of the mean scores from the incorporation table with that of the same characteristic in the importance table, the former was lower than the latter across the board. Also, the highest and lowest mean scores for the incorporation scale were similar to those of the importance scale. That is, police chiefs believed that they incorporated the positive police–public interaction element and the face-to-face police–citizen interaction elements the most ($M = 3.55$), and the leadership and management element the least ($M = 2.65$).

When the differences between the mean scores of the same elements in the importance and incorporation tables were calculated (Table 2.5), a disparity between

TABLE 2.4

Respondents' Beliefs about the Incorporation of COP Characteristics into Department Policies and Practices (N = 225)

COP Characteristics	Great Extent	Certain Extent	Somewhat	Not At All	Mean
Citizen input	93(42.3)	101(45.9)	26(11.8)	—	3.30
Broader role of the police (crime control, order maintenance, service, etc.)	88(41.1)	104(48.6)	22(10.3)	—	3.31
Personalized service (tailored policing based on local norms and values)	66(30.4)	110(50.7)	40(18.4)	1(0.5)	3.11
Face-to-face police–citizen interactions	131(61.2)	70(32.7)	13(6.1)	—	3.55
Geographic basis of assignment (24 h responsibility for smaller area)	100(45.7)	65(29.7)	43(19.6)	11(5.0)	3.16
Proactive and preventive orientation	76(35.3)	108(50.2)	30(14.0)	1(0.5)	3.20
Positive interaction between the police and the public	130(59.1)	81(36.8)	8(3.6)	1(0.5)	3.55
Police–citizen partnerships	100(46.1)	95(43.8)	21(9.7)	1(0.5)	3.35
Partnerships with other agencies	100(45.5)	94(42.7)	25(11.4)	1(0.5)	3.33
Problem-solving strategies	79(36.2)	97(44.5)	41(18.8)	1(0.5)	3.12
Restructuring the organization to facilitate COP	77(35.2)	80(36.5)	53(24.2)	9(4.1)	3.03
Leadership and management styles that place more emphasis on organizational culture and values, and less on written rules and formal discipline	33(15.1)	90(41.1)	82(37.4)	14(6.4)	2.65
The importance of quality (results, outcomes) rather than quantity (numbers of arrests made and tickets issued) of policing	50(22.8)	110(50.2)	53(24.2)	6(2.7)	2.93

Note: Scale ranged from 1 to 4, with 1 meaning "not at all" and 4 meaning "to a great extent"; percentage of respondents is given in parentheses.

the mean scores was evident across all COP characteristics. These findings indicate a discrepancy between what police chiefs perceive as important and how much each of these important elements has been incorporated. However, the biggest differences were from four elements: problem-solving strategies (.56), use of information (.52), leadership and management (.49), and proactive and preventive orientation (.45), in that order.

Several points are worth mentioning here. First, police chiefs seem to emphasize the importance of the citizen and crime prevention components over the others. All the elements that are directly related to citizen involvement and interaction, as well as crime prevention (i.e., citizen input, face-to-face interaction, proactive and prevention orientation, police–citizen partnerships, and problem-solving strategies) are viewed as more important than the other elements. This is consistent with Seagrave's (1996) findings that most police leaders defined COP as a philosophy that emphasizes police–citizen working relationships to solve crime and community problems.

TABLE 2.5

Respondents' Beliefs about the Mean Difference between the Importance and Incorporation of COP Characteristics (N = 225)

COP Characteristics	Importance	Incorporation	Difference
Citizen input	3.69	3.30	.39
Broader role of the police (crime control, order maintenance, service, etc.)	3.44	3.31	.13
Personalized service (tailored policing based on local norms and values)	3.32	3.11	.21
Face-to-face police–citizen interactions	3.81	3.55	.26
Geographic basis of assignment (24 h responsibility for smaller area)	3.34	3.16	.18
Proactive and preventive orientation	3.65	3.20	.45
Positive interaction between the police and the public	3.88	3.55	.33
Police–citizen partnerships	3.78	3.35	.43
Partnerships with other agencies	3.57	3.33	.24
Problem-solving strategies	3.68	3.12	.56
Restructuring the organization to facilitate COP	3.35	3.03	.32
Leadership and management styles that place more emphasis on organizational culture and values, and less on written rules and formal discipline	3.14	2.65	.49
The importance of quality (results, outcomes) rather than quantity (numbers of arrests made and tickets issued) of policing	3.45	2.93	.52

Second, the data suggest that the extent to which each COP characteristic is incorporated into the department policies and practices can be improved in all categories, especially in the areas of problem-solving strategies, the use of information, leadership and management styles, and crime prevention, which reveal a wider gap, compared to the others, between the importance and incorporation of COP characteristics. This study's findings confirm the outcomes of previous studies that suggest that organizational change represents strong barriers to COP (Zhao, Thurman and Lovich 1995; Glensor and Peak 1996).

Third, more can be said about the leadership and management characteristic. The data found that police chiefs saw this characteristic to be the least important element of COP and the least implemented aspect of the COP practice. For COP to be more successful, police chiefs must lead and manage their departments in ways that are conducive to a positive COP environment. As Cheurprakobkit (2001) stated, most current police officers received COP training which enhanced their understanding of COP and provided them with criteria to judge whether their police leader's leadership and management styles follow COP principles. Cheurprakobkit (2001) concluded that police executives must show their officers that they themselves understand and are committed to the COP concept, create an organizational environment that is conducive to implementing COP programs, and establish leadership skills necessary for the success of COP.

TABLE 2.6

Correlation Coefficients between Certain COP Characteristics and Internal and External Support Factors

COP Characteristics	Internal Support		External Support	
	Midmanagement	First-line Officers	Politicians	Public
Citizen input	.36**	.34**	.20**	.25**
Broader role of the police (crime control, order maintenance, service, etc.)	.30**	.24**	.26**	.33**
Personalized service (tailored policing based on local norms and values)	.24**	.33**	.19**	.17*
Face-to-face police–citizen interactions	.33**	.26**	.23**	.21**
Geographic basis of assignment (24 h responsibility for smaller area)	.28**	.31**	.28**	.23**
Proactive and preventive orientation	.37*	.39*	.23*	.30*
Positive interaction between the police and the public	.32**	.32**	.17*	.30**
Police–citizen partnerships	.40**	.35**	.37**	.40**
Partnerships with other agencies	.15*	.18**	.22**	.20**
Problem-solving strategies	.38*	.37*	.32*	.28*
Restructuring the organization to facilitate COP	.36**	.32**	.41**	.37**
Leadership and management styles that place more emphasis on organizational culture and values, and less on written rules and formal discipline	.36*	.33*	.26*	.23*
The importance of quality (results, outcomes) rather than quantity (numbers of arrests made and tickets issued) of policing	.33*	.31*	.31*	.35*

Note: $* p < .05$; $** p < .01$

Correlation analysis found no relationships, except for only a few variables, between attitudes toward the importance of COP characteristics and attitudes toward internal and external support. (The statistical results are not shown here.) However, both external and internal support was found to be correlated to every characteristic of COP (Table 2.6). The more police chiefs perceived support from their officers, local politicians, and people in the city, the more they believed they incorporated the COP characteristics into their police policies and practices.

POLICY IMPLICATIONS

Even though COP literature reveals various definitions of the term *community polic-ing*, some of which have little or no relevance, the findings of this study confirm that among police chiefs from mid-size and large cities the adoption and practice of COP ideas do exist. Most police chiefs consider every COP characteristic important and perceive support of COP from within and outside their departments. Furthermore, many departments claim their COP programs to be a great success. However, this current study reveals several interesting findings that need to be addressed pertaining to policy implications.

First, training on COP should cover some skill aspects that police leaders need to be more successful with in implementing COP programs. It appears that police chiefs surveyed in this study recognize the importance of COP principles but are unable to more fully incorporate them into their department policies. Knowing about COP through training is a good start, but knowledge about COP does not warrant a success without the necessary skills police chiefs require to facilitate the communicative, operational, and planning process with other stakeholders. It should also be true that the larger the department, the more difficult the process will be. Police chiefs may need to look at COP from two points of views: global (which is the general philosophy of COP) and specific (which is the way COP is operationalized and structured in a particular agency) (Schafer 2002). That which makes one police department a full-blown COP successor can be a major hindrance for COP in another department. In other words, police chiefs from different agencies might require different skills needed to deal with COP implementation. However, based on this study's findings, skills relating to the areas of problem-solving strategies, leadership and management, proactive and preventive orientation, and use of quantitative and qualitative information in police work are very important for police chiefs to acquire.

Second, an effective COP program should start from within. If police chiefs expect COP programs to be more successful, they must win the hearts and minds of their employees, especially first-line officers whose support for COP is perceived, according to this study, to be the lowest among other supporters. Efforts must be exerted to enrich the traditional role of patrol parallel to the COP principles. This is not only the right thing to do; it is also the most pragmatic way to gain long-term support from patrol officers. Given that these patrol officers are the ones who implement many of the police programs for the departments (including crime prevention programs and problem-solving strategies) and who directly interact with citizens, their support for COP is crucial.

Third, an effective COP program should start from the top down. As a semi-military system, police employees are for the most part rules-and-regulations-abiding officers whose duties and routines mirror their department policies. Police chiefs must recognize that their leadership and management styles can significantly affect both officers within the department as well as the people in the community. Therefore, to lead and manage the department in COP style is to set a tone for the rest of the department to follow, which enhances an organizational atmosphere that is conducive to the success of COP. A study's finding supporting this statement was revealed in Haarr's (2001) research on training in COP procedures in police academies. Haarr (2001) found that a police chief's leadership and management styles, as well as the organizational structure and environment within that police agency, would set the tone for COP, regardless of the COP training police recruits received, police recruits' preacademy experiences, or police recruits' experiences during the field-training period.

CONCLUSIONS

The present study on the attitudes toward the importance and incorporation of COP characteristics among police executives is beneficial in several ways. First, the overall high importance scores of all COP characteristics have strengthened the belief that COP will continue to be a popular practice for American law enforcement for years to come. The importance of all COP characteristics viewed by police chiefs confirm Cheurprakobkit's (2002) argument that these characteristics must be looked at in context as a whole instead of separate individual components, because many of these characteristics are inevitably interrelated and hence will affect each other. To make use of this conceptual knowledge, police chiefs must be informed of the consequences of such repercussions. Second, this study shows that attitudes toward the importance and incorporation of COP characteristics can be different and independent from each other. Such differences reveal possible incongruence between conceptual importance and perceived incorporation of COP. In other words, what seems theoretically important for COP may take much more effort to fulfill in practice. Third, an attitudinal disparity between the importance and incorporation of the same COP characteristic can provide guidance to police chiefs as to what areas should be primarily addressed. The larger the gap, the more attention police chiefs should give to narrowing it.

In sum, police chiefs will continue to be a critical part of the implementation of the COP philosophy. Police chiefs must understand the overall picture of COP and recognize the importance and impact of each COP characteristic, as well as the support they need to achieve COP goals. Whereas this is not an easy task, it should not be impossible for police chiefs to accomplish and might be the only way to enhance the likelihood of success in implementing such an innovative and dynamic concept of COP.

Future research should involve demographic variables in the analysis (e.g., educational level, experience with COP programs, race/ethnicity, types of COP training, and other important factors), which might help identify more clearly the differences between the importance and incorporation scores. Because of the various ways in which police departments incorporate COP elements into their policies and practices, a qualitative study that examines these incorporating techniques and strategies might be useful to learn. Such qualitative research should emphasize leadership style and how police chiefs make use of information, as well as problem-solving strategies that the departments use to solve and prevent crime.

REFERENCES

Barlow, H.D. (2000). *Criminal justice in America*. Upper Saddle River, NJ: Prentice-Hall.

Bradford, D., & Pynes, J.E. (1999). Police academy training: Why hasn't it kept up with practice? *Police Quarterly*, 2, 283–301.

Buerger, M.E. (1998). Police training as a pentecost: Using tools singularly ill-suited to the purpose of reform. *Police Quarterly*, 1, 27–63.

Buerger, M.E., Petrosino, A.J., & Petrosino, C. (1999). Extending the police role: Implications of police mediation as a problem-solving tool. *Police Quarterly*, 2, 125–149.

Cheurprakobkit, S. (2002). Community policing: Training, definition and policy implications. *Policing: An International Journal of Police Strategies and Management*, 25(4), 709–725.

Cheurprakobkit, S. (2001). Organizational impacts on community policing: Management issues and officers' perceptions. *Crime Prevention and Community Safety: An International Journal*, 3(1), 42–52.

Cheurprakobkit, S. (2000). Police-citizen contact and police performance: Attitudinal differences between Hispanics and Non-Hispanics. *Journal of Criminal Justice*, 28, 325–336.

Cordner, G.W. (1998). Community policing: Elements and effects. In G.P. Alpert & A. Piquero (Eds.), *Community policing: Contemporary readings* (pp. 45–62). Prospect Heights, IL: Waveland Press.

Cordner, G.E., & Jones, M. (1995). The effects of supplementary foot patrol on fear of crime and attitudes toward the police. In P. Kratcoski & D. Dukes (Eds.), *Issues in community policing* (pp. 189–198). Highland Heights, KY: Anderson Publishing.

Cox, T.C., & White, M.F. (1988). Traffic citations and student attitudes toward the police: An examination of selected interaction dynamics. *Journal of Police Science and Administration*, 16, 105–121.

Eck, J., & Spelman, W. (1987). Problem solving: Problem oriented policing in Newport News. Washington, D.C.: Police Executive Research Forum.

Glensor, R.W., & Peak, K. (1996). Implementing change: Community-oriented and problem solving. *FBI Law Enforcement Bulletin*, 65(7), 14–21.

Goldstein, H. (1987). Toward community-oriented policing: Potential, basic requirements, and threshold questions. *Crime and Delinquency*, 33, 6–30.

Green, L. (1995). Cleaning up drug hot spots in Oakland, California: The displacement and diffusion effects. *Justice Quarterly*, 12, 737–754.

Haarr, R.N. (2001). The making of a community policing officer: The impact of basic training and occupational socialization on police recruits. *Police Quarterly*, 4(4), 402–433

Kennedy, D. (1997). *Juvenile gun violence and gun markets in Boston*. Washington, D.C.: National Institute of Justice.

Kelling, G., & Moore, M.H. (1988). From political reform to community: The evolving strategy of police. In J. Greene & S. Mastrofski (Eds.), *Community policing: Rhetoric or reality?* (pp. 1–26). New York: Praeger.

Lamm-Weisel, D., & Eck, J. (1994). Toward a practical approach to organizational change: Community-policing initiatives in six cities. In D. Rosenbaum (Ed.), *The challenge of community policing: Testing the promises*, (pp. 53–75). Beverly Hills, CA: Sage Publications.

Lyons, P. (1997). Defining community policing. *Law Enforcement Management and Administrative Statistics Program Bulletin*, 4(6).

Lyons, W. (2002). Partnerships, information and public safety: Community policing in a time of terror. *Policing: An International Journal of Police Strategies and Management*, 25(3), 530–542.

Manning, P. (1984). Community policing. *American Journal of Police*, 3(2), 205–227.

Mastrofski, S. (1983). The police and non-crime services. In G. Whitaker & C. Phillips (Eds.), *Evaluating the performance of criminal justice agencies*. Beverly Hills, CA: Sage Publications.

Mastrofski, S.D, & Ritti, R.R. (1996). Police training and the effects of organization on drunk driving enforcement. *Justice Quarterly*, 13, 290–320.

Mastrofski, S., Albert, J.R., Roger, B., Parks, Robert, E., & Worden. (1998). *Community policing in action: Lessons from an observational study*. U.S. Department of Justice. National Institute of Justice

National Directory of Law Enforcement Administrators (35th ed.) (1999). Stevens Point, WI: SPAN Publishing.

Reno Police Department. (1992). *July 1992 Telephone poll*. Reno, NV: Reno Police Department.

Rich, T.F. (2001). *Crime mapping and analysis by community organizations in Hartford, Connecticut.* Washington, D.C.: Department of Justice, Office of Justice Programs, National Institute of Justice.

Rich, T.F. (1996). *The Chicago Police Department's information collection for automated mapping (ICAM) program.* Washington, D.C.: Department of Justice, Office of Justice Programs, National Institute of Justice.

Rosenbaum, D.P. (Ed.) (1994). *The challenge of community policing: Testing the promises.* Thousand Oaks, CA: Sage Publications.

Rosenbaum, D.P., & Lurigio, A.J. (1994). An inside look at community policing reform: Definition, organizational changes, and evaluation findings. *Crime and Delinquency,* 40(3), 299–314.

Sadd, S., & Grinc, R. (1994). Innovative neighborhood oriented policing: An evaluation of community policing programs in eight cities. In D.P. Rosenbaum (Ed.), *The challenge of community policing.* Thousand Oaks, CA: Sage Publications.

Schafer, J.A. (2002). "I'm not against it in theory...": Global and specific community policing attitudes. *Policing: An International Journal of Police Strategies and Management,* 25(4), 669–686.

Seagrave, J. (1996). Defining community policing. *American Journal of Police,* 15(2), 1–22.

Skogan, W., Hartnett, S., Dubois, J., Comey, J., Twedt-Ball, K., & Gudell, J.E. (2000). *Public involvement: Community policing in Chicago.* National Institute of Justice. Washington, D.C.: Government Printing.

Walker, S., & Katz, C.M. (2002). *The police in America: An introduction.* (4th ed.). Boston, MA: McGraw-Hill Companies.

Wasserman, R., & Moore, M. (1988). Values in policing. *Perspectives on policing,* No. 8. Washington, D.C.: National Institute of Justice and Harvard University.

Wycoff, M.A., & Skogan, W.G. (1994). The effect of a community policing management style of officers' attitudes. *Crime and Delinquency,* 40(3), 371–383.

Zevitz, R.G., & Rettammel, R.J. (1990). Elderly attitudes about police service. *American Journal of Police,* 9, 25–39.

Zhao, J., & Thurman, Q.C. (1997). Community policing: Where are we now? *Crime and Delinquency,* 43(3), 345–357.

Zhao, J., Thurman, Q.C., & Lovich, N.P. (1995). Community-oriented policing across the U.S.: Facilitators and impediments to implementation. *American Journal of Police,* 14(1), 11–28.

3 The Role of Citizen Surveys in Responsive Policing

Charles Burckhardt and Jim Ruiz

CONTENTS

ABSTRACT

Among the differences in performance measurement between the public and private sectors, the presence of objective feedback is lacking for public administrators. There are no sales figures, etc., in which to evaluate public programs. In fact, "objective" measures, as discussed below, may be quite misleading. The citizen survey provides managers with information about the effectiveness of their organizations in meeting the community's wants and needs. A literature review of citizen surveys, in both the policing field and public administration in general, is presented to discuss the possible benefits and uses of this subjective feedback. The goal is to lay a foundation as to how such a survey may be best implemented and used for a police agency.

INTRODUCTION

With the advent of community policing, police agencies have sought to become more responsive to their citizens' needs and to create a partnership with the community. A cornerstone of the philosophy is that the public and police jointly identify and address quality of life issues so that they can be rectified. Attendance at town hall-style meetings by police personnel, neighborhood crime watch programs, and other such initiatives have sought to create the community partnership necessary to solve and prevent crimes.

Police administrators currently review data such as reported crimes, clearance rates, and citations issued in an attempt to decide where resources should be allocated. In the absence of a business-type environment in which losses and gains are more easily determined, administrators are in need of another tool that would assist in deploying personnel and programs to a particular geographic location or problem. Without the constant feedback of sales and production figures, which are more readily found in the private sector, the police must actively solicit reviews and opinions of the public in order to provide themselves some information upon which they may make necessary adjustments to their operations.

One such tool may be the community survey that solicits information from the community to judge the department's overall performance and to make suggestions as to how it can be improved, in addition as to what the citizens feel are the problems that need to be addressed. Through the use of citizen surveys, this author believes, police administrators may be able to evaluate the effectiveness of current programs through citizens' subjective measures and possibly reallocate resources to address concerns that had previously received little or no attention.

The purpose of this paper is to provide a literature review of citizen surveys and the results of their implementation thus far. Theoretical background and past practices will be examined across the spectrum of public administration's, as well as criminal justice's, experience with the subject. Through this two-discipline approach, a greater understanding of the tool will be gained that may possibly result in the construction of a grounded, proven, and effective survey to be used for this author's organization.

A former Harrisburg, Pennsylvania, city police officer was sentenced recently for repeatedly stealing and smoking crack cocaine from the department's evidence room. One issue in this case was the theft and consumption of an illicit substance; the overriding matter was what the possible repercussions would be for the local law enforcement community. According to Dauphin County District Attorney Edward M. Marsico Jr.: "the defendant crippled many drug prosecutions and cast a bad light on law enforcement as a whole" (Decker 2005). With the increased publicity of a police officer's arrest, a concern is that local citizens will have the perception that all Harrisburg City officers are of, at the least, lower moral standards than the rest of society.

Bayley (1996, 42) reminds police administrators that the police are only as good as the public believes them to be. He indicates that in 1999, 79 percent of people had no contact with the police in the previous year; yet, it is likely that most people have firm beliefs as to how effective, good, professional, etc., their police department is. If not from personal encounters with officers, where are these beliefs rooted? Bayley suggests several sources: from trusted friends and families to media accounts of the police.

Two of the principles of perception are size and repetition (Hellriegel and Slocum 2004, 67–68). These characteristics help determine what will be noticed by an individual, and they are frequently manipulated by the media. For example, the Web site for the *Philadelphia Daily News* (2005) includes a section titled "State Cop Scandals." This link guides the reader to over 60 stories ranging from minor misconduct to sexual assaults by Pennsylvania State Police (PSP) Troopers. All of these stories had originally appeared in the newspaper, some with large and damaging front-page headlines. In addition, editorials have been added to the public relations nightmare in Philadelphia, with the *Philadelphia Daily News* calling the PSP an "insulated, undisciplined, sex-obsessed good ol' boys bureaucracy" (*Philadelphia Daily News* 2005).

With Philadelphians constantly reading stories of PSP malfeasance, in addition to the name-calling by the editorial staff, what kinds of perceptions do citizens have about troopers? It is reasonable to assume that with the size of the front-page headlines and the frequency of the paper's demands for radical change in the organization, line officers are being affected. Citizens may possibly adopt a halo effect, where they will focus on one characteristic and be blinded by that single descriptor (Hellriegel and Slocum 2004, 78). PSP Troopers may have unalterable assumptions made about them in the Philadelphia region from the paper's barrage of stories and editorials. Obviously, some effort needs to be put forth as far as personnel training and selection procedures to prevent further problems, but a larger issue is what serves as a barometer to the public's satisfaction with a particular organization.

A method is needed with which administrators can reach a true sense of the public's sentiments toward their organizations, instead of possibly biased stories and editorials. Stipak (1980) addressed the power of citizen surveys some time ago, claiming that they can create change, and that they can help managers become aware of the political climate in which they function (522).

In Goodsell's (2004) polemic on bureaucracy, he identifies citizen surveys as having an important role in a democracy. Of course, a crucial attribute of a government "of the people, by the people and for the people" is that it knows what the people want. Goodsell illustrated another important role of the citizen survey: the determination of what people truly believe about the performance of their government. He argues against the common misconception that the populace is dissatisfied with bureaucratic government. In his research, an interesting finding surfaces: people have a lower opinion of the local government, in general, than they do of specific government services (25). This leads to his belief that recent experience with specific services creates a more favorable impression with citizens, rather than relying on sources such as media, the dangers of which are indicated earlier In this chapter, and word of mouth. To this author, the findings stress the need to be in contact with the citizens and, furthermore, to gauge their opinions to allocate resources to address public desires.

Brudney and England (1982) compare outputs (objective data, such as numbers) to feedback (subjective data, such as surveys from citizens). They call attention to some of the drawbacks to citizen surveys in the public administration culture. First, survey results do not match objective measures (i.e., how much garbage was collected, police patrol miles, etc.). To this author, this highlights the need for qualitative results. Imagine a citizen who has the garbage collected in a timely manner, but the workers always leave a few pieces of rubbish behind in the street. Certainly, the number of tons hauled away may indicate success, but the citizen is dissatisfied with the added inconvenience imposed from the organization. Second, according to Brudney and England, the citizens lack sufficient knowledge of the government to judge it; this type of elitism, of course, is a parallel to literacy tests in order to vote. Brudney and England then agree with Goodsell's (2004) view that such surveys are essential in a democracy. They state: "In a society committed to democratic norms, the views of the citizenry—no matter how (ill)-conceived—are significant in themselves" (129).

In a review of current methods of performance measurement, Holzer and Yang (2004) reviewed various programs in use throughout the country at the present time.

While discussing citizen surveys, they found that the public is sometimes able to identify a core group of needs for each city service, such as response time and legal compliance of officers (23). Administrators may assume that they understand what the public's main concerns are, but they are able to reach a more definite conclusion with the use of citizen surveys. The surveys may reinforce preconceived thoughts of administrators, or possibly redirect the organization towards the true concerns of the citizenry.

In discussing the outputs of an organization, Brudney and England (1982) advise that the collector can simplify the data and choose what to report. An example of this would be the measurement of customer complaints about employee courtesy at a water company. If citizens complain to a manager about an employee's conduct, and the manager immediately addresses the issue and remedies the problem at hand, the citizens will leave satisfied, although they were upset with the employee to a degree that they reported the situation to a manager. As no "formal" measure was used, such as filing a written complaint, the number disappears if the manager does not document it. If organizations take such objective data into account for supervisory reviews, the manager may be cognizant of that and not document the confrontation.

Additionally, Brudney and England (1982) explain the dangers of managers becoming overly concerned with efficiency, the "maximization of output for a given level of input," and effectiveness, the "achievement of goals or objectives" (131). They pose that the dual goals of responsiveness and equity of service should be taken into account, as they are the essentials of a democracy. A manner in which to gauge these goals is through actively reaching out to the consumers through the medium of citizen surveys. As Whitaker agreed, "it is necessary to allow the people being served to provide standards for evaluation" (1974, 760). Whitaker calls researchers to work through the imperfections found in citizen surveys to reach the key objectives of measuring responsiveness and equity.

Morgan (1979) calls attention to the lack of free market controls over quality service in government, and the added focus that it should place on listening to the citizenry:

"In the absence of the market mechanism of price and competition, democratic governments would seem to be under special obligation to make their operations as sensitive to the public as possible" (173).

Customer complaints and praise should be given strong weight, and public administrators will need to be proactive and actively engage citizens in performance reviews. Brudney and England (1982) suggest citizen surveys, public hearings, and citizen advisory boards as means to reach these ends. The Philadelphia Police Department has embraced the citizen advisory board concept with their Police District Advisory Council (PDAC). In this program, citizens speak directly to the commissioner and command staff about issues affecting their community (Philadelphia Police Department n.d., Web site). The responsiveness of the department is seen in the public's ability to speak to the top official in a department of approximately 6,900 officers through the PDAC program.

Wells, Horney, and Maguire (2005) researched one component of Brudney and England's (1982) suggestions, citizen surveys. Seeking a deeper understanding of citizens' perceptions about the police, Wells, Horney, and Maguire (2005) examined the Lincoln, Nebraska, Police Department (LPD), which already had a citizen survey program, and sought to gauge the impact that such surveys have on an officer's behavior (courtesy and professionalism) towards citizens and the officer's performance as rated by a supervisor. The department had originally given participating officers a monthly review of citizen surveys taken for each officer. Of interest is that the officers had to consent to be involved in the surveys, so the entire department did not participate. The survey was not to be used for personnel decisions, rather, as a "professional development tool" that was seen by no one other than the officer being rated (179). This Quality Service Audit was constructed by researchers from the University of Nebraska at Omaha, a representative of the Gallup Corporation, and LPD officers, including one union representative.

The study sought to report on officer encounters with citizens who had been cited, involved in a crash, or who had been a victim of a crime. The results showed that there was no effect on the attitude of officers or on supervisor ratings for LPD officers, who knew that they were being rated by the citizen surveys. The study concludes that citizens who were cited had less favorable ratings of officers compared to those involved in crashes and who were crime victims (Wells, Horney, and Maguire, 2005, 189). This seems to call attention to the dual role of LPD officers as enforcers and helpers. Citizens may become, in a sense, victims of LPD officers when they are cited for traffic violations. Involvement in a crash or becoming a victim of a crime may be a traumatic experience, and it is possible that citizens found the officers to be the calming force in the situation. Also of importance, the study does not indicate whether the drivers involved in crashes were also in the group that was cited. Crashes frequently result in one party being cited, and having that information may have given further clarity to the results.

A change that the LPD administrators found was that officers had habitually informed crime victims that they would contact them in the future and then did not. The survey results called attention to this, as the citizens were disappointed when the officers did not follow through on the promise. There was a department-wide discussion about this issue, and it resulted in officers either following up more or not making the promise to call at all. Showing that an organization is engaging its citizens is crucial for positive relations. "Citizen surveys are a valuable source of information about how citizens perceive the police ... the mere act of surveying citizens can be viewed as part of a larger effort to improve the relationships between the police and the communities" (Wells, Horney, and Maguire, 2005, 196).

The authors also note that conducting these surveys is a sign to the LPD officers that citizens' opinions are an integral part of the organization, and that the department values their perceptions.

The notion of creating a positive environment with citizens by asking about their perceptions through surveys is echoed by other authors. Glass (n.d., 5) concluded that, among its other uses, citizen surveys indirectly send a message to citizens that the government is interested in their opinions. Watson, Juster, and Johnson (1991) reviewed the city of Auburn, Alabama, which has a citizen survey program in place. The article describes how the local news media heavily publicizes the news release of the survey's findings. The media announcements about the public's opinions would seem to be in keeping with Glass' statement, further showing to the public that its opinions are valued.

The original survey was first constructed by the Department of Political Science at Auburn University. After its completion, it was reviewed by a community group for questions that might be interpreted as somewhat biased. Watson, Juster, and Johnson (1991) point out that this review by the citizens gives the survey added credibility in the eyes of the public. The survey's reception by the media and the public echoes the Wells, Horney, and Maguire (2005) study by illustrating the public response of showing that the government cares about citizens' opinions. An added benefit, according to Watson, Juster, and Johnson (1991) is that five out of nine city council members reported using results of the citizen survey to influence their budgeting priorities. Here the government's responsiveness and how it affects the formal budgeting process is seen. The effect that disconfirmation may have had if the council members ignored the survey results is not explored, but it is assumed that it would result in negative publicity for the members, in light of the positive media coverage the survey enjoyed.

In a comparison of objective, thought of as numerical values, and subjective measures, thought of as survey research, Brown and Coulter (1983) posed a system of variables that possibly lead to various satisfaction levels with police service delivery. The authors examined the subjective variables of satisfaction with police response time, treatment of people, and perceptions of equity of protection—satisfaction with police protection in one's own neighborhood (52). It was found that the more a citizen is the victim of crime, the less satisfaction there is with response time and treatment; yet, the citizen still feels that protection is not better in other neighborhoods. Citizens who were not crime victims had a higher rating for the three subjective variables. The authors attribute this to the dichotomy of client versus consumer, with the latter being in need of police service due to negative experiences, whereas the former does not need to call for the service at all.

Brown and Coulter (1983) found that the best indicator of satisfaction is the citizen's involvement with local government; there is a positive correlation between the two. The study also contains a hypothesis that twenty years later evolves into "disconfirmation theory." The authors hypothesized that the higher a citizen's expectations of police service delivery, the lower they will become when the expectations are not met. In their closing comments, they seem puzzled about the finding and call for future research into the matter.

> Perhaps one important reason why objective service conditions do not affect satisfaction levels is that citizens interpret objective service conditions through their subjective service expectations. Citizens may evaluate what they get in terms of what they expect. Future research should explore this possibility (57).

In examining the private sector for customer satisfaction rating techniques, Van Ryzin (2004) discusses the expectancy disconfirmation model, which he claims has never before been utilized in citizen surveys. "The model views satisfaction judgments as determined—not just by product or service performance—but by a process in which consumers compare performance with their prior expectation" (434).

With organizations such as the National Academy of Public Administration and the Government Accounting Standards Board calling for more focus on citizen surveys to measure government's performance, Van Ryzin believes that there is a need for studying the surveys with this private sector theory. The private sector seems to be advanced in collecting pertinent information about its customers, as Walker (1994) states, "by monitoring sales trends and customers' buying habits, private sector managers receive almost continuous feedback" (47).

Van Ryzin (2004) utilized data from the 2001 Survey of Satisfaction with New York City Services (SSNYCS) for his study. The survey asks respondents whether their expectations for the quality of New York City services from a few years prior have been met or not. The study also asks participants to rate specific city services such as fire service, streets, etc. Van Ryzin then creates a solution to measure disconfirmation (438):

QUALITY (of service) – EXPECT (expectation) = DISCONF (disconfirmation).

The citizen's expectations from years ago will be subtracted from the perceived quality of service. This will gauge at what level, if at all, there was disconfirmation.

The finding is that what a citizen expects (EXPECT) and what they experience (QUALITY) becomes a significant determinant of the overall satisfaction judgment (Van Ryzin 2004, 442). Van Ryzin makes the recommendation that administrators should raise a citizen's expectations for the quality of city services. The author admits that performance is a significant variable in the overall process, but that the expectation level is, as well. The implications of this theory for administrators are considerable. When municipal services are facing possible cutbacks of service, administrators should not warn citizens of difficult times to come, thus implying they should lower their expectations. Based on the theory, the author suggests that a positive expectation with negative performance will lead to more negative disconfirmation than lowered expectations and positive performance. A difficulty in the theory is that administrators seem to be putting themselves in a precarious position by publicly raising expectations for a service, with the possibility that objective indicators will later show that the quality of service is declining.

Two important subissues arise in Van Ryzin's (2004) study: media coverage and use of demographics. He notes that media coverage may be a factor in a citizen's decision about satisfaction of a service. With the arrest of the Harrisburg officer, noted earlier, it seems plausible that residents of the city may weigh such a heavily publicized case into their decision of how they feel about the Harrisburg Bureau of Police. Additionally, the SSNYCS only categorized respondents geographically, by each of the five boroughs. The study does not include demographics such as race, age, and sex. Brown and Coulter (1983) had indicated that blacks had historically rated government services lower than did other groups, and which may have played a significant role in determining the results of the study. A resolution later adopted by the National Academy of Public Administration called for more focus on demographics:

"1. c) develop procedures for establishing realistic performance evaluations that take into account the influence of client characteristics, local conditions, and other factors beyond the control of program staff." (National Academy of Public Administration 1991)

Turning the focus again to police-related studies, the demographic of race is a crucial factor in citizen surveys. Engel and Calnon (2004) discuss two types of citizen surveys: information about interactions with police and those that create baselines for traffic stop data (107). The study focused on racial profiling and so information about a driver's age and race is a central variable in such a study to detect possible prejudice. Sims, Hooper, and Peterson (2002) also focused on the demographic of race, among other factors, to determine citizens' views of Harrisburg police officers. In their review of the citizen surveys, Sims, Hooper, and Peterson (2002) found that Blacks had a more positive view than did Whites. This is in contrast to Stipak's (1980) assertion that minorities have a less favorable view of government services. Sims, Hooper, and Peterson believe there may be a grudging reliance of Blacks on police, as they are the ones who are the most frequent consumers of these services.

This harkens back to the finding by Wells, Horney, and Maguire (2005) in the LPD, where those who were involved in crashes and those who were victims of crime gave higher ratings of officers than did those who were issued citations. The Blacks in the Sims, Hooper, and Peterson (2002) study may be viewing the Harrisburg officers in their "helper" role, which causes them to be seen more favorably. The main issue is that through the use of demographics, such as race, public administration can open new opportunities for understanding citizen surveys.

Another benefit of citizen surveys, according to Kelly and Swindell (2002), is that they provide another measure of job performance. As seen above, Sims, Hooper, and Peterson (2002); Stipak (1980); and Wells, Horney, and Peterson (2005) seek further knowledge in underlying, issues such as race. Kelly and Swindell (2002) suggest that objective performance measures may be closed off from realizing all sides of a given service: "Inputs, efficiencies, and outputs typically are collected and reported as administrative performance measures, while citizens' evaluations are likely to be based on outcomes that are meaningful to them" (613). If, for example, a city looks at the number of miles that its streets department plows in neighborhoods during snowstorms, it may produce a large number that administrators find indicative of effective service, in that "a lot of work" is being done. A survey may elicit a more qualitative response and rate the streets department low for reasons such as not completely plowing the street or plowing citizens' vehicles under, because the department did not give citizens adequate time or warning to move their vehicles off the street.

What Kelly and Swindell (2002) found in their review of 30 citizen surveys from various cities is that the higher the objective measure, the lower the satisfaction with the service. For example, in areas with high violent and property crime, the citizens' satisfaction declined; this occurred even in areas with high clearance rates for arrests. In addition, the more money that was spent on road maintenance, the lower was the satisfaction with the roads in the city studied. The authors believe that the more the citizens need police service, the more likely they are in a neighborhood where the police need to "do more." In areas where there is low crime, the police are called on for service less frequently; therefore, the police are being effective in that area by preventing crime altogether. The objective measure of arrests may be low, precisely because no arrests need to be made. This satisfaction with the police may be found in a subjective survey, because it is an effective method to measure crime that is not happening. Insofar as the roads are concerned, this author believes that the more spent on road repair, the more roads are closed, and citizens must take lengthy and inconvenient detours. Again, satisfaction will likely be highest when the road repair service is not needed at all.

An issue that surfaces in Kelly and Swindell's (2002) review of the surveys is that there is a lack of uniformity in the survey methods (614). It, therefore, becomes more difficult for administrators to have an objective method to survey; for example, road maintenance scores across several jurisdictions. Wholey and Hatry (1992) discussed the feasibility of performance-monitoring programs in public administration and gave the recommendation to use preexisting data to lower costs of such studies (609). An example of this is at the federal level in the form of the Uniform Crime Reports (UCR), which are crime statistics that are filed with the federal government by local and state police departments. The reporting system demands that local departments fit their reporting methods into the federal government's model, which creates the desired uniformity in reporting.

This lends itself to the option of accreditation, which is becoming a popular concept with police departments. Accreditation agencies, such as the Commission on the Accreditation for Law Enforcement Agencies (CALEA), review a police department's policies and operations, and mandates that they follow minimum, uniform policies created by the accreditation commission (CALEA, n.d., web). The benefits vary from lower insurance costs for departments to greater accountability of departmental practices. Most importantly, in terms of this chapter, is that there is a minimum level of uniformity that could be used to create some commonality in citizen surveys in the field. CALEA (2004) requires that a citizen survey be conducted a minimum of every three years, and that it survey opinions on:

> overall agency performance; overall competence of agency employees; officers' attitudes and behavior toward citizens; community concern over safety within the agency's service area as a whole; and recommendations and suggestions for improvements. (45.2.4)

Although concerns of citizen survey structure and implementation certainly validate lengthy discussion, an area that has received less attention is how well public administrators are able to predict what the citizens truly want. Melkers and Thomas (1998) thought the issue to be important, as administrators are charged with accomplishing the public's goals. The authors begin by extolling the benefits of studying managers' prediction accuracy. As stated previously, using the surveys could show managers where they have possibly fallen out of touch with the public will, and increase interest in citizen surveys by adding some type of "shock value" when the actual and predicted results are compared (328).

Melkers and Thomas (1998) performed their study in Atlanta, Georgia, and tested administrators from various departments of government, including police and water. The water department's administrators predicted citizens would be more satisfied with the drinking water than they were, and the authors attributed this to the administrators possibly relying on technical indicators of water taste that the public did not use in making their evaluations (333). Here, the difference between objective and subjective performance measures and the completely different scores they can yield is seen.

Police administrators had predicted that citizens would feel safer downtown than they actually did; the authors claim that the administrators based their assumptions on objective measures of arrests, etc. (Melkers and Thomas 1998, 331). Also, citizens felt that they were 7 or 8 percent more safe in their neighborhoods than the administrators had predicted. This suggests that administrators may have been misallocating resources to neighborhoods instead of downtown districts, or that they were not adequately publicizing their results through the media to the public. Finally, the authors address the role the news media has in creating fear in the public: "Citizen perceptions, by contrast, may reflect media reporting of crime in cities, reporting which often helps to produce an excessive fear of crime in cities" (333).

Again, the need for administrators to effectively communicate with the citizens presents itself. By creating a dialogue with citizens through surveys, and by comparing the results of those surveys compared to objective performance indicators, administrators can either redirect resources or offer proof to the public that their fears are unjustified.

CONCLUSIONS

The main focus of this chapter was to be limited to citizen surveys and issues therein. A subcategory that quickly arose was the importance of an organization's relationship with the media. As illustrated by the examples of the PSP and their failure with the *Philadelphia Daily News*, and the success of Auburn, Alabama, in the relationship with their local media, public relations should be a key concern for administrators. The research has indicated that the public may not have enough, if any, direct experience with an organization to form a grounded conclusion as to whether goals are being met; instead, media accounts, sometimes in the form of negative editorials, may fill in the void. This points out the need for administrators to engage the surrounding environment and put forth positive information and expectations about the effectiveness of their agencies.

Goodsell (2004) noted that the public is more satisfied with specific governmental programs than with the general concept of government itself. The finding suggests that administrators may need to place more effort in not only communicating their program's value to the public but in asking the public's opinion about specific programs. With shortcomings between objective and subjective measures, citizen surveys may fill the gap of understanding that administrators may currently lack. In addition, this dialogue not only improves communication that might lead to implementation of more responsive programs, but it fosters the type of community partnership that the community policing concept demands.

The benefits and drawbacks to citizen surveys have been reviewed in this paper, and this author is of the opinion that the tool is more valuable than previously thought. In the sense that it may possibly produce new ideas from the public, create greater responsiveness, and strengthen police–community bonds, the citizen survey seems to be part and parcel with the community policing concept. It seems that the basic areas addressed by the CALEA standards provide strong groundwork in addressing concerns common to all departments, in that they allow minor adjustments to be made for specific organizations while focusing on major concepts. Including some level of uniformity is a major key, as mentioned in the brief discussion on accreditation, that will lead to the creation of more meaningful statistical analyses, whose implications will not be limited to one jurisdiction due to poor formatting.

REFERENCES

Bayley, David H. (1996). *Measuring overall effectiveness.* In L.T. Hoover (Ed.), *Quantifying quality in policing*, 37–54. Washington, D.C.: Police Executive Research Forum.

Brown, Karin & Coulter, Philip B. (1983, January–February). Subjective and objective Measures of police service delivery. *Public administration review, 43*(1), 50–58.

Brudney, Jeffrey L. & England, Robert E. (1982, March–April). Urban policy making and subjective service evaluations: Are they compatible? *Public administration review, 42*(2), 127–135.

Commission on Accreditation for Law Enforcement Agencies. (n.d.). Benefits of accreditation. (n.d.). Retrieved June 10, 2005 from http://www.calea.org/newweb/accreditation%20Info/majorbenefits.htm.

Commission on Accreditation for Law Enforcement Agencies. (2004). Standards manual.

Decker, Theodore. (2005, June 16). City officer gets probation for drug thefts. *Patriot News.* Retrieved June 19, 2005, from http://www.pennlive.com/search/index.ssf?/base/news/111891383259820.xml?pennnews&coll=1.

Engel, Robin S. & Calnon, Jennifer M. (2004, March). Comparing benchmark methodologies for police-citizen contacts: traffic stop data collection for the Pennsylvania State Police. *Police quarterly, 7*(1), 97–125.

Glass, James J. (n.d.). *Citizen surveys: Powerful tools for public managers.* Auburn, AL: Center for Governmental Services.

Goodsell, Charles T. (2004). *The case for bureaucracy: A public administration polemic.* Fourth edition. Washington, D.C.: CQ Press.

Hellriegel, Don and Slocum, Jr., John. W. (2004). *Organizational behavior.* Tenth edition. Mason, OH: South-Western.

Holzer, Marc & Yang, Kaifeng. (2004). Performance measurement and improvement: An assessment of the state of the art. *International review of administrative sciences, 70*(1), 15–31.

Kelly, Janet M. & Swindell, David. (2002, September–October). A multiple-indicator approach to municipal service evaluation: Correlating performance measurement and citizen satisfaction across jurisdictions. *Public administration review, 62*(5), 610–621.

Melkers, Julia & Thomas, John C. (1998, July–August). What do administrators think citizens think? Administrator predictions as an adjunct to citizen surveys. *Public administration review, 58*(4), 327–334.

Morgan, David R. (1979). *Managing urban America.* North Scituate, MA: Duxbury Press.

National Academy of Public Administration. (1991, November 8). Performance monitoring and reporting by Public organizations. Resolution adopted at the academy's annual meeting.

Philadelphia Daily News. (2005, January 1). No radar love for state cops: State force needs outside policing. Retrieved June 1, 2005, from http://www.philly.com/mld/dailynews/news/special_packages/phillycom_front_d n/10586943.htm.

Philadelphia Police Department. (n.d.). Community Relations. Retrieved June 6, 2005 from http://www.ppdonline.org/cmty/.

Sims, Barbara, Hooper, Michael & Peterson, Steven A. (2002). Determinants of citizens' attitudes toward police: results of the Harrisburg citizen survey-1999. *Policing, 25*(3), 457–471.

Stipak, Brian. (1980, September–October). Local governments' use of citizen surveys. *Public administration review, 40*(5), 521–525.

Walker, Michael. (1994, September). Managers measure efficiency with citizen surveys. *The American city & county, 109*(10), 47.

Watson, Douglas J., Juster, Robert J. & Johnson, Gerald W. (1991, May–June). Institutionalized use of citizen surveys in the budgetary and policy-making processes: A small city case study. *Public administration review, 51*(3), 232–239.

Wells, William, Horney, Julie & Maguire, Edward R. (2005, June). Patrol officer Responses to citizen feedback: an experimental analysis. *Police quarterly, 8*(2), 171–205.

Whitaker, Gordon P. (1974, March). Who puts the value in evaluation? *Social science quarterly, 54*, 759–761.

Wholey, Joseph S. & Hatry, Harry P. (1992, November–December). The case for Performance monitoring. *Public administration review, 52*(6), 604–610.

Van Ryzin, Gregg G. (2004). Expectations, performance and citizen satisfaction with Urban services. *Journal of policy analysis and management, 23*(3), 433–448.

4 Examining the Role of the Police in Reentry Partnership Initiatives*

James M. Byrne and Don Hummer

CONTENTS

REDEFINING ROLES AND RELATIONSHIPS

The development of partnerships in law enforcement is not a new idea, but it does appear that today's police are much more likely to enter into partnerships than their predecessors, especially at the local level. One reason for this new collaborative mindset on the part of the nation's 21,143 police agencies (Maguire et al. 1998) is the adoption of community policing in many of these jurisdictions. Although a review of the research on the implementation and impact of community police reforms is beyond the scope of this chapter (for such review, see, for example, National Research Council 2004), it is worth noting that community policing programs do represent a

---

* Originally published in Federal Probation (2004). 68(2): 62–69. Reprinted with permission.

fundamental shift in strategy: rather than working alone (or in teams with other officers), patrol officers are encouraged to meet and work with community groups, personnel from social services, public health, and other criminal justice agencies to address the community's problems of crime and order maintenance.

As part of this new collaborative orientation, partnerships between police and a wide variety of agencies and community groups, including state and local corrections, are encouraged as an appropriate problem-solving strategy. Critics of community policing have pointed out that one consequence of such collaboration is to increase the span of control of police agencies, particularly in disadvantaged areas. With the help of these new "partners," local police can collect better and more detailed intelligence on residents, expand the scope of searches, and target both individuals (e.g., gang members and sex offenders) and "hot spot" areas (e.g., crack houses) for removal from the community. As Manning (2003) has pointed out, short-term gains in order maintenance in low-income, inner-city areas may be followed by long-term losses (moral, social, and political) in these same communities because of the negative consequences of incarceration on offenders, their families, and the communities in which they reside (and to which they will return). The potential for such unintended consequences must certainly be considered in the types of police–corrections partnerships highlighted in this chapter.

In addition to community policing reforms, sentencing reform can certainly be considered as another compelling impetus for police–corrections partnerships. Because of our reliance on incarceration as the "sanction of choice" for many crime categories (particularly drug offenders), we now have over 2 million inmates in custody in the United States. Last year, 600,000 inmates were released from federal, state, and local facilities—a threefold increase from just 20 years ago (RAND *Research Brief* 2003). Because of changes in "good time" provisions, tougher parole eligibility, and the establishment of mandatory minimum sentences, one in five of these new prison releasees were "max-outs," which effectively means that they returned to the community without the supervision, services, and control provided by community corrections agencies (e.g., probation and parole).

Who, if anyone, should fill this supervision, service, and control void? In many jurisdictions, the surveillance and control responsibility appears to be moving to the local police, who are likely to view prison releasees as a logical target population, especially given the "fact" that, in all likelihood, two-thirds of these offenders will be rearrested (and half will be reincarcerated) for new crimes within three years (Langan and Levin 2002). The provision of (voluntary) services for prisoners released without parole supervision is more problematic, but it does appear that both institutional and community corrections agencies are now beginning to recognize that they also need to expand their role and responsibility vis-à-vis this group of releasees. However, it is still unclear where the money will come from to fund services for these releasees who appear to be falling through the cracks of the current service provision network. Whatever the source, adequate funding for the mental health, housing, substance abuse, and public health problems of this subgroup of releasees appears to be a key to the success of the partnership. For reentry programs developed through federal grant and/or funds from private foundations, it will be interesting to "follow the money" as it flows to various partnership agencies because control of the *funding* for reentry will affect the nature, duration, and orientation (surveillance, treatment, and control) of the partnership.

An Overview of Police–Corrections Partnership Development in the United States

Parent and Snyder (1999) conducted a nationwide review of the utilization of police–corrections partnerships; in conjunction with this review, they completed site visits at 19 separate partnerships located across five states (Minnesota, Washington, Connecticut, Arizona, and California). According to the profiles included in the report, five different models of police–corrections partnerships can be identified:

1. *Enhanced supervision partnerships*, in which police and probation or parole officers perform joint supervision or other joint functions related to offenders in the community
2. *Fugitive apprehension units*, in which police and correctional agencies collaborate to locate and apprehend persons who have absconded from probation or parole supervision
3. *Information-sharing partnerships*, in which corrections and law enforcement agencies institute procedures to exchange information related to offenders
4. *Specialized enforcement partnerships*, in which police and correctional agencies, as well as community organizations, collaborate to rid communities of particular problems
5. *Interagency problem-solving partnerships*, in which law enforcement and correctional agencies confer to identify problems of mutual concern and to identify and implement solutions to them (Parent and Snyder 1999, 7)

These five models offer different strategies and problem contexts for the application of police–corrections partnerships to the myriad issues associated with offender reentry initiatives. Unfortunately, the authors of this report were unable to provide an estimate of the number of police–corrections partnerships currently in place in the United States that utilize at least one of these models.

Police–Corrections Partnerships and Offender Reentry

Partnerships between law enforcement and corrections agencies appear to be an emerging strategy adopted by several federal agencies (NIJ [National Institute of Justice], NIC [National Institute of Corrections], OJJDP [Office of Juvenile Justice and Delinquency Prevention]) that provide funding for a wide range of offender reentry initiatives at the federal, state, and local levels. In several jurisdictions, partnership development is a prerequisite for federal funding of the initiative (Taxman, Young, and Byrne 2003a). However, from where did this newfound "faith" in partnership emerge? In the absence of empirical research, it appears that program developers have turned to another source: the experience of public sector managers involved in a wide range of problem-solving scenarios. A number of recent reviews of organizational effectiveness in the public sector (see, for example, U.S. General Accounting Office 2004 for an overview) have emphasized the importance of the strategic use of partnerships to address issues involving multiple agencies and systems. According to the participants at a recent GAO forum on this issue, "to be a high-performing organization, … Agencies must effectively manage and influence relationships with organizations outside of their direct control" (GAO 2004, 9). Viewed in this light, police–corrections partnerships represent an attempt by two independent agencies to work together to solve a common problem. In the process, the question can certainly be raised: Who is influencing whom? At their core, police–corrections partnerships can be defined by the types of roles and relationships that emerge between participating organizations and agencies. In the following text, we examine "roles and relationships" across eight "model" reentry partnership initiatives identified by The Office of Justice Programs.[1] These eight program models certainly do not represent the full range of reentry programs currently available across the country,[2] but they do provide a solid analytic foundation from which we can examine the problems and potential inherent in police–corrections partnerships.

Despite fundamental differences in philosophy, background, and orientation toward offenders, police–corrections partnerships have the potential to enhance public safety, streamline service provisions, and achieve common goals such as crime reduction (Parent and Snyder 1999). They also may have unintended long-term consequences for both offenders and communities, which must be examined before we move further in this area. As described in the following text, the Reentry Partnership Initiative (RPI) is an example of a cooperative effort to maximize law enforcement and correctional resources in a meaningful way to address a specific target issue (offender reentry). Developed by the Office of Justice Programs of the Federal Department of Justice, RPI programs form a partnership among criminal justice, social service, and community groups to develop and implement a reentry process. A key component for a successful RPI program is the linking of local law enforcement with other agencies and actors responsible for offender reintegration. By working in conjunction with corrections personnel and extending the partnerships to include other agencies, police can enhance their presence in target neighborhoods and, in the process, generate support for collaborative efforts from policymakers and the general public (Parent and Snyder 1999).

In the following section, we describe the specific role of law enforcement in collaborating with representatives of corrections agencies as well as with other key actors within the RPI (community, treatment providers, victims, and offenders). In doing so, we demonstrate the pivotal role that police have in implementing a successful "shared-decision-making" partnership for offender reintegration, while also highlighting the potential problems inherent in this strategy.

IDENTIFYING THE ROLE OF POLICE AT EACH KEY PHASE IN THE REENTRY PROCESS

Local police departments have played a critical role in the development of the RPI model in several sites across the country. In an earlier review of eight "model" reentry programs completed by Taxman, Young, and Byrne (2003a), three key phases of the RPI model are described in detail: the institutional phase, the structured reentry phase, and the community reintegration phase (see Figure 4.1). Based on their detailed reviews of reentry initiatives in eight separate jurisdictions (Maryland, Vermont, South Carolina, Missouri, Florida, Nevada, Massachusetts, and Washington), we can describe and discuss the role of the police in each of these phases of reentry.[3] We have examined similarities and differences across these eight jurisdictions in the nature, type, duration, and intensity of police involvement in each phase of

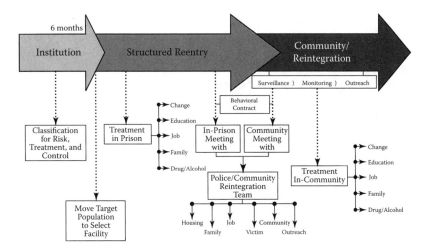

FIGURE 4.1   Reentry partnership continuum.

the offender reentry process. It is our hope that such a review will provide critical information to program developers interested in the applicability of police–corrections partnerships to the complex problems associated with offender reentry.

THE ROLE OF POLICING DURING THE INSTITUTIONAL PHASE OF REENTRY

During the institutional phase of an offender-reentry program, a number of decisions have to be made about offenders that involve local law enforcement, both directly and indirectly. Consider, for example, the selection of the target population for a new reentry program. Although the timing of the decision varied from jurisdiction to jurisdiction, local police departments have been involved in the selection of the RPI target population at several sites. The rationale underlying this strategy is fairly straightforward. The decision regarding whom to include and exclude from a particular reentry program should be made by the entire partnership, rather than one specific agency. By sharing decision-making vis-à-vis the targeting issue, program developers have increased the likelihood of police support for, and partial control of, the reentry initiative.

The dangers inherent in allowing a single agency (e.g., institutional corrections) to determine program eligibility were highlighted in the review of Las Vegas, Nevada's reentry program, in which only offenders from specific "weed and seed" areas were targeted. The police chief refused to participate in the program because of the fear that the program was tantamount to racial profiling: only neighborhoods with high minority concentration were being targeted for the partnership reentry effort.

The police chief's fear was based on the possibility or likelihood that offenders reentering these targeted neighborhoods will face much closer police scrutiny (i.e., stops, surveillance, etc.) than offenders released to other areas of the city. If such scrutiny leads to higher rearrest, reconviction, and/or return-to-prison rates for offenders released to high minority concentration areas, then the negative consequences of this "place-based" targeting decision would be substantiated. However, no such research was conducted at this site as the RPI program was only in its initial development stage. Rather than implement the reentry program and then monitor the comparative rearrest, reconviction, and return-to-prison rates of releasees citywide, the chief made a simple suggestion: expand the program beyond the initial weed and seed target sites in order to broaden the population targeted for potential police profiling.

Regardless of the specific targeting decisions made across the eight reentry programs we reviewed (Taxman, Byrne, and Young 2002), it does seem reasonable to raise the racial profiling issue and consider the implications for police–corrections partnerships. As Manning (2003, 54) recently observed,

> Racial profiling is the use of expert systems and documents that advise or encourage stopping people of a given "profile"—e.g., black teenagers; a black man in an expensive foreign car; long-haired drivers of beat-up vans; a black driver in a "white" suburban area of a city. It goes to the explicit policy-driven attempt of agencies to direct discretion and increase, for example, arrests on drug charges (Manning, 2001). Profiling of a less systematic sort is the heart of all policing—stops based on distrust, suspicion, awareness of people "out of place" in time or space, past experience, stereotyping, and other common typifications (2003, 54–55).

By targeting specific subgroups of all released offenders for inclusion in reentry programs, developers certainly increase the *awareness* of local police vis-à-vis this subgroup of returning offenders, while also changing the way police *respond* to these offenders in the community. Police in the RPI programs we visited were expected to monitor offenders' progress in the community either by direct observations (e.g., home visits and field stops) or by utilizing any combination of community information sources (e.g., victims, volunteer guardians, treatment providers, community corrections personnel, and employers). They were also expected to respond proactively to this information (e.g., increased face-to-face personal contacts, focusing on specific issues related to the victim, progress in treatment, employment, and housing), based on the notion that this type of police-initiated response might be effective, especially when it is focused on an individual offender's progress, addressing the problems that resulted in his or her most recent incarceration (i.e., substance abuse, mental illness, employment, family problems, etc.). But despite such benevolent intentions, it is certainly possible that offender targeting represents yet another manifestation of the profiling problem. Once again, it is Peter Manning (2003) who offers the most succinct summary of the research on police profiling:

> The data are overwhelming—people of color, no matter what their presence on the roads, work, or past record, are disproportionately stopped, searched, arrested, charged, and imprisoned (Meehan and Ponder 2002a,b; Walker, Spohn, and DeLone 1996) (55).

In addition to their role in offender-targeting decisions, police may also be able to assist in other decisions made during the institutional phase of RPI, such as offender classification, institutional location, and institutional treatment. Local police have information about offenders that may be shared with institutional staff involved in offender classification and placement, such as peer or gang associations, family history, and the nature of the offense committed. In addition, police at one site (Vermont) serve on local community "restorative justice" boards that review and approve the offender's institutional treatment plan within 45 days of incarceration. Although only one of the eight sites we visited included the police in decision making regarding institutional treatment (for substance abuse, anger management, and other behavioral issues), it can certainly be argued that the police have a stake in offender treatment decisions. By including police in the treatment decision-making process, Vermont's RPI program developers have given police officers an opportunity to see, firsthand, how offenders change and the value of treatment interventions throughout the system.

THE ROLE OF POLICING DURING THE STRUCTURED REENTRY PHASE

The second phase of the RPI model involves structured reentry to the community. Police have an important role in decision making during this second phase of reentry (see Figure 4.2). Typically, the structured reentry phase of RPI programs focuses on the last few months before release and the first month after release. It is during this period that an offender reintegration plan is developed and a number of basic decisions are made about when the offender will be released, whether specific release conditions will be established, where the offender will live and work, and how the offender will address his or her ongoing treatment needs. Depending on the jurisdiction we visited, police were involved in one or more of these structured reentry decision points.

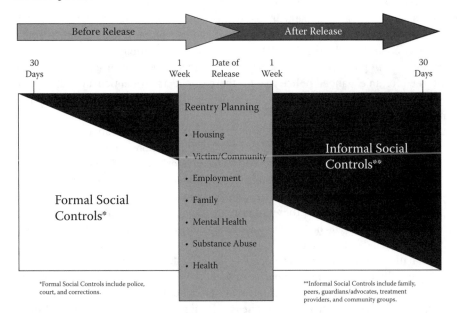

FIGURE 4.2 Overview of structured reentry phase.

Perhaps the most controversial and innovative structured reentry strategy that involves police is the use of community boards (as in Vermont) to review the offender's progress in treatment and to make release recommendations. As the local police departments are represented on these boards, they will have a say in release decisions and, in some cases, on the conditions of release. It will be interesting to track the impact of community boards on release decisions in their jurisdiction and to observe the court's response to the inevitable challenges to the authority of these community boards to essentially make early-release (i.e., parole) decisions.

In several jurisdictions, the police will meet with the offenders in prison to discuss their impending release. The purpose of this meeting is twofold: first, to explain to the offenders how local policing has changed since they were initially incarcerated because of the current emphasis on community policing (and crime prevention); and second, to let the offenders know that the police will be watching them upon release and monitoring their progress in treatment, and that they will not be anonymous. Will one meeting between the offender and a neighborhood police officer deter the offender from criminal behavior upon release? We doubt it, but there is more involved here than an attempt to "scare" an offender straight. In Lowell, Massachusetts, for example, the police meet with the offender in conjunction with the local treatment provider, who describes the types of treatment programs available for offenders returning to the community. It is a dual message—treatment and control—that the offender hears at this meeting. Equally important, the meeting establishes an essential partnership between local police and treatment providers, which will continue for the remainder of the offender's stay in the reentry program.

Another facet of the police role during the structured reentry process is the contact between the police and the offender during the first few days after the offender has been released from prison. For offenders released conditionally, police surveillance and contact serves as a supplement to probation and parole supervision. For offenders released unconditionally, police surveillance and contact represents the *only* formal offender control mechanism. Because over 20 percent of offenders nationwide leave prison *without* probation or parole supervision, there does appear to be an immediate need for an expanded police role for these offenders. We anticipate that in some RPI jurisdictions, such as the Lowell, Massachusetts (in this state, over half of prison releasees have maxed-out), police will be in contact with local treatment providers and thus will know who is—and who is not—participating in treatment, which may affect the nature and timing of police–offender interactions. In other jurisdictions (e.g., Spokane, Washington) police will meet regularly with volunteer community "guardians," who will provide assistance to offenders immediately upon release from prison (such as helping with housing, transportation, etc.), placing them in a unique position to assess offender progress during reentry. In these jurisdictions, it appears that police departments have begun to fill the void created by sentencing reform generally and mandatory sentencing in particular.

Finally, one jurisdiction developed a unique strategy for improving the community surveillance and control capacity of local police. In conjunction with the State Department of Corrections, the crime analysis unit of the Lowell police department develops "profiles" of each offender released from prison and returning to the Lowell community each month, which are displayed at roll call. These profiles include the offender's most recent picture, criminal record, gang affiliations (if any), and nature of last offense. This is certainly one possible strategy for reducing the anonymity of offenders returning to the community by increasing police awareness of the reentering offender population.

THE ROLE OF THE POLICE DURING THE COMMUNITY REINTEGRATION PHASE

The third phase of the RPI model is the community reintegration phase, which emphasizes long-term offender change, an elusive goal for the corrections system. The underlying assumption of RPI program developers is that, during this final phase of reentry, there will be a transition from formal to informal social control mechanisms, such as the offender's family, peer groups, faith-based community groups, employers, guardians, and other community members. The response of the police to reentry offenders during this final phase is likely to vary according to the behavior of the offender. For example, if the offender is employed and participating in treatment, then the police department's interaction with the offender will likely be minimal. However, offenders who have difficulty with the initial transition from prison to home will likely face much more intensive police intervention (both formal and informal). In Burlington, Vermont, and Spokane, Washington, for example, the police work in conjunction with local community corrections staff to conduct curfew checks on targeted offenders both by home visits and stops at targeted locations (e.g., bars and street corners). Police may also act informally by simply talking with at-risk offenders—those who appear to be having trouble finding a job or suitable housing, and are receiving treatment for mental health or substance abuse problems. It appears that the police have a role in the community reintegration phase that will change over time based on the behavior of the offender and the specific features of the reentry program examined.

THE POLICE AND INSTITUTIONAL CORRECTIONS

When we think about the police, it is usually in the context of offender control, not offender change. But police departments in RPI jurisdictions view their role somewhat differently: they are involved in both offender control and offender change activities. In Vermont, for example, police serve on local community boards that review and approve each offender's institutional treatment plan, which was developed by the offender (in conjunction with prison program staff) within 45 days of incarceration. They are also involved in reviewing the offender's progress in treatment and in the development of a structured reentry plan. Although Vermont is unique in terms of the police role in institutional treatment, the police are actively involved in prerelease planning in several jurisdictions (e.g., Massachusetts, Washington, and Maryland).

RPI programs require that police act in new ways toward the offender, not only upon release but also while incarcerated. For example, police officers at several sites actually visit the offender while in prison to discuss the police department's role in the reentry program. In the Lowell, Massachusetts, program, a neighborhood police officer meets with the offender in prison about a month before the offender is scheduled to return to the officer's neighborhood. Importantly, the officer does not attend this meeting alone; he or she goes as part of a neighborhood reentry team that also includes a local treatment provider. The utilization of a police–community treatment provider partnership team *within* an institutional setting represents a new role for the police in the institution. At the meeting, the neighborhood police officer describes how the police department has changed in recent years in this community, due in large part to two factors: (1) community policing and (2) more cops on the street. The officer then focuses on his or her dual role as a resource person or problem solver and community surveillance/ control officer. The "message" that the offender receives is that the police are there to help him or her, but that they will do their "helping" within the broader context of public safety. In the name of public safety, police officers will *not* allow offenders to return to the community anonymously; informal surveillance of reentry offenders will occur. Massachusetts is not the only site to employ this strategy; other sites using similar approaches include Washington, Maryland, South Carolina, and Missouri.

The police will also interact with institutional corrections staff in a wide variety of activities directly related to offender reentry. First, meetings with offenders in prison must be coordinated through the state department of corrections. Next, the development of offender profiles to be used by local police will require information to be shared by the research staffs of the releasing institution and the police department (e.g., current offenses, criminal history, institutional behavior, gang affiliations, and specific release conditions). Third, the target population selected for the program should reflect police preferences. Finally, police may participate on community boards that have a direct impact on release decisions and/or the conditions of release. In Vermont, for example, offenders are expected to develop (individual) offender responsibility plans, which are reviewed by restorative justice boards comprising a wide range of community members, including the police.

When the topic of prison release is raised, it is usually within the context of judicial and/or parole decision making. However, it can certainly be argued that police departments should have a role in release decisions as well, in such areas as the timing of the release, the offender's location in a particular community, and the determination (where applicable) of release conditions. Once again, it is Burlington, Vermont's, restorative justice model that provides the framework for this type of active police participation in the structured release process. In Vermont's RPI model, police serve on community boards that review the offender's *individual responsibility plan* approximately one month prior to the offender's proposed release date. If the offender has made progress in addressing the problem/need areas identified in the plan, then the community board will likely recommend release; but if the offender has not made sufficient progress, then the board would likely not support release. In essence, the local community board—with active police involvement—will be acting as a parole board at this site.

THE POLICE AND TREATMENT PROVIDERS

As noted earlier, the role of the police in the reentry process will change not only with respect to police–offender interactions but also in the nature and extent of police–treatment provider interactions. For many officers, this program provides them with their first opportunity to work directly and collaboratively with treatment providers. For both parties, this new partnership will likely require some intensive cross-training during the program's initial stages because both the police and the treatment provider come from quite different backgrounds and skill orientations. In such partnerships, role conflict is inevitable.

For the RPI program to be effective, this type of ongoing role conflict will have to be addressed. At one site we visited, for example, treatment staff expressed concern that offenders would not agree to participate in (voluntary) treatment programs upon release because they believed that the offenders would have trouble "trusting" the treatment providers if they arrived at the meeting along with the police. It is possible that such concerns are valid; it is also possible that they actually reflect the treatment provider's orientation toward police, not the offender's perspective. In any event, information sharing between police and treatment providers appears to be an essential feature of a reentry program, where differential police surveillance and control is triggered by an offender's progress in treatment.

THE POLICE AND COMMUNITY CORRECTIONS

In the eight programs we examined, we see indications of a fundamental change in the nature and extent of the interaction between police and community corrections personnel (e.g., probation/parole). In Spokane, Washington, for example, police and community supervision officers are physically located in the same "cop shops," where they often share information on offenders under community supervision. In Vermont, police and community corrections officers conduct joint "curfew checks" on reentry offenders, targeting specific locations in the community (e.g., bars) where offenders may be located. In Las Vegas, Nevada, community supervision officers focus exclusively on the surveillance and control aspects of community supervision. As these community supervision officers also have police "arrest" powers (and training), it could be argued that, in this jurisdiction, the line between police and community supervision officers is becoming blurred.

In Massachusetts, the Lowell police department's intelligence unit creates "posters" for each offender released to the community each month, which are hung up in the police station for officers to view at roll call. It is assumed that this information will result in an increased level of informal surveillance by police in target communities and that the results of these surveillance activities will be shared with the community supervision officers who work in this area.

In South Carolina, officers from the police and sheriff's department contact offenders immediately upon release from prison, either by phone or by home visit. The purpose of this contact is twofold: first, to demonstrate the "helping role" of police by identifying available community resources and services; and second, to reinforce the surveillance and control role of local police. It certainly appears that the role of local police is to enhance (or supplement) community supervision among conditional releasees while taking primary responsibility for those inmates released unconditionally.

THE POLICE AND THE COMMUNITY

RPI programs have affected the way police departments interact with local community residents and groups, including crime victims. At two sites—Missouri and Vermont—

neighborhood police officers sit on local community boards that make a wide range of decisions affecting offenders both directly and indirectly. In Washington, police departments work with volunteer "guardians" who assist offenders in a variety of areas (e.g., transportation, job preparation, and housing), while also acting as another set of "eyes and ears" for the police. In Vermont and Missouri, police officers serve on restorative justice boards involved in all aspects of institutional treatment and community reintegration. As these examples illustrate, the role of the police in the community has certainly been expanded to include both informal social control strategies (e.g., the use of guardians) and the pursuit of community justice initiatives. Will such an expanded police role improve the reentry prospects of offenders, or will it have potentially detrimental consequences for both the offenders and communities? At this point in the design, implementation, and evaluation process, the answer to this question is clear: we do not know. For this reason, it is important that we examine the impact of this new wave of reentry programs on both targeted offenders (e.g., rearrest, reconviction, and reincarceration) and targeted communities (e.g., crime rates, disease rates, and poverty rates).

THE POLICE AND THE VICTIM

The police play an important role in reentry not only in the areas of offender surveillance and control but also in the provision of services to victims and families of victims. Victims of crime have problems and needs that are only partially addressed when the alleged offender is arrested. An examination of clearance rates (i.e., the number of reported crimes cleared by the arrest of the offenders) reveals that most jurisdictions do a pretty good job of making an arrest when the reported crime was a crime against a person (with clearance rates usually around 50 percent); they are not nearly as effective when it is a property crime (20 percent clearance rates). As only a fraction of all arrested offenders are convicted and incarcerated, it is not surprising that community residents ask the police for help with the "offenders walking among us" (e.g., dispute resolution, formal and informal surveillance, active investigation). Because nine out of ten offenders who enter prison eventually get out, it seems logical that crime victims would ask the police for help with these offenders as well, especially when the offender has maxed-out of prison.

Victims of crime may need information on when the offender is being released and where he or she is planning to reside. They may want assistance in resolving ongoing disputes with the offender and his or her family and friends. They may also want increased police surveillance and protection. Finally, they may ask for police assistance in filing restraining orders against the offender, especially if child protection and/or domestic violence is an issue. Although getting out of prison is "good news" for the offender, it is a time of great anxiety and stress for many crime victims, friends, and family. In the past, victims could turn to community corrections for help and assistance; now, this role and responsibility appears to have moved to the police, particularly for those offenders released unconditionally from prison or jail.

THE POLICE AND THE OFFENDER

To some observers, it may seem paradoxical that police departments are now active partners in offender reentry initiatives, as these same departments were actively involved in removing these offenders from the community in the first place. To others, however, police–corrections partnerships represent an attempt to address the underlying causes of criminal behavior by focusing on a variety of individual-level and community-level problems that have been linked to criminality.

At the individual level, offenders are often afflicted with multiple problems, including drug addiction, alcoholism, communicable disease, and mental illness. As a recent RAND *Research Brief* highlighted, "... almost 25 percent of state prisoners released by year-end 1999 were alcohol-dependent, 14 percent were mentally ill, and 12 percent were homeless at the time of arrest (2003, 1)." RAND researchers go on to report that offenders released from prison have an eight to nine times higher prevalence rate for HIV (compared to the general population), a nine to ten times greater prevalence rate for Hepatitis C, a five times greater prevalence rate for AIDS, and a three to five times greater prevalence rate for serious mental illness (i.e., schizophrenia or other psychotic disorders). For many of these offenders, substance abuse has been a significant, long-standing problem (National Commission on Correctional Health Care, 2002). Unless these individual-level problems are addressed, it seems inevitable that this month's releasees will be next month's rearrests and next year's "new" prison admissions.

Of course, the types of individual-level problems just described cannot be addressed without recognizing their broader community context (see, for example, Sampson, Raudenbush, and Earls 1997). Community-level problems include unemployment, income inequality, inadequate housing, homelessness, and ineffective informal social control networks (i.e., family, school, church, neighborhood). The police–corrections partnerships highlighted in this review appear to recognize the need to address problems at both the individual and community levels. However, it is still unclear exactly how the "zero-tolerance" policing strategies commonly associated with the "broken windows" version of community policing (Kelling and Coles 1996; Bratton, Wilson, Kelling, Rivers, and Cove 2004) will coexist with RPI program initiatives designed to provide housing, treatment, services, and support to targeted offenders.[4] Ultimately, the success of police–corrections partnerships may hinge on the ability of local police to work simultaneously on crime prevention and crime control initiatives, and in the process, to resolve the conflicts inherent in current broken windows policing strategies.

A proactive, problem-solving approach is at the core of police–offender interactions in reentry jurisdictions. In the RPI model, police visit offenders in prison prior to release rather than wait until the offender is back on the street. Utilizing the latest offender-profile data, police know who are returning to their community *before* they are released. And when police interact with offenders once they return to the community, it is *before*, not after, a problem occurs or there is a call for service. It will likely take some time for offenders to realize that the role of the police in reentry jurisdictions has changed and that police are now involved in activities (related to housing, employment, and treatment) that can help them turn their lives around (Taxman, Young and Byrne 2003b). However, offenders must also recognize that the police will know where they live, who are in treatment, and whether they are employed; and that they will adjust their surveillance and control activities based on this information. It remains to be seen whether the police–offender interactions associated with reentry initiatives will have their intended effect both on individual offender change and community-level order maintenance.

CONCLUSION

The police–corrections partnerships described in this chapter represent an important shift in both the philosophy and practice of prisoner reentry. Given the inherent conflict associated with the interests of police and institutional corrections vis-à-vis offender reentry (after all, police remove offenders from the community and corrections send them "home" again, often to the same community), it is remarkable that these programs have emerged and appear to be successful, at least in terms of implementation.[5] However, a number of issues related to the expanded role of police in the offender reentry process still need to be resolved, including (1) the potential for racial profiling, inherent in offender/community targeting decisions, (2) the limits of information sharing across agencies (in particular, between police and treatment providers), and (3) the impact of this expanded role for police on both offenders released from prison or jail and the communities to which they return. Similarly, both institutional and community corrections agencies will have to consider their own need for role redefinition, particularly regarding offenders who max-out of prison and return to the community without the surveillance, services, and control provided by traditional community corrections agencies. Police departments across the eight jurisdictions we visited appear to be filling the void created by sentencing reforms, but the long-term consequences of this expanded police role—for both offenders and the communities targeted for reentry—have yet to be evaluated.

SELECTED REFERENCES

Bratton, W., J.Q. Wilson, G. Kelling, R.E. Rivers, and P. Cove (2004). This works: Crime prevention and the future of broken windows policing. *Civic Bulletin* 35: 1–14.

Byrne, J.M., F.S. Taxman, and D. Young (2002). *Emerging Roles and Responsibility in the Reentry Partnership Initiative: New Ways of Doing Business.* Washington, D.C.: National Institute of Justice.

Harrison, P. and J. Beck (2003). *Prisoners in 2002.* Washington, D.C.: U.S. Department of Justice, Office of Justice Programs, Bureau of Justice Statistics, NIC 200248.

Kelling, G. and C. Coles (1996). Fixing Broken Windows: Restoring Order and Reducing Crime in our Communities. New York, NY: Free Press.

Langan, P. and D. Levin (2002). *Recidivism of Prisoners Released in 1994.* Washington, D.C.: U.S. Department of Justice, Bureau of Justice Statistics NCI 193427.

Maguire, E. (1997). Structural change in large police organizations. *Justice Quarterly* 14: 547–576.

Maguire, E., Ju. Snipes, C. Uchida, and M. Townsend (1998). Counting cops: Estimating the number of police departments and police officers in the USA. *Policing: An International Journal of Police Strategies & Management* 21: 97–120.

Manning, P. (2003). *Policing Contingencies.* Chicago, IL: University of Chicago Press.

Manning, P. (2001). Theorizing policing: The drama and myth of crime control in the NYPD. *Theoretical Criminology* 5: 315–344.

Maruna, S. and R. Immarigeon. (Eds.) (2004). *After Crime and Punishment: Pathways to Offender Reintegration.* Portland, OR: Willan Publishing.

Meehan, A. and M. Ponder (2003a). How roadway composition matters in analyzing police data on racial profiling. *Police Quarterly* 5: 306–333.

Meehan, A. and M. Ponder (2002b). Race and place: The ecology of racial profiling African American drivers. *Justice Quarterly* 19: 399–430.

National Commission on Correctional Health Care (2002). *The Health Status of Soon-To-Be-Released Inmates*, Vol. 1. Washington, D.C.: Office of Justice Programs.

National Research Council (2004). *Fairness and Effectiveness in Policing.* Washington, D.C.: National Academy Press.

Parent, D. and B. Snyder (1999). *Police-Corrections Partnerships.* Washington, D.C.: National Institute of Justice.

Petersilia, J. (2004) What works in prison re-entry? Reviewing and questioning the evidence. *Federal Probation.* 68: 4–8.

Rand (2003). Prisoner reentry: What are the public health challenges? *RAND Research Brief.* Santa Monica, CA: RAND, RB-6013-PSJ.

Sampson, R., S. Raudenbush, and F. Earls (1997). Neighborhoods and violent crime. *Science* 227: 918–924.

Taxman, F.S., D. Young, and J.M. Byrne (2003a). *From Prison Safety to Public Safety: Best Practices in Offender Reentry.* Washington, D.C.: National Institute of Justice.

Taxman, F.S., D. Young, and J.M. Byrne (2003b). *Offender's Views of Reentry: Implications for Processes, Programs, and Services.* Washington, D.C.: National Institute of Justice.

Taxman, F.S., J. Byrne, and D. Young (2002). *Targeting for Reentry: Matching Needs and Services to Maximize Public Safety.* Washington, D.C.: National Institute of Justice.

U.S. General Accounting Office (February, 2004). *High-Performing Organizations: Metrics, Means, and Mechanisms for Achieving High Performance in the 21st Century Management Environment.* GAO-04-343SP. Washington, D.C.

Walker, S., C. Spohn, and M. DeLone (1996). *The Color of Justice.* Belmont, CA: Wadsworth.

ENDNOTES

[1] This chapter has been adapted from a report prepared for The National Institute of Justice, Office of Justice Programs. *Emerging Roles and Responsibilities in the Reentry Partnership Initiative: New Ways of Doing Business.* James Byrne, Faye Taxman and Douglas Young (Aug. 2002).

[2] For more detail on the research highlighted in this chapter, see the series of articles prepared for NIJ under grant 2000IJCX0045 and available from NCJRS.

[3] The eight case studies of model Reentry Partnership Initiative (RPI) programs were conducted in the spring of 2001 by an evaluation team directed by Faye Taxman, University of Maryland, who served as the principal investigator of the NIJ-sponsored evaluation. The site visits were conducted by Dr. Taxman (Florida, Massachusetts, South Carolina, Maryland), Dr. Byrne (Massachusetts, Vermont, Maryland, Nevada, and Washington), Doug Young (Maryland, Missouri, Washington), Meredith Thanner (Nevada, South Carolina), Dr. Anspach (Vermont), and Dr. Holsinger (Missouri). Copies of individual site evaluations can be obtained by contacting either Faye Taxman or James Byrne.

[4] Consider, for example, the problem of subway crime. Kelling has argued that the main cause of subway crime in New York City was lawlessness, not homelessness, and "it didn't take much time to end that culture once you figured out what the problem was" (2004, 8). The problem with Kelling's conceptualization is that it suggests that police can maintain order in the subway without addressing the homelessness problem of these "lawless" individuals. A very different approach to this problem would be taken by police in the reentry programs we visited; in many jurisdictions, there would be a zero-tolerance policy on homelessness among releasees from prison, not on minor subway crime.

[5] Despite the recent research attention focused on the offender reentry issue (see, for example, Maruna and Immarigeon, (2004) for an overview), we know remarkably little about the impact of adult reentry programs on either offenders or communities (see Petersilia, (2004), for a preliminary review).

5 Dilemmas Confronting Female Police Officer Promotional Candidates: Glass Ceiling, Disenfranchisement, or Satisfaction?

Thomas S. Whetstone and Deborah G. Wilson

CONTENTS

ABSTRACT

Through an analysis of data from one large Midwestern municipal police agency, this study examined some of the issues affecting the promotion of female police officers. Specifically, the issues influencing the decision concerning whether to enter the promotional process, and once a decision is made to enter the process, those factors influencing women during the promotional process, were examined. Within the agency under study, the rate of promotion for females still lags behind that for males. The study found that personal "choices" constrained by impediments from both within and outside the organization contributed to the lack of parity. Based on these findings, suggestions were made for strategies to increase the numbers of women, relative to men, in supervisory and managerial positions.

INTRODUCTION

Women in policing continue to move forward in their respective organizations albeit at a rather slow pace. Since 1893, when Mary Owens became the first woman to be given complete arrest powers by the Chicago police (Schulz 1993), women have struggled to find franchise and the opportunity to make meaningful contributions to the profession. In 1968, Betty Blankenship and Elizabeth Coffal of Indianapolis were assigned to patrol, and began to answer basic service calls. In 1970, J.V. Wilson, Chief of Police in Washington, D.C., began allowing women and men to perform the same duties (Schulz 1993).

Although the role of female police officers was expanding in terms of the breadth of responsibilities and variety of assignments, it was still rare for women to be promoted to positions that were supervisory, managerial, and of command rank in nature. This situation has continued to exist in spite of the fact that, once given the opportunity to serve in equal capacity with male officers, women have performed well, if not excelled, despite the dire predictions of more than a few police "traditionalists." Numerous studies have been published defining and discussing the various societal and organizational constraints for women in policing. Baylin (1993) observed that work and home life have heretofore been viewed as separate spheres but suggested that both are inseparable parts of a contiguous whole. These studies have illustrated the impact of both subtle and overt discrimination as well as the existence of more than a few "good ol' boy" systems. This study, built upon prior research, has examined some of the underlying reasons for the underrepresentation of women in supervisory and command positions within law enforcement organizations through an analysis of factors that affect womens' participation in the promotional process.

LITERATURE

In 1965, Felicia Schpritzer became the first woman police officer promoted to the rank of sergeant in the New York City Police Department. Although this initial promotion of a woman to a supervisory position occurred more than 30 years ago, women remain grossly underrepresented in supervisory and administrative ranks (S.E. Martin and Jurik 1996). Analyses such as those of Martin (1991) show increases in the number of women police supervisors and managers, yet these numbers remain proportionately low in comparison to their male counterparts. This inequity in representation occurs in spite of administrative efforts to achieve parity and the outstanding performance of women promotional candidates. Belknap (1996) found that women may have broken into the police profession, but they are still unlikely to become upper-level police managers. The "glass ceiling" effect has been noted within not only law enforcement but throughout the criminal justice system as well as the private sector (Belknap 1996; S.E. Martin and Jurik 1996; Moyer 1992; Rosener 1995).

Analyses of the upward mobility of women in work organizations have generally supported the theory that they are constrained by conformance with societal norms and expectations (Astin 1984). It is these same constraints that challenge women in law enforcement.

During the 1970s, police departments responded to race and sex discrimination as varied civil actions raised issues concerning entry requirements, selection criteria, and procedures regarding promotions (C. Martin 1996; S.E. Martin 1991; Potts 1983; Sulton and Townsey 1981). In some instances, court orders established affirmative action programs that directed departments to set quotas and time periods to hire and promote minorities and women.

The result of this legal intervention was an increase in the number of women police officers and minority women police officers in law enforcement agencies. The percentage of female police officers increased from 4.2 percent in 1978 to 8.8 percent in 1986. Similarly, during this same time period, the percentage of minority women police officers increased from 1.6 to 3.5 percent. With respect to representation within supervisory positions, the percentage of female supervisors also increased from 1 percent in 1978 to 3.3 percent in 1986, and minority representation among women supervisors from 20 to 33 percent during this same time period (S.E. Martin 1991). However, despite efforts to hire and promote women, their representation relative to their numbers in the general population and their representation among supervisors relative to their representation within law enforcement agencies remained low and continues to fail to meet parity with men (Belknap 1996).

The effect of forced affirmative action programs on the upward mobility of women within police departments was evident but limited. In departments with forced affirmative action programs, women accounted for 3.5 percent of all supervisors, whereas in departments with voluntarily implemented or no affirmative action programs, women accounted for 2.4 and 2.2 percent of all supervisors, respectively (S.E. Martin 1991).

These affirmative action policies influenced the upward mobility of women through various factors. One of these was the qualification of women officers for promotion. In those departments with mandated affirmative action policies, 8.3 percent of the women were eligible for promotion compared to 6 percent in departments with voluntary policies and 4.5 percent in those with no policies. This may seem to support Rosener (1995) who found that men complained that women got promoted because of affirmative action or special preference, not on merit or ability. The policies, in fact, were of more practical significance in promotional qualification than in the actual number of women promoted (S.E. Martin 1991).

Many factors have been identified as contributing to the lack of proportionate representation of women among police officers. Those difficulties reported most often by women in policing are organizational climate, discrimination, and alternative priorities of female officers (Belknap and Shelly 1993; Lanier 1996; C. Martin 1996; S.E. Martin and Jurik 1996; Poole and Pogrebin 1988; Prenzler 1995; Seagram and Stark-Adamec 1992).

Episodes of discrimination and harassment increase the difficulties women may confront in adapting to their role as police officers. The necessity to gain the support and acceptance of fellow police officers influences the rapidity with which individuals learn job skills and develop confidence in the execution of these skills (Bennett 1984; Worden 1993). Several studies have shown that women's confidence levels in carrying out certain tasks were generally lower than those of their male counterparts (Davis 1984; Wexler and Quinn 1985; Worden 1993), and that when women were unhappy or lacked commitment to their job, it was due in some part to their treatment by male counterparts (S.E. Martin 1980; Worden 1993). One study of the perceptions of women police officers found that three-fifths of the women respondents felt they had to perform better than men to receive equal credit (Belknap and Shelly 1992). Because women often lack such support, they may not feel fully empowered to carry out their duties as police officers (Worden 1993).

Many women police officers also feel they are underutilized, and this frustration affects their aspirations for promotion (Poole and Pogrebin 1988). Additionally, the lack of ease of acceptance by male officers creates a situation in which women police officers are often removed from informal and social structures within departments. This deprives them of important contacts, information, and professional relationships that can further their careers (S.E. Martin and Jurik 1996). Although much of this isolation is externally imposed by coworkers or through public perceptions, some is the result of purposive choices by women officers. Some knowingly withdraw from the social scene due to family responsibilities, whereas others remove themselves in an effort to protect their reputations (S.E. Martin and Jurik 1996; Rosener 1995).

Minority women police officers face additional stressors, a "double marginality" due their ethnicity and gender (Belknap and Shelly 1996). These officers are confronted with direct and degrading remarks about their ethnicity and gender (Morash and Haarr 1995), and have been found to feel socially isolated, apprehensive regarding backup by other police officers, concerned about the respect of the community, and reluctant to adopt a more aggressive policing style due to their personal experience as a person of color and having observed police behaviors in their communities (Belknap 1996; Belknap and Shelly 1996; Felkenes and Schroedel 1993; S.E. Martin 1994; S.E. Martin and Jurik 1996).

As Carol Martin (1996) reported in her study of the police service in the United Kingdom, women officers felt they had equal access to promotion but relatively few pursued the promotional path. S.E. Martin and Jurik (1996) found that promotions were affected by sponsorship and other factors but that opportunities should be improving because of the proliferation of collective bargaining agreements and civil service rules.

Although social expectations of males and females are becoming less "traditional," women still comprise the vast majority of child-care givers and nurturers. Many women in policing have very different priorities than their male counterparts. Women police officers' parental duties and their emphasis on family relationships may have an effect on their careers by limiting their years of duty or their perceived freedom to choose or compete with less-constrained male (and female) competitors for assignments (Poole and Pogrebin 1988; Poulos and Doerner 1996; Seagram and Stark-Adamec 1992). Research on career development theory suggests that men and women have similar career aspirations and motivations, but that women make alternative career choices based on their conformance to societal expectations and

TABLE 5.1
Gender and Racial Distribution Through
Ranks of Police Department

	Whites		Minorities		
Rank	Males	Females	Males	Females	Total
Chief	1	0	0	0	1
Deputy Chief	2	1	0	0	3
Major	3	0	1	0	4
Captain	6	1	1	0	8
Lieutenant	24	4	4	0	32
Sergeant	57	2	3	0	62
Officer	378	74	86	24	563
Total	471	82	93	24	673

in alignment with their personal upbringing. Men typically do not have to factor in such outside influences as spousal attitudes and support, family responsibilities, and child-care giving (Astin 1984). These differential priorities and the ability to make unconstrained "choices" may be interpreted as "deficiency, deviance or dysfunction" (Rosener 1995, 33), when the organizational climate presumes "one best model" for leadership and favors a more traditionally "male" approach (Rosener 1995). Baylin (1993) theorizes that work and home life cannot be viewed as separate spheres but must be seen as an essentially seamless whole if women are going to be able to compete and have access to the same opportunities as men. Women, as in Astin's and Rosener's aforementioned theories, are constrained by the norms imposed on them by society and enforced by employers, peers, spouses, and self. The essential question then remains: Can organizations be constructed so that success is not constrained by the continuing stratification and differentiation of gender roles?

METHOD

The goal of this study, presented in this chapter, was to further examine the factors that influence the promotional opportunities of female police officers; that is, their preparedness, desire, and demonstrated ability to compete for promotion.

The data used for the analysis were collected within a large Midwestern metropolitan police department. The department selected for the analysis employs over 650 sworn officers that serves a metropolitan jurisdiction of approximately 300,000 situated in a county with a total population of over 700,000.

As shown in Table 5.1, women comprised 16 percent (106) of the total of sworn personnel within the department. Minority representation was 98 percent and almost exclusively African American. Minorities comprised 18 percent (117) and minority women 4 percent (24) of sworn personnel. Only 3 percent (2) of the sergeants within the department were females, whereas at the lieutenant and captain ranks, females were closer to their proportionate representation in the department at 13 and 14 percent, respectively. At the rank of major, there were no females, but there was one female deputy chief. When all the ranks of commanding officers* were considered, there were significantly fewer females (8 percent) than males (18 percent). Based on gender representation within the department, although proportionality was approximated within two ranks, three failed to meet this criterion. Overall, neither proportionality nor parity with male counterparts was achieved.

The department has flattened the organizational structure and, through attrition, has deleted a number of supervisory and administrative positions. As such, the department has a fairly high ratio for supervisory span of control with an average of sixteen subordinates. This has been the source of some frustration for promotional aspirants because more are vying for fewer supervisory and managerial positions.

Multiple methods of data collection (triangulation) were utilized to produce more detailed and potentially insightful information. Specifically, the data were collected through two surveys (one mailed attitudinal survey and one promotional exam "exit" survey) and the conduct of focus groups.

MAILED SURVEY

All sworn personnel holding the rank of officer and who were eligible to participate in the sergeant promotional process (N = 326) were identified and sent an anonymous mailed survey, developed in cooperation with the staff services personnel in the department.

The survey consisted of a number of items requesting demographic information and perceptions concerning participation in the promotional process. The items related to perceptions of the promotional process and included those designed to elicit the reasons respondents elected to participate or not participate in the promotional process. For those respondents who reported they had elected to participate in the promotional process, an additional series of items were included in an effort to ascertain their perceptions of the process itself.

The survey was distributed via departmental mail and included a postage-paid reply envelope containing a nondepartmental address for return. Assurances were provided in the cover letter that all responses would remain confidential.

Of the 326 initial surveys mailed, 46 percent (149) were returned as useable. Because the initial surveys were mailed to promotion-eligible officers, this initial mailing represents the "population" of respondents within the agency. This initial population consisted of primarily male (86 percent) and Caucasian (80 percent) officers. The returned sample of surveys consisted of primarily male (84 percent) and Caucasian (84 percent) officers. As shown in Table 5.2, no significant differences were noted between the sample and initial population on the available demographic factors of ethnicity and gender.

Additional demographic information on the sample was garnered from the returned surveys. The sample consisted of mostly married (71 percent) or divorced (20 percent) officers. Most of these officers (61 percent) had completed at least two years of college, and almost one-third (31 percent) had completed at least a four-year

---

* Within this department, the ranks of sergeant and higher are considered to be "command officers." Although this may not be necessarily consistent with the standard categorization in other departments and scholarly works on policing, this label will be applied through the course of this chapter.

TABLE 5.2

Gender and Ethnic Characteristics

Population and Sample

	Population	Respondents
Minority Private		
Women	17 (5%)	9 (6%)
Men	49 (15%)	14 (10%)
Total Minority	66 (20%)	23 (16%)
Caucasian		
Women	29 (9%)	15 (10%)
Men	231 (71%)	109 (74%)
Total Caucasian	260 (80%)	124 (84%)
Total	326 (100%)	147 (100%)

Note: Percentages computed within parentheses and rounded.

college degree. No differences based on gender or ethnicity were noted for marital status or education.

The average age of the respondents was 39, with the ages ranging from 30 to 58 years. Their assignments were varied, though most (58 percent) were assigned to patrol within one of the five police districts overseen by the agency. The average length of time with the agency was fourteen years, though length of service ranged from five to twenty-eight years. Most respondents (47 percent) had been with the agency for seven to ten years. Longevity in the respondents' present assignment ranged from one to twenty-five years, though most (75 percent) officers had been in their present assignment for seven years or less. No differences based on gender or ethnicity were noted on the characteristics of age, longevity with the department, or longevity in current assignment.

FOCUS GROUPS

The findings from the mailed survey contained several items and issues that needed further clarification. As such, focus groups were organized as a means of collecting more qualitative information to further delineate the survey findings.

Focus group respondents were selected from promotion-eligible officers from "pools" established based on gender and ethnicity. Participants were randomly selected from these pools until a sample representative of proportionate gender and ethnic distributions, as well distribution of length of service on the department, were obtained. Length of service was used as a sample criterion to ensure that those with both short- and long-term experience with the department were included in the data collection process.

The net result was four racial/gender groups with twelve individuals in each group ranging in eligibility from one month to twenty years. Twelve participants were selected for each group to allow for attrition among the participants and yet have the capacity to retain a reasonable size group for data collection.

Each of the potential participants was sent a personal letter from the chief requesting their participation. Participants were selected from those consenting to participate based on the previously mentioned criteria, and focus groups were convened by the facilitators on two separate days. Each facilitator conducted one session with males and then another with females. During these sessions, participants discussed perceptions of the promotional process, promotional process participation or lack thereof, and the presence/absence of organizational support for promotion-seeking officers. The comments and observations from the focus groups were recorded and collated by facilitators, and the narrative comments analyzed for trends between and within the groups as well as for qualitative extrapolation of the more limited and qualitative results from the mail survey.

Exit Survey

This method of data collection consisted of administration of an exit survey immediately following the written portion of the promotional exam. The purposes of the survey were to determine the test preparation strategies of the candidates and to elicit perceptions concerning the promotional process. To protect confidentiality, all respondents were provided with the means to personally deliver their completed survey to research personnel immediately following its completion.

Seventy-two officers participated in the written portion of the promotional examination. All of these officers completed the exit survey. Most of the respondents were male (80 percent) and Caucasian (78 percent). African American women constituted 6 percent of those completing the promotional examination and therefore the exit survey.

FINDINGS

Officers from this department were a rather homogenous group. There were statistically significant gender differences on only a limited number of items. However, those items on which there were gender differences generally reflected factors that were consistent with prior research findings that women were more likely to be constrained in their occupational upward mobility by gender-specific normative expectations and responsibilities.

Promotion Eligible: No Participation in the Promotional Process

One-third (33 percent) of the respondents to the mailed survey had not participated in the promotional process. Among those survey respondents and focus group participants were those who were promotion eligible but had elected not to participate in the promotional process. The primary reasons for the decision not to participate were preference for current assignment/shift, reduction in pay, no interest in promotion, concerns with the current administration of the department, and child care/family relations.

Officers strongly identified with present assignment and shift, and were reluctant to make changes for the purposes of promotion, especially when it might mean a reduction in pay through loss of opportunities to engage in overtime work. Officers

TABLE 5.3

Factors Contributing to Decision Not to Participate in Promotional Process

	Women		Men	
Factor	Rank	Percent Reporting	Rank	Percent Reporting
Present assignment/shift	1	70	1	51
Child care/family relations	2	40	2	19
Administration bias	3	21	—	—
No interest	4	20	3	18
Salary reduction	5	17	2	19
Available openings	—	—	4	17

Note: Factors not mutually exclusive.

expressed a potentially related "lack of interest" in promotion that could be related to their preference for their current assignment over the differing and expanded responsibilities associated with the rank of sergeant. The current administration of the department and the officers' identification with administrative leadership, orientation, and direction, as well as perceived fairness of the promotional examination process itself, were concerns reported as influencing the decision not to participate. Additionally, child care and family relations were identified as inhibiting factors by the respondents. Based on the reasons identified by officers who elected not to participate in the promotional process, this group was cautious and perceived the "risks" and "costs" of promotion as exceeding the benefits.

Table 5.3 lists the top five concerns for men and women, as well as the percentage of respondents who identified these concerns as the three most important professional, organizational, and personal concerns. As shown in this table, although current assignment/shift is ranked first for both men and women, child care/family responsibilities is ranked second by 40 percent of the women, and only 19 percent of the men contributed to the ranking of that category as second in a tie with a perceived salary reduction. Clearly, the magnitude of the import of current assignment/shift and child care/family concerns is significantly greater for women. Similarly, although concerns over bias within the current administration is ranked fourth among female respondents, this item is not within the top five for men. Instead, among the men, "number of available openings" is a concern and ranked as fifth within the top five.

Women (70 percent) were more likely than men (51 percent) to report preference for their current assignment or shift as a reason not to seek promotion. Women (40 percent) were also more likely than men (19 percent) to identify child care and family relations as influential in their decision not to participate. Reduction in pay was an issue for comparable proportions of men (19 percent) and women (17 percent).

Participants within the focus groups expanded on these themes. Women within the focus groups were almost unanimous in saying that they had worked diligently to obtain their current assignment and shift and were not prepared to "give it up" for a promotion. In addition to a preference for their current assignment, the nature of supervisory ranks was viewed as "unattractive" by a majority of officers. Evidently, the benefits perceived from promotion were not great enough to exceed the risk to be taken in "giving up" the current assignment that they found satisfactory. Respondents stated they had no interest in the volume and type of paperwork required of sergeants. Many said that they signed on to do "real police work" and not "shuffle papers inside an office." Men and women differed slightly in that fewer women objected to the work itself but had reservations about having to supervise men who may harbor sexist attitudes.

Females (21 percent) were more willing than males (16 percent) to report that they did not participate in the promotional process due to a perception of a biased administration. The females opined that the administration favored males, whereas the males complained of both gender and racial reverse discrimination in promotions. Both males and females appeared somewhat pragmatic in that 16 and 13 percent felt that the number of possible openings would be insufficient to obtain a promotion. This is also an indicator of the respondent's self-assessment of their ability to successfully compete in the promotional process. In that regard, the females indicated a slightly greater degree of confidence.

Among the female respondents, child care and family responsibilities were a paramount concern. Child care and family responsibilities as factors that constrained participation in the promotional process for women were described in two primary ways. First, as noted previously, officers reported they were generally satisfied with their current assignments. Among the female respondents, this satisfaction was linked to their ability to "manage" child care and familial responsibilities along with their professional duties. For female officers, promotion would mean a change in work schedules and duties, which would have a "ripple effect" and create the need to make changes in day care, availability for children's school activities, care for children after school, and other personal adjustments related to dual-career families.*

One female focus group participant described the dilemma faced by women interested in promotion as that of a "very short window of opportunity." She explained that if women want to spend time with their children, attempts for upward mobility within the organization must be carefully scheduled to take advantage of this "window." One can enter the promotional process while the child is a toddler and obtain the rank of sergeant, with the goal of being assigned to the day shift by the time the child enters school. If this opportunity cannot or does not materialize, promotion to sergeant, while the child is in school, would result in an initial assignment to the evening shift, eliminating the ability to "tuck-in her child at night," assist with homework, and to participate in after-school activities for 2 to 3 years.†

---

* It is interesting to note that the issues related to familial and child-care responsibilities and the adjustments required for a promotion were even more salient for those women whose partners were also employed by the department. The "costs" of adjustment for a dual-career couple, when both were employed by a structured, paramilitary organization, were, no doubt, magnified by the general inability of employees within these types of organizations to easily and independently make adjustments to work schedules and assignments.

† Single-parent males shared many of the viewpoints of the female officers, as they too assume the primary responsibility for familial and child-care tasks. They had similar feelings of the need to sacrifice a "normal" family life and relationships for upward professional mobility.

Although many of these female officers would seek promotion if the conditions of promotion could accommodate family and child-care concerns, most also agreed that if they had rank, they would "give it up" to spend more time with their families. Overall, the "costs" to these women for adjustments in familial and child-care responsibilities did not exceed the "benefits" of a promotion.

Second, family and child-care responsibilities and priorities additionally magnified, among female officers, the issue noted by a majority of all respondents concerning the amount of time required to prepare for promotional examinations. Many anecdotes were provided, describing the experiences of acquaintances or partners who had taken as much as three months of vacation time to study for a promotional test. In most of the examples provided, the partner assumed total responsibility for child care and family matters to allow the candidate to prepare for the test. Most women reported they did not have the "luxury" of this type of arrangement, and therefore simply could not find the necessary amount of time required to prepare for the test.

Although the numbers of minority women in the department, and therefore participating in the survey, were too small to provide for valid statistical analysis, minority women who participated in the focus groups provided qualitative information that reinforced previous research findings of the "dual marginality" created by their ethnicity and gender. Although some of the Caucasian female officers stated that they believed male supervisors were insensitive to concerns that were generally held by female officers, this sense of "marginality" was uniformly expressed by the African-American female officers. Within the focus groups, these minority women were equally as likely to report as their Caucasian counterparts that they were satisfied with their present position, were proud of the outcomes of their professional activities, had concerns about the consequences of promotion on their ability to fulfill familial and child-care responsibilities, and did not seek promotion due to the limitations that rank would place on their ability to engage in "meaningful" work. However, the theme of frustration with stereotyping and prejudice was evident and recurring. These officers believed they had to "do twice the work to receive half the credit." Many believed that the promotional process had nothing to offer and would only result in additional frustrations due to prejudices among department personnel against women and minorities.

PROMOTION ELIGIBLE: PARTICIPATION IN THE PROMOTIONAL PROCESS

Most of the survey respondents (67 percent) reported that they had participated in a prior promotional process. More specifically, among those who had participated in a prior promotional process, 46 percent had done so during the last promotional examination for sergeant that was conducted in 1995.

Respondents who reported they had participated in a prior promotional examination process identified personal goal (26 percent), career opportunities (21 percent), salary increase (20 percent), and the desire to assume a leadership role (18 percent) as their primary reasons for participation.

Table 5.4 contains the "top four" ranked reasons for seeking promotion for the two gender groups. As shown in this table, although the rankings vary between the

TABLE 5.4

**Factors Contributing to Decision to
Participate in Promotional Process by Gender**

	Women		Men	
Factor	Rank	Percent Reporting	Rank	Percent Reporting
Career opportunities	1	27	2	20
Salary increase	2	22	2	20
Personal goal	2	22	1	26
Leadership	3	14	3	18

Note: Factors not mutually exclusive.

two groups, the differences are not extreme and interestingly enough, although one of the primary reasons for nonparticipation among promotion-eligible officers was "salary reduction," "salary increase" is the second ranked motivation for seeking promotion among both those women and men who had previously participated in the promotional process.

The reasons for participation in the promotional process are primarily professional and related to the attainment of personal and professional goals. These individuals who elected to participate in the promotional process were those who sought to further themselves and to seek more influential, i.e., leadership, roles within the agency.

Given the stringency of the promotional process and the actual or perceived time required to "study" for the promotional examination, respondents who reported that they planned to participate in the promotional process were asked whether or not they would attend preparatory sessions aimed at improving performance on the written portion of the promotional examination process. Overall, 65 percent indicated that they would attend such sessions. Gender differences were evident among these officers in that females were less likely to report they would attend written test preparation sessions than their male counterparts. Similarly, respondents were asked whether or not they would seek assistance from command officers in preparing for promotional competition. While the majority of officers (60 percent) reported they would proceed with the promotional process without counsel from command officers, women (82 percent) were less likely to report that they would do so than men (56 percent).

The lesser number of women officers who reported plans to take advantage of test preparation courses and/or "counsel" from officers of higher rank may be prompted by several factors. First, women reported greater concerns with the time required to study and prepare for the promotional process due to their more limited ability to transfer primary family and child-care responsibilities to a partner. Preparatory sessions for promotional competition only create more demands on limited available time. Second, women may additionally be more inclined to believe that they need to "make it on their own" due to their beliefs that they must work harder and more diligently than men to receive recognition and accomplishment within the organization.

The limited number of women reporting that they would seek assistance and advice from a command officer is, in all likelihood, the result of their marginality within the organization and, as reported in prior research, limited access to informal social structures and networks within the work setting. Command officers may be less approachable, less likely to be accessible for personal advice, and less inclined to be viewed as mentors and sources of personal support and guidance. As such, women simply do not view them as resources in the preparation process and/or do not access this resource.

PROMOTIONAL EXAMINATION PARTICIPANTS

Initially, 326 individuals within the department were eligible for promotion. Of this group, 72, or 22 percent, actually participated in and completed the written portion of the promotional process. As shown in Table 5.5, among those who completed the written examination, women (19 percent) were slightly higher in proportion than the proportion of women (14 percent) within the promotion-eligible group. The relative proportions of promotion-eligible candidates and those who completed the examination for each ethnic/gender group were comparable. The greatest completion rate was among Caucasian women, and the lowest among Caucasian men. When subtotals for exclusively gender categories were computed, women had a completion rate of 28 percent and men a completion rate of 21 percent—primarily due to the attrition of Caucasian men. As such, although individuals in all categories elected not to participate in the examination process, women were more likely than men to complete the written examination. Additionally, minority women were no more likely than minority men to complete the process, and slightly more likely than Caucasian men to do the same. The primary reasons for nonparticipation may necessarily be gender related, i.e., child care and family relations; however, the completion rates would suggest that it is neither gender nor a combination of gender and ethnicity itself that discourages participation in the promotion process.

Although women reported varied reasons for nonparticipation, many of which were exacerbated by the nature of the police organization and external factors such as child care and family relations, these factors did not inhibit their participation as

TABLE 5.5
Promotion-Eligible Officers and Candidates Completing Written Examination by Ethnicity and Gender

	Promotion Eligible	Completed Exam	Completion Rate
Caucasian			
Male	231 (71%)	47 (65%)	47 (20%)
Female	29 (9%)	9 (13%)	9 (31%)
Minority			
Male	49 (15%)	12 (17%)	12 (24%)
Female	17 (5%)	4 (6%)	4 (23%)
Total	326 (100%)	72 (100%)	72 (22%)

Note: Percentages computed within parentheses and rounded.

a group within the promotional process and was no more inhibited than that of their male counterparts, regardless of ethnicity.

The female officers who participated in the promotional process reported longer average periods of preparation (56 d/175 h) than men who participated (28 d/86 h). Both women and men engaged in a variety of activities to prepare for the test. Women engaged in more traditional study methods such as reviewing instructional texts and departmental policies and procedures. They were additionally more likely to report that they had engaged in their study as a solitary activity rather than using methods involving study groups and partners.

The variance in preparation and study time, as well as study methods between the gender groups, did not produce statistically significant differences in the final scores received on the written portion of the promotional exam, though the average score for women (81 percent) was slightly higher than that for men (78 percent).

CONCLUSION

Women entering the law enforcement occupation continue to face obstacles. Although women have gained in terms of their proportionate representation within police agencies, they are still generally underrepresented among sworn personnel and, more specifically, significantly underrepresented within supervisory and command ranks. This is evident nationwide among police agencies and was evident within the department used for the current research.

Although the significant underrepresentation of women within police agencies can create a situation in which there are fewer female officers eligible for promotion and therefore explains a portion of the underrepresentation of women in supervisory and command ranks, the findings of the study corroborate prior research, which shows that this is not an adequate explanation. In the department under study, the number of men eligible for promotion did exceed that of women, yet proportionately more promotion-eligible women elected to compete in the promotional process than did promotion-eligible men.

The reasons for the lack of participation in the promotional process were multiple but generally emphasized the greater participation of women in and identification of women with their familial and child-care roles. Women reported they did not participate in the promotional process because they did not have time to prepare adequately for the promotional process, preferred their current assignment, found the responsibilities associated with supervision and command unattractive, and did not want to accept the "costs" associated with promotion. In all instances, these evaluative criteria were grounded in assessments involving a comparison of familial and child-care responsibilities with the benefits of their professional role. Simply put, the priorities for these women were, by choice or ascription, family and children, and the constraints of the organizational demands and responsibilities that accompanied promotion would not permit them to adequately meet both familial and professional obligations. Although some women reported nonparticipation in the promotional process due to bias and discrimination within the organization, these were primarily African-American women officers.

When female officers elected to participate in the promotional process, they actively sought to improve their chances of passing through longer periods of preparation and study than their male counterparts. They do not, however, engage in some of the more informal means of preparation such as consultation with supervisory and command officers, neither do they engage in methods of study that would incorporate coworkers and make use of informal professional social networks. They engage in solitary preparation and study. This method of preparation is consistent with and reflects their degree of integration and identification with informal social networks and groups within the agency. They are not fully integrated into the informal social and organizational structure, and therefore do not engage in activities that would reflect or be based on this integration. Nonetheless, the outcome of their participation in the promotional process is no different from that of their male counterparts. Women participating in the promotional exam process obtain scores that are comparable to those of male participants.

These findings lend further substantiation to prior research that has described the role of women within police agencies as that of "marginal" members or "outside insiders." With respect to the ability of women to believe they should seek upward mobility within the organization, a combination of external demands and internal constraints influence their decision to seek promotion. Women police officers are still expected to be the primary caregiver and to contribute the greatest portion of support for familial and child-care responsibilities. Highly structured, paramilitary organizations maintain a traditional, albeit unrealistic, orientation that assumes that familial and work responsibilities are distinctive and independent. The ability of these organizations to provide the flexibility and alternative career ladders required of individuals who carry significant family responsibilities is seriously limited by this orientation. Although women do engage in "choices" relative to their mobility within police organizations, these "choices" are limited to those that can incorporate viable means of "juggling" both family and career and are, therefore, more limited than those "choices" available to their male counterparts.

The choices made by women concerning promotion within police agencies have serious consequences for the organization. A significant portion of qualified and viable candidates for supervisory and command positions are virtually eliminated from the pool of potential human resources when women elect not to seek promotion. Police agencies must find ways to adjust and incorporate flexibility in order to provide for a pool of the highest qualified future commanders rather than one that is necessarily biased in terms of gender. The provision of on-site child care and shift assignments that incorporate greater flexibility and the ability to more readily "change" with fellow officers, promotion preparation courses of a longer duration that would require more sessions of shorter duration, assignment of "mentors" to both male and female promotion-eligible officers, alternative "career ladders" that would promote the ability of women to obtain assignments more conducive to the fulfillment of their familial responsibilities, and more flexible policies and procedures related to child-care leave are options that should be explored. These factors, which have been found to influence the upward mobility of women within the current and prior research, are not necessarily gender dependent. Although they are more salient for women given existing gender-based social norms and expectations, they also clearly have and will continue to influence the professional careers of men as well.

REFERENCES

Astin, H. (1984). The meaning of work in women's lives: a socio-psychological model of career choice and work behavior. *Counseling Psychologist, 12*, 117–126.

Baylin, L. (1993). *Breaking the mold.* New York: Free Press.

Belknap, J. (1996). *The invisible woman: gender, crime and justice.* Belmont, CA: Wadsworth.

Belknap, J. and Shelly, J.K. (1993). The new lone ranger: police women on patrol. *American Journal of Police, 12*(2), 47–75.

Bennett, R.R. (1984). Becoming blue: a longitudinal study of police recruit occupational socialization. *Journal of Police Science and Administration, 12*, 47–58.

Davis, J.A. (1984). Perceptions of policewomen in Texas and Oklahoma. *Journal of Police Science and Administration, 12*, 395–403.

Felkenes, G.T. and Schroedel, J.R. (1993). A case study of minority women in policing. *Women and Criminal Justice, 4*, 65–89.

Lanier, M.M. (1996). An evolutionary typology of women police officers. *Women and Criminal Justice, 8*(2), 73–89.

Martin, C. (1996). The impact of equal opportunities policies on the day-to-day experiences of women police constables. *British Journal of Criminology, 36*(4), 510–528.

Martin, S.E. (1994). "Outside within" the station house: the impact of race and gender on black women police. *Social Problems, 41*(3), 383–400.

Martin, S.E. (1991). The effectiveness of affirmative action: the case of women in policing. *Justice Quarterly, 8,* 489–504.

Martin, S.E. (1980). *"Breaking and entering": policewomen on patrol.* Berkeley, CA: University of California Press.

Martin, S.E. and Jurik, N.C. (1996). *Doing justice doing gender: women in law and criminal justice occupations.* Thousand Oaks, CA: Sage.

Morash, M. and Haarr, R.N. (1995). Gender, workplace problems, and stress in policing. *Justice Quarterly, 12,* 113–140.

Moyer, I.L. (1992). *The changing roles of women in the criminal justice system: offenders, victims and professionals 2nd ed.* Prospect Heights, IL: Waveland.

Poole, E.D. and Pogrebin, M.R. (1988). Factors affecting the decision to remain in policing: a study of women officers. *Journal of Police Science and Administration, 16*(1), 49–55.

Potts, L.W. (1983). Equal employment opportunity and female employment in police agencies. *Journal of Criminal Justice, 11,* 505–523.

Poulos, T.M. and Doerner, W.G. (1996). Women in law enforcement: the distribution of females in Florida police agencies. *Women and Criminal Justice, 8*(2), 19–33.

Prenzler, T. (1995). Equal employment opportunity and police women in Australia. *Australian and New Zealand Journal of Criminology, 28*(3), 258–277.

Rosener, J.B. (1995). *America's competitive secret: women managers.* New York: Oxford University Press.

Schulz, D.M. (1993). From policewoman to police officer: an unfinished revolution. *Police Studies, 6,* 90–98.

Seagram, B.C. and Stark-Adamec, A.C. (1992). Women in Canadian urban policing: why are they leaving? *Police Chief, 59*(10), 120–128.

Sulton, C. and Townsey, R. (1981). *A progress report on women in policing.* Washington, D.C.: Police Foundation.

Wexler, J.G. and Quinn, V. (1985). Considerations in the training and development of women sergeants. *Journal of Police Science and Administration, 13,* 98–105.

Worden, A.P. (1993). The attitudes of women and men in policing: testing conventional and contemporary wisdom. *Criminology, 31,* 203–241.

6 "Difference" in the Police Department: Women, Policing, and "Doing Gender"

Venessa Garcia

CONTENTS

ABSTRACT

In this chapter, the author reviews the concept of gender "difference" in relation to the criminal justice system. The author argues that the acceptance of women as different and the practice of doing gender, although initially allowing women entrance into the police organization, has continued to keep women police in subordinate positions, and thus creates conflict. To illustrate, the author analyzes research on the history of the entrance of women into the police organization as well as their experiences and conflicts. The research reveals that without the acceptance of the doctrine that women are different and more humanistic than men, the police organization might not have accepted the issues of women and children (issues of social service) as police responsibility. However, the continuing practice of treating women police

Reprinted from *Journal of Contemporary Criminal Justice*, 19(3), 330–344, August 2003. © 2003 Sage Publications.

as different has created conflict within the police organization and worked to keep them within the lower ranks of the organization.

INTRODUCTION

According to Mary E. Hamilton (1924), New York City's first policewoman (appointed in 1918), women symbolized the mother and worked toward the protection of home and family. Although women have always performed the same types of work as men, they have historically been defined primarily by their sexual and procreative labor. This definition has cast women generally as sexual objects and particularly as mothers (Jaggar 1988). According to socialist feminism, all human adults are capable of virtually all types of labor. Both sexes can perform the labors required for basic subsistence, sexual satisfaction, and emotional nurturance. However, women have been given the sole responsibility of achieving these goals within the household, or private realm, and thus have been alienated from themselves, their children, other women, and society in general. Women's orientation has been placed on them by the patriarchal form of society, which has worked to create and maintain women's subordination.

Socialist feminism focuses on the social construction of masculine and feminine character types. Because these characteristics are the result of social practices, particularly procreative practices that are not determined by biology, they are transformable. Through a historical analysis of women's oppression, the conclusion has been made that women's liberation can only come about by creating new modes of organizing all forms of production, specifically by eliminating femininity. Gender characteristics are defined as social achievements. Therefore, to overcome women's alienation and sex-based division of labor, the private and public spheres must not be separated (Kessler-Harris 1987). Capitalism, male dominance, racism, and imperialism are intertwined; therefore, according to socialist feminists, it is important not to assume that the removal of capitalism will remove the conditions of women's experience. The removal of capitalism removes only one form of patriarchy.

Socialist feminists argue that most feminist political theories devalue the daily work of child rearing and have defined human freedom and fulfillment as the transcendence of this work (i.e., the work of women). Human nature and human society have been shaped by societal modes of organizing sexuality and procreation. To transform these traditional modes of organizing human activity, human history must be reshaped by conscious political activity. Accordingly, freedom can be achieved by transcending the sexual division of labor that exists in every area of human life, including sexuality and procreation.

Kessler-Harris (1987) argued that women's orientation, or standpoint, is determined socioculturally. However, the qualities, or identities, of women should be the standpoint of society. As Kessler-Harris has argued, women have not entered the labor market with individualistic achievement orientations. This is because they have historically been socialized with the qualities of nurturants and emotional supporters. Yet, equality in society should not require women to assume men's orientation; instead, society should assume women's orientation.

Kessler-Harris (1987) argued that to assume men's orientation would break up the family, placing the labor market first and the family second. If society integrates women's orientation into the work culture while women simultaneously resist reinforcing old gender roles, then cooperation and shared goals can be achieved within the workplace and the family concurrently. Gender is a valueless abstraction that comes to life as we fill in its meaning from time to time throughout history. The history of women's inequality has been about access, not rules. Therefore, in rewriting the rules, the challenge is focused on male structure (Kessler-Harris 1990). The adjustment comes about by revaluing the world, as well as work, through female self-interest. To create equality, we must redefine the world through the lenses of the oppressed (i.e., women).

Kessler-Harris (1987) acknowledged that her thesis is somewhat utopian, and I agree. Gender is the fundamental social interaction (DeVault 1991; Fenstermaker, West, and Zimmerman 1991; West and Fenstermaker 1993). Doing gender is always relevant to social interaction. All members of society do gender. Individuals are held gender accountable, hence the term "doing gender" (Fenstermaker et al. 1991). Gender must be accomplished in everyday interaction. It is achieved through gendered activity, most notably through work.

Historically, work has been defined by gender. The service of the nurse becomes identical to that of the wife, the mother, the clerical worker, the social worker, the waitress, the bank teller, the nun, or the policewoman. In this way, "the nursing model is feminine, the medical model is masculine" (Diamond 1978, cited in Jaggar 1988, p. 325). Within the police force, the policeman's work has been defined as one of law enforcement, whereas the policewoman's work has been one of crime prevention through moral guidance (Hamilton 1924).

Kessler-Harris (1987) argued in favour of maintaining or revaluing women's orientation (although simultaneously rejecting men's orientation), while acknowledging that the wage relation is based on gender difference (Kessler-Harris 1990). Although gender difference is fundamental to society, individuals are simply asked to shed their identities to embrace women's standpoint of nurturance and sharing. After society has shed these identities, the restructuring of the wage relation is assumed to occur.

Inequality is reinforced in such a way that definitions of women's work reinforce the orientation of women as naturally nurturant, subservient, and sexy, and women's low wages make it very likely that women will be dependent on men. Wage relations force women to endure a special form of alienation, and they are forced to exploit themselves sexually and emotionally (Jaggar 1988). It is not enough to revalue difference. That difference is fundamental is apparent when we observe the differences practiced in sex, race, age, and class. Acceptance of difference means acceptance of the status quo. To accept difference and to revalue women's orientations, the structure of society must be changed as well.

In light of this knowledge, the elimination of sex segregation in production must follow the elimination of the distinction, or difference, between masculine and feminine work as well. According to Kessler-Harris (1987), that difference should be proudly accepted. Difference has created conflict within the police organization. Furthermore, the acceptance of women as different has perpetuated the police cultural norm that having a woman's orientation makes it difficult to do a good job in policing.

THE HISTORY OF "DOING GENDER" IN POLICING

It is important to look at the history of the entry of women into the police organization to understand the sex roles women police play today. Although women were being appointed as jail and prison matrons in the 1840s, it was not until the early 1900s that women made inroads into policing (Barlow and Barlow 2000). In 1905, Portland, Oregon, hired the first woman in policing. Lola Baldwin was hired as a safety worker with arrest powers. It was not until 1910 that the Los Angeles Police Department appointed Alice S. Wells as the first sworn policewoman. By 1916, 30 cities within the United States had employed policewomen. By 1925, the number of cities grew to 210, and the number of policewomen grew to 417, although 355 women remained employed as matrons. By the 1950s, the United States saw as many as 2,610 policewomen, and by 1960, there were 5,617 policewomen (Heidensohn 1992).

The work of policewomen has been described as specialized social workers, somewhat analogous to the glorified executive secretary (Balkin 1988). Mary E. Hamilton (1924), New York City's first policewoman, described the role of the policewoman as prevention and protection. In a narration of her career and the role of policewomen, Hamilton explained that it was the woman, with her motherly qualities and instincts, who could improve the human condition. She stressed that the purpose of policewomen was not to brush off their traditional home ideals; certainly, it would be wrong to do so. Instead, they could develop their outside activities to reflect their home roles. Prevention of crime, it was realized, should be a major function of the police force. To prevent crime, however, the process had to start at adolescence, and this was the job most suitable for women. In addition, the police force was convinced that a woman could not perform an adequate job as a policewoman unless she worked as a woman and carried a woman's ideals.

Policewomen had to cooperate with men to be effective. It was understood that the policewoman's purpose was not to replace men in their occupation but to aid and assist them, quietly and unassumingly. In this manner, a policewoman could prove her services and honesty and eliminate any antagonism she may face from policemen. In fact, Hamilton described a case of a policewoman resigning her position because she was given the same detective duties as policemen. These duties were defined as improper in that they aroused among policemen suspicion and prejudice against women for all time. These duties also did not allow policewomen to engage in the kind of work women should do, and did not allow them to achieve the kind of good they were capable of. Hamilton suggested that the endeavor of a few police departments to make women equal by giving them the same duties as men was an attempt to discourage policewomen and drive them out of this male occupation.

In sum, until the 1970s, the history of the policewoman reveals duties that were custodial and were directed toward females and juveniles, whereas the policeman's duties involved punitive and arrest powers. Although Hamilton stated that the police organization realized that crime prevention must be the primary police function, this actually meant that it must be primary for policewomen but not for policemen. In essence, real police work was considered to be punitive rather than preventive (Bell 1982). The presence of policewomen was considered to be a fad that would quickly die out. With the existence of this prevalent attitude, policewomen have had to prove their competence and worth within the police organization. Bell (1982) understood that this was impossible because women were simply not accepted.

Although policewomen were being employed in larger numbers by the 1930s, their duties remained virtually unchanged. In the 1930s, policewomen were required to have a "good educational background, formal training and experience in social work, pleasant personality, and a positive attitude toward dealing with the problems of women . . . display high tolerance, common sense, sympathy, and emotional stability" (Hutzel 1933, cited in Bell 1982, p. 113). In the 1940s, police-women were expected to be college graduates and not overly feminine, aggressive, mannish, sentimental, or coldhearted (Bell 1982). In the 1950s, they were required to be dignified, sensible, tactful, sympathetic, neat, attractive, well-adjusted, and more interested in others than in themselves (Bell 1982). By the 1960s, the duties of policewomen had not changed much. They included the following: patrolling city streets, investigating public and recreational facilities to protect the morals of females and juveniles, missing persons, and juvenile delinquency (Bell 1982; Schulz 1995). However, patrolling usually involved traffic control only. In addition, in the 1970s, policewomen were warned "that they may often be the only women among men and thus may be pinched, patted, or played with. Therefore, they should not wear excessive makeup, suggestive clothing, or use abrasive language" (Anderson 1973, cited in Bell 1982, pp. 113 and 114). Yet, they were advised that maintaining their femininity would allow them to gain respect within the organization. Not only were women not accepted within the police force, had unequal and unreasonable prerequisites, and were required to be masculine and feminine simultaneously, but they were also held accountable for and allowed to be sexually harassed.

Giving an account of women's entry into policing, Heidensohn (1992) described several stages of women's role in policing. First, women served to guide moral reform, rescuing female inmates, prostitutes, juvenile delinquents, and the home-less (also see Merlo and Pollack 1995; Schulz 1995). Women served as prison and police matrons (1840 to 1910/15). Women's duties centered on issues better handled by women, such as children, female victims of sex offenses, women criminals, missing persons, and clerical work (Barlow and Barlow 2000; Feinman 1994). Following the moral reform movement, women came to be seen as specialists and pioneers (1910/15 to 1930) (also see Martin 1980). Seeking more to protect women and children and decent men, separate women's precincts were established. The third stage reflected latency and depression (1930 to 1945), when women's move-ment into the organization became stagnant during the Great Depression (Schulz 1995). Martin (1980) placed the latency stage at 1930 to 1970 because of the fact that policewomen made only minor inroads into policing. However, after World War II, the history of women in policing reflected an informal expansion (1945 to 1970). By the early 1970s, women accomplished integration (1972 to present) into the mainstream police organization (Schultz 1995). Policewomen as specialists of female and child victims and suspects were eliminated and women were integrated as *women police* (for an explanation of the usage of this term, see Barlow and Barlow 2000).

CONTEMPORARY DEVELOPMENTS OF A GENDERED ORGANIZATION

How has the history of women's entry into the police organization affected the roles and experiences of the present-day woman police? Their roles and experiences have been quite similar to women entering other male occupations. Women have repeatedly been channeled into the least desirable jobs within an occupation (Balkin 1988; Belknap 2001; Bell 1982; Berg and Budnick 1986; Kessler-Harris 1990; Reskin and Roos 1990; Wood, Corcoran, and Courant 1993). Women lawyers have been channeled into low-paying government jobs, women bankers have been channeled into teller jobs, women cooks have predominated the peripheral labor market, and within the police organization, the jobs least desired by men have been those involving women and juveniles.

According to Kessler-Harris (1990), "while abstract market goals indicate that people choose jobs, the historical record suggests that occupational segregation has been the product of deeply ingrained attitudes" (p. 121). Acker (1992) described these ingrained attitudes as gendered and interaction processes within gendered institutions. Accordingly, gender is the "patterning of difference and domination through distinctions between women and men that is integral to many societal processes" (p. 565). A gendered institution is one that has notions and symbols of gender in its processes, practices, images and ideologies, and distributions of power. The gendered process within the gendered institution constructs hierarchies, segregation, and even exclusion based on gender, although the interaction process is the medium for doing gender (pp. 567 and 568). Efforts to keep women out of male occupations have been the product of society's gender norms and have resulted in a lack of recruitment and failure to keep women in the profession, an inability or refusal to define women as competent, and to stagnate the occupational culture.

RECRUITMENT

Recruitment of women into the gendered organization of policing has been slow, and retaining women police has been an unwelcome struggle (National Center for Women and Policing 2001a). The percentage change in women police and detectives from 1970 to 1980 only increased by 2.3 percent, and from 1980 to 1988 by 4.1 percent (Reskin and Roos 1990). These are not very dramatic considering that policewomen represented only .8 percent of police personnel in 1960 and 2.7 percent in 1970 (Bell 1982). In 1973, the Crime Control Act banned sex discrimination within police organizations receiving federal aid. However, these organizations had to employ 50 or more employees and receive at least $25,000 in federal grant money to fall under the Act's jurisdiction. This meant that small rural police departments and small suburban police departments were not held accountable for sex discrimination. Furthermore, for the police departments that fell under the domain of the Crime Control Act, lawsuits had to be brought against many of them to secure equality (Bell 1982).

In 2000, among a sample of police agencies with 100 or more sworn officers, the National Center for Women and Policing (2001b) found that women represented

13 percent of all sworn officers. In 1990, this statistic was 9 percent. This represents a percentage increase of 4.9 percent within a decade, not much of an increase from that which occurred in the 1980s (a 4.1 percent increase from 1970 to 1980). Furthermore, women currently hold only 7.3 percent of top command positions.

Recruitment, however, has not come naturally for some agencies. Consent decrees mandating the recruitment of women and minorities have been a significant influence in recruitment efforts in some jurisdictions (Martin 1980; National Center for Women and Policing, 2001b). The 2000 Status of Women in Policing Survey revealed that police agencies without consent decrees reported having only 9.7 percent women sworn officers, whereas among agencies with consent decrees, women represented 14 percent of their sworn officers.

Adding to the above knowledge, research has found that advancement of women police is proportionately lower than that of policemen (Grennan and Munoz 1987). This fact may be linked to the finding that women police have a higher turnover rate than policemen (Martin 1989). The gendered institution of policing produces double standards for women, as reflected in the differential training process, sexual harassment, and performance standards (Martin and Jurik 1996). Although this has not resulted in women abandoning the field, it has continued the practice of segregating women into stigmatized assignments or specialties (Grennan 2000).

COMPETENCY

The gendered process of defining women's roles in society has resulted in the segregation of women into lower paying, less prestigious occupations. Women have been attributed feminine traits devalued by society. Accordingly, these traits are associated with one's ability or inability to perform certain jobs successfully. For the woman, it is understood that she is emotional and thus irrational, compassionate, cooperative, physically fragile, subjective, gentle, and morally superior. Women do not possess the necessary masculine traits of rationality, aggressiveness, bravery, objectivity, suspicion, and brutality required of good cops to fight crime and apprehend the enemy (Miller 1999). These cultural definitions of femininity have led to claims that women are inherently not competent to perform the police function.

The main argument against allowing women to become police officers has been that they do not have the physical strength the job requires. Without the strength it takes to fend off violent criminals, it has been argued, the presence of a woman police officer can make the difference between life and death (Charles 1981). Balkin (1988) cited several studies that found that women are no less capable than men in handling potentially violent situations.

Only one study found that women were not as good as men on patrol (Home 1980, cited in Balkin 1988, p. 32). This study was conducted to obtain evidence disputing a suit brought against a Philadelphia police department for sex discrimination. Although the study revealed that women were as persistent as men in making arrests, made the same number of arrests, and handled citizens with guns, family disturbances, and car stops better than men, the report concluded that women were not as good in patrol safety and efficiency as men. The court, however, rejected this conclusion based on the results of the study.

The argument premised on women's lack of physical strength can be rejected in light of current knowledge of domestic violence cases and response policies. It is commonly believed that domestic disturbances are the single biggest cause of officer death (Federal Bureau of Investigation, 1962 to 1985). This belief derives from FBI statistics released between 1962 and 1985. Initially, domestic disturbances were thought to cover family quarrels alone, but by 1986, the Bureau published a brief that corrected this myth and declared that the major cause of officer death was responding to "disturbance calls" (i.e., family quarrels and man with a gun) (Garner and Clemmer 1986).

Situations dealing with citizens with guns have been defined as crime fighting, whereas domestic or family violence has been defined as a private family matter. Although only a myth, most police officers still believe that domestic violence incidents are one of the most dangerous calls, or potentially dangerous calls to respond to (Dobash and Dobash 1992). Furthermore, domestic violence calls are the largest category of calls made to the police (National Center for Women and Policing 2001a). Keeping this in mind, why are women police still viewed as not physically competent for crime fighting when the actual work is not as dangerous as it is thought to be? This conclusion also becomes questionable because only about 1 percent of police work is too physically demanding for women police (Lehtinen 1976; Sherman 1973). However, Bell (1982) added that no research has proven that physical strength is related to the ability to successfully manage dangerous situations.

Currently, the police organization has shifted its focus to accept domestic violence, juvenile delinquency, and minor issues within communities as crimes worthy of police response. However, Miller (1999) argued that although the police institution combines social control and social service functions, it does so against the backdrop of masculinity while rejecting anything feminine or female. Although the police culture refuses to acknowledge these crimes as real police work, the administration has adopted response policies. Responses include mandatory arrest policies for domestic violence, special units for responding to domestic violence and juvenile delinquency, and community-policing programs. Coming full circle to the historical efforts of women police and social reformers to keep women's police work within the realm of women's issues (Barlow and Barlow 2000; Hamilton 1924; Merlo and Pollack 1995; Schulz 1995), we see that the police organization is reproducing the gendered process and women police are still doing gender.

As mentioned in the preceding text, it was not until the 1970s that women accomplished integration into the police organization. This integration has meant the official elimination of formal special women's police bureaus or specialties, though not so in practice. Today, the same work that was considered women's work prior to 1970 is cited as official crime fighting. One present-day example of the gendered process is the focus on the power of feminine traits within the police organization by the advocacy organization, the National Center for Women and Policing.

The National Center for Women and Policing (2001a) claimed that increased recruitment of women police will ultimately improve response to domestic violence. It cited a 1985 study that found that women police exhibit more concern, patience, and understanding than their male colleagues (Homant and Kennedy 1985, cited in National Center for Women and Policing 2001a, p. 25). In stressing the need to increase recruitment of women into the police force, the National Center for Women and Policing stressed the communication skills that women bring into a service-oriented style of policing. This service-oriented style of policing reveals women as less likely to use excessive force, misconduct themselves, or become cynical toward citizens. Furthermore, the National Center for Women and Policing argued that women police will not only improve response to domestic violence but their presence will also reduce sex discrimination and harassment and aid in implementing community-oriented policing.

The need to improve the image of police in the eyes of the public, as well as to prevent crime by fixing broken windows, has led to the implementation of community-oriented policing. In making an argument for the competency of women police, advocates claim that the service-oriented style of policing utilized by women police is the most desirable qualification for a police officer working under a community-policing program to possess (National Center for Women and Policing 2001a).

Police who are women have proven that they can handle these situations better than police who are men and, furthermore, that the skills of women are desirable for police work. What else is there to prove? The answer is that, historically, the notion of women doing anything outside of the home or engaging in anything other than traditional motherly or wifely behaviors has been renounced. That is, if an individual does not do gender, then he or she is rejected. A U.S. Supreme Court judge stated, "The constitution of the family organization, which is founded in divine ordinance as well as the nature of things, indicates the domestic sphere as that [to] which properly belongs the domain and function of womanhood" (*Illinois v. Bradwell*, 1873, cited in Balkin 1988, p. 32). This ideology has been revealed in studies cited by Bell (1982). Although police chiefs have determined that women police performed theft jobs as well as policemen, police officers continue to feel that women police are weak, unreliable, and not fit for patrol work.

POLICE CULTURE

There is no denying that parents socialize their daughters to possess different qualities than their sons. There is no denying that other institutions perpetuate this differential socialization, thus representing males and females as different. There is also no denying that, in the dichotomy of gender difference, society values masculinity over femininity. As with all institutions, in the gendered institution of policing, the traits most associated with success are considered to be masculine (e.g., competitiveness, aggressiveness, active persistence, and emotional detachment) (Epstein 1970). As a result of society's dichotomization of the sexes, anything other is devalued. Furthermore, if a woman does not do gender, she is rejected as deviant. As one woman put it, "If you're a woman, you have to make less mistakes … a woman must put greater effort into her work … because if you make a fool of yourself, you're a damn fool woman instead of just a damn fool" (Epstein 1970, pp. 191 and 192).

In one study on women police in Amsterdam, Van der Poel (1981) found that women police were reported to be unreliable in a fight but were put down if they displayed too much aggression. They were castigated for not staying on the job long enough but criticized as unfeminine if they showed a strong commitment to law enforcement. Women police were accused of using their sex for special treatment, yet policemen often tried to con their way out of tough assignments.

Law enforcement has always been defined as a masculine occupation. The police culture values the good pinch and backing fellow officers in dangerous crime-fighting situations (Drummond 1976). These duties are believed to require aggression and physical strength, high levels of competency, and technical abilities. However, as described by a police department social worker, the police organization has a so-called 80–20 secret (personal communication, George Patterson, January 1994). This secret is that 80 percent of a police officer's time is spent doing social-work-type jobs, such as domestic disturbances or violence, disturbances of the peace, and traffic control (Price and Gavin 1981), and 20 percent of the time is spent fighting crime, such as homicide, narcotics, kidnapping, and armed robbery. However, the police culture is such that recruits coming out of the police academy maintain an 80–20 belief that is exactly the opposite. That is, 80 percent of police work involves crime fighting, whereas 20 percent of the work involves social-work-type jobs.

Charles (1981) revealed this finding in a study on the performance and socialization of female recruits in the police academy. He found that some male recruits felt the need to belittle female success. He also found that no matter how well females did in the training process, they were still criticized and not accepted because their physical strength did not match that of males. The general ideology found in almost all of these studies is not that women are not fit to do the job; the resistance comes from the belief that women are not fit to do a man's job as well as a man, and, therefore should not make the attempt. Charles found that male recruits had preconceived notions of what women were capable of and would not accept any female success as due to the true abilities of women.

These attitudes displayed by policemen have had varying effects on women police. Wexler (1985) found that women police who displayed a neutral-impersonal role style with their male coworkers experienced the greatest amount of stress and resistance on the job. Women police who displayed a mixed-role style, using their sex to gain respect, experienced almost as much stress. However, they were able to brush the strain off with a boys-will-be-boys attitude. Women police who displayed a feminine style were concerned about being acknowledged as women and getting special treatment and protection from men. These women did not experience much stress or frustration; however, they did not interact with the policemen on a professional level. The semimasculine women police expected to be accepted as people but not to be treated as equals. Although they experienced the least amount of stress, policemen treated them as junior partners.

CONCLUSION

Doing gender within the police academy occurs also within the police department. It has also resembled the practice of doing gender within every other occupation (Fenstermaker et al. 1991; Reskin and Roos, 1990; Wood et al. 1993). Women are perceived as delicate, emotional supporters, and nurturants. This is apparent when looking at the duties of the policewoman (i.e., issues of women and juveniles). This is also apparent when looking at the conflict created by the presence of women police. If a woman acts too feminine, she is criticized for not being suitable for the job. However, if she acts too masculine, she is criticized for not acting like a woman.

The women police in Wexler's (1985) study who displayed feminine roles were doing gender. They experienced a low amount of stress and frustration; however, they were not seen as professionals. The women who did not do gender (i.e., the neutral-impersonal, the semimasculine, and the mixed style) also experienced stress and frustration, although to different degrees. However, of all these women, none was respected as a woman and none was accepted as an equal. This conflict is a result of engaging in a male occupation, the ultimate rejection of doing gender.

The practice of difference is apparent in the women police who displayed feminine-role styles. It is also apparent in the duties of the woman police. As so many researchers have found, no matter what behaviors women police display or what tasks they have accomplished, they are damned if they do and damned if they don't. Revaluing women's orientation does not reduce this conflict if the structure of the police organization is not changed. It may challenge the structure somewhat; however, to accept difference means maintaining the norms within work cultures, as well as society as a whole. Transforming the world and work through the lens of female self-interest creates a devalued men's orientation, just as women's orientation has been created in the past—only the shoe is put on the other foot. Inequality will still be prevalent. A primary condition for the adequacy of a feminist theory, indeed for the adequacy of any theory, is that it should represent the world from the standpoint of women (Jaggar 1988). However, as difference exists in sex, race, age, and class, the revamping of the world in the eyes of women's interests still creates inequality for women because not all women have the same interests.

REFERENCES

Acker, J. (1992). Gender institutions: From sex roles to gendered institutions. *Contemporary Sociology, 21,* 565–568.

Balkin, J. (1988). Why policemen don't like policewomen. *Journal of Police Science and Administration, 16,* 29–38.

Barlow, D.E., & Barlow, M.H. (2000). *Police in a multicultural society: An American story.* Prospect Heights, IL: Waveland.

Belknap, J. (2001). *The invisible woman: Gender, crime, and justice* (2nd ed.). Belmont: CA: Wadsworth.

Bell, D.J. (1982). Policewomen: Myths and realities. *Journal of Police Science and Administration, 10,* 112–120.

Berg, B.L., & Budnick, K.J. (1986). Defeminization of women in law enforcement: A new twist in the traditional police personality. *Journal of Police Science and Administration, 14,* 314–319.

Charles, M.T. (1981). The performance and socialization of female recruits in the Michigan State Police Training Academy. *Journal of Police Science and Administration, 9,* 209–223.

DeVault, M. (1991). *Feeding the family: The social construction of caring as gendered work.* Chicago, IL: University of Chicago Press.

Dobash, E.R., & Dobash, R.P. (1992). *Women, violence and social change.* New York: Routledge.

Drummond, D.S. (1976). *Police culture.* Beverly Hills, CA: Sage Publications.

Epstein, C.F. (1970). *A woman's place.* Berkeley, CA: University of California Press.

Federal Bureau of Investigation. (1962 to 1985). *Crime in the United States.* Washington, DC: Government Printing Office.

Feinman, C. (1994). *Women in the criminal justice system* (3rd ed.). Westport, CT: Praeger.

Fenstermaker, S., West, C., & Zimmerman, D.H. (1991). Gender inequality: New conceptual terrain. In R. Lesser-Blumberg (Ed.), *Gender, family and economy* (pp. 298–307). Newbury Park, CA: Sage.

Gamer, J., & Clemmer, E. (1986). *Danger to police in domestic disturbances: A new look.* Washington, DC: National Institute of Justice.

Grennan, S.A. (2000). The past, present, and future of women in policing. In R. Muraskin (Ed.), *It's a crime: Women and justice* (pp. 383–398). Upper Saddle River: NJ: Prentice Hall.

Grennan, S.A., & Munoz, R. (1987). Women as police supervisors in the twenty-first century: A decade of promotional practices by gender in three major police departments. In R. Muraskin & A.R. Roberts (Eds.), *Visions for change* (pp. 340–354). Upper Saddle River, NJ: Prentice Hall.

Hamilton, M. (1924). *The policewoman: Her service and ideals.* New York: A. Stokes.

Heidensohn, F. (1992). *Women in control? The role of women in law enforcement.* New York: Oxford University Press.

Jaggar, A.M. (1988). *Feminist politics and human nature.* Lanham, MD: Rowman & Littlefield.

Kessler-Harris, A. (1987). The debate over equality for women in the workplace: Recognizing differences. In N. Gerstel & H.E. Gross (Eds.), *Families and work* (pp. 520–539). Philadelphia, PA: Temple University Press.

Kessler-Harris, A. (1990). *The woman's wage: Historical meaning and social consequences.* Lexington, KY: University Press of Kentucky.

Lehtinen, M.W. (1976). Sexism in police departments. *Trial, 12,* 52–55.

Martin, S.E. (1980). *Breaking and entering: Policewomen on patrol.* Berkeley, CA: University of California Press.

Martin, S.E. (1989). *Women on the move: Policewomen on patrol.* Newbury Park, CA: Sage Publications.

Martin, S.E., & Jurik, N.C. (1996). *Doing justice, doing gender.* Thousand Oaks, CA: Sage Publications.

Merlo, A.V., & Pollack, J.M. (1995). *Women, law and social control.* Boston, MA: Allyn & Bacon.

Miller, S.L. (1999). *Gender and community policing: Walking the talk.* Boston, MA: Northeastern University Press.

National Center for Women & Policing. (2001a). *Recruiting and retaining women: A self-assessment guide for law enforcement.* Washington, DC: Author.

National Center for Women & Policing. (2001b). *Equality denied: The status of women in policing, 2000.* Washington, DC: Author.

Price, B.R., & Gavin, S. (1981). A century of women in policing. In D.O. Schultz (Ed.), *Modern police administration* (pp. 109–122). Houston, TX: Gulf.

Reskin, B.F., & Roos, P.A. (1990). *Job queues, gender queues: Explaining women's inroads into male occupations.* Philadelphia, PA: Temple University Press.

Schulz, D.M. (1995). *From social worker to crimefighter: Women in United States municipal policing.* Westport, CT: Praeger.

Sherman, L.J. (1973). A psychological view of women in policing. *Journal of Police Science and Administration, 1,* 383–394.

Van der Poel, S. (1981). Everybody's watching: Policewomen in Amsterdam. *Police Review, 89,* 1142–1144.

West, C., & Fenstermaker, S. (1993). Power, inequality, and the accomplishment of gender: An ethnomethodological view. In P. England (Ed.), *Theory on gender/feminism on theory* (pp. 151–174). New York: Aldine.

Wexler, J.G. (1985). Role styles of women police officers. *Sex Roles, 12,* 749–755.

Wood, R.O., Corcoran, M.E., & Courant, P.N. (1993). Pay differences among the highly paid: The male-female earnings gap in lawyers' salaries. *Journal of Labor Economics, 11,* 417–441.

Section II

Legal Issues in Police Administration

7 The Supreme Court and Police Practices: A Review of Recent Traffic Stop Cases

Craig Hemmens

CONTENTS

INTRODUCTION

The war on drugs is going strong in the United States. Those arrested on drug-related charges receive little sympathy from the public, police, or community leaders. The former Los Angeles Police Department chief, Darryl Gates, told the Senate Judiciary Committee that casual drug users "ought to be taken out and shot." Drug czar William Bennett suggested that beheading drug dealers was morally acceptable (1). These sort of comments, made by respected community leaders, can be expected to have an impact on law enforcement agencies attempting to prioritize departmental operations with limited resources.

Police departments have indeed responded to calls to "get tough" on drug crime by instituting more proactive policing methods (2–4). In particular, the war on drugs has caused police to improve their drug interdiction and apprehension techniques. An example of this is the increased reliance on routine traffic stops to investigate possible drug offenses. Police officers now frequently use a traffic infraction as a pretext to stop a vehicle so that they may then observe the actions of the driver and passengers, and possibly seek consent to search the vehicle.

Automobiles are a major drug transportation and delivery device; police have logically focused upon them. New and improved methods such as pretext stops, profiling, and roadblocks have provided police officers with better opportunities to investigate possible drug crimes. Such proactive policing is generally seen as a positive activity by police and the public, but as the police utilize increasingly intrusive means, they increase the risk of running afoul of the Fourth Amendment.

The Fourth Amendment governs police activity by prohibiting "unreasonable" searches and seizures. This begs the question: What is "unreasonable"? Reasonableness (or the lack thereof) is a moving target that is hard to pin down. It is not a bright line rule, unlike some aspects of the Fourth Amendment jurisprudence. This makes it difficult for police officers and administrators to know the outer limits of what is allowed. Proactive policing means pushing the envelope and doing everything the law allows. Good policing means not crossing the line—a difficult objective to achieve when the line keeps moving!

The Supreme Court in recent years has issued opinions in a number of cases involving police conduct during traffic stops. Although the Supreme Court has largely sanctioned police activity in this area, there are still limits to what the police can do. This chapter reviews selected recent cases involving traffic stops. It is essential that police administrators be aware of and understand Supreme Court decisions in this area, so that they can inform the patrol officers and make sure that the police are operating legally, and that any incriminating evidence police officers uncover during a traffic stop will be admissible at trial.

THE SUPREME COURT AND THE POLICE

Historically, the Supreme Court paid little attention to the activities of the state and local law enforcement agencies. There were thee primary reasons for this lack of attention: police forces remained relatively small and unorganized until the twentieth century (5), defendants in criminal cases rarely challenged the means by which police obtained evidence (6), and the Fourth Amendment, which today is the primary tool for controlling police conduct, did not apply to the activities of the state and local police (7).

It was not until 1949, in *Wolf v. Colorado* (1949), that the Supreme Court determined that the Due Process clause of the Fourteenth Amendment be "incorporated" into the Fourth Amendment and applied to state action, including the activities of state and local law enforcement agencies. During the 1960s, the Supreme Court handed down a number of decisions involving the meaning of "reasonableness" in the Fourth Amendment. Although many of these decisions provided criminal defendants with greater protections, one decision in particular, *Terry v. Ohio* (1968), provided the police with tremendous power to investigate crime. In *Terry*, the Supreme Court ruled that police could forcibly stop and frisk someone on the street based on "reasonable suspicion" that a crime had occurred. Reasonable suspicion, the Court acknowledged, required less evidence than probable cause. The Court justified relaxing the probable cause requirement by balancing the need to investigate crime against the limited invasion of privacy that a brief detention involved.

The numerous Warren Court decisions in the 1960s, including *Terry v. Ohio*, involving police practices, although harshly criticized by some police administrators at the time, have had the effect of standardizing, professionalizing, and legitimizing police investigatory practices (5–7). Significant for purposes of this discussion was the Court's consistent reliance on the balancing approach utilized in *Terry v. Ohio* and the adoption of the reasonable suspicion standard. Subsequent cases extended the reasonable suspicion standard to situations akin to pedestrian–police encounters, such as traffic stops, and the Court consistently balances the competing interests of law enforcement and individual rights in evaluating police conduct during traffic stops. The cases discussed below, pertaining to police conduct during traffic stops reveal the results of the Court's reliance on the reasonable suspicion standard and the balancing approach to Fourth Amendment jurisprudence.

TRAFFIC STOPS

Traveling by automobile is a way of life for most Americans. Traffic stops are almost inevitable by-products of this endeavor. As more than one commentator has noted, it is virtually impossible to travel by car for any appreciable length of time without committing a traffic infraction (8–10). For many citizens, a traffic stop is the only time they will interact with a police officer. The significance of this fact lies not in the small fine that may accompany a citation for a minor traffic infraction but in the use of traffic regulations by police officers as a pretext to conduct an investigation of criminal activity unrelated to the traffic stop, an investigation not based on probable cause or even reasonable suspicion.

Seizures come in several forms, including full arrest and the so-called "*Terry* stops." A traffic stop is a form of seizure (11). A police officer who observes a motorist commit a traffic infraction has probable cause to conduct a traffic stop. During this stop, the officer may investigate the traffic infraction and issue a citation. In the absence of a reasonable and articulable suspicion of further criminal activity, the scope of the seizure may not be expanded beyond the purpose of the initial stop—investigating the traffic infraction. In addition, a police officer may make a vehicle stop based on specific and articulable facts that create a reasonable suspicion of criminal activity on the part of the occupants of the vehicle. This "investigatory stop" is analogous to a *Terry* stop of a pedestrian.

A police officer may not conduct a full search of a vehicle or its occupants based on a traffic stop or an investigatory stop. This is because an investigatory stop is based on less than probable cause, which is required to conduct a full search, and because a traffic infraction does not create probable cause to investigate for possible further criminal activity. A "search incident" to a traffic stop is inappropriate, as arrest generally does not follow from a traffic infraction. Search incident to arrest requires an arrest, not merely the issuance of a traffic citation.

The Supreme Court has recently decided several cases involving traffic stops and the authority of police during these encounters, and has generally allowed the police to use the traffic stop as a means of investigating for possible additional unlawful activity. These recent cases are briefly described below.

PRETEXT STOPS

In *Whren v. United States* (1996), the Supreme Court unanimously upheld the validity of pretextual traffic stops. In doing so, the Court resolved a conflict among lower federal and state courts and held that the subjective intent of a police officer making a traffic stop is irrelevant. So long as a police officer has a valid reason to stop a vehicle, the Court said, the fact that the officer used the violation of a traffic law as a pretext, or excuse, to stop a vehicle is irrelevant. The test is not whether an officer "would have" made the traffic stop, but whether an officer "could have" made the traffic stop (12). Because the traffic infraction provided the police officers with an objective and lawful basis for making the traffic stop, inquiry into their subjective motivation for making the traffic stop is unnecessary.

In *Whren*, District of Columbia police officers on drug interdiction patrol in an unmarked car observed a vehicle stop at an intersection for approximately twenty seconds and then turn right without signaling. The police officers followed the vehicle and stopped it for the traffic infraction of stopping too long in an intersection, even though departmental regulations instructed officers on drug interdiction patrol not to conduct such traffic stops. The officers observed the passenger, Whren, in possession of crack cocaine in plain view during the stop, and he was arrested and subsequently convicted of drug possession.

On appeal, Whren claimed that the traffic stop was just a pretext to search for drugs, and that such "pretextual" stops constituted an unreasonable seizure for purposes of the Fourth Amendment. He argued that police officers used pretext stops to target members of minority groups for enforcement of drug laws, and cited a number of studies that indicated that black and Hispanic motorists were in fact stopped much more frequently for traffic offenses than white motorists (8).

The Court gave short shrift to Whren's claim that minority motorists were unfairly targeted for pretext stops, merely stating in an aside that if a defendant has evidence of intentional discrimination in the application of the law, he should file an Equal Protection claim rather than allege a violation of the Fourth Amendment. Unfortunately, this is likely a toothless remedy, as proof of an Equal Protection violation requires both a discriminatory effect and purpose. Proving a discriminatory purpose, in the absence of an officer's unlikely admission of such, may be impossible because records of traffic stops are rarely kept to document the anecdotal evidence of targeting (9).

The result of the *Whren* decision is that police officers are free to stop anyone who commits a traffic infraction even if they do so not because of concern over the traffic infraction but because they want to use the infraction as an excuse to stop the vehicle, so that they can investigate possible other crimes, for which the officer has no probable cause or even reasonable suspicion. Given the comprehensive scope of state traffic codes, *Whren* is a decision that affords the police a great deal of power vis-à-vis individual citizens. A number of studies and a mountain of anecdotal evidences support the contention that police misuse traffic regulations as a means of investigating crime, and when they do so, they often target minority drivers (8, 12–14). Indeed, the practice has become so common that it has its own slang description, DWB, or Driving While Black (15).

Whren gives police officers virtually unfettered authority to make a traffic stop, so long as they observe one of the myriad traffic infractions that are on the books. The fact that the police officer cares not about the traffic infraction but is simply using it as a pretext (or excuse) to stop a vehicle, so that the officer can conduct an investigation, is irrelevant. Assuming the investigation does not reveal any obvious signs of wrongdoing (such as the openly displayed drugs in *Whren*), the officer cannot conduct a full search of the vehicle or the occupants unless the officer obtains consent to conduct such a search.

Consent to Search a Vehicle

Citizens may waive their rights, including their Fourth Amendment rights. Police often ask a motorist stopped for a traffic infraction to waive the motorist's Fourth Amendment right to be free from unreasonable searches and seizures and consent to a search of their vehicle. However, for consent to be considered valid, it must be voluntary. There is no magic formula or "bright-line" rule for determining when consent is voluntary. Instead, courts look to the "totality of the circumstances" surrounding how the consent was obtained (7).

Although consent must be voluntary, it need not be "intelligent"; that is, there is no requirement that the state show a person who waives his or her Fourth Amendment rights and consents to a search that they have a right to refuse consent. In *Schneckloth v. Bustamonte* (1973), the Supreme Court expressly rejected the opportunity to impose a bright-line rule requiring knowledge of the right to refuse consent. In *Miranda v. Arizona* (1966), the Court determined that for a criminal suspect to validly waive the right to counsel and the privilege against self-incrimination, the waiver must not only be voluntary but intelligent, meaning that the police must inform the suspect of his rights before asking him or her to waive them. The defendant in *Schneckloth* asked the Court to extend this requirement of "intelligent" waiver to the Fourth Amendment right to be free of unreasonable searches and seizures, but the Court declined to extend the protections accorded in the Fifth and Sixth Amendment to the Fourth Amendment. This is an important distinction, and one that the police use to their advantage. Anyone who has watched a reality television show, such as Cops, must wonder why a suspect would give consent to a search that will obviously reveal incriminating evidence.

Although the Supreme Court made it clear in *Schneckloth* that the "totality of the circumstances" was the appropriate standard by which to determine voluntariness, it did not clarify the meaning of "voluntary." For instance, could a person who has been seized ever be considered to have acted voluntarily, or is there a presumption that their free will has been overborne by the police detention? Cases subsequent to *Schneckloth* have provided some guidance. In *United States v. Mendenhall* (1980), the Court determined that the standard for determining whether a person has been seized is if a reasonable person in the suspect's position would have believed that he was not free to leave. In *Florida v. Bostick* (1991), the Supreme Court stated that "a seizure does not occur simply because a police officer approaches an individual and asks a few questions ... only when the officer by means of physical force or show of authority, has in some way restrained the liberty of a citizen may we conclude that a 'seizure' has occurred."

The cumulative effect of these decisions was that police officers began to seek consent to search in a variety of encounters with civilians, including traffic stops. This request is made routinely and is not necessarily based on any particularized suspicion of drug-related activity. Specialized drug interdiction patrols utilize this tactic, as do officers on routine patrol.

In *Ohio v. Robinette* (1996), the Supreme Court, faced with an extreme example, nonetheless upheld the practice and refused to require that police officers inform motorists of their Fourth Amendment right to refuse consent to search. A sheriff's deputy on drug interdiction patrol stopped Robinette for speeding, intending, as he admitted later, to use the stop as an opportunity to seek consent to search Robinette's car. This deputy had successfully obtained consent to search 786 times the year prior to his stopping Robinette. The deputy asked Robinette to step out of the car, examined his license, issued Robinette a verbal warning about speeding, and handed back the driver's license. At this point the traffic stop was completed. The deputy did not stop there, however. He then asked: "Would you mind if I search your car? Make sure there's nothing in there?" Robinette gave his consent, a small amount of drugs was discovered, and he was subsequently convicted of felony drug possession.

On appeal, Robinette contended that once the purpose of the traffic stop (the issuance of a warning for speeding) was satisfied, the deputy could not legally detain him further for the express purpose of obtaining consent to search. The Supreme Court of Ohio agreed, and adopted a bight-line rule that once an initially valid traffic stop is concluded, a police officer must inform the motorist that their legal detention has concluded, before the police officer can endeavor to obtain consent to search. The court said that the officer should instruct the motorist that "at this time you are legally free to go" or issue a warning substantially similar. Only after this is done can a traffic stop be transformed into a consensual encounter.

The U.S. Supreme Court reversed the Ohio court's decision, holding that the Fourth Amendment does not require that a lawfully seized defendant be warned that he is free to leave, before his consent to a search is recognized as voluntary. The Court firmly rejected the rule enunciated by the Ohio court and reiterated its preference for the "totality of the circumstances" approach in determining the reasonableness of police activity involving the Fourth Amendment. The majority opinion asserted that the Court "consistently eschewed bright-line rules," and claimed that such a rule was impractical, as "it would be unrealistic to require police officers to always inform detainees that they are free to go before a consent to search may be deemed voluntary." The Court neglected to explain why requiring an officer to utter a couple of sentences would be impractical, although the opinion did acknowledge that such a requirement would not be in the interests of effective law enforcement (16).

The result of the *Robinette* decision is that police are free to attempt to turn a routine traffic stop into a full-scale vehicle search. An officer may use his authority and presence to pressure a motorist into giving consent to search. How many motorists would feel free to refuse consent when an officer has just stopped them and kindly declined to issue them a traffic ticket? Most motorists would not feel free to leave, as Robinette did not; those who felt free to leave might still be reluctant to refuse consent for fear of annoying the officer and perhaps receiving a traffic ticket after all.

Whren allows police to stop anyone for a traffic infraction regardless of their underlying motivation, and *Robinette* allows police to seek consent to search without informing a driver of the right to refuse consent. An issue unaddressed by these decisions is the impact of a traffic stop on passengers.

AUTHORITY OVER PASSENGERS

In *Pennsylvania v. Mimms* (1977), the Supreme Court determined that as a matter of officer safety, police may, as part of a traffic stop, order the driver out of a lawfully stopped vehicle. The Supreme Court determined that the police had probable cause to stop Mimms based on a traffic infraction, and that the request to exit the automobile was merely an "incremental intrusion" into the liberty of a lawfully stopped driver. The Court balanced the interests of the individual and society, and determined that that intrusion into the individual's liberty was "de minimus" and "a mere inconvenience," whereas the weight accorded to the public interest, officer safety, was "too plain for argument."

In *Maryland v. Wilson* (1997), the Supreme Court extended the *Mimms* holding to passengers, holding that a police officer who has lawfully stopped a vehicle for a traffic infraction may order an innocent passenger out of the car, along with the driver. Wilson was a passenger in a car lawfully stopped for speeding by a Maryland state trooper. After ordering the driver out of the car and asking him for his driver's license and registration, the trooper noticed that Wilson appeared nervous and sweating profusely, and ordered Wilson out of the car. As Wilson exited the vehicle, he inadvertently dropped a package of crack cocaine. The trooper seized the drugs and arrested Wilson for drug possession. Wilson sought to have the drugs suppressed as the product of an unlawful seizure, arguing that the trooper had no authority to order Wilson, a passenger not suspected of any wrongdoing, out of the vehicle. The trial court suppressed the drugs and the Maryland Court of Special Appeals affirmed it.

The Supreme Court in *Mimms* concluded that police officers could routinely order a driver out of a lawfully stopped vehicle regardless of the severity of the offense. This was based on balancing the interests in police safety against the privacy interests involved in being ordered out of a car. The Court in *Wilson* acknowledged that ordering a passenger out of a vehicle was an intrusion on the privacy interests of the passenger, but determined that, as in *Mimms*, this intrusion was minimal and greatly outweighed by the public benefit in the form of increased officer safety.

The result of the *Wilson* decision is that police are now free to order any and all passengers out of a lawfully stopped vehicle. The police may do this even though they have not observed the passenger commit a crime (or even a traffic infraction). Police need not have any articulable suspicion of wrongdoing of any sort on the part of the passenger. This provides police officers with the ability to interfere in the lives of persons who they have no reason to suspect of criminal wrongdoing.

Police can stop a vehicle for a traffic infraction even if this is a pretext to investigate for evidence of unrelated criminal activity. Additionally, they can order both the driver and the passengers out of the vehicle during the traffic stop. They may seek consent to search the vehicle and the occupants. Police officers arresting a driver may, of course, conduct a search incident of the driver, and this search extends to the passenger compartment of the car (*New York v. Belton* 1981). However, what about searching the passengers or their belongings? Such was the issue in the next case to be discussed.

SEARCH OF CONTAINERS IN THE VEHICLE

In *Wyoming v. Houghton* (1999), the Supreme Court held that a police officer who has lawfully stopped a vehicle for a traffic infraction, and subsequently developed probable cause to believe the vehicle contains illegal drugs, may search the belongings of a passenger in the vehicle even in the absence of any particularized probable cause specific to the belongings or the passenger. The Court utilized a reasonableness analysis, balancing the interests of the individual passenger against the interests of society. In this context, the Court held, there is no reason to limit the search of a vehicle to only those containers clearly in the possession of the driver. Passengers have a reduced expectation of privacy with regard to the property they transport in automobiles, and the degree of intrusiveness involved in a search of their belongings in an automobile is minimal. On the other side of the equation, society has a significant interest in permitting police officers to examine the belongings of passengers of a vehicle when there is probable cause to believe there is contraband somewhere within the vehicle.

In *Houghton*, a Wyoming state trooper stopped a car for speeding and, upon approaching the vehicle, noticed a syringe sticking out of the driver's shirt pocket. The driver admitted using the syringe to take drugs. Houghton, one of the passengers in the vehicle, was frisked, and the car was searched for drugs, based on the probable cause established when the driver admitted to illegal drug use and the automobile exception to the search warrant requirement. In the back seat of the vehicle, the trooper found Houghton's purse and opened it. Inside the purse the trooper found drug paraphernalia and a syringe containing methamphetamine. Houghton was arrested, charged, and convicted of drug possession.

At trial and on appeal, Houghton asserted that the search of her purse violated the Fourth Amendment because the trooper lacked probable cause to suspect her of carrying drugs and therefore he had no probable cause to search her purse. The Wyoming Supreme Court reversed her conviction, holding that the search of her purse exceeded the reasonable scope of the search of the car. The state court acknowledged that the trooper had probable cause to search the car, but asserted that the trooper should have known the purse did not belong to the driver, and as the police had probable cause to suspect only the driver of wrongdoing, there was no authority to examine items in the car that clearly did not belong to the driver.

This decision greatly increases the ability of police officers to search containers in lawfully stopped vehicles at the expense of the privacy interests of passengers not suspected of wrongdoing. Now virtually any container in a vehicle that is subject to search after a traffic stop may be searched even if it clearly does not belong to the driver. The Court in *Houghton* decided to issue a bright-line rule (as opposed to other cases, such as *Robinette*). Perhaps coincidentally, police benefit from the application of a bright-line rule in *Houghton* and benefit from the refusal to apply a bright-line rule in *Robinette*.

The cases so far have dealt with the authority of the police to stop vehicles and what the police can do short of an arrest. Search incident to arrest is a powerful investigatory weapon, as it allows a police officer to search the arrested person and the passenger compartment of the vehicle in which they were riding. Search incident, as the name implies, requires an arrest. Traditionally, police could not arrest a driver for a minor traffic infraction, so the only way an officer could search a vehicle during a traffic stop was through a consent search. Some states have recently changed this, however.

SEARCH INCIDENT TO CITATION (ALMOST)

The Supreme Court in *Atwater v. City of Lago Vista* (2001) upheld an arrest for a nonjailable traffic infraction that the state of Texas had classified as a misdemeanor. This decision opens the door to a search incident for many more offenses. A Texas police officer on routine traffic patrol observed Atwater and her two young children driving without wearing their seat belts. Failure to wear a seat belt is a misdemeanor in Texas, punishable by a maximum fifty dollar fine. Because there is no possibility of incarceration, it is referred to as a "citation-only offense." The police officer nonetheless chose to arrest rather than to cite and release Atwater. Texas authorizes police to arrest or cite for all offenses, even nonjail misdemeanors. Several hours after being booked and jailed, Atwater posted bail and was released. She eventually pleaded no contest to the seat belt violation and paid a fifty dollar fine. She then brought a Section 1983 suit against the officer and his employer, alleging her arrest violated her Fourth Amendment right to be free from an "unreasonable" seizure. The district court dismissed the lawsuit, and the Fifth Circuit Court of Appeals affirmed the dismissal.

The Supreme Court said it was per se reasonable for a police officer with probable cause to believe a crime has been committed in his presence to make an arrest for "even a very minor criminal offense." Justice Souter, writing for a narrow five to four majority, asserted that such an arrest was reasonable, regardless of whether or not so authorized by state law. Such an arrest is per se reasonable under the Fourth Amendment. The gravity of the offense is irrelevant in determining the authority of the police to arrest. It is important to note, however, that the opinion refers to a criminal offense, and most jurisdictions (but not Texas) treat most traffic infractions as noncriminal.

After *Atwater*, police may use their arrest authority as a pretext to conduct a search incident to arrest. *Atwater* does not authorize a "search incident to citation," as there must be both a citation and an arrest, but it does allow arrest for "minor criminal offenses." Texas chose to make failure to wear a seat belt a misdemeanor, even though there was no possibility of incarceration. Other states have similar provisions in their criminal and traffic codes. Additionally, the decision in *Atwater* rested not on state law but on the Reasonableness Clause of the Fourth Amendment. So long as an arrest is reasonable, a search may be conducted. Further, the Court's language in *Atwater* suggests that the Fourth Amendment may authorize an arrest in situations where state law does not. This gives the police tremendous discretion to arrest and then search the vehicle of persons who have done nothing more than fail to signal a lane change or wear a seat belt. Clearly, this decision is a major victory for law enforcement.

Under the preceding cases, if police can justify a traffic stop, they have a tremendous opportunity to use the stop as the foundation for additional investigation of possible criminal activity. For a traffic stop to be valid, however, the police must have evidence of some criminal wrongdoing or violation of traffic laws. What about the situation where police do not have any particularized suspicion of criminal activity on the part of a driver? A series of cases dealing with police use of roadblocks addresses this issue.

ROADBLOCKS

In *Michigan Dept. of State Police v. Sitz* (1990), the Supreme Court upheld brief roadblocks to check for possible drunken drivers. The Court in *Sitz* balanced the great public interest in removing drunk drivers from the highways against what the Court characterized as the *"de minimis"* intrusion of a brief traffic stop, and determined that random stops at roadblocks, based on less than probable cause, were reasonable. However, in an earlier case, *Delaware v. Prouse* (1979), the Supreme Court had noted that traffic stops based on less than probable cause would not be allowed for the purpose of "general crime control." These two decisions caused some confusion in the law enforcement community as police administrators sought to determine in what situations roadblocks might be lawfully employed.

Indianapolis police, relying on *Sitz*, set up roadblocks, referred to as "narcotics checkpoints," for the admitted primary purpose of catching drivers with drugs in their vehicle although police also looked for potential DWI (driving while intoxicated) offenders and checked driver license and registration papers. While a vehicle was stopped and the driver's documents examined, police walked a drug-sniffing dog around the car, looked in the vehicle windows, and sought consent from the driver to search the vehicle. If the drug-sniffing dog alerted, the police saw contraband in plain view in the vehicle, or consent to search was obtained from the driver, the vehicle would be fully examined. Indianapolis drivers brought a class action lawsuit to stop the roadblocks. The district court refused to grant an injunction, but the Seventh Circuit Court of Appeals granted it.

The Supreme Court invalidated the drug interdiction roadblocks. The Court noted that DWI checkpoints are an exception to the general rule requiring individualized suspicion, and that such exceptions were justified only when there was a great public interest at stake. Apprehension of DWI violators, the Court felt, constituted a significant public safety justification. Here, the Court asserted that the police had failed to establish a "direct public safety" justification. Drug possession is different and less likely to pose an immediate public safety issue than operating a vehicle while under the influence of alcohol. Indianapolis argued that *Whren v. United*

States (1996), which held that an officer's subjective intent was irrelevant, allowed drug checkpoint because the secondary purpose of the Indianapolis roadblocks was DWI investigation. The Supreme Court disagreed, noting that allowing such checkpoints would permit police to operate checkpoints for anything so long as they also looked for evidence of DWI. It was unclear what the Supreme Court would do if the stated primary purpose of a roadblock was DWI enforcement and the secondary purpose was to check for drugs. The Court suggested that such a checkpoint might pass constitutional muster.

In *Illinois* v. *Lidster* (2004), the Supreme Court refined the *Indianapolis* v. *Edmond* (2000) decision in holding that police may establish a roadblock to seek information about recent crimes. The case involved a roadblock set up by Illinois state police at the same spot and time of day that a hit-and-run had recently taken place. The goal of the roadblock was to contact motorists who might have witnessed the hit-and-run. Lidster was arrested and convicted of drunken driving after police at the roadblock determined he was intoxicated. He challenged the constitutionality of the roadblock, arguing that it was void under *Edmond* because the roadblock was set up to stop drivers without any individualized suspicion, and there was no significant public interest to counter the intrusion upon the individual's privacy interests.

The Supreme Court affirmed Lidster's conviction and distinguished the roadblock in this case form the roadblock invalidated in *Edmond*. The Court noted that the checkpoint was narrowly tailored to address an important investigatory need. The primary purpose of the roadblock in *Edmond* was to investigate possible criminal activity on the part of the occupants of the vehicles being stopped. Here, the primary purpose of the roadblock was to seek assistance in solving a crime. There was no attempt to investigate possible criminal activity on the part of the occupants of these vehicles. Because the primary purpose of the roadblock was not to investigate possible criminal activity on the part of the stopped motorists but rather merely to gain information about a previous crime, the roadblock did not violate the Fourth Amendment.

The result is that police may make use of roadblocks in certain situations, and any evidence of criminal wrongdoing they uncover as a consequence of the roadblock may be admitted at trial. The key is determining the primary purpose of the roadblock—if it is to conduct a general investigation of possible criminal activity by motorists, it will likely be struck down. This authority to stop individual motorists at a roadblock without any individualized suspicion gives the police tremendous authority to investigate crime.

CONCLUSION

As the preceding cases reveal, the police have increasingly relied on traffic stops in their efforts to fight the "war on drugs." The Supreme Court has repeatedly shown great deference to law enforcement interests. In so doing, the Court has retreated from its duty to provide meaningful, stringent oversight of police activities. According to the current Supreme Court, "reasonableness is the 'touchstone' of the Fourth Amendment" (*Florida v. Jimeno*, 1991). This simply means that all the Amendment requires is that police officers act rationally and pursue reasonable goals when they intrude upon individuals (9). There is no requirement that police officers always have a warrant, or even probable cause in some instances. The Court determines what constitutes reasonable police behavior by weighing the individual's privacy interest against the legitimate interests of law enforcement. Unfortunately, such a balancing test is inherently subjective and thus tends to weaken the Fourth Amendment's protections (17).

The result of the Court's increased reliance on a relaxed application of the balancing test to determine the reasonableness of police action has been a pronounced tendency by the Court to uphold virtually all police investigatory practices. If the police can identify any plausible goal that promotes law enforcement interests, the Court is likely to hold that the challenged policy is reasonable (9). Further, the message appears to be getting through to the police—just about anything goes in the war on drugs. The result is that individuals traveling the nation's highways have a circumscribed set of constitutional rights.

What all this means for police administrators is they must know how far they can push the envelope of the Fourth Amendment. They must also make sure patrol officers, the ones engaged in traffic stops, know the limits of their authority, and how they can exploit to the utmost the Fourth Amendment as interpreted by a pro–law enforcement Supreme Court. Police administrators would be well advised to consider the implications of these decisions. Proactive law enforcement requires the police to seek out new ways to uncover criminal activity and apprehend wrongdoers. The Supreme Court, as currently configured, has given the green light (pun intended) to police who seek to use traffic stops as a means of investigating possible criminal activity unrelated to the traffic stop. Police administrators should study these recent Supreme Court decisions closely and determine the appropriate parameters of police activity during traffic stops.

REFERENCES

1. Rowley, C.J. (1992). Florida v. Bostick: The Fourth Amendment: another casualty of the war on drugs, *Utah Law Review,* 1992(1992): 601–645.
2. Kelling, G.L., and C.M. Coles. (1996). *Fixing Broken Windows*, New York: The Free Press.
3. Livingston, D. (1998). Police, community caretaking, and the Fourth Amendment, *The University of Chicago Legal Forum,* 1998: 261–314.
4. Skolnick, J.H. (1998). Terry and community policing, *St. John's Law Review,* 72: 1265–1270.
5. Walker, S. (1992). *The Police in America*, New York: McGraw-Hill.
6. Harris, D.A. (1998). Car wars: The Fourth Amendment's death on the highway, *The George Washington Law Review,* 66: 557–591.
7. Kennedy, R. (1997). *Race, Crime and the Law*, New York: Pantheon Books.
   LaFave, W.R. (1996). *Search and Seizure: A Treatise on the Fourth Amendment*, St. Paul, MN: West Publishing.
8. Harris, D.A. (1998). Race and the Fourth Amendment, *Vanderbilt Law Review,* 51: 33–393.
9. Maclin, T. (1993). The central meaning of the Fourth Amendment, *William and Mary Law Review,* 35: 197–249.

10. Sklansky, D.A. (1998). Traffic stops, minority motorists, and the future of the Fourth Amendment, *The Supreme Court Review 1997*, D.J. Hutchinson, D.A. Strauss, and G.R. Stone, (eds.), Chicago, IL: The University of Chicago Press.
11. del Carmen, Rolando V. (2004). *Criminal Procedure: Law and Practice*. Belmont, CA: Wadsworth.
12. Bast, C.M. (1997). Driving while back: stopping motorists on a subterfuge, *Criminal Law Bulletin*, 33: 457–486.
13. Harris, D.A. (1994). Factors for reasonable suspicion: when black and poor means stopped and frisked, *Indiana Law Journal*, 69: 659–688.
14. Harris, D.A. (1997). 'Driving While Black' and all other traffic offenses: The Supreme Court and pretextual traffic stops, *The Journal of Criminal Law and Criminology*. 87: 544–582.
15. Harris, D.A. (2002). *Profiles in Injustice: Why Racial Profiling Cannot Work*. New York: The New Press.
16. Hemmens, C., and J.R. Maahs. (1996). Reason to believe: Ohio v. Robinette. *Ohio Northern University Law Review*, 23: 309–346.
17. Strossen, N. (1998). The Fourth Amendment in the balance: accurately setting the scales through the least intrusive alternative analysis, *New York University Law Review*, 63: 1173–1267.

CASES CITED

Atwater v. City of Lago Vista, 532 U.S. 318 (2001).
Delaware v. Prouse, 440 U.S. 648 (1979).
Florida v. Bostick, 501 U.S. 429 (1991).
Florida v. Jimeno, 499 U.S. 934 (1991).
Illinois v. Lidster, 540 U.S. 419 (2004).
Indianapolis v. Edmond, 531 U.S. 32 (2000).
Maryland v. Wilson, 519 U.S. 408 (1997).
Michigan Department of State Police v. Sitz, 496 U.S. 444 (1990).
Miranda v. Arizona, 384 U.S. 436 (1966).
New York v. Belton, 453 U.S. 454 (1981).
Ohio v. Robinette, 519 U.S. 33 (1996).
Pennsylvania v. Mimms, 434 U.S. 106 (1977).
Schneckloth v. Bustamonte, 412 U.S. 218 (1973).
Terry v. Ohio, 392 U.S. 1 (1968).
United States v. Mendenhall, 446 U.S. 544 (1980).
Whren v. United States, 517 U.S. 806 (1996).
Wolf v. Colorado, 338 U.S. 25 (1949).
Wyoming v. Houghton, 526 U.S. 295 (1999).

8 Protected Expression: Police Employee First Amendment Rights

William P. Bloss

CONTENTS

INTRODUCTION

Police employees are afforded several constitutional protections under the First Amendment to the U.S. Constitution. These include freedom of speech, expression, and association. In spite of these safeguards, the courts have permitted police employers to regulate some employee activities. This chapter examines the scope of First Amendment rights available to police employees and the circumstances in which police employers can legally regulate those workplace activities.

When courts review cases involving employee First Amendment challenges of regulatory policy or adverse employment action, they rely upon a "balancing of competing interests test" (1,2). The test weighs the government's operational needs against the constitutional rights of public employees. Whoever the court finds has the more compelling interest often prevails in the employer–employee legal dispute. Courts have bestowed authority upon police employers to enforce regulations that contribute to the effective operation of the law enforcement agency (3,4). However, employers bear the burden of demonstrating that their regulatory policies have a rational relationship to the effective operation of the government agency. If employers are unable to establish a nexus between their policy and department function, employee claims may be upheld as an unconstitutional violation of their First Amendment rights (5).

Guidelines for regulating constitutionally protected police employee activities are developed either by the courts or legislatures. First Amendment jurisprudence is formed by court decisions that determine the circumstances under which employers can regulate employee conduct in the areas of speech, expression, or association. Though the courts have not agreed on the extent of employer regulation in every instance, they have sought to balance police employee rights with the employer's need to operate an effective law enforcement agency (5,6). In fact, to legally permit the regulation of certain employee activities many courts require police employers to demonstrate that unregulated employee conduct would have an adverse impact on the agency (3,4).

EMPLOYEE FREEDOM OF SPEECH

One of the most prominent areas of the First Amendment protection claimed by police employees is freedom of speech. Courts commonly use the standard of public employee protected speech established by the U.S. Supreme Court in *Pickering v. Board of Education* (7). As police employees are treated as public employees in the court's view, the Pickering principle is considered most applicable. In *Pickering*, the Court ruled that public employees are permitted to freely speak on matters that pertain to issues of public concern or interest.

The most frequently cited case applying the Pickering standard is *Connick v. Myers* (8). In Connick, the U.S. Supreme Court stated that for employee speech to be protected as a matter of public concern, it must be "fairly considered as relating to any matter of political, social, or other concern of the community" and should be "determined by the content, form, and context of a given statement" (8 p. 146). Later, courts have concluded that police employers can only regulate employee speech that does not involve issues of public concern.

TYPES OF EMPLOYEE PROTECTED SPEECH

Though the determination of whether or not employee speech is protected is left to the courts, several types of remarks have typically been permitted. One of the more common types of speech voiced in the police workplace is employee criticism of department management or operation. This includes critical comments about management, morale, policy, procedure, pay, or other labor matters. Courts have consistently held that this type of employee remark is permissible and constitutionally protected if it is truthful, involves matters of public concern, and is not intentionally disruptive (9–11).

Further, courts have ruled that employers cannot restrict employee speech on public matters. In several cases, employers have sought to control employee public matter comments with either regulation or discipline. These efforts have been rejected by the courts who have found that such actions violate employee protected speech rights (12,13).

Other types of employee speech have also been protected by the courts. Employee views involving artistic expression, areas of expertise, or "whistle-blowing" speech are often protected from employer regulation (14).

WHISTLE-BLOWING SPEECH

Employee reporting of public official unlawful conduct has become known as *whistle-blowing* in statute and case law (15). Public employees have traditionally been protected from employer retaliation for reporting unlawful actions in a variety of areas (e.g., environmental protection, labor relations, public health and safety, and public securities). Federal law is replete with statutes affording protection to federal public employees who may suffer reprisals from employers for reporting illegal actions to law enforcement authorities (15). Though these laws are often modeled after the Whistleblower Protection Act of 1989, Congress continues to expand such statutory protections in areas of public interest (16). In 2002, Congress enacted the Sarbanes–Oxley Act to extend whistle-blowing protection to employees who report securities fraud to officials in the wake of sensational reports of corporate misconduct (17,18).

In addition to protecting federal employee whistle-blowing speech, at least thirty-eight states have enacted specific statutes that shield public employees, including police officers, from retaliation if they report illegal agency conduct to law enforcement officials (3 p. 298). Statutory provisions vary by state in terms of reporting procedures, eligible employees, available remedies, etc. Some statutes require that employees exhaust all remedies internally and others compel employees to follow procedures prescribed in the statute (19,14). However, the common ground is that these laws protect public employees from adverse employment action or reprisal as a result of the reporting of official law violations.

Police employees have been afforded considerable protection in the courts for whistle-blowing speech under the First Amendment. One federal appeals court wrote, "… an [police] employee's First Amendment interest is entitled to more weight where he is acting as a whistle-blower exposing government corruption" (20 p. 1423, 21). Though much of the whistle-blowing speech litigation involves statutes, courts using a constitutional interpretation have found such speech to be safeguarded by the First Amendment and Pickering-related case law (22). Hence, in an effort to encourage reporting and reduce official corruption, police employees have gained statutory and constitutional protection for whistle-blowing speech.

TYPES OF UNPROTECTED EMPLOYEE SPEECH

In spite of the presence of employee speech protection on public matters, not all comments are restricted from regulation. Employers are permitted to regulate or discipline employee speech that is unrelated to public matters (23). Intentionally vulgar, disruptive, or hate speech can be subject to employer discipline (24). Employee endorsement of products or services that does not involve matters of public concern is also not protected by the courts (5).

Hence, police employees are given considerable latitude in expressing their views on matters of public concern or whistle-blowing speech in the workplace. Only in areas of nonpublic concern, intentionally disruptive, vulgar, or hate speech can employers regulate and discipline employee speech.

EMPLOYEE EXPRESSION THROUGH APPEARANCE OR DRESS

First Amendment protection of expression extends beyond speech. Included in the safeguards are also nonverbal methods of expression, such as gesture, dress, or appearance. The public safety role of police agencies makes them very conscious of their community image and reputation. Thus, employers often seek to regulate the professional appearance and conduct of employees working in the community (25).

Employee grooming is one common type of appearance that can be governed by employers. The U.S. Supreme Court ruled in *Kelley v. Johnson* that police employers could establish policies that regulate employee hair grooming (26). As long as policies are not arbitrary, other grooming or appearance standards can be enforced upon employees. As an example, a Massachusetts court upheld a "no mustache ban" imposed by the Massachusetts state police (27).

Regulation of appearance can involve matters other than hair grooming. The federal Court of Appeals for the Seventh Circuit held in *Rathert v. Village of Peotone* that the police department could prohibit off-duty officers from wearing ear-stud jewelry because they had a legitimate interest in maintaining agency effectiveness, which included community image (28). In another case, the court permitted the agency to regulate the exposure of visible tattoos by a uniformed patrol officer (29). The *Riggs* court found that the officer's rights had not been violated by the department's professional appearance policy that required all tattoos be covered by uniform garments.

Following the Supreme Court's lead in *Kelley v. Johnson*, lower courts have allowed police departments to establish and enforce dress, grooming, and appearance codes upon employees (26). To regulate employee appearance, agencies must demonstrate that their rules are necessary to operate and maintain an effective police operation.

EMPLOYEE EXPRESSION THROUGH POLITICAL ACTIVITIES

There is considerable disagreement among the courts regarding political patronage by police employees. Political patronage can involve such activities as supporting or endorsing candidates, political donations, political affiliations, and participating in political campaigns. The U.S. Supreme Court has provided some guidance by deciding a few cases involving the disciplining or discharge of public employees for engaging in political activities.

PUBLIC EMPLOYEE RIGHT OF POLITICAL PATRONAGE

In *Elrod v. Burns*, the Court ruled that it was a violation of employee First Amendment freedom of expression for employers to dismiss them for engaging in political patronage if they were not involved in agency policy making (30). The *Elrod* Court recognized the importance of political loyalty among policy-making public employees, and therefore, permitted adverse employment action against them but not against those who were not involved in agency policy-making.

In another case, the Supreme Court further explained the scope of the policy maker exception. They held in *Branti v. Finkel* that if employers take adverse employment actions (e.g., dismissal, demotion, transfer, and discipline) against non-policy-making public employees for political activities, they must demonstrate that the patronage detracted from the effective operation of the agency (31). Otherwise, the Elrod–Branti doctrine holds that employers are prohibited from punishing non-policy-making employees for their political activities (30,31). Following these U.S. Supreme Court decisions, lower courts have produced mixed interpretations of the circumstances under which employers can regulate or sanction police employee political patronage.

ADVERSE ACTION AGAINST EMPLOYEES WHO SUPPORT CANDIDATES

Employees who work for elected law enforcement officials, such as sheriffs, are often subject to adverse employment action for supporting the political opposition (32). Employees who are employed by elected officials are classified as *at-will* workers and serve at the discretion of the employer. They tend to be more vulnerable to political forces in the workplace because the employer is a politician. Much of the litigation involving political patronage in the police workplace stems from these types of circumstances (5).

Some courts have prohibited employers from retaliating against employees for supporting their political opponents (33–35). Often, the political opponents lose to the incumbent sheriff, thus leaving the employee who supported them vulnerable to reprisals. In two cases, the U.S. Courts of Appeal upheld claims brought by deputy sheriffs who had been discharged for running political campaigns against their employers (36,37). Other employees, who had been transferred or demoted for supporting candidates who opposed their employers, experienced varied rulings. In *Morris v. Crow* and *Matherne v. Wilson*, the courts ruled that police employees had been improperly transferred for supporting the employer's opposition (38,39). Conversely, in *Heidman v. Wirsing*, another appeals court held that such an adverse employment action was not a violation of First Amendment protections (40). Again, in *Joyner v. Lancaster*, the Seventh Circuit found that the dismissal of a sheriff's captain for supporting a political opponent was allowable because he was in a policy-making capacity (41,42).

ADVERSE ACTION AGAINST EMPLOYEES BASED ON POLITICAL AFFILIATION

Other cases have been decided involving deputy sheriffs who suffered workplace reprisals because of their political party affiliation. The court in *Jones v. Dodson* ruled that deputy sheriffs could not be dismissed solely because of their political party affiliations (43). Several cases have emerged involving newly elected sheriffs who refuse to rehire individuals employed by their predecessor (44). In *Brady v. Fort Bend County* the court held that the new sheriff could not refuse to rehire employees, who worked for and supported his incumbent opponent, based upon their party affiliation and support of the opposition (45). However, other courts have found that if employees who supported the previous administration are sufficiently oppositional, disruptive, or abusive, the incoming sheriffs may be able to justify their refusal to rehire prior employees (46,47).

POLICY RESTRICTION OF EMPLOYEE POLITICAL ACTIVITY

Some departments try to restrict the political activities of employees through policy. In some cases, courts have decided that it was not a violation of employee First Amendment rights for policies to prohibit state police employees from running for political office or displaying political advertising on their personal property (48–50).

Courts have consistently ruled that police employers cannot take adverse action against nonpolicy-making employees for their political activities or views. Other areas of regulation of employee political patronage are less clear in the case law. Elected law enforcement officials, such as sheriffs, have been given the greatest latitude by the courts in regulating the political environment within their agency.

EMPLOYEE FREEDOM OF RELIGION

Freedom of religion is a fundamental constitutional protection that falls squarely in the First Amendment. Police employees can bring legal challenges in two areas involving their religious faith and practice.

FEDERAL ANTIDISCRIMINATION LAW

The first covers the use of federal antidiscrimination statutes, such as Title VII of the Civil Rights Act of 1964, that prohibit the discrimination against a worker based upon, among other things, their religious belief (51). Once the employee has established a prima facie case of religious discrimination, the burden then shifts to the employer to prove that the discrimination did not occur. Title VII provisions do not prevent police departments from raising questions about employee religious practices if they believe it may affect the operation of the agency (52). Rather, it specifically prohibits employee discrimination based solely on those grounds.

FIRST AMENDMENT PROTECTION

Second, employees can raise First Amendment freedom of religion legal claims against employers. In some cases, police employees are demanding that employers make some type of "reasonable accommodation" for their religious belief or practice, whereas in others, they are seeking a workplace devoid of religious coercion. Because of the principle of "separation of church and state" and constitutional protection, police departments are compelled to remain neutral and avoid an official position on religious issues in the government workplace (53). In this vein, one court ruled that employers cannot impose religious beliefs on their employees. The court in *Venters v. City of Delphi* found that the police chief's religious proselytizing, and eventual termination, of a police dispatcher for failure to adopt certain religious beliefs violated the employee's freedom of religion (54).

EMPLOYER REQUIREMENT TO MAKE REASONABLE RELIGIOUS ACCOMMODATION

Employees may seek workplace accommodations and/or exemptions based on their religious beliefs. Some courts have ruled that once employers have made work assignment accommodations, police employees cannot avoid their duty based on religious grounds. In *Rodriguez v. City of Chicago* and *Parrott v. District of Columbia,* the courts rejected an officer's request for a religious exemption from an abortion clinic duty assignment on religious grounds (55,56). The courts found that the department had offered alternative assignments to employees, and once rejected, had made the required accommodation for religious belief. Typically, if employers offer alternate duty to the employee, they have complied with any "reasonable accommodation" requirement under a freedom of religion exemption in the workplace.

Courts have, however, required police departments to make other types of reasonable accommodation for religious belief or practice when requested by an employee. In one case involving an employee's request to have Saturday as a day off to observe the Sabbath, the court in *Balint v. Carson City, Nevada* found that, although the new employee was not eligible because of seniority, the department was required to make the religious accommodation (57). In *Fraternal Order of Police Newark Lodge No. 12 v. City of Newark*, the federal appeals court held that the department could not enforce a "no beard" policy on two Muslim officers who requested exemption on religious grounds (58). The court ruled that denial of the requested exemption to permit the officers to wear beards, in compliance with Islamic mandates, violated the employee's free exercise of religion under the First Amendment.

Hence, when employers are presented with demands for exemptions or accommodations in duty assignment, shift, uniform, or days off based on religious grounds, courts require them to make reasonable accommodation that does not produce undue hardship or cost on the operation of the agency. In addition, agencies are prohibited from engaging in discrimination or imposition of adverse employment action against employees solely based upon their religious belief or practice.

EMPLOYEE FREEDOM OF ASSOCIATION

REGULATION OF EMPLOYEE SEXUAL CONDUCT

The police employee First Amendment right of association typically falls into two categories—association with persons and association with organizations. Most employee litigation involves association in personal relationships with others. Intimate relationships involving the "right to be let alone" principle dominate employee complaints brought against agencies that seek to regulate their intimate conduct (4,59). The courts have permitted employers to regulate a myriad of intimate and sexual conducts of employees as long as they can demonstrate that there is a connection between the intimate association and the effective operation, public confidence, or community reputation of the police agency (6,60). These may include fraternization, adultery, fornication, cohabitation, intimate association with minors and disreputable persons, or homosexual conduct. Regulation of these associations may stem from department policy or state statutory law (e.g., fornication, sodomy, and adultery). In circumstances where employees are violating statutory law, employers are not required to show adverse impact on the agency. They can discipline employees for proscribed conduct simply because it is a criminal violation.

Regulation of Employee Adultery

Upon showing that adulterous conduct adversely impacts the agency or violates state criminal statutes, numerous courts have permitted police employers to discipline employees for off-duty extramarital activities. Employees often challenge employer regulation of extramarital affairs as either a constitutionally protected intimate association right or claim that the off-duty activity has no effect on the operation of the agency (5,61).

Some courts have ruled that adulterous conduct is not a protected right and have permitted employers to regulate and discipline employees for engaging in misconduct (62–65). As noted, police employee relationships can affect the agency community reputation or operation.

Some employers have justified the regulation of extramarital conduct on this basis. If they can demonstrate that there is a connection between the employee's adultery and the image or effectiveness of the law enforcement agency, several courts have permitted the employer to discipline them for misconduct (6). The courts in *Baron v. Meloni* and *Smith v. Price* held that employee adulterous conduct brought disrepute upon the agency, and therefore, could be subject to discipline (66,67). In an earlier decision, one court ruled that the agency could punish employees for adultery only if they could demonstrate that the conduct discredited the department (68).

Other courts have allowed employers to discharge employees for extramarital conduct because it violates state criminal statutes that prohibit adultery (69–71). Adultery is a common intimate association conduct subject to regulation in the police workplace through policy or discipline. The majority of courts have permitted employers to regulate the behavior to avoid violation of state criminal law or disruption of the agency.

Regulation of Employee Cohabitation

Another area of intimate association employers often seek to regulate is employee off-duty cohabitation. There is much less consensus among the courts in permitting the control of employee cohabitation than exists in the area of adultery. Some courts have rejected agency termination of employees for cohabitating off duty (72,73). Similarly, in *Shuman v. City of Philadelphia*, the court found that the department could not discipline an officer for failure to answer questions about his off-duty cohabitation because it lacked any relationship to the employee's performance of his duty (74).

In some cases, cohabitation involves police coworkers and some courts have allowed employers to regulate or discipline the fraternization under the aegis of producing a disruption to the morale or effective operation of the agency (75,76). Unlike some other types of employee intimate or sexual conduct, cohabitation is more difficult for employers to regulate unless they are able to demonstrate that it has an adverse impact on the functioning of the department.

Regulation of Employee Off-duty Dating Relationships

Another off-duty conduct that falls squarely in the area of associational relationships is employee dating. Ordinarily, courts have rejected employee assertions that dating is a protected First Amendment association right. In *Jackson v. Howell*, the court held that the agency could demote an officer for dating a crime victim he met while conducting an official investigation (77). Other cases involving employee fraternization have resulted in courts supporting the dismissal or disciplining of officers for dating coworkers because it had a disruptive effect on the operation of the agency (78,79). Regulation of employee relationships can also involve fraternization with non-coworkers.

Regulation of Employee Relationships with Disreputable Persons

Several courts have permitted the regulation or disciplining of police employees for intimate relationships with disreputable or notorious persons that have a deleterious effect on the reputation or effectiveness of the agency. One of the most cited cases is *Fugate v. Phoenix Civil Service Board*, involving the termination of officers involved in on-duty sexual relations with known prostitutes (80). The *Fugate* court held that the dismissals were permissible because the conduct harmed both the community reputation and effective operation of the agency (80).

In several cases involving department policies prohibiting "unbecoming conduct," which among other things included officer intimate relationships with criminal offenders, the courts have allowed employers to restrict these activities. Courts routinely have ruled that employers can discharge or discipline officers for having intimate relations with known drug addicts, felons, or felony probationers in violation of unbecoming conduct policies (81–83). Conversely, one court in *Reuter v. Skipper*, found that an officer's relationship with an ex-felon failed to produce any safety or operational risk; therefore, the department improperly disciplined the employee for participating in the intimate relationship (84). Several other types of sexual or relational conduct may be subject to employer regulation.

Regulation of Other Types of Employee Intimate Relationships

Employees have litigated in an assortment of areas involving intimate relationships that occurred prior to becoming a police officer. The court in *Thorne v. City of El Segundo* ruled that the department could not reject an applicant because of her prior extramarital relationship (85). In another case, the court upheld the dismissal of a probationary officer who had sexual relations with a minor prior to joining the police force. As a violation of statutory law, the department was justified in discharging the officer for committing statutory rape under state statute before his employment (86).

In supporting the department's action in conducting an internal investigation into allegations that an officer had engaged in extramarital and intermarital relationships, the court in *Hughes v. City of North Olmstead* et al. found that such conduct could have a deleterious effect on department operations, and therefore, was not a violation of employee First Amendment rights (87). Another case involved two married employees who challenged the department's nepotism policy. In *Parks v. City of Warner Robins, Georgia* et al., the court upheld the nepotism policy because it found a rational relationship between the rule and agency effectiveness (88).

Regulation of Employee Homosexual Conduct

Police employer regulation of employee homosexual conduct is an unclear, yet changing, area of First Amendment and privacy jurisprudence. Some courts have permitted police agencies to dismiss employees engaged in homosexual conduct based upon either the rationale of violation of state law or effective operation of the department (6,89). Since 1986, the lower courts have relied on the doctrine of *Bowers v. Hardwick*, where the U.S. Supreme Court held that homosexual conduct was not a constitutionally protected right, thereby not shielding it from criminalization under statute (90). However, in 2003, the Court in *Lawrence* et al. *v. Texas* ruled that a Texas state statute criminalizing homosexual conduct was unconstitutional because it violates an individual liberty interest under the Due Process Clause (91). In overruling the *Bowers* holding, the Court found much of the rationale to be misguided and stated in *Lawrence* that persons had the "full right to engage in (consensual) private conduct without government intervention" (91 p.17).

One of the earliest cases involving the rejection of a civilian job applicant based on his admission of homosexual conduct is *Childers v. Dallas Police Department*. The *Childers* court ruled that the department could deny the applicant employment because of the potential negative impact on the operation of the agency (92). Using a similar rationale, the court in *Padula v. Webster* held that the FBI could reject a female special agent applicant because she was a practicing homosexual (93).

Expressing concern for the effect on the department's public reputation, the court in *Endsley v. Naes* permitted the discharge of a female deputy alleged to be a homosexual (94). Again, in *Todd v. Navarro*, the court found that the department was allowed to dismiss a lesbian deputy, ruling that homosexuals were not a protected class of persons (95). Another court in *Delahoussaye v. City of New Iberia* denied any constitutional violation in ruling that the department could refuse to reinstate a deputy alleged to have engaged in prior homosexual conduct (96).

Some courts have found that adverse employment action based upon homosexual conduct was improper. In *Buttino v. FBI*, a federal court held that the agency violated the employee's First Amendment freedom of expression by discharging a veteran agent for prior homosexual conduct discovered during an internal investigation (97). A Texas court in *City of Dallas v. England* ruled that the department could not reject an officer applicant because she admitted to being a practicing homosexual in a pre-employment polygraph (98). The department's actions were based on the fact that the conduct violates state criminal statutes prohibiting homosexual conduct.

Legal guidelines for the regulation of employee homosexual conduct are, at best, convoluted. Prior to the Supreme Court's ruling in *Lawrence* et al. *v. Texas*, the majority of the lower courts deciding cases involving the discharge of police employees alleged to have engaged in homosexual conduct upheld the department's actions (91). It appears likely that *Lawrence* will change the legal landscape regarding how departments regulate employee homosexual conduct.

EMPLOYEE ASSOCIATION WITH LABOR ORGANIZATIONS

Police employees are associated with various types of organizations, both on and off duty. Previously, it was discussed that employer regulation of employee participation with political organizations was mostly governed by the Elrod–Branti doctrine protecting nonpolicy-making employees from reprisals for their political patronage (30,31). Police employees may also become affiliated with labor organizations in the police workplace. Further, courts have found that such participation is constitutionally protected.

The courts have consistently ruled that employers cannot prohibit or restrict employee participation in labor organizations (99). In two cases, federal Courts of Appeal held that it was a violation of First Amendment freedom of association rights for police departments to restrict employee membership or participation in labor unions (100,101).

CONCLUSION

The constitutional rights of speech, expression, and association are long-standing protections outlined in the First Amendment. In order for employers to regulate employee conduct in these areas, they must demonstrate a connection between their rules and the effective operation of the agency. Though courts have given police employers the authority to regulate various employee activities, they weigh department policies and employer actions against employee First Amendment safeguards.

Employee freedom of speech is protected in the police workplace if the remarks pertain to matters of public concern or whistle-blowing speech reporting official misconduct. Speech that is vulgar or intentionally disruptive to the effectiveness of the agency is typically unprotected. Using efficient agency operation as a standard, employers are permitted to regulate appearance and some political and intimate associations. Courts have generally held that employers cannot regulate many types of nonpolicy-maker employee political activity, religious expression, and membership in labor organizations.

Although the First Amendment affords numerous constitutional safeguards, public employees, such as police officers, can be restricted from engaging in conduct or activities that interfere with the operation or public reputation of the agency. The U.S. Supreme Court has held that police employees are given lesser constitutional or privacy protections in the workplace because of their role in public safety and the need to maintain efficiency and public confidence (1,102).

Employer policies governing employee speech, expression, and association must be lawful, reasonable, and connected to agency function. To contribute to employee constitutional protection and reduce risk of litigation, employer regulation of these areas must be clearly written in policy and provided to employees through notification. Though case law and statute in First Amendment–related areas are more established than in some other areas of employment law, it is important for employers to remain abreast of changes in court doctrine and statute. As seen in *Lawrence* et al. *v. Texas,* which found state homosexual conduct laws unconstitutional, U.S. Supreme Court decisions can rapidly change interpretation of constitutional law or statute (91). Both the fluidity of American employment and constitutional law and the changing state of the police role in society compel police employers to develop and enforce policies that are current, lawful, and in the best interest of the employee and the agency.

REFERENCES

1. O'Connor v. Ortega, 480 U.S. 709 (1987).
2. W. Bloss. Warrantless search in the law enforcement workplace: Court interpretation of employer practices and employee privacy rights under the Ortega Doctrine. *Police Quarterly* 1: 57–70, 1998.
3. W. Aitchison. (1992). *The Rights of Police Officers.* 4th ed. Portland, OR: Labor Relations Press. 2000.
4. W. Bloss. Privacy issues involving law enforcement personnel: A constitutional analysis. Ph.D. dissertation, Sam Houston State University, Huntsville, TX, 1996.
5. R. del Carmen, C. Williamson, W. Bloss, J. Coons. Civil Liabilities and Rights of Police Officers and Supervisors in Texas. Huntsville, TX: Law Enforcement Management Institute of Texas, 2003.
6. W. Bloss. Police privacy rights: Dimensions of employer regulation. In J. Walker, ed. *Policing and the Law.* Upper Saddle River, NJ: Prentice-Hall. 2001, pp. 135–172.
7. Pickering v. Board of Education, 391 U.S. 563 (1967).
8. Connick v. Myers, 461 U.S. 138 (1983).
9. Gustafson v. Jones, 117 F.3d 1015 (7th Cir. 1997).
10. Verbeek v. Teller, 158 F.Supp.2d, 267 (E.D.N.Y. 2001).
11. Beach v. City of Olathe et al., 185 F.Supp.2d 1229 (D. Kansas 2002).
12. Kessler v. City of Providence, 167 F.Supp.2d 482 (D. Rhode Island 2001).
13. Walton v. Safir, 122 F.Supp2d 466 (S.D.N.Y. 2000).
14. R. Levinson. Silencing government employee whistleblowers in the name of efficiency. *Ohio Northern University L R* 23: 17–69, 1996.
15. S. Kohn. Concepts and Procedures in Whistleblowing Law, www.whistleblowers.org. 2000.
16. 5 USC § 1201 et. seq. 1989.
17. 15 USC § 7211 et. seq. 2002.
18. R. Kilroy, J. Nicholas. The Sarbanes Oxley act: The new frontier for whistleblowing claims. *Corporate Counsel* 9: 11–13, 2002.

19. T. Dworkin, E. Callahan. Internal whistleblowing: Protecting the interests of the employee, the organization, and society. *American Business L J* 29: 267–308, 1991.
20. Hughes v. Whitmer, 714 F.2d 1407 (8th Cir. 1983).
21. Brockwell v. Norton, 732 F.2d 664 (8th Cir. 1984).
22. Serna v. City of San Antonio, 244 F.3d 479 (5th Cir. 2001).
23. Cochrane v. City of Los Angeles, 222 F.3d 1195 (9th Cir. 2000).
24. Pappas v. Guilani et al., 290 F.3d 143 (2nd Cir. 2002).
25. P. Tiersma. Nonverbal communication and the freedom of speech. *Wisconsin L R* 1993: 1525–1589, 1993.
26. Kelley v. Johnson, 425 U.S. 238 (1976).
27. Weaver v. Henderson, 984 F.2d 11 (1st Cir. 1993).
28. Rathert v. Village of Peotone, 903 F.2d 510 (7th Cir. 1990).
29. Riggs v. City of Ft. Worth et al., 2002 LEXIS 1613 (N.D. Tex. 2002).
30. Elrod v. Burns, 427 U.S. 347 (1976).
31. Branti v. Finkel, 445 U.S. 507 (1980).
32. C. Singer. Conduct and belief: Public employees' first amendment rights to free expression and political association. *University of Chicago L R* 59: 897–923 1992.
33. Rogers v. Miller, 57 F.3d 986 (11th Cir. 1995).
34. Stough v. Gallagher, 967 F.2d 1523 (11th Cir. 1992).
35. Click v. Copeland, 970 F.2d 106 (5th Cir. 1992).
36. Jantzen v. Hawkins, 188 F.3d 1247 (10th Cir. 1999).
37. Perry v. Larson, 794 F.2d 279 (7th Cir. 1986).
38. Morris v. Crow, 117 F.3d 449 (11th Cir. 1997).
39. Matherne v. Wilson, 851 F.2d 752 (5th Cir. 1988).
40. Heidman v. Wirsing, 7 F.3d 659 (7th Cir. 1993).
41. Joyner v. Lancaster, 815 F.2d 20 (4th Cir. 1987).
42. Jenkins v. Medford, 119 F.3d 1156 (4th Cir. 1996).
43. Jones v. Dodson, 727 F.2d 1329 (4th Cir. 1984).
44. McBee v. Jim Hogg County, 730 F.2d 1009 (5th Cir. 1984).
45. Brady v. Fort Bend County, 145 F.3d 691 (5th Cir. 1998).
46. Rodez v. Village of Maywood, 641 F.Supp. 331 (N.D.Ill. 1986).
47. Mele v. Fahy, 579 F.Supp. 1576 (D.C.N.J. 1984).
48. Horstkoetter v. Department of Public Safety, 159 F.3d 1265 (10th Cir. 1998).
49. Krisher v. Sharpe, 763 F.Supp. 1313 (E.D.Pa. 1991).
50. Otten v. Schicker, 655 F.2d 142 (8th Cir. 1981).
51. 42 USC § 1981 et. seq. (1964); 42 USC § 2000e (1964).
52. Vernon v. City of Los Angeles et al., 27 F.3d 1385 (9th Cir. 1994).
53. S. Rosenzweig. Restoring religious freedom to the workplace: Title VII, RFRA, and religious accommodation. *University of Pennsylvania L R* 144: 2513–2536, 1996.
54. Venters v. City of Delphi, 123 F.3d 956 (7th Cir. 1997).
55. Rodriguez v. City of Chicago, 156 F.3d 771 (7th Cir. 1998).
56. Parrott v. District of Columbia, 1991 WL 126020 (D.D.C. 1991).
57. Balint v. Carson City, Nevada, 180 F.3d 1047 (9th Cir. 1999).
58. Fraternal Order of Police Newark Lodge No 12 v. City of Newark, 170 F.3d 359 (3rd Cir. 1999).
59. E. Griswold. The right to be let alone. *Northwestern University L R*, 55: 216–231, 1960.
60. W. Bloss. Privacy rights of police officers: An analysis of constitutional protections, In N. Ali-Jackson, ed. *Contemporary Issues in Criminal Justice: Shaping Tomorrows System*. New York: McGraw-Hill, 1995 pp 135–157.
61. Oliverson v. West Valley City, 875 F.Supp. 1465 (D. Utah 1995).
62. Wilson v. Swing, 463 F.Supp. 555 (M.D.N.C. 1978).

63. Fabio v. Civil Service Commission of the City of Philadelphia, 414 A.2d 82 (Cmwlth Pa. 1980).
64. Hamilton v. City of Mesa, 916 P.2d1136 (1995).
65. City of Sherman v. Henry, 910 S.W.2d 542 (Tex.App. 1995).
66. Baron v. Meloni, 556 F.Supp. 796 (D.C.N.Y. 1983).
67. Smith v. Price, 616 F.2d 1371 (5th Cir. 1980).
68. Major v. Hampton, 413 F.Supp. 66 (E.D.La. 1976).
69. Mercure v. Van Buren Township, 81 F.Supp.2d 814 (E.D.Mich. 2000).
70. Cronin v. Town of Amesbury, 895 F.Supp. 375 (D.Mass. 1995).
71. Suddarth v. Slane, 539 F.Supp. 612 (D.C.Va. 1982).
72. Swope v. Bratton, 541 F.Supp. 99 (W.D.Ark. 1982).
73. Briggs v. North Muskegon Police Department, 563 F.Supp. 585 (W.D.Mich. 1983).
74. Shuman v. City of Philadelphia, 470 F.Supp. 449 (E.D.Pa. 1979).
75. Kukla v. Village of Antioch, 647 F.Supp. 799 (N.D. Ill. 1986).
76. Shawgo v. Spradlin, 701 F.2d 470 (5th Cir. 1983).
77. Jackson v. Howell, 577 F.Supp. 47 (W.D. Mich. 1982).
78. Puzick v. City of Colorado Springs, 680 P.2d 1283 (Colo.App. 1983).
79. Struck v. Hackett, 668 A.2d 411 (Me. 1995).
80. Fugate v. Phoenix Civil Service Board, 791 F.2d 736 (9th Cir. 1986).
81. Riveros v. City of Los Angeles, 49 CalRptr.2d 238 (1996).
82. Merrifield v. Illinois State Police, 691 N.E.2d 191 (Ill.App. 4 Dist. 1998).
83. Wieland v. City of Arnold, 100 F.Supp.2d 984 (E.D.Mo. 2000).
84. Reuter v. Skipper, 832 F.Supp. 1420 (D.Or. 1993).
85. Thorne v. City of El Segundo, 726 F.2d 459 (9th Cir. 1983).
86. Fleisher v. City of Signal Hill, 829 F.2d 1491 (9th Cir. 1987).
87. Hughes v. City of North Olmstead et al., 93 F3d 238 (6th Cir. 1996).
88. Parks v. City of Warner Robins, Georgia et al., 43 F3d 609 (11th Cir. 1995).
89. W. Bloss. Privacy rights of police officers: A constitutional analysis of compulsory workplace HIV/AIDS disease testing and lifestyle preference. Paper presented at the annual meeting of the Academy of Criminal Justice Sciences, Louisville, KY. 1997.
90. Bowers v. Hardwick, 478 U.S. 186 (1986).
91. Lawrence et al., v. Texas 123 S.Ct. 2472 (2003).
92. Childers v. Dallas Police Department, 513 F.Supp. 134 (N.D.Tex. 1981).
93. Padula v. Webster, 822 F.2d 97 (D.C.Cir. 1987).
94. Endsley v. Naes, 673 F.Supp. 1032 (D.Kansas 1987).
95. Todd v. Navarro, 698 F.Supp. 871 (S.D.Fla. 1988).
96. Delahoussaye v. City of New Iberia,937 F.2d 144 (5th Cir. 1991).
97. Buttino v. F.B.I., 801 F.Supp. 298 (N.D.Cal. 1992).
98. City of Dallas v. England, 846 SW2d 957 (App. 3 Dist. 1993).
99. Police Officers' Guild v. Washington, 369 F.Supp. 543 (D.D.C. 1973).
100. Mescall v. Rockford, 655 F.2d 111 (7th Cir. 1981).
101. Latino Officers Association, New York v. The City of New York, 196 F.3d 458 (2nd Cir. 1999).
102. National Treasury Employees Union v. Von Raab, 489 U.S. 656 (1989).

9 Americans with Disabilities Act and Law Enforcement: Legal and Policy Implications for Law Enforcement Administrators

Lisa S. Nored

CONTENTS

INTRODUCTION

In 1990, Congress enacted the Americans with Disabilities Act (ADA) to protect the rights of disabled yet qualified citizens. The primary objective of the ADA is relatively simple and straightforward: the elimination of discrimination against persons with disabilities in a variety of contexts, including employment, transportation, communications, education, recreation, institutionalization, health services, voting, and access to public services. Although the underlying legislative intent and objective of the legislation is apparent, actual implementation of the mandate has been more elusive.

Moreover, implementation of the ADA is presumably more challenging in some professions than others. Research suggests that implementation has proven especially complex, although not impossible, within public safety professions, including law enforcement.

Law enforcement administrators are primarily charged with maintaining a qualified and skilled law enforcement force. This task, however, has become increasingly more challenging during the last two decades. Slonaker et al. (2001) suggest that "[t]hose charged with staffing police organizations will likely agree that attracting and retaining qualified personnel is more challenging today than at anytime in the recent past."[1] Much of this difficulty is attributable to the additional burden of ensuring that law enforcement agencies implement various laws regarding employment discrimination, including Title VII, the Age Discrimination in Employment Act (ADEA), and the ADA, each of which has intricacies, ambiguities, and interpretative quagmires of its own. Complicating implementation of these laws is the fact that the courts and the Equal Employment Opportunity Commission (EEOC) often render conflicting decisions regarding an employer's obligations. Thus, achievement of statutory and policy goals is a complex and frustrating process for many police administrators.

As such, this chapter is intended to be a practical tool for the modern law enforcement administrator. Its purpose is to provide law enforcement administrators with a basic overview of the ADA and the accompanying administrative responsibilities and obligations. Greater understanding and appreciation of the ADA mandate will, in turn, alleviate much of the difficulty with regard to successful implementation of the Act.

ASSESSMENT OF IMPLEMENTATION OF THE ADA MANDATE

In general, studies have attempted to predict or analyze whether the goals of the ADA have been or will be successfully implemented in the United States.[2] Bishop and Jones (1993) attempted to "forecast whether current conditions favor successful implementation of the ADA," and suggested "that the ADA is on track in terms of accomplishing its goals."[3] Despite the encouraging prediction, subsequent research efforts revealed the difficulties experienced in actual implementation of the ADA. Generally, researchers and policy analysts recognize the difficulty in full and satisfactory implementation of the ADA. For example, Percy (1993) observed:

> Since passage of the act, states and municipalities across the nation have been scrambling to achieve compliance through such actions as studying and revising policies pertaining to disability rights, taking physical inventories of public buildings and facilities, reviewing employment policies, and responding to complaints about ADA violations.[4]

According to Condrey and Brudney (1993),

> Title 1 of the ADA falls into the category described by Matland as 'experimental implementation'—policy areas characterized by high policy ambiguity and low policy conflict. Policies with clear and widely supported goals but with unclear means of implementation take on experimental characteristics .... This statement describes Title 1 of the ADA: The personnel-related portion of the legislation called for increased

employment of persons with disabilities but was vague and nonprescriptive regarding how to attain this goal.[5]

In light of the apparent difficulties surrounding ADA implementation, Condrey and Brudney (1993) surveyed municipal personnel directors of all cities in the United States with a population of fifty thousand or greater to gather data with regard to the following areas: obstacles to municipal ADA implementation, accommodation of various occupational classifications, comparison of employment characteristics, preparing for ADA implementation, perceived importance of ADA implementation, personnel modifications and the ADA, and steps taken to accommodate workers with disabilities.

In general, the research indicated high levels of implementation of the personnel-related aspects of the ADA. Moreover, despite budgetary constraints and vague regulations, municipalities have made great efforts to accommodate individuals with disabilities. Personnel managers indicated a positive view of the ADA and its mandate.

Of interest, however, were the findings regarding public safety occupations. Survey respondents reported that making a reasonable accommodation was significantly more difficult for public safety occupations such as law enforcement officers and firefighters as compared to professional, technical, or clerical positions. As a result, law enforcement administrators, faced with the inherent difficulty of accommodating current or potential employees, must be familiar with their responsibilities under the ADA.

THE ADA AND LAW ENFORCEMENT ADMINISTRATION

The unique nature of law enforcement makes one pause when considering the practical implication of implementing the ADA. The public expects law enforcement to serve and protect the community. Given the mental, emotional, and physical demands of the law enforcement profession, strict compliance with the ADA is difficult. Despite this difficulty, a quick review of the statute reveals that "... no one is above the law when it comes to complying with the ADA and the Rehabilitation Act—not even federal, state, or local law enforcement agencies."[6]

As such, police managers must understand the basic obligations of the ADA in order to make effective, nondiscriminatory personnel decisions. Yet, a basic understanding is not easily obtained as the obligations imposed by the ADA originate from a variety of sources. For example, although the statutory mandate provides the overall directive regarding disability-based employment discrimination, employers must be familiar with regulations and policy promulgated by the EEOC, as well as case law that interprets both statutory and administrative directives. As such, the following discussion provides guidance from these sources in an effort to provide law enforcement administrators with a general understanding of the ADA as well as those issues that are crucial to effective implementation within the law enforcement profession.

THE ADA MANDATE

In 1990, Congress enacted the ADA in order to protect individuals with disabilities from discrimination in certain situations, specifically employment, transportation, communications, education, recreation, institutionalization, health services, voting, and access to public services.[7] Within the employment context, employers may not "discrimin[ate] against a qualified individual with a disability because of the disability of such individual in regard to the job application procedures, the hiring, advancement, or discharge of employees, employee compensation, job training, and other terms, conditions, and privileges of employment."[8] "To this end, the Act requires employers to 'make reasonable accommodations to the known physical or mental limitations of an otherwise qualified individual with a disability who is an applicant or employee, unless [the employer] can demonstrate that the accommodation would impose an undue hardship on the operation of the employer's business.'"[9]

Employers should first examine the statute to determine whether they are obligated to implement and enforce the ADA. In general, a "covered entity" within the ADA is defined as an employer, employment agency, labor organization, or joint labor-management committee.[10] An employer is defined by the Act as "any one of more individuals, governments, governmental agencies, political subdivisions, labor unions, partnerships, associations, or corporations that in some way affect commerce and has fifteen or more employees."[11] Exemptions from the ADA exist for "small employers, United States government, Indian tribes, and tax-exempt membership clubs."[12]

An individual with a disability is considered "qualified" under the ADA if that person "with or without reasonable accommodation, can perform the essential functions of the employment functions of the employment position that such individual holds or desires."[13] The ADA recognizes three types of situations that give rise to a disability: (1) a physical or mental impairment that substantially limits one or more of the major life activities, (2) a record of such an impairment, or (3) being regarded as having such an impairment."[14]

The third situation is problematic and creates troublesome issues for employers. Essentially, if individuals are treated as if they have a disability, they are entitled to the protections of the ADA. Thus, the actions of the employer (or potential employer) may result in the extension of the ADA to an individual who otherwise would not meet the threshold qualifications for ADA protection. As such, employers must carefully and correctly assess whether an individual has a disability.

However, the majority of cases fall within the first situation—a disability that limits major life activities. These include functions such as caring for oneself; performing manual tasks; and walking, seeing, hearing, speaking, breathing, learning, and working.[15] Moreover, EEOC guidelines suggest use of the following factors to determine whether an impairment substantially limits a major life activity: the nature and severity of the impairment, the duration or expected duration of the impairment, and the permanence or expected permanence of the impact.[16]

Thus, individuals who fall within one of these categories are clothed with the protection of the ADA if they are qualified for the position and able to perform the essential functions of the position. However, employers are not required to hire individuals who lack the "prerequisites for the position, such as possessing the appropriate educational background, employment experience, skills, licenses, etc. ..."[17] Moreover, the ADA prohibits employers from utilizing standards, criteria, or methods of administration ... which have the effect of discrimination on the basis of a disability.[18]

IDENTIFICATION OF ESSENTIAL FUNCTIONS

If an individual satisfies employment qualifications, the appropriate inquiry then shifts to an evaluation of whether that individual can perform the essential functions of the position with or without reasonable accommodation. As such, employers should take care to identify the essential functions of each and every position in order to properly make personnel decisions. When identifying essential functions, employers should evaluate the function that is required, as well as its relationship to a particular position.

Most courts that have considered this issue have held that an essential function is one that is fundamental or necessary, rather than marginal or only occasionally required.[19] However, frequency of performance does not end the inquiry regarding whether a particular function is properly deemed essential. For example, the Seventh Circuit Court of Appeals suggests that "functions may be essential even if not frequently performed."[20] Further, the ADA indicates that "consideration shall be given to the employer's judgment as to what functions of a job are essential, and if an employer has prepared a written description before advertising or interviewing for the job, this description shall be considered evidence of the essential functions of the job."[21]

As a proactive measure, police managers should identify essential job functions of every position within their department. Case law is particularly helpful in illustrating functions that have been considered essential to employment as a law enforcement officer. The following have been identified by courts as essential job functions within the law enforcement profession:

1. Operation of a motor vehicle to police specifications[22]
2. Safe handling of firearms[23]
3. The ability to make a forceful arrest[24]
4. Firing a weapon[25]
5. Evidence collection[26]
6. Ability to shoot in the Weaver stance[27]
7. Patrol by foot or automobile[28]
8. Direction of traffic[29]
9. Enforcement of traffic regulations[30]
10. Honesty and law-abiding character[31]

In a more recent decision, the Eighth Circuit Court of Appeals held that attendance at work is a necessary function, and therefore concluded that an employee who was unable to come to work on a regular basis due to his disability was unable "to satisfy any of the functions of the job, much less the essential ones."[32]

REASONABLE ACCOMMODATION

In general, the ADA requires reasonable accommodation for disabled applicants or employees. As such, although accommodation is required, reasonableness is the appropriate test to utilize when considering alteration of the workplace environment. The reasonableness of the accommodation must be evaluated in light of the nature of the employment as well as the ability of the employer to provide it.

Reasonable accommodation has been defined as a "change in the workplace environment or in the way of doing business that permits the disabled to enjoy equal employment opportunities and benefits."[33] Although general guidelines are provided, a review of the relevant case law and EEOC guidelines reveal that reasonable accommodation, like other ADA-related issues, is typically decided on a case-by-case basis.[34]

According to the ADA, reasonable accommodation may include "(A) making existing facilities used by employees readily accessible to and usable by individuals with disabilities; and (B) job restructuring, part-time or modified work schedules, reassignment to a vacant position, acquisition or modification of equipment or devices, appropriate adjustment or modification of examinations, training materials, or policies, the provision of qualified readers or interpreters, and other similar accommodations for individuals with disabilities."[35] However, if an accommodation will present an undue hardship to an employer, such as unreasonable cost, extensive or substantial alteration, or the accommodation would fundamentally alter the nature of the business, the employer is not obligated to provide the accommodation. Moreover, accommodations may be denied if the employee poses a direct threat to the health and safety of the employee or others.

If employers are aware of a disability during the application phase or after an offer has been made to a qualified applicant, either because the disability is obvious or the applicant voluntary discloses, employers have a duty to offer reasonable accommodations to assist in completing the application and interviewing process.[36]

Likewise, employers must provide reasonable accommodation for established employees. The ADA directs employers to consider the following when accommodating a disabled employee in their current position: flexible work schedules, equipment modification, job restructuring, and ensuring accessibility to employment facilities.[37] Extraordinary efforts that constitute an undue hardship on employers, or require employers to eliminate essential job functions, are not required.

Situations may arise where the employer is unable to accommodate the employee within his/her current position. Job reassignment is allowed, but not required by the ADA. Moreover, employers are not required to create new positions, displace fellow employees, or promote disabled employees.[38]

Many law enforcement agencies create "light duty" work assignments for officers who become disabled while on the job. The creation of light duty work assignments is not required by the ADA. Moreover, the primary danger of establishing light duty positions is the potential for creating a legal expectation in continued light duty assignment.[39]

Administrators should recognize that accommodation of disabled employees may have important collateral effects on fellow employees. For example, in many employment settings, including law enforcement agencies, seniority is a factor in placement and promotion. As such, law enforcement administrators must carefully consider the effects of reasonable accommodation upon the seniority rights of fellow employees.

This issue was addressed in *U.S. Airways, Inc. v. Barnett*, where the U.S. Supreme Court addressed the interaction between the obligation to accommodate disabled employees and the seniority rights of other employees.[40] In *Barnett*, the employee suffered a back injury and requested reassignment. However, the requested position was the subject of seniority-based employee bidding. The employee requested that an exception to the seniority rules be made in order to accommodate his disability. After review, the Supreme Court held that a violation of seniority rights of other employees was not required by the ADA's mandate for reasonable accommodation.

Although administrators must willingly accommodate the disability of a qualified applicant or employee, the accommodation is only required to be reasonable. Administrators should understand that the ADA mandate has both logical and necessary boundaries. Without such limits, it would become impossible to efficiently operate in most employment settings. As noted by the Seventh Circuit Court of Appeals, reasonable accommodation is not the equivalent of "a perfect cure for the problem."[41] Thus, the ADA is not designed to thwart the mission of employers but rather to seek a workable balance between the objectives of employers and the right of disabled employees to effectively participate in the workforce.

QUESTION AND ANSWER: WHAT MAY EMPLOYERS ASK?

With the exception of obvious and apparent disabilities, in order to accurately assess whether a potential or established employee is entitled to accommodation under the auspices of the ADA, employers must obtain information. However, the means by which an employer may gather such information is governed by statute, case law, and EEOC guidelines. As such, there is a complex combination of sources that govern the timing and nature of disability-related inquiry by employers. The following discussion, although not exhaustive, will address common areas of concern regarding disability-related inquiry by employers.

Disability-related inquiry is defined by the EEOC as "a question or series of questions likely to elicit information about a disability."[42] This includes questions that are likely to elicit information regarding the nature or extent of a disability.[43] The timing of the inquiry largely determines the nature and extent of inquiry allowed by the ADA.

During the application and interviewing process, employers may not make direct disability-related inquiries.[44] Employers, however, may inquire whether an applicant will need any special accommodation for the application or interviewing process.[45] Moreover, employers may ask applicants about nonmedical qualifications and skills required to perform the job. Questions about alcohol and drugs are acceptable only if they seek to elicit information about current use, not about a past or current addiction. Such stringent guidelines are calculated to insure equal access to the application and interviewing process.

Once an offer of employment has been made, employers enjoy more freedom to inquire about the presence of a disability. Generally, employers may make disability-related inquiries with little restriction as long as questions are posed to all offerees and any elicited information remains confidential.[46] Disability-related inquiries may also be made of current employees as long as the inquiries are job-related and consistent with job necessity.[47] "An inquiry is job-related if and employer has a reasonable belief, based upon objective evidence, that employees' ability to do their job is impaired, or that employees pose a direct threat because of the condition."[48] This belief may be based on a deterioration of work performance or attendance records, an employee's request for accommodation for a disability, or if the employee is returning from medical or workers' compensation leave.[49] Thus, these situations may legitimately give rise to employer concerns regarding an employee's ability to perform job functions.

Due to the unique nature of public safety professions, law enforcement employers, unlike other professions, may inquire whether "police officers are taking prescription medications which may pose a direct threat to the safety of the officer or others."[50] Inquiries may be made regarding medications that may impair the officer's judgment, ability to properly use a firearm, or to operate a motor vehicle.[51]

MEDICAL AND NONMEDICAL EXAMINATIONS

In light of the demands of the profession, law enforcement applicants and employees are subject to a variety of medical and nonmedical examinations regarding their ability to perform job functions. Public safety requires an officer who is fit, both mentally and physically, to meet the unique demands of law enforcement. For example, officers are typically expected to take and pass polygraph examinations, vision acuity tests, annual physical fitness examinations, firearms qualification and certification, drug testing, and personality inventories. However, when administering tests that measure an individual's ability to perform job-related functions, employers must determine whether the evaluation is considered a medical examination.

The ADA is clearly implicated when medical examinations are required. A medical examination is defined by the EEOC as a test that seeks information about individuals' physical or mental impairments or health. If a particular examination meets the following criteria, it is likely to be considered a medical examination.

1. Examinations that are interpreted by health professionals
2. Examinations that are administered in a medical setting, administered with medical equipment, or invasive
3. Examinations that are used by employers for the purpose of identifying disabilities or determining their nature or extent
4. Examinations that are specifically designed to reveal disabilities or impairments
5. Examinations that measure an individual's responses to performing tasks, rather than simply the ability to perform those tasks[52]

As with disability-related inquiries, the timing of medical examinations is important. According to the ADA, prior to an offer being made, job applicants may not be required to undergo medical examinations.[53] However, employers may inquire whether an applicant can perform job-related functions.[54]

Moreover, certain nonmedical examinations may be required. For example, departments may require applicants to undergo testing for illegal drug use, physical agility, physical fitness, psychological testing that is not aimed at discovering mental illness or defects, and polygraph examinations that do not contain disability-related questions.[55] Employers may require medical certification demonstrating that the applicant can safely undergo such testing.

Once a job offer has been extended to the applicant, departments may require medical testing as long as it is required of all applicants and test results are confidential.[56] As such, this is the appropriate time to evaluate the impact of an applicant's disability. At times, a disability may require that the offer be revoked. If so, the ADA will require employers to justify the revocation. Sufficient justifications for withdrawal of employment offers are inability to accommodate the disability, the applicant is unable to perform job-related tasks or those constituting a business necessity, and applicants who pose a direct threat to health or safety.[57]

Generally, employees are not subject to medical examinations unless the employer reasonably believes that the employee cannot perform job-related functions.[58] Thus, if the medical examination is job-related and a matter of business necessity, it may be administered.[59] However, within the various public safety professions, the EEOC and the courts have held that periodic medical examinations may be conducted even when there is no objective evidence that the employee is unable to perform job functions.[60] The underlying rationale of such decisions indicates judicial awareness that undetected medical problems of public safety personnel may constitute a direct threat to the safety of the officer or others. Administrators must, however, be prepared to demonstrate that periodic medical examinations are necessary and that the scope of the exam is limited to job-related issues.

THE ADA AND LAW ENFORCEMENT:
A SELECTIVE REVIEW OF CASE LAW

The ADA has given rise to a plethora of litigation regarding the interpretation of its mandate. The following is a selective review of case law particularly relevant to law enforcement administrators. However, it is not intended to contain an exhaustive review of all judicial decisions that interpret the ADA.

In ADA cases, the complainant bears the burden of establishing that a disability exists, that the employee is able to perform the essential functions of the position with or without accommodation, and that an adverse employment action occurred due to the disability.[61] As such, the aggrieved applicant or employee must demonstrate that he or she meets the threshold requirements under the ADA in order to proceed with litigation.

The Supreme Court has held that "the ADA allows employers to prefer some physical attributes over others and to establish physical criteria."[62] " ... [A]n employer is free to decide that physical characteristics or medical conditions that do not rise to the level of an impairment—such as one's height, build or singing voice—are preferable to others, ..."[63] However, impairments that constitute a disability must be accommodated. The determination of disabilities for purposes of the ADA is far from an exact science; however, guidance is found in the following cases.

In *Kapache v. City of San Antonio*, the Fifth Circuit Court of Appeals indicated that employers must conduct individualized assessments of employees when determining whether the employee is able to perform the essential functions of the job.[64] After passing a background investigation and a written test, Kapache, an applicant for the position of a San Antonio police officer, filed suit after the City determined that he was unable to perform the essential functions of his job due to insulin-treated diabetes mellitus (ITDM). Specifically, the City concluded that Kapache would be unable to drive safely with his condition and therefore constituted a direct threat to the health and safety of others. Recognizing the current medical debate over the safety of driving with this condition, the Fifth Circuit revised its earlier ruling allowing for wholesale exclusion of applicants with ITDM, and required individualized assessments to be made on a case-by-case basis prior to exclusion.[65] As such, mere diagnosis or existence of a particular condition is insufficient in and of itself to conclude that an individual is disabled according to the ADA.

Examples of other conditions that have been accepted as disabilities for purposes of the ADA are as follows: posttraumatic stress disorder, bipolar disorder, blindness, delusional paranoid disorder, loss of use of extremity, degenerative joint disease, epilepsy, asthma, tuberculosis, alcoholism, and drug addiction. "Based on current case law, law enforcement officers and applicants need to realize that courts are rather narrowly interpreting what constitutes a protected disability in cases involving law enforcement positions."[66]

Currently, there is a great amount of confusion regarding alcohol and drug addiction with regard to the ADA. However, the statute and case appear to be fairly clear on the subject. Although alcoholism and drug addiction are considered to be disabilities, the actual use of alcohol and/or drugs, which results in impairment to employment performance, is not a disability for purposes of the ADA. Moreover, the ADA specifically allows employers to adopt policies and procedures, such as drug testing, to determine whether a person continues to use alcohol or drugs.[67]

A review of conditions that have not been found to be disabilities is also informative. For example, poor judgment, irresponsible behavior, and poor impulse control; temporary conditions; or conditions alleviated by medication are not protected by the ADA. Moreover, the majority of courts and the EEOC have concluded that the mere fact that a condition impairs a person's ability to perform a particular job does not necessarily mean that the individual is disabled.[68] However, the question remains whether a person is disabled when his or her condition disqualifies the person's employment in an entire profession, i.e., law enforcement. The resolution of this issue will turn on "whether the position of police officer is truly its own job classification in and of itself, or whether it is merely one of the many possible jobs in the field of law enforcement."[69]

OVERSIGHT AND ENFORCEMENT OF THE ADA MANDATE

The EEOC is the public agency that is primarily responsible for the interpretation and enforcement of the ADA.[70] In addition, the EEOC promulgates regulations that interpret the ADA. These regulations serve as excellent guides for administrators, human resource practitioners, and legal advisors.

The EEOC is also the entity that is responsible for the investigation of ADA-related complaints by current or prospective employees as well as for providing an administrative tribunal for the resolution of those complaints. ADA complaints may be filed by aggrieved individuals or by the EEOC. If there is insufficient evidence, the EEOC will dismiss the complaint. However, the result of an EEOC investigation does not preclude the individual from filing a civil suit against the employer.[71] If the EEOC concludes that there is "reasonable cause" to believe a violation has occurred, efforts will be made to resolve the matter through conciliation, which is utilized in lieu of litigation.[72]

If conciliation is unsuccessful, with the exception of governmental entities, the EEOC may bring a civil action against the employer. In addition, as with complaints that result in EEOC dismissals, individuals may still elect to bring a civil suit against the employer and may recover monetary damages, unless the individual has negotiated or received a settlement.

Private enforcement against employers is an alternative method of enforcement for aggrieved applicants or employees. However, the U.S. Supreme Court in *Board of Trustees of the University of Alabama, et al., v. Patricia Garrett, et al.*, 531 U.S. 356 (2001) seriously undermined the application of the ADA to the states and held that suits in federal courts by state employees to recover money damages due to the failure of the state to comply with Title I of the ADA are barred by the Eleventh Amendment. Specifically, the Court held that Congress failed to properly abrogate state immunity when drafting and enacting the ADA. To properly abrogate, Congress must identify constitutional violations of the Fourteenth Amendment and fashion a remedy appropriate to the violation.

Following a review of relevant authority, the Court emphasized that the due process clause of the Fourteenth Amendment does not require special protections or accommodations for disabled citizens, but rather that the state act rationally. Moreover, the Court held that Congress failed to identify a pattern of irrational employment discrimination by the states against disabled applicants or employees. In fact, in committee, the record indicates that Congress was most concerned with private sector discrimination against the disabled. As such, the Court concluded that the constitutional prerequisites for congressional abrogation of the Eleventh Amendment were not satisfied.

However, despite the damage inflicted by *Garrett*, aggrieved state employees are not without legal recourse. The ADA is "applicable to the States which can be enforced by the United States in actions for money damages, as well as by private individuals in actions for injunctive relief under Ex Parte Young, 209 U.S. 123 (1908)."[73] The Supreme Court also noted the availability of remedies provided by state laws for persons with disabilities who experience discrimination in the employment setting. Moreover, local employees were not affected by the Garrett decision as the Eleventh Amendment immunity does not extend to local governmental units such as cities and counties as of yet.[74]

The judiciary has also been called upon to determine the appropriate manner in which to resolve claims made pursuant to the ADA. Due to the expensive and time-consuming nature of litigation, arbitration has become a popular and effective alternative to litigation. Arbitration allows parties to a legal dispute to select qualified individuals to serve as a tribunal for the purpose of determining legal rights. With few exceptions, the decision of the arbitrator is binding on the parties and considered final. Arbitration is increasingly used in a variety of contexts including, but not limited to, the following areas: domestic relations, contract disputes, labor relations, product liability, and Securities and Exchange complaints.

The Federal Arbitration Act (FAA) was enacted by Congress in 1947 and expresses a clear preference for the use of arbitration in a variety of federal cases. The FAA provides that arbitration agreements in contracts, including employment contracts, are valid, irrevocable, and enforceable. This provision, coupled with the fact that binding arbitration agreements are increasingly included in employment contracts, raises the question of the effect of these agreements on ADA complaints and the remedies that may be pursued by the EEOC.

In *Equal Employment Opportunity Commission v. Waffle House, Inc.*, 122 S.Ct. 754 (2002), the U.S. Supreme Court addressed these issues.[75] In this case, the EEOC, acting on a complaint from a Waffle House employee, investigated the matter and concluded that there was cause to believe a violation had occurred. Conciliation failed, and the EEOC filed a suit against Waffle House seeking compensatory damages and injunctive relief. Waffle House requested that the matter be submitted to arbitration as provided in the employment contract entered into with the employee.

The Supreme Court held that the EEOC was not a party to the arbitration agreement and therefore was not bound by its provisions. Thus, the EEOC could file suit in federal court seeking damages from the employer. However, EEOC remedies may be limited if the employee, independent of the EEOC, accepts a settlement or elects to litigate.

CONCLUSION

Modern law enforcement administrators are faced with myriad challenges. In order to maintain an effective police force, administrators must attract and retain qualified and skilled officers. Navigation of the modern employment process is a complicated endeavor given the variety of federal, state, and local laws and the applicable administrative regulations. In order to effectively serve, police administrators must understand the obligations that exist under a variety of federal laws, including the ADA.

REFERENCES

1. Slonaker, William M., Wendt, Ann C., and Kemper, Michael J., Discrimination in the ranks: An empirical study with recommendations, *Police Quarterly*, Vol. 4, Issue 3, September 2001.
2. Condrey, Stephen E. and Brudney, Jeffrey, L., The Americans with Disabilities Act of 1990: Assessing its implementation in America's largest cities. *American Review of Public Administration*, Vol. 28, Issue 1, 1998; Percy, S. ADA, disability rights, and evolving regulatory Federalism. *Publius: The Journal of Federalism*, Vol. 23, 87–105, 1993; Bishop, P.C. and Jones, A.J., Jr. Implementing the Americans With Disabilities Act of 1990: Assessing the variables of success. *Public Administration Review*, Vol. 53, Issue 2, 121–128.
3. Bishop, P.C. and Jones, A.J., Jr. Implementing the Americans with Disabilities Act of 1990: Assessing the variables of success. *Public Administration Review*, Vol. 53, Issue 2.
4. Percy, S. ADA, Disability rights, and evolving regulatory federalism. *Publius: The Journal of Federalism*, Vol. 23, 87–105, at 101, 1993
5. Condrey, Stephen E. and Brudney, Jeffrey, L., The Americans With Disabilities Act of 1990: Assessing Its Implementation in America's Largest Cities. *American Review of Public Administration*, Vol. 28, Issue 1, 1998.

6. Byers, Keith A., No One is Above the Law When it Comes to the ADA and the Rehabilitation Act-Not Even Federal, State, and Local Law Enforcement Agencies, 30 Loy. L.A. L. Rev. 977, 1997.

7. 42 United States Code Annotated §12101.

8. 42 United States Code Annotated §12101

9. Board of Trustees, et al. v. Patricia Garrett et al., 531 U.S. 356 (2001).

10. 42 United States Code Annotated § 12111 (2).

11. 42 United States Code Annotated § 12111 (2).

12. 42 United States Code Annotated § 12111.

13. 42 United States Code Annotated 12111 (8).

14. 42 United States Code Annotated §12102 (2).

15. 29 Code of Federal Regulations §1630.2.

16. 29 Code of Federal Regulations §1630.2.

17. 42 United States Code Annotated § 12102.

18. Board of Trustees of the University of Alabama, et al. vs. Patricia Garrett, et al., 531 U.S. 356, 360-61 (2001); 42 United States Code Annotated § 12112.

19. 29 Code of Federal Regulations §1630.2.

20. Doner v. City of Rockford, IL., 77 Fed. Appx. 898, 901 (7th Cir. 2003).

21. 29 Code of Federal Regulations §1630.2. (quoting 42 United States Code Annotated 12111 (8).

22–31. Gonzales V. City of New Braunfels, 176 F3d 834 (5th Cir. 1999).

32. Epps v. The City of Pine Lawn, 353 F.3d 588, 593 (8th Cir. 2003).

33. Epps v. City of Pine Lawn, 353 F.3d 588 (8th Cir. 2003).

34. See generally, Hogarth v. Thornburgh, 833 F.Supp. 1077 (S.D.N.Y. 1933); Coski v. City of Denver, 795 P.2d 1364 (Colo.Ct. App. 1990); Siefken v. Village of Arlington Heights, 65 F3d 664 (7th Cir. 1995); Stewart v. County of Brown, 86 F.3d 107 (7th Cir. 1996).

35. 42 United States Code Annotated §12111(9).

36. United States Code Annotated §12111(9).

37. United States Code Annotated §12111 (9).

38. Enforcement Guidance: Reasonable Accommodation and Undue Hardship Under the Americans with Disabilities Act. EEOC 1999.

39. Colbridge, Thomas D., The Americans with Disabilities Act, *FBI Law Enforcement Bulletin*, September, 2000.

40. 2002 WL 737494.

41. Stewart v. County of Brown, 86 F.3d 107, 112 (7th Cir.1996).

42. Colbridge, Thomas D., The Americans with Disabilities Act: A Practical Guide for Police Departments, *FBI Law Enforcement Bulletin*, January 2001, Vol. 70, Issue 1(23) and ADA Enforcement Guidance: Preemployment Disability-Related Questions and Medical Examinations.

43. Colbridge, Thomas D., The Americans with Disabilities Act: A Practical Guide for Police Departments, *FBI Law Enforcement Bulletin*, January 2001, Vol. 70, Issue 1(23); and ADA Enforcement Guidance: Preemployment Disability-Related Questions and Medical Examinations.

44. Colbridge, Thomas D., The Americans with Disabilities Act: A Practical Guide for Police Departments, *FBI Law Enforcement Bulletin*, January 2001, Vol. 70, Issue 1(23); and ADA Enforcement Guidance: Preemployment Disability-Related Questions and Medical Examinations.

45. Colbridge, Thomas D., The Americans with Disabilities Act: A Practical Guide for Police Departments, *FBI Law Enforcement Bulletin*, January 2001, Vol. 70, Issue 1(23); and ADA Enforcement Guidance: Preemployment Disability-Related Questions and Medical Examinations.

46. Colbridge, Thomas D., The Americans with Disabilities Act: A Practical Guide for Police Departments, *FBI Law Enforcement Bulletin*, January 2001, Vol. 70, Issue 1(23); and ADA Enforcement Guidance: Preemployment Disability-Related Questions and Medical Examinations.

47. 42 United States Code Annotated 12112 (d)(4)(A); 29 Code of Federal Regulations 1630.14(c).

48. Colbridge, Thomas D., The Americans with Disabilities Act: A Practical Guide for Police Departments, *FBI Law Enforcement Bulletin*, January 2001, Vol. 70, Issue 1(23); and ADA Enforcement Guidance: Preemployment Disability-Related Questions and Medical Examinations.

49. Colbridge, Thomas D., The Americans with Disabilities Act: A Practical Guide for Police Departments, FBI *Law Enforcement Bulletin*, January 2001, Vol. 70, Issue 1(23); 29 Code of Federal Regulations Pt. §1630.14 (c) and Watson v. City of Miami, 177 F.3d 932 (11th Circuit 1999).

50. Colbridge, Thomas D., The Americans with Disabilities Act: A Practical Guide for Police Departments, *FBI Law Enforcement Bulletin*, January 2001, Vol. 70, Issue 1(23).

51. Colbridge, Thomas D., The Americans with Disabilities Act: A Practical Guide for Police Departments, *FBI Law Enforcement Bulletin*, January 2001, Vol. 70, Issue 1(23); ADA Enforcement Guidance: Preemployment Disability-Related Questions and Medical Examinations of Employees Under the Americans with Disabilities Act, Notice No. 915.002.

52. Colbridge, Thomas D., The Americans with Disabilities Act: A Practical Guide for Police Departments, *FBI Law Enforcement Bulletin*, January 2001, Vol. 70, Issue 1, 23; ADA Enforcement Guidance: Preemployment Disability-Related Questions and Medical Examinations of Employees Under the Americans with Disabilities Act, Notice No. 915.002.

53. 42 United States Code Annotated § 12112(d).

54. 42 United States Code Annotated § 12112 (d).

55. Colbridge, Thomas D., The Americans with Disabilities Act: A Practical Guide for Police Departments, *FBI Law Enforcement Bulletin*, January 2001, Vol. 70, Issue 1(23); ADA Enforcement Guidance: Preemployment Disability-Related Questions and Medical Examinations of Employees Under the Americans with Disabilities Act, Notice No. 915.002.

56. 42 U.S.C. 12112 (d)(3).

57. Colbridge, Thomas D., The Americans with Disabilities Act: A Practical Guide for Police Departments, *FBI Law Enforcement Bulletin*, January 2001, Vol. 70, Issue 1(23); ADA Enforcement Guidance: Preemployment Disability-Related Questions and Medical Examinations of Employees Under the Americans with Disabilities Act, Notice No. 915.002.

58. Colbridge, Thomas D., The Americans with Disabilities Act: A Practical Guide for Police Departments, *FBI Law Enforcement Bulletin*, January 2001, Vol. 70, Issue 1(23); 42 United States Code Annotated 12112 (d)(4)(A).

59. 42 United States Code Annotated 12112 (d)(4)(A).

60. Sutton v. United Air Lines, Inc., 527 U.S. 471, 490 (1999).

61. Epps v. City of Pine Lawn, 353 F.3d 588 (2003).

62. Sutton v. United Air Lines, Inc., 527 U.S. 471, 490 (1999).

63. Sutton v. United Air Lines, Inc., 527 U.S. 471, 490 (1999).

64. Kapache v. City of San Antonio, 2002 U.S. Lexis 17961 (5th Cir.).

65. Kapache v. City of San Antonio, 2002 U.S. Lexis 17961 (5th Cir.).

66. Byers, Keith A., No One is Above the Law When it Comes to the ADA and the Rehabilitation Act-Not Even Federal, State, and Local Law Enforcement Agencies, 30 Loy. L.A. L. Rev. 977 (1997).

67. 42 United States Code Annotated§ 12114.

68. 29 Code of Federal Regulation 1630.2 (j)(3)(I).

69. Byers, Keith A., No One is Above the Law When it Comes to the ADA and the Rehabilitation Act-Not Even Federal, State, and Local Law Enforcement Agencies, 30 Loy. L.A. L. Rev. 977, 1007 (1997).

70. 29 Code of Federal Regulations § 1639.

71. 29 Code of Federal Regulations §1601.19.

72. 29 Code of Federal Regulations §§ 1601.24 and 1601.27.

73. Board of Trustees of the University of Alabama, et al., v. Patricia Garrett, et al., 531 U.S. 356 (2001).

74. Board of Trustees of the University of Alabama, et al., v. Patricia Garrett, et al., 531 U.S. 356 (2001); Lincoln County v. Luning, 133 U.S. 529, 533 (1890).

75. 177 S.Ct. 754 (2002).

10 Law Enforcement Employment Discrimination Based on Sexual Orientation: A Selective Review of Case Law

R. Alan Thompson and Lisa S. Nored

CONTENTS

ABSTRACT

Homosexuality has been the subject of discrimination from Biblical times through the present. Homosexuals continue to experience pervasive forms of discrimination, including denial of employment that they may be otherwise qualified to obtain. One profession that is particularly open in its discrimination against homosexual employees is law enforcement. This chapter traces the development of homosexuals' rights as they specifically relate to employment in law enforcement. Examples of common arguments raised by police administrators to justify such actions are examined, with each illustrated by an example from relevant case law. Finally, areas in which the law has begun to provide greater protection for the employment rights of homosexuals are identified.

INTRODUCTION

Sodomy and related homosexual acts have been the subject of countless religious, moral, and legal prohibitions throughout the course of history. For example, the Old Testament refers to such acts between two men as an "abomination" for which both parties "shall be put to death" (Leviticus 18: 22). This early code created the foundation for many of today's moral attitudes and legal sanctions regarding such behavior. During the 17th and 18th centuries, homosexuals were tortured, tried, and publicly executed. Suspected homosexuals were castrated before being put to death in Nazi Germany (Heger 1994). Although Western society no longer endorses such harsh sanctions, homosexuals continue to experience various forms of discrimination. For example, they are precluded from military service. They may also be denied custody of their adoptive or biological children, the opportunity to serve as youth group leaders, and access to fair and equal employment opportunities.

Generally speaking, homosexuals assert their individual and collective interests in these areas on the basis of First Amendment rights to freedom of speech, religion, association, and privacy. The Fourteenth Amendment rights to due process and equal protection also come into play. Despite such assertions, the judiciary remains reluctant to broadly accept these views. Instead, judges choose to rule against the rights of homosexuals based upon the firmly held Judeo–Christian belief that same-sex behavior is immoral and, thus, violates "natural law." A morally conservative approach to resolving claims of discrimination on the basis of sexual orientation may seem appropriate in certain "sensitive" contexts. For instance, the Supreme Court recently upheld an organization's right to deny membership to gays (*Boy Scouts of America v. Dale*, 2000). However, the Court may not take a similar stance in other situations. More specifically, it would seem reasonable to suggest that the opportunity to obtain fair and equal employment should not be abridged solely by conservative notions of morality. Rather, both the judiciary and employers should assess each individual's ability to perform the essential tasks associated with the job without regard to sexual orientation. This more objective standard has not yet been realized, due in large part to the blind application of conservative moral philosophy and judicial precedent developed in contexts outside the domain of contemporary employment law.

In sum, conservative moral pressure has created an environment in which homosexuals are denied status as a protected class when it comes to employment law. As a result of persistent unwillingness to confront and remediate employment discrimination on the basis of sexual orientation, affected individuals and support groups have begun to challenge prevailing legal standards in ever-increasing numbers. Outside of the military, one conspicuous profession that historically has discriminated against homosexual employees is law enforcement (Leinen 1993). Given the blatant manner in which these agencies often mistreat homosexual applicants and existing personnel, coupled with their general refusal to ameliorate such long-standing practices, embittered and protracted litigation is undoubtedly bound to occur. For this reason, agency administrators must become sensitized to and well-informed about emerging developments in this particular area of employment law. To meet this need, this chapter examines the development of employment law as it specifically applies to homosexuals within the law enforcement field. This objective is accomplished through selective review of relevant Supreme Court, federal, and state cases. Special attention is given to the various arguments litigants frequently raise in these types of discrimination cases. Finally, the chapter concludes with a general overview of the existing legal landscape and its effect on contemporary police employment practices.

JUSTIFICATIONS FOR DISCRIMINATORY HIRING PRACTICES

There are a number of arguments that law enforcement officials rely upon when they justify discriminatory hiring practices against suspected or admitted homosexuals. One viewpoint is that there is no right to privacy for homosexual acts and, therefore, it is not a behavior protected from discrimination. Another fear is that homosexual employees may constitute a security risk to the agency because of their propensity to sympathize with similarly situated individuals. Other worries are that homosexuals may disrupt the working atmosphere by creating disharmony among fellow employees. A fourth position is that the policies and employment practices of law enforcement agencies, for the most part, are shielded from judicial review either through the application of previous case law, or legislative action such as the Administrative Procedures Act (APA). A fifth objection is that homosexuals who do not make their sexual preference publicly known may constitute an additional security risk by exposing themselves to threats of blackmail or extortion. Of course, there is concern in some jurisdictions that homosexuals are habitual lawbreakers and, thus, unsuitable for employment as law enforcement officers. Finally, employing homosexuals may lead to the public perception that the agency tacitly approves such behavior.

Law enforcement agencies use these arguments to defend themselves from claims of employment discrimination. In fact, the various justifications to rationalize employment discrimination against homosexuals vary considerably from case to case so that these arguments often merge with one another. Because a case-by-case approach fails to elucidate each of these justifications, it instead becomes necessary to consider each argument in turn.

HOMOSEXUAL RIGHTS AS INTERPRETED
BY THE U.S. SUPREME COURT

The rights of homosexuals are often couched in several different contexts, one of which is the right to privacy. The leading opinion on this matter is *Bowers v. Hardwick* (1986). There, the U.S. Supreme Court was asked to determine the constitutionality of a Georgia criminal statute prohibiting sodomy and regulating homosexual conduct. Ultimately, the Court rejected the assertion that the statute violated the right to privacy. The majority held that the right to privacy did not include homosexual conduct. The reasoning was that such protection traditionally applies only to activities of a marital, familial, or procreative nature. Because homosexual sodomy, according to the majority opinion, bore no relationship to any of these three interests, the right to privacy was not implicated. In other words, the right to privacy does not protect same-sex conduct.

The *Bowers* decision firmly established the principle of law that there exists no fundamental right to engage in homosexual sodomy. A fundamental right, wrote Justice White, is one that is "deeply rooted in this nation's history and tradition" (*Bowers v. Hardwick*, 1986, p. 194). The Court further held that because homosexual acts historically were condemned rather than protected by society, it was "facetious" to assert that such a right should be considered "implicit in the concept of ordered liberty" (*Bowers v. Hardwick*, 1986, p. 194).

LEGAL IMPLICATIONS OF *BOWERS*

The Supreme Court decision to let the Georgia statute stand clearly emphasized deference to prevailing moral attitudes. Although not directly adjudicating the issue of employment discrimination against homosexuals, the case nonetheless served as a legal watershed upon which future cases would be predicated. Furthermore, the decision has forced lower courts to interpret for themselves on a case-by-case basis the more specific issues that tend to arise when adjudicating claims by homosexuals in other contexts. Narrow interpretations of the *Bowers* opinion by lower courts have resulted in the general rule of law that homosexuals, as a class, are not entitled to any special privileges or rights. Broader interpretations, on the other hand, have granted limited equal protection rights to homosexuals in certain highly specific situations. It is, however, the narrow view that lower federal and state courts typically embrace in settling employment discrimination claims against law enforcement agencies.

ARE HOMOSEXUALS A PROTECTED SOCIAL CLASS?

One specific question the Supreme Court failed to resolve in the *Bowers* case was whether or not protected status should be conferred upon homosexuals as members of a "suspect" or "quasi-suspect" class. The distinction between these two levels of treatment is sometimes vague. A *suspect class* of individuals is one that has experienced a history of discrimination or oppression to such an extent that it deserves an increased level of protection with regard to constitutional due process or equal protection claims. The Court's failure to confer protected status upon homosexuals, combined with the conclusion that same-sex conduct does not fall within the right to privacy, has resulted in denial of various due process and equal protection rights that are extended routinely to such groups as racial minorities, females, and handicapped persons.

If the *Bowers* court had determined that a privacy right was affected or that homosexuals constituted a protected social class, a higher level of scrutiny would apply to any due process or equal protection claims that were raised. Thus, cases involving either a fundamental right or members of a suspect class require lower courts to strictly scrutinize the government's actions and underlying motivations. Under this standard, the government, as a defendant, bears the burden of demonstrating the existence of a compelling interest, and that the policy, law, or regulation at issue has been tailored narrowly to achieve that interest. As the descriptive label implies, strict scrutiny is the most difficult level of constitutional review to satisfy. Had the *Bowers* court, hypothetically speaking, determined that homosexuals were either members of a quasi-suspect class (a designation generally limited to matters of gender, age, or illegitimacy) or that the case involved an important (but not fundamental) constitutional right, it would have applied a standard known as *intermediate scrutiny*. This level would require the government to demonstrate that an important state interest is at stake, and that the law, ordinance, or regulation in question is substantially related to achieving that interest. As the *Bowers* case failed to satisfy the criteria for consideration under these two standards, it fell instead within the purview of what is known in legal circles as *rational basis review*. This level of scrutiny requires only that the government prove some rational basis for the law, ordinance, or regulation in question. Obviously, the rational basis test is the least difficult to overcome, thereby increasing the chances that the government will prevail. At present, most cases involving claims by homosexuals are assessed utilizing this least demanding of the three standards.

CHILDERS V. DALLAS

The earliest case specifically addressing the practice of open employment discrimination against homosexuals within the law enforcement context was *Childers v. Dallas Police Department* (1981). Childers, an employee with the Dallas Water Department, had become eligible under the then-existing civil service guidelines to apply for a transfer of assignment into the position of a property storage clerk for the city's police department. This job involved handling property and drugs seized by the police, as well as the occasional processing of evidence at crime scenes.

A question arose during Childers' initial interview with the property supervisor regarding his sexual preference and affiliation with a church whose aim was to provide religious outreach services to the gay community. Childers answered honestly about his sexual interests. At that point, the interviewer determined him to be unfit for employment. This decision was based upon Childers' admission of being a habitual lawbreaker under the state's sodomy law and the fact that he might pose a security risk by warning other homosexuals of impending police raids. As a result, Childers was rejected from consideration for the position with no explanation given.

Later, Childers reapplied for the property room position and was interviewed again by the same police supervisor. The officer did not remember Childers' previous interview, but Childers reminded the interviewer of his identity and same-sex preference. Childers asked why he had not been hired previously. He was told flatly that the decision was directly linked to his participation in two church-sponsored public marches. A discussion ensued in which Childers expressed the view that religion should not affect his job performance. The interviewing supervisor then told Childers that he would have to have a high tolerance for jokes and that he would not be hired because of the emotional strain that this atmosphere would place upon him. The supervisor also cited the department's security interests. Childers agreed with the supervisor that it would be preferable to cite reasons other than his sexual orientation in official documentation as to why he was not selected for the position. The two ultimately agreed to indicate that he had been offered the job but that Childers had turned it down.

As a result of this perceived discriminatory conduct, Childers subsequently brought suit against the agency, the chief of police, and the supervising officer who had interviewed him. Childers claimed they had violated his First and Fourteenth Amendment rights. The federal district court hearing the claim considered several important questions. The first issue was whether or not the department had abridged Childers' First Amendment right to freedom of religion. The court held that there was no evidence to indicate that the department's refusal to hire was based solely upon Childers' religious beliefs, adding that "the mere fact, however, that an activity [such as participation in gay demonstrations] ... comes under the auspices of a church does not mandate a finding that that activity is constitutionally protected" (*Childers v. Dallas Police Department* 1981, p. 139).

A second concern was whether or not the department's refusal to hire Childers violated his First Amendment rights of freedom of expression and association. Here, the court expressed sympathy noting that the type of activity in question—namely, educating the community as to the plight of homosexuals—was "a clear example of the associational activity singled out for protection under the First Amendment" (*Childers v. Dallas Police Department*, 1981, p. 139). Having determined that an associational right was at stake, the court sought to determine the extent to which the department had a justifiable reason to burden that right or exact a penalty for its exercise by denying public employment because of it.

The court applied a post hoc balancing test requiring Childers, the injured party, to demonstrate that he had been denied employment because of the expression in question. The department, on the other hand, was required to prove that such expression would have prevented its efficient operation. Although Childers satisfied his initial burden, the court ultimately ruled in favor of the department's interests. The court explained that law enforcement officers must be "beyond reproach" and that an employee's participation in such actions would likely undermine the agency's legitimate need for obedience and discipline among personnel (*Childers v. Dallas Police Department*, 1981, p. 139). The court further suggested that the types of activities in which Childers engaged could very well discredit the agency, present a potential security risk, expose him to harassment by fellow workers, and even promote unrest and disharmony among coworkers.

Childers also raised procedural and substantive due process claims. In addressing the procedural due process claim, the court required Childers to establish that the agency's action deprived him of a protected property or liberty interest. On this point, the court held that the policies and procedures of both the Civil Service Commission and the Dallas Police Department neither guaranteed nor entitled Childers to a promotion or transfer. Rather, these regulations merely determined eligibility for promotion or transfer. In light of Childers' own admissions regarding his participation in homosexual conduct, an activity clearly prohibited by Texas law, he could not claim any entitlement to the promotion being sought. In other words, the court found that transfer denial had not deprived Childers of any constitutional liberty.

With regard to the substantive due process claim, Childers was unable to establish that the types of activities in which he engaged were protected by an absolute right to privacy. When it finally reached his equal protection claim, the court swiftly concluded that homosexuals were not a protected social class nor had Childers been deprived of a fundamental constitutional right. As such, established standards of constitutional scrutiny only required that the governmental action at issue be rationally related to a legitimate state interest. Based upon Childers' inability to establish that he had been treated differently from other similarly situated individuals, the equal protection claim was also dismissed.

Despite the fact that the *Childers* case was resolved prior to the Supreme Court decision in *Bowers*, it has serious implications for the future evolution of employment law in this area. Primarily, it reinforced the view that homosexuals do not constitute a protected social class. Second, *Childers* identified several basic arguments that law enforcement agencies and administrators tend to assert when defending their actions in employment discrimination suits filed by homosexuals. In the cases that have been decided since then, law enforcement agencies have begun to assert and expand these initial arguments more strongly. The various cases that follow serve to illustrate this point, beginning first with the assertion that homosexual conduct has the potential to jeopardize agency credibility and security interests.

HOMOSEXUALS AND THE FEDERAL BUREAU OF INVESTIGATION

The hiring practices of the Federal Bureau of Investigation (FBI) were challenged shortly after *Bowers* was decided. In the case of *Padula v. Webster* (1987), the plaintiff was rejected as an applicant for a special agent position due to her same-sex preference. The federal district court that originally heard Padula's claim entered summary judgment for the government, and she subsequently appealed.

During retrial, Padula argued that the Bureau violated its own hiring policies as well as the Constitution. Specifically, she argued that the FBI had established an open practice and policy of hiring individuals as special agents despite their sexual orientation. Padula offered a series of letters the FBI had sent to various law schools as proof. The Bureau, however, argued that it had established no such policy and that its hiring decisions were made on a case-by-case evaluation of an individual's overall conduct and not just his or her sexual orientation alone.

In resolving this dispute, the appellate court first addressed whether it even had jurisdiction to review Padula's claims. Relying upon its interpretation of the APA, the court determined that historically Congress had committed hiring and policy decisions of this type to the Bureau's discretion, thereby shielding such matters from judicial scrutiny. The court further ruled that the letters in question did not make sexual preference irrelevant in hiring decisions. Instead, they only assured potential applicants that the screening process would remain fair.

In resolving Padula's equal protection claim, the appeals court noted that governmental actions, despite being relegated by law to agency discretion, are subject to judicial review only in instances where violation of a constitutional right has occurred. The question then became one of determining whether or not homosexuals constituted a protected social class. Relying upon the recently decided *Bowers* case, which had rejected the assertion that homosexual conduct was a fundamental right protected by the First Amendment's privacy clause, the court applied a ratio-

nal basis test, concluding that the Bureau's specialized functions rationally justified consideration of homosexual conduct in hiring matters. Specifically, the court
recognized that hiring agents who would violate the laws of roughly one-half the
states would undermine the FBI's credibility as a law enforcement agency. The court
further agreed with the notion that many of an agent's duties are related to matters of
counterintelligence, classified information, and national security. To the extent that
agents are secretive in their same-sex preferences, they may become targets of blackmail and extortion. In essence, the court expressed concern with the possibility that
a secret lifestyle may expose an agent, fellow agents, and perhaps even the nation to
unnecessary risk. All things considered, the appellate court affirmed the decision
of the lower court. Thus, the holding allowed the FBI to discriminate legitimately
against applicants on the basis of same-sex orientation.

TERMINATION AS A FORM OF EMPLOYMENT DISCRIMINATION

Both the *Padula* and *Childers* cases asked the judiciary to determine whether an
agency's refusal to hire prospective employees on the basis of sexual orientation
constituted discriminatory conduct prohibited by law. In both instances, the courts
hearing these cases gave broad deference to agency interests. They did not, however, have occasion to address the question of whether or not termination from
employment on the basis of same-sex preference also constituted a prohibited form
of discrimination. However, this issue would arise later in other notable cases. One
such case dealt with the dismissal of a sheriff's deputy, whereas a second situation involved the FBI's response to discovering a homosexual within its existing
ranks. Unlike previous cases centering on pre employment hiring practices, which
tend to manifest a fairly consistent rule of law, the following two cases do not.
Consequently, both become important examples of the distinctions the judiciary
frequently draws in balancing governmental interests against those of existing
homosexual employees.

The plaintiff in *Todd v. Navarro* (1988) was an admitted lesbian. She was
employed by the Broward County Sheriff's Office as a correctional officer for
approximately 2 1/2 years. During the latter period of her employment, Todd
maintained a simultaneous sexual relationship with two female coworkers. Upon
discovery of the relationship by colleagues, Todd alleged that those two individuals and other employees conspired to circulate inflammatory and damaging statements throughout the agency about her same-sex preference. Shortly thereafter,
disciplinary charges were filed against Todd, citing her lesbianism and alleging
various instances of misconduct, resulting in a 14-day suspension without pay.
Upon returning to duty, Todd claimed to have been faced with harassment, verbal
abuse, and revelation of her lesbianism to inmates. She believed these efforts were
intended to motivate her resignation. Before being given the opportunity to do so,
however, she was dismissed from employment on charges of absenteeism, malin-
gering, and failure to perform.

Todd brought suit against the Broward County Sheriff and 13 individuals, claiming violations of her Fourteenth Amendment equal protection and due process rights
as they specifically related to the termination decision. At trial, the Sheriff's Office

asserted that Todd's dismissal was not based upon her lesbianism. Even if sexual preference was the basis for the dismissal, homosexuals were not a protected class under existing case law. Therefore, all the agency had to do was demonstrate that its action was reasonably related to a legitimate governmental interest.

This defense tactic effectively shifted the burden of proof back to Todd to show that her termination was arbitrary and irrational. Unable to satisfy this requisite criteria, the court dismissed Todd's equal protection claim, and the defendants received judgment as a matter of law. Because Todd was unable to establish a protected property interest in continued public employment, her due process claim was also dismissed.

The decision in *Todd* had the temporary effect of legitimating termination as a legal form of employment discrimination against homosexuals. Perhaps not surprisingly, lower courts hearing similar claims relied heavily upon this case. Only four years later did this general standard and practice shift as the result of a federal case involving the FBI and one of its existing special agents.

In *Buttino v. Federal Bureau of Investigation* (1992), the plaintiff with 20 years of service was dismissed following an anonymous tip that he was gay. The Bureau conducted an internal investigation into the allegation and promptly revoked Buttino's security clearance. Because agents are required to have top-secret clearance, a criteria Buttino was no longer able to satisfy, he was terminated from employment.

Buttino filed suit in federal district court alleging that the FBI had violated his equal protection rights. In essence, Buttino's equal protection challenge was twofold. First, he argued that revocation of his security clearance, the purported reason for his dismissal, was arbitrary and irrational. Second, he claimed that the decision to terminate him was unconstitutional to the extent that it was based solely upon his sexual orientation.

In seeking to determine whether or not the revocation of Buttino's security clearance was justified, the district court hearing the case applied its interpretation of both the APA and existing case law. This analysis led to the conclusion that although security clearance matters typically were shielded from judicial review, the Bureau's actions in this particular case were nonetheless highly questionable. Specifically, the court was disturbed not only by the Bureau's apparent interest in actively rooting out homosexual agents but the fact that Buttino's case seemed to have been handled disparately when compared to other, more serious policy infractions. Ultimately, the district court concluded that a pervasive antigay policy existed within the FBI and this atmosphere discriminated against Buttino in the revocation of his security clearance. Consequently, the court held that Buttino had presented adequate evidence to suggest that his termination had been based largely, if not solely, upon his sexual orientation.

In considering Buttino's second claim that the termination decision was based solely upon his same-sex preference, the court applied the rational basis test. Buttino was required to bear the initial burden of demonstrating that the action in question was arbitrary and irrational. The Bureau, on the other hand, had to show that its actions were rationally related to a legitimate governmental interest. The court tempered this approach, however, by adhering to recent precedent set forth in *Pruitt v. Cheney* (1992). In *Pruitt*, the U.S. Supreme Court held that any argument set forth by the government that merely gives effect to prevailing social prejudices should be rejected automatically. In other words, the court was restricted to performing an "active" type of rational basis review (*Pruitt v. Cheney*, 1992, p. 1165). As such, the government must prove a rational basis for its policy.

Utilizing this modified approach, the district court expressed serious reservations as to the rationale underlying the FBI's policy against homosexual agents. For example, the court acknowledged the contradiction between the Bureau's policy encouraging homosexual agents to be "open" about their preferences while, at the same time, remaining discreet in conduct. The court also rejected the assertion that Buttino's same-sex preference made him a potential target for blackmail or extortion. Buttino had granted the Bureau unrestricted permission to disclose his homosexuality to anybody it so desired.

These concerns, along with the Bureau's inability to relate its antigay policy to any legitimate governmental interest, resulted in Buttino receiving summary judgment. An apparent and lasting effect of the decision in this case has been a widening of the legal protections available to homosexuals confronted with employment discrimination at the hands of law enforcement agencies. Although regarded by many observers as a drastic split from the case law incorporated under *Bowers* and its progeny, the *Buttino* decision has prevailed due to the district court's use of a modified criteria for the rational review test.

DENIAL OF EMPLOYMENT BASED UPON STATUTORY PROHIBITIONS

In the same year that *Buttino* was decided, the Dallas Police Department again found itself in court responding to a claim of employment discrimination based upon an applicant's same-sex orientation. The case originated when a female applicant, Mica England, was rejected from further consideration on the basis of her admitted same-sex preference revealed during a screening interview. England subsequently brought suit against the State of Texas, the City of Dallas, and its chief of police claiming that both departmental policy and existing state law prohibiting homosexual conduct violated several constitutionally protected rights, namely those of privacy, equal protection, and freedom of association.

The gist of England's claim was that the Texas law prohibiting homosexual conduct was unconstitutional. Because of this statute, the Dallas Police Department denied her employment, which she was otherwise qualified to obtain. In Texas, homosexual conduct and its related acts are prohibited jointly by Chapters 21.06 and 21.01 of the penal code, which reads, in relevant part:

> A person commits an offense if he engages in deviate sexual intercourse with another individual of the same sex. Deviate sexual intercourse is defined as: (a) any contact between any part of the genitals of one person and the mouth or anus of another person, or; (b) the penetration of the genitals or the anus of another person with an object (Texas Penal Code Ann., 1999, 43.21).

The Dallas Police Department, following what it believed to be a constitutional statute enacted by the state legislature, had incorporated this language into its code of conduct and policy requisites for employment of new officers. Because the state's highest court had never addressed the law's constitutionality, the Police Department maintained that its policy of rejecting homosexual applicants should be allowed to stand on three grounds. First, because a court had not overturned or repealed the statute, the agency should not be compelled to alter its policies nor forced to hire individuals who are admitted and habitual lawbreakers. Second, the department asserted that employing homosexuals not only creates the public perception that it tacitly approves of such criminal behavior but that doing so also exposes the agency to extreme criticism regarding its overall effectiveness and productivity. Finally, both the department and its chief argued that they should be summarily dismissed from the suit because the agency had acted in good faith and merely maintained a policy it believed to conform with existing state law.

After review, the District Court of Travis County concluded that it lacked the requisite jurisdiction to determine whether or not the State should be included as a defendant in the case. Accordingly, the State was summarily dismissed. Second, and perhaps most importantly, the trial court ruled that the state law regulating homosexual conduct was unconstitutional. Third, a permanent injunction was issued prohibiting the department from enforcing the statute and from denying employment to applicants based solely upon sexual orientation or for admitted violations of the law in question.

As one might expect, the City of Dallas appealed this adverse ruling to the next tier of judicial review. Once again, the City was unsuccessful in defending its antigay hiring policy that had been predicated on state law (*City of Dallas v. England*, 1993). To make matters more complex, the final resolution of this case was intertwined with *Morales v. State of Texas* (1991). In *Morales*, the plaintiffs sought an injunction against prosecutions pursuant to Tex. Penal Code Ann. 21.06, alleging that the prohibition against sodomy violated the constitutional right to privacy under the Texas Constitution. The trial court agreed and declared the statute unconstitutional and enjoined its enforcement. The Court of Appeals affirmed this holding. However, the state's high court reversed this short-lived victory for homosexual rights based upon what it stated was a lack of jurisdictional authority over criminal statutes by a lower civil court. Moreover, the plaintiffs in *Morales* were unable to demonstrate that they suffered concrete injury. Thus, they were unable to satisfy equitable requirements for injunctive relief (*Texas v. Morales*, 1994, p. 946).

Unlike the *Morales* plaintiffs, the Supreme Court of Texas concluded that Mica England had suffered "the concrete injury that the Plaintiffs in Morales alleged they would suffer" and, therefore, equitable injunctive relief was proper (*Texas v. Morales* 1994, n.5). However, the Texas Supreme Court acknowledged that it did not address the merits of the *England* case because the City failed to file the necessary motion for rehearing that would have triggered the jurisdiction of that Court. In essence, the *England* case "died on the vine" due to a procedural or jurisdictional error. None of the substantive issues, such as whether or not the prohibition against same-sex behavior was unconstitutional, could be addressed. As of this writing, no further judicial action has been taken on the matter, leaving this question wholly unresolved in the state of Texas.

MAKING SENSE OF THE DIFFERENCES

With little room for disagreement, the *Buttino* decision and, to a lesser extent, the initial ruling in the *England* matter constitute a dramatic break from the well-established judicial perspectives that have been relied upon for decades in adjudicating claims of employment discrimination based upon same-sex orientation. *Bowers* and its progeny, on the other hand, are classic examples of how the judiciary has interpreted individual constitutional rights more strictly. Those decisions are formulated upon the philosophy that homosexuals have no inherent right to engage in or express their preference for same-sex behavior. They are indicative of the traditionally conservative approach that the legal system has taken in adjudicating both the individual and collective claims of this group. In contrast, the *Buttino* and *England* decisions have created an avenue by which more liberal-minded courts, if they so choose, may approach the legal questions surrounding this difficult issue.

CONCLUSION

The issue of employment discrimination against homosexuals extends well beyond the law enforcement context to many other professions, both public and private. The body of case law surrounding this issue continues to evolve as the subtle effects of the *Buttino* and *England* decisions are evaluated for their long-term implications. It is anticipated that most cases on this topic will be won at the state level for two reasons. First, state courts generally extend greater freedom and protection to individuals than do federal courts on such issues. Second, the APA traditionally shields the policies of federal law enforcement agencies from judicial scrutiny. This growth of case law at the state level will proliferate and eventually influence federal decisions in cases of employment discrimination against homosexuals. Until such time, however, it appears that most federal courts will adhere to *Bowers* and subsequent case law, while continuing to regard *Buttino* as an anomalous departure from accepted precedent and conventional judicial philosophy.

In any event, the wide degree of discretionary administrative power that traditionally has been extended to local law enforcement agencies will erode to the point where they are no longer allowed to discriminate against individuals manifesting a same-sex preference. As increasing numbers of jurisdictions begin to enact broad antidiscrimination laws and repeal statutes that prohibit same-sex behavior, state and lower-level courts will begin to adopt more liberal criteria for evaluating homosexuals' claims of discrimination. This shift in ideology will, no doubt, be facilitated by increased political activism and pressure intended to illuminate the individual and collective plight of homosexuals.

REFERENCES

Heger, H. (1994). *The men with the pink triangle: The true life and death story of homosexuals in the Nazi death camps.* Boston, MA: Alyson.
Leinen, S. (1993). *Gay cops.* New Brunswick, NJ: Rutgers University Press.
Leviticus. *The holy bible, old testament.*
Tex. Penal Code Ann. 43.21 (1999).

CASES CITED

Bowers v. Hardwick, 478 U.S. 186 (1986).

Boy Scouts of America v. Dale, 530 U.S. 640 (2000).

Buttino v. Federal Bureau of Investigation, 801 F.Supp.298 (N.Dist.CA 1992). See also, *Buttino v. Federal Bureau of Investigation*, 1992 U.S. Dist. Lexis 21919 (order granting Buttino's request for class certification).

Childers v. Dallas Police Department, 513 F.Supp. 134 (N.D. Tex.1981), *affirmed*, 669 F.2d 732 (5th Cir.1982).

City of Dallas v. England, 846 S.W.2d 957 (1993).

England v. State of Texas et al., No. 484,697 (200th Jud.Dist., February 11, 1992).

Morales v. State of Texas, No. 461, 898 (200th Jud.Dist., March 15, 1991).

Padula v. Webster, 822 F.2d 97 (D.C. Cir.1987).

Pruitt v. Cheney, 963 F.2d 1160 (1992), *cert. denied*, 506 U.S. 1020 (1992).

Texas v. Morales, 869 S.W.2d 941 (1994).

Todd v. Navarro, 698 F.Supp. 871 (S.D. Fla.1988).

Section III

The Role of Empirical Research, Education and Training, and Technology in Police Administration

11 The Importance of Theory to Police Research and Practices

Barbara Sims

CONTENTS

INTRODUCTION

Theories of crime and delinquency have provided a plethora of explanations as to why people break the law. Beginning with Beccaria in 1764, classical theory argues that crime is the result of an individual's free will, and to reduce crime, punishment must be swift and certain. Lomboros's biological theory in the late 1800s suggested that criminals were born that way, and that one could determine who was, and who was not, a criminal simply by examining certain physical characteristics of an individual. The early 1900s were the heyday of the Chicago School and such sociologists as Edwin Sutherland, Clifford Shaw, Henry McKay, and others. This group of theorists suggested that both classical and biological theory were overreaching in their underlying assumptions, and that crime was the result of a bad environment. Social process theorists, on the other hand, viewed crime and delinquency as the result of modeling other people's behavior (social learning theory) or a function of not being bonded to society and its major social institutions (social control theory). Other theorists began to suggest, in the 1960s or so, that criminologists/sociologists were asking the wrong questions. Instead of asking why people commit crime, conflict and/or critical theorists argued that a closer examination needed to occur related to power and resources of the ruling class, illuminating the very processes involved in society's law making and reaction to law breaking.

Although much of this early work in theory sought to explore crime causation and its correlates, a parallel effort has developed through the years related to the more general field of police studies. Within this genre, researchers have used a variety of theories to explain certain police-related phenomena. The purpose of this chapter is to explore some of those studies that have used (1) Tittle's control balance theory, (2) Turk, Chambliss, Vold, and others' assumptions grounded in conflict theory, (3) Barlett's schema theory, (4) Merton's strain theory, (5) angry aggression theory, and (6) social interactionism theory.

CONTROL BALANCE THEORY

Hickman et al. (2001) used control balance theory (Tittle 1995) to study decision making by police officers. A random sample of Philadelphia police officers was surveyed about how they would react to witnessing misbehavior by fellow officers. Two scenarios were described to the sampled officers: the first dealing with the respondent coming upon a fellow officer who drove his vehicle into a ditch because of being intoxicated, and witnessing another officer letting the intoxicated officer off without any action taken; in the second, the respondent witnessing the punching of a captured fleeing suspect by a fellow officer. Respondents were asked whether they would report the behavior of the two officers in these scenarios, using concepts operationalized from control balance theory as key independent variables, controlling for basic demographic characteristics. Questions from Regoli's (1976) police cynicism scale and Krejei, Kvapil, and Semrad's (1996) ethics scale were also included in the survey. One final question was controlled for respondents' perceptions of the punishment that might be given to the misbehaving officer (with a scale of 1–6, were 1 = verbal reprimand and 6 = dismissal).

According to Hickman et al. (2001, 498):

> The central premise of control balance theory is that the amount of control to which one is subject relative to the amount of control one can exercise (the control ratio) affects not only the probability that one will engage in a deviant act, but also the specific form or type of deviance. When these two forces of control are balanced, the theory predicts conformity. As the amount of control one can exercise exceeds the amount of control to which one is subject (a control surplus), the theory predicts an increasingly autonomous form of deviance. As the amount of control to which one is subject exceeds the amount of control one can exercise (a control deficit), the theory predicts an increasingly repressive form of deviance.

Although the control ratio might be strongly predictive of a person's behavior, Tittle (1995) posits that motivation, constraint, and opportunity play equal roles in the production of deviance. All individuals have a desire for autonomy and are driven by human drives. Most of us, however, are constrained by either internal or external controls. If we are motivated enough such that our desires run roughshod over our constraints, and if an opportunity presents itself, our control ratio could tip the scales one way or the other.

If an officer's control ratio is unbalanced, deviant behavior could result should the situation present an opportunity (e.g., provocation by a citizen, or the myriad situations that are part of police work, such as often working in isolation and in unsupervised situations). Further, police officers often get ambiguous orders, and navigating the many policies and procedures in place can be overwhelming. Given the nature of the police subculture, the situation is further exacerbated. Officers are likely to be predisposed to go along with the unofficial street-level rule book, and the control ratio internal to each officer could be the deciding factor when it comes to the extent to which the officers will react to engaging in acts of deviance associated with their jobs, or willing to turn their heads when witnessing deviant on-the-job acts by their fellow officers.

Hickman et al. (2001) used an earlier point made by Van Maanen (1978) about the moral contest that occurs when citizens challenge the police. These altercations are seen by officers not only as threats to their authority but also to the integrity of the state itself. The extent to which officers will use force against citizens is often directly related to the degree to which they believe their authority is being challenged.

The authors also pull from Westley's (1956) now-classic work on the so-called *blue wall of silence* among police officers. In his work, he found that most officers reported they would not testify against a fellow officer, and some reported they actually would lie under oath to protect their peers. Next, Westley (1956) sought to understand better why officers would risk a perjury charge. He found that the fear of informal sanctions often outweigh the risk of formal sanctions. How an officer is perceived by fellow officers is a strong motivating factor to keep quiet or even lie about a fellow officer's misbehavior. A second reason is related to closing ranks to protect the overall image of police as portrayed by the media. Because of negative media, police realize that many citizens hold them in contempt. In turn, police become contemptuous of citizens and react to them in open expressions of that resentment (Westley 1956). When we add to this mix the fact that new recruits are indoctrinated into this secrecy mold early on in their careers, we have a situation that is ripe for the maintaining of silence.

Hickman et al. (2001) also use Herbert's (1998, 347) six normative orders—"sets of generalized rules and common practices oriented around a common value." These include the law, bureaucratic control, adventure/machismo, safety, competence, and morality. Officers have laws to follow but, at the same time, are allowed a certain amount of street-level discretion. They also are limited by the organizational bureaucracy of the police agency. In many cases, a supervisor is called to the scene and must make the final decision about a course of action. Although some officers enjoy immensely the danger element involved in some police work, others try to avoid such machismo works. When it comes to dangerous situations, preserving his/her life moves to the forefront of the officer's thinking. Also, keeping citizen bystanders safe is another factor that influences police officers' decisions about what actions to take. Officers are also expected to show evidence of the effectiveness (competence) of their work (number of tickets, arrests made, etc.), and this can also influence their decision making. Finally, Herbert's (1998) sixth normative order, morality, addresses the sometimes-held perceptions by police officers that they are the good guys and thus responsible for maintaining the larger value system of society.

In their study, Hickman et al. (2001) asked respondents to rate the amount of influence each of 12 items has over how they do their job. They used a 4-point scale consisting of 1 = no influence, 2 = some influence, 3 = lots of influence, and 4 = total influence. The response options also included qualifying statements such as "This has some influence over how I do my job; most of the time it is up to me, but sometimes I have to do this" (Hickman et al. 2001, 510).

After the respondents read the two scenarios (described earlier in this section), they were asked to answer questions about whether they would report a fellow officer engaging in such behavior. A 5-point Likert scale was used with 1 = definitely to 5 = definitely not. A decision to report misbehavior is viewed by the authors as a rejection of the police cultural norm of silence. From control balance theory, Hickman et al. (2001, 511) hypothesize that "officers with control deficits will be more likely to report a fellow officer's behavior."

Hickman et al.'s (2001) findings related to the first scenario (intoxicated officer) can be summarized as (1) the deficit segment of the control balance ratio is positively and significantly related to the likelihood of reporting a fellow officer, (2) non-white respondents were more likely to report a fellow officer, (3) officers who exhibited lower levels of cynicism were more likely to report a fellow officer, (4) officers with stronger attitudes toward ethics were also more likely to report a fellow officer, and (5) officers who believed that a higher level of punishment would result for the offending officer should the action be reported were more likely to say they would report a fellow officer.

In scenario two (punching a suspect who was down after fleeing police), the control deficit was significant, and (1) older respondents were more likely to report a fellow officer as were non-white and female officers, and (2) officers who exhibited lower levels of cynicism, with stronger attitudes toward ethics, and estimated that higher levels of punishment would be forthcoming, were more likely to report fellow officers.

Hickman et al. (2001) conclude that it might behoove agencies to increase officer autonomy. This is based on how their data were coded, but the bottom line is that a clearer articulation of the police role is called for. Problem-oriented and/or community policing actually calls for a move away from a continual, direct connection between the field officer and his/her supervisor. Greene et al. (1999) discovered that officers who have moved to a community policing model enjoy the new-found sense of autonomy, which, in turn, leads to an increase in job satisfaction. The end result is better police performance (Greene et al. 1999).

CONFLICT THEORY AND POLICING

Much has been written about the relationship between poverty and other social phenomena, and drug use and trafficking. Mosher (2001) discusses the issue from a somewhat different angle and from a conflict theoretical perspective. Turk (1969), for example, has pointed out the relationship between race/ethnicity and society's official reaction to drug use and sales. When subordinate groups are thought to be a threat to the social order, they will systematically be overrepresented in official crime statistics. Quinney (1970) has argued that laws are directed at controlling the perceived lack of control mechanisms in certain groups of the population. In communities that are diverse, with several different racial/ethnic groups, police may enforce the law more punitively. Further, with an increase of non-whites in any given community, police may perceive an increase in the threat of crime within those communities. Jackson and Carroll (1981), for example, have shown a direct and positive correlation between the numbers of minorities within a city and expenditures by the police, as well as the number of sworn personnel.

Using drug possession and drug trafficking data for 187 U.S. cities for the year 1989, Mosher (2001, 94) was able to demonstrate that "racial composition has a strong independent effect on drug possession arrest rates that is not attributable to racial/ethnic-specific deprivation, thus providing support for the assertions of conflict theory." Related to trafficking arrests, the author was able to demonstrate that the "percentage of Blacks exerts a strong and statistically significant positive effect on trafficking arrest rates, which is not attenuated when the race/ethnic-specific economic deprivation factors are added to the equation" (Mosher 2001, 96).

From a conflict perspective, the disproportionate representation of minorities in drug-related arrests has very little to do with a misplaced perception that minorities are more likely to engage in drug use than their white counterparts. Data from the National Institute on Drug Abuse, for example, shows just the opposite. Whereas whites comprised 77 percent of the estimated 13 million users of illicit drugs in the United States, blacks/African Americans comprised only 15 percent (Mosher 2001). Lockwood, Pottieger, and Inciardi (1995) have estimated that 50 percent of the 479,000 identified crack cocaine users were white, 36 percent Hispanic, and 36 percent Black/African American. Further, there is no evidence that whites participate in trafficking to any lesser extent than do blacks/African Americans (Lusane 1990). Blumstein (1993, 5) has concluded that "There is no clear indication that racial differences in arrests truly reflect different levels of activity … and so it is reasonable to presume that a large part of the difference is attributable to enforcement patterns and practices."

Common sense tells us that police are going to catch more people behaving illegally in the inner cities, as opposed to out in the suburbs, if they take a proactive approach to policing within urban neighborhoods. This is akin to findings that show that intensive supervision on parole actually produces an increase in parole revocations. Chambliss (1994) argues that intense supervision of minorities by police is nothing less than *institutional racism* because police have decided that drug use and trafficking is a black/African American male phenomenon. Examples abound, and one of the most well known is New York's Operation Pressure Point. Under this policy, drug dealers (primarily black/African American) are arrested on the scene when buyers (whites from the suburbs) are scared off and told not to come back to that neighborhood (Mosher 2001). This policy exacerbates the problem of portraying both dealers and users as primarily black/African American.

Conflict theorists conclude that the disparate treatment of minorities in the war on drugs has forever damaged the already fragile foundation of social institutions within the inner cities. Bertram et al. (1996, 37) have suggested that the war on drugs will "inevitably aggravate the conditions that encourage drug abuse, addiction, and dealing in the first place."

In that same vein, conflict theory has been used to explain the killing of citizens by police officers. Researchers have examined the existence of a relationship between the social status and/or race of the deceased and the number of police killings (Knoohuizen, Fahey, and Palmer 1972; Takagi 1974). Goldkamp (1976) includes the conflict perspective as one of two possible theories of homicides caused by the police, with the second theory related to the disproportionality of minorities represented in serious/violent crime. Whereas the former basically argues that the police perceive minorities as more violent than whites, e.g., a labeling perspective, the latter seeks to dispel stereotyping by police officers. From this perspective, and as pointed out by Goldkamp (1976, 177), "more minorities are killed by police because more minorities are involved in violence, and that neither prejudice nor discrimination figures in."

Testing the so-called "danger-perception" theory, MacDonald et al. (2001) added a second possibility: that homicides by police increase during a time of an upsurge in certain types of homicides. During times of a higher number of robbery-related homicides, police killings will be higher. Conversely, when homicides are up due to "love triangle" homicides, homicides by police will be lower. This is related to the danger-perception hypothesis because police do not view the latter situation as particularly threatening to the general order of society, whereas they do view the former as such.

The findings by MacDonald et al. (2001) support their hypothesis that although the danger-perception theory might play a role in homicides by police, their "ratio-threat" hypothesis, described earlier, plays a stronger role. They state, "We found that the average monthly counts of police killings of civilians, homicides caused by love triangles, and justifiable citizen homicides do not differ greatly from one another" (MacDonald 2001, 168). They further suggest that, in addition to examining homicides by police through intensive investigations related to the circumstances surrounding a specific event, police administrators might use both the danger-perception and the ratio-threat perspectives to situate such incidents within the larger societal perspective.

Schema Theory

Robinson (2000) has used Barlett's (1932) schema theory to examine a change in police officers' perceptions of incidents of domestic violence. In 1932, Barlett discovered that the more the mind is exposed to certain knowledge, it develops a generic cognitive representation of those situations. Schema, then, help us organize our thoughts and perceptions about the world around us. Researchers have found that types of schemata can have an effect on the way criminal justice personnel process clients. How probationers are processed, for example, depends on whether they perceive their client as a gang member, a female welfare fraud, a dumb hillbilly, etc. (Lurigio and Carroll 1985).

Although some may argue that the use of schemata in their everyday interactions with citizens could allow police, probation/parole, or corrections officers do their jobs more effectively, and perhaps more efficiently, others are cautious. It is true that experience is a good teacher, and these officers have become experts of sorts when it comes to making the right call in their *sizing up* of their clients. On the other hand, preconceived notions could be seen as biasing officers, and play a negative role in the practitioner/client relationship. Either way, schemata theory provides a "general framework for demonstrating the active and reflexive nature of decision making and gives a sense of the large roles that learning, socialization, and experience play" in the decision-making process of criminal justice personnel (Robinson 2000, 604).

In her own work with schemata, Robinson (2000) examined the effect of somewhat radical changes in police policies toward domestic violence changing their schemata about such incidents, and subsequently their actual on-the-job behavior. Prior to the 1980s, violence between intimate partners was seen as a private matter, and assault within the home was handled much differently from assaults between strangers. As Robinson (2000, 606) notes, "officers were to handle these calls with the main goal of settling the parties down and restoring order." Arrest was to be used only when no other option appeared to be possible. In the late 1990s, police departments began to implement mandatory arrest policies, and today's policies "make it clear that domestic violence is considered criminal conduct rather than disorderly conduct and they specifically mandate that officers make arrests when probable cause exists in domestic disturbances" (Robinson 2000, 607). This new direction in policy can be viewed in some sense as a liability issue, and officers who once were able to use their discretion on the scene of a domestic violence situation now are told to follow the policy exactly as written, and much in-service training deals specifically with this one issue (Robinson 2000).

With this new direction in domestic violence policies came the creation of a new set of schemata among police officers. Robinson (2000) argues, however, that the time period in which officers were socialized within the police subculture could determine the influence that this new policy might have on any changed schemata associated with them. It could be that the socialization process of some officers is so strong that any attempt to restructure their thinking about domestic-violence-related calls for service would be a futile process.

Robinson (2000) hypothesized in her study that (1) there will be a significant difference in officers' arrest decisions based on whether their schemata were formed before or after the domestic violence policy change and (2) there will be a significant difference in the perceptions of officers toward domestic violence victims based on whether their schemata were formed before or after the domestic violence policy change. In a study, a sample of 115 police officers were placed into two different groups: officers hired before a change in the domestic violence policy, and those hired after the new pro-arrest policy.

As part of the study, the officers were ordered by the Chief to complete a domestic violence case summary form that collected data on information used to determine if probable cause existed, the cooperativeness of the victim, and whether the officer attributed certain characteristics to the victim (e.g., considered the victim to be someone who abuses substances). The form also collected extralegal documentation such as whether the parties were living together, and the gender, race/ethnicity, and time of hire of each officer.

Robinson (2000) found that whether the victim and perpetrator were living together significantly increased the chances of a decision to make an arrest as did whether the officer believed the victim had a substance abuse problem. Other significant predictors of whether an arrest occurred included race (white officers more likely than minority officers to make an arrest) and whether a witness was present. Of primary importance, however, is the fact that there were no significant differences found between the two groups. This means that officers hired before the change in the policy have changed their domestic violence schemata, even in light of the strong pull of the police subculture and/or the socialization process. For domestic violence advocates, this should come as good news. Even when officers did not believe that victims would cooperate and that the case was not likely to be prosecuted, they still made an arrest when probable cause was present. Robinson (2000, 617) concludes that "schemata are active processes that may be revised or tuned contingent on exposure to new information."

STRAIN THEORY AND POLICE CYNICISM

In 1967, Niederhoffer used strain theory to develop what has come to be called a police cynicism scale. Merton (1938) proposed that a state of confusion (anomie) can develop when individuals are encouraged to achieve certain cultural goals but are not given the means through which to achieve those goals. Niederhoffer (1967) used strain theory to explain feelings of frustration that police officers might experience as policing moved away from a more traditional model towards a more professional model. In the middle of conflicting directives, or other ambiguities inherent in broad-scale changes, cynicism among officers could develop. Through a twenty-item additive scale, Niederhoffer examined cynicism among 220 New York City police officers, testing eleven hypotheses based on his theoretical arguments about what might be related to police officer cynicism. The major findings from his study indicated that lower levels of cynicism were found for younger officers new to policing, that levels increased over time, but they leveled off after a certain number of years in policing. The level of cynicism expressed by more experienced officers, however, according to Niederhoffer (1967), never reached the lower levels experienced by them when they first entered the field of policing.

Niederhoffer's work has been replicated, but with ambiguous results (Hickman, N.L. Piquero, and A.R. Piquero 2004). Regoli (1976), for example, surveyed 324 police officers from nine different agencies, and through factor analysis, was able to show that Niederhoffer's original unidimensional scale actually broke out into a five-factor solution. On the other hand, Hou et al. (1983) confirmed Niederhoffer's original scale. In 1987, Langworthy examined over twenty-one studies using the cynicism scale and found several inconsistencies, leading him to call into question the reliability and validity of Niederhoffer's original scale.

Addressing the issue of reliability, Hickman N.L. Piquero, and A.R. Piquero (2004) used Niederhoffer's cynicism scale on a sample of 499 Philadelphia police officers. The original purpose of that study was to examine the nature of police integrity. The earlier work on the cynicism scale by Regoli (1976) was revisited, and Hickman et al. (2004) used such questions as "Police supervisors are very interested in their subordinates." "When you get to know the department from the inside, you begin to think that it is a wonder that it does one-half as well as it does." "When a police officer appears before the Police Board of Inquiry, the officer will probably be found guilty even when he/she has a good defense." The authors used a 5-point Likert scale (strongly disagree, disagree, neutral, agree, and strongly agree) and, using item response theory, were able to demonstrate a reliable scale, although some of the items exhibited gender and race bias, and some of the items had to be deleted in order to improve the reliability of the scale (Hickman et al. 2004). After these adjustments to the original scale, they were able to show that cynicism did increase after years in service, and that police behavior actually is correlated with police attitudes. The authors suggest that future studies pay more careful attention to measurement issues, as these issues greatly influence outcomes.

ANGRY AGGRESSION THEORY AND EXCESSIVE USE OF FORCE

Police use of excessive force has received much attention in the police studies literature. Much of the theoretical foundations associated with these studies come from either a police subculture perspective or a personality disorder perspective (Griffin and Bernard 2003). The police subculture theory argues that the working environment of police officers is influenced greatly by police codes of deviance, secrecy, silence, and cynicism, and can be traced back to the early work of Westley in the 1950s and 1960s. Westley (1969, 216) suggested that police organizations create a subculture of violent people within the ranks, and that an officer "uses violence illegally because such usage is seen as just, acceptable, and, at times, expected by his [sic] colleague group." As noted by Walker (1999) and others, the subculture of police theory could be overreaching by creating a forced dichotomy between those who are not caught up in the police subculture and those who are. Rather, many see the world of policing as anything but monolithic in nature, with many roles being adopted by officers (Griffin and Bernard 2003).

The personality disorder theory assumes that a certain type of individual is drawn to the world of policing: an individual that is predisposed to using violence, and who comes to policing with a preexisting cynical, bigoted, and suspicious nature (Balch 1972). Adorno (1950) was one of the first to point out that many police officers come to policing not being able to tolerate people who do not do what they tell them to do, referring to this as the *authoritarian model of policing*. Rhead et al. (1970, 58) have argued further that police officers exhibit "a greater degree of paranoid ideation, and a greater tendency to act out" than individuals who are not working in the world of policing.

Critics of the personality disorder theory, however, argue against such a notion that police officers are individuals who seek out policing because they are looking for excitement based on a predisposed bent toward acting violently. Trojanowicz (1971), for example, was able to demonstrate that police officers are not much different from everyday citizens, with Bayley and Mendelsohn (1969) finding that when it comes to diagnosing police officers using personality disorder scales, they are no different from the average citizen. Finally, MacNamara (1967) found that younger police officers actually were less cynical than a group of surveyed community leaders. Griffin and Bernard (2003, 8) conclude that "both theories of police subculture and theories of individual police officer characteristics have thus, independently, failed to adequately explain police officer use of extralegal force."

Griffin and Bernard (2003, 4) define *extralegal force* as that used by police officers "to achieve legal goals when nonforceful means to achieve those goals are readily available to the officer." In other words, they distinguish between unnecessary force, used by a well-meaning officer who is incapable of "dealing with the situations they encounter without needless or too haste resort to force" (Griffin and Bernard 2003, 5), and extralegal force, the "willful and wrongful use of force by officers who knowingly exceed the bounds of their office" (Fyfe 1989, 465).

Griffin and Bernard (2003) developed an alternative theory for explaining extralegal force by police officers. Angry aggression theory "is based on a large and well-established body of biological and psychological research about physiological arousal, which is the body's fight-or-flight response to being threatened" (Griffin and Bernard 2003, 8). Bernard (1990) first used this theory to explain violent responses to seemingly unimportant and insignificant insults between people in highly urbanized areas. Rather than being a function of a personality disorder or a function of a subculture of violence, angry aggression results from structural characteristics such as poverty and racial discrimination (Bernard 1990). Further, when chronically aroused people "are socially isolated in a particular environment, the environment itself becomes quite dangerous because everyone sees threats everywhere and responds aggressively to threats" (Griffin and Bernard 2003, 8).

The angry aggression model begins with the on-the-job stressors experienced by police officers ("danger, citizen hostility, internal and external political pressures, media relations," etc.) (Griffin and Bernard 2003, 15) and moves into an argument that, generally speaking, most officers are never afforded adequate opportunities to assist them in dealing with these stressors. This inability to reduce the stress in their lives leads to a "chronic physiological arousal of police officers" where they are left with two options: learn to cope on their own or respond to seemingly minor or nonexisting threats as very real and calling for increased aggression on the officer's part (Griffin and Bernard 2003, 16).

This is the hallmark of the angry aggression theory: individuals are quick to become physically aroused and thus more likely to engage in violent, explosive behavior, even when others around them see no real threat or insult on the parts of people who are the brunt of the violence. In other words, police officers who become chronically aroused and use extralegal force are irrationally taking out their frustration on the more visible and vulnerable target, as opposed to lashing out at the true basis of their stress (e.g., frustration with what they perceive as public perceptions of police officers or problems with supervisors and/or coworkers, etc.).

In the end, Griffin and Bernard (2003) do not suggest that police subculture and personality disorder theories should be dismissed out of hand. Rather, they suggest that the angry aggression theory could explain the police culture itself when it comes to acts of violence used against citizens. Of course, future research will need to be conducted to test this theory, so there are no indicators at this time as to how successful it will be in the empirical arena.

SOCIAL INTERACTIONISM AND DISRESPECT FOR THE POLICE

It has been argued that the manner in which an individual and/or suspect interacts with the police greatly influences police behavior during contacts with citizens (Van Maanen 1978). Several studies have indicated a correlation between a suspect's demeanor and subsequent police behavior (Mastrofski, Reisig, and McCluskey 2002;

Sykes and Clark 1975; Worden and Shepard 1996). As pointed out by Reisig et al. (2004), very little effort has been made to examine what might influence a suspect's demeanor in the first place. Using social interactionist theory, these researchers seek to determine the predictors of attitudes and behaviors displayed by both the public and the police when they come in contact with each other (Reisig et al. 2004).

The social exchanges between individuals, either verbally or nonverbally through a person's body language, constitute interactionism. The presence of some third party can greatly change the manner in which one person interacts with another, as can the need to protect one's social standing or perceived reputation (Reisig et al. 2004). Certain factors thrown into the mix can break down any inhibitions a person might hold, e.g., the presence of alcohol or drugs in the individual's system. All of these factors come together and work simultaneously to influence how any person will react in the presence of another. This is particularly true of police contact, and one might argue that social interactionism might take a less positive turn when one throws in some sense of an individual feeling the need to right some wrong, e.g., thinking that somehow justice has not been done (Reisig et al. 2004).

Reisig et al. (2004) tested the social interactionism theory as it relates to suspects' demeanor toward the police through a series of field observations with researchers teaming up with patrol officers. A total of 6,500 citizen contacts were observed in Indianapolis and 5,500 in St. Petersburg. They report contact time ranging from less than a minute to up to several hours. In the end, researchers were able to collect sufficient data for the study using 3,128 encounters between the citizens and 298 police officers.

To measure the "disrespect toward the police," Reisig et al. (2004) developed a dichotomous variable: passive and active. Passive disrespect is associated with the ignoring of the officer's request by the citizen, and active disrespect involves name calling and other insulting gestures or comments. Police behavior was measured along two different constructs. The first construct, coercion, was measured using a Likert scale ranging from 0 (officer used no force) to 4 (officer used force to take down a suspect). The second construct, police incivility, was measured using a dummy coded variable, where 1 = police were disrespectful and 0 = police were not disrespectful (Reisig et al. 2004).

Reisig et al. (2004) found support for interactionist theory. First, suspects did not respond to the police in a disrespectful manner even when they were provoked by the police. Second, when it came to high levels of police use of force, however, many suspects responded in kind, leading the authors to conclude that perhaps the suspects felt as though they had nothing to gain by complying beyond a certain point (Reisig et al. 2004). Third, after controlling for neighborhood characteristics, African American suspects did not respond to the police any differently from white suspects. This means that disrespectful behavior toward police is more likely a function of community structure than it is the background racial/ethnic characteristics of a suspect (Reisig et al. 2004). If police officers understand the dynamics between one's environment and the way suspects may or may be acting toward the officer, perhaps more volatile situations could become less so with the officer taking the more "moral" high ground when those circumstances present themselves (Reisig et al. 2004).

SUMMARY AND CONCLUSIONS

This chapter sought to illustrate several examples of how theory has been applied in police studies that are published in peer-reviewed scholarly outlets. It should be pointed out that there are many more such examples than those used here. Future research might include a more in-depth look at those additional examples and an effort made to directly apply findings from those studies to the field of policing. It is suggested here that several useful policy implications can be extrapolated from those studies reviewed earlier, some of which have been alluded to already.

First, perhaps police need clearer directions when it comes to exactly what role it is that society wants them to play in local communities. In the same vein, some degree of autonomy might prove worthwhile, with police expressing a higher level of satisfaction associated with their work when they do feel that the traditional power and authority hierarchy has been slightly flattened.

Second, and from a conflict perspective, perhaps it is time that we think more carefully about *who gets policed more* across U.S. communities. This is a direct reference to the nation's war on drugs, a war in which the police are the first line of contact with both the enemy and citizen casualties. Not much can be done here without a general overhaul of the system, but conflict theorists would argue that there are some things that could be done at a more micro level to make the system more equitable while we wait for that change to occur.

Third, the schemata theory suggests that police can change their thinking about certain issues, and that this change in thinking can bring about a change in officers' behavior. This remains so even when controlling for the police subculture that has such a strong hold on officers. Through careful training and education, adjustments can be made and officers can learn to react differently in light of a new policy or regulation.

Fourth, through role playing, officers could learn how better to respond to suspects who appear agitated and who pose a potential threat to the officer or innocent bystanders. Police supervisors should watch for signs of chronic physiological arousal, continuing to search for ways to reduce on-the-job stress experienced by a majority of police officers.

Fifth, interactionist theory suggests that several key factors come into play when officers come in contact with a citizen suspect. What is key to this interaction, however, is the role that the local environment plays in the decision by a suspect to respond negatively to an officer who is either using too much force than called for or who is behaving in a way that is not civil. Both the police and the suspect are very much influenced by the structural characteristics of their surroundings, and it would be good if officers could keep that in mind when deciding how to handle a street-level incident. Recall that the schemata theory has shown remarkable results in changing an officer's attitude and subsequent behavior in light of new information through education and training.

In sum, theory, research, and policy together comprise an important triangle with far-reaching implications for the world of policing. What is left now is for academics to better present evidence-based facts to police practitioners and supervisors, and perhaps to the criminal justice student with plans for making a career out of policing.

REFERENCES

Adorno, T. 1950. *The Authoritarian Personality*. New York: Harper.

Balch, R. 1972. Police personality: Fact or fiction? *Journal of Criminal Law, Criminology, and Police Science*, 63: 106–119.

Bartlett, F.C. 1932. *Remembering*. London: Cambridge University Press.

Bayley, D. and H. Mendelsohn. 1969. *Minorities and the Police*, New York: Free Press.

Bernard, T. 1990. Angry aggression among the truly disadvantaged. *Criminology*, 28: 73–96.

Bertram, E., M. Blachman, K. Sharpe, and P. Andreas. 1996. *Drug War Politics: The Price of Denial*. Berkeley, CA: University of California Press.

Blumstein, A. 1993. Making rationality relevant: The American Society of Criminology presidential address. *Criminology*, 31, 1–16.

Chambliss, W. 1994. Policing the ghetto underclass: The politics of law and law enforcement. *Social Problems*, 41, 177–194.

Fyfe, J. 1989. The spkit-second syndrome and other determinants of police violence. In R. Dunham and G. Alpert (eds.) *Critical Issues in Policing*. (pp. 465–479). Prospect Heights, IL: Waveland.

Goldkamp, J.S. 1976. Minorities as victims of police shootings: Interpretations of racial disproportionality and police use of deadly force. *The Justice System Journal*, 2: 68–183.

Greene, J.R., M. Hickman, K. Henderson, R. Stokes, W. Pelfrey, and A.R. Piquero. 1999. *Measuring What Matters: Assessing Community Policing in Philadelphia*. Final report to the National Institute of Justice, Washington, D.C.

Griffin, S.P. and T.J. Bernard. 2003. Angry aggression among police officers. *Police Quarterly*, 6(1): 3–21.

Herbert, S. 1998. Police subculture reconsidered. *Criminology*, 36(2): 343–369.

Hickman, M.J., A.R. Piquero, B.A. Lawton, and J.R. Greene. 2001. Applying tittle's control balance theory to police deviance. *Policing*, 24(4): 497–519.

Hickman, M.J., N.L. Piquero, and A.R. Piquero. 2004. The validity of Niederhoffer's cynicism scale. *Journal of Criminal Justice*. 32(1): 1–13.

Hou, C., A. Miracle, R.D. Pool, and R.M. Regoli. 1983. Assessing determinants of police cynicism in Taiwan. *Police Studies*, 5: 3–7.

Jackson, P. and L. Carroll. 1981. Race and the war on crime: The sociopolitical determinants of municipal police expenditures in 90 non-Southern U.S. cities. *American Sociological Review*, 46(3): 290–305.

Knoohuizen, R., R.P. Fahey, and D.J. Palmer. 1972. *The Police and Their Use of Fatal Force in Chicago*. Chicago, IL: Chicago Law Enforcement Study Group.

Krejei, P., J. Kvapil, and J. Semrad. 1996. The relation between job satisfaction, job frustration, and narcissism and attitudes toward professional ethical behavior among police officers. In M. Pagon (ed.) *Policing in Central and Eastern Europe*, College of Police and Security Studies, Slovenia.

Langworthy, R. 1987. Police cynicism: What we know from the Niederhoffer Scale. *Journal of Criminal Justice* 15: 17–35.

Lockwood, D., A. Pottieger, and J. Inciardi. 1995. Crack use, crime by crack users, and ethnicity. In D. Hawkins (ed.) *Ethnicity, Race, and Crime: Perspectives Across Time and Place* (pp. 214–234). Albany, New York: SUNY Press.

Lurigio, A.J. and J.S. Carroll. 1985. Probation officers' schemata of offenders: Content, development, and impact on treatment decisions. *Journal of Personality and Social Psychology*, 48: 1112–1126.

Lusane, C. 1990. *Pipe Dream Blues*. New York: Beacon Press.

MacDonald, J.M., R.J. Kaminski, G.P. Alpert, and A.N. Tennenbaum. 2001. The temporal relationship between police killings of civilians and criminal homicide: A refined version of the danger-perception theory. *Crime and Delinquency*, 47(2): 155–172.

MacNamara, J. 1967. Uncertainties in police work: The relevance of police recruits' backgrounds and training. In D. Bordua (ed.) *The Police: SixSociological Essays* (pp. 163–252). New York: John Wiley.

Mastrofski, S.D., M.D. Reisig, and J. McCluskey. 2001. Police disrespect toward the public: An encounter-based analysis. *Criminology*, 39: 519–552.

Merton, R.K. 1938. Social structure and anomie. *American Sociological Review,* 3: 672–682.

Mosher, C. 2001. Predicting drug arrest rates: Conflict and social disorganization perspectives. *Crime and Delinquency*, 47(1): 84–104.

Myer, M.W. 1980. Police shootings at minorities: The case of the Los Angeles police. *Annals of the American Academy of Political and Social Science*, 452: 98–110.

Niederhoffer, A. 1967. *Behind the Shield*. New York: Doubleday.

Quinney, R. 1970. *The Social Reality of Crime*. Boston, MA: Little, Brown and Company.

Regoli, R. 1976. An empirical assessment of Niederhoffer's police cynicism scale. *Journal of Criminal Justice*, 4, 231–241.

Reisig, M.D., J.D. McCluskey, S.D. Mastrofski, and W. Terrill. 2004. Suspect disrespect toward the police. *Justice Quarterly*, 21(2): 241–269.

Rhead, C., A. Abrams, H. Trosman, and P. Margolis. 1970. The psychological assessment of police candidates. In A. Neiderhoffer and A. Blumberg (eds.) *The Ambivalent Force: Perspectives on the Police*. Waltham, MA: Ginn.

Robinson, A.L. 2000. The effect of a domestic violence policy change on police officers' schemata. *Criminal Justice and Behavior*, 27(5): 600–624.

Sykes, R.E. and J.P. Clark. 1975. A theory of deference exchange in police-civilian encounters. *American Journal of Sociology*, 81: 584–600.

Takagi, P. 1974. A garrison state in a democratic society. *Crime and Social Justice*, 1: 27–33.

Tittle, C. 1995. *Control Balance: Toward a General Theory of Deviance*. Boulder, CO: Westview Press.

Trojanowicz, R. 1971. The policeman's occupational personality. *Journal of Criminal Law, Criminology, and Police Science*. 62: 551–559.

Turk, A. 1969. *Criminality and the Legal Order*. Chicago, IL: Rand McNally.

Van Maanen, J. 1978. The asshole. In V. Kappeler (ed.) (1995) *The Police and Society* (pp. 307–328). Prospect Heights, IL: Waveland Press.

Walker, S. 1999. *The Police in America: An Introduction*. (3rd ed.) New York: McGraw-Hill.

Westley, W.A. 1956. Secrecy and the police. *Social Forces*, 34: 254–257.

Westley, W.A. 1969. Violence and the police. In R. Quinney (ed.). *Crime and Justice in Society*. Boston, MA: Little, Brown.

Worden, R.E. and R.L. Shepard. 1996. Demeanor, crime, and police behavior: A reexamination of the police services study data. *Criminology*, 34: 83–106.

12 Technology Applications: Tools for Law Enforcement

Vicki S. Williams and Barry O. Williams

CONTENTS

INTRODUCTION

To do any job correctly, one must have the right tools for that specific job. No one can change a flat tire using a knitting needle or a spoon. Over the years, there have been tools officers had to have in order to perform their law enforcement duties. There were tools of communication like radios and call boxes, tools of investigation like cameras and fingerprint kits, and tools of surveillance like video and audio pickups. Increasingly, newer, more specific tools have been developed using emerging technologies. These innovations enhance the old tools and make some new tools possible. These new tools take the officer from a local to a global environment with a flick of the switch. They have the potential to improve communication and information sharing, crime investigation and prevention, and public and officer safety.

COMMUNICATION AND INFORMATION SHARING

COMMUNICATION

Without communication, our global vision would quickly break down. Without communication, the officer is isolated and must work with and make decisions based on what is possibly incomplete information. Radios were a partial solution but only offered a connection to the station and other officers on duty—who had their radios turned on. Vehicle and driver's license checks had to go through the station dispatcher, and the officer waited for the results. While he or she waited, a lot of things could happen.

Today, many patrol cars carry laptop computers (Mobile Computer Terminals, or MCTs) that are connected to databases that allow on-the-spot checks of vehicle registration and driver identification. Many states have installed onboard systems for cruisers. For example, the Pennsylvania State Police have deployed this type of technology in their Initial Mobile Office (IMO) project (1), installing approximately 1,200 data terminals and wireless mobile data software in police vehicles. Through these terminals, officers can access the Commonwealth Law Enforcement Assistance Network (CLEAN) (2) and National Crime Investigation Center (NCIC) databases, as well as the National Law Enforcement Telecommunications System (NLETS), searching for information on vehicle registration, driver's licenses, state criminal histories, and stolen or wanted files. An officer can obtain information through the Pennsylvania Justice Network (JNET) or other state database information systems. The NCIC system allows for national searches on a number of parameters such as serial, vehicle identification number (VIN), license plate, and hull numbers on stolen articles, including firearms. Knowing almost immediately whether the driver of the car a trooper is approaching might be wanted or dangerous is critical to officer safety.

The system also provides Global Positioning System (GPS) information for relaying location information, access to an online version of the *Criminal Justice Manual*, and a word processor for writing and filing reports while still in the field. Unlike radios, these wireless transmissions are encrypted and not subject to being picked up by the public on police-frequency scanners. They afford the officer the ability to remain on the scene, remain in contact, and remain informed.

Along with these mobile offices, officers have access to standard communications technologies such as e-mail and cell phones. E-mail has made possible rapid inter- and intra-agency contact and response capabilities that, before, only faxing could provide. In e-mail, images of original items with color and fairly good detail can be transmitted as attachments to e-mail notes in a matter of seconds. This makes possible sharing almost any type of information over distances, locally and globally. Cell phones allow voice access in the field, giving investigators freedom of movement and the ability to obtain and share information as needed, regardless of location. Some cell phones even allow receipt and transmission of e-mail messages and include small digital cameras to transmit digital images. All in all, today's law enforcement officers literally have the world at their fingertips regarding communication. Using any or all of these communications technologies, inquiries can go from the crime scene in Maine or Oregon to the FBI in a matter of seconds, and even to INTERPOL if necessary.

With the increase in availability of communications satellites and satellite phones, the range of communication expands around the entire globe, offering access to and from anywhere, even the most remote region. Add a video camera, and the satellite videophone brings the remote transmission into the station. Sensitive satellite videophone transmissions must be electronically encrypted, yet another function of technology and an area of research and development.

INFORMATION SHARING

The Internet and the World Wide Web (WWW) offer a vast source of information and an opportunity to share information. Using any Web search engine such as Google or Yahoo, a search on the term *law enforcement* results in approximately 15,000,000 hits, or occurrences, of the term on the WWW. Many of these are news media sites and merely mention the phrase, some are job recruiting sites, and many are vendor sites offering equipment and services for sale. Others, however, are sites designed for law enforcement officers, such as PoliceOne.com, The National Association of Police Organizations (NAPO) Web site, and the Web site of the Federal Law Enforcement Training Center of the U.S. Department of Homeland Security http://www.fletc.gov/. In this Web site alone, there is a page of links to more than fifty other related Web sites that have been determined to be useful.

Most states such as Florida, Pennsylvania, Louisiana, and California maintain a state law enforcement Web site with areas for public relations information topics and password-protected areas for official access. According to an Associated Press (AP) news story (3) in 2000, the Florida Department of Law Enforcement (FDLE) launched a Web site that allows an Internet search to see whether vehicles, vehicle parts, license plates, boats, and guns are stolen. With all this data at one's fingertips, the first concern becomes how to separate useful, reliable, and relevant information from the irrelevant and unreliable. The next concern is one of security.

Although e-mail, data transfer, wireless phones, and Internet transmissions improve the officer's ability to send and receive vital information anywhere and at any time, it is also open for interception by unapproved personnel. Security steps to be taken include authentication and encryption protocols. The federal government maintains several Web sites dealing with computer security such as the Federal Agency Security Practices (FASP) Web site sponsored by the National Institute for Standards and Technology (NIST) and its Information Technology Laboratory (ITL). This site (http://csrc.nist.gov/fasp/index.html) outlines and discusses the FASP, which include data encryption standards.

Simply put, encryption is the electronic scrambling and descrambling, coding and decoding of information, or making the readable unreadable and then readable again. Encryption began as simple alphanumeric substitutions but has evolved into a complex electronic process. It is the use of mathematical algorithms to prevent or greatly reduce the ability to intercept and read electronic data. Currently, four cryptographic algorithms, the Data Encryption Standard (DES) with its 56-bit key, the Triple DES Algorithm (4), the Advanced Encryption Standard (AES), and the Skipjack are widely used. But AES, approved by the Federal Information Processing Standards (FIPS) in 2001, is the algorithm of choice. According to FIPS Publication

197 (5), the AES algorithm is a symmetric block cipher that can use cryptographic keys of 128, 192, and 256 bits to encrypt and decrypt data in blocks of 128 bits.

Although encryption can protect sensitive data during transmission, it is a two-edged sword. It can be used positively in intelligence and law enforcement to prevent unauthorized interceptions, but it can also be used by those attempting to avoid the law (6). Encryption can be put to negative uses such as disguising smuggling, drug trafficking, or terroristic communications. The National Security Agency's (NSA) Signals Intelligence (SIGINT) unit and the Information Assurance Directorate are charged with monitoring international (they use the term "foreign") airwaves for unusual transmissions and keeping U.S. national information safe from harm. This includes setting standards for all secure systems and developing or identifying encryption algorithms.

CRIME INVESTIGATION AND PREVENTION

BIOMETRICS ANALYSIS

Thanks to the Crime Identification Technology Act (CITA) of 1998, assistance is available to states to establish or upgrade criminal justice information systems and identification technologies. This includes most biometrics systems such as finger-print and DNA identification and matching, voice prints and iris patterns, as well as facial dimensions recognition and clay model reconstruction. Technology aids in dealing with suspected criminals using digital fingerprinting and photography as well as DNA classification.

Fingerprinting is done not with paper and ink but with a scanner known as a Livescan (Tenprinter) (7). The officer uses the scanner, on location, to collect, read, match, and compare digital fingerprints and transmit the records to a central repository. The record can be immediately available to other agencies. The prints collected can be compared to other fingerprint record databases using the Integrated Auto-mated Fingerprint Information System (IAFIS or AFIS). The IAFIS provides major savings in time and effort. Established in the 1990s, the IAFIS can search the million or so national fingerprint records on file in roughly thirty minutes compared to the painstaking work of a fingerprint classifier's sixty five years. This makes it pos-sible to identify a person, criminal or victim, even when only a partial set of prints can be obtained. The Royal Canadian Mounted Police (RCMP) in British Columbia have a similar system, Computerized Arrest and Booking System (CABS), which also captures images of identifying marks such as scars and tattoos.

In addition to fingerprint identification, DNA matching has been increasingly used as a tool in crime investigation. Technology has made it possible to more quickly get DNA sample results and search millions of records for a match. Like IAFIS, the FBI maintains a database of DNA records called the Combined DNA Index System (CODIS). CODIS maintains a three-tiered structure with separate local, state, and national (National DNA Index System, or NDIS) databases to provide flexibility within the laws of individual states.

Within the CODIS files are more than 1.5 million DNA records mostly from convicted felons, as well as hundreds of records from missing persons, relatives of missing persons, and unidentified human remains. However, although DNA samples are collected from suspected terrorists, they are not currently included in the NDIS records. What all this means is that there are roughly 175 crime labs across the entire United States, the FBI crime lab, and the U.S. Army crime lab uploading DNA evidence available for investigation and identification assistance. The FBI's CODIS Web site claims to have aided in almost 11,000 investigations to date with more than 3,000 forensic hits or matches and 7,000 offender hits.

Retinal and voice recognition are gaining acceptance for both authentication and identification. Neither can be easily replicated and used fraudulently. Retinal recognition is based on the unique pattern of blood vessels in the retina of the eye (8). Like fingerprints, no two persons share the same retinal patterns. Scanners compare the retinal patterns to a file image and identify matches or misses. Voice recognition has become sophisticated enough to reject a tape-recorded password attempt and is safer than PINs and passwords, which can be written down or forgotten. This has great potential for use in checking up on an offender incarcerated at home. Imagine a computer dialing up the telephone number on a random schedule, recording and analyzing the voice, then delivering a message of acceptance or rejection of the voice match. Voice recognition can be used to control inmate facilities to allow or deny access to cells and other areas. Unlike other biometrics that require fancy and expensive scanners to be placed in vulnerable locations, voice recognition requires only a microphone and the computer software to analyze it. Keys can be lost and passwords can be overheard, so voice recognition is an ideal method of classifying, identifying, and authenticating.

SURVEILLANCE

Cameras are impacting the everyday life of officers as well. Digital still cameras allow images of a suspect or victim or "hot" property to be transmitted to agencies, providing more rapid identification when compared to other images on record. It can be used to take photos of a crime scene and then have the images enlarged, enhanced, or the contrast adjusted to analyze their contents better. Video cameras in police cruisers are providing valuable evidence (not to mention television entertainment) and improving officer safety. Now that officers often patrol alone, the on-board camera can record the incident as a witness. This evidence can protect the officer against false claims and aid in identifying suspects who leave the scene. Video cameras are also valuable as security camera. New technologies enable image enhancement, with computer examination of images caught on security tapes aiding in criminal identification. Although disallowed as evidence at times because of the possibility of digital tampering, it is now possible to better determine whether digital files have been altered. As a result, in Canada, the British Columbian Supreme Court now allows as evidence digital images captured during a crime that have been enlarged or enhanced if they are found to be critical.

ELECTRONIC AND COMPUTER CRIME

Just as technology can prevent or solve a crime, criminals can use technology to commit a crime. Computers can be used to hack into a company's computer system and alter information or transfer documents and falsify transactions. Similarly, computer backup tapes can be intercepted or stolen, exposing thousands of people to computer fraud and identity theft (9).

Several Californian universities have experienced security breaches and discovered them only when the computer monitoring system identified unauthorized software in the system. This software was collecting personal data on employees and students. In Pennsylvania, a prospective student hacked into a university's server just to see the status of his application. Another hacker monitored passwords, social security numbers and U.S. Secret Service e-mail for over a year through a cell phone company's servers. Laptops storing personal information as well as sensitive data have been stolen from hospitals, companies, and even from supposedly secure government sites. The offenses range in severity from curiosity to premeditated felony.

The Universal Press International (UPI) (10) and AP (11) reported that several major companies have been hacked and that thousands of individuals' personal information, credit card numbers, and checking account numbers were stolen and sold. In another instance, tapes being transported from a major banking company to a credit reporting company disappeared en route. These news agencies claim identity theft cost an estimated $550 million in 2004.

Many of these computer crime activities can be traced through the use of Computer Forensic Analysis or postmortem intrusion analysis (12). This process involves reading the activity logs and time stamps, and tracking down the traces left behind in the invaded system. The U.S. Department of Defense Computer Forensics Laboratory maintains a unit called Intrusions and Information Assurance Solutions (http://www. dcfl.gov/dcfl/dcfl.htm) that is dedicated to tracking down computer criminals and identifying system breaches. Electronic log files can be transmitted to them for analysis.

PUBLIC AND OFFICER SAFETY

BODY ARMOR

Body armor has come a long way from chain mail suits and flak jackets. Now made of metal alloys and ceramics, body armor's effectiveness and comfort will continue to improve as lighter and stronger materials are developed. However, any technology breakthroughs will be limited by two key variables: types of material used and their arrangement within the armor (13). The highest levels of protection are afforded by armor that is made up of a hard layer of steel or ceramic backed by soft layers of material such as Kevlar. Ceramic hard layers and Kevlar soft materials are the best materials available in the market today. The optimal arrangement of these materials within the armor has been determined over the last 30 years using experimentation and trial-and-error experience that has not changed in recent years. Therefore, it is logical to predict that only the introduction of new, stronger, lighter materials will increase the effectiveness of today's body armor. Examples of new body armor material due in the near to far future include Vectran, a space-age material used in the landing system of the last Martian lander and is five to ten times stronger than steel.

Liquid armor is one of the newest technologies being developed at the U.S. Army Research Laboratory (14). It is both light and flexible and will allow the officer to be more mobile, and will not hinder an individual from running or aiming a weapon. Further, because it is flexible, the armor can be used to protect body areas that presently cannot be protected. Liquid armor works by shear thickening. It is composed of extremely small hard particles suspended in a liquid that easily conforms to the shape of the body and flexes well with it. During normal body movement, the liquid is very deformable and flows. However, once a bullet impacts the liquid armor, it instantly changes into a rigid material that prevents the projectile from penetrating.

Other researchers are looking at spider silk fiber and carbon nanotechnology. Goats have been genetically engineered to produce the chemical constituents of spider silk, and the resulting material is called Biosteel. A strand of Biosteel can be up to five to twenty times stronger than an equivalent strand of steel. Additionally, the latest candidate for body armor is carbon nanotubes, which promise to be even stronger than spider silk. Carbon nanotube thread is still rare, and fabric is even rarer. Although expensive now, in time prices should fall and make carbon nanotubes a viable fiber for body armor. In all, body armor is being developed that should give the user extra protection through strength without the extra weight.

FIREARMS

Smart Gun is a term used to identify a handheld or shoulder-fired weapon that utilizes an electronic technology to deactivate the firearm when anyone other than the authorized users attempt to discharge the weapon. With the use of this technology, a dramatic reduction in the number of officer injuries and deaths resulting from the use of the officer's own weapons could be expected. Presently, a reliable and instantaneously activated firing pin locking/unlocking system does not exist, but progress is being made.

Early Smart Gun development began with Colt in the late 1990s with its unsuccessful startup called iColt to work solely on Smart Gun technologies. One system focused on having the officer enter a PIN code into the weapon and another required the officer to wear a transponder ring or belt to allow firearm activation. Currently, several companies have also pursued the possibility of incorporating a fingerprint scanner into the weapon for recognition, with limited success. As the reader can imagine, problems with these types of security systems abound. No officers in a crisis situation could afford to take the time necessary to activate their weapons with a PIN number, nor would they want an assailant to remove their transponder ring and then shoot them with their own firearm. Last, fingerprint scanners hold promise, but miniaturization and costs are significant factors that hinder their implementation in Smart Guns.

A promising new line of Smart Gun research has come from the field of biometrics, more specifically, dynamic handgrip recognition. New Jersey Institute of Technology (NJIT) has patented a pressure sensor gun grip using piezoelectric sensors and an integrated circuit to distinguish each user in a matter of a few milliseconds. NJIT has data that indicates that an individual can be identified by his or her unique grip even wearing gloves or in harsh conditions. Fine tuning the technology is the biggest obstacle. Currently, mechanical failure rates for handguns are about one in twenty thousand rounds expended; unfortunately, the best, most expensive biometrics equipment still has an error rate of about one in a thousand. So, the development still has a long way to go. The development goal is to reduce false acceptance (unauthorized user permitted to use the weapon) and false rejection (authorized user denied use) to less than one in a thousand rounds expended.

POLICE VEHICLE DESIGN

Technology can also help protect the officer while in a police vehicle. Research is ongoing to improve vehicle design to better protect officers during high-speed rear-end collisions. Ford created a Crown Victoria Police Interceptor (CVPI) Technical Task Force to investigate how to improve officer safety in their CVPI and implemented a "Police Officer Safety Action Plan" (15). Various manufacturers are studying the use of fuel bladder tanks and fire-suppression systems like those used in racecars to minimize the risk of fire. However, according to Ford's CVPI Web page, as of April 2005, no fuel tank bladder has been approved for use on their CVPI. Another safety approach the task force is investigating is the addition of tank and rear axle component shields. Computer-aided models simulate the impact forces of a high-speed collision and allow nondestructive testing of trial components before destructive testing in the lab.

SUMMARY AND CONCLUSIONS

Technology is all around us and has the potential for changing our lives on a daily basis. From computer imaging to night-vision scopes, from computer recreation of crime scenes to satellite communications, the law enforcement officer has a treasure trove of tools to use in fulfilling the responsibilities of the job (16). Never before could officers be in constant communication with the entire enforcement network or have such sophisticated methods for identifying both victim and criminal. Realizing the vast scope of the applications of technology in law enforcement, the authors have not tried to present here a comprehensive inventory of all possibilities, but only attempted to raise awareness of the vastness of that scope and the possibilities for tomorrow.

REFERENCES

1. Pennsylvania State Police. The Mobile Office. Available at http://www.psp2.state.pa.us/iims/MobileOffice.htm.
2. Pennsylvania State Police. C.L.E.A.N. The Commonwealth Law Enforcement Assistance Network. Available at http://www.psp2.state.pa.us/bts/clean.htm.
3. Associated Press. Online Law Enforcement Plan Started. In LECTC Law Enforcement & Corrections Technology News Summary (October 12, 2000). Available at http://www.nlectc.org/justnetnews/10192000.html#story1.
4. Advanced Encryption Standard (AES), Data Encryption Standard (DES), Triple-DES, and Skipjack Algorithms. Available at http://csrc.nist.gov/cryptval/des.htm.
5. National Institute of Standards and Technology (NIST). (2001). Advanced Encryption Standard (AES). Federal Information Processing Standards Publication 197. Available online at csrc.nist.gov/publications/fips/fips197/fips-197.pdf.
6. Olson, D. (2000). Analysis of criminal codes and ciphers. *Forensic Science Communications* 2(1), January 2000. Available online at http://www.fbi.gov/hq/lab/fsc/backissu/jan2000/olson.htm.

7. Identix Incorporated. (2005). Technology and Trends: Finger Biometrics. Available online at http://www.identix.com/trends/finger.html.

8. Das, R. (2005) An Application of Biometric Technology: Retinal Recognition. Available online at http://www.informatik.uni-augsburg.de/~kimjongh/biometrics/retinal.pdf.

9. Icove, D., Seger, K., & VonStorch, W. (1995). *Computer Crime: A Crimefighter's Handbook*. Sebastopol, CA: O'Reilly and Associates.

10. *The Washington Times* (April 7, 2007). Laptops Stolen with Info on School Workers. Available online at http://washingtontimes.com/20070407-111158-1181r.htm.

11. Wired (March 28, 2005). Thief Swipes More than a Laptop. Associated Press. New York. Available online at http://www.wired.com/politics/security/news/2005/03/67052.

12. Farmer, D. & Venema, W. (2005). *Forensic Discovery*. Boston, MA: Addison Wesley.

13. Arris, T. (2005). How Body Armor Works. Available online at Howstuffworks http://people.howstuffworks.com/body-armor.htm.

14. Johnson, T. (2004). Army Scientists, Engineers Develop Liquid Body Armor. Available online at http://www.military.com/NewsContent/0,13319,usa3_042104.00.html.

15. Ford Motor Company Crown (2002). Victoria Police Interceptor (CVPI). Available online at http://www.cvpi.com/cvpi_tech_task_force.htm.

16. Justice Technology Information Network (n.d.). Law Enforcement: Technology Resources Available online at http://www.nlectc.org/links/lelinks.html#subCat16.

13 Understanding the Use and Abuse of Statistics

Randy Garner

CONTENTS

INTRODUCTION

Statistics are all around us and have become intertwined with our lives. We read the sports box scores, we hear about the latest opinion poll on television, or we learn that four out of five dentists recommend something or other. In policing, we have a whole host of local, state, and national crime statistics: UCR, NIBRS, NCVS, …, and the acronyms keep on coming. In addition to this parade of numbers, we are also trying to make sense of a host of graphs, tables, figures, and other such items—each trying to persuade us to a particular understanding. The purpose of this chapter, however, is not to get mired in the details of statistical equations or complicated formulae. It is not mathematics or detailed theory that we are concerned with here; it is providing a better understanding of some of the general principles and definitions of the statistical process and offering a number of cautions on how to become more informed consumers of statistical information.

From a basic perspective, let us realize that a *statistic* is really just a numerical figure or value that represents or summarizes some measurable characteristic or some type of relationship. In other words, it is not the number itself, but the underlying meaning that is of importance. By definition, *statistics* is the area of mathematics that deals with collecting, organizing, and analyzing numerical data. Statistics is merely a tool to use in dealing with data. Generally, there are two broad categories of statistics: descriptive and inferential.

Descriptive statistics are the more general summarizing and organizing procedures that allow us to describe information in a more accessible or structured way. For example, you may hear a report that the average crime index score on a particular measure is eighty-eight. First, recognize that this number alone is meaningless without some form of context or understanding of what it is supposed to represent. Is this a good score? Is it a bad indicator? Is it like golf where a higher number spells doom? One must have some general understanding of what this value means. Second, realize that once you do know what such a score might represent, you will also appreciate that having a single number, in this case eighty-eight, is a much more efficient way of describing the information than to read a report that simply lists the thousands of rating responses that were generated by a crime survey. By way of example, what if you wanted to know how hot it typically gets in Houston, Texas, in the month of August? Today, a quick check with the local chamber of commerce or a host of Web sites will get you not only the average August temperature but also a report of the average rainfall, humidity, wind, etc. Now, imagine a time when there were no descriptive statistics. Instead we simply had "Fred" observing the weather each day and recording it in his logbook. Now, one day you wonder about the August temperature in Houston, so you call Fred. As there are no descriptive statistics to summarize this information, Fred offers to send you copies of the hundreds of pages of weather observations for each day in August that he has collected over the last 30 years. Not exactly an efficient or appealing proposition, but this clearly demonstrates the value of descriptive statistics.

The second general area of statistics is *inferential statistics*. This is frequently a much more complex process, in which data are collected and analyzed from a smaller group or sample and the results are generalized or *inferred* to a larger group. The key here is not only the proper use of statistical technique but also the careful selection of the smaller sample being used. Inferential statistics are the real "workhorse" of many types of information to which you are exposed. For instance, in our crime poll example given earlier, it is likely that only a small subset or sample of people were asked about their opinions regarding crime. This information was then analyzed and generalized to the larger population. For example, if this was a statewide crime poll, it is unlikely that you could actually ask every person in the entire state to provide his or her input. However, through careful sampling techniques, you can ask a properly selected subgroup of residents, whose responses can be expected to be reflective of the general sense of crime across the state. Of course, with this type of procedure there is great potential for problems and biases.

MAY I HAVE A SAMPLE PLEASE?

The key to accurately generalizing information to larger groups is in the careful systematic sampling of what statisticians call a population. A *population* is the complete group of individuals, objects, or items being measured. In the case of our hypothetical statewide crime poll, this would be every person in the entire state. Think about trying to ask every person in the state of Texas or California about his or her opinion on crime. Clearly, this would be an impossible task. However, because we continue to maintain an interest in public opinion about crime, we must attempt to find a way to accurately measure this issue. This is where the *sample* comes into play. If we utilize a sound sampling procedure, we should get a general sense of the topic of interest in the larger population. By way of illustration, think of passing by the Cookie Hut at the local mall. Frequently, they will offer you a sample of their latest cookie product. By sampling this cookie, you will be able to tell if you like the product or not; there is no need to eat the entire batch of cookies to make this determination (although this could be tempting on occasion). As long as the cookie you consumed was representative of the whole batch, you can be reasonably confident in your judgment.

In populations of people, a *representative sample* (one that is likely to capture the characteristics of the population) is one in which every member of the population has an equal chance of being selected. Of course, the topic of interest often influences the dynamics and definition of the population. For example, if we are interested in only the opinion of crime issues among college freshmen in the state, then our population of interest becomes a more specific group—not the entire residents of the state. If we are interested in the opinions of police officers on the effectiveness of some new crime-reduction initiative, then our population becomes all of the licensed police officers in the state. However, this brings up another important point. It might be that we are only interested in the opinions of those licensed police officers who work for an agency of a certain size. Alternatively, we might only want information about officers of a certain rank or those who serve in a particular division. You can see that with each new specification, the population is redefined and, in this case, reduced. The important point is to clearly identify your population of interest. Only once this is known will you be able to begin the process of random selection of a sample. It is essential to always keep in mind that the ultimate goal is not to collect numbers or data but to be able to make an accurate inference about the characteristics of the larger population—as generalized from a smaller sample. Remember, statistics are merely a convenient way to convey information in an orderly manner.

SAMPLING WOES

As many may have already guessed, even trying to randomly sample the entire population of a state would be a daunting task. First, you would have to try to find a list of everyone—no easy task and not very realistic. Researchers often use vehicle registration records, birth records, driving records, phone books, property ownership records, and other such means in an attempt to capture the population. However, even the best approach will exclude large numbers of individuals. As a result, we must simply try to do the best possible job in identifying the most numbers of individuals in our population of interest and accept that the process is imperfect. Even with these limitations, it is a far better approach than to simply poll a few people who happened to be conveniently available. Not surprisingly, statisticians call this a *convenience sample* and recognize that it has significant limitations in generalizing any information received to the larger population. Unfortunately, much of the information we might receive in the media is based on such potentially biased sampling practices, and the information conveyed is not likely to be representative of the overall population.

Consider trying to predict the outcome of a major metropolitan citywide election by simply polling a few people in your neighborhood who conveniently happen to be in their yards one sunny afternoon. Think of all the reasons that this sample may not be a good one. Ask yourself, "Did everyone in the city get an equal chance of being selected?" The answer, of course, is "No." Not only were you merely examining the opinions of those in your immediate neighborhood but you were asking only those who were outside and available at a particular time, on a particular day. You might also ask, "Do those who were conveniently available differ in some particular characteristic that would not be reflective of the larger citywide population?" The answer is "Of course." First, they were only the conveniently available people on that particular day at that particular time who live in your immediate neighborhood. Further, because research demonstrates that neighborhoods tend to cluster by socioeconomic and other such defining factors, the responses obtained here might be vastly different from those in the neighborhood across the tracks.

THE LIGHT AT THE END OF THE SAMPLE

The process becomes more manageable when the population is narrowly defined and more easily identified. For example, if we want to send a survey to a random selection of the registered voters in a particular county, such information is readily available. However, assuming we get a good response rate and useful data, the information we derive from the sample should only be generalized to the registered voters in the city—not voters all across the state. During my time as a police chief, I routinely sent quality of service surveys to a random selection of those persons who had requested or received police service each month (interestingly, this even included those who had received citations). By the use of a computer random number generation program, a strictly random sample of individuals was selected and mailed a survey. Because everyone who had requested or received police services had an equal chance of being selected, this was a truly random sample, and, given we had a good return rate, the information could be expected to be representative of the opinions of most other people who had also received police service but were not a part of the survey. This information was very useful in identifying potential concerns, and, most importantly, reinforced that we were generally doing a good job. However, this scenario also points to at least two particular problems that may still give us difficulty: return rate and response bias.

POINT OF NO RETURN

Even though we have carefully identified our population and have painstakingly followed the procedures for creating a truly random sample, we are still not sure who will actually send the questionnaire back. Of course, there are several techniques to increase the return rate, such as making sure the information is anonymous (or in other cases confidential), having the form include a postage-paid envelop that is addressed for return (so they do not have to pay to respond), making sure the format of the survey is easily understood and can be completed quickly, and so on. However, despite their best efforts, many researchers indicate that a response rate of 50 to 60 percent is extraordinary (of course, the topic, the relevance to the person receiving the survey, and other circumstances can have an effect on this number). Frequently, response rates as low as 30 percent are found. In such cases, we must wonder what might be different about those individuals who chose not to return the survey. For example, if we had a low response rate in our police quality of service questionnaire (despite our wonderful sampling technique), the results could be suspect. What if only those who had positive things to say returned the survey? What if only the elderly returned the survey? What if only a particular group, classification, or category (whatever that might be) returned the survey? The point is that if we have low response rates, we are not sure how those individuals who did not respond differ from those who did—and that introduces room for bias and error.

WHAT SHALL I SAY?

Another concern is what researchers call "response bias." Certain people may be predisposed to respond in a certain way. For example, receiving a survey from the police department has the potential to be alarming for some individuals. They may think that if they report anything bad, some sort of reprisals might be forthcoming. Even when given assurances of anonymity, people may still believe there is a way to track them down, and thus, they will either not return the form or provide only the type of answers that they believe the department may want to hear. Others may simply view the survey as an inconvenience, and, if they chose to respond at all, may make quick judgments without thoughtful reflection, or may simply provide all "neutral" answers. In the case of the most popular questionnaire format, the Likert-type index, subjects may be asked about a particular issue and then will be presented with a series of five to seven categories to indicate their opinion on the matter. For example, in a 5-point scale, a person may be provided with a statement such as "Your interaction with an officer of the City Police Department was generally positive." The respondents are then asked if they "strongly agree," "somewhat agree," "neither agree nor disagree," "somewhat disagree," or "strongly disagree." Unfortunately, some individual may simply select the same response for each question.

As we can see, this is a very complex process. We need to know *why* we are doing the survey in the first place to ensure that we identify our population of interest, so we can follow an empirically sound sampling procedure that results in a truly random sample that can be generalized to the larger group, providing us some useful understanding about the subject at hand. Not the simplest of tasks. Of course, we must also ensure that we have a properly developed survey that is easily understood, pleasingly formatted and designed, can be finished in a short amount of time, and will be completed and returned by the largest number of nonbiased respondents possible. Now you can see why major research firms and polling institutions get big bucks for their efforts. However, a great deal of the information that we are exposed to on a daily basis was not collected by such careful and scrupulous means. In fact, frequently information is collected in a very haphazard manner or is intentionally biased. Because it is so difficult and costly to do it correctly, there are a great many ways in which information is collected and presented that is downright misleading, and in the case of certain influence peddlers, done so intentionally. An examination of the ways in which statistics can be used and abused will be the subject of the remainder of this chapter.

AN AVERAGE RESPONSE

One of the most confusing and often misunderstood terms we find in statistical reporting is the word "average." The problem is that this term can have many different meanings. Although most people assume that "average" refers to the *arithmetic mean*, where you add all the values and divide by the number of scores used in the calculation (for example, adding all three of your test grades and dividing by three to get your average test grade for a class), there are actually many types of averages, including geometric averages, quadratic averages, harmonic averages, and so on. One thing such terms usually have in common is that they are all measures of *central tendency*. In other words, the statistic is trying to represent the center or "middle" of some distribution or group. In addition to the mean (discussed previously), the two other most frequently used measures of central tendency are the mode and the median. The *mode* simply identifies the most frequently occurring score. It is relatively easy to determine because it is obtained by observation rather than calculation. For example, consider a series of crime poll scores such as 88, 76, 66, 88, 49, 56, and 45. (Of course, we are using ridiculously small samples just to make the point.) Upon inspection, you would be able to say that the mode is 88, as this is the only number that appears more than once. You might compare this with the mean, which would be 66.8. Again, keep in mind that we still do not know what these numbers really mean, but we are already able to see that these are both very different numbers, and both can be correctly identified as an average.

Now let us add the median to the mix. The *median* is merely the midpoint of all the scores. In the preceding example, we would reorder the numbers from lowest to highest: 45, 49, 56, 66, 76, 88, and 88. Notice that the central number, or midpoint, is 66—almost the same as our mode. However, consider what would happen if we included six additional scores to our data set, three higher and three lower. For example, consider the following crime poll scores: 16, 20, 21, 45, 49, 56, 66, 76, 88, 88, 88, 88, and 89. Notice that the mode and median remain the same, as the number 88 is still the most frequently occurring one, and number 66 remains at the midpoint. However, our mean is much more sensitive to extreme scores and now becomes 54. As a result of our example, we can accurately say that we have an average crime poll score of 88, 66, or 54, depending on the spin we want to put on the numbers. For the sake of argument, let us assume that a low number represents a low concern about crime and few incidences, whereas a high number represents a greater concern about the crime and an increase in number of offenses. If you were the chief of police, which number would you report to the city council? If you wanted it to look like things were going well, you might want to use the mean (54). However, if you needed to argue for more resources to combat an increasing concern over crime, you might want to use the mode (88). (Of course, this latter strategy could also adversely impact your job!)

The point is that both scores could be accurately reported as the average result because of the confusion over the term. Of more concern is when individuals intentionally misuse statistics to persuade. The most appropriate course of action would be to report not only the mode, median, and mean of the crime poll results but also reveal other important information as well, such as the sampling issues discussed previously, and the range. (Actually, one also should report other important statistical information such as the variance and standard deviation, but that discussion is left for another time.) The *range* is merely the distance between the smallest and largest score. For example, in our crime poll, the range would be 73—quite a large difference, which informs us that there was variation in the responses. In other words, not everyone had the same general opinions. Why is the range important? One could make the argument that the average temperature in the Mojave Desert and Houston are nearly the same for a given month, let's say 68°. However, it is the range that may provide you with more useful (and possibly survival) information. Whereas the range in Houston temperature is only 18°, the range in temperature in the desert may be 102! You would be freezing at night and melting during the day, but would still report an average temperature of 68°.

AVERAGE ALERTS

Clearly, when we see a report of the average something or other, we should be cautious. In order to be a more informed consumer of statistical information, we should ask questions rather than merely accept the offerings of others who may be intentionally trying to misinform or bias us. When we hear about averages, we should ask the following questions:

- What type of average are they talking about? Mode? Median? Mean? Other?
- How was the sample selected? Did everyone in the population of interest have an equal chance of being selected?
- Was the sample size large enough to reasonably represent the larger population?
- How were the questions asked?
- What was the return rate or refusal rate?
- What was the range, variance, or standard deviation of the information presented?
- Is there any information that is obviously missing from the report?

Questions such as these help us to better interpret the information for ourselves, rather than rely on the potentially biased information that may be presented, especially by those who are intentionally trying to persuade us.

JUST AN AVERAGE EXAMPLE

What if I told you that a recent national publication reported that the average salary of police chiefs in the United States was $102,340.15? In addition to this being a suspiciously precise number, I might imagine that it is not what you would have expected. Considering that most police agencies in the United States have fewer than 15 officers, this seems to be an extremely large and unanticipated amount. Further, as we consider our "average alerts," we realize that we do not know much about what this number really means or how it was derived. Instead of merely accepting it as true—because it was, after all, reported in a national publication—we should begin to ask questions. What kind of average is this? Was every police chief in the United States sampled? If not, how was the sample collected? Was the sample large enough to represent the entire population of U.S. police chiefs? How were the questions asked and how many people actually responded?

A quick glance at the article reveals that none of these questions are answered, and, furthermore, the article itself was a very biased piece addressing the cost of policing—especially police administration. It seems clear that the missing information and lack of detail in sampling procedures would require us to discount this report. How was this number generated? Given the paucity of information, we cannot really say for sure; it might even have just been made up. Maybe, the surveys were only sent to very large police agencies in the United States, or only chiefs from the largest departments chose to respond. The point is, such a suspiciously precise and intuitively inaccurate number should not be accepted at face value. When confronted with such information, we should immediately put on our statistical detective hat and run through our "average alert" process. Notice, in this case, as with many others, that there really is no statistical information reported at all—just a number. This is an equally important point to remember: much of the chicanery that goes on in the reporting of statistical information occurs in the inaccurate presentation and errone-ous assumptions presented—not the math. In fact, it may be that the salary number presented earlier was a correctly calculated mean of a few individuals who actually responded from large agencies. So, it is not the math that is the problem per se but the culmination of all of the biasing influences we have discussed previously, including poor methodology, poor sampling, lack of representativeness, and biased response rate, as well as the author's intentional omission of this important information and the improper inferences that have been drawn from the flawed process.

THE PROBLEM WITH PERCENTAGES

In addition to the misunderstandings (intentional or otherwise) over averages, proba-bly the second biggest area of statistical confusion deals with percentages. For exam-ple, if one were to read in the newspaper that crime is up by 200 percent, we again need to put on our statistical detective hat and try to decipher what is really being said. Where did this number come from? What is it being compared to? Is this 200 percent of all crime, or some specific category? What exactly is this a percentage of? Again, all of the types of cautions mentioned previously should be considered.

What if we were talking about a relatively small community that had only one burglary in the previous year? This year, however, there were three burglary reports. Not exactly a crime wave—but it does result in a 200 percent increase in reported burglaries for this year. Again, it is important to put all of this into context, as the number itself is meaningless without perspective. First, we should recognize that this is only two more burglaries than occurred in the previous year, and it deals only with the category of *burglary*, not all crime as was initially reported. Further, realize that it also describes reported burglaries. In fact, there may have been no increase in actual burglaries in this community; it was just that previous ones were not reported to the police. Again, making sure you understand what a particular number really means is very important.

As it relates to actual math, percentages are often problematic. Let me give you one very important aspect of percentages that will always help with your interpretation of this information: You can *increase* something by more than 100 percent, but you cannot *decrease* something by more than 100 percent. For example, if you have $50 and I give you $100, your "worth" has increased by more than 100 percent. However, if you have $50, I can only take 100 percent of what you have—the $50.00; there is no more to take. Alternatively, you might experience a 150 percent increase in your electric bill, but your bill cannot be reduced by more than 100 percent—unless you have devised a way for the power company to pay you for using their electricity. Reported crime can rise by over 100 percent, but it cannot decrease by more than 100 percent. So, if you see a report that claims crime is down by 150 percent, you should know something is fishy.

A funny example involves the story of a man who, while walking down the road, spots a $10.00 bill and puts it in his pocket. He already had a $20.00 bill, so his wealth has increased by 50 percent. Unfortunately, his pocket had a hole in it, and the $10.00 bill was lost. He concludes, however, that he is still ahead! After all, his earlier wealth had increased by 50 percent, to $30.00; so the loss of the $10.00 bill represents a decrease of only 33 percent —therefore he is still ahead by 17 percent! Of course, this is all statistical chicanery, but it helps one to visualize the point.

Another cautionary example involves a newspaper account that reported a 50 percent cut in wages for part-time workers at a particular business due to the slumping economy and sales. Assume that you were earning $20,000; a 50 percent cut would result in your now earning only $10,000. After several months, the economy was rebounding, and the business owners indicated they were increasing wages by 50 percent to restore the earlier cut. However, remember that the starting point has now changed. Earlier, a 50 percent cut of $20,000 resulted in a new wage of $10,000. So we begin the "restoration" by increasing the new wage (in reality a new starting point) by 50 percent. As a result, the pay for these workers will increase to $15,000. As one can see, this is a full $5,000 less than the workers were originally making. To say that you have first cut wages by 50 percent and then later increased them by 50 percent may sound like everything is back to normal, but the problems associated with understanding percentages can reveal a much different story.

Lastly, percentages are not usually something that can be added or averaged, especially when they come from many different sources. For example, we may have experienced a 10 percent increase in housing, a 12 percent increase in food costs, and a 3 percent increase in energy expenses. However, we cannot simply add these items together and declare that living costs have increased by 25 percent (although I have seen this type of inaccurate reporting a number of times). To do so is sheer nonsense. Remember that the percentages of each individual area (housing, food, energy, etc.) are based on a unique number not directly related to the others. For example, a 12 percent increase in food cost may represent only $10.00; however, a 3

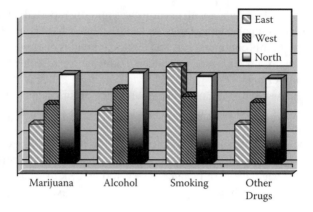

FIGURE 13.1   Substance use by campus.

percent increase in energy cost may be twice that much—we do not know the starting point or actual dollar amount for each individual area or what that percentage means in relative terms. Similarly, one cannot conclude that, because there is a 12 percent decrease in burglaries, a 13 percent decrease in robberies, and a 75 percent reduction in homicides, overall crime has been reduced by 100 percent. Again, this is just nonsense, but such reporting has been found in official information and media accounts all across the country.

FALLACIOUS FIGURES

Having covered two of the main sources of statistical confusion, let us now turn our attention to another problem that confounds the accurate interpretation of numerical information: graph and chart abuse. For an example, consider a graph of reported drug use by campus (see Figure 13.1). Of the three campuses in the district, marijuana use, drinking, and other drug use (with the exception of smoking) has been more frequently found at the north campus. As a result, if one were considering which campus to enroll one's child, this information may be used in deciding to send the child to the east or west campus, with the east campus having the lowest rate for all categories except smoking. However, a more careful examination of this graph reveals that there is no unit of measure given. In other words, the heights of the bars in this graph are not able to be interpreted. We do not know what they represent. This is a very typical trick that is often used to misrepresent data. By contrast, look at the graph depicted in Figure 13.2. Remember that these are the same data, but now we have some understanding of what the graph actually means. We now know that the number of incidents are relatively few by examining the ordinate or y-axis that runs vertically.

This information was missing from the previous graph, which thus presented a potentially misleading picture—literally and figuratively. Keep in mind that we still need much more information in order to properly interpret this graph. For example, what period of time does this represent? How were these data collected? Do these represent self-report information from students on their substance use, or are they reflective of disciplinary cases of those who got caught? As you can see, more infor-

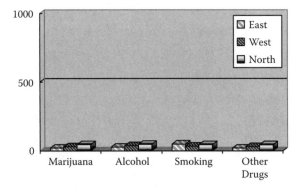

FIGURE 13.2 Substance use by campus.

mation gives us a great deal more insight in interpreting these data. You may ask, why is this information not always reported? Easy; it is usually either ineptitude or intentional attempts to persuade or mislead. Consider the graph of the number of citizen complaints received by a police agency over the period of a year (see Figure 13.3). First, recognize that without other information we do not know if these are sustained complaints, severe complaints, formal complaints, written complaints, or any other complaints. However, for the sake of example, let us assume that this graph simply measures the number of overall complaints received by a particular police agency distributed over four quarters.

Let us also assume that the police chief asked for this graph to present at a meeting of community leaders. At first glance, this may not look very favorable; after all, observe how high the bars appear. It may give the impression that there are lots of complaints against officers, and that may not reflect kindly on the chief and his or her policies. As a result, the chief decides to do a little chart doctoring before heading out to the community meeting. It is not that the actual information has changed, but the way in which it is presented certainly has. Figure 13.4 shows the same data

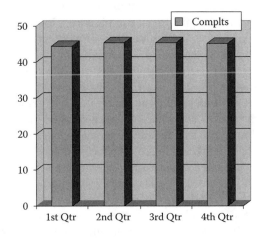

FIGURE 13.3 Departmental complaints.

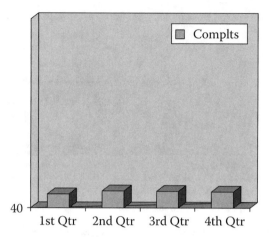

FIGURE 13.4 Departmental complaints.

presented in bar-graph format, but notice the difference in appearance. Now it seems that citizen complaints are a rarity.

Notice what has been done to present a more favorable picture; the vertical axis has been relabeled so that the bottom of the graph represents a lower limit of 40 complaints. In other words, there have to be more than 40 complaints in a given quarter for it even to register on the graph. Again, this is a visual representation of data that can be misleading. If one were to quickly glance at this chart—which is usually the case with most of us—one would not immediately observe a very substantial problem. Although the graph is not inaccurate, it can clearly be misleading. Of course, if you were the chief, you might consider making similar graphical representations if it made you and your department look better. The problem is that once someone calls attention to this potentially misleading tactic, the credibility of all information coming from that department can come into question.

Though there are several ways to present misleading graphs and figures, one final graph tactic that must be considered involves mixing height with area (e.g., height x width = area). For example, look at Figure 13.5. Here, we have a symbol that represents the number of dollars stolen in property crimes during two comparative years. (Of course, the statistical detective in us automatically wonders why these particular years were chosen.) Notice that the symbol on the left is of a certain height, similar to a bar graph and representing a particular amount of money. However, now let us look at the height of the symbol on the right. This symbol clearly demonstrates an increase in lost dollars, as measured by its height; but it also, misleadingly, has a larger area (remember your high school geometry). At first glance, it appears that the losses are much greater than they actually may be, simply as a result of not accounting for the increase in the area of the symbol used to depict the dollars stolen. This is a case in which the graph may make things appear worse than they actually are. Although the actual dollars stolen, as represented by the height differential, is a rather modest increase, the increased area of the symbol gives the illusion that the losses might be much greater. Of course, this technique can be used to take advantage of this effect as well. Consider the impres-

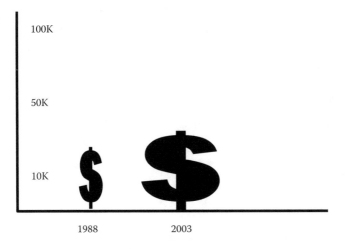

FIGURE 13.5 Dollars lost.

sion created if this graph were to be relabeled as an indication of profit increases between two fiscal quarters. Again, the increase is modest, but the graphical representation may lead an unsuspecting individual to form an inaccurate conclusion that the profits were greater than they actually were.

DIGITAL DISCUSSION AND CONCLUSIONS

There are a great many techniques and tactics that can be used by those who may want to misrepresent the truth, and we have only scratched the surface. However, even this short chapter demonstrates the importance for us all to become better consumers of statistical information and not simply accept information at face value. We must question the quality of the sample, the rigor of the method, and the logic of the statistical information reported. We must be better detectives in determining what data we choose to accept, and asking questions such as those in the average alerts section can be a great start. Further, we must recognize that statistics can be a helpful tool in deciphering data or a deceptive device subject to misuse and misinterpretation. Statistical information without proper context is relatively meaningless. If a community reports that they have reduced their crime rate by 50 percent, the first question to ask is, 50 percent of what? Even if statistically correct, does it really make a difference? For example, if there were two reported thefts last year, but only one this year—is that really significant in a practical sense? Remember the mantra, "A difference is only a difference if it makes a difference." If a denture cleaner reports that it removes 23 percent more stains, what does that mean? Is it 23 percent more than doing nothing? Is it 23 percent more than simply letting dentures soak in water? Is it 23 percent more than their old product? What is being represented here? If the Traffic Institute reports that more accidents occur in clear weather, then clear weather is more dangerous—a very big warning bell should be ringing in your head. Although a part of that information might be technically true, consider that much more driving is done in clear weather than bad, so, of course there will be more accident opportunities during this time. In this case, one has to wonder if such a statement was due to ignorance or insidiousness. Either way, you should now be armed with the awareness and determination to be a more vigilant and cautious consumer of statistical information.

REFERENCE

Garner, R. (2004). *Mythical Means and Other Little White Lies of Statistics.* Prescient Press.

14 The Impact of Distance Learning

Doug Dailey

CONTENTS

INTRODUCTION

Distance education can be defined in various ways. Perraton (1988) defines distance education in an informal, straightforward way as "an educational process in which a significant proportion of the teaching is conducted by someone removed in space and/or time from the learner." Wells and Minor (1998) similarly define it as "a process in which teachers use audio, video, and computer technology to convey instructional material from one location to students at remote sites." Simonson, Smaldino, Albright, and Zvacek (2003) define it as "institution-based, formal education where the learning group is separated, and where interactive telecommunications systems are used to connect learners, resources, and instructors."

There are four components to the latter definition. First is the concept that distance education is institutionally based, which is what differentiates it from self-study. Although the "institution" referred to in the definition is usually a traditional educational school or college, increasingly there are emerging nontraditional institutions that offer education to students at a distance. One example of this type of nontraditional institution is the Federal Law Enforcement Training Center located in Glynco, Georgia, which used to train federal law enforcement officers, offering both traditional on-site and off-site classroom-based courses as well as Internet-based courses.

The second component of the above definition is the concept of *separation* of the teacher and student. Although generally we tend to think of separation in terms of geographical distance, it can be separation in time as well. Traditional education takes place at the same time in the same place, typically the regular self-contained classroom that is usually lecture-based and teacher-centered. Different-time, same-place education means that individual learning occurs in a learning center or that multiple sections of the same class are offered so students can attend the class in the same place at a time they choose. This is education that is available at different times to students in the same place, such as the media center or computer lab at a university.

Telecommunications systems allow instruction to take place in different places at the same time. Often, television is used to connect the local classroom with the teacher and students to learners at a distance. The author taught distance education classes for two years at Eastern Kentucky University in Richmond, Kentucky, using closed-circuit broadcast video. Classes were held at one of five interchangeable sites and broadcast to the remaining four other sites. Students at the remote sites used television video and two-way audio to participate in the classes. Student evaluations from the remote distance learning classes were not statistically different from evaluations from students at on-campus classes.

Satellite, compressed video, and fiber-optic systems are increasingly used for same-time, different-place education, which is also called *synchronous* distance education. The distance education classes taught at Eastern Kentucky University, primarily to police administration and criminal justice majors, is one example of synchronous distance learning. Students can also learn at different times and in different places. In other words, learners choose when and where to learn and when and where to access instructional materials. This approach is called *asynchronous* distance education. *Asynchronous* distance education means that instruction is offered and students access it at separate times or anytime it is convenient to them. This form of distance learning is the most advantageous to students, particularly those with full-time jobs, as it allows them to continue their education without worrying about conflicts between work and school.

Interactive telecommunications is the third component of the Simonson et al. Interaction can be synchronous or asynchronous, i.e., at the same time or at different times. Interaction is critical, but not at the expense of content. In other words, it is important that learners be able to interact with each other, with the resources of instruction, and with their teacher. However, interaction should not be the primary characteristic of instruction but should be available, commonplace, and relevant. In the author's opinion, based on his experience teaching in distance education with Eastern Kentucky University, this interaction between student and teacher is of utmost importance. Whether teaching takes place in a classroom setting or via some form of distance media, student engagement is the key, and the key to engagement is interaction. Without that interaction between student and teacher, it is difficult for learning to take place. Students must be highly motivated to work completely on their own, completing a course, traditional or nontraditional, without some form of interaction with an instructor.

Telecommunications can be defined as "communicating at a distance." The words *telecommunications system* imply some form of electronic media, such as television, telephone, and/or the Internet, but this term need not necessarily be limited to only electronic media. The definition can include communication via the postal system (correspondence study), and other nonelectronic methods of communication.

The final concept of Simonson et al. definition relates to the idea of *connecting* learners, resources, and instructors. There must be a forum that allows instructors to interact with learners and that provides resources to be available for learning to occur. Resources should be organized into learning experiences that promote learning, including resources that can be observed, felt, heard, or completed.

GROWTH OF DISTANCE EDUCATION

Distance education has been applied to a variety of programs serving numerous audiences via a wide variety of media. Some use print, some use telecommunications, and many use both.

The last ten years has seen an explosive growth in distance education. According to the U.S. Department of Education, in 1995 there were 690 two- and four-year higher education institutions that offered degree programs in distance education. This number increased 73 percent to 1190 in 1997–1998, a number that represented 44 percent of all two- and four-year institutions of higher education (National Center for Education Statistics 1999). The Internet was the medium of choice for most institutions providing distance education. The use of interactive and one-way prerecorded video declined slightly between 1995 and 1998, dropping from 57 to 56 percent and 52 to 48 percent, respectively, indicating that most of the growth in distance education involved use of the Internet (National Center for Education Statistics, 1999).

According to the U.S. Department of Education, in 1999, distance education was being considered by almost 90 percent of higher education institutions larger than 10,000 students (Simonson et al. 2003). Distance learning is viewed by the U.S. military as a cost-efficient way to deliver technical training to a large number of soldiers. The development of new weapon systems and other advanced technologies further increases the demand for this type of training. The army's Interactive Teletraining Network, the navy's Video Teletraining Network, and the air force's Teleteach Expanded Delivery System all provide distance education for military personnel.

In addition to the military impetus, there are some societal changes contributing to the growth of distance education. Increasing complexities of the environment of some occupations require a corresponding increase in education to stay abreast of competition and to advance in one's occupation or profession. For instance, a significant number of law enforcement agencies in this country require continuing education of their line officers and administrative personnel. In a nationwide survey of law enforcement personnel, Brenner and Dailey (2004) found that 54 percent of administrators responding to the survey reported that their agencies had a continuing education requirement.

Another factor relevant to the increase in distance learning classes and institutions that offer them is the increased demand for flexible scheduling from those whose daily routines do not coincide with the traditional campus schedule, particularly those students like law enforcement officers who must work on rotating shift schedules. Most students with full- or part-time jobs cannot attend classes during the day, and those classes offered at night are relatively restricted and tend not to cover the required courses to fulfill degree requirements. In addition, older students sometimes have to juggle full-time jobs with child-rearing responsibilities, which may further restrict educational opportunities.

Demographic studies of distance education students (Moore and Kearsley 1996, Hardy and Boaz 1997) indicate that most are between the ages of 25 and 50, two-thirds are female, over half are married, and the majority work full-time while taking courses. Of the approximately 200 distance education students the author has taught the past 3 years, most have been older than traditional students, approximately half were male, half female, and more than half had either part-time or full-time jobs while attending classes. Most were police administration or criminal justice majors, and approximately 5 percent were full-time law enforcement personnel.

THEORY

There is an ongoing debate about whether distance learning is inherently better than classroom-based instruction. The argument is that the medium that carries the message somehow improves either the content of the message or the ability of the student to absorb it. However, a majority of current research (Crane 1984, Batey and Cowell 1986, Hezel 1996, Johnston 1987, Moore 1989, Wells and Minor 1998), indicates that distance learning students do not learn any more or any better than traditional students. Clark (1983) wrote in the Review of Educational Research:

> The best current evidence is that media are mere vehicles that deliver instruction but do not influence student achievement any more than the truck that delivers our groceries causes changes in nutrition ... only the content of the vehicle can influence achievement. (p. 445)

The *type* of media used in education does not directly affect learning. Clark (1994) argued that educators should not claim that technology-based learning, such as modern distance education systems, has any inherent advantage over other methods of learning.

Media does have certain advantages, however, not the least of which is that it allows students to take advantage of educational opportunities across time and space. Instructional media, such as that used in video teleconferencing, is excellent for storing educational courses and delivering them almost anywhere. However, media is *not* inherently responsible for a learning effect. Learning is *not* enhanced because instruction is media based. What *does* promote learning, in the author's opinion, is the content of the instruction and the involvement of the learner in the educational experience. If the student is engaged, and the course content is relevant and substantial, then the medium used is irrelevant. Some distance educators claim, however, that distance education is the best way to learn. If we assume for the moment that this is true, the primary relevant factor is the student's ability to modify the time and place of learning because it allows students to acquire knowledge when and where it is most relevant to them.

RESEARCH AND DISTANCE EDUCATION

Much of the research in distance education is of the media comparison type. This is to be expected given the rapid development of distance education technology. In a technologically driven society, with each new advance in technology, the temptation is to conduct media comparison research on the chance that the new technology might truly bring about higher student achievement. However, media comparison studies indicate that no inherent significant difference exists in the achievement effectiveness of media (Clark 1983, Whittington 1987). The specific medium used does not matter, at least in terms of knowledge gained.

Cheng, Lehman, and Armstrong (1991) compared the performance of graduate-level students enrolled in traditional classrooms and nontraditional teleconference classrooms. There were 25 graduate students in the on-campus class, and the off-campus teleconference group included 28 graduate-level in-service teachers. The groups differed significantly only in age; the off-campus teleconference students were older than the traditional classroom-based students. Results, using a standard pretest–posttest, indicated no significant difference in overall course performance between the two groups.

Bruning, Landis, Hoffman, and Grosskopf (1993) compared achievement results in an interactive video conference course in high school Japanese with a traditional class. The video conference course originated in Nebraska and was transmitted to 170 schools (911 students) the first year, 255 schools (1157 students) the second year, and 259 schools (1330 students) the third year. The achievement test administered by the researchers was designed to measure how well the students listened and the foreign-language writing skills of each student.

The evaluation test at the end of the first two years indicated that the achievement of students in the video conference classes was significantly higher than that of students in the traditional schools for both listening and writing. The researchers noted that the students in the distance classes were generally older and seemed to be more highly motivated, and this, according to the researchers, may have had a significant impact on their achievement, much more than the fact that they learned at a distance.

DISTANCE EDUCATION AND THE MILITARY

The effectiveness of distance learning in the military was investigated by Bramble and Martin (1995). Standard multiple-proficiency, criterion-based, and achievement tests were given to the 275 military personnel taking the five courses. Pretests and posttests were administered in four of the five courses. The participants who did not pass the first tests were allowed a second chance at taking the proficiency tests; after the second tests, all students reached acceptable performance levels. Students in all five courses were asked if they thought that distance learning was as effective as live instruction. In four out of five classes, 75 percent or more responded in the affirmative. The researchers came to the conclusion that distant and local learners can achieve at the same level, and that distance education is an effective method for delivering instruction that works.

PERCEPTIONS OF THE DISTANCE EDUCATION STUDENT

The satisfaction of the distance student is an important factor related to success in interactive distance courses. Biner, Dean, and Mellinger (1994) found that relevant factors included satisfaction with the instruction given, the technology used, course management, and on-site personnel. The researchers concluded that assessment of learner satisfaction with the above factors was essential to the overall success of a distance learning program.

According to the researchers, a primary factor related to satisfaction with course management is the amount of information the students receive about the distance learning course. The typical distance learning student begins the course at a disadvantage due to the lack of information they receive, compared to traditional on-campus students. The distance student is generally completely dependent upon the on-site coordinator for information relating to the course and the technology used for communication, etc. The on-site coordinator is extremely important for another reason, and that is that he or she is the primary liaison between the instructor, the students, and the institution. A competent, intelligent on-site coordinator can easily mean the difference between a successful distance class and an unsuccessful one. Student evaluations of distance education classes taught by the author as well as others (Moore 1995, Workman and Stenard 1996, Hardy and Boaz 1997) reveal the importance of site coordinators to provide such streamlined support as advising, liaison to the main campus, and troubleshooting for both technical and administrative problems.

Faculty information is critical to distance students. As most students are unable to regularly visit the main campus, they should be provided with phone numbers and e-mail addresses of their instructor, teaching assistants, and technical support personnel by the instructor, the on-site coordinator, or both.

Hardy and Boaz (1997) sent out a survey to approximately 200 distance learning students. One of the questions in the survey was, "Do you feel the administration at the sending end demonstrates an understanding of your needs as a distance student?" Many of the respondents indicated that their institutions failed to provide the necessary support. The most common complaint noted related to nontechnical issues such as material distribution, financial considerations, overall communication, and knowledge of the institutions' policies and procedures. "Students commented that materials often arrived late or not at all. Others received their materials by fax, which was unreadable. Students were equally frustrated with (lack of knowledge about) the process of sending in assignments" (Hardy and Boaz 1997, p. 43).

Communication was another problem noted by the researchers. Many students responded by indicating that there was a lack of quality communication between themselves and the sending campus, which often led to a variety of problems, including failure to complete the course. These students did not know who to contact when technological problems occurred or when course materials did not arrive on time.

Trying to maneuver around the institution's bureaucracy, whether registering for classes, signing up for on-campus housing, or attempting to obtain financial support, is a frustrating problem known to any college student, but it can be especially frustrating for students studying at a distance. The amount of time and effort needed to reach the right person in the right department to overcome a particular problem can be overwhelming. Several distance education students in the survey commented that even when they found the right person to talk to, they were treated as second-class citizens because they were not taking classes on campus.

Interaction is the key to the success of any class—traditional or nontraditional (Haaland and Newby 1984; Young, Barnes, and Lowery 1995; McHenry and Bozik 1995). These researchers studied interaction and concluded that it is critical to the success of a student in both face-to-face instruction and distance education. Therefore, they recommend that instructors integrate interaction in their instruction by encouraging student interaction and supporting the proper use of equipment so that every student at each site may participate in classroom activities to the fullest.

POLICE AND DISTANCE EDUCATION

Faced with constant modifications to existing laws, limited personnel, and shrinking budgets, police departments nationwide are looking to distance education as one possible solution to a training problem. The officers at the University of Central Florida recognized the problem and came up with a solution—laptops for each officer with wireless capability, and an online training program comprising two major components: a publicly accessible part and a password-protected component within WEBCT, the online management program at the University of Central Floriday (UCF) (Walton 2004). The Field Training Officer, together with the police administrators and representatives from the education department at the university, are presently designing an online training program for the university police.

The University of Dayton Law School, together with the Rural Law Enforcement Tech Center, surveyed law enforcement agencies nationwide to obtain information on distance education. Results from the survey indicated that although 93 percent of the responding agencies had Internet access, only 42 percent currently use the Internet for training. Approximately one-third of responding officers who had previously used Internet training preferred it to traditional classroom-based training. Police administrators who responded to the question "What percentage of your officers have participated in Web-based training?" indicated that over half of the agencies had less than 5 percent of officers participating. Of the agencies, 18 percent indicated that between 10 and 49 percent of their officers participated, and 30 percent had participation between 50 and 100 percent (Brenner and Dailey 2004). It is apparent that agencies have the ability to do Internet training, but there is some resistance on the part of police administrators. Supporting evidence for this is the fact that 82 percent of law enforcement administrators responding to the direction, "Please rate the following types of training methods in the order of which method you find most beneficial" chose "Attending seminars/workshops" as their number one choice, and only 3 percent chose "Web-based virtual training" as the most beneficial. However, almost half (44 percent) indicated that either Web-based training or Web-based seminars would be among the top three choices. So, although law enforcement administrators would prefer obtaining training through attendance at seminars and conferences, they do apparently realize that Internet-based training is a viable alternative.

A joint project between the National Law Enforcement and Corrections Technology Center in Anchorage, Alaska, the Rural Law Enforcement Technology Center in Hazard, Kentucky, and the Federal Law Enforcement Training Center in Glynco, Georgia allowed 250 police officers nationwide to register for online Internet courses provided by Federal Law Enforcement Training Center (FLETC). The course selection included 37 courses related to law enforcement procedures, as well as several hundred covering other general topics including business administration. The officers were allowed to take as many of the courses as they wanted, or as few, and the cost was completely covered by the two Centers. A total of 125 officer-students registered for the classes through the Alaskan Center, and the other half registered with the Kentucky Center. Generally, students who lived and worked west of the Mississippi River were placed into the Alaskan list, and those east of the River were placed on the Kentucky list.

The project ran from June of 2003 until June of 2004. The Kentucky officers completed a total of 962 classes, with 55 out of 125 (44 percent) not completing at least one class and 70 (56 percent) completing at least one Internet class during the year. The average completion per officer was 7.7 overall, and 13.7 classes per officer among of those who completed at least one class. The Alaskan officers completed a total of 788 classes, with 45 percent not completing any and 55 percent (69 officers) completing at least one. The officers averaged 6.3 classes, with 11.4 per officer among those who completed at least one class—slightly below that of the eastern law enforcement students (Andrews and Dailey 2004). The fact that almost half of each group failed to complete at least one class may be explained by the answers to a short survey given to the officers. Respondents to one of the questions, which asked about problems with the courses, noted that the "introductory" course, which explained how the officers were supposed to use the system, was, in the words of one of the students, "least user-friendly and most aggravating." Another officer-student noted that, if any of the other officers had not completed any or all of the courses, it was probably due to the introductory course. Generally, the respondent officers liked the flexibility of the Internet courses, which allowed them the opportunity to receive the training at their convenience. Of the respondents, 42 percent indicated that the law enforcement courses, overall, would help them in the regular performance of their duties and 45 percent indicated that the Weapons of Mass Destruction course was the best course offered among the law enforcement courses available (Andrews and Dailey, 2004).

CONCLUSIONS

In the experience of this author, distance education is a viable method of instruction but not inherently more beneficial than other methods, including traditional classroom-based instruction. Clark (1994) and others argue that learning is more influenced by the *content* in a medium than by the *type* of medium used. Research on the subject has determined that no significant differences exist between the different types of media used for learning. Any differences between the media used will be primarily economic. The designer must make a selection between media based primarily on economic factors, not other factors. He or she must choose the less expensive and most cognitively efficient way of transferring knowledge to the prospective students. Based on the requirements of a given situation, certain media may be more efficient for certain students, learning goals, and tasks.

BIBLIOGRAPHY

Andrews, M., and Dailey, J. (2004). *Survey of the FLETC Officer Program: 2004*. National Law Enforcement and Corrections Technology Center (in publication).

Batey, A., and Cowell, R. (1986). *Distance Education: An Overview*. Portland, OR: Northwest Regional Educational Laboratory. (ERIC Document Reproduction Service No. ED 278 519).

Biner, P.M., Dean, R.S., and Mellinger, A.E. (1994). Factors underlying distance learner satisfaction with televised college-level courses. *The American Journal of Distance Education*, 8(1): 60–71.

Bramble, W.J., and Martin, B.L. (1995). The Florida teletraining project: Military training via two-way compressed video. *The American Journal of Distance Education*, 9(1), 6–26.

Brenner, S., and Dailey, J. (2004). *Survey of Law Enforcement Agencies*. Washington, D.C.: National Law Enforcement and Corrections Technology (in publication).

Bruning, R., Landis, M., Hoffman, E., and Grosskopf, K. (1993). Perspectives on an interactive satellite-based Japanese Language Course. *The American Journal of Distance Education*, 7(3), 22–38.

Carnevale, E. (2000). Survey finds 72% rise in number of distance education programs. *Chronicle of Higher Education*, January 7, A57.

Cheng, H.C., Lehman, J., and Armstrong, P. (1991). Comparison of performance and attitude in traditional and computer conferencing classes. *The American Journal of Distance Education*, 5(3), 51–64.

Clark, R.E. (1983). Reconsidering research on learning from media. *Review of Educational Research*, 53(4), 445–459.

Clark, R.E. (1994). Media will never influence learning. *Educational Technology Research and Development*, 42(2), 21–29.

Crane, V. (1984). *Student Uses of the Annenberg/CPB Telecourses in the Fall of 1984*. Chestnut Hill, MA: Research Communications.

Cyrs, T.E. (1997). *Teaching and Learning at a Distance: What it Takes to Effectively Design, Deliver, and Evaluate Programs*. New Mexico State University, San Francisco, CA: Josey Bass Publishers.

Haaland, B.A., and Newby, W.G. (1984). Student perception of effective teaching behaviors: An examination of conventional and teleconference based instruction. In Parker, L. & Olgren (Eds.) *Teleconferencing and Electronic Communications III*. Madison, WI: University of Wisconsin–Extension, Center for Interactive Programs.

Hardy, D.W., and Boaz, M.H. (1997). *Teaching and Learning at a Distance: What It Takes to Effectively Design, Deliver, and Evaluate Programs*. New Mexico State University, San Francisco, CA: Josey Bass Publishers.

Hezel, R. (1996). Coordinated statewide telecommunications: An essential ingredient of distance learning. *Educational Journal*, October 10(10), J-4–J-8.

Johnston, J. (1987). *Electronic Learning: From Audiotape to Videodisc*. Englewood Cliffs, NJ: Lawrence Erlbaum Associates.

McHenry, L., and Bozik, M. (1995) Communicating at a distance: A study of interaction in a distance education classroom. *Communication Education*, 44, 362–370.

Moore, M. (1989). *Effects of Distance Learning: A Summary of the Literature*. Washington, D.C.: Office of Technology Assessment Contractor Report, Congress of the United States.

Moore, M., (1995). The five C's of the local coordinator. *American Journal of Distance Education*, 9(1), 1–5.

Moore, M.G., and Kearsley, G. (1996) *Distance Education: A Systems View*. Belmont, CA: Wadsworth.

National Center for Education Statistics. (1999). *Distance Education at Postsecondary Education Institutions 1997–1998* (p. 51). Washington, D.C: U.S. Department of Education.

Peak, K. (1991). Criminal justice in the outland: The methods and promise of distance education. *Journal of Criminal Justice Education*, 2(1), 133–137.

Perraton, H. (1988). A theory for distance education. In D. Sewart, D. Keegan, & B. Holmberg (Eds.), *Distance Education: International Perspectives* (pp. 34–45). New York: Routledge.

Simonson, M., S. Smaldino, M. Albright, and S. Zvacek. (2003). *Teaching and Learning at a Distance: Foundations of Distance Education*, 2nd ed. NJ: Merrill Prentice Hall.

Walton, E. (2004). From books to Bytes: A tale of police training transformation. *Campus Law Enforcement Journal* 34(1): 25–28.

Wells, J., and Minor, K. (1998). Criminal justice students' attitudes toward distance learning as a function of demographics. In Moriarty, L. & Carter, D. (Eds.) *Criminal Justice Technology in the 21st Century* (pp. 47–60). Springfield, IL: Charles C. Thomas.

Whittington, N. (1987). Is instructional television educationally effective? A research review. *The American Journal of Distance Education*, 1(1), 47–57.

Workman, J.J., and Stenard, R.A. (1996). Student support services for distance learners. ED, *Education at a Distance*, 7, 18–22.

Young, D.B., Barnes, F.M., and Lowery, B.R. (1995) Distance education: How to begin. *Journal of Criminal Justice Education,* 6(2): 299–309.

Section IV

Special Topics in Police Organization, Management, and Administration

15 Professional Courtesies: To Ticket or Not to Ticket

John Kleinig and Albert J. Gorman

CONTENTS

INTRODUCTION

It is well known that police do not normally ticket each other. If a police officer is pulled over for speeding or driving under the influence, and it becomes known (police officers have a way of making it known) that he or she is a police officer, then the chances of a ticket being issued or an arrest being made will plummet.[1] Maybe the officer will be given a warning, maybe he will be escorted or taken home, and maybe nothing will happen—the process will be more like that of checking an admission ticket.[2] Police officers know this, and it can sometimes create a difficult situation. In one jurisdiction, the problem of officers driving home under the influence became so serious for a neighboring jurisdiction that a formal letter was sent to its headquarters, warning that the practice could no longer be tolerated and that formal action might have to be taken in future.[3]

THE SCOPE OF PROFESSIONAL COURTESIES

How far such courtesies extend is not altogether clear. Both with respect to the class of beneficiaries and the nature of the courtesies, there is variation and vagueness. On- and off-duty officers from one's own jurisdiction will almost always have such courtesies extended to them. But then there is also a potentially larger class of people to whom such courtesies are frequently extended: officers from other jurisdictions,[4] retired officers, the immediate and not so immediate families of officers, and so on, extending sometimes to members of other groups whose affiliations are generally of a work-related kind.[5] With respect to the kinds of courtesies involved, officers with whom we have spoken sometimes draw an informal distinction between administrative and criminal violations. Speeding, parking, and drunk-driving offenses are seen as administrative breaches; burglary and armed robbery would almost certainly be viewed as criminal.[6] Disorderly conduct, domestic, and some sexual assaults frequently occupy a gray area.[7]

Professional courtesies are not, of course, the exclusive preserve of police. As the name indicates, they are endemic to professional life, and their analogues are no doubt found in other occupations and contexts. Doctors and lawyers quite often assist each other—and their families—without or at reduced charge, or provide them with speedier service than they might otherwise have received.[8]

The case of what are termed police "courtesies," however, might appear to be different. In part, this may be because police are seen as public servants and not as private entrepreneurs. Even if it is allowable for others, as private service providers, it is not for the police to show this kind of favoritism. Thus, police who pledge allegiance to the Law Enforcement Code of Ethics vow never to "permit personal feelings ... or friendships to influence [their] decision ... [and to] enforce the law courteously and appropriately without fear or favor." As beneficiaries of a public payroll, they owe impartial treatment, making distinctions only where relevant distinctions can be drawn. Whereas impartiality may be optional for private professionals, it is mandatory for police officers.

There is, however, another more important reason why we might want to distinguish police courtesies. Police are pledged to enforce the law, and failure to do that just because an offender is a fellow officer is a violation of one of the central requirements of their office. Discretion is one thing; favoritism another.

ARE POLICE SPECIAL?

Notwithstanding these apparent differences, one is hard put to find police officers willing to advocate the ticketing of fellow officers in situations in which a ticket would have been issued had the violator been an ordinary citizen.[9] Quite the contrary. In one of the few "public" statements on the issue, Phil Caruso, the New York City president of the Patrolmen's Benevolent Association, is on record as telling his membership "You Don't Summons Another Cop."[10] On the surface, at least, this looks patently unfair. So what makes for the difference? Does whatever it is justify such partiality? And if so, what limits ought to be observed?

We have heard or can think of several possible arguments[11]:

(1) *Not just police*: Police often become self-defensive about the breaks they give each other, and one strategy of defense is to claim that they are not the exclusive beneficiaries of such practices. Clergy, doctors, judges, and sometimes political figures are accorded similarly privileged treatment by police officers. Presumably, this is meant to show that there is nothing specially self-serving about the courtesies, and, therefore—whatever else one might say—that they carry no moral taint.

But this is surely too quick a conclusion to draw, for it presumes that the practice of "forgiving" clergy, doctors, and others is itself defensible. Moreover, it assumes that the reasons for going easy on clergy, doctors, and others shows that police are not acting self-interestedly.

In the case of clergy and doctors, it is quite likely that there exists a certain affinity or fellow feeling. Police officers have to work with clergy and doctors, particularly in crisis situations, and in some cases at least, there are fairly deep ties between the church and police. In departments in which there are appreciable numbers of Irish and Italian police, as is the case in a number of large U.S. cities, the connections may be quite substantial, and the courtesies extended may be very considerable.[12] Police and doctors both understand and have to deal with the messy end of human life, and so, despite the enormous social differences,[13] an empathy exists, such that a warning is more likely to result than a ticket.[14]

At best, the affinities between police, clergy, and doctors show why courtesies extended to one group might also be extended to another. They do not show that they are justifiably extended to any group. Later we will see how the group cohesion argument [see (3) below] might be employed to accommodate all three.

The situation of judges and political representatives is probably different.[15] Police have to work with judges, and alienating them may create problems in the courtroom. In the case of politicians, there is probably little love lost between them and the police. That is probably because of what police often see as political interference with their work. Politicians, whether through the legislative process or through personal influence, can and do affect the working conditions, prospects, and lives of police officers, and extending "courtesies" to them might seem the prudent or expedient thing to do.[16]

Expediency is not a very good reason for making an exception in favor of judges or the politically influential. It is more like bowing to a veiled threat or acceding to what is "politic" than making a wise judgment about what would be the most appropriate thing to do. We must, however, recognize that a great deal of public life is conducted under constraints of these kinds, and, as a matter of social fact, it is hardly surprising that police respond as they do.

(2) *The exercise of allowable discretion*: That police are not rigidly bound to enforce all the laws all the time, and that they have some discretion about how to enforce them need not be argued here.[17] Whatever the public relations face of police work, we all know the reality is one that requires and, indeed, accepts that police exercise some discretion about how they fulfill their social tasks.

Police do not ticket every violator of traffic regulations. Sometimes they ignore, sometimes they warn, sometimes they ticket, and sometimes they may even arrest. And so the exercise of a discretion that refrains from ticketing a fellow officer need not automatically violate any reasonable expectation we may have of police. Indeed, provided that they issue enough tickets to give substance to the traffic regulations, there may be few constraints on the considerations that ought to influence the decision not to ticket. Ergo, it might be argued, the nonticketing of fellow officers remains within the boundaries of allowable discretion.

But acceptable discretion is not an arbitrary power, even though it may sometimes need no powerful basis. Granted, police may exercise discretion. But why in this way in these cases? If scarce police resources make it a bad investment to focus on certain kinds of traffic violations or on traffic violations in certain situations, that may well be a reason for going easy on certain violators or even for not enforcing the law at all. If someone is speeding because he is trying to get emergency medical assistance or because he is on a deserted country road, that may be a reason for not issuing a ticket. The exercise of favorable discretion may be justified here.[18]

However, what is it about a fellow officer that makes it appropriate to exercise favorable discretion in his case? Does it not constitute the same kind of favoritism that one finds in nepotism, bias, and partisanship, the very partiality that police vow to avoid in their role as law enforcers?

Sometimes police do endeavor to show why, in the case of a fellow officer, they feel justified in exercising favorable discretion. It may be said, for example, that police know how to handle a car at high speeds. Or that if they have had a few too many drinks, that is understandable and excusable—given the stresses of the job. A compassionate response is called for, and another officer is able to give it.

We do not wish to deny that considerations like these are sometimes relevant. We doubt, however, whether they are overriding.[19] And they are hardly sufficient to justify the steady practice of letting fellow officers off. Courteous "discretion" is not grounded in some contingent circumstance of a case but simply in the identity of the violator. Some police officers can handle cars better than others, and though some stresses may come from the job, others do not. Something more needs to be said than the discretionary argument appears able to provide. What we need to find is not some situational factor that enables one to say "I won't ticket you ..." on a particular occasion, but a different kind of factor, associated with a person's identity as a police officer, that will explain and justify a general practice of favorable discretion. The discretionary argument, in other words, does not explain—or justify—the refusal to ticket as a "professional courtesy."

There is, however, one group-related factor that might be adduced in favor of the discretionary argument. Were it arguable that police violators would suffer more or disproportionately if summonsed or formally dealt with, this could be taken into consideration in deciding whether a summons or arrest was warranted. It is not uncommon for violators of traffic rules to plead that a summons will cause them excessive hardship (they will lose their license, their job depends on having a license, etc.), and it could well be the case that police who are convicted of certain traffic violations (say, of driving under the influence or of breaching the law—without good reason—while on duty[20]) will experience some form of departmental discipline in addition to any legal costs. Although it may not be inappropriate for an officer to respond to the motorist who pleads such hardship by asserting "Well, you knew what the risks were before you drove, and you must therefore be willing to accept the consequences," there is also a place for deciding that "a break" would be warranted. Justice may sometimes be tempered with mercy.[21]

But this argument is still not broad enough, because many traffic offenses will not expose officers to more serious hardship than other citizens. And even if they did, it could be argued, at least in some cases, that by virtue of their work police were under some special duty to avoid violations.

There is one further possibility.[22] If the purpose of ticketing traffic violators is not to penalize every violator but only a number sufficient to give motorists a significant reason for driving carefully, then it might be argued that a police officer who is upholding his end (or fulfilling his "quota") should have a very broad discretion about how he selects those who will not be ticketed. What injustice will be involved if his colleagues are favored?

But fairness can be comparative as well as noncomparative. Were the officer to make up his "quota" ("observe the norm") by ticketing minority violators and going easy on others, we would be rightly concerned. Should it not be a matter of some concern, also, that fellow officers are let off as a matter of course? More importantly, if a select group is excluded from sanctions, then the deterrent function that might serve to broaden the officer's discretion will be undermined. For police officers will then know that they can violate traffic regulations with impunity.

(3) *Group cohesion*: To understand professional courtesies generally, and police courtesies in particular, we must focus on the fraternal bonds that exist between members of these groupings.[23]

In general, police share in a special kind of camaraderie. They are coparticipants in a fellowship of risk and fear. They are guardians of the thin line that separates civilization from the jungle. As they would probably express it, they are constantly putting their lives on that line, and a sense of mutual dependence becomes central to their perseverance and well-being. They can cope with the demands of their job only because of the supportive "familial" relations that they develop with their partners and fellow officers.[24] In such an environment, there are things one might properly do for partners and colleagues that one would not, and need not, do for others. "Giving them a break" is one of them. And there are things one would not do to partners and colleagues that one might and should do to others. "Ticketing a fellow officer" is one of them. Officers who chose to ticket another officer would show themselves to be, at the very least, jerks, lacking in feeling for the interdependent and communal nature—the "brotherhood"—of police work.

In a sense, professional courtesies are cut from the same fabric as the code of silence that operates in professional life generally, and most dramatically in police work. Police professional courtesies constitute one of those group- and morale-maintaining gestures that police make to keep themselves going in what is generally perceived to be an alien and hostile environment. It is, as Caruso puts it, "one of the things that police can do for one another." It is a benefit, one that police are in a distinctive position to offer, and one that would not normally be given to others. Although a police officer who gave a ticket to a fellow officer would hardly be guilty of betrayal, he would be thought to show himself lacking in the fraternal attachments with which loyalty is associated.[25]

Although the foregoing may help to explain the reluctance of police officers to ticket each other, it does not automatically justify such a practice. Just as the code of silence may serve to discredit, as well as to unite, police, so too, it might be claimed, does the failure to issue tickets in circumstances in which they would otherwise have been issued. Though it will manifest and strengthen the bonds that sustain them, it will also reinforce the view that police constitute "an exclusive fraternity granted special privileges and immunities from the laws which [they] enforce."[26]

In the circumstances under consideration (a traffic violation) police are likely to think that a ticket would not be justified. This is partly a reflection of the way in which they see the offenses in question. These violations are seen as administrative rather than criminal. In a really bad case, they might consider reporting the incident to a superior and having a letter written to the officer's commander. But in the usual traffic cases, in which we are all likely to have been violators from time to time, internal reporting of this kind would be "sure to cause the officer more inconvenience, embarrassment, and punishment than a speeding summons would cause."[27] Even issuing a ticket in cases in which only a fine would result might be considered to convey an inappropriate message about the relationship that ought to exist between police officers. What a fellow officer needs, it might be claimed, is not judgment but a gesture of understanding and support. Admonition may sometimes be appropriate but not a response that takes it "out of the family." Family problems should be settled in the family and not by recourse to outside parties.

In addition to destroying the intimacy that exists between police officers, ticketing also upsets an equality of status that they share. An officer who tickets another is effectively putting himself above the other.[28] True, circumstances may arise when such a differential may be required if, for example, the officer has committed a serious felony. But in that case, it might be argued, the offending officer has effectively surrendered his claims as an officer of the law. Put in another way, officers who commit felonies are likely to jeopardize the lives and/or careers of their buddies, and thereby disqualify themselves from protection.

We believe that the argument from group cohesion—one that is usually cast in familial terms—is central to understanding the professional courtesies that police show to each other. It has to be taken seriously by those who object to the form it takes in exempting fellow officers from traffic summonses. The significance of such courtesies lies not so much in the freedom that they give officers to ignore certain regulations (or at least to treat them pragmatically) as in the role that they have in expressing and reinforcing officer solidarity. The benefit is psychosocial rather than material (though in some cases, presumably, officers are saved from substantial financial and other burdens).

HAZARDS OF PRIVILEGE

However, just because a practice has developed and has acquired a significant psychosocial meaning for the members of a group, it does not follow that it is justified or that it should be tolerated. There are, of course, differences between practices that have not been established and those that are already deeply entrenched. There are costs to the removal or dismantling of a practice that need not be considered when contemplating it futuristically. Nevertheless, there are several possible reasons why the status quo ought not to be accepted wholesale and unthinkingly, and why it may be appropriate for police to rethink the wisdom of what they have embraced.

(1) *A form of corruption*: The giving of professional courtesies, at least of the kind envisaged, might be considered a form of corruption. For does not the exemption of fellow officers just because they are fellow officers represent a corrupt misuse of discretionary authority?

If we understand corruption to mean some misuse of authority for the purpose of advantaging oneself, then it may not be immediately obvious that any corruption is involved. A police officer who waves on or merely reprimands another officer is unlikely to benefit personally. It is not like taking a twenty dollar bribe.

However, there are indirect benefits of which an officer must be aware. There is little doubt that as a group—and therefore, for the most part, individually—officers benefit from a situation in which such a practice exists. Because of the reciprocity involved, it is unlikely that the apprehending officer would himself be ticketed were he to violate a speeding requirement—something that at some time or other he or she will probably do. The knowledge that this is so may well, and often clearly does, affect the way in which a police officer copes with traffic regulations. Understood in this way, the refusal to ticket a fellow officer may be seen as a form of petty corruption. It is a form, however, that police are likely to excuse as a "reward" or "recognition" for the generally tough job they are called on to do—a kind of loosening of the collar. Or, as it has been put: "Surely shoveling society's shit is worth something."[29] "Something," of course, need not mean an exemption from traffic summonses, and it needs to be shown that the practice does not constitute a form of corruption, even if only a petty one.

But the indirect benefits are social, as well as individual. This partisan use of police authority maintains and reinforces the fraternal bonds that for police, as individuals, makes the job tolerable and even engrossing. For this reason the benefit is not likely to be viewed as corrupt. Such courtesies are owed as part of the fraternal order to which one is privileged to belong. Ticketing a fellow officer is not the kind of thing one does. Family and other intimate group members ipso facto deserve different treatment from others. Or, as American Express is fond of saying, "Membership has its privileges." It is not for nothing that the practice is described as a "professional courtesy." The person who makes no distinction between friends and strangers, between family and outsiders, between members and nonmembers is not being impartial. That person lacks a certain kind of moral sensitivity or at least a sense of relational appropriateness.

There is something to this. We accept and indeed expect that people will give favored treatment to family and friends—to their own. One may give one's children benefits that one does not extend to others. We may even relieve them of burdens that we would expect others to bear. But there is a limit to such privileged treatment. Some discriminations are unseemly and others may be flatly wrong. We need to ask whether notticketing is one of the partialities that officers might properly extend to those who stand in a special relationship to them.

The issuing of a ticket need not deny the existence of a special relationship, any more than the withholding of a benefit from one's child need show a failure of intimacy. A parent and issuing officer may do what they believe they have to do with a heavy heart—in the case of a police officer, with a sense of sorrow not only that a fellow officer has violated the laws he is sworn to uphold, but also that one has the responsibility of taking action against a "brother." Hard choices may need to be made when the obligations that are embedded in intimate or professional relationships come into conflict with other obligations one has, either generally or by virtue of one's role. Are there reasons for thinking that the exemption of fellow officers from summonses goes beyond what is an appropriate favoritism?

(2) *The beginning of a slippery slope*: In many discussions of police corruption, it is argued that corrupt police do not usually start that way, but begin with little things like accepting gratuities, perks, free meals, and so on, and then gradually slip into more serious compromises.[30] Professional courtesies may be thought to be among those little things that set one on the slope of serious corruption. One reason why it may be considered appropriate to include such courtesies in their number is that they constitute violations (albeit minor) of a commitment. Police officers who expect or receive favored treatment shows themselves willing to compromise, and the only issue is: How far will they go?

To some extent, this way of putting the slippery slope argument presumes that the officer involved will recognize this kind of professional courtesy as a compromise, even though a minor one. But as we have indicated, that is not always the case. Many officers do not see it that way, any more than they see favoring their own children over others as compromising some principle of impartiality. The principle of impartiality does not require that one's own children should be treated the same as others'. *Pace* William Godwin, there is some magic in the pronoun "my."[31] And where officers do not see the extension of such professional courtesies as compromising, the issue of their being softened up for more serious violations will not really arise. Maybe officers do not draw the line where others draw it, but crossing it is not an option.

There is, however, another way to construe the slippery slope argument—one that does not require this perception.[32] And, as many police officers do not see the extension of professional courtesies as a compromise, it may be more relevant to the present situation. The claim here, basically, is that these kinds of professional courtesies blur certain clear distinctions or, to use a legal metaphor, dim certain bright lines, and make it very difficult for officers to come to appropriate decisions in other cases in which the circumstances differ only "by degree." The point is not that it is always wrong, but that the distinction between what is allowable and what is wrong becomes so difficult to draw that one "slips" into making greater and greater concessions. What should one do if the fellow officer is not only speeding but driving recklessly? Or if he is only speeding, but then tries to avoid apprehension and must be hotly pursued?[33] Or if he has an accident in which only property damage is involved? What if the person who is stopped is the officer's spouse or child, or the chief's nephew or golfing partner? An officer who is prepared to count a fellow officer as "family"—and therefore entitled to concessions—is going to have to decide how much the family can tolerate and how big the family really is, and those may be hard calls. True, police are constantly called upon to make discriminating and discretionary judgments, but some judgments, it might be said, serve to blur the vision rather than to aid one's visual acuity.

As the "family" is extended, the courtesies are also likely to have an effect on others' respect for the police. It is at least understandable—whether or not justifiable—that police should give their own a break. But if that privilege is then extended to others, it will increasingly appear that what is important is not what one has done, but who one is or knows.[34] Police can do without that.[35] Indeed, the very fact that relatives and friends of officers should try this ploy suggests that they already believe that "connections" will count. Such exploitation of the system already shows a certain cynicism about, if not contempt for, the integrity of the police.

(3) *The responsibilities of a public servant*: Apart from the fact that the professional courtesies that we have referred to appear to involve police in a violation of their oath of office,[36] they also sit uncomfortably with the "public" nature of their employment. Unlike many professionals who are privately employed and who may therefore be accorded a great deal of discretion about the way in which and the conditions under which they provide their services,[37] police are paid from the public purse and are, ultimately, answerable to that public for the way in which they exercise their authority and, hence, their discretionary power. In their case, discrimination in favor of their own and certain others becomes much more problematic. By placing themselves (as it would appear) above the law, they subvert the democratic traditions they are required to uphold under a rule of law.

The point here is not to question the appropriateness of fraternal bonding among police, but to ensure that such bonding is structured within the framework that sustains democratic police authority. What is often seen as one of the dangers of police acceptance of gratuities—a skewing of the delivery of police services toward those who are "good" (i.e., offer discounts or freebies)—is here realized through bonds and affinities that should be checked by the rule of law. The point is not to deny police discretion in the form of a power to selectively enforce the law but to yoke such discretion to the values that are served by the law. Fundamental among such values is equality before the law. Police are citizens under law, as well as agents of the law. And any preferential treatment they give should be grounded in differences that can be socially acknowledged. The partisan treatment of violations by fellow officers finds little resonance in our social ideology and is explicitly forbidden by the oath whereby police signal their role obligations.

Intimate bonds are, of course, generally recognized and supported by the law. And, if the law should eschew or seek to undermine familial relationships, that may be a reason for breaking it. But in this respect, police bonds are not analogous to familial relationships. The latter have a certain social priority; at one level they are what civil society seeks to protect and promote. The institution of policing is, in this respect, secondary; it is an agent of civil society. Important though the bonding of police officers may be, it must nevertheless remain subject to the more limited social ends that it serves.[38]

CONCLUSION

The issue of professional courtesies is more complex than it might at first appear. For although the extension of such courtesies may express the selfish self-interest of a privileged group, they need not do so. They may, instead, be more accurately seen as one distinctive expression of the intimate bond that exists between members of many groups, including those familial arrangements that we consider central to our social being—a bond that we acknowledge and seek to preserve through our political and other regulatory structures. We not only may but ought to favor our own, for by them we have been supported, through them we have our identity, and on them we continue to depend.

But familial traditions and obligations and their analogues do not ipso facto take priority over all others, and in the case of police not ticketing fellow officers, we have symbolically, at least, a compromise of the egalitarian and democratic commitment that goes with the public nature of their employment and service.

This tension between particularist and impartial or universal values is deeply embedded in police professional courtesies, and it is difficult to see how it can be resolved. Active resistance to the practice will surely depress morale and breed defiance. Condonation of the practice is incompatible with the impartial discharge of responsibility that police are authorized and expected to provide. The relative silence that surrounds it probably testifies to its ethical awkwardness. We could probably be content with that were such courtesies limited to what might be easily seen as administrative offenses.[39] But they inevitably creep outward, and in so doing, create a problem not only for those who are to enforce the law but also for those whom the law is supposed to protect. Showing professional courtesy may not be the worst thing that police officers do, but neither may it do much to enhance their reputation within the wider community.

ACKNOWLEDGMENTS

This chapter was originally prepared while John Kleinig was a fellow in professional ethics in the Program in Ethics and the Professions, Harvard University. Earlier drafts benefited from the comments and assistance of Juan Albornoz, Arthur Applbaum, Allan Brett, Howard Cohen, Michael Cullina, Peter Dodenhof, William Heffernan, Colin Honey, Marie Rosen, Dennis Thompson, Steven Wasserman, and Kenneth Winston.

NOTES

[1] In some jurisdictions we might extend this to violations of parking regulations. Police officers who display a departmental or association badge or some other identifier in their windows are unlikely to be ticketed.

[2] We have heard of the keys being taken or even being thrown away, so that the offender will sober up before continuing on his way. But see the account given in Robert Daley's *Prince of the City*, New York: Berkeley Books, 1981, p. 300.

[3] The motivation for this is not exactly clear. It may simply have been concern for the danger posed to other travelers. However, we suspect that the volume was becoming such that it would become inevitable that an accident would occur, that it would come out in the aftermath that the officer had been stopped but permitted to continue. It would create the kind of scandal that the media love but police departments hate.

[4] There is an interesting footnote discussion of interjurisdictional ticketing in Michael T. Charles *Policing the Streets*, Springfield, IL: Charles C Thomas, 1986, p. 145, in which the author reports on a training academy discussion of the issue. Although the instructor did not wish to say outright that "officers don't ticket officers," the implicit moral of the story was that they don't/shouldn't.

[5] Bumper stickers, decals on windows, and police union cards in wallets occasion the question: "Are you on the job?" The reply: "No, but my uncle is, and my grandfather used to be a police officer" is very often sufficient to qualify one for such courtesies. In New York City, faculty members from John Jay College of Criminal Justice, where many officers enroll for degrees, are sometimes exempted from a traffic violation if they have a college sticker in the window. Naturally, the more tenuous the relationship the more unpredictable is the courtesy. There is a sad case reported in *Prince of the City* in which a police officer who has been fired finds that he can no longer call on his associations (p. 196).

[6] Although see the case reported in Mike McAlary's *Buddy Boys* in which a police officer is caught in a stolen/borrowed car (New York: G.P. Putnam's Sons, 1987, pp. 94–97). In *Prince of the City*, p. 191, it is made clear that a police officer caught with a bale of marijuana in his car would have been "given a break" had the find not been recorded and the investigating officers not worried that their integrity was being tested.

[7] On domestic violence, see Jacob R. Clark, Policing's dirty little secret? Spouse abuse by police sparks concern—and a Federal Lawsuit, *Law Enforcement News*, XVII, 334 (April 15, 1991), 1, 10.

[8] In some places, this practice has been almost discontinued, and it is frequently limited.

[9] There is, naturally, a practical problem about saying whether, if the person apprehended had been an ordinary citizen, a summons would have been issued. There will probably be many cases in which it is difficult to know how the police officer would have exercised his or her discretionary power. For instances of or arguments concerning police ticketing police, see Stuart M. Wise, "Cop After Cop," *The National Law Journal*, V (June 13, 1983), p. 47, col. 1 (reporting a ticketing incident in Hawaii), and Allen P. Bristow, *You ... And the Law Enforcement Code of Ethics*, Santa Cruz, CA: Davis Publishing Co., pp. 53–56 (a case study advocating impartial enforcement of the law).

[10] Reported in "Around the Nation," *Law Enforcement News*, XV, 296 (July 15, 1989), p. 2, col. 2. Caruso is reported to have stated that the "courtesy" should be extended to officers in other jurisdictions, to their families, and to retired officers. When asked to defend his position on a local radio program, Caruso stated: "This is one of the things we can do for one another that costs the taxpayer no money, that really infringes on nobody's rights or authority or anything like that."

[11] We have found very few discussions of this issue. For the most part, it exists as oral tradition. See, however, the accounts given in Michael T. Charles, *Policing the Streets*, pp.108–110; and, briefly, in Edward A. Thibault, Lawrence M. Lynch, and R. Bruce McBride, *Proactive Police Management*, second edition, Englewood Cliffs, NJ: Prentice-Hall, 1990, p. 34.

[12] See, for example, their characterization by ex-police-officer-turned-novelist William J. Caunitz in *One Police Plaza*, New York: Bantam Books, 1985. Also Connie Fletcher, *What Cops Know*, New York: Villard, 1991, pp. 4–5.

[13] The economic differences, however, should not obscure what are often moral and political convergences.

[14] We have encountered other explanations as well: The belief that doctors, because of the preoccupying nature of their work, are excusably distracted; a desire to be held in high regard by doctors; and an affinity mediated by the "tradition" of male police officers marrying female nurses. The latter might account for the special favor sometimes given to nurse violators (see Charles, *Policing the Streets*, p. 117).

[15] Lawyers, too, sometimes receive privileged treatment. Perhaps because police must often deal with lawyers, especially in adversarial situations, they do not want to aggravate the tensions that are often felt between the two. Lawyers can do police a lot of damage, and they can cause a lot of trouble, too. Police can do without that kind of grief.

[16] Even in an era that proclaims a separation between police and politics, there is still room for a great deal of interference by politicians (whether federal, state, or local) in police activity.

[17] We should, however, note that selective enforcement raises more difficult issues than discretion about the way in which laws are to be enforced. Police, generally, have a more definite and less discretionary obligation to enforce the law than one concerning the way in which the law should be enforced. See John Kleinig, "Selective Enforcement and the Rule of Law," *Journal of Social Philosophy*, xxix, 1 (Spring, 1998), 117–131.

[18] Discretion can also be exercised unfavorably, though, as there is a presumption in favor of enforcement, the decision to enforce will not usually be considered discretionary. However, if the reason why a police officer issues a ticket in a particular case is the need to meet a quota, we might well consider that an unjustifiable exercise of discretion, particularly if it is a case for which a favorable discretionary judgment might have been acceptable or expected. See, "Green Bay Cops Cry 'Foul' Over Alleged Traffic Ticket Quotas," *Law Enforcement News*, XVII, 332 (March 16, 1991), 7, 15.

[19] Certainly they should never be thought so overriding that the behavior is treated lightly. Any violator whose behavior cannot be directly justified should at least be reprimanded.

[20] In the Hawaiian case reported in note 9, the on-duty officer was ticketed for driving his squad car at 89 mph in a 35-mph zone without using his turret lights or siren. His reason, apparently, was that he was in a hurry to pick up a colleague's mail.

[21] For an example, see Charles, *Policing the Streets*, pp. 106–107.

[22] Suggested by Dennis Thompson.

23 This is also the opinion of Thibault, Lynch, and McBride, *Proactive Police Management*, pp. 33–34.

24 The use of familial terminology to refer to fellow officers is pervasive: "I sleep with my wife, but live with my partner" (from the film version of *Prince of the City*; cf. pp. 173–174). Sometimes police speak of being "married" to their partners.

25 Thus, Bristow, commenting on the aftermath of ticketing a fellow officer (which he recommends), observes: "Your action may cause temporary lack of cooperation or animosity between your department and that of the driver. It may also embarrass your superiors in their social and professional relationships with their counterparts at conventions or meetings," *You ... And the Law Enforcement Code of Ethics* (p. 55).

26 Ibid. For such a reaction, see the case reported by Carla Hinton, in which an off-duty Oklahoma City police officer was exempted, as part of departmental policy, from a traffic citation after an accident ("Preferential City Policy Criticized," *The Daily Oklahoman*, May 24, 1991, p. 1).

27 Bristow, *You ... And the Law Enforcement Code of Ethics*, p. 56. He warns against such action in the case of an infraction of which we are all guilty from time to time, and says that it is likely to be invested with greater significance than it really has, and to cause disproportionate trouble for the officer in question. There is another reason why this scenario is unlikely: An officer who attempted to take this route could well find himself in trouble. He would show himself to be uncollegial, and for this would expose himself to a retaliatory reprimand for not enforcing the law! An interesting case, in which police executives were involved, is reported in Charles, *Policing the Streets*, p. 145, n. 17.

28 The situation is made even more problematic if the officer who is apprehended is a higher-ranking officer.

29 There is some evidence that many citizens are not too disturbed by this practice. There are probably several reasons for this: For many, it is just one of the perks and peccadillos that goes with the job—like the perks and peccadilloes that go with their own jobs (the personal telephone calls, free stationery, etc.). It is also seen as unimportant next to the serious crime that police are there to protect us from. Finally, it may well reflect a desire that many citizens have that *they* be shown some favorable treatment by police. Police who ticket police will almost certainly ticket other citizens. Police who do not ticket police just may be lenient with us.

30 For a well-known statement of this position, see Lawrence Sherman, "Becoming Bent," reprinted in Frederick A. Elliston and Michael Feldberg (eds.), *Moral Issues in Police Work*, Totowa, NJ: Rowman and Allanheld, 1985, pp. 253–265. Although the argument has its weaknesses (see, Michael Feldberg, "Gratuities, Corruption, and the Democratic Ethos of Policing: the Case of the Free Cup of Coffee," in ibid., pp. 267–276) there does seem to be a fair bit of anecdotal evidence to support Sherman's claims. See Robert Leuci's (*The Prince of the City*) account of his descent into corruption in Myron P. Glazer, "Ten Whistleblowers and How they Fared," *Hastings Center Report*, 1983, or William Gallagher's (*Buddy Boys*) account in the videotape "I Used to be a Cop" (John Jay College of Criminal Justice, City University of New York).

31 Godwin constructs a story in which Archbishop Fénelon and his mother are trapped in a burning building, and he can save only one. Whom should he save? Godwin opts for the archbishop, as the one likely to contribute more to the general happiness. "What magic," he asks, "is in the pronoun 'my' that should justify us in overturning the decisions of impartial truth?" (*Enquiry Concerning Political Justice*, Vol I). Godwin's example gained so much notoriety that by the third edition "father" had been substituted for "mother."

32 Writers on the slippery slope argument rarely distinguish between its "logical" and "psychological" forms. For a brief statement of the distinction, see James Rachels, *The End of Life*, Oxford University Press, 1985, pp. 172–180.

33 Albert Gorman knows of a case in which, shortly after the end of the evening tour, two on-duty officers called off a hot pursuit, figuring that "it must have been an officer on his way home."

34 An officer of John Kleinig's acquaintance was called to a case in which the teenage daughter of his partner (the daughter also happened to be the girlfriend of the chief's son) was injured in an accident with another vehicle. The driver of the other vehicle recognized the daughter, and apparently his first words on being approached by the officer were: "I know I'm going to get screwed, because her father's a cop and you cops don't write other cops tickets." He was right. He was charged with failing to take proper precautions when exiting from a driveway (though he was, in fact, entering it), and the daughter was let off, even though it was clear to all present and from skidmarks that the daughter's car had been driven round a corner at excessive speed. As he put it to Kleinig: "Really it was the only choice. I couldn't sacrifice the relationships with my friends or at least didn't feel I could at the time." What struck Kleinig about this case is that the officer in question, although troubled by his action, had a reputation for being absolutely straight.

[35] We have evidence that some police groups have become sufficiently troubled by what *they* would regard as the abuse of a privilege to tighten up their eligibility criteria. We know of at least one case in which police officers' private cars are issued with specially pressed license plates, on which FOP (Fraternal Order of Police) is stamped, along with the branch number, and the wives (and only the wives) of officers are given distinctive pendants to indicate to any apprehending officer how "family" they are.

[36] Many professional courtesies in other areas involve no violation of rules, internal or external, though occasionally there are parallels. Doctors sometimes prescribe nonmedically-indicated drugs for colleagues. Or they may falsify details on a report to ensure that personally embarrassing information will not become public. Sometimes, of course, doctors agree to falsify records for their regular patients, (for insurance, reimbursement, or employment purposes). The point of a professional courtesy, however, is that these things will be done almost "as a matter of course."

[37] Though even that discretion has come increasingly under challenge, especially where it has been used to make race-, gender-, or sex-based discriminations. And in the case of doctors or lawyers who are benefiting from public funding or the use of public facilities, the discretion may be limited even further.

[38] There was, therefore, a particular poignancy about the case of a police officer who was dismissed after leaving his desk (without permission) so that he could help his family who were being threatened by rapid flooding ("Police Officer Faces Dismissal for Loyalty to Family in Storm," *New York Times*, September 29, 1987).

[39] There are similarities between police professional courtesies and the more general practice that exists in many institutions, in which employees remove paper clips, pads, and pencils for personal use. Although such practices are strictly unjustifiable, an organization that seeks to prevent this from occurring is likely to have morale problems. At the same time, there is a problem of drawing the line.

16 At What Price a "Freebie?" The Real Cost of Police Gratuity Acceptance

Jim Ruiz and Christine Bono

CONTENTS

ABSTRACT

There has long been a debate among academics and police practitioners as to the level of danger represented by police officer acceptance of what has often been classed as "minor gratuities." Some claim that police acceptance of gratuities is harmless and may, in fact, strengthen the bond between the police and the public.[11] On the other hand, others warn that allowing or ignoring police gratuity acceptance may well lead to greater levels of corruption. The authors, one retired from the New Orleans Police Department, take the view that gratuity acceptance not only leads to other deviant behavior by police officers, but that gratuities can amount to 30% or more of an average police officer's annual salary. As such, police gratuity acceptance represents a greater threat to police integrity, corruption, and deviant behavior than has previously been considered.

INTRODUCTION

Criminal justice has long struggled for acceptance and legitimacy in the larger academic community. Conceived in the bosom of the Law Enforcement Assistance Administration (LEAA), Criminal Justice is still striving to break the academic shackles of "Handcuffs and Nightsticks 101." Since those early years, the ranks of those teaching criminal justice have grown with former and retired practitioners from the fields of policing, law enforcement, courts, corrections, and probation and parole. The lead author traveled the path of practitioner-turned-academic and was long protective of policing issues when raised in the classroom, defending police deviant behavior and minor police corruption as either innocent and inconsequential or actions necessary to get the job done.

However, as he progressed through academia, he came to the realization that the police deviant behavior he had once considered necessary, innocent, and inconsequential was, in fact, harmful and detrimental to policing and the public they are sworn to protect and serve. One of the police behaviors long considered deviant or corrupt by some that he defended and regularly took part in was the practice of police acceptance of gratuities. It is the position of the authors that police acceptance of gratuities is a harmful and degrading practice that should be actively discouraged.

We will demonstrate that what many consider minor gratuities are not minor in that they can easily amount to 30% or more of an average police officer's annual salary. This discussion will also include (1) how the acceptance of gratuities is the first test of whether the rookie can be trusted before moving on to greater levels of police deviant behavior; (2) gratuity's contribution to the corruption of noble cause; (3) gratuities as exploitation: whether they are given as a sign of respect or fear; (4) gratuities as double-dipping; and (5) gratuities as entitlement and how top police administrators are beginning to acknowledge the corrosive effect of police acceptance of gratuities.

POLICE AS PROFESSIONALS

Those in policing have long desired that their work be considered and classed a "profession." Although numerous writers in criminal justice have referred to policing as a profession,[2] the matter of policing as a profession is still in debate.[3]

Those in the field of policing desire recognition as professionals, but does the presentation and acceptance of gratuities occur in the "acknowledged professions of law, medicine, and education" as it does in policing?[4] The answer would seem to be no.

The dichotomy of the situation is that police officers desire the recognition of a "professional," yet they strive to retain the perks that ordinarily accompany those occupations that would not be classified as professions as listed by Walker (1999). Occupations that regularly accept gratuities or tips include table servers, bellboys, doormen, hair stylists, cab drivers, parking attendants, sky caps at airports, and pizza delivery persons, just to name a few. Under this rubric, it would seem that police acceptance of gratuities moves them away from the classification of a "professional" and more toward trade or craft workers.

THE GRATUITY

Gratuities often lead to things like kickbacks (bribery) for referring business to towing companies, ambulances, or garages. Further up the scale comes pilfering, or stealing (any) company's supplies for personal use. At the extreme, opportunistic theft takes place, with police officers skimming items of value that won't be missed from crime scenes, property rooms, warehouses, or any place they have access to. Theft of items from stores while on patrol is sometimes called "shopping."[4]

Definitions and descriptions of the term "gratuity" have been given by many different authors.[55] However, a simplistic approach to the definition or description may be that it encompasses an expression or gesture that represents gratitude indicating that a gratuity would be no more than a token of appreciation for a job well done.[66]

Often, however, the form a gratuity takes can influence opinions and actions of those who accept them, whether it be a gift, a service, or cash. The monetary value is a strong determinant of whether a gratuity is acceptable or not. August Vollmer, considered one of the founding fathers of police professionalism, was an adamant critic of police acceptance of gratuities. He believed that officers who accepted free coffee should be fired.[7]

Some believe that corruption can not be present in the absence of money.[87] Others believe that even things considered trivial, such as a free cup of coffee, should not be condoned.[98] Yet, it has been recognized that gratuities can and are given with ulterior motives.[10] It has been noted that "What makes a gift a gratuity is the reason it is given; what makes it corruption is the reason it is taken."[119] This interpretation could encompass most, if not all, gratuities. Said another way, it appears to suggest that even if a gratuity is offered without a hidden motive, the reason the officer accepts it can make it wrong. If we accept this view, then when police officers accept gratuities or "freebies" from a giver with corrupt intent, have they not tainted themselves and unnecessarily placed themselves, their careers, and their departments in a precarious position?

CODES OF CONDUCT

Nearly all police departments flatly prohibit their personnel from accepting gratuities. For example, the Philadelphia Police Department speaks directly to this issue in their Statement of Ethical Principles. The department defines ethics as a word that "encompasses the standard of conduct governing all members of a profession."[12] It informs its members that they "bear the public trust" and the importance for them to "protect the safety and the rights of fellow members of society."[13] They are admonished not to abuse that authority.

> Two basic constraints limit use of this authority. First, it is wrong for police to use their office for personal profit or gain, wrong for them to accept any favor which places their own advantage above the welfare of the public. Second, it is wrong for officers to violate the Constitution or laws in performance of their work.[14]

Regarding the acceptance of gratuities, the Philadelphia Police Department frames the problem as a matter of personal and departmental integrity instead of corruption.

Integrity

> The public demands that the integrity of its law enforcement officers be above reproach. The dishonesty of just one officer may impair public confidence and cast suspicion upon the Department as a whole. Succumbing to even minor temptations can generate a malignancy which will ultimately destroy an individual's effectiveness and which may well contribute to the corruption of fellow officers. Officers must scrupulously avoid any conduct which might compromise their integrity or the integrity of those with whom they work. No officer should seek or accept any special consideration or privilege, nor anything of value for which others are expected to pay, solely because they are police officers, or for performing their duty in some manner inconsistent with the highest regard for integrity.[15]

The International Association of Chiefs of Police (IACP) Code of Ethics speaks directly to the prohibition on police acceptance of gratuities but will be addressed in-depth later. The United Nations Code of Conduct for Law Enforcement Officials also speaks to the problem police acceptance of gratuities.

Article 7

> Law enforcement officials shall not commit any act of corruption. They shall also rigorously oppose and combat all such acts.

Commentary:

> (a) Any act of corruption, in the same way as any other abuse of authority, is incompatible with the profession of law enforcement officials. The law must be enforced fully with respect to any law enforcement official who commits an act of corruption, as Governments cannot expect to enforce the law among their citizens if they cannot, or will not, enforce the law against their own agents and within their agencies.

(b) While the definition of corruption must be subject to national law, it should be understood to encompass the commission or omission of an act in the performance of or in connection with one's duties, in response to gifts, promises or incentives demanded or accepted, or the wrongful receipt of these once the act has been committed or omitted.

(c) The expression "act of corruption" referred to above should be understood to encompass attempted corruption.[16]

The fact that major police departments, the IACP, and the United Nations recognize the danger to the integrity and performance of police officers is captured in their own words. Indeed, the danger represented by this seemingly innocent practice could be a threat to the Social Contract.

THE SOCIAL CONTRACT

Olsen (1965) noted that "governments are unavoidable features of human societies" in that they afford safety for its citizens by means of the social contract. However, such protection can only occur by means of coercion.[17] Reiman (1985) defines the social contract as

> embodying a general test of the legitimacy of the acts and rules of public agencies of law enforcement, namely, that such acts or rules must be such that the limits on citizens' freedom that they bring must result in a net increase of that freedom all told.[18]

Referring to the ramifications of the social contract for modern policing, Reiman holds that any application of coercion by police that impedes and jeopardizes freedom of the people, instead of increasing and safeguarding it, breeds the exact circumstance "that coercive legal agencies are meant to remedy."[19] Dunham and Alpert (2001) note that "if the police use their authority and force in an exploitive fashion, it would literally undermine their own justification, because it would subject citizens to precisely the sort of risks they were given special powers to prevent."[20]

Police must be held accountable for their use of coercive power, and that accountability needs to be to the general public and not simply to others in policing or law enforcement.[21] This is critical because the power and privilege to use coercive force is "owned by the public and loaned to police officers for specific reasons, and it must be exercised under specific conditions."[22]

In fact, under the democratic model of policing, one major function of the police is to guarantee citizens their rights.[23] Reiman stated "if law enforcement threatens rather than enhances our freedom, the distinction between crime and criminal justice is obliterated."[24]

Dunham and Alpert observed that some people given positions of power and authority "will begin to use that power and authority to exploit others."[25] This has been called the great dilemma of state.[26] The real challenge is "to have the state and keep it tame, or from exploiting its citizens."[27] This has been referred to as "the great dilemma in policing."[28]

The question has been asked, "How can we authorize a police force to maintain our safety, insure that our laws are obeyed, and keep officers from using that force illegitimately?"[29] Quinney noted that "a society is held together by force and constraint ... [that] values are ruling rather than common, enforced rather than accepted, at any given point in time."[30] Dunham and Alpert observed that "we need the police to have a civilized society, to insure safety from being harmed by insiders, and to make sure we contribute to other needed public goods."[31] Controlling the police is a prime factor when contrasting a police state to a democratic state.

> In a police state the citizens do not have adequate control over the police. The police are therefore able to use their monopoly on physical force to exploit citizens. In a democratic state, the people have maintained more control over the police, so that the police cannot exploit them.[32]

Regarding the manner in which police power was relegated, early policing in London depended upon strict organizational power, whereas, on the other hand, American policing turned on unofficial control or personal power. Said another way, American police brought into existence their own authority in their jurisdiction, rather than relying on the legitimacy of the establishment such as parliamentary law. "The personal, informal [American] police officer could win the respect of the citizenry by knowing local standards and expectations. This meant that different police behavior would occur in different neighborhoods."[33]

A DIFFERENT APPROACH TO GRATUITIES
AS AN INCIPIENT CORRUPTER

> Police officers out on the street have a perspective that directly influences how they apply morality, and they use the law to enhance that application.[34]

Most textbooks and training in police academies take the "Reefer Madness"[35] approach to police acceptance of gratuities. Just as "Reefer Madness" presented an unrealistic image of marijuana use, it is just as unrealistic to portray police acceptance of gratuities as the unequivocal first step on that slippery slope to greater levels of police corruption. We claim to have "zero tolerance" for police disregard of department regulations, except for acceptance of gratuities, as well as other police deviant and/or corrupt behavior. The disregard for enforcement of the anti-gratuity acceptance regulations is allowed despite the fact that two major investigations into police corruption, the Mollen Commission in New York and the investigation into the Rampart Division in Los Angeles, cited the danger of this practice. Added to this are the voices of reform-minded chiefs of police who have openly acknowledged the danger presented by police gratuity acceptance and their efforts to eradicate it.[36] We have "zero tolerance" marijuana use and seatbelt violations. Why do these restrictions exist? The answer is that violation of these tenets or laws could cause harm or lead to harm. With the awareness of the danger presented by the potentially corrupting and definitely the degrading practice of police acceptance of gratuities, why can we not have "zero tolerance" for police acceptance of gratuities?

One of the reasons offered by some police and academics is that there would be no way to stop it anyway. So why try? This seems to be a poor excuse. If the same position had been taken during the police professionalization movement, major corruption would still be rampant. Truth be told, it can be controlled, and there are police administrators involved in that fight.[37]

POLICE ECONOMIC CORRUPTION

Economic corruption in American policing and efforts at reform date back to the late 19th century.[38] Grafting and extortion were pervasive principal forms of corruption in the early 20th century. [39] Police officials accepted bribes to look the other way, allowing various racketeers to prosper. Graft was taken as payment for allowing prostitution, gambling, and illegal liquor sales.[40]

Established in 1893, the International Association of Chiefs of Police (IACP) has been a driving force in the professionalization and reform of American policing. Considered foremost in this effort was exercising control of street officers.[41] To this cause, they established the International Association of Chiefs of Police (IACP) Law Enforcement Code of Ethics.[42] The Code is not silent on the topic of police acceptance of gratuities.

> I will never act officiously or permit personal feelings, prejudices, political beliefs, aspirations, animosities or friendships to influence my decisions. With no compromise for crime and with relentless prosecution of criminals, I will enforce the law courteously and appropriately without fear or favor, malice or ill will, never employing unnecessary force or violence and never accepting gratuities.[43]

Ordinarily, when this section of the Code is cited, attention is paid only to the phrase "never accepting gratuities." Indeed, the first line of the Code vows that the officer will not "permit personal feelings ... or friendships to influence my decisions." We suggest that personal feelings, friendships, and police indebtedness develops between police officers and givers of gratuities because of the shear magnitude and frequency represented by the annual amount received. It is difficult to imagine how a police officer could accept daily gratuities from merchants and employees of merchants that amount to thousands of dollars annually without establishing personal feelings, friendships, and indebtedness to them.

It was the experience of one of the authors that merchants and employees of merchants who gave gratuities to the police were quick to remind him of their generosity when stopped for a traffic violation or some minor infraction of the law. At the very least, the givers of gratuities expected to be treated with deference when it came to answering calls for service. Police officers who espouse otherwise are either being less than honest or they worked in cities with loving philanthropists.

PUTTING THE "SQUEEZE" ON RECALCITRANT
BUSINESS OWNERS WHO REFUSE TO "POP"

Police officers across the United States have created an "argot" or police lexicon that is foreign to persons not in police circles. "Much police argot revolves around (1) citations to the penal law, (2) words and phrases that are coded and phrased so that they can be heard without ambiguity over a radio, and (3) criminal and street jargon laced liberally with obscenities."[44] For example, attempts have been made to beatify police acceptance of gratuities by claiming that it is a way for persons in the business community to pay the debt they perceive they owe to police officers for doing their job.[45]

If police officers possessed the same reverence for the exchange that this implies, it would seem that the transaction would be approached in a respectful and humble manner. This is not the case. Locations that provide gratuities for the police are said to "show love," or, more commonly, "pop."[46] When referring to locations that are reluctant to provide gratuities, officers say they "badge" their way to a price break, "flex muscle" or wear the "blue discount suit."[47] It was one author's experience that police officers rarely went for coffee or lunch to places other than those that provided free or discounted coffee and food. In police slang, "If you got not pop, you got no cop."[48] Aside from the numerous restaurants in the French Quarter and Central Business District that "showed love," all fast-food restaurants recognized the "blue discount suit."[49]

IT'S TIME TO TEACH THIS ASSHOLE A LESSON

When one of the authors graduated from the police academy, the concept of "field training officers" had not been instituted. Field training was something you received from whomever you happened to be riding with at the time. As the "extra man," he was assigned to a two-man car whenever one of the regular officers assigned to that car was off, sick, or on vacation. He was once assigned to an officer for two weeks because the regular partner was on vacation. One day they stopped for lunch at a small restaurant bordering the Central Business District and the French Quarter. His partner, an older officer, had always taken him to places where the meals were either free or half-price. He was kind enough to let the author know what the situation was before going in. This particular restaurant, he said, was free.

At the end of lunch, the owner came to the table with a bill. He told them he was sorry, but that he could no longer give free lunch to the police. The older officer's face turn to stone as the owner walked away. Looking back on it now, it is easy to see that two dynamics had come into play. First, the owner had embarrassed the older officer in the presence of a rookie. Second, it was a slap in the face and a challenge to the older officer. The bill was paid and not a word said. However, once in the police car the older officer said, "It's time to teach this asshole a lesson." Turning to the rookie [me], he said, "We'll deal with this tomorrow."

The restaurant was very popular not only for walk-ins but for others who drove. One of the biggest headaches in the Business District/French Quarter is finding a place to park legally on the street. This restaurant, like most others in the area, was surrounded by freight zones, crosswalks, and fire hydrants. In short, there wasn't a legal place to park for blocks. Customers had taken to parking in freight zones, crosswalks and too close to fire hydrants because it was commonly known that the police did not give parking tickets near this restaurant. That changed.

The following day the author and the older officer issued over 12 parking citations to vehicles illegally parked near the restaurant. It was not known if the owners of the cited vehicles were, in fact, in the restaurant. However, the older officer explained to the author, "We won't have to get many." The following day another ten citations were issued in the same location. The next day at roll call, the older officer was given a message to stop by the restaurant and see the owner. When we arrived, the owner came out to our car. However, instead of an angry tirade, the owner apologized for what he called a "misunderstanding" and asked us to please come in and eat in his restaurant any time—free.

It has been noted that "noble-cause corruption" can take various shapes. One of the forms is called the "magic pencil."[50]

> The magic pencil is a form of noble-cause corruption in which police officers write up an incident in a way that criminalizes a suspect. It is a powerful tool for punishment, and in the hands of a value-based decisionmaker—and that's what police are—it carries the weight of the United States' massive criminal justice system. It proves the maxim that the pen is mightier than the sword.[51]

One needs only follow the daily news to keep abreast of the latest scandals in which police officers have lied under oath, tampered with evidence, or participated in a host of other violations. Should we be surprised when that same "magic pencil" is used to show an "asshole" restaurant owner the error of his ways?

AND THEN THERE WAS BARRY

Barry[52] owned a small restaurant and bar located in the heart of the "wino section." He was a good businessman and to my knowledge was as straight as they come. Many police officers who worked in the district ate and drank at Barry's and always for half-price. Barry was also located close enough to federal and city office buildings to bring in a heavy lunch crowd. Despite the downtown location, his food was known to be very good and reasonably priced. Although he never said it, Barry wanted only one thing from the police in exchange for discounted food and drink. He wanted the phone number for the straight line into the district station, a privilege given to a select few who "pop" for the police. He did not want to have to wait for his turn for service.

Barry learned long ago that when he called the Communications Division at headquarters he received slow response. By providing police officers half-price food and drink, he was given access to the district desk sergeant's direct line. If a problem were to arise and police officers were not in the business to handle the situation (which was a rare occasion), he would call directly to the station and the desk sergeant would put out the call immediately. The response was also immediate. Why? Because we felt obligated to someone who "liked" the police. So what's the bottom line?

The bottom line is the simple fact that good business people do not give away profit without a motive. The motive for Barry was simple. He wanted police around (1) to show the uniform in his businesses, which were open 24 hours, (2) because of the neighborhood, and (3) if no officer was on scene when needed, one would come immediately when he called. And on those occasions when he did call, response time could be counted in seconds, and it was common for multiple cars to respond.

MEET "BROTHER GASTON"

The first Christmas after one of the author's graduated from the police academy, he was introduced to "Brother Gaston."[53] Brother Gaston managed a handful of seedy, but not illegal, strip clubs that operated outside of the French Quarter. During the year leading up to Christmas, he had answered calls at Brother Gaston's clubs on numerous occasions. At Christmas time, Brother Gaston would put in a call to the station telling the desk sergeant to have all of the officers assigned to the district to pass by for their Christmas present.

There was a corridor in the back that connected all of the bars, and Brother Gaston's office was in that corridor. On top of his desk was a pile of $50 bills, and as each officer entered, Brother Gaston would give them a $50 bill and say "Merry Christmas." Then the officers were directed to the liquor closet and told to take whatever they desired.

Fifty dollars and a bottle of Wild Turkey would be considered a sizeable Christmas present even by today's economy, much less in 1968. But should the police have declined Brother Gaston's present simply on the basis that he ran seedy strip clubs? Would not the positive community relations created by Brother Gaston's indebtedness to the police[54] be in jeopardy if that gift were refused?

As the years passed, I watched fellow officers perfect the art of "mooching" at Christmas time. Their technique was to walk into bars and say loudly, "Ho, ho, ho. Merry Christmas." This was a clear hint to the owner that the officers were there to collect their presents. It became a game or competition between officers to see which car could bring in the most. The winner was a team who received over 50 bottles of liquor on one shift. Naturally, any cash gifts remained untold.

SHERMAN'S SLIPPERY SLOPE INDIVIDUAL-LEVEL CORRUPTION

> The slippery-slope metaphor recognizes the importance of police peers in encouraging corruption and the role played by the secretive elements of police culture. The slippery-slope argument resonates well in the moral environment of policing—it allows problems of corruption to be conceptualized in terms of personal responsibility and moral weakness.[55] (p. 67)

Sherman's slippery slope metaphor holds that after an officer engages in minor illegal or corrupt behavior, greater levels by that police officer become easier to perform.[56] "The officer has learned how to rationalize illegal and inappropriate behavior and can rationalize more serious wrongdoing."[57] Sherman described slippery slope corruption as "becoming bent."[58] However, it would be incorrect to claim that all officers become bent.[59] Only in those locales where "grafting subcultures"[60] are already engaging in some form of economic corruption will this take hold.[61] "Grafting subcultures are groups or cohorts of officers who are already 'bent' and they socialize new officers into corrupt activities."[62] An example of one such grafting subculture can be found in the scenario presented by Kania,[63] a then-NYPD training officer. He told of how he intentionally brought a rookie officer to establishments that gave gratuities even though he knew that the young officer did not want to accept gratuities. He continued this activity until on one occasion the rookie was called an "asshole" by the owner of an eating establishment in the presence of Kania and anyone else within earshot.[64]

> The argumentative officer was called an "ass-hole" to his face and, in my opinion, had earned the label for his rigid refusal to accept an inconsequential discount. In the few months left of that inflexible but ethical officer's appropriately short, difficult, but uncorrupted, police career, he found it necessary to bring a bag lunch and eat in the car while his "corrupted" partners ate at discount in neighborhood eateries.[65]

Although this may seem a matter of little consequence to some, others note that this ritual indoctrination of gratuity acceptance by rookie police officers has a more insidious purpose. It is called "The Mama Rosa's Test."[66]

THE MAMA ROSA'S TEST

> A new recruit and his training officer are eating at Mama Rosa's cafe. Soon they are joined by other officers. At the end of the meal, they prepare to leave; the rookie has his money in his hand and asks how much should he leave. The veterans tell the rookie to shut up and put his money away. It seems the cops have been eating free forever and the place has never been held up, unlike other restaurants in the neighborhood. Mama Rosa is very appreciative of this. The rookie insists that he wants to pay for the meal, but he is told to shut up and not jeopardize a good thing.

> Here is the test. If the rookie goes along, he is tainted. He loses his virginity. If he doesn't play ball at Mama Rosa's, he won't be trusted as a team player. If he does, his next step is to test him in the field. This might include dropsy testimony, or backing up another officer in court that makes an honest mistake by supporting his partner's version of events. This is how it happens. A test at the restaurant, then a test in the field.[67]

The Mama Rosa's Test boils down to a test of a rookie's loyalty to brother and sister officers, and it serves as a first measure of his or her willingness to violate departmental rules and regulations. Gilmartin noted that "[L]oyalty becomes more important than integrity."[68] Kania provided an excellent example of what happens to officers who do not pass the Mama Rosa's Test.[69]

Crank and Caldero's slippery slope notion corresponds to Sherman's slippery-slope concept of economic corruption but with two notable distinctions.

> 1. First, the test is not intended to prepare the rookie for a "grafting subculture." It's a test of his loyalty to the group. Recall that Mama Rosa is appreciative of what the police do. There is no extortion involved. If Mama Rosa has not been burglarized, although the surrounding restaurants have been burglarized, then the police are preventing crime by eating at Mama Rosa's. They are doing a moral good.

> 2. The second test involves supporting another officer's version of events. Again, it's a loyalty test. Note that the second test has two components. The first is loyalty: Will the rookie go along when the stakes are raised? The second is the good-end: Officers are trying to do something about crime. That is, it involves a commitment to the noble cause. What the second test shows us is that police loyalty to each other and commitment to the noble cause are intertwined phenomena. It's part of the reason that police

will protect each other with such passion. Their beliefs and their loyalty are linked together. The brotherhood (sisterhood) is familial, a bond of loyalty and morality.[70]

Crank and Caldero's model of slippery slope corruption is similar to Sherman's. However, it varies in modest but significant ways. They describe the stages as follows:

1. *Free meals.* This is not to test willingness to graft but whether an officer is going to be loyal to other officers in the squad. This is the Mama Rosa's Test.

2. *Loyalty backup.* Here, an officer is tested to see if he or she will back up other officers. This is more involved because officers may have to "testily" (give false testimony), dropsy (removing drugs from a suspect during a pat-down and then discover them in plain sight on the ground) [Or retain them for encounters with "assholes" or known drug dealers or habitual criminals and "discover" the contraband on them.], the shake (similar to dropsy, only conducted during vehicle stops), or stiffing a call (When police officers call up and report a crime as if a citizen had seen one. Used to justify unlawful searches).

3. *Physical violence against citizens.* This is more serious because an officer who is violent against a citizen risks death, injury, citizen retaliation, or leaving marks that are traceable and thus provide evidence of violent police behavior.

4. *Flaking drugs.* This is a much more serious form of noble-cause corruption. In this example, cops add drugs to create a more serious crime, or they plant drugs on someone to make a case. Though some police may get involved in this, it is not very common. It is more serious because cops have to be engaged in ongoing crime—carrying narcotics—in order to commit these acts. Cops engaged in flaking drugs consequently tend to have small loyalty cohorts.[71] (p. 74)

Crank and Caldero hold that noble-cause corruption and economic corruption are intimately connected to one another. "Once started, a police officer may move back and forth across the two lines."[72] Also connected to "noble-cause corruption" are police cynicism,[73] noble-cause violence,[74] and the "Dirty Harry" problem.[75]

NOBLE CAUSE CORRUPTION

[Noble cause corruption] is corruption committed in the name of good ends, corruption that happens when police officers care too much about their work. It is corruption committed in order to get the bad guys off the streets, to protect the innocent and the children from the predators that inflict pain and suffering on them. It is the corruption of police power, when officers do bad things because they believe that the outcomes will be good.[76]

What has long been portrayed as the innocent acceptance of gratuities by police has much more serious undertones than previously realized. Economic corruption differs from noble cause corruption, yet they are alike in other ways. Economic or material reward corruption has been defined as, "whatever the officer receives through the misuse of his or her authority ... some tangible object, either cash, services, or goods that have cash value."[77]

Whereas material or economic corruption results in personal aggrandizement, noble-cause corruption has its roots in individual standards of righteousness. We believe, as do others,[78] that a relationship exists between noble-cause corruption and economic or material-reward corruption.

Police accountability has long been the aim of police reformers. "Men and women who are police officers have absolutely no identity or power as police officers outside the law. Police officers are creatures of law, their powers are described and limited by law, and if they operate outside the law, they become criminals just as everyone else and should be punished."[79]

Noble-cause corruption offers police officers an alternative method of viewing the police/law relationship. Officers acting under the guise and defense of noble-cause corruption engage their personal standards of morality when enforcing the law. In essence, they believe their actions to be on a moral plane that exists above the law. They are no longer law enforcers. Instead, they become lawmakers who twist and distort the law to fit their own moral criterion.

> If the police act on their own moral predispostions in pursuit of good ends, then whatever they do must be good itself. In such an ethical environment, efforts to control the behavior of police are viewed as disloyal. If police are the law, what they do must be right. If they accept a free dinner in order to safeguard a restaurant, it is because society owes it to them. If they mistreat suspects, it is because they are above the law, and suspects get what they deserve.

We hold that noble-cause corruption becomes a portal for economic- or material-reward corruption and vise versa. "Where noble-cause corruption flourishes, material-reward corruption cannot be far behind."[80]

> It is our belief that noble-cause corruption is a more widespread and significant problem today than economic corruption in American police departments, and that noble-cause corruption is increasing in United States police organizations today.[81]

POLICE AUTHORITY AND DISCRETION

> In a formal sense the police are authorized to enforce the law, and only to enforce the law. More specifically, they are required to enforce the law at all times and in every case. Yet there are so many laws, and so many violations of them, that the police are compelled to set priorities about which laws to enforce and which violations to overlook. In this sense, the police are given discretion in their role as law enforcers to choose from several options regarding how and when to enforce *particular laws* [authors' emphasis].[82]

> Unchecked authority operating in an ethical vacuum is a central component of all police corruption.[83]

The law enforcement aspect of policing can range between 5%[84] to 19%[85] of what police officers actually do. Their primary responsibility is to maintain order and keep the peace. In this role, police officers are granted wide-ranging discretion in how they perform these duties.[86]

That police officers possess authority and the discretion of when and if to exercise that authority requires application of good judgment because policing is fraught with ethical dilemmas.

Most people are influenced by personal feelings, be they good or bad. Police officers are no different, but they must be constantly on guard that their personal feelings do not interfere with the discharge of their duty. "Officers have to ask themselves whether their choices are influenced by prejudice or hostile personal feelings toward some individuals or members of a group; whether their actions are motivated by a sense of duty, personal gain, or mere convenience."[87] What it boils down to is fundamental fairness. Police officers are obliged to treat "similarly situated people in similar ways."[88] But are those eating and drinking establishments that provide gratuities treated equally when it comes to police coverage and police presence?

ENTITLEMENT

One of the central traits to values deterioration is the development of a culture of perceived "entitlement."[89]

Entitlement is the manner in which some police officers explain away and self-vindicate inappropriate conduct. The view that preferred treatment or exemptions should be given embodies entitlement. "Entitlement can take many forms and can appear at initial review to be a relatively benign issue. Closer scrutiny can demonstrate the essential malignant nature of entitlement."[90]

Entitlement is the notion that because a person is a police officer, special rights are part of the job. Policing is an authority-based system with an almost limitless possibility to abuse that authority, and it demands unwavering attentiveness to prevent abuse of that authority. This mindset can produce a belief that "you owe us cops for all we put up with on the streets to serve and protect you."[91]

When values are discussed in policing circles, oftentimes the philosophy of entitlement is omitted. When police acceptance of gratuities is addressed without addressing entitlement, it sidesteps the more central question of the possible impact of police gratuity acceptance and its impact on basic police values. Preaching abstinence of gratuities and the notion of the "slippery slope" to experienced police officers will usually be greeted with snickering and closed minds.

On the other hand, discussing entitlement affords police officers the knowledge key to discern "independent values-based decisions."[92] A discussion of this nature allows examination of whether the free or discounted meal is an innocent assertion of appreciation or represents a conditional gratuity such as, "if I keep the cops in my restaurant the added security is good for business."[93] Over and above the provision of security for the business, police administrators should examine whether the free or discounted meals produce a conviction in their officers that the standard of accountability applied to the general citizenry does not apply to the police.

Discounting of basic values is relatively easy for those officers assigned to some not-so-savory beats. "What harm is there in accepting a free meal compared to the carnage these suspects at my last call just dealt to society?" or "Because of all the garbage we put up with on the streets, what's the big deal about a little speeding or a free meal?"[94] is an easy way for officers to rationalize entitlement to gratuities.

"Entitlement is the precursor belief that leads to wrongful acts ranging from minor to felonious."[95] Police administrators are also recognizing the danger of entitlement in police acceptance of gratuities.[96]

FEAR OR RESPECT?

The questions in the minds of many police officers accepting gratuities are usually, "What does this guy want?" and "Am I willing to go the distance, or will he or she ask for too much?" Regrettably, the only time that police officers learn the answers to these questions and discover the true motive(s) of the givers is when the giver calls in their marker. It is at this point that officers must decide just how far they are willing to go.

In the classroom, one of the authors brings up the proposition heard quite so often that "People do not respect police officers anymore." The question propounded to the students was whether respect is the true emotion of this proposition, or is there another word that is more appropriate for the feeling that many citizens have toward police officers? The example given in class concerns a person driving on an interstate highway exceeding the speed limit when suddenly a police vehicle is seen on the median of the highway. The statement is then made that the students would slow their vehicles out of respect for the police officer. Invariably, laughter will erupt as they admit that they slow down out of fear and not respect. We suggest that it is entirely possible that some givers of gratuities may do so out of fear of what might occur if they do not, or for fear that they will experience a repeat negative episode with police officers.

Said another way, givers bestow gratuities out of fear of how they may be treated if the flow of gratuities is interrupted or how their business might be affected if they do not give the gratuities that police officers have come to expect. As demonstrated earlier, one of the most potent weapons in the fear-generating arsenal of any police officer is the "magic pencil" and the ticket book. Indeed, there exists no greater soft underbelly for merchants than for their customers to come and go without fear of receiving a parking citation.

For police officers wishing to "convince" a recalcitrant merchant that gratuities would be in his or her best interest, it is not necessary to target his or her business directly. A better strategy is to "hang paper" [police terminology for writing tickets] in an area close to the targeted business. This way the owner would get the message indirectly, and the officers are simply citing violators. The effectiveness of this tactic has already been demonstrated. A gratuity given out of fear is not a gift. It is tribute or extortion.

GRATUITIES, EXPLOITATION, OR EXTORTION?

Precisely because police have wide-ranging authority and the latitude to exercise it in relatively unsupervised ways, they also have ample opportunity to exploit their authority.[97]

Policing is a most unique occupation. It is rare to find a job that offers such a high degree of authority, power, and autonomy. When an officer leaves the station to begin a tour of duty supervision, what there is of it, consists of the sergeant or lieutenant monitoring radio transmissions and the occasional encounter on the street. In such an environment, the potential to exploit their authority, power, and autonomy is omnipresent.[98]

The degree to which police officers take advantage of their power and autonomy to engage in serious economic crime is a matter of conjecture. However, it has been noted that "there is scarcely an officer in uniform who has not taken a free cup of coffee or a discounted meal."[99] Clearly, a free cup of coffee or a discounted or free meal taken only *once* could hardly be considered exploitation. Therefore, we must define exploitation. Exploitation has been characterized as follows:

> Acting on opportunities, created by virtue of one's authority, for personal gain at the expense of the public one is authorized to serve. The elements of exploitation then are:

> - A position of authority
> - An opportunity for personal gain created by that position
> - A causal relationship between the gain and the cost[100]

Cohen (1986) noted that the three conditions listed above exist when a police officer accepts free coffee or a free or discounted meal.[101]

Some police chiefs have staked out the position that acceptance of a free cup of coffee is equal to taking a television from a department store,[102] and there is a growing chorus of top police executives who are taking an active role in discouraging police gratuity acceptance.[103]

Generally, it is not uncommon for officers who decline gratuities (Yes, they do exist), not to criticize other officers who do. Cohen points out that officers who decline gratuities do not view the action as a moral dilemma. "From their point of view, if taking free coffee is a sin at all, it is an extremely minor sin."[104]

The question we raise is whether police acceptance of gratuities should be classified as exploitation of police authority. Cohen recognized this when he wrote, "This issue is important not as a way to encourage us to condemn the free cup of coffee but to understand what it is about the exploitation of authority that makes it a violation of our moral sensibilities."[105]

In all instances when police officers accept gratuities, the opportunity to do so exists only because of the authority possessed by the police. Cohen noted:

> It is the authority to investigate crimes, keep public order, write traffic citations, and protect merchants that creates the opportunities for "taking." Thus, it is not merely taking, but the taking *in an official capacity*. This feature is an important element of exploitation.[106]

Clearly, the term "exploitation" implies a grave moral violation, and some may deem it unsuitable for police acceptance of gratuities. The argument presented by most officers attempting to justify the taking is usually accompanied by the claim "that the police do not behave any differently toward those who offer the gratuities than they do toward other citizens."[107] This was not the experience of the gratuity-taking author. In fact, there was always a feeling of indebtedness toward givers even if they were an employee. Nearly all other police officers observed by the gratuity-taking author reacted in the same fashion.

BLINDED BY THE "FREEBIE"

It was one author's experience that gratuities were such a part of the policing landscape that no real attention was paid to the departmental regulation their prohibition. But is it possible that the practice can become so common or "inconsequential" that a potential violation of law goes unnoticed? In the following scenario, Kania describes an encounter with a short-order cook.

> I tried to argue the short-order cook out of giving me a free meal on a night-watch. The cook would have none of it and refused payment. I even reminded the cook that the owner only gave a percentage discount. In response, the cook replied that the owner did not work the midnight crowd, and had a lot less to be grateful to the police for. The short-order cook was grateful to the police; he felt that he was in a state of indebtedness to the police. The gratuities were not gifts given in expectation of future rewards, but, as Leach had explained, in repayment of the debt already owed by the late night cook.[108]

This is a prime example of how habit/custom and entitlement can seduce those with authority power and authority. Both the short-order cook and Kania knew that the owner discounted food to the police by 50%. Yet, the cook took no payment for the meal because of his "indebtedness" to the police. Was not the cook giving away that which was not his to give? If the answer is yes, then did not the cook commit a theft from his employer? Knowing that the cook was giving what was not his to give, did Kania not become the receiver/consumer of the fruit of this theft? Although we are certain Kania would not intentionally become a party to a violation of law, was this not the case? Therein lies the danger. Officers become blinded to a violation of law by what appears on the surface a genuine display of gratitude.

AT WHAT PRICE A "FREEBIE?"

When discussion occurs about police acceptance of gratuities, the focus is usually about free coffee, sodas, or a free or discounted meal. Rarely has the discussion been framed in the context of a portion of a police officer's annual income. Cohen once suggested that "The value of what is taken in the gratuity cases can mount up as well. If value alone determined the seriousness of taking gratuities, we might end up with an equation of 400 cups of coffee to the television sets."[109] Indeed, our contention is that the annual take of common police gratuities could reach between $8,000 to $10,000 or more.

One of the authors actively engaged in the acceptance of police gratuities. During that period, NOPD salary was very low. In fact, were it not for gratuities in the way of food and cigarettes, there was always "too much month at the end of the money."[110] Table 16.1 contains the dollar amount of gratuities that were commonly taken equivalent to 2003 prices.

The cost of the various gratuities was calculated on a 50-week work year and an 8-hour 7:00 AM–3:00 PM shift. The coffee/soda was calculated on the assumption of two breaks per 8-hour shift. It was the experience of one author that a great deal more was consumed during a shift. But for the purposes of this chapter we will adhere to the standard breaks. We will also suggest an average of $1.00 per coffee or soda despite the fact that most "designer coffees" may cost three to four times as much. Two cups of coffee or two sodas purchased 247 times would cost $494.00. It

TABLE 16.1
List of Common Gratuities

Gratuities	Cost per Use	Number of Times Spent per Year	Annual Cost
Coffee/soda	$1.00 per day	494	$494.00
Doughnuts	3 @ .60 = $1.80 per day	247	$444.60
Lunch	$6.00	247	$1,482.00
Cigarettes	$3.85	520	$2,002.00
Alcohol	4 @ $6.00	416	$2,496.00
Laundry	3 pants @ $11.75	50	$587.50
	5 shirts @ $7.50	50	$375.00
Movie theater	$8.00	104	$832.00
Total annual gratuities	**$8,713.10**		

was commonly held that there was no need in paying for something when it could be obtained free; hence, it was always the habit to wait until the shift began to have breakfast. Doughnuts were a natural with the morning coffee and three could be consumed easily. Krispy Kreme doughnuts, considered the standard by most connoisseurs of the pastry sciences, cost about 60 cents. Three doughnuts costing $1.80 multiplied by 247 days totals $444.60.

Working in the French Quarter/Business District allowed access to many high-priced restaurants and hotels whose managers/owners were happy to welcome uniformed officers for lunch. Needless to say, lunch would be quite costly. Instead of calculating the cost of these meals, we will suggest that a modest lunch could be purchased for an average of $6.00. A $6.00 lunch purchased 247 times in a year would total $1,482.00.

The author was a smoker who averaged about a pack and a half a day, or roughly a carton of cigarettes per week. In order to acquire enough to last a week including days off, it was necessary to visit several different "Stop-N-Rob" [convenience] stores because it wasn't considered good form to get more than one pack per day from each one. If possible, every effort was made to show up every other day. Because of the variation of cigarette prices across the United States, we have chosen a $3.85[111] cost per pack. Smoking one carton a week would cost $38.50. That multiplied by 52 weeks totals $2,002.00.

Whether on- or off-duty, finding free alcohol was never a problem in New Orleans, particularly in the French Quarter. At my last duty station, there was one bar that served on- or off-duty officers all the alcohol they wanted at no charge. In establishing the cost and amount, we asked classes of criminal justice students three questions. First, "What type of alcohol would the average person drink if price was no object?" Second, "How many drinks would the average person order per night out if price was no object?" Third, "How many times per week would the average person frequent an establishment that provided free alcohol?"

Most students indicated they would order mixed drinks, if they did not have to pay for them. As most mixed drinks cost between $5.00 to $8.00, we settled at

TABLE 16.2

Gratuities as a Portion of an Officer's Annual Salary

Total annual gratuities	$8,713.10
Tax & benefits on total @ 30%	$2,613.93
Total gratuity gross income	$11,327.03
National police officer gross salary	$34, 556.00
Percentage of annual salary	33%
Weekly gratuity take	$217.83
Monthly gratuity take	$943.92

$6.00 per drink. When asked how many drinks they would consume each outing if they were free, most responded three to five. We chose the median of four drinks per night. In answering the third question, many students responded "every night!" Although this might be the case for some, we chose a more conservative frequency of two nights a week. Four mixed drinks at $6.00 each amount to $24.00. Going out twice a week per year totals 104 multiplied by $24.00 is $2,496.00.

Finding a laundry that provided free dry cleaning was never a problem. Conservatively averaging the cleaning of three pairs of uniform pants at $11.75 and five shirts at $7.50 per week by 50 weeks totals $962.50.

Free entry into most movie theaters requires only that police identification be presented which usually admitted the officer and his or her significant other. Most first-run theaters cost about $8.00, and the students indicated that they would go on average twice a week totaling $16.00. Sixteen dollars multiplied by 52 weeks totals $832.00. It should be noted that this estimate does not take into account free admission to special events such as football and basketball games. Nor does it account for special needs items like tires, general auto repair, prescription glasses, etc. Clearly, the total amount is much higher than this conservative estimate represents.

Without a doubt, gratuities significantly increase a police officer's annual income. Table 16.2 lists the total annual gratuities, the average salary of a police officer in the United States, the percentage of the officer's annual salary accounted for by gratuities, and the weekly and monthly take for gratuities.

The total annual gratuities for the average police officer is multiplied by 30% to determine the additional income necessary to net $8,713.10. These two figures are summed to arrive at the total gross income. With an average national police gross salary of $34,556, the total gross gratuity income increases the gross salary over 33% to $45,883.03. The reader is reminded that the gratuities listed are those most commonly accepted and by no means represents an exhaustive list. Considering other gratuities accepted for auto parts or repairs, equipment rentals, sporting events, eyeglasses, etc., gross gratuity income could easily reach 40% or more of a police officer's annual salary. When viewed in this light, it is difficult to understand how police acceptance of gratuities can be classed as a minor inconsequential infraction of the rules best left unenforced or ignored.

ARE GRATUITIES "DOUBLE DIPPING?"

Another disturbing aspect of the "security" arrangement between police officers and merchants is double dipping. Few, if any, police departments require their officers to take lunch or coffee breaks so as they are "off the clock." Said another way, when officers take coffee or lunch breaks, they are still on the department payroll. However, during this same time period their concurrent roles of public police officers and providers of private security to a single business, sets up a situation in which they are being compensated by two separate entities. There can be little doubt that their acceptance of gratuities constitutes payment for their presence in the business. This being the case, these officers are being paid twice, once by the department and once by the merchant.

This raises serious questions as to the equitable delivery as well as distribution of police services to *all* citizens. Indeed, the question might be raised as to the merchants who do not feel this compelling desire to demonstrate gratitude and indebtedness. Are they not being denied access to these "special services" simply on the basis of their failure to experience the epiphany of overwhelming desire to express their undying gratitude and indebtedness?

Considering the amount taken annually in gratuities, might it not set up conflict of interests if it came to a matter of providing services to the public or the merchant? In this dual role as public servant and private protector, Barlow asks, "When police officers serve private interests, will they also be as diligent, professional, and alert in serving public interests?"[112] Asked another way, how can we be certain that police officers will administer the law fairly in a situation involving a dispute between a citizen and the giver of a gratuity?

DISCUSSION

Police corrupt behavior appears to be an on-going theme in the news media. For example, there have been six major investigations in New York alone since 1994.[113] Between April 1994 and March 1995, four New Orleans police officers were charged with murder in four separate cases, and between January 1, 1993, and June 30, 1994, 19 New Orleans police officers received lesser criminal charges. [114] In Florida, 15 Miami police officers implicated in the Miami River case were charged with drug sales, home invasions, robbing motorists, and conspiring to murder witnesses.[115] And these are not isolated cases.

Across the nation, police deviant and corrupt behavior has been reported in Atlanta, Boston, Chicago, Detroit, Indianapolis, Los Angeles, Minneapolis, New Orleans, New York, Philadelphia, Portland, Providence, San Francisco, and Washington, D.C.,[116] just to name a few. Is it logical to conclude that major police deviant and corrupt behavior blossoms in full flower completely devoid of any mode of progression? Can we accept the premise that police officers begin corrupt careers by dealing drugs, robbing citizens, and committing murder? Is that the way persons not in policing begin criminal careers?

Having had the opportunity to view numerous criminal records, it was the experience of one author that the vast majority of criminal careers began with petty offenses and progressed steadily to major offenses: The Slippery Slope. Most police officers as well as persons working in criminal justice will generally agree that this is the usual mode of progression. This being so, why should it be any different for police officers?

CONCLUSION

At times the best contribution a philosopher can make to the debate on an important public issue is to express the problems clearly enough so that discussion can progress. This is particularly true when the issue has become mired in cliches that push our thinking down the same roads to the same dead ends. Not that philosophers have nothing substantive to contribute to such debates; we, too, have solutions to propose and defend. But on some issues no one (philosophers included) will make much progress until we stop trading the conventional wisdom that passes for solutions and reconsider the way in which we have posed the problem.[117]

The bottom line is that there is no free lunch. Nor is the acceptance of gratuities by police officers a minor affair when it can account for 30% or more of their annual income. Whenever businesspersons cut into their profit margin by giving systematic gratuities to anyone, there must exist substantial motivation to do so. When police officers take gratuities, they know that there is an ulterior motive to the giving. However, when the annual take represents such a significant amount of an officer's annual salary, can the practice be considered minor and inconsequential?

Regrettably, gratuities are not given with the best interests of police officers in mind, but rather in the best interest of the giver. Nor are they given because of any overwhelming feeling of indebtedness merchants have to the police. If we buy into the "Lake Woebegone" of concept of indebtedness or gratitude, then we would fail to face the real and true nature of what nearly all police gratuities represent.

Can we be so cavalier as to arbitrarily dismiss the logical progression from minor gratuity to major corruption? The claim is boldly made that marijuana is a gateway drug, and although not everyone will progress to more potent addictive drugs, the position of the U. S. government is "zero tolerance." This position is taken despite the fact that the government is well aware that those who merely experiment with or are only occasional marijuana users will not progress to more dangerous and addictive drugs.

Yet, in light of the Mollen Commission findings and the investigation into the Los Angeles Rampart Division Scandal, both of which cited the danger of police acceptance of gratuities, most police administrators, some academics, and some police-turned-academics continue to maintain the position that gratuity acceptance is of no consequence and should be left to the officers themselves to decide whether or not to (1) take a gratuity and (2) have the clairvoyance to divine the motive of the giver as benign.

It is our position that we must take the responsibility to protect our police officers even if it is to protect them from themselves. We would not allow anyone we truly cared about to engage in an activity that could cause them serious harm. Friends do not let friends drive drunk. When intoxicated persons makes the decision to drive, those individuals believe that they are up to the task. Do all drunk drivers become involved in traffic accidents? Although it is difficult to discern what percent of the population has driven over the legal limit, would it not be safe to say that the number is substantial? Despite the fact that many operate vehicles while over the legal limit and do not injure themselves or anyone else, we prohibit such behavior because of the potential for injury and loss of life.

It has been recognized that police acceptance of gratuities can and does occur under circumstances when the giver does have ulterior motives, and the officer(s) receiving such gratuities are aware of these motives yet take the gratuities anyway. By knowingly allowing such exchanges to occur, are we not failing to fulfill our obligation to protect our officers even as they protect us?

We send our young officers out with no real understanding of the gravity of their authority and minimal concepts of ethics or knowledge of the true nature of the temptations with which they will be faced. We expect them to be paragons of virtue while often toiling in the midst of the worst society has to offer. We do little to prepare them for this or to impress upon them the sacred trust bestowed upon them and how important the exercise of that authority is. Attempting to wrap this corrupt and evil practice in a cloak of moral, ethical, and philosophical respectability would be the same as a painter applying fresh paint to wood known to be infested with termites inside.

ENDNOTES

1   Richard Kania, Should we tell the police to say "yes" to gratuities? 7 *Criminal Justice Ethics* 37–49 (1988).
2   Larry Gaines, Victor E. Kappeler, & J.B. Vaughn, *Policing in America*, 1997., Clemens Bartollas & Larry D. Hahn, *Policing in America,* 1999., Kenneth J. Peak, *Policing America*, 1997., Samuel Walker, *The Police in America*, 1999., Larry Miller & Michael Braswell, *Human Relations and Police Work,* 1993., Robert Trojanowitz, Victor E. Kappeler, Larry K. Gaines, & Bonnie Buequeroux, *Community Policing: A Contemporary Perspective*, 1998., Hill, Dean Champion, & George Rush, *Policing the Community*, 1997., Herman Goldstein, *Problem-Oriented Policing*, 1990., Randy L. Lagrange, *Policing American Society*, 1993., Robert H. Langworthy & Lawrence P. Travis, *Policing in America: A Balance of Forces*, 1999., Victor E. Kappeler, Richard D. Sluder, & Geoffrey P. Alpert, *Forces of Deviance: Understanding the Dark Side of Policing*, 1998.
3   Walker, supra note 2, at 28. According to the dominant school of thought, professional status consists of three basic dimensions: professional knowledge, professional autonomy, and the service ideal. A profession is characterized by a complex and esoteric body of knowledge capable of being codified and applied to social problems. Professionals are then experts who have mastered that body of knowledge through intensive training. Professionals hold a monopoly on the right to use their expertise and to exclude others from dealing with their area of interest. Professional autonomy comes with monopoly status: they assume the responsibility for not only maintaining standards of performance, but also for generating new knowledge in the field. In return for their monopoly power, professionals commit themselves to a service ideal. Their activities are not directed toward self-gain but toward the interests of their clients and the general public".
4   http://faculty.ncwc.edu/toconnor/205/205lect11.htm

5   Bartollas & Hahn, *supra* note 2, D.L. Carter, *Drug-Related Corruption of Police Officers: A Con-temporary Typology,* 18 *Journal of Criminal Justice* 85–98 (1990), John S. Dempsey, *An Introduction to Policing,* 1999., Vern L. Folley, *American Law Enforcement,* second edition, 1976., Gaines, Kappeler & Vaughn, *supra* note 2, D.A. Hansen, *Police Ethics,* 1973., Hill, Champion, & Rush, *supra* note 2, Kania, *supra* note 1, Kappeler, Sluder, & Alpert, *supra* note 2, John Kleinig, *The Ethics of Policing,* 1996., Lagrange, *supra* note 2, Langworthy & Travis, *supra* note 2, Harry W. More & O.R. Shipley, *Police Policy Manual: Personnel,* Springfield, Illinois, 1987., P.V. Murphy, *Corruptive Influences in Government Police Management,* second edition, 52, 73 (Bernard L. Garmire, 1982)., Corruption in the Criminal Justice System (Agenda I-75 Series), (1974)., Knapp Commission Report on Police Corruption, New York (1973)., Peak, *supra* note 2, T. Prenzler & P. Mackay, Police gratuities: what the public think, 14 *Criminal Justice Ethics* 15–25, (1995)., A.E. Simpson, *Police Corruption: A Selective Review of the Literature and the Theory,* 1976., Walker, *supra* note 2.

6   Kleinig, supra note 5.

7   Carte. G. (1986). August Vollmer and thee origins of police professionalism. Pp. 3-9 IN M. Pogrebin and R. Regole (eds.) Police administrative issued: Techniques and functions. Millwood, NY: Associated Faculty Press.

8   Folley, supra note 5.

9   Prenzler & Mackay, supra note 5.

10 Leonard, J. (2002, October 12). Paying a price for freebies; Merchants' handouts and discounts for police are a tradition that some chiefs want ended, calling them unseemly and compromising. Los Angeles Times, p. A.1.; RICHARD KANIA, Should We Tell the Police to Say "Yes" to Gratuities? 7 CRIMINAL JUSTICE ETHICS 37-49 (1988).From Kania P. 42

The position I am proposing here does not assume that all gratuities are offered in a spirit of genuine gratitude. Certainly it seems unlikely that they would be. Some givers give with ulterior motives, just as the police academy warnings have suggested. An equally serious concern is that the gifts are offered out of a sense of obligation, habit, or worse still, necessity.

In some cities the practice of gathering in gifts is undertaken with the zeal of collecting on a 100 percent commission basis. The merchants likewise view the visiting police officers as free-lance tax collectors.

The ethical quality of an exchange is a relative matter, requiring some understanding of the intentions and perceptions of both the giver and the recipient.

11 Kleinig, supra note 5, at 165.

12 Philadelphia Police Department: Statement of Ethical Principles. http://www.ppdonline.org/ppd_ethics.htm.

Philadelphia Police Department: Statement of Ethical Principles.

In one of its definitions, the word "ethics" encompasses the standard of conduct governing all members of a profession. Police exist to preserve law and order. The Greek philosopher Plato wrote that good government is wise, brave, temperate and just. This statement of ethics for police officers establishes broad standards to help police accomplish their mission in a manner which comports with good and wise government.

Citizens who earn their police badges voluntarily bear the public trust. They are faithfully charged to protect the safety and the rights of fellow members of society.

To provide these special protections, police officers carry special powers. They have the authority to investigate other people, to abridge their normal liberties, and to use force when necessary.

Two basic constraints limit use of this authority. First, it is wrong for police to use their office for personal profit or gain, wrong for them to accept any favor which places their own advantage above the welfare of the public. Second, it is wrong for officers to violate the Constitution or laws in performance of their work.

Officers must also bring to their work personal qualities which can spring only from within their personal fabric. They must appreciate and care for the needs of the people they serve. They must exercise common sense in a manner that conveys common decency. They should never render themselves needlessly to danger; they should maintain their physical fitness and their skillfulness in using the tools of their work.

Fulfilling this public trust is demanding work. It brings disappointment, weariness, and stress. These are the facts of life in this profession each officer has chosen. But it also provides officers the opportunity to contribute in an immeasurable way to the common good.

The Philadelphia Police Department is obligated to provide the best training and support for its officers throughout their careers. The Department will strive to the utmost to provide clear policies and adequate resources for every officer to accomplish the work we have accepted together.

Integrity

The public demands that the integrity of its law enforcement officers be above reproach. The dishonesty of just one officer may impair public confidence and cast suspicion upon the Department as a whole. Succumbing to even minor temptations can generate a malignancy which will ultimately destroy an individual's effectiveness and which may well contribute to the corruption of fellow officers. Officers must scrupulously avoid any conduct which might compromise their integrity or the integrity of those with whom they work. No officer should seek or accept any special consideration or privilege, nor anything of value for which others are expected to pay, solely because they are police officers, or for performing their duty in some manner inconsistent with the highest regard for integrity.

Respect for Rights

A broad range of rights and privileges are afforded each individual by law and nature. Liberty is maintained for the most part by our constant attention toward preservation of a consistent exercise of these rights and privileges and through mutual respect for every person's exercise of his or her rights and privileges. However, the police officer must contend with a persistent flow of personal conflicts, both legal and illegal. To resolve these differences, the police enforce a body of laws within the Constitution's assurance that all of us—regardless of economic status, sex, race or creed—receive equal and fair treatment. In so doing, officers often face ambiguous situations, particularly in trying to protect the rights of a victim and an accused. To carry out this mission, police officers have the power to search and arrest, to use force, and to investigate and incarcerate. As police, we must use these tools properly with no abuse of our authority. Decency, security, and liberty all demand that government officials observe strict limits to their awesome powers. A government of laws cannot exist when its servants fail to observe the law's own boundaries. Any government official who disobeys the rigorous demands of law in turn disturbs the public order which all of us are sworn to uphold.

Use of Force

In a complex urban society, officers daily confront situations where control must be exercised to affect arrests and to protect public safety. Control is achieved through advice, warning and persuasion, or by the use of physical force. Force may not be used unless other reasonable alternatives have been exhausted or would be clearly ineffective under the particular circumstances. When the use of physical force is necessary, using baton, pepper spray, firearms or other means, it must be exercised only when, and in the manner, authorized in the Department's policies. Decisions as to when and how to use force must be consistently made and exercised throughout every neighborhood of this City.

Courtesy

Effective law enforcement depends on a working partnership and a community of interest between the Department, its officers and the public they serve. The practice of courtesy in all public contacts encourages understanding and appreciation. Discourtesy breeds contempt and resistance. Most of the public are law-abiding citizens most of the time; they rightfully expect fair and courteous treatment by Department employees. While the urgency of a situation might preclude the ordinary social amenities, discourtesy under any circumstance is indefensible. The practice of courtesy by an officer is entirely consistent with the firmness and impartiality that characterizes a professional police officer.

13   Philadelphia Police Department: Statement of Ethical Principles. http://www.ppdonline.org/ppd_ethics.htm.

14   Philadelphia Police Department: Statement of Ethical Principles. http://www.ppdonline.org/ppd_ethics.htm.

15   Philadelphia Police Department: Statement of Ethical Principles. http://www.ppdonline.org/ppd_ethics.htm.

16   Internet May 25, 2003. http://www.freedomtocare.org/page125.htm. United Nations Code of Conduct for Law Enforcement Officials, G.A. res. 34/169, annex, 34 U.N. GAOR Supp. (No. 46) at 186, U.N. Doc. A/34/46 (1979).
      Article 1

Law enforcement officials shall at all times fulfill the duty imposed upon them by law, by serving the community and by protecting all persons against illegal acts, consistent with the high degree of responsibility required by their profession.

Commentary:

(a) The term "law enforcement officials," includes all officers of the law, whether appointed or elected, who exercise police powers, especially the powers of arrest or detention.

(b) In countries where police powers are exercised by military authorities, whether uniformed or not, or by State security forces, the definition of law enforcement officials shall be regarded as including officers of such services.

(c) Service to the community is intended to include particularly the rendition of services of assistance to those members of the community who by reason of personal, economic, social or other emergencies are in need of immediate aid.

(d) This provision is intended to cover not only all violent, predatory and harmful acts, but extends to the full range of prohibitions under penal statutes. It extends to conduct by persons not capable of incurring criminal liability.

Article 2

In the performance of their duty, law enforcement officials shall respect and protect human dignity and maintain and uphold the human rights of all persons.

Commentary:

(a) The human rights in question are identified and protected by national and international law. Among the relevant international instruments are the Universal Declaration of Human Rights, the International Covenant on Civil and Political Rights, the Declaration on the Protection of All Persons from Being Subjected to Torture and Other Cruel, Inhuman or Degrading Treatment or Punishment, the United Nations Declaration on the Elimination of All Forms of Racial Discrimination, the International Convention on the Elimination of All Forms of Racial Discrimination, the International Convention on the Suppression and Punishment of the Crime of Apartheid, the Convention on the Prevention and Punishment of the Crime of Genocide, the Standard Minimum Rules for the Treatment of Prisoners and the Vienna Convention on Consular Relations.

(b) National commentaries to this provision should indicate regional or national provisions identifying and protecting these rights.

Article 3

Law enforcement officials may use force only when strictly necessary and to the extent required for the performance of their duty.

Commentary:

(a) This provision emphasizes that the use of force by law enforcement officials should be exceptional; while it implies that law enforcement officials may be authorized to use force as is reasonably necessary under the circumstances for the prevention of crime or in effecting or assisting in the lawful arrest of offenders or suspected offenders, no force going beyond that may be used.

(b) National law ordinarily restricts the use of force by law enforcement officials in accordance with a principle of proportionality. It is to be understood that such national principles of proportionality are to be respected in the interpretation of this provision. In no case should this provision be interpreted to authorize the use of force which is disproportionate to the legitimate objective to be achieved.

(c) The use of firearms is considered an extreme measure. Every effort should be made to exclude the use of firearms, especially against children. In general, firearms should not be used except when a suspected offender offers armed resistance or otherwise jeopardizes the lives of others and less extreme measures are not sufficient to restrain or apprehend the suspected offender. In every instance in which a firearm is discharged, a report should be made promptly to the competent authorities.

Article 4

Matters of a confidential nature in the possession of law enforcement officials shall be kept confidential, unless the performance of duty or the needs of justice strictly require otherwise.

Commentary:

By the nature of their duties, law enforcement officials obtain information which may relate to private lives or be potentially harmful to the interests, and especially the reputation, of others. Great care should be exercised in safeguarding and using such information, which should be disclosed only in the performance of duty or to serve the needs of justice. Any disclosure of such information for other purposes is wholly improper.

Article 5

No law enforcement official may inflict, instigate, or tolerate any act of torture or other cruel, inhuman or degrading treatment or punishment, nor may any law enforcement official invoke superior orders or exceptional circumstances such as a state of war or a threat of war, a threat to national security, internal political instability or any other public emergency as a justification of torture or other cruel, inhuman or degrading treatment or punishment .

Commentary:

(a) This prohibition derives from the Declaration on the Protection of All Persons from Being Subjected to Torture and Other Cruel, Inhuman or Degrading Treatment or Punishment, adopted by the General Assembly, according to which: "[Such an act is] an offence to human dignity and shall be condemned as a denial of the purposes of the Charter of the United Nations and as a violation of the human rights and fundamental freedoms proclaimed in the Universal Declaration of Human Rights [and other international human rights instruments]."

(b) The Declaration defines torture as follows:

" ... torture means any act by which severe pain or suffering, whether physical or mental, is intentionally inflicted by or at the instigation of a public official on a person for such purposes as obtaining from him or a third person information or confession, punishing him for an act he has committed or is suspected of having committed, or intimidating him or other persons. It does not include pain or suffering arising only from, inherent in or incidental to, lawful sanctions to the extent consistent with the Standard Minimum Rules for the Treatment of Prisoners."

(c) The term "cruel, inhuman or degrading treatment or punishment" has not been defined by the General Assembly but should be interpreted so as to extend the widest possible protection against abuses, whether physical or mental.

Article 6

Law enforcement officials shall ensure the full protection of the health of persons in their custody and, in particular, shall take immediate action to secure medical attention whenever required.

Commentary:

(a) "Medical attention," which refers to services rendered by any medical personnel, including certified medical practitioners and paramedics, shall be secured when needed or requested.

(b) While the medical personnel are likely to be attached to the law enforcement operation, law enforcement officials must take into account the judgment of such personnel when they recommend providing the person in custody with appropriate treatment through, or in consultation with, medical personnel from outside the law enforcement operation.

(c) It is understood that law enforcement officials shall also secure medical attention for victims of violations of law or of accidents occurring in the course of violations of law.

Article 7

Law enforcement officials shall not commit any act of corruption. They shall also rigorously oppose and combat all such acts.

Commentary:

(a) Any act of corruption, in the same way as any other abuse of authority, is incompatible with the profession of law enforcement officials. The law must be enforced fully with respect to any law enforcement official who commits an act of corruption, as Governments cannot expect to enforce the law among their citizens if they cannot, or will not, enforce the law against their own agents and within their agencies.

(b) While the definition of corruption must be subject to national law, it should be understood to encompass the commission or omission of an act in the performance of or in connection with one's duties, in response to gifts, promises, or incentives demanded or accepted, or the wrongful receipt of these once the act has been committed or omitted.

(c) The expression "act of corruption" referred to above should be understood to encompass attempted corruption.

Article 8

Law enforcement officials shall respect the law and the present Code. They shall also, to the best of their capability, prevent and rigorously oppose any violations of them. Law enforcement officials who have reason to believe that a violation of the present Code has occurred or is about to occur shall report the matter to their superior authorities and, where necessary, to other appropriate authorities or organs vested with reviewing or remedial power.

Commentary:

(a) This Code shall be observed whenever it has been incorporated into national legislation or practice. If legislation or practice contains stricter provisions than those of the present Code, those stricter provisions shall be observed.

(b) The article seeks to preserve the balance between the need for internal discipline of the agency on which public safety is largely dependent, on the one hand, and the need for dealing with violations of basic human rights, on the other. Law enforcement officials shall report violations within the chain of command and take other lawful action outside the chain of command only when no other remedies are available or effective. It is understood that law enforcement officials shall not suffer administrative or other penalties because they have reported that a violation of this Code has occurred or is about to occur.

(c) The term "appropriate authorities or organs vested with reviewing or remedial power" refers to any authority or organ existing under national law, whether internal to the law enforcement agency or independent thereof, with statutory, customary or other power to review grievances and complaints arising out of violations within the purview of this Code. (d) In some countries, the mass media may be regarded as performing complaint review functions similar to those described in subparagraph (c) above. Law enforcement officials may, therefore, be justified if, as a last resort and in accordance with the laws and customs of their own countries and with the provisions of article 4 of the present Code, they bring violations to the attention of public opinion through the mass media.

(e) Law enforcement officials who comply with the provisions of this Code deserve the respect, the full support and the co-operation of the community and of the law enforcement agency in which they serve, as well as the law enforcement profession.

17   Olsen, M. (1965). The logic of collective action. Cambridge: Harvard University Press.

18   Reiman, J. (1985). The social contract and the police use of deadly force. In Frederick A. Ellison and Michael Feldberg (Eds.) Moral issues in police work, pp. 237-249. Savage, MD: Rowman and Littlefield Publishers, p. 246.

19   Reiman, J. (1985). The social contract and the police use of deadly force. In Frederick A. Ellison and Michael Feldberg (Eds.) Moral issues in police work, pp. 237-249. Savage, MD: Rowman and Littlefield Publishers. p. 240.

20   Dunham, R. G. and Alpert, G. P. (2001). The foundation of the police role in society. In R. G. Dunham and G. P. Alpert (Eds.) Critical issues in policing: Contemporary readings. pp. 1-16, Cincinnati: OH: Waveland Press, p. 4.

21   Dunham, R. G. and Alpert, G. P. (2001). The foundation of the police role in society. In R. G. Dunham and G. P. Alpert (Eds.) Critical issues in policing: Contemporary readings. pp. 1-16, Cincinnati: OH: Waveland Press, p. 4.

22   Reiman, J, (1985). The social contract and the police use of deadly force. In Frederick A. Ellison and Michael Feldberg (Eds.) Moral issues in police work, pp. 237-249. Savage, MD: Rowman and Littlefield Publishers, p. 246.

23   Dunham, R. G. and Alpert, G. P. (2001). The foundation of the police role in society. In R. G. Dunham and G. P. Alpert (Eds.) Critical issues in policing: Contemporary readings. pp. 1-16, Cincinnati: OH: Waveland Press, p. 4.

24   Reiman, J. (1985). The social contract and the police use of deadly force. In Frederick A. Ellison and Michael Feldberg (Eds.) Moral issues in police work, pp. 237-249. Savage, MD: Rowman and Littlefield Publishers, p. 241.

25   Dunham, R. G. and Alpert, G. P. (2001). The foundation of the police role in society. In R. G. Dunham and G. P. Alpert (Eds.) Critical issues in policing: Contemporary readings. pp. 1-16, Cincinnati: OH: Waveland Press.

26   Stark, R. (2000). Sociology. New York: Wadsworth Publishing Company.

27   Dunham, R. G. and Alpert, G. P. (2001). The foundation of the police role in society. In R. G. Dunham and G. P. Alpert (Eds.) Critical issues in policing: Contemporary readings. pp. 1-16, Cincinnati: OH: Waveland Press.

28   Dunham, R. G. and Alpert, G. P. (2001). The foundation of the police role in society. In R. G. Dunham and G. P. Alpert (Eds.) Critical issues in policing: Contemporary readings. pp. 1-16, Cincinnati: OH: Waveland Press.

29   Dunham, R. G. and Alpert, G. P. (2001). The foundation of the police role in society. In R. G. Dunham and G. P. Alpert (Eds.) Critical issues in policing: Contemporary readings. pp. 1-16, Cincinnati: OH: Waveland Press.

30   Quinney, R. (1970). The social reality of crime. Boston: Little Brown, and Company. (p. 9-10).

31   Dunham, R. G. and Alpert, G. P. (2001). The foundation of the police role in society. In R. G. Dunham and G. P. Alpert (Eds.) Critical issues in policing: Contemporary readings. pp. 1-16, Cincinnati: OH: Waveland Press, p. 2.

32   Dunham, R. G. and Alpert, G. P. (2001). The foundation of the police role in society. In R. G. Dunham and G. P. Alpert (Eds.) Critical issues in policing: Contemporary readings. pp. 1-16, Cincinnati: OH: Waveland Press.

33   Uchida, C. (2001). The development of the American police: An historical overview. In R. G Dunham and G. P. Alpert (Eds.) Critical issues in policing: Contemporary readings. pp. 18-35, Cincinnati: OH: Waveland Press, p. 24.

34   A statement from a police officers in Crank, J. and Caldero, M. (2000). Police ethics: The corruption of noble cause. Cincinnati, OH: Anderson Publishing, p. 65.

35   Internet May 25, 2003. A propaganda film from 1936 that has become a cult hit because of its dated outlook on marijuana use, Reefer Madness is the height of camp entertainment. Framed as a "documentary," the film is narrated by a high school principal imparting his wisdom and experiences with the demon weed. The bulk of the film focuses on almost slapstick scenes of high school kids smoking pot and quickly going insane, playing "evil" jazz music, being committed, and going on a murder spree. Meant to be an important and affecting cautionary tale, this dated black-and-white film's true value is in its many entertaining moments of unintended hilarity. —Robert Lane (This text refers to the VHS tape edition.) http://www.amazon.com/exec/obidos/tg/stores/detail/-/dvd/6305066795/reviews/104-1831590-5087906#63050667957480

36   Leonard, J. (2002, October 12). Paying a price for freebies; Merchants' handouts and discounts for police are a tradition that some chiefs want ended, calling them unseemly and compromising. Los Angeles Times, p. A.1.

37   Leonard, J. (2002, October 12). Paying a price for freebies; Merchants' handouts and discounts for police are a tradition that some chiefs want ended, calling them unseemly and compromising. Los Angeles Times, p. A.1.

38   Berman, J. (1987). Police administration and progressive reform: Theodore Roosevelt as police commissioner of New York. New York: Greenwood Press.

39   Walker, S. (1984). Broken windows and fractured history: The use and misuse of history in recent police patrol analysis. Justice Quarterly, 1: 57-90.

40   Berman, J. (1987). Police administration and progressive reform: Theodore Roosevelt as police commissioner of New York. New York: Greenwood Press.

41   Fogelson, R, (1977). Big-city police. Cambridge, MA: Harvard University Press.

42   As a law enforcement officer, my fundamental duty is to serve the community; to safeguard lives and property; to protect the innocent against deception, the weak against oppression or intimidation and the peaceful against violence or disorder; and to respect the constitutional rights of all to liberty, equality and justice.
      I will keep my private life unsullied as an example to all and will behave in a manner that does not bring discredit to me or to my agency. I will maintain courageous calm in the face of danger, scorn, or ridicule; develop self-restraint; and be constantly mindful of the welfare of others. Honest in thought and deed both in my personal and official life, I will be exemplary in obeying the law and the regulations of my department. Whatever I see or hear of a confidential nature or that is confided to me in my official capacity will be kept ever secret unless revelation is necessary in the performance of my duty.
      I will never act officiously or permit personal feelings, prejudices, political beliefs, aspirations, animosities, or friendships to influence my decisions. With no compromise for crime and with relentless prosecution of criminals, I will enforce the law courteously and appropriately without fear or favor, malice or ill will, never employing unnecessary force or violence and never accepting gratuities.

I recognize the badge of my office as a symbol of public faith, and I accept it as a public trust to be held so long as I am true to the ethics of police service. I will never engage in acts of corruption or bribery, nor will I condone such acts by other police officers. I will cooperate with all legally authorized agencies and their representatives in the pursuit of justice.

I know that I alone am responsible for my own standard of professional performance and will take every reasonable opportunity to enhance and improve my level of knowledge and competence.

I will constantly strive to achieve these objectives and ideals, dedicating myself before God to my chosen profession … law enforcement.

(Internet   May   28,   2003.   http://www.theiacp.org/documents/index. cfm?fuseaction=document&document_id=95)

43   (Internet   May   28,   2003.   http://www.theiacp.org/documents/index. cfm?fuseaction=document&document_id=95)

44   Thibault, E. Lynch, L, and McBride, R. (2001). Proactive police management. Upper Saddle River, NJ: Prentice-Hall, p. 19.

45   Kania, R., Should we tell the police to say "yes" to gratuities? *Criminal Justice Ethics,* 37-49 (1988).

46   Leonard, J. (2002, October 12). Paying a price for freebies; Merchants' handouts and discounts for police are a tradition that some chiefs want ended, calling them unseemly and compromising. *Los Angeles Times,* p. A.1.

47   Leonard, J. (2002, October 12). Paying a price for freebies; Merchants' handouts and discounts for police are a tradition that some chiefs want ended, calling them unseemly and compromising. *Los Angeles Times,* p. A.1.

48   Leonard, J. (2002, October 12). Paying a price for freebies; Merchants' handouts and discounts for police are a tradition that some chiefs want ended, calling them unseemly and compromising. *Los Angeles Times,* p. A.1.

49   Fast-food restaurants that commonly gave police free or discounted food are Burger King, McDonald's, Arby's, Wendy's, Popeye's Fried Chicken, Kentucky Fried Chicken, and Taco Bell, just to name a few.

50   Crank, J. and Caldero, M. (2000). Police ethics: The corruption of noble cause. Cincinnati, OH: Anderson Publishing, p. 72.

51   Crank, J. and Caldero, M. (2000). Police ethics: The corruption of noble cause. Cincinnati, OH: Anderson Publishing, p. 72.

52   This is not the real name of the person.

53   This is not the real name of the person.

54   Kania, R., Should we tell the police to say "yes" to gratuities? *Criminal Justice Ethics,* 37-49 (1988).

55   Crank, J. and Caldero, M. (2000). Police ethics: The corruption of noble cause. Cincinnati, OH: Anderson Publishing, p. 67.

56   Sherman, L. (1985). Becoming bent: Moral careers of corrupt policemen." pp. 253-265 in F. Elliston and M. Feldberg (eds.) Moral Issues in Police Work, Totowa, NJ: Rowman & Littlefield Publishers.

57   Crank, J. and Caldero, M. (2000). Police ethics: The corruption of noble cause. Cincinnati, OH: Anderson Publishing, p. 66.

58   Sherman, L. (1985). Becoming bent: Moral careers of corrupt policemen. pp. 253-265 in F. Elliston and M. Feldberg (eds.) Moral Issues in Police Work, Totowa, NJ: Rowman & Littlefield Publishers.

59   Crank, J. and Caldero, M. (2000). Police ethics: The corruption of noble cause. Cincinnati, OH: Anderson Publishing, p. 66.

60   Graft is defined as "the acquisition of money, position, or other profit by dishonest or questionable means (as by actual theft or by taking advantage of a public office or a position of trust or employment to obtain fees, perquisites, profits on contracts, or pay for work not done or service not performed) : illegal or unfair practice for profit or personal gain." Webster's Unabridged Dictionary On-Line May 27, 2003, http://collections.chadwyck.com/mwd/htxview?template=basic. htx&content=ftfram.htx&ALL=Y&ACTION=BYOFFSET&div=2&OFFSET=12703642&FILE= ./session/1054157376_16370&SEARCH_NO=default.

61   Sherman, L. (1985). Becoming bent: Moral careers of corrupt policemen. pp. 253-265 in F. Elliston and M. Feldberg (eds.) Moral Issues in Police Work, Totowa, NJ: Rowman & Littlefield Publishers.

62   Crank, J. and Caldero, M. (2000). Police ethics: The corruption of noble cause. Cincinnati, OH: Anderson Publishing, p. 66.

63   Kania, Richard E. (1988). Should we tell the police to say "yes" to gratuities? *Journal of Criminal Justice Ethics,* Summer/Fall pp. 37-49.

64   From Kania P. 42

I had a junior officer assigned to me for training, a officer of unquestionably strong moral character who accepted the academy creed at face value. He steadfastly refused even the most minor discounts from restaurateurs and twice became embroiled in arguments over the matter in my presence. On the second occasion, the argument actually became heated, and the inflexible officer accused the restaurant owner of trying to corrupt the police force. At that point, the officer was verbally evicted from the establishment and told not to return. The argumentative officer was called an "ass-hole" to his face and, in my opinion, had earned the label for his rigid refusal to accept an inconsequential discount. In the few months left of that inflexible but ethical officer's appropriately short, difficult, but uncorrupted police career, he found it necessary to bring a bag lunch and eat in the car while his "corrupted" partners ate at discount in neighborhood eateries. This deviation from the unethical" behavior of his peers served to provide the businesses of his patrol sector less on-site protection than was provided by the "corrupt" police who continued to accept meal discounts in the spirit in which they were offered. Although an isolated cases does not an empirical proof make, it does illustrate one of the possible consequences of rejecting a minor gratuity, originally offered in a spirit of genuine gratitude.

65   Kania, R., Should we tell the police to say "yes" to gratuities? *Criminal Justice Ethics,* 37-49 (1988), p. 42.

66   Crank, J. and Caldero, M. (2000). Police ethics: The corruption of noble cause. Cincinnati, OH: Anderson Publishing, p. 73.

67   Crank, J. and Caldero, M. (2000). Police ethics: The corruption of noble cause. Cincinnati, OH: Anderson Publishing, p. 73.

68   Gilmartin, K. Ethics based policing: Undoing entitlement. http://www.rcmp-learning.org/docs/ecdd1220.htm. Downloaded 6-18-2003.

69   Kania, R., Should we tell the police to say "yes" to gratuities? *Criminal Justice Ethics,* 37-49 (1988), p. 42.

70   Crank, J. and Caldero, M. (2000). Police ethics: The corruption of noble cause. Cincinnati, OH: Anderson Publishing, p. 73-74.

71   Crank, J. and Caldero, M. (2000). Police ethics: The corruption of noble cause. Cincinnati, OH: Anderson Publishing, p. 74.

72   Crank, J. and Caldero, M. (2000). Police ethics: The corruption of noble cause. Cincinnati, OH: Anderson Publishing, p. 75.

73   Crank, J. and Caldero, M. (2000). Police ethics: The corruption of noble cause. Cincinnati, OH: Anderson Publishing, p 40.

Cynicism is closely tied to noble cause. Cynicism's different facets tap specific ways in which the noble cause becomes jaded. One cannot, for example, fully understand cynicism toward the courts unless it is also recognized that many police view the courts as too lenient, morally bankrupt, over-run with lawyers, and without the courage to actually do something about the bad guys. In other words, the courts, when viewed cynically, are seen as hindering police efforts to carry out their commitment to the noble cause. And herein lie the seeds of noble-cause corruption.

As cynicism toward the courts increases, officers sometimes decide that they will have to act on their own to insure that criminals are attested, booked and found guilty. Cynicism toward the courts thus leads to noble cause corruption in the form of testimonial deception and lying

74   Crank, J. and Caldero, M. (2000). Police ethics: The corruption of noble cause. Cincinnati, OH: Anderson Publishing, p. 37.

When we think of police brutality, we sometimes imagine it as the unreasoned, vicious power of the state acted out against an individual citizen. Part of the reason we haven't learned how to control it is because we have failed to understand how it can be rooted in the way in which police relate to victims—protecting the public, doing something meaningful for other people. What reformers have failed to realize is how this kind of police violence is deeply rooted in our democratic traditions.

To overlook this dimension of violence is to fail to understand the roots of much of what is called brutality. If we fail to recognize that police smell the victim's blood, we have no hope to control the use of violence by police officers. The victim's blood mobilized them. The more we want our street officers to reflect a democratic ethics, to be committed to the poor and care about the downtrodden, the more we open the door for noble-cause violence.

75   Crank, J. and Caldero, M. (2000). Police ethics: The corruption of noble cause. Cincinnati, OH: Anderson Publishing, pp. 42-46.

Karl Klockers (1983) presented the noble-cause dilemma in terms of what I widely called the "Dirty Harry Problem." When should an officer commit a dirty act to achieve a good end? Klockers presented a thorough experiment. He described a then-popular movie titled *Dirty Harry*. Klockers described the following scene:

A 14-year-old girl has been kidnapped and is being held by a psychopathic killer. The killer, "Scorpio," has struck twice. He demands $200,000 ransom to release the girl, who is buried with just enough oxygen to keep her alive for a few hours.

"Dirty" Harry gets the job of delivering the ransom money. Scorpio reneges on the deal and lets the girl die. Scorpio escapes, but Harry tracks him down. He confronts Scorpio on the 50-yard line of a football field. Harry shoots him in the leg while Scorpio is trying to surrender.

As the camera draws back from the scene, Harry stands on Scorpio's bullet-mangled leg to torture a confession of the girl's location from him.

In the incident, there is a good end, an effort to save the life of an innocent victim of kidnapping. There is also bad means, extorting a confession using third-degree torture tactics. There is also the connection between the end and the means—as Klockers (1991) notes, a means that can be justified if "what must be known, and, importantly, known before the act is committed, is that it will result in the achievement of a good end."

Klockers presented a compelling argument that the "Dirty Harry" problem is at the core of the police role. He identified four elements of police culture that predispose police to believe that they are dealing with guilty people, even in the absence of evidence, and this justify the corruption of noble cause.

Klockers: Elements of Police Culture that Predispose Guilt

The operative assumption of guilt. The police tend to assume guilt as a working premise of their craft. Officers believe that any questionable or furtive behavior they witness is evidence of some concealed offense.

The worst of all possible guilt. Police, Klockers observed, are obliged not only to make an operative assumption of guilt but to also think that the person is dangerously guilty." ... the premise that the one who has the most to hide will try hardest to hide it is a reasonable assumption for interrogation" (1983). Consequently, it is imperative that police rapidly find out the underlying truth. This perspective justifies the use of the third degree.

The great guilty place assumption. Police are expose to highly selective samples of their environment. Places are criminogenic, and the wise policeman sees danger where there might be none apparent to less suspicious eyes.

The not guilty (this time) assumption. When a random stop of a motorist proves unwarranted, a vehicle search finds nothing, or an interrogation fails, police do not conclude that the person is thereby innocent. Most people have committed numerous crimes for which they have not been caught. Sometimes a little additional pressure will bring out an undisclosed truth that is being hidden by a seemingly innocent citizen.

76   Crank, J. and Caldero, M. (2000). Police ethics: The corruption of noble cause. Cincinnati, OH: Anderson Publishing, p. 2.

77   Barker, T. (1996). Police ethics: Crisis in law enforcement. Springfield, IL: Charles Thomas Publishers, p. 25.

78   Crank, J. and Caldero, M. (2000). Police ethics: The corruption of noble cause. Cincinnati, OH: Anderson Publishing, p. 75.

79   Pomeroy, W. (1985). The sources of police legitimacy and a model for police misconduct review: A response to Wayne Kerstetter. pp. 183-186 in W. Geller (ed.) Police leadership in America: Crisis and Opportunity. New York: Preager.

80   Crank, J. and Caldero, M. (2000). Police ethics: The corruption of noble cause. Cincinnati, OH: Anderson Publishing, p. 76.

81   Crank, J. and Caldero, M. (2000). Police ethics: The corruption of noble cause. Cincinnati, OH: Anderson Publishing, p. 67.

82   Elliston, F and Fieldberg, M. (1985). Authority, discretion, and the police function. In Frederick Elliston and Michael Fieldberg (Eds.). Moral issues in police work. pp. 11-13. Savage, MD: Rowman and Littlefield Publishers, p. 11.

83   Gilmartin, K. Ethics based policing: Undoing entitlement. http://www.rcmp-learning.org/docs/ ecdd1220.htm. Downloaded 6-18-2003.

84   Lilly, R. (1978). What are the police now doing? Journal of Police Science and Administration, 6, 51-53.

85   Scott, E. (1981). Calls for service: Citizen demand and initial police response. Washington, DC: National Institute of Justice.

86   Elliston, F and Fieldberg, M. (1985). Authority, discretion, and the police function. In Frederick Elliston and Michael Fieldberg (Eds.). Moral issues in police work. pp. 11-13. Savage, MD: Rowman and Littlefield Publishers, p. 11.

87   Elliston, F and Fieldberg, M. (1985). Authority, discretion, and the police function. In Frederick Elliston and Michael Fieldberg (Eds.). Moral issues in police work. pp. 11-13. Savage, MD: Rowman and Littlefield Publishers, p. 11.

88   Elliston, F and Fieldberg, M. (1985). Authority, discretion, and the police function. In Frederick Elliston and Michael Fieldberg (Eds.). Moral issues in police work. pp. 11-13. Savage, MD: Rowman and Littlefield Publishers, p. 11.

89   Gilmartin, K. Ethics based policing: Undoing entitlement. http://www.rcmp-learning.org/docs/ ecdd1220.htm. Downloaded 6-18-2003.

90   Gilmartin, K. Ethics based policing: Undoing entitlement. http://www.rcmp-learning.org/docs/ ecdd1220.htm. Downloaded 6-18-2003.

91   Gilmartin, K. Ethics based policing: Undoing entitlement. http://www.rcmp-learning.org/docs/ ecdd1220.htm. Downloaded 6-18-2003.

92   Gilmartin, K. Ethics based policing: Undoing entitlement. http://www.rcmp-learning.org/docs/ ecdd1220.htm. Downloaded 6-18-2003.

93   Gilmartin, K. Ethics based policing: Undoing entitlement. http://www.rcmp-learning.org/docs/ ecdd1220.htm. Downloaded 6-18-2003.

94   Gilmartin, K. Ethics based policing: Undoing entitlement. http://www.rcmp-learning.org/docs/ ecdd1220.htm. Downloaded 6-18-2003.

95   Gilmartin, K. Ethics based policing: Undoing entitlement. http://www.rcmp-learning.org/docs/ ecdd1220.htm. Downloaded 6-18-2003.

96   Leonard, J. (2002, October 12). Paying a price for freebies; Merchants' handouts and discounts for police are a tradition that some chiefs want ended, calling them unseemly and compromising. *Los Angeles Times*, p. A.1.

97   Cohen, H. (1986). Exploiting police authority. *Criminal Justice Ethics*, 5(2), pp. 23–30.p. 23

98   Cohen, H. (1986). Exploiting police authority. *Criminal Justice Ethics*, 5(2), pp. 23–30.p. 23

99   Cohen, H. (1986). Exploiting police authority. *Criminal Justice Ethics*, 5(2), pp. 23–30.p. 23

100 Cohen, H. (1986). Exploiting police authority. *Criminal Justice Ethics*, 5(2), pp. 23–30.p. 23

101 Cohen, H. (1986). Exploiting police authority. *Criminal Justice Ethics*, 5(2), pp. 23–30.p. 23

102 Cohen, H. (1986). Exploiting police authority. *Criminal Justice Ethics*, 5(2), pp. 23–30.p. 23

103 Leonard, J. (2002, October 12). Paying a Price for Freebies; Merchants' handouts and discounts for police are a tradition that some chiefs want ended, calling them unseemly and compromising. *The Los Angeles Times*, p. A.1.

104 Cohen, H. (1986). Exploiting police authority. *Criminal Justice Ethics*, 5(2), pp. 23-30.p. 23

105 Cohen, H. (1986). Exploiting police authority. *Criminal Justice Ethics*, 5(2), pp. 23-30.p. 23

106 Cohen, H. (1986). Exploiting police authority. *Criminal Justice Ethics*, 5(2), pp. 23-30.p. 26

107 Cohen, H. (1986). Exploiting police authority. *Criminal Justice Ethics*, 5(2), pp. 23-30.p. 26

108 RICHARD KANIA, Should We Tell the Police to Say "Yes" to Gratuities? 7 *Criminal Justice Ethics* 37–49 (1988), p. 39.

109 Cohen, H. (1986). Exploiting police authority. *Criminal Justice Ethics*, 5, (2), pp. 23-30.p. 24.

110 http://www.pagedepot.com/martystuart/hamelmn%2D2%2D13%2D03%2Dar.htm.

111 http://tobaccofreekids.org/research/factsheets/pdf/0202.pdf

112 Barlow, H. (2000), Criminal Justice in America?

113   Bannish, H. and Ruiz, J. (2003). The antisocial police personality: A view from the inside. International Journal of Public Administration, 26 (7), 831–881.

114   Bannish, H. and Ruiz, J. (2003). The antisocial police personality: A view from the inside. International Journal of Public Administration, 26 (7), 831–881.

115   Bannish, H. and Ruiz, J. (2003). The antisocial police personality: A view from the inside. International Journal of Public Administration, 26 (7), 831–881.

116   Bannish, H. and Ruiz, J. (2003). The antisocial police personality: A view from the inside. International Journal of Public Administration, 26 (7), 831–881.

117   Cohen, H. (1985). Authority: The limits of discretion. In Frederick Elliston and Michael Fieldberg (Eds.). Moral issues in police work. pp. 27-42. Savage, MD: Rowman and Littlefield Publishers, p. 27.

17 Supervising the Undercover Function

Michael L. Arter

CONTENTS

INTRODUCTION

The undercover function of law enforcement has been referred to as a necessary evil often required to address specific issues of concern in many agencies. Generally speaking, the same principles of supervision applied throughout law enforcement, and discussed in the preceding chapters, are applicable to effectively supervise and manage undercover officers and the undercover function. However, there are several unique characteristics of this function, and of the officers who are assigned in this capacity, which can make effective supervision both demanding and challenging. Prior to discussing the unique supervisory challenges that can be encountered in the undercover function, it is necessary to define the term "undercover" and discuss some current trends and specific needs of those assigned into the undercover capacity.

THE EVOLUTION OF THE UNDERCOVER ROLE

Historically, the undercover role has been characterized as either "deep cover" or "light cover." Deep cover involves a continuing role over an extended period of time, with the firm establishment of an alter identity supported by prepared documents to establish a history for the officer portraying the role. Deep cover assignments often require the officer to live the role in a hostile environment, and usually involve a long-term commitment on the part of both the officer and the sponsoring agency. On the other hand, light cover operations usually do not require the officer to live an extended identity, but involve short term portrayals in the role as required for operational or intelligence purposes. Officers working light cover operations typically do not live a separate life in establishing the undercover persona, and perform other duties in support of the undercover unit when not in the role.

Whereas both deep cover and light cover assignments were used extensively during the peak of the so-called war on drugs in the '80s and '90s, more recently the use of the deep cover officer has all but disappeared in the vast majority of local police agencies. Larger departments may utilize a semideep cover role to target specific areas of interest of concern, but generally do not commit the same resources that had been expended in the past decades. The majority of state level agencies that had used deep cover operations on a fairly routine basis also have limited the use as the exception rather than the rule. Information on the actual use of deep cover officers by federal agencies is difficult to obtain. Unofficially, agents within the Drug Enforcement Administration (DEA) report the use of long-term undercover operations are a thing of the past. However, considering the current focus on terrorism and national security interests, it can be intuitively inferred that deep-cover operations are still a frequently utilized investigative tool by other agencies within the federal arena.

Administrators and supervisors in departments that no longer utilize the undercover function provide differing rationales for abandoning the undercover role. Effective undercover operations are manpower and resource intensive, producing minimal gains for the resources expended. The risks involved for both the undercover officer and the sponsoring department can exceed the expected benefits of long-term operations. Additionally, the recognition that the "best" undercover officers often are the most difficult to supervise causes many administrators to reevaluate the prior focus on the extensive use of undercover operations. These factors, combined with the ever-increasing need for the responsible accounting of scarce resources, have resulted in the evolution of investigative techniques that maximize nonpolice resources (such as informants) and exploit the general self-interested nature of the targeted offending populations.

Although long-term undercover operations are not as commonplace as in the past, the vast majority of departments maintain narcotic units and vice units that utilize short-term undercover operations, or what has been termed as "spontaneous" undercover operations, based upon strategic intelligence or specific information. Additionally, many departments have responded to intensified public concern regarding vice activities such as prostitution and gambling by employing undercover operatives on both sides of the issue, either offering, or seeking, the activity in question. With the growing emphasis on the exploitation of our children and the use of the Internet by sexual predators and pedophiles, many larger local agencies and state level agencies have expanded investigation strategies to employ online undercover officers.

Each of these assignments entail unique factors and requirements that can make effective supervision difficult. Additionally, as the perception among many administrators is that the agency does not get involved in the historical perception of the undercover function, allocations for training in this area have been shifted to other areas of need. Accordingly, the officers who do function in the spontaneous roles, or vice roles, often are not provided the training required to effectively and safely perform the assignment.

As mentioned earlier, the principles and goals of effective supervision for virtually any assignment within law enforcement are basically the same. Supervisors are seeking efficiency, effectiveness, and both the physical and emotional safety of every officer for whom they are responsible. The challenge often found in supervising the undercover function lies in how supervisors and the administration define efficiency and effectiveness, and at what levels they are willing to sacrifice individual officer safety or emotional well being. Many times efficiency is recognized by administration and management by the number of arrests or cases presented for prosecution. Effectiveness might be gauged by the lack of complaints against an officer in amassing his efficiency record. This supervisory challenge is often aggravated by the type officer who self-selects into undercover assignments.

THE UNDERCOVER OFFICER

Officers who function in an undercover capacity differ from officers in other assignments in several ways. The majority of officers who are assigned to undercover duties volunteer, or self-select, into these positions. This in itself can be an issue of concern for a supervisor, as the reasons officers may request assignment into an undercover unit can impact the style, and level, of supervision that may be required to successfully manage each officer. Often the stereotypical image of the undercover officer must be addressed for new officers entering an undercover unit in order to eliminate any misconceptions that often permeate the agency's informal lines of communication.

Some of the reasons given for requesting assignment into the undercover function include seeking to mediate the impact of a serious social issue such as controlled substances or other vice activities, seeking the perceived respect inherent in the position, an attraction to the autonomy and power such assignments provide, and seeking to prove themselves capable of attaining a higher level of performance and discipline. Historically, the undercover assignment often was viewed as a stepping stone to advancement within the agency as the successful completion of an undercover tour of duty emphasized the officer's ability to adapt, innovate, interact, and accomplish demanding requirements. Officers seeking advancement within the traditional hierarchical police structure often sought an undercover assignment as a means of speeding up the process through high visibility cases and the recognition and achievement that can come from a successful undercover tour of duty.

Many officers rotate into an undercover unit, serve several years and return to more routine duties or transfer into a different investigative assignment. When comparing the officers in the undercover function to officers in other assignments within policing, one thing becomes fairly obvious. The officer in the undercover function appears to be driven by different workplace needs than are the majority of the more routinely assigned officers, or those officers assigned to the more traditional investigatory functions. The job expectations placed upon the undercover officer by others within the agency, and by the officer himself, can be an intense source of pressure and stress when these expectations are not realized. The inherent stress in under-cover assignments will be addressed later in this chapter.

UNDERCOVER INVESTIGATIONS

By their nature, undercover investigations are more proactive than are those in other investigative assignments. Although investigators in homicide may be lim-ited by information, evidence, and numerous other factors beyond their control, undercover officers are responsible for developing the required evidence against targeted persons, locations, or organizations. The successful closure of assigned cases may be the standard by which reactive investigations are assessed; how-ever, proactive investigations, such as vice and drugs, are assessed by the num-ber and quality of cases developed and processed for prosecution. The rationale for these assessment criteria assumes that because drugs and vice are at such "epidemic" levels, the effective undercover officer should be limited in the number of cases only by the individual (or team) ability to locate, identify, and apprehend guilty parties. The inability to maintain expected levels of successful cases is often viewed by administration (as well as by the officers) as a failure in this assignment.

Homicide investigators certainly would not be viewed as ineffective if the num-ber of active cases fell below the number that could be managed effectively. How-ever, vice investigators who did not maintain a consistent number of active cases would likely be viewed as not being effective by administration and not working hard enough to identify, locate, and apprehend offenders. A lack of active cases in homicide is a good thing that needs to continue. A lack of active cases for the under-cover officer is a "slump" that needs to be corrected.

This perception regarding the limitless number of cases available to the innova-tive and effective undercover officer can be an enormous source of stress for both undercover officers and those who supervise them. With the inferred association between the number of cases and effectiveness, pressure often is perceived to develop cases that normally may not have been viewed as effective utilization of resources. This pressure often results in a modification of individual and unit criteria by which cases may be actively pursued. Each of these unique and inherent factors involved in undercover investigations present an environment which can be conducive to actions and behaviors that are neither consistent with departmental policies and procedures, nor in compliance with the professional code of ethics.

CHALLENGES OF SUPERVISION

ETHICS AND MORAL COMPASS

Ethical conduct is an issue of concern throughout law enforcement. However, in the undercover function there is even more concern for sound ethical behavior. The numerous temptations and pressures inherent in the undercover function require more than mere dependence on the individual officer's moral compass or conscience. Equally important in the close working nature of undercover units, is the impact that unethical or immoral actions can have on the other officers in the unit, as well as to the overall reputation of the unit or agency. For these reasons, ethics must be viewed as both an individual and supervisory responsibility.

Officers who enter the undercover function do so with a sincere sense of purpose sworn to uphold the duties of office and with no intentional design to violate ethical responsibilities. However, the desire to do the right thing and excel in the undercover assignment often can result in the unintentional displacement of the moral compass in the utilitarian name of serving the greater good of the majority. Rationalization, justification, and minimization may be employed to mitigate ethically questionable actions or behaviors. The individual officer and the first-line supervisor each must be accountable for ethical behaviors and moral responsibility.

The pressures of the undercover assignment, in conjunction with the inherent nature of such assignments and the numerous temptations and opportunities for unobserved and unreported activities, can be overwhelming for those pressured by individual needs, or unit and agency expectations. The sense of isolation that often accompanies working in undercover assignments can create a synergy that fuels individual need and the desire to achieve. Handling informants, "buy" funds, the opposite sex, and alcohol use are each areas in which undercover officers are extremely vulnerable for rationalizing ethically unsound actions and behaviors. Additionally, the labels applied to those who are targeted in undercover assignments often allows for the justification of the misuse of force through physical, emotional, or social abuse directed toward those who have been socially stigmatized as unworthy of ethical treatment.

Supervisors who hold every officer accountable for unethical behavior, who do not allow the maltreatment of any individual, and who lead by example are often the most respected and effective supervisors in the undercover function. The undercover function requires the same level of close contact by the supervisor with subordinates to monitor all activities of case development, intelligence gathering, and investigation as all other assignments. Due to the nature of the undercover function, it is necessary to delegate the authority required to perform effectively. However, responsibility cannot be delegated and remains with the supervisor.

UNDERCOVER STRESS

Undercover assignments have been an attractive and prized reward for many dedicated and conscientious police officers, who have proven themselves to be capable and reliable under stressful and demanding circumstances. These assignments have historically been coveted by officers and investigators alike, and are viewed by many as a stepping-stone to professional advancement and personal achievement. Some officers prosper during and after undercover assignments, as they effectively utilize the energy created by the undercover experience and turn potentially harmful stress (distress) into beneficial stress (eustress). Unfortunately, this is not the case for every officer who functions in an undercover assignment.

Undercover assignments differ significantly from routine police duties, and some would argue that undercover operations can be one of the most stressful assignments in policing. Undercover work has been described as "physically, intellectually, and emotionally demanding."[1] The fear of discovery while in the undercover role, the inherent potential for violence and retaliation from targeted individuals, and the professional embarrassment of "failing" in the role and losing face among peers and superiors, are major factors in the mind of the undercover officer and can be intense sources of stress for those who function in the undercover capacity.

The perceived intense pressure to succeed in undercover assignments produces an additional strain that is not present for officers assigned to routine duties. Undercover assignments can require a large expenditure of agency resources and manpower. Subsequently, supervisors and administrators place great emphasis on the success of these costly operations. Many officers assigned to undercover duties have a proven track record of prior successful duty assignments and have earned their way into becoming an undercover operative. Intense pressure is placed upon these officers by both supervisors and the officer themselves to produce the same results they have shown in prior assignments. However, the same rules and levels of supervision they operated under before may no longer be in effect. Many officers facing these pressures find it necessary to cut Constitutional corners in order to meet the self-imposed demands or the perceived demands of superiors. A study of undercover officers in 1999 reported that violations of the due process rights of suspected drug dealers and users were commonplace, and included such actions as "unlawful entry, illegal searches, long periods of detainment, and threats bordering on extortion."[2]

In general, the investigative function is not as closely supervised as patrol and other line functions. Investigations often are supervised by the case management approach, and the level of supervision is based on the complexity and visibility of the case in question. The deeper the undercover assignment, the more difficult supervision becomes, and the easier it can be for the undercover officer to control what information is (and is not) passed on to the supervisor. It is important in the supervision of the undercover function for supervisors to require continual reporting of case development progress and investigative strategies being employed in order to maximize the information that is passed up the chain and minimize activities and behaviors that may be inconsistent with effective investigative techniques.

Undercover assignments can intensify the emotional stressors inherent in the law enforcement profession. The desire to succeed in the undercover function is one of the most frequently reported stressors among undercover officers.[3] Unfortunately, officers who are not perceived as being successful in their assignment, either by themselves or by others, may succumb to feelings of shame and embarrassment, withdraw inside themselves, or lash out against offenders out of fear, frustration or displaced anger. Some of the most prevalent issues affecting those assigned in the undercover capacity include a lack of adequate training, lack of effective supervision, perceived demands of the assignment, and the omnipresent desire to excel as an undercover operative.[4] Each of these have implications for the supervisor of the undercover function.

In addition to the inherent stressors of undercover work, officers can also experience levels of alienation from society, as well as from their departmental peers. The anger and resentment experienced by undercover officers may lead to a self-alienation, which exacerbates previous feelings and contributes synergistically to experiential stressors. It might not be uncommon for officers in these situations to abandon their personal value systems and to substitute a modified value system implemented as a means of self-survival. This modified value system may provide a rationalization for their actions, in many ways similar to the techniques of neutralization described by Sykes and Matza, which may be employed as a means of repelling feelings of self-betrayal and self-condemnation.[5] Actions counter to a caring and trusting relationship may be justified as a required part of the job. Actions taken against targeted individuals may be justified as "just desserts" or the penalty for being a "one of those" people. As the process continues, courtroom testimony may be replaced by "testilying" in order to make the case and protect the actions taken during the undercover assignment. Officers may utilize these, or similar, "justifications" with the sincere belief that there is no harm being done, as only drug dealers or other criminals are being affected, and a greater good is being served.

Administrators and bureaucrats may ignore the warning signs and attribute problematic behaviors to individual weaknesses or the "rotten apple" theory. This theory in law enforcement suggests that certain officers turn "rotten" and no longer serve the best interests of the police organization or the communities they serve. Failure to identify and remove the rotten apple can result in the contamination and spoilage of the other apples in the barrel. It falls on the shoulders of the first-line supervisor to be aware of the total officer to understand the individual officer's needs and personality. The recognition of changing personality, attitudes, and behaviors can be a key factor in preventing outcomes that are inconsistent with the undercover mission or not in the best interest of the agency or community.

THE TOTAL OFFICER APPROACH

Although the undercover function can be a unique and challenging environment, the sound and effective supervision techniques identified and explicated throughout this text are applicable in the supervision of undercover officers. The primary distinction for the supervisor of the undercover officer is to recognize and understand the primary needs of those who function in the undercover capacity.

UNDERSTANDING THE UNDERCOVER OFFICER

The "top down" policing approach, which has been the mainstay of policing organizations for decades, does not appear conducive to instilling the respect and appreciation often demanded by those in the undercover function. In general, line officers in undercover assignments respect those supervisors who themselves have served in undercover assignments and have an understanding of the nature of the duties required to be successful in such assignments. Undercover officers who are supervised by those who have never experienced the undercover role are often very vocal regarding displeasure with such supervision as the following comments from active undercover officers indicate.

> They don't have any experience and they are trying to
> tell us how to do our jobs. That causes problems.

> The biggest stressor in this office, you know, you have
> supervisors that come in and have never worked or even
> seen drugs before supervising our unit.

... it is more comfortable knowing that a person that is
running an undercover operation has been involved in
undercover work. You know, your life depends on his
judgment.

... there is a lack of understanding about maybe what we
do. I don't think they actually understand, sometimes, the
actual dangers.

"Here [in vice] this is different because they [supervisors]
can't see what you do. Even though they can read it, they
don't live it. They can't have that feeling.

Consequently, a "bottom up" approach to supervision can be more effective and
can better meet the needs of both the officers assigned, as well as the supervisor of
the undercover function. By allowing the line officers to have a voice in the decisions
that might be more unilateral in the prevailing supervisory paradigm, the lines of
communication are more efficient and the concerns of each officer can be expressed
in an environment more conducive to officer safety, while at the same time meeting
the primary responsibilities of supervision: efficiency and effectiveness.

As a group, line officers in the undercover function exhibit a more personal focus
on their performance and job satisfaction than do line officers in other assignments. As
stated previously, this has much to do with the proactive nature of investigations in undercover assignments and the demands to "produce" cases. This more personal approach
can be both an advantage and a disadvantage to the supervisor of such units. A more
personal approach to investigations, along with the competitive nature of police officers
in general (and undercover officers specifically), provides inherent motivation to perform to the highest levels of expectations within undercover units. Conversely, however,
this motivation, if left without adequate supervision, can result in the misallocation of
resources by pushing cases past logical ending points, pursuing cases in the expectation
of greater results than may be realistic, and the misuse or mishandling of informants and
intelligence. It is not uncommon for the desire to make the big case to replace sound logic
and common sense, as the following comments from undercover officers indicate.

I often did it [took unnecessary risks]. I just wanted to
succeed in the deal.

I violated policy because I just wanted to make the case.

I realized that if they wanted to do something to me, how
quickly could my people have gotten to me, but I did it
because I just wanted the deal to go.

TEAM FOCUS VERSUS INDIVIDUAL ACHIEVEMENT

One of the subtle, but dramatic, phenomena that can occur in the undercover function
appears in the isolation of some officers from their peers, friends, and family. Often

this isolation is a defense mechanism employed to mediate individual and professional stressors which can overwhelm many assigned in the undercover function. Officers often feel more comfortable working alone and resist the team approach to case development and management. This isolation can be detrimental to the individual officer, as well as to the efficient and effective attainment of the unit's goals and the agency's overall mission. A team-focused philosophy in case development and management is much more conducive to enhance unit cohesiveness, maximize manpower and other scarce resources, and minimize the impact of individual coping strategies which often are maladaptive in nature and inconsistent with effective supervision.

An important portion of the team focus approach involves the identification and measurement of the unit's success. By focusing on the achievements of the team while still recognizing individual effort as part of team accomplishments, both the team concept is reinforced and the individual officer is given the attention and recognition that is expected and required from the workplace.

Although it is difficult to overcome the traditional measures of success used in law enforcement in general, and undercover units specifically, success should be measured by quality over quantity. Historically, although contrary to both common sense and the earliest principles of policing established by Sir Robert Peel, success in policing has been measured by the number of arrests, or the number of cases brought into the system. When success is measured by numbers alone, quality cases are sacrificed in order to show success through numbers. This concept may be justifiable in traffic enforcement or even in reactive investigations in which the factual circumstances are established. However, in proactive investigations in which the factual circumstances are limited to the evidence developed and not the evidence presented at the scene, it can be easy for the officer seeking success in the undercover assignment to make numerous smaller cases as opposed to one large case that could have greater implications. This phenomenon of quantity over quality is frequently seen in agencies across the United States in the use of "sweeps" for targeted offenses. This strategy involves the arrest of numerous offenders at one time for offenses that occurred over an extended period of time, or by throwing a wide net over a known area of concern and arresting everyone within the area in a zero tolerance approach to enforcement. Both strategies are effective in creating public awareness and support for police activities but have little value on effectively mediating any given social problem. Quality is sacrificed for quantity.

RECOGNITION

Regardless of how success is measured in the agency or unit, it is imperative that the line officers be recognized for their achievements within the team concept. Individual recognition is highly appropriate and effective in meeting the workplace needs of the individual and enhancing unit solidarity. Recognition and acceptance by coworkers is one of the highest workplace needs for most individuals.[6] This recognition can be an even higher need for occupations such as undercover assignments where performance is more proactive and, therefore, more personal in nature. As Hans Selye stated, "man must have recognition; he cannot tolerate constant censure, for that is what—more than any other stressor—makes work frustrating and harmful."[7]

Recognition from peers, as well as from superiors, is crucial to achieving the psychological rewards everyone seeks from the work environment in order to fulfill the basic human needs of achievement, self-purpose, pride, and competence. Effective supervision and management can be a highly effective way to meet these needs and subsequently provide the psychological rewards sought by each of us.

CONCERN FOR THE INDIVIDUAL OFFICER

Although performance and success should be assessed from a team perspective, the nature of police work in general, and undercover assignments specifically, demand an examination and evaluation of the individual officer's experiences and needs. Workplace stress is a highly subjective and complex phenomenon that is influenced by multiple factors at many different levels. Even those officers who are experiencing adequate acceptance and recognition may be dealing with personal issues that warrant the need for periodic assessment. Undercover officers should be evaluated periodically in order to ascertain if the cumulative nature of experiential or other duty-related stressors is causing adverse consequences in the officer's personal, social, or professional life. The very closeness that is a desirable benefit developing naturally in undercover units also can be a negative characteristic of such units if that closeness results in the rationalization of actions and behaviors, or overlooks key signs indicative of cumulative or chronic stress.

Following the whole-officer approach, supervisors should be aware of personal issues of concern to the officer, including the officer's social and family situations. Personal relationships have significant impact on the ability of any police officer to perform his/her duties in an effective and professional manner. This can be even more dramatic in the case of undercover officers when the assignment requires focus, and distracting personal issues can be both dangerous and inconsistent with the objective of lawful evidence accumulation.

The total-officer approach to supervision should not be viewed as intrusive or beyond the scope of workplace responsibility. Showing interest in the individual as a fellow officer and an important component of the unit and agency presents a higher workplace consideration than merely a nine-to-five mindset observed in many organizations. Supervision of the undercover function requires more than meeting minimum expectations and requirements. The stakes are higher in undercover assignments, and an effective supervisor can make the difference between success and failure at both the unit and individual levels.

SUMMARY

Supervision of the undercover function requires more attention and consideration than other first-line supervisory positions. The nature of the officers who function in undercover assignments, as well as the nature of the requirements for success in the undercover role dictate a more inclusive and holistic supervision strategy. The proactive nature of undercover investigations creates an environment that can be detrimental to the unit goals and agency mission if left unchecked or if allowed to function without adequate supervision and guidance.

The nature of undercover assignments requires a supervisor with knowledge and understanding of the specific issues of concern for the undercover officers. Those who function in an undercover capacity differ from officers in other assignments, in that the focus is on different workplace needs. Ethical issues have more importance in undercover assignments due to the nature of the duties and the additive components of stress and temptation. Stress often overwhelms many who are assigned to undercover duties. The desire to meet expectations and the fear of failure in the assignment, as well as the stressors inherent in policing in general, can all have both an additive and synergistic effect on officers involved in such assignments.

The bottom-up approach to supervision, coupled with supervisors who have worked undercover assignments, appears to be a more effective strategy for those who supervise the undercover function. The team focus approach can take pressure off the individual to succeed and allow for more efficient and effective case development and management, focusing on quality over quantity.

Recognition for achievement is an important responsibility for any supervisor and is even more significant in undercover units due to the proactive and personal approach to investigations. Acceptance and recognition in the workplace can go far to meet the higher psychological rewards we all seek from the work environment. In conjunction with recognition, the undercover supervisor must evaluate those in his charge to ensure the cumulative nature of the numerous administrative and experiential stressors do not result in adverse consequences in any aspect of the officer's life. Focusing on the total officer directly benefits the officer, the unit, and the agency, and indirectly benefits the community being served.

REFERENCES

1. Macleod, A.D. (1995). Undercover policing: A psychiatrist's perspective. *International Journal of Law and Psychiatry,* 18(2), 239-247.
2. Stevens, D.J. (1999). Corruption among narcotic officers: A study of innocence and integrity. *Journal of Police and Criminal Psychology,* 14(2), 1–10.
3. Arter, M.L. (2005). Undercover and under stress: The impact of undercover assignments on police officers. (Doctoral dissertation, Indiana University of Pennsylvania, 2005). *Dissertation Abstracts International,* 66(02), 769.
4. Stevens, D.J. (1999). Corruption among narcotic officers: A study of innocence and integrity. *Journal of Police and Criminal Psychology,* 14(2), 1–10.
5. Sykes, G.M. and Matza, D. (1957). Techniques of neutralization: A theory of delinquency. In H.N. Pontell (Ed.), *Social deviance: Readings in theory and research* (pp.152–156). Upper Saddle River, NJ: Prentice Hall.
6. Shostak, A.B. (1980). *Blue-collar stress.* Reading, MA: Addison-Wesley.
7. Selye, H. (1974). *Stress without distress.* Philadelphia, PA: Lippincott.

18 Law Enforcement Responses to Ethnic Street Gangs

Pamela Preston

CONTENTS

ABSTRACT

There are a multitude of strategies designed to deal with the problem or issue of street gangs in the United States. Programs run the gamut from prevention (aimed at the very young) through suppression (designed to stop existing gang members and activity) to legislation (which attempts to make gang activity illegal and prosecutable). However, not all gangs are the same; they are a reflection of the culture (whether racial/ethnic or social class) of their members. As such, a one-size-fits-all strategy is inappropriate. This chapter looks at the varied types of ethnic street gangs and the programs currently (and historically) used in gang prevention/suppression, and discusses the potential effectiveness of various programs for different types of street gangs/street gang members.

Although street gangs have existed in the United States since at least the early 1800s, they have only recently diversified their criminal activities. Gangs are, and always have been, for the most part, ethnically based. However, until the mid-to-latter part of the 20th-century gang activity for one ethnic group in an area would decrease with the rise of another (generally more recent) ethnic gang; for example, the Irish street gangs ran the Five Points area of New York City until the rise of the Jewish street gang, who ruled Five Points until the Italian street gangs moved in. As new gangs moved in, they tended to take over the criminal enterprises their predecessors engaged in.

However, increased immigration to the United States, and within the United States beginning in the 1940s, led to the concurrent existence of many different ethnic street gangs in many major cities of the United States, all competing for resources and criminal opportunities. This chapter looks at the history and criminal activity of different ethnic street gangs and general law enforcement practices directed at fighting street gangs, and makes some suggestions as to the appropriateness of various types of programs to different ethnicities of street gangs.

A BRIEF HISTORY OF ETHNIC* STREET GANGS

OUTLAW MOTORCYCLE GANGS

The first outlaw motorcycle gang (OMG) made its appearance in 1945. The Pissed Off Bastards of Bloomington were made up of former GIs and later changed its name to the Hell's Angels. Currently, there are about 900 different clubs in the United States with many thousands of members found in all states. Outlaw motorcycle gangs can also be found in Europe, Australia, and Asia. Major OMGs include the Hell's Angeles, Outlaws, Pagans, and Bandidos.

Outlaw Motorcycle Gangs are involved in diverse illegal and legal business activities. Some OMGs are running strippers, drink hustlers, and prostitutes, and are producing adult videos (which they franchise through the Mafia). OMGs have long hired themselves out as private security (with tragic results at Altamont in the early 1970s), and as debt collectors to the Mafia. They are involved in the narcotics trade, including methamphetamine production and sale, marijuana sales, and the illegal prescription drug business, including valium and vicodan. Other economically driven crimes include the purchase and sale of illegal weapons, arson, loan sharking, forgery and counterfeiting, and welfare fraud. Some law enforcement agencies report that OMGs are involved in motorcycle thefts and the selling of parts or entire bikes; however, this may not be widespread, as statistically Harleys and Indian motorcycles are the least-often stolen motorcycles. The more organized and successful OMGs

---

* For the purposes of this chapter, ethnicity refers to culture, rather than race. Culture is defined to include race, religion, and social class.

(like the Hell's Angels, Pagans, etc.) also reinvest their illegal profits in legitimate businesses, including catering companies, motorcycle repair, wrecking yards, real estate, hotels, investment firms, bars, towing companies, and even ice cream shops. This reinvestment makes it possible for OMGs to be prosecuted under RICO (Racketeer Influenced and Corrupt Organizations Act) and leads them to be classified as organized crime, rather than street gangs.

SKINHEADS

The earliest Skinhead gangs formed in England in the late 1960s. These gangs arose out of the amalgamation of two working-class subcultures; the white Mods and the West Indian Rude Boys. These early Skins were white working-class youth who felt that the Mods had lost touch with their roots. Early gangs were multiracial, adopting a truly working-class look (jeans, bomber jackets, and boots) and embracing Rude Boy music (Ska and Rocksteady). The first wave of Skins focused on drinking, football, and fighting. Racism did not become a part of Skin lifestyle until the 1970s; however, Skins and blacks remained (and have remained) on good terms in the United Kingdom. The second wave of skins directed their hatred towards the East Indian community, whom the Skins perceived were moving into their working- and lower-class neighborhoods. Skin culture in the 1970s and 1980s divided into two distinct tracts or philosophies: the apolitical or Oi! Skin whose main focus was traditional working-class concerns like drinking, fighting, and shagging (although some Oi! Skins became leftists, environmentalists, and animal rights activists) and the politicized hardcore Skins, who were recruited by England's answer to the KKK; the National Front. The United States got its first media view of Skins when a small number of racist Skins made an appearance on the Donahue show in 1984. Although most Americans continue to associate Skinhead culture with racism, there are both racist and antiracist (SHARP or Skinheads Against Racial Prejudice) Skins in both the United States and Great Britain, and the Skinhead look has become very popular among European gays. Although not technically Skinhead, Straightedge gangs (gangs that don't do drugs or engaged in casual sex) have adopted much of the Skinhead style.

Skinhead criminal activity is not primarily economically motivated. Fighting is the most common criminal activity (assault), with racist Skins attacking minorities, SHARPs attacking racist Skins and vice versa, and straightedge gangs attacking any gang engaging in alcohol, drug, or tobacco use or casual sex. Racist Skins engage in anything from malicious mischief/vandalism to murder, generally targeting racial minorities or gays. Skins and SHARPs are involved in drug and alcohol use and abuse. Racist Skins that have allied themselves with supremacist or militia groups may be recruited into economically driven crime (such as bank robbery) by the organization to help support it.

CRIPS AND BLOODS

Crip and Blood sets (gangs) originated in Los Angeles in the late 1960s/early 1970s. The Crips formed when Raymond Washington (originally a member of the Avenue Boys) moved to Washington High School and formed his own gang. The origin of the name Crip is unclear; it may have come from the fact that Washington used a cane or wheelchair, from the movie *Tales from the Crypt*, or from Kryptonite (the gang started with the name "Superman"). Bloods originated as the Piru Street Boys and Westside Pirus, which were formed by Centennial High School students Silvester Scott and Benson Owens. *Blood* is actually an umbrella term to denote gangs that are not a Crip set, and as such, Bloods (unlike Crips) limit their infighting, as their main function is protection from Crips.

Prior to the 1980s Crip and Blood criminal activity was fairly localized. Sets financed their activities through armed robbery and car thefts. The 1980s saw the rise in importance of drugs as a main source of income for the sets, and territory assumed new importance, as territory was essentially a set's sales franchise. At this time, Crips and Bloods also started to engage in highly skilled and organized bank and jewelry store robberies that required surveillance. They also initiated the one-minute robbery as a way of maximizing profits and minimizing risk; the one-minute robbery involved taking everything possible from the target (such as a jewelry store) within the time frame of 60 seconds, then getting out. This minimized the robber's chances of being caught. As the 1980s wore on smaller local gangs were annexed by larger Blood and Crip sets, and by the early 1990s they had extended their territory to 39 states and 69 cities outside of California. The most successful Crip and Blood leaders have moved into organized crime, reinvesting their profits into legitimate businesses.

PEOPLE AND FOLK NATION

People and Folk Nation are multiracial, culturally African-American gangs initially formed in Chicago. Folk Nation formed in 1979 when the Black Gangster Disciples and Simon City Royals (the largest African-American and white gangs, respectively) formed an alliance with 20 other gangs in the city, signing a nonaggression treaty. People Nation formed later that year as a protective measure when the Vice Lords and Latin Kings formed an alliance with 16 other local gangs. People and Folk nation gangs are the most politically oriented of all street gangs. The Vice Lords (People Nation) community redevelopment activities in Lawndale in the late 1960s and the Gangster Disciples (Folk Nation) political wing 21st Century Vote were/are the highest profile political activist organizations out of the Chicago gang scene.

Criminal activity of People and Folk Nation gangs run the gamut from car thefts, large-scale drug activity and, through their military contacts, weapons purchasing, stealing, smuggling, and selling.

JAMAICAN POSSES

Jamaican Posses first appeared in Kingston, Jamaica, in the mid-1970s. They were employed by both the leftist and rightwing political parties to get out the vote. By the 1980 elections, Michael Manley's leftist party was getting warfare and weapons training from Cuba, and the Jamaican Labour Party (right wing) was receiving the same from the CIA. The JLP won the 1980 election, but by this time, the gangs had become so violent in Kingston that the government decided to eradicate all gangs, including their supporters. Posse members who survived immigrated to the United States in the 1980s, initiated the crack business there on a large scale, and professionalized it.

In addition to the drug business (crack, cocaine, and marijuana), posses are involved in firearms trafficking of weapons obtained through legal purchase, straw purchase, theft, home invasion robberies, hijacking, military theft, and/or mail theft, with the bulk of weapons acquired in southern states and sent to New York City for subsequent distribution throughout the United States and Jamaica. Money obtained through drugs or weapons is then laundered. Posses will launder money through street vendors, transport 55-gallon barrels full of money into Jamaica; work with airline employees or currency couriers to transport money out of the United States; hide cash in new cars purchased with cash; send money by Express Mail and Western Union or through banks and legitimate companies, and place bets with illegally gotten cash at racetracks. Jamaican street gangs are also involved in immigration fraud, including counterfeit documents (green cards, etc.), illegal immigration via cruise ship, and sham marriages with U.S. citizens.

Asian Gangs

Chinese

The first Chinese street gang was formed in the 1950s in San Francisco by second-generation Chinese Americans. The first immigrant Chinese gang was the Wah Ching and formed as a means of protection for immigrant Chinese youth from American-born Chinese gangs. Wah Ching continued to grow and spread along the West Coast. The first East Coast Chinese gangs formed about a decade later, from the juvenile branch of the On Leong Tong, the On Leong Youth Club, later know as the White Eagles. East Coast Chinese gangs are more numerous and appear more (at least outwardly) violent than West Coast gangs. They are active throughout New York City, and major gangs include the Flying Dragons (under the control and protection of the Hip Sing Tong), Ghost Shadows (associated with the On Leong Tong), Tong On Boys (working in New York, Philadelphia, and Portland, ME, and with the Tung On Tong), Fuk Ching (involved in the immigrant smuggling ship *The Golden Venture*), the Green Dragons, Born to Kill (ethnically Vietnamese), White Tigers (a subsidiary of Ghost Shadows), and Gum Sing.

Chinese street gangs on both coasts have diversified criminal interests. Extortion is often a primary money-making venture, and involves forced contributions from neighborhood merchants, discounted merchandise, sales of raw materials and equipment to merchants, protection, lucky money, and forcing business owners to install video poker machines. Chinese street gangs are also involved in immigrant smuggling, home and business invasion robberies, credit card fraud, commodity scams, prostitution (generally of Korean or Vietnamese women who must work off their illegal immigration costs), kidnapping for ransom, drug trafficking (especially heroin), and money laundering.

Korean

Korean street gangs are believed to be a result of culture conflict and family conflict, as many Korean youth at least partially assimilated into American society, whereas their parents retained the old customs. Korean street gangs initially appeared on the East Coast (New York City) and West Coast (Los Angeles). Recently immigrant youth formed gangs in New York City, Washington, D.C., Denver, Chicago, and Los Angeles. The first California Korean Street gang was American Burger (AB) initially formed to protect Korean youths from assaults by gangs of other ethnicities. Other Korean gangs found in the Los Angeles area are Burger King (BK) and Korean Killers (KK). There are also independent Korean girl gangs, including a female offshoot of Burger King called IBK (Innocent but Killers aka Innocent Bitch Killers) and a female offshoot of Korean Killers called KGK (Korean Girl Killers). Korean street gangs work with Japanese Yakuza.

Criminal activities of Korean street gangs include production and sale of crystal methamphetamine ("ice") and extremely well-organized home and business invasion robberies, a favorite business target being Korean-owned jewelry stores. Rounding out their profit-oriented criminal activities are burglary, extortion, and the theft of autos and auto parts. Korean gang members have also been prosecuted and convicted of sexual offenses against women of their community. Gang rape is a relatively common form of initiation into the gang; however, these seldom come to the attention of the authorities as the victims and their families are reluctant to report them.

Southeast Asian

Southeast Asian street gangs include Vietnamese, Viet-Chin (ethnic Chinese from Vietnam), Laotian, and Cambodian members. Original gangs were created along ethnic lines (gangs were exclusively Laotian, Cambodian, etc.), but as the second generation Southeast Asian entered gang life, these barriers broke down. Southeast Asian gangs are more prevalent on the West Coast than on the East Coast, although Tiny Rascals Gangsters sets have been found in the Northeast and Born to Kill is originally a New York gang. Many Southeast Asian gangs follow a military model, imported to the United States with the fall of Saigon and the immigration of many Vietnamese military personal friendly to the U.S. military to the States. Southeast Asian gang membership also tends to be fluid, with members drifting in and out for the commission of specific crimes. Southeast Asian independent girl gangs also exist, affiliated with male gangs, but also functioning as an independent gang. They will challenge, fight, and kill rival gang members, whether male or female. Some all-male Southeast Asian gangs even have a female leader.

Southeast Asian street gangs introduced the home invasion robbery to the United States. These are well organized (often using a female associate to gain entrance to the house), involving small number of participants, arming all members, binding and gagging victims and keeping them in a single location, and using intimidation. Home invasion robberies were considered extremely profitable, as most Vietnamese immigrants were unlikely to keep their money and valuables in a bank. More recently, Southeast Asian gangs have moved into the theft of computer chips, which are small, easily transported, difficult to trace, and auctioned off or sold at computer swap shows. Obsolete chips are also stolen as they include some type of precious metal. Additionally, Southeast Asian gangs are involved in auto and auto part theft, drug trafficking (crack and heroin), gambling, prostitution (massage parlors and escort services), and extortion.

LATINO GANGS

The "official" Los Angeles Latino Street gang formed in 1909 was called the Alpine Street gang. The Mexican Revolution of 1910–1940 led to an increase in Mexican immigration to the United States and helped fuel the development of more and more powerful Latino Street gangs in the Southwest. The most powerful Latino gang, Maravilla (named after a barrio in east Los Angeles) was formed in the 1940s. This gang would later form the nucleus of the Mexican Mafia. Tensions between whites and Latino gang members escalated in the 1940s with the Sleepy Lagoon murder trial (which many in the Mexican-American community felt was fixed to allow for the incarceration of gang members) and erupted into rioting in June 1943, when sailors on leave in Los Angeles attacked "zoot-suited" Latino youth, who engaged in retaliatory strikes by gang members. In the 1950s, Latino gang members moved into the suburbs, and some gangs became "Puro Chicano," open only to nonmixed race (exclusively Mexican-American) members. Second-generation Latino gang members appeared in the 1960s, and at this time Latino gangs became involved in the drug trade. Latino prison gangs also started recruiting street gang members at this time. Firearms became common in these gangs in the 1970s, and the prison mentality/philosophy filtered into the street gangs as well. In the 1970s the LAPD also cracked down on older gang members ("Veteranos"), leading to a marked change in Latino gang culture in the 1980s. Latino gangs of the 1980s moved into the cocaine business, and by 1988 there were 450 Latino gangs and 50,000 Latino gang members in Los Angeles County alone. In the early 1990s Central and South American Latino gangs made their appearance in Southern California, and continued immigration from this area has led to an increasing number of gangs and of gang members from Central and South America.

Latino gangs tend to be the most territory-oriented of all street gangs, and much of their violent crime is a result of territorial warfare. However, Latino prison gangs, particularly the Mexican Mafia, have for many years worked with street gangs who serve as their agents on the outside. Latino street gangs deliver drugs (marijuana, cocaine, and heroin), collect money, and act as enforcers for prison gangs, taking a cut of the profit. Street gang members have also been known to intimidate witnesses who testify (or are going to testify) against Mexican Mafia or "Nuestra Familia" members or even kill them. Some gangs are involved in nonviolent, nondrug- oriented businesses, such as counterfeit identification, payroll checks, credits cards, and bus passes.

LAW ENFORCEMENT RESPONSES TO GANGS

The Office of Juvenile Justice and Delinquency Prevention (2000) identifies seven approaches to dealing with gangs. These include: (1) prevention programs, aimed at stopping gangs from developing and stopping youth from gang involvement, (2) intervention programs designed to pull at-risk youth away from gangs and to decrease criminal behavior by active gang members (3) suppression programs, which reduce the criminal activity of gangs and gang members through prosecution and incarceration, (4) integrative programs, which use some combination of prevention, intervention, and suppression, (5) multiagency programs which combine federal, state, and local agencies to combat gangs, (6) comprehensive programs, which adopt an holistic approach, and (7) antigang legislation.

PREVENTION PROGRAMS

Prevention programs, as earlier stated, attempt to prevent the formation of gangs and to stop youth from joining gangs. Community organization projects focus on neighborhoods. The Chicago Area Project, developed in the mid-1930s, was the first to try to restructure neighborhoods to block the formation of youth gangs, the philosophy being that disorganized communities facilitated gang formation and involvement, and institutional (family, economic, education) organization was the key to preventing gangs and crime. The House of Umoja, formed in the 1970s, was created in Philadelphia to provide familial and spiritual support to urban youth, the same benefits previously supplied by gangs. Although empirical support for the Chicago Area Project is limited, it remains popular. The House of Umoja has been fairly successful in transforming young men into successful citizens.

Although community organization projects focused on fixing the community with the assumption that youth would then fix themselves, more recent programs provide services and support of at-risk youth. These programs tend to be focused on lower-income areas and public housing projects. Some examples of this type of program include The Beethoven Project for mothers and infants located in Chicago, The Neutral Zone (recreational facility) in Washington State, and the Community Outreach Program, developed in St. Paul, MN, to work with its rapidly expanding Asian community.

Early childhood programs identify at-risk youth (prior to gang involvement) and attempt to attract youth (usually elementary-school aged) away from gangs and to improve social skills, while simultaneously training parents how to monitor behavior, use punishment effectively, use positive reinforcement, and manage family crises. Some programs (Syracuse University Family Development Research Project, High-Scope Perry Preschool Project) started as early as preschool and included educational, child care, and health services to at-risk families, adding regular home visits.

In response to growing gang presence in public schools, many have adopted gang prevention programs of their own. Some programs involve increased police and other capable guardian presence, such as Passport in Visalia, CA. Many youth give protection from others as a motivation for joining gangs; some European cities (Bergen, Norway, and Sheffield, England) have adopted antibullying programs, with varying degrees of success (more successful with younger children). The Gang Resistance Is Paramount (Paramount, CA) program offers support to parents in trying to prevent gang involvement by their children, courses on gang behavior, and activity for second- and fifth-grade students, and a follow-up program at the high school level. The Gang Resistance Education and Training Program (GREAT) teaches middle school students about crime, victimization and their rights, cultural sensitivity, conflict resolution, meeting social needs, drugs, responsibility, and goal setting. Data on the effectiveness of the GREAT program has yet to show a measurable reduction in gang involvement (Esbensen 2001).

INTERVENTION PROGRAMS

Intervention programs are designed to pull gang members out of gangs, and decrease the severity and frequency of crime by gang members. One of the earliest forms intervention program was the detached-worker program. The New York City Youth Board was one of the earliest examples of this type of program, utilizing former gang members to go out into the streets and work with the gangs, providing counseling and advocacy, or whatever it would take to lure youth out of the gangs. Other detached-worker programs include the Midcity Project (Boston), Group Guidance Project (Los Angeles), and the Ladino Hills Project (East Los Angeles). Empirical studies point to a lack of positive effect by these programs, part of which may be due to the varied and noncomplimentary program objectives.

The next wave of intervention programming was crisis intervention. This type of program, pioneered in the 1970s, involved sending detached workers to work in gang areas, rather than assign them to a specific gang or group of gang members. Workers in these programs did not provide general social services; rather, they patrolled areas of gang activity attempting to diffuse violent or potentially violent situations. The pioneer program was Crisis Intervention Network out of Philadelphia. Later programs included Los Angeles' Community Youth Gang Services and the Crisis Intervention Services Project out of Chicago. Crisis Intervention programs have been criticized as, at best, at temporary solution to gang violence, neglecting the underlying social causes of gang formation and involvement.

Several intervention programs have focused on transitioning gang members from illegal to legal means of income production. Two Los Angeles-based programs that have been effective in reducing gang membership and gang activity are Homeboy Industries and Jobs for a Future. Jobs for a Future is a more traditional operation that places gang members in jobs within their communities. Homeboy Industries and Homeboy Bakeries manufacture, produce, and market goods (including breads). Proceeds from both programs fund various community services. Interestingly, many gang members and associates/at-risk youth state they would give up the retail drug business in exchange for wages not far above the minimum wage being paid in fast food establishments and, in fact, gang activity has been reduced in areas with these and similar programs.

Intervention programs that focus on changing the social and economic conditions prevalent in gang neighborhoods appear to be more successful than what can be considered Band-Aid approaches, which seek to limit violence be fail to address the root causes of gang involvement and criminality. Those programs that provide alternative means of economic attainment (either through jobs within the community or through the creation of businesses operated by gang and former gang members), such as Homeboy Industries, do decrease gang involvement and violence. Detached-worker and crisis intervention programs, while decreasing the violence, do not appear to have any lasting or long-term positive effects on gang activity. Some support for community/social institution redevelopment is shown in Hagedorn's (2001) study of gangs and social structure in Milwaukee.

Suppression Programs

Suppression programs focus on the reduction of gang activity, generally through the use of law enforcement and correctional systems. Suppression programs, while in existence since the late 1970s, gained momentum and public support with the rise in gang violence associated with the developing crack business of the 1980s. Perhaps the most high-profile of these operations is the Los Angeles Police Department's Community Resources Against Street Hoodlums (CRASH) unit. CRASH is characterized by police sweeps of neighborhoods in which the arrest gang members and likely gang members for any number of offenses. Arrestees would be taken to a mobile booking station, where most were subsequently released without charges. CRASH has been notoriously inefficient; Operation Hammer (1988) involved the arrest of more than 1400 individuals, only half of whom were gang members, resulting in 60 felony arrests, and only 32 charged. The CRASH unit came under scrutiny for civil rights violations and criminal behavior. The Los Angeles City Civil Gang Abatement program (Los Angeles City Attorney Gang Prosecution Section, 2001) also broaches concerns about civil rights violations against gang members.

Conversely, the Los Angeles County Sheriff Department's Operation Safe Streets has been more successful. Operation Safe Streets identified the most active and high-profile gang within a given area, and focused its resources and activity on that gang. Officers formed a relationship with the gang members that reduced the anonymity necessary to successful gang behavior, and made it possible to officers to work with gang members to move them out of the gang life style. The combination of thorough knowledge of the gang and humanitarian concern (absent in the CRASH unit sweeps) with law enforcement practices that were fair but still firm led to a decrease in gang activity and positive community and gang reaction to the Sheriff's Department.

The Office of Community Oriented Policing Services (COPS) has supported a number of gang-suppression programs. These programs run the gamut from strictly deterrence and suppression to a combination of suppression and intervention. The majority of programs (Antigang Initiative in Dallas, TX, and Youth Firearms Violence Initiatives in Inglewood, CA, Salinas, CA, and Milwaukee, WI) utilize some combination of law enforcement saturation of gang areas and enforcement of curfew and truancy laws. The Youth Firearms Violence Initiative in Seattle, WA, includes aggressive law enforcement working with schools, tracking of the most violent youth in the area, and provision of services.

Some agencies are starting to rely on sophisticated tracking, mapping, and identification systems. These allow law enforcement to identify where the gangs are, where the violence occurs, and the availability of services in these areas. The Orange County Sheriff's Department (Orange County, CA) has perhaps the most sophisticated gang tracking systems in the country. The Gang Incident and Tracking System (GITS) includes a centralized database that creates geomaps of gang crime, location of gang members' homes, and types of community interventions based on data from 22 cities.

Multiple Technique Strategies

These gang suppression strategies involve cooperation between the community and community policing. Community policing programs, such as the Community Action

Team (Reno, NV), involve minority community representatives, political leaders, and representatives from service agencies within the targeted community working with local law enforcement to target the most serious gang offenders and develop intervention and prevention programs for gangs members not yet considered hardcore. Community residents can provide feedback to the program through a local advisory board.

In some areas, local universities work in tandem with the community to stem emerging gangs and gang activity. Developed initially for small cities, the programs can be modified to work in larger cities. The Community-University Model for Gang Intervention and Delinquency Prevention in Small Cities, originally developed for Racine, WI, suggests six steps for dealing with the early stages of gang development. They include (1) a true commitment to the youth in the area through addressing local issues such as lack of recreation and services and an understanding of the underlying socio-economic structure, (2) an assessment of gang development in the area, to include input from all sources, (3) networking with community and neighborhood to create a gang response that reflects the community, (4) identification of a local resource (such as college or university) to study the gang and obtain funding for the study, (5) dissemination of information outside the community in order to expand the network and possible sources of funding, and (6) creation of master plan with long-term goals.

MULTIAGENCY INITIATIVES

Multiagency programs involve multiple law enforcement agencies pooling their knowledge and resources in order to better fight gangs. Most often this involves cooperation between federal, state, and local agencies across their jurisdictional boundaries; however, in some instances, this involves collaboration between different types of crime control agencies within local boundaries.

The Los Angeles Metropolitan Task Force and Boston Gun Project are examples of the former. The Los Angeles program is led by federal agencies, including the ATF and the FBI. The federal agencies provide money for purchases and informants, the use of federal laws, and logistic support. The Boston program, unlike the Los Angeles program, is not completely suppression oriented. While working with the ATF, the Boston Police Department attempts to control the illegal gun market; however, probation also works to enforce the terms of probation for youth, and street workers (police, probation, social services) work to resolve conflicts among youth and provide social services. Kennedy (2001) states that this program's effectiveness is heightened by the concurrent use of community policy strategies.

Orange County, CA, has instituted a program involving same-level collaboration among agencies. The Tri-Agency Resource Gang Enforcement Team (TARGET) includes the Orange County Sheriff's Office, local law enforcement, the Orange County District Attorney's Office, and Orange County Probation. This program, which is suppression oriented, targets the most serious and violent street gang members. TARGET, now operating in eight cities, has been quite successful, as indicated by the near-elimination of gang crime in specific targeted spots. Although this can result in the simple movement of gangs into other neighborhoods, Kent and Smith (2001) point out that it appears to be an effective technique in smaller communities.

COMPREHENSIVE APPROACHES TO GANG PROBLEMS

Comprehensive approaches to gang control are less unidimensional than multiagency programs, which tend to focus on the suppression of gang violence and gang activity. These programs address structural issues such as community disorganization, in addition to gang suppression. The Comprehensive Community-Wide Approach to Gang Prevention, Intervention, and Suppression has programs in Mesa, AZ, Tucson, AZ, Riverside, CA, Bloomington, IL, and San Antonio, TX. The basic characteristics of the program included coordinated gang suppression, community mobilization, social intervention, and academic, economic, and social opportunities for older gang members, as well as modification of existing law enforcement agencies. This holistic approach to gang control emphasizes to everyone (law enforcement, the community, local agencies, families, and individuals) that they are all affected by, and can bring about change to, the community.

LEGISLATION

Legislation as a means of gang suppression has been becoming increasingly popular, both at the federal and the local level. Aimed at gang suppression, most legislation includes penalty enhancements that allow for increased sanctions for gang related offenses, including drug trafficking, assault, robbery, auto theft, and less serious crimes such as conspiracy, and aiding and abetting.

Street gangs and gang members have been prosecuted under the Racketeer Influenced and Corrupt Organizations Act (RICO). Usually used against adult organized crime and to prosecute the highest ranking adults in these organizations, youth members of street gangs have in some cases been prosecuted under this act. States have also enacted their own laws designed to suppress gangs and gang activity. California's STEP Act (Street Terrorism Enforcement and Prevention) allows law enforcement to gather evidence on specific gangs that fit STEP's definition of a gang. Gang members are then notified that they are known to be members of the specified gang. This allows enhanced penalties against gang members whenever they are involved in any criminal activity. The California model has been adopted by several other states, including Louisiana, Florida, Georgia, and Illinois. Cities and other local jurisdictions have also adopted laws designed to suppress gang activity. Gang abatement measures include statutes prohibiting flashing of gang signs, wearing gang colors, and insulting rival gangs. Law enforcement agencies are able to obtain injunctions against gangs to prevent them from congregating in public areas. Many cities enact and enforce curfews as a means to reduce gang activity. However, the effectiveness of curfews has not been established, and the constitutionality of curfew laws has come into question in recent years

YOUTH GANG PROGRAM APPLICABILITY TO ETHNIC STREET GANGS

Given the diversity of history and criminal activity of ethnic street gangs, it is unreasonable to assume that any one program can serve as a panacea for the street gang problem. Rather, law enforcement must take into account both the culture the street gang derives from, and the primary criminal activities of that gang, before adopting any antigang program or initiative.

Traditional ethnic street gangs, which are mainly concentrated in socially disorganized areas (barrios, ghettos, etc.), have been the focus of the majority of youth gang programs. Prevention programs, which focus on tracking youth away from gangs while simultaneously improving the effectiveness of social institutions (including family) in the youths community; intervention programs diverting youth from legal to illegal means of income attainment; suppression programs relying on mapping, tracking, and identification; aggressive suppression of gangs; community-oriented policing programs; and multiple technique strategies incorporating many of these programs are best suited to those street gangs concentrated in a neighborhood or small area. These types of programs may have some success combating traditional territorially oriented Latino/Chicano gangs, some African American gangs, and small Skinhead groups.

However, these programs will not be effective against those gangs that are not territorial. Asian gangs (Chinese, Korean, and Southeast Asian) were the first to not fit the traditional street gang mold. Asian gang members are more likely to come from intact families (both parents present) than other gang members. Many Asian street gang members come from relatively affluent neighborhoods, and have parents who are small business owners. They may also be exceptional students and have applied to and been accepted by top-level universities. They or their parents are able to afford nice cars and expensive computer equipment. Asian street gangs (especially Korean and Southeast Asian) are not geographically tied down. Gang membership can also be fluid, with gang members coming together for the commission of a particular crime, then going their separate ways when finished. Criminal activity is also not limited to a single area; rather, these gangs may take to the road, committing crimes throughout the country before separating. Multiagency programs involving many levels of law enforcement (local, state, and federal agencies) would be most effective against this type of gang, given the regional and/or national focus of their gang activity. Additionally, legislation such as RICO could prove effective against these types of gangs as much of their activity (and interstate activity) could be prosecuted as organized crime.

It is important to remember that ethnic street gangs are a diverse lot, driven by different motives, and a product of different causal factors. As such, law enforcement strategies must be customized with respect to the type of gang being dealt with. One-size-fits-all youth gang programs, while they may have been appropriate in the past, are not applicable to the street gangs of the 21st century.

REFERENCES

Chin, K. (1996). *Chinatown gangs: extortion, enterprise, and ethnicity.* Oxford University Press, New York.

Curry, G.D. and Scott, H.D. (1998). *Confronting gangs: crime and community.* Roxbury Publishing Company, Los Angeles, CA.

Esbensen, F.-A. (2001). The National Evaluation of the Gang Resistance Education and Training (G.R.E.A.T.) Program. *The modern gang reader.* Eds. Miller, Jody, Maxson, Cheryl L., and Klein, Malcolm W. pp. 289–302. Roxbury Publishing Company. Los Angeles, CA.

Fearn, N.E., Decker, S.H., and Curry, G.D. (2001). Public policy responses to gangs: evaluating the outcomes. *The modern gang reader*. Eds. Miller, Jody, Maxson, Cheryl L., and Klein, Malcolm W. pp. 330–344. Roxbury Publishing Company, Los Angeles, CA.

Grennan, S., Britz, M.T., Rush, J., Barker, T. (2000). *Gangs: an international approach.* Prentice Hall, Upper Saddle River, NJ.

Hagedorn, J.M. (2001). Gangs, neighborhoods, and public policy. *The modern gang reader*. Eds. Miller, Jody, Maxson, Cheryl L., and Klein, Malcolm W. pp. 262–274. Roxbury Publishing Company. Los Angeles, CA.

Kent, D.R. and Smith, P. (2001). The tri-agency resource gang enforcement team: a selective approach to reduce gang crime. *The modern gang reader*. Eds. Miller, Jody, Maxson, Cheryl L., and Klein, Malcolm W. pp. 303–308. Roxbury Publishing Company. Los Angeles, CA.

Kleinknecht, W. (1996). *The new ethnic mobs: the changing face of crime in America.* The Free Press, New York.

Landre, R., Miller, M., Porter, D. (1997). *Gangs: a handbook for community awareness.* Facts on File, New York.

Long, P.D.P. and Ricard, L. (1996). *The dream shattered: Vietnamese gangs in America.* Northeastern University Press, Boston, MA.

Pope, C.E. and Lovell, R. (2004). Gang prevention and intervention strategies of the boys and girls clubs of American. *Understanding contemporary gangs in America: an interdisciplinary approach*. Ed. Petersen, Rebecca D. pp. 354–353–367. Prentice Hall, Upper Saddle River, NJ.

Sachs, S. (1997). *Street gang awareness.* Fairview Press, Minneapolis, MN.

Valdez, A. (2000). *Gangs: a guide to understanding street gangs.* LawTech Publishing Co., San Clemente, CA.

Vigil, J.D. (2000) *Barrio gangs: street life and identity in Southern California.* University of Texas Press, Austin, TX.

Westin, J. (2001). Community policing: an approach to youth gangs in a medium-sized city. *The modern gang reader*. Eds. Miller, Jody, Maxson, Cheryl L., and Klein, Malcolm W. pp. 315–319. Roxbury Publishing Company. Los Angeles, CA.

19 Outlaw Motorcycle Gangs: National and International Organized Crime

Thomas Barker

CONTENTS

INTRODUCTION

The popular image—or myth, if you will—surrounding outlaw bikers has been that of social misfits on the seat of a stripped-down Harley, driven by freedom of the road, wind whipping in their long hair: outsiders showing their contempt for society through drinking, drug taking, and deviant sexual acts—just "good ole boys" living up to the patch they wear, bearing the acronym FTW ("fuck the world"). One researcher, a member of an OMG (outlaw motorcycle gang) for two years (1973–1974), describes outlaw motorcycle gangs (there is a separate gang known as the "Outlaws," which will be discussed below) as a subculture whose members, "referring to themselves as 'One Percenters,' operate within the 'saloon society' milieu of lower-class taverns, and either cannot or will not 'fit in' conventional social life" (Quinn, 1987: 47). The name "One Percent" reportedly comes from a statement in the 1940s by the president of the American Motorcycle Association stating that one percent of the bikers were the ones causing trouble for all bikers. George "Baby Huey" Wethern (1978), former Oakland Hell's Angels (HA) vice president and one of the first of many biker informers, relates the results of a 1960 statewide meeting of all California Hell's Angels leaders and leaders of other rival clubs such as the Gypsy Jokers, Road Rats, Galloping Gooses, Satan's Slaves, the Presidents, and the

Mofos. The purpose of this meeting was to form a united front against police harassment. The leaders decided to unite themselves under the One Percenter patch in order to distinguish themselves from pretenders and weekenders like the members of the American Motorcycle Association. Wethern says that he and Sonny Barger, president of the HA Oakland chapter, were the first to get the diamond-shaped One Percent patch.

In the formative years of the late 1950s and early 1960s, the Hell's Angels developed cultural traditions that would define them and other OMGs for years. They were white supremacists with a definite antiblack attitude (the motto for membership: "No niggers, no cops, no snitches"); they were male chauvinists, treating women, except their "old ladies" (wives or current girlfriends), as sexual objects not worthy as members of the club, only property of the club; and they held meetings governed by rules, including parliamentary procedures. Wethern (1978) reports that even the charismatic leader Ralph "Sonny" Barger occasionally lost the vote on some issues of club business. The cultural tradition of "brotherhood" which embodied such statements as "Angels Forever," "Forever Angels," "Angels Come First," "No Snitches," and other expressions/mottos of mutual support, camaraderie, and "love" between equals would later reveal itself to be more illusionary than real.

There was an early recognition of public deviant sexual activities: for example, white wings worn on the cut-off jacket for having public cunnilingus with a menstruating white women, black wings for the same act on a menstruating black women, and brown wings were given for having public sodomy with a man. These died out, as did the display of Nazi memorabilia. The most vivid account of the deviant sexual activities of the early Hell's Angels is contained in the autobiography of "Buttons," the first English Hell's Angel (Mandelkau, 1971). Buttons, in the first of many OMG "crooks books," describes his visit to California to become a Hell's Angel, including the gang sodomy of a male homosexual and other deviant acts. Buttons returned to England and established the first Hell's Angel chapter with himself as president.

In one of the first scholarly works on OMGs as organized crimes, the author, using Cressey's definition of organized crime, said that:

> ... One Percenters reject the standard of the other ninety-nine percent by the adoption of outlandish uniforms with Nazi German trappings to instill fear; performing of weird initiation rites (including the performance of deviant and outlandish sexual acts witnessed by other members, and the commission of criminal acts); gaining the respect of law-abiding groups through fear and intimidation. (Hill, 1980: 27)

This description of OMGs is as outdated as Cressey's definition of organized crime. It contains some elements of current OMG members and groups (rejection of society's norms, initiation rites, fear and intimidation) and is far off the mark on the rest. The infiltration of undercover police officers into OMGs, including some who have become "officers," demonstrates that such initiation rites as deviant sexual acts and criminal behavior are not required. Furthermore, the wearing of Nazi Germany trappings has become a thing of the past as OMGs, particularly the Hell's Angels, have "cleaned up" their image as they moved into organized crime activities.

TWENTY-FIRST-CENTURY OUTLAW MOTORCYCLE GANGS

At one time, bikers who described themselves as One Percenters may have lived the life of drinking binges, brawls, and rowdiness described above. As stated, this is not an accurate portrayal of One Percenters in the twenty-first century. According to the Los Angeles Police Department, OMG are organizations whose members use their membership in a motorcycle club as a basis for criminal activities (Haut 1999). Many OMG have evolved into highly sophisticated organized crime groups nationally and internationally. Many American-based OMGs have written constitutions, by-laws, and hierarchical leadership structures, and the members pay dues and attend regular meetings. Lavigne (1999) reports that Hell's Angels spend as much time at meetings as corporate executives. Meetings are held at all levels of the organization, chapter, regional, West Coast, East Coast, and world. Veno (2002) reports that clubs meetings and other mandatory runs and obligations causes many Australian bikies (bikers) to leave the clubs because they do not have a life of their own.

The minutes of many OMG meetings have been confiscated during police raids and used in prosecutions, particularly RICO cases. Lavigne (1999) has copies of the Hell's Angels' and Bandidos' minutes in several of his books. They reveal interesting facts about the clubs (gangs) internal operations and overseas expansion, as well as disturbing intelligence on law enforcement operations. As Lavigne (1999) opines, the police keep their operations secret, not even telling their wives, but because of administrative red tape the paperwork for budgets and overtime approval is handed over to civilian clerks whose desks and computers are accessible to everyone in the office. For that matter, anyone who has worked for a police bureaucracy, particularly in an undercover operation, knows of the problems presented by the Insistence of "paper shufflers" on receipts for reimbursements of expenses (see Pistone 1987). Imagine the reaction by criminals and gangsters to an undercover operative asking for a receipt of a meal, taxi, or other expense. There are "ritualists" in every bureaucracy, including law enforcement.

Many OMGs have incorporated and trademarked their gang logos. The Hell's Angels have trademarked their name and organization's classic Death's head logo. Their intellectual property lawyer sued Marvel Enterprises, Inc., for putting out a comic book titled *Hell's Angels* (McKee 2001). Marvel was forced to change the comic's name to *Dark Angel* and pay the Hell's Angels $35,000. At the suggestion of the federal mediator, the money was donated to Ronald McDonald House Charities, because Marvel balked at giving it to the Hell's Angels. They have sued or threatened to sue others for using the name or the logo, including a Southern California porn producer who made a film titled *Hell's Angels: Demon of Lust*. The Hell's Angels sued Yves Lavigne and the English and French publishers after the publication of his first book on the motorcycle club, *Taking Care of Business,* because of an artist rendition of the Death's head on the cover (Lavigne 1996). The English-language publisher of the book declared bankruptcy to get out of the suit. The French-language publisher settled with Hell's Angels and agreed never to publish another book on them.

Outlaw motorcycle gangs have been called the "only organized crime group developed in the United States (without ethnic ties) that is being exported around the world" (Smith, 1998, p. 54). One law enforcement expert on OMGs says that "Biker gangs are the only sophisticated organized crime groups that we export from the United States" (Trethewy and Katz 1998). They have established ties and working relationships with traditional OC groups such as La Cosa Nostra, Columbian cartels, and even the Chinese Triads (Haut, 1999; Trethewy and Katz 1998). OMG members have acted as hitmen for traditional OC groups (Smith 2002). Interpol includes OMGs with Mafia-type organized crime organizations because of their highly structured hierarchies, internal rules of discipline, codes of "ethics," and diversity in illegal and legitimate affairs (Kendall, 1998).

Research into the activities of OMGs is a difficult endeavor because, as a criminal group, they are dangerous, secretive, do not grant access to outsiders, and do not publish histories (other than on Web sites) and membership lists. Nevertheless, there have been some published sources (academic, court cases, law enforcement/government reports, popular literature, and numerous "crooks books") of their exploits and actions. They have, contrary to their stated hatred for snitches/informants and allusions to brotherhood, turned on one another when the going got tough and long prison sentences loomed, especially with the advent of RICO prosecutions. They have been penetrated by undercover police officers on several occasions. And, the majority of the groups maintain Internet Websites, an excellent source of chapters and affiliates. This work is based on a review of these sources, interviews and associations with current and past OMG members, and interviews with law enforcement officials. These sources document that since their origins in the early 1940s, United States OMGs have become highly organized criminal networks motivated more by criminal interests than by hedonistic pursuits. Specifically, this work deals with the three major American-based OMGs with international connections: the Hell's Angels, the Outlaws, and the Bandidos.

OUTLAW MOTORCYCLE GANGS AS ORGANIZED CRIME

It appears from Wethern's (1978) accounts of the early Hell's Angels that their first movement into organized crime began with the control of psychedelic drugs in the San Francisco Haight Street district in the early 1960s. By the end of the 1960s, the Hell's Angels had moved from a club where the members held unskilled labor jobs to their holding full-time jobs as Hell's Angels and drug pushers (Wethern 1978). Wehtern and his "crew" handled the psychedelic drugs, another Angel ran the mescaline traffic, and Sonny Barger controlled heroin and cocaine. New members and chapters were chosen based not solely on biker values, although the prospect had to have a reputation as an outlaw, but it was more important that they could contribute to the drug trade: Could they provide a drug route link, manufacture a drug, supply chemicals, or distribute drugs in an untapped area? (Wehterhn, p. 102) There were numerous biker outlaws that wanted to join and cash in on the available money. Drug dealing Hell's Angels were buying new Harleys, luxury cars like Cadillacs, Corvettes, and Jaguars; numerous automatic pistols and machine guns, and even, exotic animals, such as lions. Membership climbed to 500 in 21 chapters (ten in California, eight out of state, and three international—in Switzerland, England, and West Germany). It was during this same period (1968) that the Oakland Chapter performed its first execution when a member was killed for stealing President Sonny Barger's coin collection (Wethern 1978). So much for brotherhood. The new members came in with little respect for the brother rhetoric. As Wehtern states, " ... lots of the younger guys lived by an every-man-for-himself ethic, and keeping an individual reputation, body, and finances intact became more important than club unity (p.166)." During this same time period, other OMGs were following the Hell's Angels into the drug trafficking arena in their areas.

The media was turning the gangs and many of their members, such as Barger, into celebrities. Numerous biker movies were produced with gang members as extras and technical consultants. None of the 1960s biker movies lost money (Stidworthy 2003). The bikers were usually cast as free spirits fighting against abusive cops or Rednecks. However, the much-publicized murder of a black man accompanying a white women at the Rolling Stones concert at Altamont Park in California resulted in a change in their tactics and the public façade of the biker gangs.

In the 1970s the already established biker began to clean up their images (the Hell's Angels banned rape because it was bad for public relations) and through expansion and growing sophistication, escalated their move into diverse criminal operations (Reid 1981; Haut 1999). Their lower profile attracted less attention from the media. However, some law enforcement agencies began to recognize biker gangs as organized crime groups. In 1979 the leader of the Hell's Angels, Sonny Barger, sensing the law enforcement push to eliminate them, gave the following reason for law enforcement efforts:

> First of all, we're a virtual army. We're all across the country, and now we're in foreign countries also. And they [law enforcement] have no idea how many of us there are. We have money, many allies that are outlaw bikers that are not Hell's Angels, that would probably do anything we asked them to, if something happened. Like a revolution. Or anything like that. (quoted in Levigne, 1987: 27).

In 1979, the government's first attempt against the Hell's Angels as a criminal organization under RICO was a dismal failure. In a trial where the government paid a former HA $54,000 and gave him immunity for six murders, the defense was that their acts where individual acts and not organization acts, the jury could not reach a verdict, and the judge declared a mistrial. A second trial also ended in a hung jury, and all charges were dropped against Barger and 17 other Hell's Angels (Lavigne 1987; Barger 2000).

The FBI began investigating OMGs, particularly the Hell's Angels, in 1981 under its Organized Crime Program. A 2-year undercover investigation by an FBI agent, begun in 1982 and known as Operation Roughrider, involved eleven Hell's Angels chapters in seven states (Operation Roughrider 1985). At that time the *Hell's Angels* had 64 chapters in 13 countries. Drugs confiscated during this operation included: methamphetamine, cocaine, marijuana, hashish, PCP, and LSD. A 1982 RICO (racketeer influenced corrupt organization) prosecution against *Outlaws MC* members from Florida, Georgia, North Carolina, and Tennessee involved white slavery and transporting women across state lines for immoral purposes (Smith, 2002).

In 1981, an investigation by the Fayetteville, North Carolina, Police Department into thefts of Harley-Davidson motorcycles and insurance fraud led to a local *Hell's Angels* chapter (Johnson 1981). The investigation resulted in arrests in twenty states. A 1982 law enforcement report listed the criminal activities of major motorcycle gangs as manufacturing and distribution of narcotics, prostitution, weapons-related violations, extortion, murder, arson-for-hire, pornography, protection rackets, loan sharking, interstate transportation of stolen property and stolen vehicles, and insurance fraud (Davis 1982).

In 1986, a nationwide raid targeting OMGs by the Bureau of Alcohol, Tobacco, and Firearms (BATF) resulted in the arrest of four chapter presidents of the "Big Four" (Hell's Angels, Outlaws, Bandidos, and Pagans) and presidents of some of the affiliated gangs such as the Devil's Disciples, Diablos, and Trampers. This crackdown, the largest operation by the BATF up to that time, resulted in the seizure of sawed-off shotguns, hand-held machine guns, silencers, rifles, handguns, ammunition, hand grenades, and dynamite, as well as drugs (cocaine, marijuana, and PCP) (Anonymous [b] 1986).

The profits from these illegal activities were being invested in legitimate businesses. The movement of OMGs into drug trafficking, an inherent international criminal market, resulted in the exportation of American-based OMGs beyond the boundaries of the United States. For that matter, American gangs have been involved in the international drug trade since the early 1920s, when Arnold Rothstein, a Jewish gangster, began importing drugs from overseas (Katcher 1959).

INTERNATIONAL EXPANSION

> They [Hell's Angels] started out wanting to control street corners in 1948, cities in the mid-60s, states in 1970s, countries in 1980s, and now the world.
>
> **Yves Lavigne (1999: 610)**

Lavigne's statement maybe be more hyperbole than reality; the Hell's Angels and other OMGs maybe not be interested in world domination. However, they are certainly involved in world expansion. Interlocking networks with OMGs in other countries allowed American-based OMGs to link common criminal enterprises and the benefits derived from these. These United States gangs have entered the global marketplace of crime. The international implications of OMGs were recognized by the law enforcement community in the early 1980s (Doughtie 1986). In a 1984 report from the General Secretariat of Interpol the Hell's Angels and Outlaw motorcycle gangs were reported to have chapters in Canada (Interpol, 1984). The Hell's Angels were said to be the only motorcycle gang with chapters in twelve countries (seven Western European countries (Great Britain, West Germany, Netherlands, Denmark, Switzerland, France, and Austria), Australia, New Zealand, Japan, Canada, and the United States. Since that report was issued, the Hell's Angels have expanded and the other U.S. OMGs have established chapters in other countries (discussed below).

In 1991, Interpol created Operation Rockers to deal with the rapid expansion of OMGs throughout the world (Smith 1998). Named after the banners on top and bottom of the gang's colors, Project Rockers (still in operation) has the following objectives:

- Identify motorcycle gangs that are engaged in continuous criminal activities.
- Identify each gang's membership, hierarchy, modus operandi and specific criminal activity.

- Correlate the information for analysis and dissemination.
- to assist member countries in the exchange of criminal intelligence information.
- Identify specific contact officers within the NCBs (Interpol's National Central Bureau in member countries) and law enforcement agencies having expertise with outlaw motorcycle gangs.

As of 2000, in addition to the United States, there are twenty-eight countries cooperating in Operation Rocker. These countries include all those with current chapters of the Hell's Angels. A Project Rocker Newsletter was initiated in 1998 (McClure 2000). This newsletter contains international OMG activities from reports from NCBs and other intelligence sources. There is also a yearly meeting of those involved in Operation Rocker. Operation Rocker has had some success in dealing with OMGs, but it has not stopped their expansion. There is also the International Outlaw Motorcycle Gang Investigators Association which, among other purposes, was "organized to promote training and development of law enforcement professionals involved in the investigation of non-traditional organized crime groups, primarily outlaw motorcycle gangs … " (www.iomgia.com).

AMERICAN-BASED OMGs WITH INTERNATIONAL CHAPTERS—THE BIG THREE

The police call it a gang … . We call it a club.

Ralph Hubert ("Sonny") Barger, 1983 (quoted in Lavigne, 1987: 42)

The actual number of American OMGs is probably unknowable, One Percent motorcycle clubs/gangs fluctuate as clubs combine or are taken ("patched over") over by other gangs or put out of existence by law enforcement authorities. Chapters of the larger gangs generally lose their chapter status when the number of members on the street—not in the Big House (prison)—drop below six. For example, the Hell's Angels passed a rule in 1968 that if a charter (chapter) gets below six members it has to dissolve (Lavigne 1999: 487). The Big Five—Hell's Angels, Outlaws, Bandidos, Pagans, and Sons of Silence—are the most numerous, criminal, and violent. The Pagans, although an organized crime group, do not have any international chapters and the Sons of Silence, according to their Website, have only one international chapter. Sources tell the author that there are other Sons of Silence chapters outside the United States. Nevertheless, the discussion will focus on the Big Three—Hell's Angels, Outlaws, and the Bandidos.

HELL'S ANGELS MOTORCYCLE CLUB/GANG

The *Hell's Angels* (HA) are the most prominent and numerous international motorcycle gang. They are also known as "Local 81" after the placement of the letters H (8) and A (1) in the alphabet, the "Red and White," and "The Big Red Machine." Supporters and known associates are allowed to wear Local 81, Red and White, and Big Red Machine patches, but not *Hell's* (without the apostrophe) *Angels* which is a registered logo worn only by patched members. The first chapter of the *Hell's Angels* formed in San Bernardino, California, March 17, 1948. However, this chapter of disaffected World War II veterans, known as the "Pissed Off Bastards of Bloomington," bears little resemblance to the *Hell's Angels* of today. According to Ralph "Sonny" Barger, the first president of the Oakland Hell's Angels, the former national president, and some say the de-facto leader of today's *Hell's Angels*, he and his fellow bikers formed the *Hell's Angel's* in April of 1957 without knowing that other Hell's Angels chapters existed in California (2000: 30). Barger says that the Oakland chapter members were much younger than the other chapters—eighteen to twenty-one with the other chapters closer to twenty-six. This further demonstrates that the *Hell's Angels* of today were not the evolution of World War II combat vet as is the popular myth. It wasn't long before Barger amalgamated the other chapters into his Oakland chapter.

Sonny Barger is without a doubt the person responsible for the growth and expansion of the *Hell's Angels* into organized crime and outside the United States (Lavigne 1987; Veno 2002). Lavigne, no fan of the *Hell's Angels* or Barger, refers to the Hell's Angels as "white trash on wheels" and says that "Sonny Barger does for the *Hell's Angels* what Lee Iaccoca does for Chrysler Corp … " (Lavigne 1987: 15). This growth and expansion is not without problems with the law. Barger in his book lists 21 arrests since 1957, including several convictions and prison sentences (Barger 2000: 257–260). His last conviction was in 1987 in the United States District Court for the Western District Court of Kentucky (No. 87-00154). He was convicted of conspiracy to violate federal explosives, firearms, and arson laws, and for knowingly converting a copy of the official law enforcement intelligence manual regarding the identities and personal data on members and associates of the Outlaws Motorcycle Club (EPIC manual), in full knowledge that it was stolen. Barger served fifty-nine months in prison. This case evolved out of an attempt to kill members of the *Outlaws* for murdering a Anchorage, Alaska, *Hell's Angel* in Louisville, Kentucky. The interesting thing about this case is that the evidence was gathered by a trusted friend and fellow *Hell's Angel* who had been an FBI informer for years. So much for brotherhood and loyalty.

The current national president, George Christie, Jr., was recently sentenced to three years probation for conspiracy to sell drugs (Anonymous [a] 2002). His ex-wife and his son, also a *Hell's Angel,* pleaded guilty and no contest to charges arising out of an indictment accusing them, along with Christie, Jr., of stealing drugs from a U.S. Air Force base and selling them to school-age children (Associated Press 2003).

The *Hell's Angels'* Website lists thirty chapters in the United States. However, the author knows that all American chapters are not listed, including one in Kentucky. Arthur Veno, the self-described "only academic in the world who has made it [the study of outlaw motorcycle clubs] his focus [2002: 2]," says that there are 65 chapters in North America and 35 chapters in other countries. Only those chapters with individual Web sites are listed. The HA's first expansion outside the United States occurred in 1961 (Auckland, Australia). The first European chapter was established in London in 1969, followed by Zurich in 1970, Hamburg in 1973, and a Paris chapter in 1981 (Haut 1999). At the present time, the *Hell's Angels'* Web site lists chapters in 23 countries (United States, Canada, Brazil, Argentina, South Africa,

Australia, New Zealand, Spain, France, Belgium, Holland, Germany, Switzerland, Lichenstein, Austria, Italy, England/Wales, Finland, Norway, Denmark, Greece, Bohemia/Czech Republic, and Portugal), and two hang-around chapters in Russia and Chile (http://www.hells-angels.com/charters.htm).

In 2002, the vice president of the Arizona Nomads Chapter of the *Hell's Angels* was sentenced to 180 months in prison for conspiracy to possess with intent to distribute methamphetamine (U.S. Attorney General District of Arizona 2002). The case involved procuring methamphetamines from *Hell's Angles* members in South Africa and distributing it in Massachusetts and New Mexico. The president of the same Hell's Angels Nomads Chapter was sentenced to sixty months.

The *Hell's Angels* are a particular crime problem in Canada. Canadian authorities consider the *Hell's Angels* to be one of the most powerful and well-structured criminal organizations in Canada (CISC, 2000). The HA have at least eighteen chapters in Canada. There have been organized biker gangs in Quebec since the early 1930s; however, biker gangs were not a problem until the *Hell's Angels* arrived (Alain 1995).

The Canadian Hell's Angels seem to be a particularly vicious and brazen organization. In 2002, the Quebec *Hell's Angels* president Maurice "Mom" Boucher was convicted of two counts of first-degree murder for ordering the deaths of two prison guards in an attempt to intimidate the Canadian criminal justice system (Macafee 2002). This was the second trial for Boucher on these charges. The first trial ended in an acquittal, but a new trail was ordered after the Supreme Court of Canada heard an appeal from the prosecution.

Canada uses the *Hell's Angels* as the touchstone in defining outlaw motorcycle gangs. According to the Provincial Court in Alberta, an outlaw motorcycle gang has the following features (quoted in Haut 1999, p. 28):

- A structure based on that of the Hell's Angels
- Rules and principles that allow for the use of extreme violence in the best interests of the gang and its members
- Very strict membership conditions that require applicants to prove their "worth"
- Associates who provide services to the gang or connect it to other gangs
- The "colors" (sleeveless vest with club patch on the back), which are the most important aspect for the members
- Use of fortified clubhouses
- The gathering of information about enemies, i.e., other gangs and the police
- Involvement in criminal activities, which are the gangs' *raison d'etre*

These chapters and associates with puppet clubs and alliances with other organized crime groups make the *Hell's Angels* a national priority for Canadian law enforcement. The Quebec *Hell's Angels* were involved with La Cosa Nostra and the Columbian drug cartels in an attempt to smuggle tons of cocaine into Europe (Smith 1998). The Canadian HAs are involved in the following criminal activities: importation and distribution of cocaine, the production and distribution of methamphetamines, the cultivation and exportation of high-grade marijuana, the illegal trafficking of firearms and explosives, the collection of protection money from both legitimate and illegitimate businesses, fraud, money laundering, and prostitution. In 2001 their nine-year war with the Quebec *Rock Machine Motorcycle Club* had lead to 160 deaths, including innocent bystanders. The *Rock Machine* has recently become patched *Outlaws*, another American-based and worldwide OMG and a bitter enemy of the *HA*. The *Outlaws* (to be discussed more thoroughly below) have had a presence in Canada since the late 1970s (Reid, 1981).

The Nordic chapters of the *Hell's Angels* and the *Bandidos* (American-based) were involved in violent warfare in the late 1990s (Brown 1999, Lavigne 1999). The battles, waged with weapons such as explosives and shoulder-fired antitank missiles, led to eleven deaths and numerous injuries to innocent bystanders. They were fighting over the sharing of the criminal market in Scandinavian countries. Brown (1999) states that the open seas of the Nordic countries are ideal for drug activities.

The *Hell's Angels* Germany Chapter was established in 1973 and quickly became an object of investigation by the Hamburg police. They were suspected of being involved in narcotics trafficking, extortion, illegal possession of firearms, and assault. After an 18-month investigation, simultaneous raids in August 1983 in West Germany, the United States, and Switzerland led to the arrest of fifteen HA members and thirteen associates (Sielaff 1988). Thirteen HA were convicted.

The *Hell's Angels* have been a problem in Australia for over twenty years. In the 1980s HA chapters and puppet gangs were involved in narcotics, prostitution, major armed robberies, movement of arms and explosives, fencing, and assaults and murders (Reid 1981). The Melbourne Chapter had strong connections with the Oakland, California, HA as early as the late 1970s. Other American-based OMGs, the *Outlaws* and the *Bandidos*, have chapters in Australia. The *Gypsy Jokers* are the largest OMG in Australia. Although, the *Gypsy Jokers* are an Australian-based motorcycle gang, there has been a *Gypsy Jokers* motorcycle gang with chapters in Washington and California since the early 1960s. Veno reports that when the American *Gypsy Jokers* learned of the Australian *Gypsy Jokers* they invited them to the United States and after a night of partying the two gangs affiliated with one another. OMGs are a major organized crime problem in Australia, leading to the formation of a National Task Force, Panzer, to deal with them (http://www.nca.gov.au/html/pg_TskFce.htm).

THE OUTLAWS MOTORCYCLE CLUB/GANG

According to their national Website, the *Outlaws MC* is the oldest and first One Percent motorcycle club, disputing the claims by their bitter rival, the *Hell's Angels* (http://www.outlawsmc.com/history.html). They claim to have been established in 1935 as the McCook Outlaws Motorcycle Club "out of Matilda's Bar on old Route 66 in McCook, Illinois, outside Chicago." In 1950 the club's name was changed to the Chicago Outlaws. In 1963, the Outlaws MC became an official member of the One Percenter Brotherhood of Clubs, the first true One Percenter club east of the Mississippi. The Website states that in 1965 the club became the *"Outlaws Motorcycle Club Nation."*

Since their 1935 beginning in Illinois, the *Outlaws* have grown into one of the largest motorcycle clubs worldwide and one of the largest (maybe second behind the *Hell's Angels*) OMG in the world. The *Outlaws* list 66 chapters in 17 U.S. states (Illinois, ten; Connecticut, one; Florida, nine; Georgia, four; Indiana, three; Kentucky, one; Maine, one; Massachusetts, five; Michigan, six; New Hampshire, two; New York, two; North Carolina, four; Ohio, six; Oklahoma, one; Pennsylvania, two; Tennessee, four; and Wisconsin, five). Reportedly, the Outlaws are the largest motorcycle gang in Florida. In addition to these U.S. chapters there are seven chapters in Canada. Worldwide, the *Outlaws* have 83 chapters in 11 countries outside the United States: Australia, fourteen; England, fourteen; Wales, two; Belgium, six; Germany, thirty-three; Ireland, three; Norway, three; Sweden, one; Italy, one; Poland, five; and Thailand, one. In any city or country where the Hell's Angels have chapters there has been continual warfare between the gangs.

The *Outlaws* are affiliated with the *Bandidos* but dislike/hate the *Hell's Angels*. *Outlaws* proudly wear patches signaling their hatred for the *Hell's Angels*—AHAMD (All Hells Angels Must Die) and ADIOS (Angels Die in Outlaw States). The animosity between the two OMGs apparently started on July 4, 1979. The two gangs were involved in a violent struggle for control over the drug and prostitution markets in Charlotte, North Carolina. Each gang was absorbing and patching-over the existing gangs when on July 4, 1979, five members of the Outlaws were massacred in their clubhouse. This was the worst mass killing in Charlotte's history. The killings are still unsolved, but the Outlaws and law enforcement authorities believe the Hell's Angels are responsible. Many Outlaws wear a 7-4-79 patch to remember the date and their hatred for the Hell's Angels.

Law enforcement sources say that drug trafficking is the *Outlaws* main source of income (National Alliance of Gang Investigators Association [NAGIA], n.d.). The NAGIA reports that "Canadian Blue," diazepam, is manufactured in Ontario, Canada, and smuggled into the United States for distribution. The same source says that Florida *Outlaw* chapters buy cocaine from Columbian and Cuban sources for distribution in the United States. Florida and Georgia chapters also manufacture their own methamphetamine.

The International president of the *Outlaws*, Harry Joseph "Taco" Bowman, was recently convicted of racketeering, conspiracy to murder, and various drug and firearms offenses (*United States v. Bowman*, 2002). He was tried and sentenced to life in prison after two years on the run and a place on the FBI's Ten-Most-Wanted List. Court testimony revealed that Bowman lived in an affluent Detroit suburb, sent his children to private schools, and drove an armored plated Cadillac. The Ottawa *Outlaws* with 14 patched members are said to be involved in drug trafficking, prostitution, and nude dancing agencies (RCMP 1999). Recently, a member of the *Outlaws* pleaded guilty in London, Ontario, to participating in a criminal organization (Sims, 2003). The Canadian *Outlaws* have an uneasy truce with the dominant *Hell's Angels* groups.

THE BANDIDOS MOTORCYCLE CLUB/GANG

The *Bandidos MC* was formed in Houston, Texas, in 1966 by the late Donald Eugene Chambers. He formed this biker gang to control drug trafficking and prostitution in Texas. Since that time, the *"Bandido Nation"* has been called by the National

Alliance of Gang Investigators (NAIGA) the fastest growing OMG in the United States with thirty U.S. chapters and one in Australia. There is no date on the NAIGA report, but it must have been several years ago because the *Bandidos* have certainly lived up to the growth prophecy. According to their national Web site, the *Bandido Nation* has eighty-five U.S. chapters in thirteen states (New Mexico, thirteen; Texas, twenty-seven; Louisiana, four; Washington, thirteen; Alabama, two; Mississippi, two; Colorado, three; South Dakota, three; Nevada, two; Wyoming, one; Arkansas, one; Montana, one; Oklahoma, one; a "National Chapter–U.S."; and a "Nomads Chapter–Everywhere") (http://www.bandidosmc.com). The Nomads Chapter is reportedly made up of long-time members who act as a security element, taking care of counterintelligence and internal discipline. The Website also states that "More Are Coming."

The *Bandido Nation* list 73 chapters in 13 countries outside the United States: Canada, four, Australia, twelve; Belgium, one; Denmark, twelve; Finland, two; France, five; Germany, twenty-six; Italy, two (probationary); Luxemborg, one; Norway, five; Sweden, three; Tailand, two (probationary), and the United Kingdom, two.

As stated earlier, the *Bandidos* and the *Outlaws* are affiliated. They list each other as links on their Websites, and they socialize together. There are reports that the *Outlaws* provide the *Bandidos* with drugs for resale, participate in joint criminal ventures, and own property and legitimate businesses together. They are also united in their hatred for the *Hell's Angels*.

In 1996, an explosion occurred at the Copenhagen, Denmark, headquarters of the *Hell's Angels,* killing one and injuring twenty (Associated Press 1996). Reportedly, the bombing was part of the 2-year struggle between the HAs and the *Bandidos* over the drug market in Denmark, Finland, Norway, and Sweden. The *Hell's Angels* established a chapter in Denmark in 1977. They were the only American-based OMG until 1993 when the *Bandidos* established a chapter in 1993, setting off what has been called the Nordic Wars. In 1996 a shootout broke out between the two rival gangs in the Copenhagen airport (Brown, 1999). The fight between the HAs and the *Bandidos*, mentioned earlier, over the Canadian drug traffic led to the shooting death of a Quebec *Bandidos* in 2001 (Harris and Lanthier 2001).

CONCLUSION

There are other American-based OMGs that represent organized crime threats, particularly the *Pagans* which have, at this time, no International chapters. However, the *Pagans* have had ties with other international organized crime groups, such as the Mafia and the Columbian cartels. The *Pagans* have also waged a 40-year battle with the *Hell's Angels*. There latest battle occurred in Plainview, New York, in February 2001. The knife-and-gun fight resulted in one death, twelve persons injured, and seventy-three *Pagans* arrested. One *Hell's Angels* was arrested and charged with murder. He was acquitted at trial on the grounds of self-defense.

There are also other American-based OMGs such as the Sons of Silence, the Mongols, the Avengers, the Black Pistons, and the Vagos, which have chapters in one or more countries outside CONUS. The Sons of Silence list a chapter in Germany. The national treasurer (a millionaire accountant) of the Sons of Silence was recently charged and convicted of being a drug kingpin (Anonymous 2002). The approximately 200-member Mongols MC has 21 chapters in this country and several chapters in Mexico. They were recently involved in a violent shootout with the Hell's Angels in Harrah's Casino in Laughlin, Nevada, that left three dead. The Black Pistons, official supporters of the Outlaws according to their Web site, have twenty-one chapters in the U.S., seven in Canada, and one in Germany. The ATF reports that the 200-member Vagos have chapters in California, Nevada, Hawaii, and Mexico. The ATF says that this OMG uses smaller networks of motorcycle gangs and associates to distribute firearms and controlled substances. The Avengers MC claims to have chapters in Michigan, Ohio, Florida, Indiana, and West Virginia. They also claim to have a chapter in Malta. The national president of the Avengers, Thomas M. "Foot" Khali, was recently convicted of RICO violations racketeering, and two counts of distributing marijuana (U.S. v. Khalil 2002). However, the Big Three—the Hell's Angels, the Outlaws, and the Bandidos—have made major expansion efforts into countries through out the world. As they have patched-over existing biker gangs in these countries, they have engaged in violence and gained in influence and wealth. There is every reason to believe that their expansion efforts will continue as long as the profits are there.

REFERENCES

Alain, M. (June, 1995). The rise and fall of motorcycle gangs in Quebec. *Federal Probation*. 59(2).

Anon. a. (2002) OMG Discussion. Hell's Angel leader, ex-wife and son get probation in drug-selling case. http://www.gligic.org/OMG/00000007.htm.

Anon. b. (1986). U.S. Takes Action Against Motorcycle gangs, leaders. *Organized Crime Digest*. May, 1986.

Anonymous. (2002). 10-year probe fingers cycle gang financier. *Organized Crime Digest*. March 1, 2002.

Associated Press. (1996). Explosion at Hells Angels headquarters; one reported dead. File://A:HA7.htm.

Associated Press. (2003). Hell's Angel Boss Guilty. http://www.dimmockreport/haboss-guilty.htm

Barger, R. *Hell's Angels: The life and times of Sonny Barger and the Hell's Angels Motorcycle Club*. New York, William Morrow.

Brown, P. (1999). Nordic Motorcycle Gangs, *ICPR*: 474–475.

Doughtie, J. A. (August, 1986). Motorcycle Gang Investigations: A Team Effort. *FBI Law Enforcement Bulletin*, 19–22.

CISC. (2000). Outlaw Motorcycle Gangs. *Criminal Intelligence Service Canada-2000*.

Davis, R. H. (1982). Outlaw Motorcyclists: A problem for law enforcement, *FBI Law Enforcement Bulletin.*: 13–22.

Harris, K. and Lanthier, A. (2001). Killings spark biker war fears. *Ottawa Sun* .August 14, (2001).

Hatcher, L. (1959). *The Big Bankroll: The Life and Times of Arnold Rothstein*. New Rochell, N.Y. Arlington House.

Haut, F. (1999). Organized crime on two wheels: Motorcycle gangs, *ICPR*: 474–475.

Hill, T. (1980). Outlaw motorcycle gangs; a look at a new form of organized crime. *Canadian Criminology Forum*. 3(Fall): 26–36.

Interpol. (1984). Motorcycle Gangs, *ICPO-Interpol General Secretariat.*

Johnson, W.C. (1981). Motorcycle Gangs and organized crime, *The Police Chief:* 32–33, 78.

Katcher, L. (1959). *The Big Bankroll: The Life and Times of Arnold Rothstein.* New York. Da Capo Press.

Kendall, R. E. (1998). The International Problem of Criminal Gangs, *ICPR:* 469–471.

Lavigne, Y. (1987). *Hell's Angels: Taking Care of Business.* Toronto, Canada. Random House.

Lavigne, Y. (1996). *Hells Angels: Into the Abyss.* Toronto, Canada. Harper Collins.

Lavigne, Y. (1999). *Hells Angels at War,* Harper Collins, Toronto, Canada.

Mandelkau, J. (1971). *Buttons: The Making of a President.* Sphere Books Limited. London.

McClure, G. (2000). The Role of Interpol in Fighting Organized Crime, *International Criminal Police Review*-No. 481.

McKee, M. (2001). On the side of the Angels. *American Lawyer Media* (April 23, 2001).

Macafee, M. (2002). Biker trials, not turf wars, will dominate scene in 2003, experts say. (http://cnews.canoe.ca/CNEWS/Law/Bikers/2002/12/19/8224-cp.html).

National Alliance of Gang Investigators Association. (No Date). Motorcycle Gangs. *NAGIA.*

Operation ROUGHRIDER. (May 15, 1985). After three years on the road, FBI arrests "Angels" in nationwide raid. *Narcotics Control Digest, 4–5.*

Pistone, J. D. (1987). *Donnie Brasco: My Undercover Life in the Mafia.* New York: New American Library.

Quinn, J. F. (1987). Sex role and hedonism among members of "outlaw" motorcycle clubs, *Deviant Behavior,* 8:47–63.

Reid, K. E. (1981). Expansionism-Hell's Angels Style, *Police Chief.* 48(5): 38–40, 69, 78.

Sielaff, W. (1988). Organized Criminal Activity in the Federal Republic of Germany, *The Police Chief.* November, 76–79.

Sims, J. (2003). Outlaws a 'criminal organization.' *Sun Media, January 17, 2003.* http://cnews.ca/CNEWS/Law/Bikers/2003/01/17/12050.html.

Smith, B. W. (1998). Interpol's "Project Rocker" Helps Disrupt Outlaw Motorcycle Gangs, *Police Chief.* September, 54–56.

Smith, R. C. (2002). Dangerous motorcycle gangs: A facet of organized crime in the Mid Atlantic Region, *Journal of Gang Research,* 9(4): 33–44.

Stidworthy, D. (2003). *High on the Hogs.* Jefferson, North Carolina. McFarland & Company.

Trethewy, S. and Katz, T. (1998). Motorcycle Gangs or Motorcycle Mafia?, *The Police Chief,* 66(4): 53–60.

U.S. v. Bowman. (2002). *U.S. 11th Circuit Court of Appeals-U.S. v Bowman No. 01-14305.*

U.S. v. Khalil. (2002). *US Court of Appeals-U.S. v Khalil No. 00-3626.*

United States Attorney General District of Arizona. (June 18, 2002). Press Release Number 2002–109.

Veno, A. (2002). *The Brotherhoods: Inside the Outlaw Motorcycle Clubs.* Crows Nest NSW, Australia: Allen & Unwin.

Wethern, G. (1978). *Wayward Angel.* Richard Marek. New York.

20 Physical Fitness in Policing

Jeffery C. Lee

CONTENTS

INTRODUCTION

Police officers are not constantly engaged in strenuous physical activities. However, there are occasions when officers have to exert a maximum amount of effort for significant periods of time. Foot pursuits, subduing resistive subjects, and removing people from dangerous areas or crashed vehicles are a few examples of these activities.

Police officers have been described as athletes. One researcher compared police work to competing in a heptathlon. The events of the heptathlon include: a three-mile cross-country run, target shooting, obstacle course, rope climb, 100-meter sprint, bench press, and chin-ups. It has been suggested that police officers train as heptathletes in order to perform at optimum levels (1). Police officers often go from a sedentary routine to duties requiring great athleticism at a moment's notice (2). If police officers are to be called on to perform athletic tasks, then a certain level of fitness must be maintained.

Researchers have identified several athletic physical demands that are placed on law enforcement officers. Officers are frequently required to run, sometimes for durations of over two minutes. Climbing and jumping are two of the demands that were identified. Officers may climb fences or stairs and jump over obstacles to reach citizens in need, or to pursue fleeing suspects. Officers are also called upon to lift, carry, drag, or pull heavy objects. Finally, officers use force to overcome resistance; this use of force requires stamina for maximum exertion (3).

Some suggest that police work is not a physically demanding job. However, officers need to maintain fitness levels that allow them to perform these demanding activities when called upon to do so. An officer's ability to perform demanding activities is critical, and in some circumstances may mean the difference between life and death (4).

Given this call for police officers to be physically fit, one may ask whose responsibility it is to ensure that appropriate fitness levels are maintained. Certainly, the individual officer should share in the responsibility. The officers owe it to themselves, their families, and the people they serve to be physically fit. However, the police agencies have some responsibility to ensure that sufficient fitness levels are maintained. Agencies should create physical fitness programs that are staffed with fitness coordinators who are qualified to provide training and education to teach officers how to achieve and maintain physical fitness. Furthermore, these programs should be supported by policy and management to ensure their success (5).

One study indicated that officers want to be physically fit and favor departmentally sponsored fitness programs (6). Therefore, a comprehensive wellness programs may be important to the recruitment and retention of good officers (7). In a time when police agencies are in competition with each other for good officers, agencies may find that the inclusion of a comprehensive wellness program in the benefits package is a valuable recruiting tool. Furthermore, it has been suggested that wellness programs be an essential requirement for agency accreditation (8).

FITNESS IN THE POLICE WORKPLACE

In 1978 a comprehensive study concluded that police officers were unfit. We often think that the risks associated with police work are associated with threats from suspects; however, this study produced data indicating that medical or health conditions were the primary causes of death among police officers. Furthermore, medical and health conditions caused the majority of early retirements. Heart-related conditions were the single greatest cause of early retirement. In sum, the health condition of police officers in general, and heart-related conditions in particular, seriously impacts the number of officers who die or are retired early. Many of these health conditions may be avoided with a fitness or conditioning program (9).

Since 1975, police officers' fitness levels have been compared to the general population. Many researchers reported that officers are often at low levels of fitness when compared to the general population. A recent study reported that only 24 percent of local law enforcement officers were not overweight, 43 percent were categorized as overweight, and 33 percent were considered obese. Furthermore, the study reported that almost 60 percent of the officers were categorized as having "poor" or "very poor" fitness levels (10). In other studies, police officers were compared to inmates. Inmates were reported as having higher work capacity and cardiovascular endurance than police officers. Inmates were also found to have lower body weights, fat, blood pressure, and cholesterol than officers (11). In 1980 campus police officers' fitness levels were compared to college students. The officers were less fit and had more body fat than students. Furthermore, the officers ran less distance in the 12-minute run test, and performed fewer pull-ups and sit-ups than the students (12). In a study conducted in Australia similar results were found. Officers were found to exercise inadequately, to be overweight, and to have symptoms of stress. Forty-eight percent of the male officers and forty percent of the female officers reported excessive alcohol use. The study concluded that police officers in Australia have unhealthy lifestyles (13). Although officers often perceive themselves to be in good health, they routinely score lower on fitness tests when compared to other groups (14).

Although veteran police officers have below average fitness levels, two studies reported that police recruits tend to have average fitness levels. Recruits often show normal muscular strength and endurance levels, and good flexibility. They also perform in a range of moderate to high cardiovascular fitness, and body fat was rated from fair to excellent (15). If police recruits tend to be at average- to above-average fitness levels, then it can be concluded that something changes during their careers to cause them to be less fit than the general population, as well as criminals.

NATURE OF POLICE WORK

Many of the physical tasks that police officers are called to perform are not routine and are performed infrequently; in fact, quite often police work has been described as sedentary (16). Many police officers have desk jobs. For example, some police officers and most investigators work in an office at their desk. Patrol officers may also be thought of as having a desk job. Patrol officers spend much of their time sitting in a patrol vehicle that is equipped with a computer and a telephone, much like a typical desk in an office (17). Unfortunately, the sedentary nature of police work requires insufficient activity to maintain high levels of fitness for physically demanding incidents. For example, a mailman who walks a route every day is able to maintain fitness levels to perform the tasks that are required. On the other hand, police work is mostly sedentary, and day-to-day activities do not allow officers to maintain fitness levels to perform the strenuous job tasks that may be essential but infrequent. A sedentary job coupled with a sedentary lifestyle can cause police officer fitness levels to decline (18).

Police work has been described as an occupational field with very high stress levels. Police officers have significantly high levels of premature death, heart disease, coronary risk, and digestive disorders. All of these disorders are stress-related. Police officers have to contend with stressors such as shift work, fear, and danger. Other reported stressors officers often contend with are poor pay and insufficient training. It also can be stressful for officers to deal with the frustrations of the criminal justice system, such as the adversarial court system, prison overcrowding, and a lack of public support. An often-overlooked source of stress for officers is the agency itself. Officers often feel that their supervisors or command staff do not adequately support them. In fact, many officers view the stress generated by their departments as more problematic than that stemming from dealing with the public (19).

Officers' eating habits often contribute to their poor health. They frequently eat at fast-food restaurants, where food is often high in fat but low in nutritional value. Officers often eat their meals in a hurry in order to get back in the rotation to answer calls. A lack of regularly scheduled meal breaks may also lead to overeating. Eating more nutritional meals on regular schedules and at a slower pace would be beneficial to officers (20).

FITNESS PROGRAM CONSIDERATIONS

There are several issues that police administrators should consider when making decisions about fitness programs. Program goals and implementation strategies are important. Administrators should also consider what type of leadership is necessary and if medical screenings are necessary. Another consideration is the type of motivation strategies that are to be used and if fitness standards are to be a part of pre-employment screening, maintenance, or both. The type of program, cost of the program, and manner in which the results are measured and evaluated are other important considerations.

GOALS

There were two primary goals of fitness programs identified in the literature. The first primary goal was to get officers fit. Secondly, officers should be taught skills to maintain desired fitness levels. It is important that officers be prepared to stay active throughout their lives (21). By being prepared to stay active throughout their lives, officers may be able to enjoy physical activities in retirement. Secondary goals of cardiovascular disease prevention, detection of warning signs of officers at risk, and offering exercise prescriptions have also been identified (22). Once an agency establishes the goals of a fitness program, then individualized goals for officers must be considered. Goal-setting helps officers answer the question, "Where should I be, realistically?" The Cooper Institute recommends that fitness assessments be conducted to determine the officers' fitness levels. Raw scores are compared to norms and standards that indicate one's relationship to others of a similar age and gender. Scores are converted to levels of "very poor," "poor," "fair," "good," "excellent," or "superior." Goal levels should be set no higher than one level above the current raw score. It is recommended that goals be made too easy rather than too difficult. This is a very important aspect for adherence to the training program. Personalized contracts can be made to improve adherence to attain goals. These contracts involve the officers' giving themselves small rewards for accomplishing their stated goals (23).

IMPLEMENTATION

There are several factors that should be considered when implementing a fitness program. Budget appropriators are often the first obstacle that has to be overcome. Fitness program advocates should prepare documentation for the appropriators to provide them with information on the benefits of fitness programs. If advocates can provide documentation that programs save money by reducing absenteeism, lost time due to light duty assignments, or early retirements, appropriators may be inclined to fund them (24).

Next, administrators need for the officers to support and buy into the fitness program. A wise administrator will not ignore collective bargaining in this process. Many officers may be fearful of fitness standards and resist or stall implementation efforts. An evolutionary approach is recommended. It is unreasonable to demand unfit officers to meet high fitness standards overnight. This process involves mandatory fitness testing as well as education. Then, officers should be given exercise prescriptions based on current fitness levels. Once officers have their prescriptions they are afforded an opportunity to participate in voluntary training sessions. After standards have been developed, officers are then tested against the standard. Reinforcement systems are formed to encourage maintenance or to assist those who fall below the standard. Time frames for adherence to the standard should be negotiated and stated. Giving officers ownership in program development will assist in a smooth implementation process (25).

LEADERSHIP

Effective program leadership is critical for the success of a police fitness program. However, it is unfeasible for law enforcement agencies to employ academically trained exercise physiology experts to manage fitness programs. Therefore, the use of physical fitness coordinators who can provide a human link between physical fitness programs and officer participation is recommended. Coordinators should be able to serve as fitness role models. Role modeling is essential for changing the culture of an agency. Furthermore, they must be proficient in the skills and competencies associated with the physical fitness program. Proper selection, training, and certification for the position of physical fitness coordinator are essential. Often physical training instructors are defensive tactics instructors with no training in physical education. Courses have been developed that prepare police fitness instructors with the skills and concepts to develop and implement fitness programs safely. These courses should include principles of conditioning, curriculum development strategies, fitness assessment techniques, exercise techniques, evaluation techniques, and safety procedures. Without coordinators who are properly trained and certified, programs may fail (26).

MEDICAL SCREENING

Medical screenings are an important part of fitness programs. The purpose of medical screenings is to review existing information to see if there are any risks to exercise. The Cooper Institute suggests that screenings function as a check to ensure safety. If the screenings indicate any potential medical complications, fitness tests should not be performed. One simple and validated screening questionnaire is the PAR-Q test. Screenings may also include blood pressure checks and the three-minute step test. Proper medical screenings can help prevent litigation for any injuries or medical complications that may result from fitness testing. Sophisticated medical screenings may be used for officers over 40 or officers that have certain risk factors like high blood pressure, obesity, or diabetes (27). Some contend that agencies may consider making professional medical screenings a part of regular fitness assessments. It should be noted that thorough medical screenings by doctors are expensive. Often medical screenings are a part of pre-employment selection, and candidates may be required to pay for them.

MOTIVATION

Police administrators should ask themselves what motivates officers to adhere to fitness programs. Self-responsibility and reinforcement are key factors for adherence (28). Administrators must decide if departmental fitness programs are going to be mandatory or voluntary. Programs with mandatory standards need considerable legal scrutiny (29), particularly when these standards may be the basis of personnel actions such as assignment, dismissal, or promotion. Voluntary wellness-oriented programs that focus on benefits to employees are less likely to experience challenges. However, voluntary programs often do not have the lasting success that mandatory programs do (30). Another intrinsic aspect of motivation is incentives. Certainly, officers should be self-motivated, but reinforcements in the form of incentives may contribute to higher adherence rates. Many of the common incentives offered to officers include additional leave time, on-duty workout time, pay bonuses, fitness club memberships, and special recognition such as T-shirts and awards (31).

PERSONNEL

Several questions may be asked concerning personnel. What personnel should fitness programs affect? Should all types of officers be required to meet fitness standards? Should they be a part of only pre-employment selection or should officers be required to maintain fitness levels beyond recruitment and academy training?

Several researchers reported on the use of fitness tests for pre-employment screening. Some advocate the use of fitness tests in pre-employment selection, suggesting that the tests be used to assess a recruit's ability to train for job task-tests (32). Pre-employment screening for appropriate levels of fitness may also serve to prevent or reduce injuries during academy training (33). Others have advocated the use of pre-employment fitness screenings as an alternative to maximum age requirements (34).

In 1982 a study revealed that officers' fitness levels diminished significantly after the academy (35). Given officers' reduction in fitness levels after the academy, police administrators should consider fitness maintenance programs. However, it seems illogical to select police officers on the basis of physical fitness and abilities and then to have no requirement that minimum fitness and abilities be maintained. It is essential for police agencies to implement fitness maintenance programs to achieve fitness goals. Agencies may be guilty of negligent retention or failure to train when it comes to unfit officers. It has even been suggested that employees be contractually obligated to maintain adequate fitness levels (36). There have been many examples where fitness maintenance programs have improved officers' fitness and performance (37).

Type of Programs

There is some disagreement in the literature as to what type of program is best. Most programs can be categorized as fitness/conditioning programs, abilities/job task programs, or a combination of these. There are advantages and disadvantages to each.

The fitness/conditioning-type programs are thought of as being more cost effective, easier to administer, and somewhat familiar to the participants. Most fitness programs follow the Cooper Institute's model that has national norms and is easy to score and evaluate. The Cooper Institute suggests a fitness battery of 1.5-mile run, 300-meter run, vertical jump, one repetition maximum bench press or maximum push-ups, and the 1-minute sit-up test. They claim that these tests measure underlying fitness and predict an officer's ability to perform essential and critical physically demanding job tasks regardless of age, gender, or handicap condition. It has been reported that the fitness/conditioning programs are subjected to fewer legal challenges because norms are based on age and sex. There are equal passing rates for males and females; therefore, protected classes are not failed at higher rates (38). However, fitness and conditioning programs validity maybe scrutinized because two tests that are designed to measure the same thing may have different results. For example, push-ups and bench presses measure upper body strengths. If officers can pass a push-up test, but not a bench press test, defensibility of the test comes into question.

Job simulation or abilities programs also have certain advantages. Primarily there is a link between the exercise and real life job tasks. These tests are good predictions of essential job task performance. Although it is difficult to develop a job simulation test, it is easy to develop minimum standards by field-testing adequately performing officers. These tests usually have a single absolute standard without separate norms. Unfortunately, this almost always has an adverse effect on females because they pass at a lower rate. Another disadvantage is that these types of tests do not address the total well being of a person (39). One example of a job-tasks program is the Physical Abilities Test (PAT) that includes this eight-task test battery:

1. Exiting vehicle/open trunk
2. First two-hundred-twenty-yard run
3. Obstacle course
4. Dummy drag
5. Obstacle course
6. Second two-hundred-twenty-yard run
7. Dry fire weapon
8. Place item in trunk and enter vehicle

The cut-off time for passing this test is 6 minutes and 4 seconds. These test components measure the fitness dimensions of dexterity, flexibility, stamina, strength, and cardio-vascular condition. A field test, as a part of the validation process, was conducted using a random sample of officers from Florida. Ninety-eight percent of the officers passed the test (40). This may indicate that the PAT is able to predict who may perform essential physical job tasks as their validation claims; however, the question remains if it is an indication of physical fitness.

Therefore, some may advocate fitness testing over abilities testing because officers that are in poor health may still pass the abilities test. Furthermore, officers may have a variety of job assignments, such as patrol, investigations, or administration, that may have different essential job tasks. In other words, job-tasks testing for patrol officers may be different than the testing for investigators. Regardless of the officers' assignment, the fitness/conditioning model can be used to assess all officers.

Advocates of the abilities or job simulation system most often cite that these tests are more accurate in predicting the ability to do police work. Physical fitness does not guarantee that someone will be able to adequately perform tasks that are essential to police work. Furthermore, these advocates report that abilities tests are more defensible than fitness tests because of their job-relatedness (41).

Some researchers and administrators call for programs to include both fitness and abilities components. The developers of the POPAT (Police Officer's Physical Abilities Test) claim that it tests both fitness and ability. However, it should be noted that one study revealed that only sixteen percent of the females passed the POPAT test, while sixty-eight percent of the males passed (42). An argument may be made that the POPAT is discriminatory to females.

Cost

Most police departments' budgets are limited. It can be difficult to fund new programs, in spite of the cost-reducing benefits of fitness programs. However, certain cost-saving techniques may be helpful in getting programs started. Some departments have formed partnerships with schools that have fitness equipment. Officers may use local academy facilities to train even after graduation. Furthermore, departments could save money by training law enforcement personnel to conduct fitness assessments and to manage and evaluate programs. The literature suggested that fitness programs pay for themselves and provide long-term savings to agencies (43).

MEASURING RESULTS AND EVALUATIONS

There are two important issues to be considered in measuring the effectiveness of fitness programs. The first and most important is whether the program is improving the health and fitness scores of the officers. The evaluator should determine if officers' cholesterol and blood pressure levels, dietary trends, tobacco habits, and levels of obesity are improving. The second is whether the program is saving money in health-care costs. A database should be formed that tracks health-care-related information such as absenteeism, injuries, insurance claims, and workers' compensation claims. Any positive effects can be documented and presented to justify the program (44).

LEGAL ISSUES

When police administrators are considering the implementation of fitness programs for their departments, they must examine certain legal issues. Administrators should be aware of two important cases. First, in *Tennessee v. Garner* (1985) the United States Supreme Court's ruling restricted the police's use of deadly force in apprehending fleeing felons. Therefore, under certain circumstances, officers may opt to allow a suspect to flee and attempt to apprehend him or her at a later time or officers may pursue the suspect. A practical implication of this ruling is that officers should be in adequate physical condition to pursue fleeing suspects and subdue certain levels of resistance without depending on their firearms. In *Parker v. District of Columbia* (1988), the United States District Court of Appeals for the District of Columbia addressed police officers' physical fitness and agencies' responsibility. In this case, an unfit officer who was not physically able to affect an arrest resorted to the use of deadly force. The court found that a pattern of deliberate indifference existed in training, discipline, and supervision. Based on this ruling alone, police administrators should implement fitness programs and adequately monitor the fitness levels of their officers.

HISTORICAL REVIEW OF LEGAL CHALLENGES

Following the reform era, police departments introduced civil service standards for selection of officers. For many years police departments contended that assaults on police and officers' ability to control crowds, use police equipment, and gain respect and a psychological advantage were based on an officer's size (45). Therefore, the only physical requirement used in the selection of police officers was based on height and weight standards. As we know today, these standards adversely affected the employment of women and some ethnic groups with small body sizes. Once Title VII of the 1964 Civil Rights Act was made applicable to law enforcement, people began to challenge these standards as being discriminatory (46). There have been several legal challenges to height and weight standards. These challenges alleged that these standards were discriminatory in nature. Many agencies attempted to defend these standards. Police administrators argued that these standards were bona fide qualifications; however, their arguments universally failed when challenged (47). Therefore, height and weight standards were found to be discriminatory to women and certain ethnic groups. This violated Title VII of the 1964 Civil Rights Act.

To replace the height and weight standards, police departments began to implement physical abilities testing or job tasks testing. Many of these tests include tasks such as running, climbing stairs, lifting and dragging body dummies, jumping hurdles, and scaling walls. The courts tended to encourage the development of job tasks tests but have failed to support them. Primarily, the courts often criticized and rejected the validation of the physical abilities/job tasks test. For example, in *Officers for Justice v. Civil Service of San Francisco* (1975), the court ruled that the San Francisco Police Department used an inadequate job validation procedure. The procedure was criticized because of inadequate sampling, low response rate, and confusing questionnaire items. Furthermore, the San Francisco Police Department test resulted in only two of the 166 eligible female applicants passing, whereas 573 of 906 male applicants passed. The court found these results to be prima fascia evidence of discrimination. In *United States v. City of Philadelphia* (1979) the court rejected the validation process of the city's fitness test because the job tasks analysis did not focus on frequency, importance, or skill levels for the tasks and duties. In 1980 the court rejected the validation of Toledo Police Department's physical agility test. The process was found to be "intuitive." The process involved establishing cut-off scores through the use of experts who would review events and make a determination of a cut-off score. This process was viewed as abstract and difficult to link to job tasks (*Harless v. Duck,* 1980). In light of these rulings some departments still utilize job tasks testing. Many researchers reported on successful validation efforts; however, they also pointed out the difficulties associated with validating physical ability or job tasks tests (48). Therefore, some may view that physical abilities or job tasks tests are no more valid or dependable than the old height and weight standards. There are no global physical fitness tests for law enforcement officers and physical abilities or job tasks tests may not be able to be successfully defended as job-related measures until comprehensive validation studies have been conducted.

With the many reported difficulties associated with physical abilities/job tasks testing, many departments began to adopt the fitness/conditioning model. This model typically consists of running, sit-ups, push-ups, bench press, and flexibility testing. These tests tend to predict overall fitness; however, it may be difficult defending them as job-related, which is an Equal Employment Opportunity Commission (EEOC) guideline as argued in *Thomas v. City of Evanston* (1985). For example, it can be argued that a police officer does not have to perform sit-ups on the job. Therefore, sit-ups may not pass the job-relatedness guideline of the EEOC. The Cooper Institute, which is a leading authority in public safety fitness training, responded to that argument by suggesting that ample data exist that support fitness components as being predictive in performing tasks associated with police duties like pursuits, dodging, lifting, dragging, pushing, jumping, crawling, and use of force. They suggested that a test battery of a 1.5-mile run, 300-meter run, vertical jump, one repetition maximum bench press or push-up, and 1-minute sit-ups would be able to predict the ability to perform physical police tasks. Furthermore, in *United States v. City of Wichita Falls* (1988) the United States District Court recognized that officers are similar to athletes and upheld the city's testing for cardio-fitness, body composition, flexibility, and dynamic and absolute strength.

The Cooper Institute collects data on the general population norms that are age- and gender- specific for these tasks. Using age- and gender-specific norms may minimize the adverse impact on women and older officers that is associated with the job tasks model. However, the age- and gender-specific norms utilized with the fitness/ conditioning model can be problematic. The Civil Rights Act of 1991 forbade the use of gender-adjusted norms for selection and promotion. To further complicate the matter, if departments choose to use norms based on females' scores, males will pass at a higher rate, thus violating Title VII of the 1964 Civil Rights Act (49). However, it should be noted that in *Powell v. Reno* (1997) age- and gender-specific scores were successfully defended. Although men and women were tested at different cut-off scores, the United States District Court for the District of Columbia supported the tests because they were found to represent the same level of fitness.

The Americans with Disabilities Act (ADA) shifted the focus to a person's ability to perform essential job functions. Fitness testing tends to evaluate a person's health and level of physical fitness. It is arguable whether it evaluates a person's ability to perform essential tasks. Subsequently, the Civil Rights Act of 1991 and the ADA may force administrators to abandon fitness and conditioning testing and return to job-tasks testing (50).

LIABILITY

Given the confusion and problems associated with implementing fitness programs it becomes evident why administrators may tend to avoid fitness programs. There are two levels of concern over the liability of implementing a fitness program. The first level of concern is potential negligence by a department in delivering the fitness program. In addition to the liability associated with test validation and standard development, there is also an issue of officer safety (51). Departments are concerned about the safety of their employees and may minimize the risk associated with fitness training by adopting well-written policies for the fitness program. Furthermore, agencies should employ trained fitness coordinators to offer exercise prescriptions and training on proper exercise techniques. Fitness coordinators should also supervise workout areas to minimize risks to officers. However, administrators must be aware of the risks for potential worker's compensation claims for injuries incurred during fitness training.

Police administrators may apply a five-point test that determines benefits eligibility. First was whether an injury occurred during work hours. Time spent working out at the department's fitness centers may be considered "during work hours." Second was whether the injury occurred on the employer's premises. Third was whether the employers initiated the employees' exercise program. Fourth was whether the department executed any control or direction over the program. Last was whether the department stands to benefit from the employees' participation in the exercise program. Departments may reduce their liability in worker's compensation benefits by making exercise and recreation programs voluntary and by having participants sign waivers of benefits. However, in the case of death, participants cannot waive the rights of dependents. Therefore, it stands to reason that departments may incur some risks for worker's compensation benefits for injuries resulting from officers' participation in fitness programs. Waivers may be obtained; however, they may not totally release the department from liability (52).

The second level of liability is associated with negligence for not having fitness programs. It is understandable why some police administrators have avoided implementing fitness programs out of fear of legal challenges that may land them in a courtroom defending their actions. However, many researchers cite the relevance of *Parker v. District of Columbia* (1988) as an example of an agency's being negligent for not requiring a physical fitness program for officers to police administrators. Agencies can be liable for negligent hiring of unfit officers. They may also be liable for negligently training officers to perform their jobs. Furthermore, agencies that fail to supervise officers to ensure that they can meet the physical demands of the job can be liable. Lastly, those agencies that negligently retain those who cannot meet the physical demands of the job can be held liable (53).

Police administrators should also note that the courts have upheld laws allowing monetary compensation for families of officers who have heart disease. The high rate of law enforcement heart disease and hypertension made the officers deserving of the benefit according to the courts. A Virginia law recognized cardiopulmonary disease of law enforcement officers as being automatically job-related. This presents agencies with tremendous liability concerns over worker's compensation and disability claims (54).

CONCLUSION

Almost all researchers agree that police officers need to be physically fit, because there may be times when officers need to be able to exert maximum efforts. Police work is often sedentary in nature, without sufficient physical activity to maintain level of fitness for exertive efforts or general health. Many writers suggest that police officers should be at least as fit as the general population.

There seems to be some controversy in the literature as to how fit police officers are. A majority reports that police officers have below average fitness levels. A review of the literature suggested that officers achieve an acceptable measure of physical fitness during academy training. However, without fitness maintenance programs, these gains achieved in the academy decline rapidly.

Many departments claim to have fitness programs. However, most do not have comprehensive wellness programs that address fitness, stress management, mental health, diet and nutrition, and alcohol and chemical dependency. In fact most departmental fitness programs are a part of pre-employment selection. It is illogical to use fitness standards as a part of selection, without any maintenance requirements.

A frequently debated issue in police fitness centers on testing. Some researchers suggest that physical abilities tests be used. These tests attempt to simulate actual job tasks. Other researchers recommend fitness and conditioning tests using the Cooper program. Physical abilities tests are criticized because they do little to tell about total well being. Fitness tests are criticized because they do not correlate to job tasks. These criticisms often arise when defensibility is discussed. Litigation is likely to come from officers who do not meet standards, officers who have been injured, the families of officers who have died as a result of their lack of physical fitness, or citizens who have been harmed as a result of officers' not being physically fit.

REFERENCES

1. Rhyan, S. An 8 week strength training for police heptatheletes. *Strength and Conditioning, 18*(6), 31–33, 1996.
2. Schultz, R. & Acevedo, A. Ensuring the physical success of a department. *Law and Order, 48*(12), 34–37, 2000.
3. Hoffman, R. & Collingwood, T.R. *Fit for Duty.* Human Kinetics: Champaign, IL, 1995.
4. Lee, J.C. Police Fitness: The Effects of Activities, Service, Limitations, and Programs on Fitness and Retirement. Unpublished doctoral dissertation, University of Southern Mississippi, Hattiesburg, 2003.
5. Collingwood, T.R. Implementing programs and standards for law enforcement physical fitness. *Police Chief, 55*(4), 20–24, 1988.
6. Ness, J.J. & Light, J. Mandatory fitness standards. *Police Chief, 59*(8), 74–78, 1992.
7. Church, R.L. & Robertson, N. How state police agencies are addressing the issue of wellness. *Policing: An International Journal of Police Strategies and Management, 22*(3), 304–312, 1999.

8. Ness, J.J. & Light, J. Mandatory fitness standards. *Police Chief, 59*(8), 74–78, 1992.

9. Price, C.S., Getteman, L.R., & Kent, D.A. *Physical fitness programs for law enforcement officers: A manual for police administrators*, National Institute for Law Enforcement and Criminal Justice: Washington, D.C., 1978.

10. Lee, J.C. Police Fitness: The Effects of Activities, Service, Limitations, and Programs on Fitness and Retirement. Unpublished doctoral dissertation, University of Southern Mississippi, Hattiesburg, 2003.

11. Copay, A.G. & Charles, M.T. Police academy fitness training at the Police Training Institute, University of Illinois. *Policing: An International Journal of Police Strategies and Management, 21*(3), 416–431, 1998.

12. Klinzing, J.E. Physical fitness status of police officers. *Journal of Sports Medicine and Physical Fitness, 20*(3), 291–296, 1980.

13. Richmond, R.L., Wodak, A., Kehoe, L., & Heather, N. *How healthy are the police a survey of lifestyle factors.* School of Community Medicine: University of New South Wales, Australia, 1998.

14. Pealo, W. The Effectiveness of Two Stages of Wellness Intervention upon the Royal Canadian Mounted Police Officers in the Victoria Subdivision. Unpublished doctoral dissertation, University of Alberta, Canada, 1991.

15. Copay, A.G., & Charles, M.T. Police academy fitness training at the Police Training Institute, University of Illinois. *Policing: An International Journal of Police strategies and Management, 21*(3), 416–431, 1998.

16. Lee, J.C. Police Fitness: The Effects of Activities, Service, Limitations, and Programs on Fitness and Retirement. Unpublished doctoral dissertation, University of Southern Mississippi, Hattiesburg, 2003.

17. Lee, J.C. Police Fitness: The Effects of Activities, Service, Limitations, and Programs on Fitness and Retirement. Unpublished doctoral dissertation, University of Southern Mississippi, Hattiesburg, 2003.

18. Lee, J.C. Police Fitness: The Effects of Activities, Service, Limitations, and Programs on Fitness and Retirement. Unpublished doctoral dissertation, University of Southern Mississippi, Hattiesburg, 2003.

19. Anderson, G.S., Litzenberger, R., & Plecas, D. Physical evidence of police stress. *Policing: An International Journal of Police Strategies and Management, 25*(2), 399–420, 2002.

20. Hoffman, R. & Collingwood, T.R. *Fit for Duty.* Human Kinetics: Champaign, IL, 1995.

21. Lee, J.C. Police Fitness: The Effects of Activities, Service, Limitations, and Programs on Fitness and Retirement. Unpublished doctoral dissertation, University of Southern Mississippi, Hattiesburg, 2003.

22. Johnston, J.H. & Hope D.P. Physical fitness assessment and educational plan-law enforcement administrators must contend. *Police Chief, 48*(1) 16–17, 1981.

23. Hoffman, R. & Collingwood, T.R. *Fit for Duty.* Human Kinetics: Champaign, IL, 1995.

24. Jones, G.R. Health and fitness programs. *FBI Law Enforcement Bulletin, 61*(7), 6–11, 1992.

25. Collingwood, T.R. Implementing programs and standards for law enforcement physical fitness. *Police Chief, 55*(4), 20–24, 1988.

26. Collingwood, T.R. Physical fitness leadership in law enforcement. *Police Chief, 55*(4), 30–32, 34, 37, 1988.

27. Jones, G.R. Health and fitness programs. *FBI Law Enforcement Bulletin, 61*(7), 6–11, 1992.

28. Cooper Institute. *Physical Fitness Specialist Course Manual.* Dallas, TX, 2001.

29. Jones, G.R. Health and fitness programs. *FBI Law Enforcement Bulletin, 61*(7), 6–11, 1992.

30. Ness, J.J. & Light, J. Mandatory fitness standards. *Police Chief, 59*(8), 74–78, 1992.

31. Lee, J.C. Police Fitness: The Effects of Activities, Service, Limitations, and Programs on Fitness and Retirement. Unpublished doctoral dissertation, University of Southern Mississippi, Hattiesburg, 2003.

32. Wilson, D. & Bracci, R. Police agility test-another look at pre-employment screening. *Law and Order, 30*(8), 36–38, 1982.

33. Regali, J.E. Athletic injuries: a comparative study of municipal/county basic police cadets at the Maine criminal justice academy. *Journal of Police Science and Administration, 16*(2), 80–83, 1988.

34. Mostardi, R.A., Porterfield, J.A., King, S., & Urycki, S. Pre-employment screening and health management for safety forces-methods and techniques. *Journal of Orthopedic and Sports Physical Therapy, 11*(9), 398–401, 1990.

35. Turner, D.J. Evaluation of Prescriptive Physical Fitness Programs Used by the Police Department of the City of Calgary. Unpublished doctoral dissertation, University of Oregon, Eugene, 1982.

36. Strobel, C.T. & Bryant, M. Physical fitness a fiscal prescription. *Police Chief, 48*(8), 40–41, 1981.

37. Lee, J.C. Police Fitness: The Effects of Activities, Service, Limitations, and Programs on Fitness and Retirement. Unpublished doctoral dissertation, University of Southern Mississippi, Hattiesburg, 2003.

38. Cooper Institute. *Physical Fitness Specialist Course Manual.* Dallas, TX, 2001.

39. Rafilson, F.M. Candidate physical fitness testing. *Law and Order, 48*(3), 99–101, 2000.

40. Florida Department of Law Enforcement (FDLE). Physical Abilities Testing Procedures. Florida Department of Law Enforcement Web site: http://www.fdle.state.fl.us. cjst/Publications/PAT.htm (accessed August 2002).

41. Lee, J.C. Police Fitness: The Effects of Activities, Service, Limitations, and Programs on Fitness and Retirement. Unpublished doctoral dissertation, University of Southern Mississippi, Hattiesburg, 2003.

42. Rhodes, E.C. & Farenholtz, D.W. Police officers physical abilities test compared to measures of physical fitness. *Canadian Journal of Sport Sciences, 17*(7), 228–233, 1992.

43. Lee, J.C. Police Fitness: The Effects of Activities, Service, Limitations, and Programs on Fitness and Retirement. Unpublished doctoral dissertation, University of Southern Mississippi, Hattiesburg, 2003.

44. Jones, G.R. Health and fitness programs. *FBI Law Enforcement Bulletin, 61*(7), 6–11, 1992.

45. Lee, J.C. Police Fitness: The Effects of Activities, Service, Limitations, and Programs on Fitness and Retirement. Unpublished doctoral dissertation, University of Southern Mississippi, Hattiesburg, 2003.

46. Gaines, L.K., Falkenberg, S., & Gambino, J.A. Police physical agility testing: an historical and legal analysis. *American Journal of Police, 12*(4), 47–65, 1993.

47. Maher, P.T. Police physical abilities test: can they ever be valid? *Public Personnel Management, 13*(2), 173–183, 1984.

48. Lee, J.C. Police Fitness: The Effects of Activities, Service, Limitations, and Programs on Fitness and Retirement. Unpublished doctoral dissertation, University of Southern Mississippi, Hattiesburg, 2003.

49. Gaines, L.K., Falkenberg, S., & Gambino, J.A. Police physical agility testing: an historical and legal analysis. *American Journal of Police, 12*(4), 47–65, 1993.

50. Gaines, L.K., Falkenberg, S., & Gambino, J.A. Police physical agility testing: an historical and legal analysis. *American Journal of Police, 12*(4), 47–65, 1993.

51. Cooper Institute. *Physical Fitness Specialist Course Manual.* Dallas, TX, 2001.

52. Eickhoff-Sherenk, J. Legal claims in worksite fitness programs. Paper presented at the Annual Meeting of the Society for the Study of the Legal Aspects of Sport and Physical Activity, Branson, MO, 2001.

53. Lee, J.C. Police Fitness: The Effects of Activities, Service, Limitations, and Programs on Fitness and Retirement. Unpublished doctoral dissertation, University of Southern Mississippi, Hattiesburg, 2003.
54. Lee, J.C. Police Fitness: The Effects of Activities, Service, Limitations, and Programs on Fitness and Retirement. Unpublished doctoral dissertation, University of Southern Mississippi, Hattiesburg, 2003.

21 Retiring the Old Centurion: Life after a Career in Policing— An Exploratory Study

Jim Ruiz and Erin Morrow

CONTENTS

ABSTRACT

Research in policing usually begins with the application process and continues throughout the career. However, little research has been conducted on what happens to police officers after retirement. This part of a larger study begins with a review of the available literature on the general effects of retirement as it pertains to the general population in contrast to police officers. Findings indicate that police officers suffer higher levels of job-related health problems, depression, suicide, and employment issues. Longevity also appears to be shorter, but this is debatable.

THE PROBLEM

Often when a police officer begins his or her career, little thought is directed toward retirement. For the most part, an officer is happy to have been hired into an occupation perhaps dreamed about since childhood. Although aware of the retirement system, it may seem too distant to warrant serious attention. As time passes and the officer begins to approach the mid-point of his or her career, notice is finally taken by some officers long past retirement age, even 30 to 40 years past, who are still working in the department.

Although police and law enforcement officers encounter many unpredictable situations, perhaps one of the most stressful is retirement.[1] Most, if not all, of police and law enforcement officers have either heard stories or can provide antidotal evidence of officers who have retired only to find menial employment, marital discord, depression, alcohol abuse, premature death, or suicide. The lead author retired from the New Orleans Police Department where these were commonly held beliefs among the rank and file. "In most occupational groups, and especially the very physically active occupations, there is the apocryphal story, with often real examples, of John Doe who only lived a year beyond retirement."[2]

The inspiration for this research occurred over 20 years ago just prior to the lead author's retirement. When he reached retirement age, he met one of his police academy classmates and jokingly asked, "What are you still doing here? Why haven't you retired?" His classmate responded in all seriousness, "Man, where would I go? What would I do?" This is a common problem that most police officers face when approaching retirement. They have spent their lives in an occupation in which retirement age is an impediment for future policing and law enforcement opportunities. Although there are opportunities in private security, they tend to be line-level positions such as security guards and department store loss prevention officers. The working environment of police officers also has a tendency to be an impediment to future employment. Because policing is prone to generate health problems (i.e., high blood pressure, elevated cholesterol, etc.), potential employers are not eager to hire a health risk.

There are many beliefs commonly held by police officers concerning retirement. For example, most believe that along with physical health problems, longevity, marital discord, depression, and suicide plague retired police officers. These topics will be reviewed in an attempt to ascertain current research findings on these and other issues that retired police officers face.

WHO CARES?

There is little impetus to conduct research on retired police and law enforcement officers for three reasons. First, it is not a topic that grabs headlines or public interest such as terrorism, racial profiling, high-speed chases, and excessive or deadly force. Academics are drawn to "hot" topics because they are more likely to provide researchers with opportunities for grants and publication. Second, this is not a topic that excites the media and without some exposure, the general public is not aware of the problems. Third, police administrators and city managers are not eager for police retirement research to be made public for fear that it may uncover liability issues.

Chandler[3] acknowledged that police and law enforcement agencies are especially drawn to hot issues devoid of good research and evaluation. Bartol[4] posited that hot issues "have included missing children campaigns, voice stress analysis, use of psychics, ritualistic crimes, and satanic cults. Good research eventually brings fad-like behavior in check."

This research is important because, first, society has an obligation to see to the latter years of those who placed themselves in harm's way for decades in order to preserve the peace and order that we all take for granted. Second, this research will not only contribute to the quality of life, health, and well-being of our police and law enforcement officers, but it will hopefully generate research interest, better address the root causes of these difficulties, and perhaps eliminate or minimize their negative influence.

RESEARCH METHOD

Because of his negative retirement experience from the New Orleans Police Department, the lead and his co-author began an inquiry to explore the existing literature on pre- and post-retirement experiences of police and law enforcement officers in the United States. Surprisingly, we learned that little research has been directed toward this topic in traditional criminal justice literature. Only one study[5] was located, and it centered on state police officers: a cohort that most urban and suburban police officers would agree do not handle the type nor magnitude of calls for service as they do.

Interestingly, research does exist on retired police officers outside of the United States. For example, studies were conducted in Australia,[6a,b] Canada,[7a,b] and Ireland.[8] Because of the lack of relevant literature on retired U.S. police officers, the authors expanded their search to include the disciplines of psychology, public health, public administration, and sociology. These searches produced literature on serving police and law enforcement officers, but not retired officers. They did, however, contribute greatly to retirement issues facing the general public, which made comparisons possible.

In a search of the dissertation abstracts for police and law enforcement retirement issues, three sources were located that focused on preretirement training,[9] preretirement educational needs,[10] and preretirement planning.[11] However, two suffered from small sample sizes,[12a,b] and the results of other[13] were inconclusive.

This study has three main objectives: (1) to determine available literature on retired police officers in the United States and abroad; (2) to review the existing literature to ascertain if retired police officers experience the same employment, marital, medical, and psychological difficulties experienced by the lead author and many of his compatriots; and (3) to perform an exploratory comparison of the problems faced by retired police officers and those of the general public to determine if differences exist.

ON BECOMING A POLICE OFFICER

When applicants enter the policing occupation, they experience a sudden transmogrification from civilian to police officer. This change is powerful. As one officer put it, "Police work gets in your blood. You become it, and it becomes you."[14] Violanti[15] noted that the police socialization process "attempts to instill a sense of superhuman emotional strength in officers."

Policing is distinguished by a requirement for absolute dedication to the occupation. It is "more an avocation than an occupation."[16] Researchers observed that the excitement and adventure of policing can result in an addiction to the work.[17a,b] Pointing to what he called the "brotherhood of chemistry," Gilmartin[18] posited that police work can create "a psychological as well as social dependency." He also proffered some disturbing effects of police work.

> Officers quickly adapt to excitement and danger and become psychologically depressed in calm or normal periods. Police officers become listless and detached from anything unrelated to police work. At home, they feel uneasy and have difficulty adjusting to the role of spouse, father, or friend. Some officers begin to treat their families like suspects on the street, unable to separate police work from their personal life.[19]

THE ROLE OF THE POLICE SUBCULTURE

"It's a cop thing. You wouldn't understand."[20]

Many groups from differing social backgrounds exist within a culture. They may have customs, beliefs, morals, and judicial procedures that differentiate them from the central culture. These members are said to belong to a subculture. "The police are set apart from other occupational groups and members of society by their unique role and social status. Therefore, some scholars have adopted a collateralization perspective of the police as a unique occupational subculture."[21]

The police subculture is mainly responsible for what has come to be known as the "police worldview." "Worldview" refers to the way that a group views the world and their place in it.[22a,b] Under this aegis, police officers develop a biased viewpoint which influences the way they perceive circumstances and incidents they encounter[23] or "distinctive ways to view the world."[24] The "police worldview" sets in motion the "we/they" or "us/them" configuration. Police officers view themselves as *insiders*, with a unique knowledge of their work. On the other hand, members of the general population are considered *outsiders* at best and "assholes"[25] at worst, and they are treated suspiciously.[26] Few occupations have the breadth of autonomy as do our police and law enforcement officers. Bannish and Ruiz[27] note that autonomy is of such importance that "attempts to restrain police autonomy are seen by police officers as an effort to undermine police authority."

Opler[28] observed that members of a group sustain "dynamic affirmations" that reveal themselves as cultural themes. In the subculture of policing, two themes are found to maintain equilibrium or correspond with one another: police *isolation* and *solidarity*.[29] "*Isolation* is an emotional and physical condition that makes it difficult for members of one social group to have relationships and interact with members of another social group."[30] Cain,[31] Harris,[32] Manning,[33] Reiss and Bordua,[34] Sherman,[35] Skolnick,[36] and Westley[37] all observed the division between the police and society. This self-imposed police isolation is a normal consequence of the interaction between the ethos of secrecy, the police worldview, police suspiciousness, and unusual working hours.[38]

> Social isolation becomes both a consequence and a stimulus. Police officers find that constraints of schedule, of secrecy, of group mystique, and of growing adaptive suspiciousness and cynicism limit their friendships and relationships in the nonpolice world.[39]

When recruits graduate from the police academy, "they become members of a closed society."[40] This closed society or subculture places many expectations or ethos upon its members. Kappeler et al.[41] noted that police maintain three ethos: bravery, autonomy, and secrecy. These attributes are the bedrock of police social character because they are considered to be unequivocally linked with the assumed and actual hazards of policing.[42] Never backing down in the face of danger must be openly displayed to their peers. Bouza[43] noted that "coward is such a powerful epithet that, even in a profession accustomed to the rawest of language, it is a word that is used very sparingly. Compounding matters, police officers are haunted to express their feelings openly. Crank[44] noted that "cops do not emote," which paves the way for isolation and the desire for autonomy.

The ethos of secrecy has many aliases. For example, the "blue wall of silence,"[45] the "blue curtain,"[46] "the code of silence,"[47] and the "code of the blue fraternity"[48] are only a few of the terms used to describe police secrecy. Walker and Katz[49] noted that secrecy serves group solidarity in that it acts "as a shield against attacks from the outside world." In fact, 73 percent of police officers interviewed by Westley[50] believed the general public to be hostile toward the police. The loyalty code and isolation that foster the code of silence also serve to build a solid wall between the police and the public they are hired to protect. In fact, most officers view the public as an annoyance rather than the community they are pledged to serve.

> This attitude is powerfully reinforced on the job when recruits become full-fledged officers and interact with the public every day. It creates strong pressures on police officers to ally themselves with fellow officers, even corrupt ones, rather than reaching out to the public to create supportive and productive relationships with the communities they serve.[51]

The police subculture also fosters the theme of *solidarity*.[52a–e] Solidarity and loyalty are natural outgrowths of police officers' wishes to protect themselves from conceived perils and what they view as public disdain.[53] Police *learn* how to behave and what to think from their shared experiences with other police officers.[54]

However, police loyalty appears to dissipate upon retirement. Although some "professional courtesy" may still exist between active and retired officers (i.e., not issuing a citation for a traffic violation), that is about the extent of former courtesies. When police officers retire, they are no longer viewed as members of the closed society, and they have few friends or associates outside of policing. Hence, they lose the solidarity and loyalty they held dear, and the isolation that served them well during their careers has a negative effect upon retirement.

TWENTY-FOUR HOURS A DAY, SEVEN DAYS A WEEK

For years, municipal officials struggled with issues surrounding the off-duty employment of police officers. Pursuant to the generally accepted wisdom, police officers are considered to be on the job twenty-four hours a day. In many cases, they must supplement their incomes by seeking secondary employment. Hence, Alabama law implicitly recognizes the need for officers to accept off-duty employment (see Sections 6-5-338 and 36-25-5[c], Code of Alabama 1975).[55]

Following are statements from police officers describing their perceptions of being on the job 24 hours a day.

Being a police officer is one of those jobs that defines you as a person. I am a police officer 24 hours a day, and if I see a crime while I am off duty, I have to respond (Granger, 2004:2).[66]

Being a police officer affected my home life obviously because I have four boys and I guess I'm strict with them because I don't want to see them on the opposite side of the law. So I don't let them get away with things some parents might let their kids get away with. It's harder for them but you're a police officer 24 hours a day, you get calls at home from friends, friends of friends for legal questions. That is your job as well as your lifestyle.[56]

Being a police officer is not just a job, it truly is a lifestyle. You are introduced to people by your job more than you are as a person—"Hi, this is Glenn. He's a police officer." All of your friends and neighbors treat you differently after you join the police department. You are considered to be a police officer twenty-four hours a day and seven days a week, and you are told that you are held to a higher standard than the rest of the public.[57]

I'm not gay all the time—only when I go out to pubs—but I'm a police officer 24 hours a day.[58]

These perceptions place an added dimension to the on-duty stress of police officers. Rather than feeling the pressure of their occupation only while on duty, police officers are compelled to maintain their role even while off-duty. The lead author also experienced this first-hand, and although it has been twenty years since his retirement, he still employs tactical driving techniques, scans the driver and license plates of on-coming vehicles, and when in public is aware of persons entering an establishment. This just can't be turned off.

ALCOHOL CONSUMPTION

Richmond et al.[59] questioned whether police officers exhibit higher health risks due to their tendency to cope with stress through alcohol consumption. Although their intention was to promote further research on the positive effects of stress intervention to create a decline in addictive habits, the analysis provides important insight on the rates of alcohol and tobacco use among police officers.

The Australian Health and Medical Research Council defines excessive drinking as exceeding 28 drinks per week for men and 14 drinks for women. Binge drinking is considered when men have more than eight drinks in one sitting and women have six or more drinks, two or more times per month.[60]

Richmond et al.'s[61] assessment was conducted on 954 New South Wales (Australia) police officers. Through the use of five separate focus groups, the study revealed that forty-eight percent of males and forty percent of females drank alcohol excessively, with those of the highest risk being between the ages of eighteen to thirty-nine years old. Males reported drinking an average of 17.9 drinks per week and females 8.1 drinks. Excessive drinking was significantly more prevalent among male than female officers but tended to increase with age among female officers.

The drinking habits among police aroused concern. When compared to the rates of alcohol consumption by the Australian general population, 10.5 percent of men and 7 percent of women were classified as excessive drinkers. Australian police officers displayed alcoholic liver disease deaths of 1.2 percent, which is twice that of the country's general population.[62]

Richmond et al.[63] postulated three theories as to why excessive drinking is more prevalent among police than other occupations. First, men employed in male-dominated industries tend to drink heavier than in areas with a more balanced or a majority female workforce. Second, female police feel under pressure to emulate their male colleagues by keeping up with their drinking habits. Drinking at the end of shifts is viewed as an important part of the police culture. Third, shift work, conflict with management, limited job commitment, occupational stress, and a hierarchical police culture emphasizing conformity are all identified as important factors associated with excessive alcohol consumption.

Kohan and O'Connor[64] surveyed the possible correlation between job satisfaction, job stress, life satisfaction, self-esteem, and alcohol consumption among 122 police officers. They noted that mental health and well-being are related to work-related constructs, and emotional experiences are characterized through two labels: positive affect (PA) and negative affect (NA), which represent temporary mood states. A high PA score is associated with extroversion and a zest for life, whereas a low PA signifies fatigue and lethargy. A high NA score indicates distress or feeling upset, nervous, and tense, whereas a low NA describes feeling peaceful and relaxed. In their study, job-related variables (i.e., global satisfaction, perceived stress, and intention to quit) were examined in relation to PA, NA, life satisfaction, self-esteem, and alcohol consumption among police officers.

Kohan and O'Connor[65] recognized that most studies of police officers focus on high NA dimensions (distress and anxiety). Their most significant correlating factor with a high NA was related to alcohol consumption and job stress. Of the 122 officers surveyed, the median frequency of drinking among them was a "few times a month."[66] The mean number of ounces of alcohol consumed per sitting was .91 (2.3 ounces of 40 percent alcohol). The findings confirmed previous observations that alcohol consumption is associated with NA among police officers. Kohan and O'Connor[67] noted that PA is rarely explored in relation to substance abuse, but may be critical in determining coping strategies among alcohol abusers.

Woolston[68] found that compared to the general population, 25 percent of police officers are likely to die of cancer and fifty percent are more likely to die of cirrhosis of the liver. Violanti, Vena, and Petralia's[69] cohort also documented a significantly elevated risk of dying from cirrhosis of the liver. They observed that liver disease is especially threatening to retiring officers because the mortality risk increased 3.3-fold for those with over 30 years of service.

People who report the highest levels of satisfaction during employment are also those who enjoy a fulfilling retirement.[70] However, coping with dissatisfaction and job stress through alcohol not only leads to a disappointing career and retirement, but also creates an early onset of preventable health disorders. Rehm[71] concluded that retirement ranked ninth as a cause of stress in the United States. Because a high percentage of police officers adopt behaviors such as substance abuse, it would logically follow that retirement can become a psychological and physical personal disaster, especially if alcohol is used as a common coping device.

TOBACCO USAGE

Richmond et al.[72] noted that when compared to the general population, a higher percentage of police officers smoke. They reported that 27 percent of male and 32 percent of female police officers smoke, more than the general population at 24 percent and 21 percent. The trend was particularly noticeable among older policewomen. Almost half of the policewomen over 50 were smokers or double that of the 18- to 29-year-old age group.[73]

Of the respondents who smoked, Richmond et al.[74] found that 27 percent of men and 32 percent of women smoked over a pack of cigarettes a day. They also discovered a significant relationship between alcohol and tobacco use in the New South Wales study, indicating that light, moderate, and heavy smokers were more likely to be excessive drinkers. A 1995 study published by the Australian Bureau of Statistics found that lung cancer deaths were more common among police (7 percent) than the general population (5.4 percent).[75]

Violanti et al.[76] found that 40 percent of United States police officers smoke cigarettes, and they have a significantly higher mortality risk for esophageal cancer. Woolston[77] noted that death rates from esophageal cancer were two to three times higher for police officers than the general population. He indicated that smoking is also linked to officers having higher rates of hypertension and diabetes. Schaefer and Helm[78] reported that of the North Carolina officers who suffered heart attacks in 1996, 46 percent were smokers.

In a study of Canadian police officers, Anshel[79] found that those who often use alcohol and tobacco as a coping mechanism are more likely to suffer frequent and severe health problems as they age when compared to officers who practice more constructive coping strategies.

DIET AND EXERCISE

The stress of policing can also take its toll on officers who are not dependent on alcohol or tobacco. Psychological exhaustion, poor sleep habits, unhealthy diets, and infrequent exercise are all precedent to an aging process fraught with health problems. Police appear to have a high prevalence of unhealthy lifestyle behaviors, which results in excess morbidity and mortality.

Violanti et al.[80] stated that the long-term psychological effects of the policing occupation, in combination with unhealthy lifestyle habits, increase health risks for American officers. In their longitudinal study, they found that the average age of death for a police officer is sixty-six years old. According to a 2001 Department of Health and Human Services survey, Americans live an average of 77.2 years.[81]

Richmond et al.[82] found that eight out of ten (87 percent) New South Wales police officers reported at least one unhealthy lifestyle factor, with one-fifth (19 percent) reporting more than three factors, including drinking, smoking, weight problems, lack of exercise, and stress. Over half of the officers questioned admitted to being overweight. Richmond et al.[83] also found that one-fifth of men (21 percent) and one-quarter (24 percent) of women never exercised. Respondents older than 30 years were most likely to report not exercising at all in the previous three months, and males in their 40s reported never exercising.

Ongoing psychological stress and frustration can lead to anxiety, depression, low self-esteem, and a loss of self-control.[84] The long-term effects can be devastating to a successful career as well as satisfaction with retirement. Richmond et al.[85] found that twenty percent of police admitted to having stress symptoms, and 12 percent of policemen and 15 percent of policewomen reported feeling moderate to intense feelings of stress. However, 71 percent of the police reported that their work was stressful.[86] By coping with stress through destructive lifestyle habits, occupational stress is strongly correlated with coronary heart disease.[87]

Poor and unhealthy lifestyle trends (i.e., unpredictable shift work, inadequate diet, and poor exercise habits) can lead to police officers manifesting higher than normal rates of heart disease. Woolston[88] found that retired police officers were twice more likely than nonofficers of the same age to suffer from heart disease.

Heart disease among police officers is the single greatest cause of early retirement and the second greatest cause of limited duty assignments in police agencies.[89] When Schaefer and Helm[90] conducted an informal study of the incidence of heart disease among North Carolina police officers, they found that the officers had a 35 percent increased risk when compared to the state's general population. Lack of adequate exercise and frequent consumption of fast food contributes to health problems of more experienced and retired police officers. Of the 168 officers in North Carolina who suffered from heart attacks in 1995, 76 percent did not participate in fitness programs, 53 percent had elevated cholesterol levels attributed to saturated fat intake, 60 percent were overweight by more than 16 pounds, and 46 percent had high blood pressure.[91]

Violanti et al.[92] found that 76 percent of police officers have elevated cholesterol, 26 percent have elevated triglycerides, and 60 percent have elevated body fat in addition to elevated mortality risks from colon and digestive cancers. Officers are also more likely to suffer from high blood pressure, a disease strongly related to stress.[93]

FAMILY EFFECTS OF A POLICING CAREER

Jackson and Maslach[94] documented the relationship between job-induced emotional exhaustion and the disruption of family life when they surveyed 142 couples in which the husband was a police officer. Each officer responded to the Maslach Burnout Inventory, which assesses feelings of emotional exhaustion, personal accomplishment, and depersonalization. Their spouses were asked to describe the officer's interactions with the family and their techniques employed to cope with occupational stress while at home. The officers described feelings of mild to moderate emotional exhaustion on a monthly basis, moderate feelings of depersonalization several times a month, and moderate to strong feelings of personal accomplishment several times a month. Jackson and Maslach[95] reported that 27 percent of variance in the quality of family life could be accounted for by the husband's burnout.

Police officers also dealt with stress noticeably through smoking, drinking, withdrawal from others, and finding alternate activities for distracting themselves. Their coping behaviors correlated with the quality of family life, because withdrawing socially or depending on substances negatively affected marital satisfaction. Jackson and Maslach[96] pointed out that unless these lifestyles are altered, the compounding stress and family disruption could lead to personal disaster for the officer, including health problems, psychological ailments, and social disorders.

Janik and Kravitz[97] observed that police officers were more likely than factory workers to have their personal lives affected by job experiences. Officers were reported to become tough and aggressive when dealing with their families, to question them more, mistrust them, and be less capable of emotional involvement. The former husband of a female police officer stated, "It's as if you become a cop twenty-four hours a day, you treat everyone commanding, suspicious, paranoid. She'd gone into the cop role so much that she regarded any challenge to her authority as an attack."[98]

Although Janik and Kravitz[99] did not examine work shift changes as a source of marital stress, O'Neill and Cushing[100] concluded that the constant change of an officer's work shifts has a significant impact on marriage. The unpredictable work schedule disrupts planning and attending social events, which contributes to increased friction and emotional distancing within the family. Jackson and Maslach[101] reported that dysfunctional family and marital relationships inhibit open and trusting partnerships and contribute to high divorce rates among police officers.

In a 1994 study of officer satisfaction after retirement, Goldfarb[102] found a significant number of marital-difficulty complaints. Although only a pilot study of domestic effects following an officer's retirement, Goldfarb found that out of 64 officers who responded to a questionnaire, there was a significant correlation between retirement not being as the officer expected and subsequent marital difficulties; 21.89 percent of the retired group reported dissatisfaction with their marriage that was either absent or minimal prior to retirement.

The national divorce rate in the United States is roughly 50 percent; however, an estimated divorce rate among police officers ranges from 60 to 75 percent.[103] Among couples in which the spouse is a police officer, their turbulent relationships are highly related to job stress transferred into the home front. Goldfarb[104] noted that out of 14 suicides committed by New York City police officers, 12 (86 percent) were going through a divorce or a relationship breakup. Police officers experiencing a divorce are five times more likely to commit suicide than officers in stable marriages.[105]

CYNICISM, STRESS, AND DEVIANCE

Cynicism, "an attitude of contemptuous distrust of human nature and motives,"[106] is not only well-entrenched in police officers and the department but it also affects the public's view of policing. This ideology has a direct effect on how police recruits view their position. Skeptical views not only scar the department's accomplishments but also tarnish the community's sense of well-being, which is an officer's duty to provide.

Policing is recognized as one of the most stressful occupations due to community upheaval, dangerous situations, the media's lack of acknowledgment, little or no organizational compassion, and inadequate social support. This reality creates an "us versus them" attitude, lending resentment towards the general public and compelling police officers to rely only on each other.[107]

Withdrawal from the civilian population happens when officers depend solely on each other for social outlets. This occurs when they believe that they alone understand how the criminal justice system works, and how every one outside their subculture is a potential criminal.[108] Police officers tend to have relatively few friends outside their department, which can place additional strain on officers and their families. "Cops tend to feel very uncomfortable outside the company of other officers. They tend to be very clannish."[109] As a result, they lose the capacity to enable constructive coping skills when faced with stressful situations.

A career compounded with emotional dysfunction can lead to excessive alcohol and tobacco use, deadly stress-related health disorders, domestic upheaval, and even suicide. These behaviors and psychological stressors are likely to emerge when faced with retirement, especially when foreseeing future negative financial situations and second careers. A career immersed in the police subculture can create an unstable, helpless, and depressed individual upon retirement. Retirement may represent the loss of one of the most meaningful sources of instrumental control in an officer's life—the work role.[110]

According to Violanti, Vena, Marshall, and Petralia,[111] "Stressors reported as inherent in police work are danger, shift work, public apathy, boredom, a sense of uselessness, and dealing with misery and death." Officers tend to build up years of resentment, frustration, and cynicism through repeated negative press, inadequate community support, disappointing court systems, skeptical views of society, and unsatisfactory family relationships. This pessimistic routine may eventually lead to social isolation within the police department among peers who reinforce shared values and negative images.

> It all comes down to the same old song. No one else is going to look out for you—maybe not "look after" but "care" about you, except maybe your friends. To the department you're just there when it needs you, and when it doesn't—you're on your own. You're replaced. They've got another officer, and he's young, and he's ready, and he can't wait to be a cop for the city.[112]

"Police stress often leads to the development of cynicism."[113] Bannish and Ruiz[114] observed how the occupational demands made on police create stress, including depersonalization, authoritarianism, organizational protection, and danger preparation:

- Depersonalization results in stress because officers are faced with people at their worst most, if not all of the time, and they are supposed to react to job-related incidents differently from social situations.
- Authoritarianism also causes stress because the officer must follow laws, rules, and regulations that may, at times, provide little discretion for making his/her own decisions. Organizational protection involves the police officer's need to act in a socially acceptable way in the public's eye.
- Danger preparation causes much stress because the police officer believes that his/her life is on the line every day that s/he is on duty.

"Cynicism is generated by feelings of dissatisfaction with the law and results in police officers becoming isolated and manifesting a hatred for society as a whole."[115] Police deviance, on the other hand, occurs when stress is high because officers view it as a way to reduce job demands. Although cynicism rather than deviance is more likely to occur, both traits intensify officers' stress levels.[116] Cynicism and stress result in police officers retreating from society and displaying antipathy to idealism.[117] Because police officers believe that they are the only ones who can understand their plight, they do not keep company with non-police persons.[118] "Such isolation is also common among persons with antisocial personality disorders who believe that all relationships are traps. They have virtually no concern for others, similar to the police officer who sees all people as evil."[119]

Griffin and Ruiz[120] suggest that when police engage in deviant behavior, it is more a result of the "rotten barrel" than the "rotten apple." Stated differently, police deviant behavior is a result of exposure to the unique police subculture and working environment rather than a consequence of lone personal deviance. This proposition is supported by other researchers who maintain that police behavior is learned through training and exposure to the singular environment of policing.[121a,b]

Lahue, Ruiz, and Clark[122] propose a link between depression, aggressive behavior in police and law enforcement officers, and low levels of serotonin. They posit that research on prolonged exposure to low serotonin levels has found a propensity to aggressive behavior, depression, alcohol abuse, and suicide. They suggest that these traits are commonly found in police officers due to a career of exposure to low levels of serotonin in their day-to-day work.

POST-TRAUMATIC STRESS DISORDER IN POLICING:
THE SILENT WALKING WOUNDED

Many events have the potential to be distressing, and an inability to deal with them can leave an officer potentially at risk for developing post-traumatic stress disorder (PTSD).[123] The presence of PTSD in police officers varies. For example Wilson, Poole and Trew[124] found PTSD present in five percent of the police officers in the Royal Ulster Constabulary, and Carlier, Lamberts, and Gersons-Berthold[125] found 7 percent in their sample of 262 traumatized police officers. Perhaps more telling, they discovered that 34 percent experienced post-traumatic stress symptoms or subthreshold PTSD. Of particular interest to this study, Carlier et al. reported that the acuteness of the trauma endured as a major predictor of post-trauma stress symptoms up to one year later. According to Patterson et al.,[126] "In order to function normally within a macho environment, police officers may use avoidance to help deal with intrusive phenomena resulting from a traumatic experience."

Liberman, Best, and Metzler[127] found that exposure to traumatic events was not a requirement for the presence of PTSD in police officers. They observed that routine occupational stress exposure carried a significant risk for psychological distress in police officers, and they were surprised to find it to be a strong predictor of PTSD. Harvey-Lintz and Tidwell[128] studied Los Angeles police officers after the 1992 civil unrest and discovered that seventeen percent experienced PTSD symptomatology and were twice as likely to use avoidance coping strategies of their counterparts without symptomatology. A study conducted by Robinson, Sigman, and Wilson[129] of suburban police officers found robust correlations between on duty-related stress, somatization, and symptoms of PTSD. In fact, 13 percent of the officers met the diagnostic criteria for PTSD.

UN-BECOMING A POLICE OFFICER

As a social animal, man seeks meaningful and satisfying human connections with others … . The quest to achieve connectedness is inseparable from social and cultural life, and in many respects it underlies the sense of connectedness and comradeship felt by members of the police subculture. Where the psychic struggle for connectedness fails or when images of connectedness are unavailable, alternative images of separation arise. These images of separation are kind of a psychological precursor for the idea of death, and they develop through the same kind of process that leads to images of connection. In the police context, images of separation also figure prominently in officers' struggles around retirement.[130]

One's social identity is commonly associated with a chosen occupation. The policing occupation is often separates its members from the general citizenry. Nearly all interactions, both social and occupational, remain internal. This is often the case because of the common bond and occupational hazards shared universally by police officers. For example, the nearly constant low level of stress characteristic of policing punctuated with occasions of extreme stress and shift work all draw officers closer to one another. Because of the intense social bonding, it would be reasonable to expect that departure from such an employment could amplify the apprehension and problems generally associated with retirement.[131]

One's occupation often defines "social location and social worth."[132] In some circles, to be unemployed is to lack social worth. Additionally, retirement not only represents the end of a career, "it is frequently the termination of personal and social worth."[133] With retirement comes a change in a person's social distinctiveness as well as social value. "The disruption is sometimes so severe as to have retirement perceived as a prelude to death, a definition that may at times become self-fulfilling."[134]

Following are statements from police officers explaining the impact that leaving policing had on them.

> It's like belonging to a big club. I was one of the guys, I did my job. Everyone in the station respects you and you get along good with the sergeants and lieutenants. Suddenly, all of that is gone and you are on the outside looking in. I felt so different. I called the guys almost every day to see if they still related to me the same way. I visited the station, wondering what was going on and wanting to be part of the action. I played golf with the guys, went to all the parties. Somehow, it wasn't the same. I wasn't one of them anymore. It's hard to explain. I retired, but I couldn't let go of this strong attachment.[135]

> Giving back that badge and gun was one of the most difficult moments in my life. I cried for months.[136]

One interviewee remarked how he had attended several golf tournaments for serving and retired officers and found that during the social activities afterwards the still-serving officers sat separately from the retired officers and avoided discussing with them what was happening in "the job."[137]

Kim and Moen[138] conducted a longitudinal study of retirement transitions and its long-term psychological well-being among 458 married men and women. The subjects, aged 50 to 72 years old, were either still employed at their primary jobs, retired, or had retired two years previous to the study. They found that being "continuously" retired (over two years) related to greater symptoms of depression. To understand the overall psychological well-being of retirees, the researchers enforced the importance of "role theory" as being primary in relation to retirement adjustment. Men and women who retire from their careers are vulnerable to feelings of role loss which can lead to psychological distress. When employment is crucial to one's identity, the loss of that status produces a decline in morale and an increase in depressive symptoms. Some careers become an identifying factor to one's self-image, such as that of police officers.[139]

Research on the challenges that police officers face upon retirement is scarce. However, retirement relates closely to the satisfaction factors that Kim and Moen[140] document, such as prior level of psychological well-being, spouse's circumstance, changes in personal control, marital quality, subjective health, and income adequacy. Research appears to support the proposition that police officers are especially unique in their retirement due to the lifestyle and culture experienced during their career.

Unlike U.S. secret service agents who have the option to retire and return as full-time investigators, most police officers realize that they face an uncertain future. Forcese and Cooper[141] found that "employment opportunities are few" for retired police officers. Many indicated that policing provided little in the way of career mobility and their overall lack of post-high school education provided few occupational alternatives. "The most distinguishable post-retirement job was related to security (approximately 25 percent)."[142] They also found that police officers failed to plan for retirement and "fully one-quarter indicated no preparation whatsoever."[143]

The most successful retirees in the Forcese and Cooper[144] study were those whose "retirement was career detachment." For example, those who viewed the policing occupation as just a "job" were more successful in retirement than those professionally and psychologically committed to what most police officers refer to as "The Job." Patterson et al.[145] note that "throughout their service, police officers operate within an organized bureaucratic system that is predictable and familiar. Upon leaving this system, unless the family system provides organization and predictability, then the retiree may experience some discomfort."

MORTALITY

Raub[146] questions the assumption that police officers are destined to have shorter life spans than the general population. He found that retired officers from the Illinois, Ohio, Arizona, and Kentucky state police live just as long, if not longer, than the population as a whole. Raub assumed the shorter than average life expectancy of police is related to research surrounding the effects of stress on higher incidences of health problems. Comparative studies of health disorders between police officers and other occupations do not exist.[147]

Raub[148] compared 732 Illinois state trooper retirees to the civilian population with the average amount of service at retirement being 26.4 years. It was found that younger retirees (40 to 54) did not live as long as expected, whereas retirees 55 and older lived longer than expected.

Overall, retirees from Illinois, Ohio, Kentucky, and Arizona had life expectancies equal to or exceeding normal. Even greater differences were seen when the age of retirement was 55 or older. Also, deaths of disabled retirees were no different than expected based on disability life mortality tables.

SUICIDE

When faced with retirement, an officer may experience overwhelming helplessness at the thought of ending a membership within the policing subculture and resent emerging into a disliked community. The deprivation of this company equates to abandoning absolute protection and defined identity, and occupying a world perceived as a threat.

More often than not, police officers maintain an ambivalent relationship with their chosen occupation. Although they struggle to stay with a job that became a part of them, they find it difficult to leave. "Retired officers are generally not prepared to become 'civilians.'"[149]

Separation from the police subculture can be a frightening and depressing experience, despite the many benefits of retirement. Retiring police officers may face intense psychological pressure because of the striking difference between the police officer and civilian roles. This apprehension, in combination with increasing age (a universal suicide factor), stems from a perceived loss of power, prestige, self-definition, and hero status. During this time, some officers turn to alcohol and/or contemplate suicide. Gaska[150] concluded that retired officers are especially vulnerable to the temptation of suicide.

The verbal bravado often expounded by officers approaching retirement may suddenly cease as the reality of leaving hits. Many officers experience a crisis that Violanti (1996)[151] termed as "retirement identity crisis." He also noted that police officers "develop a cynical attitude about police work, complain incessantly about administration, dislike their work, and feel trapped in their jobs because of pensions. On the other hand, they struggle with separation from the close identity they developed towards police work."[152] Violanti[153] notes that these officers do not enjoy their retirement. The bitterness and cynicism that they previously had is carried into retirement and a negative view of life follows. Consequently, these officers become high suicide risks.

Violante[154] listed three factors that complicate police retirement: age, barriers to retirement, and changing circumstances. Officers realize that if they wait past age 45, they will experience difficulty securing another job. Barriers such as "financial obligations, mortgages, or college tuition" force them to stay. Promotions or a transfer to a plush assignment may well be incentives to remain.[155]

Policing has often been considered at high-risk for employee suicide. In 1950, the Department of Health, Education, and Welfare found that the mortality rate for police officers was the highest of all stressful occupations.[156] According to McCafferty,[157] "police officers, because of the stress they endure, are prone to depression, alcoholism, anxiety disorders, all of which are associated with increased suicide." Fell and Wallace[158] found that police officers in the United States have the third highest suicide rates when compared to 130 other occupations.

Violante et al.[159] studied suicide rates of police officers in Buffalo, New York, between 1950 and 1990. They found that there were no significant differences between retired officers and other occupations. However, suicides "were significantly higher in officers just prior to retirement." Police suicides in New York City were double that of the city's general population and significantly higher than suicide rates of all public service employees.[160] In the first nine months of 1995 alone, the NYPD endured 11 police suicides in a department of 38,000 officers.[161] Vena, Violanti, Marshall, and Fiedler[162] found that white male police officers displayed a proportionately higher suicide risk than all other municipal employees. Their research also noted that although overall police mortality is decreasing, suicide rates in large cities (i.e., Chicago and New York) surpass the line-of-duty deaths.

Janik and Kravitz[163] examined the demographics, experiences, instances of substance abuse, and stress factors that possibly influence officers to take their own lives. It was assumed that the suicide attempts referred to in the officer's fitness-for-duty evaluations occurred within their years of police service due to the researchers' logic that if suicide attempts occurred prior to applying with the department, the applicant would not have passed the psychological requirements for employment. Janik and Kravitz[164] found that 55 percent of the officers documented in their fitness-for-duty evaluations had attempted suicide. The two most significant influences preceding their suicide attempts were marital problems and suspension from the department.

The validity of suicide rates among police officers is questionable, creating difficulty in adequately researching the topic. Common obstacles faced by researchers is that officer suicide reports are not collected, not released, or misclassified as accidental or undetermined deaths.[165] Again, the strength of the police subculture continues this misrepresentation because of their belief that the stigma of suicide tarnishes their superior image. Misclassifying police suicide allows the deceased officer to receive burial with honors and allows the surviving family members to receive the officer's insurance and benefits. Therefore, those psychological stressors that lead to the thought of death, as well as the suicide itself, are avoided or ignored.

Violanti[166] attempted to assess the sensitivity, specificity, and predictive value of official police suicide rates when compared to municipal workers. All deaths classified as suicide, accidental, or undetermined were validated by a medical examiner for inclusion in the cohort. The findings showed that police suicide rates were less sensitive than rates of municipal workers and had a less predicative value. Violanti[167] claims the nonrecognition of mental health and survivors of suicide is a public health issue that needs to be resolved, and this can be accomplished only through a more universal approach to assuring validity in suicide reports. Hem, Anne, and Oivind[168] also recognized the methodological problems that plague research on police suicide and noted that sample sizes were often too small to consider accurate results.

Other areas of concern are a general misunderstanding as to the very nature of police work, and that stress in policing may be more location specific. For example, the public generally characterizes police work as highly dangerous, when in reality the majority of police confront high-risk situations infrequently.[169] The location of the studies also raises concern over suicide validity rates. Previous studies are based on limited police populations within the United States, without recognizing that local and regional variance in suicide can affect the study's outcome.[170] Previous research has also failed to designate appropriate comparison groups. By comparing police officers to the general population, the research creates a "healthy worker effect." Due to the occupational requirements, police officers are selected in accordance of strict criteria, creating a labor population with stronger healthy worker effects. It is not feasible to compare suicide rates among police officers to those of the general population that contain the unemployed and mentally ill.[171]

Hem et al.[122] acknowledge the possibility of flawed research indicating that police officers are at high-risk for suicide, and conducted a systematic review of the worldwide literature on police. Overall, they found no data on suicides to indicate that police had significantly more, or they found inconsistent results throughout reviews. Hem et al.[173] were confident that pre-retired and retired police are at a tenfold increase in risk of committing suicide. Further, suicide rates among police are relatively stable in comparison to the United States population, with one exception: police officers with 30 or more years of duty have a higher suicide rate. Hem et al.[174] could not find conclusive data to support the position that police rates of suicide are exceptionally high; the only consistent findings were the correlated risk of suicide upon retirement among officers.

TABLE 21.1
Federal Bureau of Investigation (FBI) and Police Department (PD) Suicides in Selected Cities

Force	Years	Suicides	Line of Duty Deaths	Size of Force	Percentage over National Suicide Rate
FBI	1993–1998	18	4	11,500	116.6
New York City PD	1985–1998	87	36	40,000	29.1
Chicago PD	1990–1998	22	12	13,500	50.9
Los Angeles PD	1990–1998	20	11	9,668	75.5
San Diego PD	1992–1998	5	0	2,000	197.5

In a study to determine whether there were significant differences between the rates of suicide between the general population and police officers, Gaska[175] found that a significant difference existed between retired police officers compared to members of the general population in the same age group. Gaska's study of suicide among 4,000 retired Detroit police officers found that the rate for these officers was 334.7/100,000 yet the general population rate was 11.1/100,000. The suicide rate for retired officers jumped to 2,616/100,000 due to disability. Of particular note was that 66 percent of suicides among retired police officers were listed as natural or accidental. This was normally practiced to protect the department and family members, so it is reasonable to assume that other departments would adopt this practice for the same reasons.

Hackett and Violante[176] note that by "the very nature of the law enforcement profession, stresses that can lead to suicidal thinking are many." Because of the nature of the police and law enforcement occupation, officers are exposed regularly to personal danger as well as encountering murder, rape, and other tragedies which put them at increased risk for suicide.[177] In fact, according to Turvey,[178] more police officers take their own lives than fall victim to felons or other deaths that occur in the line of duty. Table 21.1 exemplifies this problem.

FINANCES

The transition to retirement is a combination of emotional and financial adjustments. Durkheim's "social anomie" is applicable to the emotions provoked upon retirement. Social anomie is defined as a personal crisis experienced while moving from one culture to another: from blue-collar worker to manager, from having little money to sudden wealth, from working to retirement. It is a time when the ground beneath one's feet does not feel solid.[179]

Bradley[180] found that it can take years for a person to move from a life that once was to one that is now free to create. Initially, retirement is an overwhelmingly fragile time, especially because satisfaction is based largely on having enough money. The Bureau of Labor estimates that individuals require an income of approximately 70 to 80 percent of their working salary to maintain the same standard of living upon retirement.[181]

Even though retirement can be perceived more as an emotional transition than a significant financial experience, what one can afford that will provide for the new environments, goals, and values will ultimately predict one's overall personal satisfaction. Retirement can open doors for unexpected life changes and financial issues once the new lifestyle is established. Frustration and depression are common when retirees feel financially overwhelmed and their new lifestyle is not affordable.[182]

Police officers must embrace financial planning in order to create a fulfilling retirement. A study involving Canadian officers[183] found that their retirement anxiety revolved primarily around income factors rather than "changed social circumstances or inactivity." This is the mindset that many officers have, as reflected in their decision to remain employed with the department past their retirement dates.[184]

Rehm[185] also found that remaining with the department actually harms one's retirement fund contributions. He discovered that a captain serving additional time would only increase his/her personal retirement fund by $40 per month. This is less than minimum wage at a part-time job. Continuing with the department past retirement is a poor financial decision, and experienced police officers are worth significantly more in the open job market. The anxiety that occurs upon ending a policing career also emerges from the stress of securing future employment. The authority insured with wearing the badge, the unpredictable excitement, and the family-like structure of the department may convince the officer that no other career can deliver similar satisfaction.

McCormick[186] noted that a retiring officer might feel inadequate in the open job market due to a perceived lack of commercial skills. Officers may believe they are not qualified for other employment options because all they know is how to be a police officer. According to Goldfarb,[187] "If you are what you do, and you don't, you AIN'T!" This mentality makes it very difficult for officers to leave their badge behind and embrace a new career.

Police officers are especially unique in their post-retirement opportunities because they can often retire at a younger age than the general population. They also leave their career with an abundance of skills that would be beneficial in applying for another line of work such as experience in interacting with a variety of people, making split-second decisions, and being proficient in conflict resolution.[188]

Administrators must take steps to prepare their officers for retirement. Rehm[189] noted that less than 15 percent of police agencies in the United States provide retirement counseling. Ironically, police agencies are trained in mobilizing resources and developing operational plans for various crisis situations but fall short at developing the well-being of their own employees.

The American Association of Retired Persons offers job placement for retiring officers free of charge.[190] Rehm[191] believes that for optimal efficiency, retirement planning should occur five years before eligibility. Agencies should train officers in job hunting skills such as resume preparation, interview techniques, and letter writing. Departments should also encourage their officers to contemplate further education, and they should assist the officer in locating financial assistance to do so. Rehm[192] also suggests cost-effective placement for retired officers. He believes that agencies should consider rehiring a limited number of retirees as civilian employees, which would allow the department to retain valuable assets as well as eliminate in-depth training required for a newly hired employee. Agencies could use retired officers for specialty programs such as community policing, special problem assignments, and internal affairs investigations. This cost-effective approach frees active-duty officers for other assignments, creates a valuable training environment for younger officers assigned to work with the retirees, and allows retired officers to enter a new phase of their careers within a familiar organization.

POST-EMPLOYMENT SCREENING

Prior to being hired, police officers must pass strict physical and psychological exams. During their career, most officers are required to have yearly physicals. However, few, if any, departments require their officers to submit to regular psychological exams in the same manner. Because of this deficiency, it is not possible to know how many officers suffer from untreated depression. On the other hand, if police officers do seek treatment, they become labeled as emotionally defective, and "it is this label that seems to be the kiss of death within law enforcement."[193] To escape this disgrace, officers may avoid treatment and are almost certain to transfer to "the Rubber Gun Squad."

Gettys[194] found that police psychologists do little by way of research. Chandler[195] is an ardent advocate of police psychologists becoming knowledgeable and active in conducting research. In a national survey of 152 police psychologists, Bartol[196] found that although they perform pre-employment screenings and fitness-for-duty evaluations, these are usually conducted only after an incident or a series of incidents occur that cause police administrators concern. Bartol also determined that none performed periodic evaluations to check for changes in scores attained during pre-employment screening. "Traditionally, law enforcement has used psychologists on an "as needed" basis rather than for systematic human resource development and prevention."[197] This suggests that the increasing range of existing psychological services is not scientifically being incorporated into policing. The challenge will convince police administrators and police unions that psychological services aimed at prevention and intervention is, in the long run, more beneficial for everyone rather than reacting after a tragedy has occurred.

CONCLUSION

In May of 1985, the lead author retired from the New Orleans Police Department. At that time the department had no pre-retirement training or assistance. Retirement was completely different from entry into the police department. Although it is easy to remember the date of graduation from the police academy and the swearing-in ceremony with all its pomp and circumstance, no such ceremony existed upon retirement. Retirement consisted of appearing in the personnel office and advising a clerk of the desire to retire. A folder was presented with forms to complete, and in about ten minutes it was over.

One minute he was a platoon commander in a large police department. The next minute that status was gone with no transition, no ceremony, and no thanks for all the time spent away from family on weekends, holidays, and emergencies. It was over. One minute he was an "insider." The next he was no longer a part of the policing brotherhood. As such, he instantly became what most police officers believe the general public to be, and what Van Maanan[198] wrote about—and the belief to which he subscribed during his time in uniform. He had become one of the "Assholes."

There has long been a need for assistance as police officers approach retirement. Johnson[199] noted that police officers face special problems when retiring. Because they can retire before the age of 50, they are able to begin another career. Johnson observed that retirement for police officers can be traumatic and even fatal, and departments should assist their personnel in planning for the future. He recommended that a counseling program be provided to help officers prepare for a second career, and that this planning begin five years prior to retirement.

Johnson[200] also called for police department training divisions to bear the responsibility of preparing employees for separation and training for another vocation through in-house programs or community-based educational services. The significant other should be included in retirement planning, especially when officers retire at an early age. Such programs can boost the morale of the mid-tenure officer by demonstrating that the department cares. Of particular interest is a service offered in Ireland to retired police officers. Patterson et al.[201] noted that "all police retirees have access to their local police voluntary welfare group, which arranges meetings and outings for police pensioners."

Policing is notorious for its selective subculture among the officers, the ideals they possess about themselves, and the civilian world they must face. This macho culture inadvertently creates a lack of constructive coping skills and an unwillingness to admit weakness. Analysis of the police organization shows that more often police officers turn to self-destructive coping techniques rather than healthy options, and these habits are only intensified when faced with the decision to retire. Literature on police retirement notes that officers are apprehensive about retiring and may stay on in the department past their retirement date, or they spend their retirement overwhelmed with physical and psychological problems. The most disturbing aspect of police during retirement is their vulnerability to commit suicide.

To a police officer, retirement equates a loss of one's identity, the demise of a sympathetic social support group, and dealing with the aging process. Retirement also means facing the consequences of their lifestyle while employed. These may be fatal health ailments, substance abuse problems, disabling psychological disorders, and unsupportive or failed personal relationships.

Traditionally, police administrators have paid little or no attention to the plight of their officers after retirement. Moreover, precious little is done to prepare police officers for the virtual free-fall they may experience emotionally and socially upon retirement. In order to address this, programs and assistance should be offered early on, before retirement. Police organizations must recognize that stress counseling and positive coping techniques for officers should be embraced both while they are members of the department and after retirement. Only through caring and appropriate preparation can there be hope for long and enjoyable retirements.

REFERENCES

1. Newman, D., Rucker-Reed, M. Police stress, state-trait anxiety, and stressors among U.S. Marshals. *Journal of Criminal Justice, 32,* 631–641, 2004.
2. Forcese, D., Cooper, J. Police retirement: Career succession or obsolesce? *Canadian Police College Journal 9,* 413–424, 1985.
3. Chandler, J. *Modern Police Psychology: For Law Enforcement and Human Behavior Professionals.* Springfield, IL: Charles C. Thomas, 1990.
4. Bartol, C. *Police Psychology: Then, Now, and Beyond. Criminal Justice and Behavior, 3,* 78–79, 1996.
5. Raub, R. *Police Officer Retirement: The Beginning of a Long Life.* Illinois State Police, IL Division of Administration, 1987.
6a. Richmond, R., Kehoe, L., Hailstone, S., Wodak, A., Uebel-Yan, M. Quantitative and qualitative evaluations of brief interventions to change excessive drinking, smoking, and stress in the police department. *Addiction, 94,* 1509–1521, 1999.
6b. Richmond, R., Wodak, A., Kehoe, L., Nick, H. Research report: How healthy are police? A survey of life-style factors. *Addiction, 93,* 1729–1737, 1998.
7a. Forcese, D., Cooper, J. Police retirement: Career succession or obsolesce? *Canadian Police College Journal, 9,* 413–424, 1985.
7b. Rehm, W. Retirement: A new chapter, not the end of story. *FBI Law Enforcement Bulletin, 65,* 6–12, 1996.
8. Patterson, M., Poole, D., Trew, K., Harkin, N. The psychological and physical health of police officers retired recently from the Royal Ulster Constabulary. *Irish Journal of Psychology, 22,* 1–27, 2001.
9. Lynch, K. Retirement satisfaction of Florida police officers as related to pre-retirement training and other variables. Dissertation Abstracts: University of South Florida http://wwwlib. umi.com/dissertations/gateway (accessed June, 2001),1997.
10. Storch, J. A description of the preretirement educational needs of potential first career retirees from a major metropolitan police department. Pub No: 9136450 Columbia University Teachers College, http://wwwlib.umi.com/dissertations/gateway (accessed June, 2005), 1991.
11. Dimond-Smith, S. The relationship between pre-retirement planning and satisfaction with retirement among law enforcement officers. 8315108 United States International University. http://wwwlib. umi.com/dissertations/gateway (accessed, June, 2005), 1983.
12a. Storch, J.A description of the preretirement educational needs of potential first career retirees from a major metropolitan police department. Pub No: 9136450 Columbia University Teachers College, http://wwwlib.umi.com/dissertations/gateway (accessed June, 2005), 1991.
12b. Dimond-Smith, S. The relationship between pre-retirement planning and satisfaction with retirement among law enforcement officers. 8315108 United States International University. http://wwwlib. umi.com/dissertations/gateway (accessed, June, 2005), 1983.
13. Lynch, K. Retirement satisfaction of Florida police officers as related to pre-retirement training and other variables. Dissertation Abstracts: University of South Florida http://wwwlib. umi.com/dissertations/gateway (accessed June, 2001), 1997.
14. Violanti, J. *Police Suicide: Tactics for Prevention.* Charles Thomas: Springfield, IL, 2002, 67 pp.
15. Violanti, J. *Police Suicide: Tactics for Prevention.* Charles Thomas: Springfield, IL, 2002, 67 pp.
16. Forcese, D., Cooper, J. Police retirement: Career succession or obsolesce? *Canadian Police College Journal, 9,* 414, 1985.

17a. Gilmartin, K. Hypervigilance: A learned perceptual set and its consequences on police stress. In *Psychological Services for Law Enforcement*, Reese, J., Goldstein, H., Eds., U.S. Government Printing Office: Washington, DC, 1986, pp. 443–446.

17b. Van der Klok, B. *Psychological Trauma*. American Psychiatric Press: Washington, DC, 1987.

18. Gilmartin, K. Hypervigilance: A learned perceptual set and its consequences on police stress. In *Psychological Services for Law Enforcement*, Reese, J., Goldstein, H., Eds., U.S. Government Printing Office: Washington, DC, 1986, pp. 443–446.

19. Gilmartin, K. Hypervigilance: A learned perceptual set and its consequences on police stress. In *Psychological Services for Law Enforcement*, Reese, J., Goldstein, H., Eds., U.S. Government Printing Office: Washington, DC, 1986, pp. 443–446.

20. Crank, J. P. *Understanding Police Culture*. Anderson: Cincinnati, OH, 1998, 13 pp.

21. Kappeler, V., Sluder, R., Alpert, G. *Forces of Deviance: Understanding the Dark Side of Policing*. Waveland Press: Prospect Heights, IL, 1998, 88 pp.

22a. Benedict, R. *Patterns of Culture*. Houghton Mifflin: Boston, MA, 1934.

22b. Redfield, R. *The Primitive Worldview and its Transformations*. Cornell University Press: Ithaca, New York, 1953.

23. Skolnick, J. *Justice Without Trial: Law Enforcement in a Democratic Society*. Macmillian, New York, 1994.

24. Kappeler, V., Sluder, R., Alpert, G. *Forces of Deviance: Understanding the Dark Side of Policing*. Waveland Press: Prospect Heights, IL, 1998, 89 pp.

25. Van Maanen, J. The asshole. In *Policing: A View from the Street,* Manning, P., Van Maanen, J., Eds., Goodyear, Santa Monica, CA, 1978, pp. 221–238.

26. Kappeler, V., Sluder, R., Alpert, G. *Forces of Deviance: Understanding the Dark Side of Policing*. Waveland Press: Prospect Heights, IL, 1998.

27. Bannish, H., Ruiz, J. The antisocial police personality: A view from the inside. *International Journal of Public Administration*, *26*, 838, 2003.

28. Opler, M. Themes as dynamic forces in culture. *The American Journal of Sociology*, *51*, 198–206, 1945.

29. Kappeler, V., Sluder, R., Alpert, G. *Forces of Deviance: Understanding the Dark Side of Policing*. Waveland Press: Prospect Heights, IL, 1998, 100 pp.

30. Kappeler, V., Sluder, R., Alpert, G. *Forces of Deviance: Understanding the Dark Side of Policing*. Waveland Press: Prospect Heights, IL, 1998, 100 pp.

31. Cain, M. *Society and the Policeman's Role*. Routledge and Kegan Paul: London, 1973.

32. Harris, R. *The Police Academy: An Insider's View*. John Wiley: New York, 1973.

33. Manning, P. The police: Mandate, strategies and appearances, In *The Police and Society: Touchstone Readings*, Kappeler, V., Ed., Waveland Press: Prospect Heights, IL, 1995, pp. 97–125.

34. Reiss, A., Bordua, D. (1967). Environment and organization: A perspective on police. In *The Police: Six Sociological Essays*, Bordua, D., Ed., John Wiley: New York, 1967, pp. 215–227.

35. Sherman, L. Learning police ethics. *Criminal Justice Ethics, 1*, 10–19, 1982.

36. Skolnick, J. *Justice Without Trial: Law Enforcement in a Democratic Society*. Macmillian, New York, 1994.

37. Westley, W. Violence and the police. *American Journal of Sociology, 59*, 34–41, 1965.

38. Kappeler, V., Sluder, R., Alpert, G. *Forces of Deviance: Understanding the Dark Side of Policing*. Waveland Press: Prospect Heights, IL, 1998.

39. Bahn, C. Police socialization in the eighties: Strains in the forging of an occupational identity. *Journal of Police Science and Administration*, *12*, 392, 1984.

40. Ozee, K. (2001). Retirement Options and Quality of Life of Retired Illinois State Police Officers. Dissertation Abstracts: Walden University 2001, file:///Users/jmr33/Documents/Old%20Centurian/ozee1safari.html (accessed May, 2005).

41. Kappeler, V., Sluder, R., Alpert, G. *Forces of Deviance: Understanding the Dark Side of Policing*. Waveland Press: Prospect Heights, IL, 1998.

42. Kappeler, V., Sluder, R., Alpert, G. *Forces of Deviance: Understanding the Dark Side of Policing*. Waveland Press: Prospect Heights, IL, 1998.

43. Bouza, A. *The Police Mystique: An Insider's Look at Cops, Crime, and the Criminal Justice System*. Plenum Press: New York, 1990, 71 pp.

44. Crank, J. P. *Understanding Police Culture*. Anderson: Cincinnati, OH, 1998, 183 pp.

45. Mollen, M. *Commission Report, Commission to Investigate Allegations of Police Corruption and the Anti-Corruption Procedures of the Police Department*. The City of New York: New York, 1994.

46. Walker, S., Katz, C. *Police in America: An Introduction*. McGraw-Hill: Boston, MA, 2002.

47. Westley, W. *Violence and the Police*. MIT Press: Cambridge, MA, 1970.

48. More, H. *Special Topics in Policing*. Anderson: Cincinnati, OH, 1998.

49. Walker, S., Katz, C. *Police in America: An Introduction*. McGraw-Hill: Boston, MA, 2002, 428 pp.

50. Westley, W. *Violence and the Police*. MIT Press: Cambridge, MA, 1970.

51. More, H. *Special Topics in Policing*. Anderson: Cincinnati, OH, 1998, 284 pp.

52a. Banton, M. *The policeman in the Community*. Basic Books: New York, 1964.

52b. Harris, R. *The Police Academy: An Insider's View*. John Wiley: New York, 1973.

52c. Skolnick, J. *Justice Without Trial: Law Enforcement in a Democratic Society*. Macmillian, New York, 1994.

52d. Stoddard, E. The informal code of police deviancy: A group approach to blue collar crime. In *The Police and Society: Touchstone Readings*, Kappeler, V., Ed., Waveland Press: Prospect Heights, IL, 1995, pp. 185–206.

52e. Westley, W. *Violence and the Police*. MIT Press: Cambridge, MA, 1970.

53. Kappeler, V., Sluder, R., Alpert, G. *Forces of Deviance: Understanding the Dark Side of Policing*. Waveland Press: Prospect Heights, IL, 1998, 101 pp.

54. Kappeler, V., Sluder, R., Alpert, G. *Forces of Deviance: Understanding the Dark Side of Policing*. Waveland Press: Prospect Heights, IL, 1998, 87 pp.

55. Alabama League of Municipalities. *New POST rules*. http://www.alalm.org/New%20POST%20Rules.html (accessed June, 2005).

56. Sudbury Region Police Museum. Police are People Too! Police at Home. http://www.virtualmuseum.ca/pm.php?id=exhibit_home&fl=0&lg=English&ex=00000217 (accessed June, 2005).

57. Norstrem, G. Do Cops Really Like Donuts? http://www.merriampark.org/POST/may02/donut.htm (accessed June 2005).

58. Burke, M. (1995, December). Identities and disclosures: The case of lesbian and gay police officers. *The Psychologist* 1995, http://www.academicarmageddon.co.uk/library/BUR.htm (accessed June, 2005).

59. Richmond, R., Kehoe, L., Hailstone, S., Wodak, A., Uebel-Yan, M. Quantitative and qualitative evaluations of brief interventions to change excessive drinking, smoking, and stress in the police department. *Addiction, 94,* 1509–1521, 1999.

60. Richmond, R., Kehoe, L., Hailstone, S., Wodak, A., Uebel-Yan, M. Quantitative and qualitative evaluations of brief interventions to change excessive drinking, smoking, and stress in the police department. *Addiction, 94,* 1509–1521, 1999.

61. Richmond, R., Kehoe, L., Hailstone, S., Wodak, A., Uebel-Yan, M. Quantitative and qualitative evaluations of brief interventions to change excessive drinking, smoking, and stress in the police department. *Addiction, 94,* 1509–1521, 1999.

62. Richmond, R., Kehoe, L., Hailstone, S., Wodak, A., Uebel-Yan, M. Quantitative and qualitative evaluations of brief interventions to change excessive drinking, smoking, and stress in the police department. *Addiction, 94,* 1509–1521, 1999.

63. Richmond, R., Kehoe, L., Hailstone, S., Wodak, A., Uebel-Yan, M. Quantitative and qualitative evaluations of brief interventions to change excessive drinking, smoking, and stress in the police department. *Addiction, 94,* 1509–1521, 1999.

64. Kohan, A., O'Connor, B. Police officer job satisfaction in relation to mood, well-being, and alcohol consumption. *The Journal of Psychology, 136,* 307–318, 2002.

65. Kohan, A., O'Connor, B. Police officer job satisfaction in relation to mood, well-being, and alcohol consumption. *The Journal of Psychology, 136,* 307–318, 2002.

66. Kohan, A., O'Connor, B. Police officer job satisfaction in relation to mood, well-being, and alcohol consumption. *The Journal of Psychology, 136,* 307–318, 2002.

67. Kohan, A., O'Connor, B. Police officer job satisfaction in relation to mood, well-being, and alcohol consumption. *The Journal of Psychology, 136,* 307–318, 2002.

68. Woolston, C. A Dangerous Beat. http://www2.vhihealthe.com/topic/cops, 2000 (accessed July, 2003).

69. Violanti, J., Vena, J., Petralia, S. Mortality of a police cohort: 1950–1990. *American Journal of Industrial Medicine, 33,* 366–373, 1998.

70. Goldfarb, D. An Instrument for Predicting Retirement Satisfaction in Police Officers: A Pilot Study. 1994, http://www.heavybadge.com/retire.htm (accessed July, 2003).

71. Rehm, W. Retirement: A new chapter, not the end of story. *FBI Law Enforcement Bulletin,* September, *65,* 6–12, 1996.

72. Richmond, R., Kehoe, L., Hailstone, S., Wodak, A., Uebel-Yan, M. Quantitative and qualitative evaluations of brief interventions to change excessive drinking, smoking, and stress in the police department. *Addiction, 94,* 1509–1521, 1999.

73. Richmond, R., Kehoe, L., Hailstone, S., Wodak, A., Uebel-Yan, M. Quantitative and qualitative evaluations of brief interventions to change excessive drinking, smoking, and stress in the police department. *Addiction, 94,* 1509–1521, 1999.

74. Richmond, R., Kehoe, L., Hailstone, S., Wodak, A., Uebel-Yan, M. Quantitative and qualitative evaluations of brief interventions to change excessive drinking, smoking, and stress in the police department. *Addiction, 94,* 1509–1521, 1999.

75. Richmond, R., Kehoe, L., Hailstone, S., Wodak, A., Uebel-Yan, M. Quantitative and qualitative evaluations of brief interventions to change excessive drinking, smoking, and stress in the police department. *Addiction, 94,* 1509–1521, 1999.

76. Violanti, J., Vena, J., Petralia, S. Mortality of a police cohort: 1950–1990. *American Journal of Industrial Medicine, 33,* 366–373, 1998.

77. Woolston, C. A Dangerous Beat. http://www2.vhihealthe.com/topic/cops, 2000 (accessed July, 2003).

78. Schaefer, P., Helm, M. The Incidence of Heart Disease in North Carolina Officers. Fall, 1996, http://www.jus.state.nc.us/NCJA/w-08-99tip.htm (accessed July, 2005).

79. Anshel, M. A conceptual model for implications for coping with stressful events in police work. *Criminal Justice and Behavior, 27,* 375–400, 2000.

80. Violanti, J., Vena, J., Petralia, S. Mortality of a police cohort: 1950–1990. *American Journal of Industrial Medicine, 33,* 366–373, 1998.

81. Social Security eNews. Long Live Americans. May 2003, http://www.ssa.gov/enews/2003/may/enews2003may.htm (accessed June, 2005).

82. Richmond, R., Kehoe, L., Hailstone, S., Wodak, A., Uebel-Yan, M. Quantitative and qualitative evaluations of brief interventions to change excessive drinking, smoking, and stress in the police department. *Addiction, 94,* 1509–1521, 1999.

83. Richmond, R., Kehoe, L., Hailstone, S., Wodak, A., Uebel-Yan, M. Quantitative and qualitative evaluations of brief interventions to change excessive drinking, smoking, and stress in the police department. *Addiction, 94,* 1509–1521, 1999.

84. Violanti, J., Aron, F. Police stressors: Variations in perception among police personnel. *Journal of Criminal Justice, 23,* 287–294, 1995.

85. Richmond, R., Kehoe, L., Hailstone, S., Wodak, A., Uebel-Yan, M. Quantitative and qualitative evaluations of brief interventions to change excessive drinking, smoking, and stress in the police department. *Addiction, 94,* 1509–1521, 1999.

86. Richmond, R., Kehoe, L., Hailstone, S., Wodak, A., Uebel-Yan, M. Quantitative and qualitative evaluations of brief interventions to change excessive drinking, smoking, and stress in the police department. *Addiction, 94,* 1509–1521, 1999.

87. Richmond, R., Kehoe, L., Hailstone, S., Wodak, A., Uebel-Yan, M. Quantitative and qualitative evaluations of brief interventions to change excessive drinking, smoking, and stress in the police department. *Addiction, 94,* 1509–1521, 1999.

88. Woolston, C. A Dangerous Beat. http://www2.vhihealthe.com/topic/cops, 2000 (accessed July, 2003).

89. Quire, D., Blount, W. A coronary risk profile study of male police officers: Focus on cholesterol. *Journal of Police Science and Administration, 17.* 89–94, 1990.

90. Schaefer, P., Helm, M. The Incidence of Heart Disease in North Carolina Officers. Fall 1996, http://www.jus.state.nc.us/NCJA/w-08-99tip.htm (accessed July, 2005).

91. Schaefer, P., Helm, M. The Incidence of Heart Disease in North Carolina Officers. Fall 1996, http://www.jus.state.nc.us/NCJA/w-08-99tip.htm (accessed July, 2005).

92. Violanti, J., Vena, J., Petralia, S. Mortality of a police cohort: 1950–1990. *American Journal of Industrial Medicine, 33,* 366–373, 1998.

93. Woolston, C. A Dangerous Beat. http://www2.vhihealthe.com/topic/cops, 2000 (accessed July, 2003).

94. Jackson, S., Maslach, C. After-effects of job-related stress: Families as victims. *Journal of Occupational Behaviour, 3,* 63–77, 1982.

95. Jackson, S., Maslach, C. After-effects of job-related stress: Families as victims. *Journal of Occupational Behaviour, 3,* 63–77, 1982.

96. Jackson, S., Maslach, C. After-effects of job-related stress: Families as victims. *Journal of Occupational Behaviour, 3,* 63–77, 1982.

97. Janik, J., Kravitz, H. Linking work and domestic problems with police suicide. *Suicide and Life-Threatening Behaviour, 24,* 267, 1994.

98. Gibbs, N. Officers on the Edge. *Time,* September 1994, 63.

99. Janik, J., Kravitz, H. Linking work and domestic problems with police suicide. *Suicide and Life-Threatening Behavior, 24,* 267, 1994.

100. O'Neill, J., Cushing, M. *The Impact of Shift Work on Police Officers.* Police Executive Research Forum: Washington, DC, 1991.

101. Jackson, S., Maslach, C. After-effects of job-related stress: Families as victims. *Journal of Occupational Behaviour, 3,* 63–77, 1982.

102. Goldfarb, D. An Instrument for Predicting Retirement Satisfaction in Police Officers: A Pilot Study. 1994, http://www.heavybadge.com/retire.htm (accessed July, 2003).

103. Goldfarb, D. An Instrument for Predicting Retirement Satisfaction in Police Officers: A Pilot Study. 1994, http://www.heavybadge.com/retire.htm (accessed July, 2003).

104. Goldfarb, D. An Instrument for Predicting Retirement Satisfaction in Police Officers: A Pilot Study. 1994, http://www.heavybadge.com/retire.htm (accessed July, 2003).

105. Goldfarb, D. An Instrument for Predicting Retirement Satisfaction in Police Officers: A Pilot Study. 1994, http://www.heavybadge.com/retire.htm (accessed July, 2003).

106. Graves, W. Police cynicism: Causes and cures. 1996, http://www.fbi.gov/publications/leb/1996/june964.txt (accessed July, 2003).

107. Graves, W. Police cynicism: Causes and cures. 1996, http://www.fbi.gov/publications/leb/1996/june964.txt (accessed July, 2003).

108. Graves, W. Police cynicism: Causes and cures. 1996, http://www.fbi.gov/publications/leb/1996/june964.txt (accessed July, 2003).

109. Gibbs, N. Officers on the Edge. *Time,* September, 1994, 63.

110. Kim, J., Moen, P. Retirement, transitions, gender, and psychological well-being: A life-course, ecological model. *The Journal of Gerontology, 57B*, 212–222, 2002.
111. Violanti, J., Vena, J., Marshall, J., Petralia, S. A comparative evaluation of police suicide rate validity. *Suicide and Life-Threatening Behavior, 26*, 81–82, 1996.
112. Barker, J. *Danger Duty, and Disillusion: The Worldview of Los Angeles Police Officers*. Waveland Press: Prospect Heights, IL, 1999, 151 pp.
113. Bannish, H., Ruiz, J. The antisocial police personality: A view from the inside. *International Journal of Public Administration, 26*, 844, 2003.
114. Bannish, H., Ruiz, J. The antisocial police personality: A view from the inside. *International Journal of Public Administration, 26*, 845, 2003.
115. Bannish, H., Ruiz, J. The antisocial police personality: A view from the inside. *International Journal of Public Administration, 26*, 845, 2003.
116. Violanti, J., Marshall, J. The police stress process. *Journal of Police Science and Administration, 11*, 389–394, 1983.
117. Graves, W. Police cynicism: Causes and cures. 1996, http://www.fbi.gov/publications/leb/1996/june964.txt (accessed July, 2003).
118. Graves, W. Police cynicism: Causes and cures. 1996, http://www.fbi.gov/publications/leb/1996/june964.txt (accessed July, 2003).
119. Bannish, H., Ruiz, J. The antisocial police personality: A view from the inside. *International Journal of Public Administration, 26*, 845, 2003.
120. Griffin, C., Ruiz, J. The sociopathic police personality: Is it a product of the "rotten apple" or the "rotten barrel?" *Journal of Police and Criminal Psychology, 14*, 28–37, 1999.
121a. Skolnick, J. *Justice Without Trial: Law Enforcement in a Democratic Society*. Macmillian: New York, 1994.
121b. Stoddard, E. The informal code of police deviancy: A group approach to blue collar crime. In *The Police and Society: Touchstone Readings*, Kappeler, V., Ed., Waveland Press: Prospect Heights, IL, 1995, 185–206.
122. Lahue, L., Ruiz, J., Clark, P. Serotonin: What role does it play in the making of a "rotten apple?" *Journal of Police and Criminal Psychology, 14*, 20–28, 1999.
123. American Psychological Association [APA]. *Diagnostic and Statistical Manual of Mental Disorders*. American Psychiatric Association: Washington, DC, 1994.
124. Wilson, F., Poole, A., Trew, K. Psychological distress in police officer following critical incidents. *Irish Journal of Psychology, 18*, 321–340, 1997.
125. Carlier, I., Lamberts, R., Gersons-Berthold, P. Risk factors for posttraumatic stress symptomatology in police officers: A prospective analysis. *Journal of Nervous and Mental Disease, 185*, 498–506, 1997.
126. Patterson, M., Poole, D., Trew, K., Harkin, N. The psychological and physical health of police officers retired recently from the Royal Ulster Constabulary. *Irish Journal of Psychology, 22*, 2, 2001.
127. Liberman, A., Best, S., Metzler, T. Routine occupational stress and psychological distress in police. *Policing: An International Journal of Police Strategies and Management, 25*, 421–439, 2002.
128. Harvey-Lintz, T., Tidwell, R. Effects of the 1992 Los Angeles civil unrest: Post Traumatic Stress Disorder symptomatology among law enforcement officers. *The Social Science Journal, 34*, 171–183, 1997.
129. Robinson H., Sigman M., Wilson J. Duty-related stressors and PTSD symptoms in suburban police officers. Psychological Reports 1997, *81*, 835–845.
130. Henry, V. *Death Work: Police, Trauma, and the Psychology of Survival*. Oxford University Press: New York, 2004, 55 pp.
131. Forcese, D., Cooper, J. Police retirement: Career succession or obsolesce? *Canadian Police College Journal, 9*, 413, 1985.

132. Forcese, D., Cooper, J. Police retirement: Career succession or obsolesce? *Canadian Police College Journal, 9,* 413, 1985.
133. Forcese, D., Cooper, J. Police retirement: Career succession or obsolesce? *Canadian Police College Journal, 9,* 413, 1985.
134. Forcese, D., Cooper, J. Police retirement: Career succession or obsolesce? *Canadian Police College Journal, 9,* 413, 1985.
135. Violanti, J. *Police Retirement: The Impact of Change.* Charles Thomas: Springfield, IL, 1992, 75 pp.
136. Stuccio, D. Email retrieved June 15, 2005. (a former Sgt. with the Syracuse, New York Police Department)
137. Patterson, M., Poole, D., Trew, K., Harkin, N. The psychological and physical health of police officers retired recently from the Royal Ulster Constabulary. *Irish Journal of Psychology, 22,* 22, 2001.
138. Kim, J., Moen, P. Retirement, transitions, gender, and psychological well-being: A life-course, ecological model. *The Journal of Gerontology, 57B,* 212–222, 2002.
139. Kim, J., Moen, P. Retirement, transitions, gender, and psychological well-being: A life-course, ecological model. *The Journal of Gerontology, 57B,* 212–222, 2002.
140. Kim, J., Moen, P. Retirement, transitions, gender, and psychological well-being: A life-course, ecological model. *The Journal of Gerontology, 57B,* 212–222, 2002.
141. Forcese, D., Cooper, J. Police retirement: Career succession or obsolesce? *Canadian Police College Journal, 9,* 419, 1985.
142. Forcese, D., Cooper, J. Police retirement: Career succession or obsolesce? *Canadian Police College Journal, 9,* 422, 1985.
143. Forcese, D., Cooper, J. Police retirement: Career succession or obsolesce? *Canadian Police College Journal, 9,* 420, 1985.
144. Forcese, D., Cooper, J. Police retirement: Career succession or obsolesce? *Canadian Police College Journal, 9,* 422, 1985.
145. Patterson, M., Poole, D., Trew, K., Harkin, N. The psychological and physical health of police officers retired recently from the Royal Ulster Constabulary. *Irish Journal of Psychology, 22,* 21, 2001.
146. Raub, R. *Police Officer Retirement: The Beginning of a Long Life.* Illinois State Police, IL Division of Administration, 1987.
147. Raub, R. *Police Officer Retirement: The Beginning of a Long Life.* Illinois State Police, IL Division of Administration, 1987.
148. Raub, R. *Police Officer Retirement: The Beginning of a Long Life.* Illinois State Police, IL Division of Administration, 1987.
149. Violanti, J. *Police Suicide: Epidemic in Blue.* Charles C. Thomas, Springfield, IL, 1996, 48 pp.
150. Gaska, C. *The Rate of Suicide, Potential For Suicide, and Recommendations for Prevention Among Retired Police Officers.* 1980, Wayne State University, http://wwwlib.umi.com/dissertations/gateway. (accessed June, 2005).
151. Violanti, J. *Police Suicide: Epidemic in Blue.* Charles C. Thomas, Springfield, IL, 1996.
152. Violanti, J. *Police Suicide: Epidemic in Blue.* Charles C. Thomas, Springfield, IL, 1996, 49 pp.
153. Violanti, J. *Police Suicide: Epidemic in Blue.* Charles C. Thomas, Springfield, IL, 1996.
154. Violanti, J. *Police Suicide: Epidemic in Blue.* Charles C. Thomas, Springfield, IL, 1996.
155. Violanti, J. *Police Suicide: Epidemic in Blue.* Charles C. Thomas, Springfield, IL, 1996.
156. Janik, J., Kravitz, H. Linking work and domestic problems with police suicide. *Suicide and Life-Threatening Behavior, 24,* 267–274, 1994.
157. McCafferty, F. Stress and suicide in police officers. *Journal of The American Medical Association, 85,* 238, 1992.

158. Fell, R., Richard, W., Wallace, W. Psychological job stress and the police officer. *Journal of Police Science Administration, 8*, 139–143, 1980.

159. Violanti, J., Vena, J., Marshall, J., Petralia, S. A comparative evaluation of police suicide rate validity. *Suicide and Life-Threatening Behavior, 26*, 79, 1996.

160. Janik, J., Kravitz, H. Linking work and domestic problems with police suicide. *Suicide and Life-Threatening Behavior, 24*, 267–274, 1994.

161. Horvitz, L. Can police solve their epidemic of suicide? *Insight*, November 9–11, 1994.

162. Vena, J., Violanti, J., Marshall, J., Fiedler, R. Mortality of a municipal worker cohort: III. Police officers. *American Journal of Industrial Medicine, 10*, 383–397, 1986.

163. Janik, J., Kravitz, H. Linking work and domestic problems with police suicide. *Suicide and Life-Threatening Behavior, 24*, 267–274, 1994.

164. Janik, J., Kravitz, H. Linking work and domestic problems with police suicide. *Suicide and Life-Threatening Behavior, 24*, 267–274, 1994.

165. Violanti, J. *Police Suicide: Epidemic in Blue*. Charles C. Thomas, Springfield, IL, 1996.

166. Violanti, J. *Police Suicide: Epidemic in Blue*. Charles C. Thomas, Springfield, IL, 1996.

167. Violanti, J. *Police Suicide: Epidemic in Blue*. Charles C. Thomas, Springfield, IL, 1996.

168. Hem, E., Anne, M., Oivind, E. *Suicide in police — A critical review. Suicide and Life-Threatening Behavior, 31*, 224–233, 2001.

169. Hem, E., Anne, M., Oivind, E. *Suicide in police — A critical review. Suicide and Life-Threatening Behavior, 31*, 224–233, 2001.

170. Hem, E., Anne, M., Oivind, E. *Suicide in police — A critical review. Suicide and Life-Threatening Behavior, 31*, 224–233, 2001.

171. Hem, E., Anne, M., Oivind, E. *Suicide in police — A critical review. Suicide and Life-Threatening Behavior, 31*, 224–233, 2001.

172. Hem, E., Anne, M., Oivind, E. *Suicide in police — A critical review. Suicide and Life-Threatening Behavior, 31*, 224–233, 2001.

173. Hem, E., Anne, M., Oivind, E. *Suicide in police — A critical review. Suicide and Life-Threatening Behavior, 31*, 224–233, 2001.

174. Hem, E., Anne, M., Oivind, E. *Suicide in police — A critical review. Suicide and Life-Threatening Behavior, 31*, 224–233, 2001.

175. Gaska, C. *The Rate of Suicide, Potential For Suicide, and Recommendations for Prevention Among Retired Police Officers.* 1980, Wayne State University, http://wwwlib.umi.com/dissertations/gateway. (accessed June, 2005).

176. Hackett, D., Violanti, J. *Police Suicide: Tactics for Prevention*. Charles C. Thomas: Springfield, IL, 2003, 8 pp.

177. Hackett, D., Violanti, J. *Police Suicide: Tactics for Prevention*. Charles C. Thomas: Springfield, IL, 2003.

178. Turvey, B. *Police Officers: Control, Hopelessness and Suicide*. Knowledge Solutions: Los Angeles, CA, 1997.

179. Bradley, S. Retirement: A major life transition. *Journal of Financial Planning, 5*, 34–36, 2001.

180. Bradley, S. Retirement: A major life transition. *Journal of Financial Planning, 5*, 34–36, 2001.

181. Rehm, W. Retirement: A new chapter, not the end of story. *FBI Law Enforcement Bulletin, 65*, 6–12, 1996.

182. Bradley, S. Retirement: A major life transition. *Journal of Financial Planning, 5*, 34–36, 2001.

183. Rehm, W. Retirement: A new chapter, not the end of story. *FBI Law Enforcement Bulletin, 65*, 7, 1996.

184. Rehm, W. Retirement: A new chapter, not the end of story. *FBI Law Enforcement Bulletin, 65*, 6–12, 1996.

185. Rehm, W. Retirement: A new chapter, not the end of story. *FBI Law Enforcement Bulletin, 65,* 6–12, 1996.
186. McCormick, M. Resolving retirement issues for police officers. March 2003, http://www.cji.net/clera/CJI/CenterInfo/lemc/papers/Resolving%20Retirement%20Issues%20for%20Police%20Office rs.pdf (accessed June, 2005).
187. Goldfarb, D. An Instrument for Predicting Retirement Satisfaction in Police Officers: A Pilot Study. 1994, http://www.heavybadge.com/retire.htm (accessed July, 2003).
188. Rehm, W. Retirement: A new chapter, not the end of story. *FBI Law Enforcement Bulletin, 65,* 6–12, 1996.
189. Rehm, W. Retirement: A new chapter, not the end of story. *FBI Law Enforcement Bulletin, 65,* 6–12, 1996.
190. McCormick, M. Resolving retirement issues for police officers. March 2003, http://www.cji.net/clera/CJI/CenterInfo/lemc/papers/Resolving%20Retirement%20Issues%20for%20Police%20Office rs.pdf (accessed June, 2005).
191. Rehm, W. Retirement: A new chapter, not the end of story. *FBI Law Enforcement Bulletin, 65,* 6–12, 1996.
192. Rehm, W. Retirement: A new chapter, not the end of story. *FBI Law Enforcement Bulletin, 65,* 6–12, 1996.
193. Hackett, D., Violanti, J. *Police Suicide: Tactics for Prevention.* Charles C. Thomas: Springfield, IL, 2003, 61 pp.
194. Gettys, V. *Police and Public Safety Psychologists: Survey of Fields of Study, Activities and Training Opportunities.* Paper presented at the annul convention of the American Psychological Association, Boston, MA, August 1990.
195. Chandler, J. *Modern Police Psychology: For Law Enforcement and Human Behavior Professionals.* Charles C. Thomas: Springfield, IL, 1990.
196. Bartol, C. Police psychology: Then, now, and beyond. *Criminal Justice and Behavior, 3,* 70–89, 1996.
197. Scrivner, E. *The Role of Police Psychology in Controlling Excessive Force.* U.S. National Institute of Justice: Washington, DC, 1994, 30 pp.
198. Van Maanen, J. The asshole. In *Policing: A View from the Street,* Manning, P., Van Maanen, J., Eds., Goodyear, Santa Monica, CA, 1978, pp. 221–238.
199. Johnson, K. The missing link in police education: Retirement counseling. *FBI Law Enforcement Bulletin, 47,* 28–31, 1978.
200. Johnson, K. The missing link in police education: Retirement counseling. *FBI Law Enforcement Bulletin, 47,* 28–31, 1978.
201. Patterson, M., Poole, D., Trew, K., Harkin, N. The psychological and physical health of police officers retired recently from the Royal Ulster Constabulary. *Irish Journal of Psychology, 22,* 21, 2001.

22 Police–Community Consultation in Australia: Working with a Conundrum

John Casey and Margaret Mitchell

CONTENTS

INTRODUCTION

Casey and Trofymowych (1999) identified a *community consultation conundrum* in policing that resulted from two apparently opposing dynamics: consultation with relevant communities is recommended as a core strategy to promote accountability, and to strengthen intelligence-driven approaches to the management of crime, while at the same time, evaluations of consultation indicate widespread dissatisfaction on the part of both police and community participants with the processes and the outcomes of consultation. These contradictory dynamics have formed the backdrop for the implementation of consultation processes in Australian policing.

The conundrum has continued to vex policing agencies in Australia and overseas. Important new initiatives in consultation have been launched at the same time as evaluations of consultation in policing and other public service areas continue to identify the weaknesses in the model and the implementation of initiatives (Newburn and Jones 2002, Myhill et al. 2003, Myhill 2006). Given that consultation is based on a series of contested concepts, such as *community, representation,* and *participation* (see Wilson 1992), and that evaluations tend to focus primarily on subjective assessments by stakeholders, it is not surprising to find that there continues to be little consensus about the outcomes. Those working with police consultation in Australia can at least take heart in the fact that it appears to operates with the same contradictions in policing overseas (Skogan et al. 2000, Myhill et al. 2003) and in other public sector agencies in Australia (see National Institute of Governance 2004 for a discussion of consultation in urban planning, and Ipsos 2005 for human services).

This chapter examines the current efforts by the Victoria Police and the New South Wales Police* (NSWP) to consult with local communities. In Victoria, there have been four recent evaluations that address consultation issues, and this chapter summarizes the evidence from those evaluations. The chapter also reports an internal survey conducted by NSWP in 2002 that audited all forms of external consultation involving NSWP police officers.

The focus of the chapter is generally on local-level consultation that covers a small locality or suburb, and on consultation targeted at a specific social or minority groups (immigrant communities, youth, gay, and lesbian, etc.), particularly where this correlates in some way with locality (e.g. because of ethnic enclaves or specific attempts to dialogue with local youth). The chapter does not directly address higher-level consultation and oversight processes such as police boards, policy advisory groups, or departmental-level liaison with specific target groups. In many jurisdictions outside Australia higher-level and local-level consultation processes often coincide, particularly where the police department is relatively small and is contiguous with a specific locality. However, as this chapter is written in the context of policing in Australia where the single police agencies in each state are relatively large organizations, there is a significant institutional distance between local-level and higher-level consultative processes.

DEFINITION: WHAT IS COMMUNITY CONSULTATION?

For the purposes of this chapter, consultation refers to the processes used to promote any outside input into policing policy and strategy involving individuals or organizations (Casey and Trofymowych 1999). This is a deliberately broad definition, given that consultation occupies little more than a conceptual space determined by the confluence of two continuums: (a) the degree of control of activities by police or outsiders and (b) the source of the information used the consultation process. Figure 22.1 represents the conceptual space occupied by consultation and indicates the possible location of various consultative activities.

Consultation abuts at one end to processes such as police public relations, which merely serve to communicate a police agenda, and at the other end to community or citizens' initiatives, such as protest or vigilante activities, which are clearly outside police control. The "balance point" in the definition is that there is significant outside

---

* Victoria and New South Wales are two of the eight states/territories in Australia. Each state/territory is a single jurisdiction with only one police agency (i.e. there are no town, city or county police in Australia). Victoria Police has 11,000 uniformed officers and 3,000 civilian staff; New South Wales has 13,300 officers and 3,500 civilians.

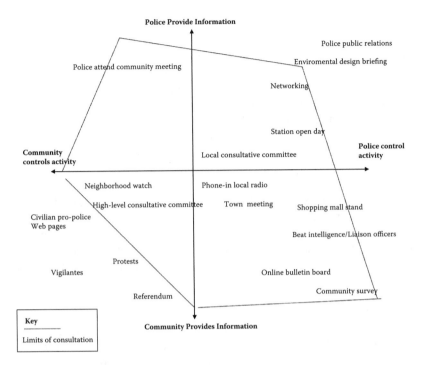

FIGURE 22.1   Consultation. (*Adapted from* Casey, J. & Trofymowych, D. (1999).)

input into policing, whereas at the same time the police organization maintains some level of control over the process involved.

Another common use of the term *consultation* locates it within a "ladder of partic-ipation" (Arnstein 1969), which describes different levels of community involvement in the public policy process and the delivery of public services. In the classic Arnstein ladder, consultation is located half way between manipulation at the bottom of the lad-der and citizen control at the top. Similarly, Davis and Bishop (2001) identify a range of participation processes that include consultation, partnership, and consumer control. In these approaches, consultation is conceptualized as one point along a continuum, somewhere between merely informing and creating full partnership. The choice of the term *consultation* to describe external input into policing may seem to imply a deliberate choice to position activities along a participation continuum, but the reality is somewhat more haphazard. "Poor" consultation process are essentially public rela-tions exercises, whereas "rich" consultation processes in effect become the basis for partnerships and joint governance of on-going projects or programs.

It should also be noted that although *community* consultation implies nongovern-ment input—from individuals, advocacy groups, and community organizations— many of the processes discussed in this chapter, in fact, include the participation of other government departments, such as social services, education, health, and public safety, as well as from other tiers of government, particularly local govern-ments. What is presented as community consultation is often, in effect, interagency and intergovernmental coordination processes, and the distinction between whole-of-government and community consultation approaches may not always be clear.

Moreover, the term *consultation* is often used interchangeably with terms such as *engagement, dialogue, involvement,* and *participation*, although these latter terms— in particular, *participation*—generally imply the broader range of activities included in the participation continuums outlined above (see Myhill 2006).

There is a "patchwork quilt of day-to-day consultations" (Morgan in Hughes 1994, p. 262), that can include the full range of techniques identified in Figure 22.1, as well as a range of newly emerging policy participation processes such as citizens' juries, televoting, and deliberative conferences, which are just starting to be used by police (Ward 1995, Myhill et al. 2003). However, almost all discourses on consultation quickly focus on the single technique of consultative committees. Community consultative committees—variously called *customer councils, local safety committees,* etc.—are by far the most common form of consultative structures (Ward 1995, Myhill et al. 2003), and debates about their efficacy quickly dominate any discussions about consultation.

Police community consultation committees vary greatly in their functioning between jurisdictions and between localities within the same jurisdiction. In addition to the issues of control and information flow that determine the definitions outlined above, there are a number of key parameters that determine differences between committees:

- *Coverage.* Committees may cover local government areas, neighborhoods, or even a single shopping street or business precinct, or they may be focused on a specific target group such as youth or ethnic minorities.
- *Ownership/control.* The "ownership" of the committee (in terms of who initiates, chairs, hosts, provides administrative support, etc.) may reside with the police or with other agencies. In the Australian context, local governments are taking an increasing role in crime prevention, and they often initiate local liaison processes that become the primary means of consultation between police and the wider community.
- *Appointment/selection of members.* Members of the committee may be appointed by controlling authorities or selected through a range of processes that may include elections.
- *Open versus closed participation.* Attendance, voice, and vote at the meetings may be restricted to appointed/selected members or may be open to the public.
- *Relationship to other processes.* The committee may be a stand-alone consultation committee or may be connected to related activities such as Neighborhood Watch and other crime prevention programs.
- *Focus of activities.* The committees may have different primary focuses, such as information exchange, development of local safety strategies, or the management of public safety and crime prevention programs.

Whichever format the committee takes, it must demonstrate its legitimacy as a valid consultation process through its capacity to measure the pulse of public safety and crime concerns in that community. In order to achieve this, committees often employ a range of other consultation processes (surveys, town meetings) to gather additional input into their deliberations, and they often sponsor or manage projects that engage the police and community in joint problem solving (see for example, Johnston et al. 2002).

CONSULTATION IN POLICING

The U.K. Scarman Report (Scarman 1981) is generally seen as the impetus for the wider use of community policing strategies in Britain and Australia. Lord Scarman investigated three days of rioting in the London neighborhood of Brixton in 1981, and while he acknowledged that the root cause of the rioting was poverty and inner city deprivation, he attributed a large part of the blame on the deteriorated state of relations between the police and the primarily black-Caribbean Brixton community. This was both a result of on-going reactive policing tactics and also a response to a specific "accelerator event," Operation Swamp, in which police had targeted Brixton in a way that was seen as harassing young Carribeans.

In the Scarman Report, the recommendations about policing were only one section of a slew of recommendations that included policy reform in the areas of housing, education, and employment. Moreover, consultation was only one part of the police-related recommendations that sought to address a range of issues related to working with minority groups (recruitment, training, and addressing prejudice) and the handling of public disorder. The recommendations regarding consultation called for the establishment of statutory liaison committees and exhorted the police and the community to work positively to establish relations of mutual trust and respect. As a result of the report, consultation became enshrined in U.K. legislation. The U.K. Police and Criminal Evidence Act 1984 created the legal responsibility for the police to consult, and this was confirmed more than a decade later through the 1998 Crime and Disorder Act, which placed an obligation on local authorities and the police, in partnership with other agencies, to audit and consult.

In the United States, the 1980s saw the more widespread acceptance of community policing philosophies that emphasized the need for greater dialogue with the community. However, given the fragmented nature of policing in the United States, including the existence of thousands of police departments serving small local areas, the structure of consultation processes differed considerably between police departments. Many larger police departments have district advisory committee and "beat meetings" (Skogan et al. 2000), which are the equivalent of the consultation structures created as a result of the Scarman Report in Britain.

Consultation is not in itself a process or practice separate from other more global policing developments such as *community policing, policing by consent,* and the notion of a police *service* (as opposed to *force),* which, by definition, imply dialogue with and legitimation by the communities and citizens policed (Findlay 2004). Moreover, consultation is intimately related to other contemporary labels now commonly associated with policing such as *problem-solving, proactive, cooperative, partnership, participation, reassurance,* and *local priority,* and it is the basis of a range of strategies considered to be *social* and *preventive* responses to crime and disorder, which are part of the *multilateralization* of policing (Bayley and Shearing 2001).

There is also widespread awareness of an operational necessity to maintain an open dialogue with the communities served. Despite popular media representation of intrepid sleuths deciphering mystifying clues, crime is mostly solved by information gathered in the community from cooperative citizens and informants (Findlay 2004, Dixon 2005), and consultation processes can foster the trust needed to ensure that citizens do cooperate. The current move to strengthen intelligence-driven policing seeks to combine the "objective" data generated by centralized crime mapping with the community intelligence provided by local input, and the possible information flow from consultation processes can be a key to achieving this input (Maguire and John 2006). However, there are real questions about how community consultation can be reconciled with intelligence gathering. Lyons (2002) argues that "until we learn to police in ways that build trusting relationships with those communities where criminals or terrorists can more easily live insulated from observation, no amount of additional funding or legal authority will increase the capacity of our police to gather the crime and terror-related information we desperately need" (p. 530). Working closely with communities, while at the same time observing members of these communities as potential objects of suspicion, arguably produces dissonance in frontline police.

The rise of police consultation has coincided with broader shifts in the relations between state and nonstate institutions. The crisis of faith confronting both representative democracy and Weberian notions of efficiency in the public service have lead to a "legitimation gap," which Western democracies have sought to bridge through new public management and governance processes (Davis and Weller 2001). An integral part of these new processes is the increased emphasis on the role of community, civil society, and citizens in both policy development and service delivery, which have resulted in profound changes in the way in which all public sector organizations operate. The notion of public agencies directly providing services has given way to approaches that seek greater stakeholder involvement in policy processes, more transparent accountability of public services, and stronger public–private partnerships in service delivery. Internally within government, there is also an increased emphasis on collaboration between agencies and whole-of-government approaches (Bayley and Shearing 2001, Fleming and Rhodes 2004).

Consultation has not been without its critics. As Casey and Trofymowych (1999) noted, criticisms of consultation can be classified as ideological, structural, or operational. Ideological critiques reject what they see as the tokenism of consultation, with progressives claiming that it mainly serves to stifle dissent, whereas conservatives see it as pandering to special interests and diverting police from core policing tasks. Structural criticisms focus on the difficulties of reaching the most marginalized sectors of society, on the uneven power relationships between police and those being consulted, and on internal police procedures, which do not necessarily reward consultation efforts. Operational criticism is focused on performance indicators and the difficulties of documenting the direct impact of consultation.

Do police themselves support consultation? Yates et al. (1997) in a study on the level of support for various community policing strategies, including consultation, among officers in England and the United States see "significant support" for a range of measures. However, their interpretation of the findings appear to be a case of seeing the glass as half full, given that the significant support they identify is expressed in the following terms: "Well in excess of one third to one half of police officers popularly support the community policing philosophy" (Yates et al. 1997, p. 113). Similarly, Gennaro et al. (2005) found that police middle managers were "ambivalent" about community policing; they adopted the philosophy but appeared unwilling to the make organization changes necessary to support it.

CONSULTATION IN AUSTRALIAN POLICING

Police in Australia have tended to operate at some distance from the communities they serve and have lacked a tradition of local community access to police decisions (Bayley 1986). However, Australian police agencies could not remain at the margin of the international changes in both policing and public management, and so a range of community policing initiatives were begun in the mid-1980s. In 1986, Bayley noted that, although the then NSW Police Commissioner John Avery had called for the establishment of community consultative councils in his 1981 book *Police, Force or Service?* (published three years before he became commissioner) and a 1985 Commission of Inquiry into Victoria police had recommended the establishment of local liaison committees, until then "nothing along those lines [had] been created anywhere in Australia" (Bayley 1986, p. 22).

However, from the late 1980s, all Australian jurisdictions have developed consultation structures, although there have not been any moves to create U.K.-style legislative provisions. Current Australian consultative activities are based solely on policies and guidelines internal to policing. The Australasian Police Ministers' Council, the coordinating body of those with political responsibility for policing in each Australian state and New Zealand has declared that a key strategy is to "consult and collaborate on policy development and service delivery" (Australasian Police Ministers' Council 2005: Strategy 2.2.2).

VICTORIA*

Victoria is the Australian police jurisdiction that has made consultation most central to its operating philosophy. In 1998 Victoria police embarked on a major strategic realignment known as Local Priority Policing. The goal of Local Priority Policing was to ensure that the local community became an active participant in shaping police service priorities. As stated by the then Chief Commissioner, the first two of seven key characteristics of Local Priority Policing were:

- The community significantly influences which services are provided.
- Local service issues are the prime focus (Victoria Police 1999)

Local Priority Policing was implemented in three phases: Phase 1 was a Statewide Management Model, Phase 2 was a Service Delivery Model, and Phase 3 was a Community Consultation Model. Through the Statewide Management and the Service Delivery Models, Victoria police aligned the district-level operational boundaries to coincide with local government boundaries and gave local managers more

---

* The following section on Victoria Police is based on cited evaluations and a series of confidential interviews with key stakeholders.

control over specialist services. Through the Community Consultation Model, structures were established to promote community input (Victoria Police 2004).

As part of the Community Consultation Model, each District Inspector was responsible for the establishment of a Local Safety Committee (LSC) as the key local-level component of the Local Priority Policing strategy. The LSCs were established in 2000 as a means of identifying local crime and public safety issues, as a conduit for input by local agencies into policing initiatives, and as a forum for police to account for local strategies and practices. The LSCs were implemented against the background of the prior existence of the Police Community Involvement Program, first established in 1981; Neighborhood Watch, established in 1983; and of Police Community Consultation Committees (PCCC), a network of community consultation structures first launched in 1991 as the primary consultation mechanism under previous Victoria government crime prevention initiatives such as the Safer Cities and Shires program. There was also a wide array of previously established community safety committees and other community-based crime prevention programs that had been instituted by other public organizations such as local governments, social service agencies, and nongovernmental organizations.

The membership of LSCs comprises a range of appointed representatives from local government, from local offices of statewide agencies and nongovernment organizations, and some community representatives. The LSCs were not intended as forums for grassroots community representation; instead, they are seen more as local government area level "management committees" for local crime prevention and community safety activities (Victoria Police 2004: 17). LSCs generally seek to involve senior staff from participating agencies that focus on strategic issues and high level interagency collaborations. A core task of the LSCs was the development of a community safety plan. The aims of the LSC were:

- Identify and satisfy validated local community needs and expectations.
- Involve the public in shaping policing services and action plans.
- Develop effective partnerships with the community to prevent crime and improve community safety.
- Improve community perception of crime and public safety.
- Increase public confidence in the accountability professionalism and integrity of police;
- Provide information on police decision making.

District Inspectors were given flexibility to implement LSCs according to local conditions and local experiences with previous consultation. As a result, in some districts pre-existing consultation structures took on LSC responsibilities, and a range of different linkages were created between the new LSCs and existing PCCCs and Neighborhood Watch. Even though LSCs were to be the key component of the Community Consultation Model, District Inspectors were required to institute other mechanisms for consultation and for strengthening their knowledge of the local community, including the development of community profiles that documented the demographics and the security concerns of their districts.

TABLE 22.1
Research Projects on Consultation

Research Project (Bibliographic Reference)	Researchers	Focus and Aim
Evaluation of Community Consultation Model of Local Priority Policing (Victoria Police 2004).	Victoria police. Internal evaluation by Corporate Management Review Division	Evaluated the Community Consultation component of Local Priority Policing; focused on the LSCs and directly related consultation and fact-finding activities.
Evaluation of Police Community Consultation Committees (PCCCs) (Martin Bonato and Associates 2003).	Crime Prevention Victoria (a division of the State Department of Justice) contract to private consultants Martin Bonato and Associates	PCCCs and related activities
Evaluation of community governance in crime prevention and community safety (Armstrong and Rutter 2002; Armstrong, Francis and Totikidis 2004, Totikidis, Armstrong and Francis 2005).	Crime Prevention Victoria and Victoria University, joint researchers. Funded by the Australian Research Council.	On-going evaluation that targeted a range of governance processes. Some of the research has ended up focusing on LSCs, although the 'ownership' of the four committee that are the subject of the 2005 paper are attributed more to local government than to Victoria Police.
Evaluation of local government Community Safety Officers (CSOs) (Sutton, Dussuyer and Cherney 2003)	Crime Prevention Victoria and Melbourne University, joint researchers, Funded by the Australian Research Council.	Did not directly deal with the work of the Victoria police community consultation structures, but a 2003 paper from the project provided some assessment of these structures

Although Victoria police now appear to downplay the "brand" aspect of Local Priority Policing (it tends to appear in lower case in current Victoria Police documents, except when referring to the 1998 initiative), it is still very much a core philosophy and its structures are still in place. The LSCs continue to be one of the current Chief Commissioner's flagship initiatives under a strategic plan known as "The Way Ahead" (Victoria Police 2003).

In recent years, there have been four separate research projects which have evaluated the LSCs, the PCCCs, and the community governance of community safety and crime prevention programs. All four were based on survey techniques and focused on assessments of the outcomes by current participants in the processes. Table 22.1 provides the details of the research projects.

The combined findings of the four evaluations give a comprehensive picture of the operation of community consultation in Victoria. The evaluations of LSCs and

PCCCs are considered first, given the overlap between these two police-initiated structures, and subsequently the evaluations of community governance structures are used to contrast the "internal" structures.

The LSC and PCCC Evaluations

Both evaluations highlighted that there is considerable variation in how LSCs and PCCCs operate and how they interact with other consultation mechanisms. As a result of these variations, LSCs and PCCCs were able to respond to local conditions and generally garner positive reviews. Those interviewed for the PCCC evaluation noted that when they were introduced by Victoria police in 1991, they were an important and ground breaking initiative at the forefront of a shift to a community policing philosophy. The evaluation concluded that some PCCCs have strong, committed, active, and long-term memberships that have been very productive with limited resources. The LSCs, established almost a decade after the first PCCCs, were seen as being able to fulfill a commitment to extend the existing community consultation by building on the past experiences.

The LSC evaluation concluded that they have helped drive the wider community consultation initiatives and promote a wide range of community safety and crime prevention programs, as well as assisting in attracting funding. The two reports found that both PCCCs and LSCs had significantly enhanced relationships with other government departments, local government, and organizations within the community The LSC evaluation found that there is majority support within police ranks for the LSC initiative as a key component of community consultation. A conflation of a number of survey questions in the report indicates that some 50 to 55 percent of officers considered LSCs to be very valuable or generally valuable; some 20 to 30 percent considered the value limited by quality; 15 percent consider them of little value; and no one considered them to be of no value.

But both reports also indicate that, despite the successes, there is also widespread concern about the functioning of consultation. The signature phrase in relation to the PCCCs was:

> The supporters of PCCCs were able to identify many useful projects and initiatives but most PCCCs appear to have been limited by lack of sustained interest and funds or inability to increase the reach of the committee to incorporate the views of local communities with common interests or concerns. In an attempt to identify outputs and outcomes of PCCC the reviewer found a great deal of scepticism and inability to articulate significant outcomes, even from some PCCCs regarded as model performers by their peers. [Martin Bonato and Associates 2003: 9]

The conclusion was that most PCCCs have not achieved sustained, effective consultation and information exchange with broad representation from local citizens. Most PCCCs had limited reach into the community due to lack of time and resources, and the skills and knowledge on how to approach the wider community were sometimes lacking in committees. Some senior police do not believe PCCCs have a significant impact on their work; whereas some acknowledge the value of the interactions on committees and relationships built, the impacts are generally not considered substantial in terms of their own operational targets.

The subsequent introduction of LSCs somewhat complicated the situation for PCCCs. The evaluation of PCCCs found that their role was "severely challenged" with the implementation of LSCs, as many of the stated aims and objectives of the two committees remain the same or similar, despite the theoretical division between the more grassroots focus of PCCCs and the focus of the LSCs on creating inter-agency forums of managers. In theory LSCs are supported at the local level by a network of PCCCs and Neighborhood Watch Groups (Victoria Police Annual Report 2001/2002), but it appears that in practice the connection is at best loose, and there is no formal requirement for PCCCs to report to LSCs. According to the PCCC evaluation, "there is a palpable divide between many LSCs and PCCCs leading to confusion and at times animosity and rivalry" (Martin Bonato and Associates 2003, p v). Some PCCCs have been disbanded or absorbed into LSCs or other local structures and those that remain are not necessarily complying with requirements or expectations originally laid down for PCCCs. In some instances, however, the continued existence of PCCCs allow the replication of the LSC structure at a lower level so supervisory and frontline staff also have the opportunity to participate in consultation and coordination structures.

There appeared to be a significant division of opinions about the relationship between the PCCCs and LSCs, with many of those surveyed seeing a complementary role but also many considering that the PCCCs are now redundant and should be disbanded. There was consensus that PCCCs need to be realigned within the newer and broader community safety and crime prevention infrastructure, particularly with Local Priority Policing as it now operates within the Victoria police and within a whole-of-government approach to community involvement in service planning and delivery. At the time of the evaluations the PCCCs and the LSCs were operating through different units within the Victoria Police Department and there was only limited coordination between the two structures.

While LSCs were more an integral part of Local Priority Policing, they were still hampered by structural difficulties in the model, and there were few mechanisms to link consultation with other operational process. The LSC evaluation found that the Victoria Police Department's internal cultures, and current management processes such as COMPSTAT, continued to tie reward and recognition more to reactive crime-fighting approaches than to preventive approaches and to the pursuing cross-agency synergies. There continued to be operational staff, particularly district inspectors, who still had not embraced community consultation and/or did not have the skills or commitment to promote successful processes. Moreover, other government agencies weren't always prepared to participate in the LSC process, sometimes because their boundaries were not aligned, requiring a single agency representative to sit on multiple committees or because they feel their expertise was not used.

Both the LSC and PCC evaluations identified key elements for successful consultation. For the LSCs, the most successful outcomes were observed in long-established forums with mainly local government leadership, but there were also successful police-driven LSCs. Successful consultation appeared to emerge in response to pressing urban issues, such a drug problems or youth violence, and where such triggers did not exist there appeared to be less incentive to maintain the structures. Success of community consultation was also dependent on the commitment and capacities of key individuals, usually district inspectors, and terms like *enthusiasm, leadership, skill,* and *level of expertise* were used to identify success factors for individual LSCs. The report drew a distinction between "reporting" and "action" LSCs, with committees that helped create on-going crime-prevention activities being seen as the ones that were more successful. For action-oriented LSCs, their capacity to obtain funding for initiatives was seen as the key to success. Similarly, the features of successful PCCCs included: strong leadership through a local "champion"; a clear direction and a sense of purpose; representative membership and continuing attendance; effective chairing of meetings; the availability of resources to support the committees work; and a strong sense of having achieved results.

Both reports made recommendations for strengthening the work of the LSCs and PCCCs, which include the following*:

1. The importance of local flexibility. The LSC evaluation recommended that committees not necessarily be required to use the LSC name, and the PCCC evaluation recommended that they be an optional form of consultation and that any decision to create/continue or discontinue a PCCC should be made with reference to the views and needs of the relevant local community. As part of this flexibility, both reports emphasized the need for all consultation processes to define their purpose, principles, goals, objectives, and performance measures, as well as the rights and responsibilities of members.

2. The need for central coordination and sufficient resources. Both reports called for greater coordination between LSCs, PCCCs, and other consultation processes, and the PCCC evaluation called for greater formalization of the relationship between LSCs and PCCCs.

3. The need for dissemination of information about consultative process and good practices. Both reports called for a range of measures, including regular state-wide forums of staff involved in consultation, the improvement of training materials, and greater presence on the internet and other means of communication by Victoria police.

4. The need for integrated performance reporting. Both reports stressed that consultative processes should be better integrated into performance management at all levels. There was particular emphasis on the need to incorporate the outputs and outcomes of consultation into performance processes such as COMPSTAT.

5. The need for skills training. The reports noted that consultative committee members, both police and external, need ongoing training and development in the role, function, focus, and process of committees, and on establishing, maintaining and achieving results from partnerships.

6. The need for varied consultation processes. The reports recommended the use of processes such as surveys, focus groups, inviting people to attend meetings on a short-term basis, or joining existing committees with projects initiated by other groups.

---

* At the time of writing of this chapter, Victoria Police has put into place a number of processes to implement these recommendations.

Evaluation of the Community Governance of Crime Prevention

Three preliminary reports of the joint Crime Prevention Victoria–Victoria University research project on the governance of crime prevention have been published (Armstrong and Rutter 2002; Armstrong, Francis and Totikidis 2004, Totikidis, Armstrong and Francis 2005). The 2004 and 2005 papers focused on the work of LSCs, and whereas they noted that LSCs were launched by the police minister and chief commissioner in 2000, almost no other mention or analysis is made of the role of Victoria police or of the Local Priority Policing approach. From data in the tables and the responses to survey questions about chairing, funding and reporting of the committees, it appears that the "ownership" of the LSCs is attributed more to local councils than to Victoria police. This attribution of ownership to local councils is not inconsistent with the flexibility accorded to by the Victoria police to district inspectors, which allowed them to build on existing local structures when implementing LSCs under Local Priority Policing, but it is also a reflection of an apparent lack of clarity by the researchers about the drivers of the LSCs and perhaps of "turf wars" over ownership.

The 2004 report on the determinants and inhibiters of community governance focused on LSCs and indicated that:

> The conclusions are that the LSCs are very effective in generating networks of people. They had input into local government safety plans, and were able to bring diverse resources together to successfully tackle local issues. Limitations to their success were lack of leadership, infrequent meetings, lack of objectives and lack of seniority in the members of participating partners ... and data sharing was limited [Armstrong, Francis and Totikidis 2004].

The results of the 2005 report are also generally positive. Almost eighty-three percent of LSC members surveyed agree with the statement that LSCs facilitates partnerships between agencies, whereas 55 percent had a strong sense of achievement from their participation and 54 percent believed that the LSC was very successful in preventing crime.

Evaluation of Local Government Crime Prevention Officers

The Crime Prevention Victoria–Melbourne University research project did not directly address the work of Victoria police consultative structures, but in assessing the work of the local government based Community Safety Officers (CSOs), it provided some insight to the work of these structures (Sutton, Dussuyer and Cherney 2003). As is to be expected, given the nature of the work of CSOs, the issue of consultation and interagency collaboration by Victoria police surfaced a number of times in the report. LSCs were cited both as the community safety network group that CSOs were most involved with (sixty-three percent of respondents who were members of groups) and the most effective community safety and crime prevention partnerships (34 percent of respondents rate the LSCs as very effective and 53 percent rate them as somewhat effective); Victoria police Inspectors and Victoria Police Crime Prevention Officers were cited as the first and third, respectively, most important contacts in the work of CSOs; and Victoria police were seen as the most active agency in crime prevention. LSCs were seen as generally being effective and working well, but a lack of resources and the lack of relevant experience of members were seen as issues. The effectiveness of partnerships for community safety and crime prevention (in which LSCs which were seen as most effective) were viewed in terms of their capacity for creating change and utilizing scare resources, their adoption of a strategic approach, their ability to add to the core knowledge base of the participants, achieve outcomes, and commitment from members.

NEW SOUTH WALES

Consultation with its communities is a key component of the strategic direction of the New South Wales police (NSWP). This commitment was reaffirmed in the recommendations of the Royal Commission of Inquiry into New South Wales Police (Wood 1997), which emphasized the importance of the organization's not being isolated from the community it serves. The Royal Commission recommended that "each patrol commander ... put into effect such form of Community Consultative groups or strategies for community feedback as best meet its needs," and "that the effective establishment and use of community consultation be regarded as an important aspect in the ongoing assessment of the performance of patrol and regional commanders" (Wood 1997, p. 368).

In 2002, Mitchell and Urquhart conducted an audit of all means by which NSWP was represented externally on committees, working parties and other consultation structures (Mitchell and Urquhart, 2002)*. The project was initiated after an initial scoping of the roles and responsibilities of senior staff to act as public spokespersons found that there was no complete listing of the consultation structures on which NSWP officers serve. Requests for information were sent from the commissioner to officers of superintendent rank and above, and to executive directors seeking information about the representation by officers on the bodies in which NSWP participated. These senior officers then delegated the request to officers within their command who participated in these structures. The request asked for the name of the consultation structure, the NSWP officer who attended, who provides administrative support (i.e., who was the holder of the agendas, minutes, and outcomes of the meetings), what was its general purpose, and any other comments. The request was deliberately kept simple in order to maximize the responses.

The results indicated that there were over 2,500 separate consultation and meeting structures in which primarily sworn officers, and some civilian staff, regularly participated. Given that the survey documented all structures, it included a range of statutory or required committees that dealt with whole-of-government and inter-agency matters, and these consultation structures were primarily attended by senior officers. There were also working parties and groups set up to deal, usually in the short term, with a particular emergent or critical crime or legislation issue the deliberations about which required external input and/or cooperation. In addition there are numerous specific-focus committees dealing with such issues as local youth,

---

* These data, and the analysis and discussion of these data, have been previously presented at two conferences (Mitchell 2003, Casey and Mitchell 2003).

domestic violence, aboriginal matters, drug issues or school liaison. Each geographical area also appeared to have its own structures dealing with the broad range of community crime and safety matters, including small business and representatives from chambers of commerce. It was evident from the results of the survey that NSWP was fulfilling its commitment to consult with the community and that, as a result, an enormous amount of police time was spent on these necessary consultative groups. Each meeting of such groups requires research, review, and preparation and often yielded recommendations and outcomes that needed to be acted upon. Included also were meetings on programs of long standing such as Neighborhood Watch, most of which were attended by one or more police representatives and could take place as frequently as bimonthly.

Apart from obtaining an overview of the large number of committees and consultative structures, other insights into the processes were derived. It was found that the police representative may not always be the same individual. This appeared to be the direct consequence of the fact of shift work, pressure of more urgent police work, the frequent changes in responsibility and location that characterizes much of police work, illness, vacations, and other reasons why a delegate or new representative would be sent. The occasions when this did not occur were when community consultation was part of the officer's job, such as meeting with the Aboriginal Community Liaison Officers, Youth Liaison Officers, and Crime Prevention Officers. Even here there was movement in jobs with new staff being appointed to these posts.

Often, other than at high-level peak meetings attended by senior government officials and senior police commanders where resolutions and agreements could be reached and committed to, police representatives attending the meetings were often not, nor could they be, those with the necessary decision-making authority. It was also the case that there was some fluidity in the participants from the community, this also leading to some problems of discontinuity.

This review of NSWP community consultation, in addition, demonstrated a degree of duplication of effort. Importantly, it was also apparent that there was little coordination, across the police organization or among interested parties within the organization, of the rich information emerging from these structures. To achieve that outcome would be a mammoth task in such a large organization. There was no overarching system to centrally manage issues and solutions as they emerged, to incorporate information about interagency projects and programs, to share good practice from other law enforcement agencies, or to provide consistent guidance on corporate issues.

Some of characteristics of community consultation suggested that rationalization of the number of community consultation structures might be advisable. However, it was found that these structures were considered important to the participants and, in general, both community and police members felt that to amalgamate one process with another, or to disband it, would result in a loss of "voice" by the community. It is evident that consultation with the community and the community's engagement with the police are both seen as an important component of civic engagement.

The information gathered through this survey offered a concrete opportunity to maximize the benefits of the consultative structures. Another common theme of the responses was that technological solutions, i.e., computerized solutions, were sought to address the problems of inconsistent attendance by police representatives, and lack of coordination of the issues and outcomes of the various consultative structures. As a first step, the main themes of the consultations were documented, which included such issues as transport, traffic, housing, rural crime matters, police input into community planning through the Safer by Design program, and relationships with minority groups such as gay and lesbian community issues or particular ethnic groups. By far the greatest number of committees and consultation exercises concerned mental health issues and matters concerning youth.

These themes were then designated as Key Policing Issues and were used as a basis to augment the already-existing NSWP Corporate Spokesperson Program. The Corporate Spokesperson Program had been in place with NSW police as a corporate initiative to ensure that a senior officer was dedicated to a particular area of policing and could therefore support and lead change and new programs, and also speak to the media on topics in that area. Through analysis of the community consultation themes, a strategic plan of portfolios, each with a spokesperson selected according to that person's areas of interest, their expertise, and their corporate responsibilities was developed. The Corporate Spokesperson Program then had a comfortable strategic fit with the range of community consultation structures and facilitated information sharing. Internal corporate Web pages, called Knowledge Maps, were also enhanced and developed under the name of the theme and the relevant corporate spokesperson. These "maps" contained policy and practice information, and as much information as was available about relevant structures and standing committees for community consultation. Through this online mechanism, those attending consultation meetings were able to access a consistent and current resource that reflected corporate knowledge and understanding of an issue. In addition, representatives could feed back discussions from consultation to influence future corporate directions. The drawback of course, is the considerable amount of effort in research and time—as is the case with any Web site—to ensure currency. Nevertheless, its aim was to solve some of the issues that had emerged from the survey and to overcome potential frustration that may have been felt about whether time spent in consultation was productive. Although there was a clear and energetic commitment to consultation by managers and commanders, each clearly sought more efficient and effective ways to achieve its purposes.

The review also raised many questions. Consultation is "required" and considered essential so that the community may have input into operational matters, but are face-to-face committee meetings the best way to achieve that goal? In other words can "local policing solutions for local crime problems" actually be achieved through a committee? Efforts need to continue not only to find more efficient and effective ways to consult but also to address some ideological issues to ensure that consultation is not seen as a "soft" option that takes time from real policing. Any review of consultation also inevitably raises the question discussed earlier in this chapter about who is being consulted. Of what community or community interests are the participants "representative" and is this meeting what those requiring that police consult with their communities (such as Justice Wood in the Royal Commission recommendations) intended?

CONCLUSIONS

In 1999, Sarre and Tomaino observed that:

> What is conceptualized in theory, however, many not translate well into practice. Asking police to become problem-solvers and expecting them to be constantly engaged in widespread community consultation involves a fundamental challenge to police leadership and culture. Given the current culture, reward structure and community expectations, translating rhetoric into reality has proved to be a formidable task. [p. 103]

The case studies of Victoria and NSW presented in this chapter suggest that perhaps Australian policing has started to surmount the "formidable task." Considerable challenges remain, but there also seems to be a majority opinion that police agencies have made significant strides in the move to incorporate community consultation as an institutional commitment. Some twenty-five years after the Scarman Report inaugurated consultation as a major policing strategy in Britain and Australia, the conclusion is that it has become a key element in strengthening the relationship between police and the wider civil society. Even though Casey and Trofymowych (1999) suggested that consultation may be under threat as a tactic as politicians and communities demanded more measurable outcomes, it appears to have become even more consolidated as a core policing strategy over the last five years.

As consultation is evaluated in a wide range of government services, we find that another conclusion is that policing is certainly not doing any worse than many other agencies. A recent review of the consultation by the ACT Planning Department concluded that it was "characterized by strengths worth retaining and building on ... but also by low levels of trust and confidence among stakeholders ... [and it was] not always conducted in a transparent and accountable way ... and was subject to problems in communications and the effective dissemination of information" [National Institute of Governance 2004]. The Victorian Department of Human Services in an evaluation of its consultation process concluded that 63 percent of nongovernmental agencies they dealt with were very satisfied with the processes, 20 percent were neutral, and 18 percent were dissatisfied (Ipsos 2005). These figures are similar to the Victoria police figures quoted above.

In 1990, at an Australian Institute of Criminology on community policing, the acting director of the Institute posed the question of how we get police organizations to take such approaches seriously (Wilson 1992). At the same conference Moir (1992) asked whether it was possible for police to use consultation processes to work with communities to become coproducers of public order, and Sarre (1992) asked why evaluation of community policing does not occur. Fifteen years later, those questions perhaps have not yet been fully answered, but there are crucial differences that need to be considered. In 2005, community policing philosophies and the consultation processes that underpin them are entrenched as core policing strategies. In fifteen years we have moved from wondering if community policing and consultation will be implemented, to a situation where we are now looking back at their implementation and evaluating their continued development.

We can conclude that, despite possible shortcomings as both a local priority setting mechanism and a means of intelligence-gathering, consultation continues to garner success as a process that creates dialogue and interchange on local crime and disorder issues and serves to assist polices in meeting local accountability and oversight imperatives. Although the link to crime reduction of these outcomes may be hard to measure, these are an important value in themselves. Fleming (2005) questions the current wisdom that Neighborhood Watch programs are of little practical use by reframing the criteria for their assessment of in terms of relationship building, community participation, and reassurance, and these criteria can also be applied to consultation programs in general.

It is unlikely that police agencies will abandon consultation in the near future, as it continues to form an integral part of a wider movement of citizen participation and public sector reform. It establishes legitimacy with key stakeholder communities such as business and community elites, local activists, and specific ethnic and racial communities, and it continues to be an integral part of the new public management and governance frameworks that are being applied to policing. Public police no longer have a monopoly on policing (Bayley and Shearing 2001), and they now function within a framework of continual democratic dialogue with the communities they serve (Fleming and Rhodes 2004, Myhill 2006). Consultation processes continue to be essential for mobilizing support for the police among the "middle and respectable working classes" (Squires 1998) and for responding to the consumerist rhetoric that dictates perceptions of effectiveness and demands an ethos of service and responsiveness to clients.

Despite its flaws, consultation continues to reinforce the current agenda of *serving the community* and provides the basis for intelligence-driven and problem-solving approaches to policing. Consultation is a lynch pin of both operational effectiveness and public accountability, and there continues to be widespread support for consultation, which accepts the contradictions found by researchers and commentators. Considering the great effort that is expended on consultation, police agencies should be continually exploring creative and flexible approaches, including using the many technical solutions now available, to ensure that consultation goals are being met.

BIBLIOGRAPHY

Armstrong, A. & Rutter, A. (2002). *Evaluating the success of a crime prevention strategy targeting community capacity and participation.* Paper presented to Australasian Evaluation Society International Conference, Wollongong Australia, October–November 2002. Retrieved August 5, 2006 from http://www.evaluationcanada.ca/distribution/20021030_armstrong_anona_rutter_anthea.pdf.

Armstrong, A., Francis, R., & Totikidis, V. (2004). *Managing Community Governance: Determinants and inhibiters.* Paper presented to 18th ANZAM Conference, Dunedin, December 2004.

Arnstein, S.R.(1969). A ladder of citizen participation. *Journal of the American Institute of Planners*, 35(4), 216–224.

Australasian Police Ministers' Council (2005). *Directions in Australasian Policing 2005–2008.* Australasian Police Ministers' Council. Retrieved July 18, 2006 from http://www.acpr.gov.au/pdf/Directions05-08.pdf.

Bayley, D. & Shearing, C. (2001). *The New Structure of Policing: Description, Conceptualisation, and Research Agenda.* Washington, D.C.: National Institute of Justice. Retrieved August 5, 2006 from http://www.ncjrs.gov/pdffiles1/nij/187083.pdf.

Bayley, D.H. (1986). *Community Policing In Australia: An Appraisal.* Australasian Centre for Policing Research, Report Series No. 35. Retrieved August 11, 2005 from http://acpr.gov.au/pdf/ACPR35.pdf.

Casey, J. & Trofymowych, D. (1999). *Twenty years of community consultative committees: Is it possible to solve the conundrum?* Paper presented to the History of Crime, Policing and Punishment Conference Australian Institute of Criminology, December 9–10, 1999, Canberra. Retrieved August 5, 2006 from http://www.aic.gov.au/conferences/hcpp/caseytro.html.

Casey, J. & Mitchell, M. (2005). *Twenty-five years of community consultation: Working with a conundrum.* Paper presented to Australian and New Zealand Society of Criminology Conference, Wellington. February 8–11, 2005. (Unpublished).

Davis, G. & Bishop, P. (2001). Developing consent: consultation, participation and governance. In Davis & Weller (Eds.). *op. cit.*

Davis, G. & Weller, P. (Eds.) (2001). *Are You Being Served? State Citizens and Governance.* Sydney: Allen and Unwin.

Dixon, D. (2005). Why don't the police stop crime? *Australian and New Zealand Journal of Criminology,* 38(1) 4–24.

Findlay, M. (2004). *Introducing Policing: Challenges for Police and Australian Communities.* Melbourne: Oxford University Press.

Fleming, J. & Rhodes, R. (2004). *It's situational: the dilemmas of police governance in the 21st century.* Paper presented to the Australasian Political Studies Association Conference University of Adelaide. Retrieved February 5, 2006 from http://www.adelaide.edu.au/apsa/docs_papers/Pub%20Pol/Fleming%20%20Rhodes.pdf.

Fleming, J. (2005). Working together: Neighbourhood watch, reassurance policing and the potential of partnerships. *Trends and Issues in Crime and Criminal Justice* No. 303, Australian Institute of Criminology, Canberrra. Retrieved August 11, 2005 from http://www.aic.gov.au/publications/tandi2/tandi303.html.

Gennaro, V., Walsh, F., William, F., & Kunselman, J.C. (2005). Community policing: The middle manager's perspective. *Police Quarterly,* 8(4), 490–511.

Hughes, G. (1994). Talking cop shop? A case-study of police community consultative groups in transition. *Policing and Society,* 4, 253–270.

Ipsos. (2005). DHS — *Partnership Survey 2005: Statewide Report.* Ipsos Consulting Report for Victorian Department of Human Services. Retrieved September 6, 2006 from: http://www.dhs.vic.gov.au/pdpd/partnership/downloads/2005_partnership_survey_report.pdf.

Lyons, W. (2002). Partnerships, information and public safety: Community policing in a time of terror. *Policing: An International Journal of Police Strategies and Management,* 25(3): 530–542.

Maguire, M. & John, T. (2006). Intelligence led policing, managerialism and community engagement competing priorities and the role of the National Intelligence Model in the U.K. *Policing and Society,* 16(1), 67–85.

Mitchell, M. (2003). *Perceptions of Crime and Community Responsiveness.* Australian and New Zealand Society of Criminology Conference, Controlling crime: Risks and responsibilities, October 1–3, 2003, Sydney Australia. (Unpublished).

Mitchell, M. & Urquhart, J.D. (2002). *Representation of NSW Police on meetings, committees, working parties, councils and other bodies,* Operational Policy and Programs, NSWP, Sydney, NSW. (Unpublished).

Moir, P. (1992). *Community Policing: Questioning some basic assumptions.* In J. Vernon & S. McKillop (Eds.). *op.cit.*

Martin Bonato and Associates (2003). *Report from Review of Police Community Consultative Committees.* Crime Prevention Victoria. (Unpublished confidential paper.)

Myhill, A., Yarrow, S., Dalgleish, D., & Docking, M. (2003). *The role of police authorities in public engagement*, Home Office Online Report 37/03. Retrieved December 11, 2005 from http://www.homeoffice.gov.uk/rds/pdfs2/rdsolr3703.pdf.

Myhill, A. (2006) Community engagement in policing, Lessons from the literature. U.K. Home Office. Retrieved December 11, 2005 from http://police.homeoffice.gov.uk/news-and-publications/publication/community-policing/Community_engagement_lit_rev.pdf.

National Institute of Governance. (2004). *Review of Stakeholder Engagement in ACT Planning.* National Institute of Governance. Retrieved August 5, 2006 from http://www.actpla.act.gov.au/publications/reports/nig-report.pdf.

New South Wales Police (2006). *NSW Police On-Line: PACT Page.* Retrieved August 5, 2006 from http://www.police.nsw.gov.au/community_issues/pact.

Newburn, T. & Jones, T. (2002). *Consultation by Crime and Disorder Partnerships.* Home Office Police Research Series Paper 148. Retrieved January 11, 2005 from http://www.homeoffice.gov.uk/rds/prgpdfs/prs148.pdf.

O'Malley, P. (1997). The politics of crime prevention. In O'Malley, P. & Sutton, A. (Eds.). *Crime Prevention in Australia.* Sydney: The Federation Press.

Sarre, R. & Tomaino, J. (1999). *Exploring Criminal Justice: Contemporary Australian Themes,* South Australian Institute of Justice Studies, Adelaide.

Sarre, R. (1992). Community policing — success or failure? Exploring different models of evaluation. In J. Vernon & S. McKillop (Eds.). *op.cit.*

Scarman, Lord Leslie (1981). *Report of an Inquiry by the Right Honourable The Lord Scarman into the Brixton Disorders of 10–12 April 1981,* Her Majesty's Stationary Office, London (also published as *The Scarman Report,* London, Pelican Books, 1982).

Skogan, W.G., Hartnett, S.M., DuBois, J., Comey, J.T. Twedt-Ball, K., & Gudell J. E. (2000). *Public Involvement: Community Policing in Chicago.* National Institute of Justice Research Report. Retrieved November 18, 2005 from http://www.ncjrs.org/pdffiles1/nij/179557.pdf.

Squires, P. (1998). Cops and customers: Consumerism and the demand for police services. Is the customer always right? *Policing and Society,* 8, 169–188.

Sutton, A., Dussuyer, I., & Cherney, A. (2003). *Assessment of Local Community Safety and Crime Prevention Roles in Victoria,* Crime Prevention Victoria and Department of Criminology, University of Melbourne (Unpublished).

Totikidis, V., Armstrong, A., & Francis, R. (2005). *Local safety committees and the community governance of crime prevention and community safety,* Paper presented to the Beyond Fragmented Government: Governance in the Public Sector conference, Victoria University, Melbourne, August 15–17, 2005. Retrieved August 5, 2006 from http://www.businessandlaw.vu.edu.au/conferences/psc_proceedings/Totikidis_VUREF.pdf.

Vernon, J. & McKillop, S. (Eds.) (1992). *The police and the community: Proceedings of a conference held 23–25 October 1990,* Australian Institute of Criminology, Canberra. Retrieved January 11, 2005 from http://www.aic.gov.au/publications/proceedings/05/.

Victoria Police (1999). *Strategic Development Department, Continuous Improvement Handbook.* Melbourne: Victoria Police.

Victoria Police (2003). *The Way Ahead: Strategic Plan 2003–2008.* Melbourne: Victoria Police. Retrieved August 5, 2006 from http://www.police.vic.gov.au/files/documents/352_The-Way-Ahead-Strategic-Plan-2003-2008.pdf.

Victoria Police (2004) *Evaluation of Local Priority Policing Phase Three — The Community Consultation Model,* Victoria Police Corporate Management Review Division, Melbourne. (Unpublished confidential paper.)

Ward, J. (1995). *Facilitative Police Management.* Melbourne: Partnership Press.

Wilson, P. (1992). Avoiding the dangers and pitfalls of community policing: ten questions that need to be addressed. In J. Vernon & S. McKillop (Eds.). *op.cit.*

Wood, J.R.T. (1997). *Royal Commission into the NSW Police Service, Final Report, Vol. II.* Sydney: Government Printer. Retrieved August 5, 2006 from http://www.pic.nsw.gov.au/Reports_List.asp?type=Royal.

Yates, D.L., Pillai, V.K., & Humburg, J.D. (1997). Committing to the new police-community partnerships in the United States and England. *Policing and Society*, 7, 99–115.

Improving Impact: Evidence-Based Policing or Fostering Community Participation through Action Research and Communities of Practice?

Catherine Layton and Christine Jennett

CONTENTS

ABSTRACT

Evidence-based practice has a high profile in medicine and associated professions, and, more recently, in policy-making and policing. In this chapter, we argue that this model has limitations in the crime prevention context. Eck[1] suggests that problem-oriented policing is a more useful approach. This, too, has its problems, in that there is an insufficient focus in the literature on how to engage with the communities, which is integral to the success of the problem-oriented process. We outline how an action-research approach can overcome these limitations and offer examples of the outcomes of taking this approach. Finally, we suggest how police managers might use communities of practice to foster the development of action-research projects in crime prevention.

INTRODUCTION

Our reflections in this chapter are based on teaching crime prevention to master's degree students and on educational consultancy work for the New South Wales Police, undertaken with crime prevention officers. The evidence-based approach to any profession involves reflexive praxis as information from social life is analyzed, an intervention is planned, and implemented and an output sought. It is a process typical of late modern society where the risks of daily living, such as those posed by crime, must be managed. Those who advocate the approach assert its validity through references to the scientific method, but such an assertion is at odds with the critique of the value of the scientific method that characterizes the late modern social world.

Those who advocate the scientific method to deal with social problems tend to blame managers or frontline police officers for failing to take it up in their practice. In this chapter we argue that reasons for nonadoption of the scientific method may lie in the nature of practice in a complex social world. We argue that *process* is the central issue. The relevant processes involve relationships of equality between diverse stakeholders, with diverse histories, standpoints, and interests. Action research seems to us to be an appropriate problem-solving methodology that foregrounds process, enabling the practitioner to become a collaborative researcher with other stakeholders in social problems. Ways of fostering a climate in which action research projects can grow are to be found in the literature on communities of practice.

EVIDENCE-BASED POLICING

Evidence-based policing is a recent development, arising out of a similar drive for improved practice in medicine, where it is described as a scientific approach having great promise in that it de-emphasizes intuition, unsystematic experience, and general theoretical assumptions about the causes of problems as sufficient grounds for decision-making.[2] The Evidence-Based Medicine Working Group argues that this scientific approach to professional practice represents a paradigm shift.[3]

The turn to evidence-based practice has also been very attractive in crime prevention, perhaps owing to the influence that scientific management has had on the functioning of police. It is clear that the approach has worked for a range of crime problems, and in particular for evaluation of crime interventions, as exemplified in the work of the Campbell Collaboration.[4] We thus have no quarrel with turning to research, but do take issue with the universal applicability of the scientific model and the capacities of those without a background in science in general, and research in particular, to conduct the necessary appraisals, particularly given that reactive work and high workloads predominate in those areas with the most significant crime problems.[5]

Sherman[6] interprets the paradigm as referring to whole-of agency activity, not individual practice, and links it with Deming's qualitative management approach. He summarizes the relevance of the medical model of evidence-based practice, saying that

> … just doing research is not enough and [that] proactive efforts are required to push
> accumulated evidence into practice through national and community guidelines. These
> guidelines can then focus in-house evaluations of what works best across agencies,
> units, victims, and officers. Statistical adjustments for the risk factors shaping crime
> can provide fair comparisons across police units, including national rankings of police
> agencies by their crime prevention effectiveness [Sherman 1998: 1[7]].

This suggests that evidence-based policing offers techniques that can be applied across the board, and that communities have no role in the process; it is a top-down activity. This perspective is used in U.K. Home Office research,* which is mostly aimed at police managers.

EVIDENCE-BASED PRACTICE

The evidence-based approach is an example *par excellence* of reflexivity; information drawn from social life is analyzed and fed back to us as participants in social life, modifying our actions. It is a process typical, writes Giddens,[8] of late modern societies, where the risks of daily living, now affected by events and people far beyond those immediately experienced by us, need to be managed. It is interesting that the validity of the approach is asserted through references to the scientific method[6] against a hum of unmentioned dissent about the value of positivist assumptions about the social world.[9–13] Evidence-based practice is a late-modern strategy for practice in a post-modern world where such strategies are questioned.

The focus of evidence-based practice is fundamentally managerial, about establishing the most effective strategies for intervening in the social world for the least possible cost. Given the required scale of the research underpinning evidence-based practice and the scientific standards applied to establish the most useful evidence (see Sherman[6]), the model is also *researcher-centered*, rather than *practitioner-centered*. Practitioners are expected to provide the studies upon which researchers will build, and are expected to draw on the principles established through the researchers'

---

* The Home Office is a U.K. government department responsible, among other things, for policing in
England and Wales. The Home Office undertakes a huge range of research to inform their policies and
measure the impact of their initiatives.

activities in conducting their practice. This does occasionally happen, but the most common use of research is tactical.[14] Sherman[6] notes that, even in medical practice, doctors rarely turn to research in the desired manner, and special supports and processes are needed for evidence-based approaches to become embedded in practice.

The failure to turn to research in medical practice is likely to be an even greater issue in policing, which has historically been very suspicious of outsider views on policing, including researchers' perceptions.[15] Even though there are, indeed, areas of police work that have been affected by research findings, there is little to suggest that a turn to research has become embedded in either managerial practice, through its concern with outcomes rather than outputs (arrest rates),[6] or at the coalface.

A further problem lies in the appeal to science and to the scientific method as the means of social progress. It is intuitively appealing but ignores the conceptual presuppositions that generate the processes of inquiry in the first place (which are inevitably skewed), the ways in which the narrowing of any study for practical or for other purposes mean that there will always be the possibility of conflicting evidence, that data always requires interpretation, and that, in many instances, progress is made when mistakes are identified, rather than when things run as expected.[16]

Although the tendency is to blame the managers, or to blame the people at the coalface, for their failure to adopt an improved approach to their work, the reasons for nonadoption may lie elsewhere altogether. It is possible that the reasons have far more to do with the nature of practice in a complex social world than ignorance, suspicion, conservatism, or recalcitrance. The problem may lie in the action choices as they unfold for people in specific, unpredictable situations, and in the relationship between knowledge and action.

The issue lies in what it is to be a human being—far more than in cognition and reason.[17–18] Faced constantly with new situations—similar to, but never exactly the same as, those one has encountered before; people have to improvise, trying to "guesstimate" the responses of others and their interpretation of their actions or remarks.[19–21] The practitioners have to take account the affordances of the context as they understand them at that moment.[18]

Novices will turn to the rules, and maybe even theory, although there is plenty of evidence that novice practitioners actually focus on the strategies that will help them survive/save face, such as checking what others in the immediate environment are doing and leaving those they are in contact with to deal with their own survival.[22] Expertise brings with it the capacity to "reflect-in-practice,"[2] a process that is likely to draw in emotional, as well as rational, cues as to which improvisations are most likely to have the desired effect.[24–27]

Thus, when a group of local people come together to deal with a crime problem, the context is one of multiple uncertainties and improvisations. The way in which these are worked out has been characterized as a process of group "forming, storming, norming, and performing."[28] These phases are about relationships more than they are about product. Ignoring them, and assuming the problem itself or research are sufficient to guide action and outcomes has the potential to deny the importance of community commitment to, and involvement in, addressing a problem.

Also ignored is the role of chance conjunctions in determining the outcome of a particular project. Becker[29] illustrates the important role that *chance* plays in people's lives and actions, and finds it curious that academics, whose lives, like anyone else's are so much affected by chance, place such faith in science and rational order. When people get together to address a crime problem, if the process is to be a collaborative one rather than a consultative process with minimal impact on an already established direction, much will inevitably depend on who likes whom, what shared interests and values there are, the resources to which people happen to have access and so on.

Given these premises, then, where does the evidence drawn from an evidence-based approach to policing come into action? It will potentially come in to the problem-solving processes used, be this SARA (Scanning, Analysis, Response, Assessment), PROCTOR (PRoblem, Cause Tactic/Treatment Output, Result), or through *action research*. The difficulty with SARA and PROCTOR is that they are fundamentally rational approaches to problem solving, which can be undertaken without drawing on communities as equal participants in the action. Only action research recognizes that the participants in the research have a vital role to play in the processes of problem-solving, as well as the outcomes.

EVIDENCE-BASED CRIME PREVENTION

Let us now look at how this might relate to crime prevention practice. Crime prevention is a relatively new term which is applied to a wide range of activities, and it has subtle and ambiguous meanings.[30] Moreover, as with criminology generally,[31] it draws on a wide range of conflicting disciplines to try to address a wide spectrum of crimes in a wide variety of ways. Nor should we forget Crawford's[32] reminder that crime prevention is somewhat problematic for practitioners, in that it is an activity which results in noncrime. However, distinguishing whether a reduction in crime is actually a consequence of a particular intervention is inherently extremely complex and elusive. Sherman's[33] view of crime prevention as being defined by consequences (the number of criminal events and the number of offenders) shows a far more narrow focus than the several suggested by Hughes.[34] Hughes discusses reform, deterrence, or protection, and prevention of social harms or the promotion of social goods, such as community building.

Eck points out that many interventions are small scale and tailored to individual contexts, and goes on to delineate an evaluation process, within the context of problem-oriented policing, that shares many characteristics with the action research process.[35] He sees the *problems* as being practitioners' lack of relevant theories (a difficult hurdle to leap, given the historical preference for the practical over the theoretical in policing), low quality analyses, and a failure to look at what others are doing (the aim of evidence-based policing). We would also add that policing style may be as important as substance, as Sherman and Eck[36] remark that a striking recent finding is the extent to which police bad manners create a risk factor for crime.

However, the advantages of problem-oriented policing that Eck[1] identifies include the fact that theory and practice can be integrated. Practitioners will generate solutions that will work better than off-the-shelf solutions. Problem-oriented policing is a practical tool, not requiring an academically rigorous approach; it increases accountability, and it is suited to changing circumstances—circumstances that will change as a consequence of the intervention. He concludes, in relation to small-scale projects, that "adherence to rigorous evaluation criteria is misguided."[37]

PARTNERSHIPS IN CRIME PREVENTION

Alongside the impetus for evidence-based policing has been an increasing reliance on the use of partnerships to develop and implement crime prevention initiatives. This focus on partnerships extends and deepens early concerns about the distance between police and the community[38] and goes beyond processes such as Neighborhood Watch to require real, active partnerships in which power is shared.[39] Crime, like any other social problem, is increasingly recognized as having multiple causes that cannot be addressed in a piecemeal fashion. Indeed, partnerships between agencies are currently seen as the most effective way to develop and implement effective crime prevention initiatives, so the fostering of participation is an inherent requirement of the crime prevention officer's job. Bright[40] outlined the issues relating to multiagency partnerships as being a means to overcome the vertical silos of public agency objectives and services, a means of reducing the costs associated with reactive rather than proactive approaches to crime, and an uncertain process, given that the responsibility for multiagency partnerships is dispersed. Consequently, it is not always easy to show that multiagency partnerships really add value.

It is in the *processes of partnerships* that the issues lie. Community policing, and problem-oriented policing, both of which imply relationships with people outside of policing, have had uneven implementation and evidence-based policing may yet follow suit. This is related to the lack of attention to process and to the particular demands of partnerships. Contact with police, for communities, is generally characterized by the lecture/guest-speaker model, where groups listen to an expert and have the opportunity to ask questions.

This model of contact with communities is just one form of participation on a "ladder" of participation.[41] We have not included all of Arnstein's[41] eight categories here because some of her distinctions are too fine to be useful. The categories of participation that we consider to be useful are manipulating/providing, informing, consulting, partnering, delegating, and community control.

The most tokenistic and least participative approach is that of *providing for others' needs* without asking them what they need, and *manipulations* which include handpicking "'worthies" who will toe a particular line. Bull and Stratta's research on consultative committees[42,43] indicates that the latter is often the case, and that it is also a matter of drawing solely on established organizations. *Informing* people (that is, the lecturer/guest-speaker model) is the first step to legitimate participation, although it is a one-way street. *Consulting* with people (through conducting surveys and certain types of neighborhood and public meetings, and so on—common practices in crime prevention) is one step higher, but the ultimate decision still rests with those who have the power. *Partnering* involves negotiations about power, and developing an appropriate balance between partners. It is in this situation that crime prevention workers need to be particularly clear about what they can legitimately offer, and when, how, and to whom they should be listening. So, too, with *delegating*, in which individuals or subgroups have decision-making power and are accountable for their decisions and actions. The highest degree of participation comes with *community control*.

The more participative the process, the more the crime prevention worker needs to pay attention to networks and stakeholder participation. *Networks* involve the development and maintenance of positive relationships with diverse players who have the potential to contribute something of mutual value, and who are drawn from both inside and outside of policing. The good relationships upon which networks depend are characterized by information exchange, trust, and confidence (which are underpinned by treating people with respect and empathy, adhering to organizational values and standards, competent performance, and a capacity to adapt to differing social and cultural environments—matters of style). Networking also involves being a conduit linking people in the network *to each other* (with due regard to potential conflicts of interest or values), as well as conscious attention being paid to the establishment and maintenance of the network. Particular attention may well need to be paid to those who might not routinely have the opportunity to contribute to the prevention or reduction of crime, but whose contributions are likely to inform actions in ways that would not otherwise be possible, that is, stakeholders. Stakeholders generally fall into one or more of the following categories:

- Those whose **interests** are affected by a problem, plans or strategies, as well as those whose **activities** contribute to it
- Those who control or influence the **management** of the problem
- Those who possess important **information or expertise** in addressing the problem[44]

ACTION RESEARCH

It seems to us that action research provides a methodology that enables the crime prevention officer to focus on both collecting *evidence* and the *process* by which it is collected, and on how social change interventions are planned, implemented, and evaluated. It helps us escape the limitations of separatist models of the relationship between research and practice, which demand intermediaries to ensure each can influence the other.[14] In contrast, it allows for the development of crime prevention workers as what Leigh[45] has termed "practitioner-researchers" (see also Jennett et al.[46] for application to the policing context).

There are many varieties of action research, some invoking the scientific method and some the interpretive method in order to justify the validity of their approach. Two types of action research which are appropriate for police officers to address crime prevention issues are (1) organizational action research (as outlined by Coghlan and Brannick[47]) and (2) community-based action research (as depicted by Stringer[48] and Dick[13,49]).

Action researchers are *change agents*. Traditional academic researchers work to create knowledge but action researchers work to produce both action and knowledge outcomes. According to Coghlan and Brannick[42]:

> Action research works through a *cyclical process* of consciously and deliberately: (a) planning; (b) taking action; (c) evaluating the action, leading to further action and so on [Coghlan and Brannick 2001: xi; emphasis added].

Action research is appropriate when the research topic is an unfolding series of actions over time in a given group, community, or organization, and the members wish to study their own action in order to change or improve the working of some aspects of the system—and study the process in order to learn from it. Hence, action research is akin to experiential learning (Kolb 1984) and reflective practice (Schön 1983).[50]

Action research involves all stakeholders (not their representatives) in defining the problem to be researched, planning the research, reviewing the findings, and planning an intervention to address the problem, evaluating its success and subsequent cycles as necessary. It provides stakeholders with the experience of ownership of the project and, hence, they will be committed to it, but this will only happen if all stakeholders respect each other's interests and points of view, and negotiate a way forward rather than impose a plan with which some stakeholders are not happy. Stringer says that participation is most effective when it achieves the following:

- Enables significant levels of active involvement
- Enables people to perform significant tasks
- Provides support for people as they learn to act for themselves
- Deals personally with people rather than with their representatives or agents[51]

Community-based action research relies upon the "type, nature, and quality of relationships." Therefore, the establishment and maintenance of "positive working relationships" is crucial. Stringer[43] characterizes the necessary relationships for community-based action research as ones which:

- Promote feelings of equality for all people involved
- Maintain harmony
- Avoid conflicts, where possible
- Resolve conflicts that arise, openly and dialogically
- Accept people as they are, not as some people think they ought to be
- Encourage personal, cooperative relationships, rather than impersonal, competitive, conflictual, or authoritarian relationships
- Be sensitive to people's feelings[52]

In order for relationships to have these characteristics, they require effective communication. Stringer cites Habermas' four fundamental conditions that need to be met in order to facilitate effective communication:

Understanding: The receiver can understand what is being communicated.
Truth: The information is accurate and is not a fabrication.
Sincerity: The communicator is sincere in his or her attempts to communicate and has no hidden agendas.
Appropriateness: The manner, type, and form of communication are appropriate to the people, the setting, and the activity.[53]

Writers about action research set out a series of stages through which a research project must go in order to be a transparent, collaborative and, therefore, democratic, process of inquiry and evaluation. Stringer's[54] urging for researchers to "look, act, and think" is the most simply articulated version of it. Coghlan and Brannick[55] present an action research cycle that involves a pre-step—context and purpose—and four basic steps: diagnosing, planning action, taking action, and evaluating action.

It should be noted that action research is political by its very nature, and Coghlan and Brannick remark that:

> Political forces can undermine research endeavors and block planned change. Gaining access, using data, and disseminating and publishing reports are intensely political acts.[56]

Action research can threaten people because it is rigorous, examining everything, questioning everything, listening to everyone, advocating reflection on what is found, then taking action, which involves everybody who will be affected by the action (social change). Its strength is the sense of commitment to and ownership of the proposed change that its collaborative approach engenders. Its weakness is that if the processes are not handled well there can be backlashes and blocking behavior on the part of those who feel that the proposed action will not be in their interests. Coghlan and Brannick argue that:

> … you need to be politically astute in deciding to engage in action research, becoming what Buchanan and Badham (1999) call a "political entrepreneur." In their view, this role implies a behavior repertoire of political strategies and tactics, and a reflective self-critical perspective on how those political behaviors may be deployed. Buchanan and Boddy (1992) describe the management of the political role in terms of two activities, performing and backstaging. *Performing* involves you in the public performance role of being active in the change process, building participation for change, pursuing the change agenda rationally and logically, while backstage activity involves recruitment and maintenance of support and the reduction of resistance. *Backstaging* comprises skills at intervening in the political and cultural systems, through justifying, influencing and negotiating, defeating opposition and so on.[64]

Importantly, because action research in community contexts involves ongoing monitoring of projects and processes, and allows for adjustments to both, as issues, information, and even blockages emerge, chance factors may play a far more significant role than would be the case for less participative and organic approaches.

ACTION RESEARCH FOR CRIME PREVENTION STUDENTS

Dick[13,49] argues that the "action" part of "action research" involves change, which requires flexibility and participation, and the "research" part depends upon high quality data and accurate interpretations (whether or not this data is derived from positivist research). The goal is achieving change, and, as such, there are various interpersonal processes to be managed (preplanning, which is where relationships are negotiated and built; planning, where what is to be done is decided; and action and ongoing monitoring), all of which may need revisiting as a project progresses.

Dick's formulation of the action research process, with its focus on building and sustaining relationships productive of change has been used for several years in a subject, "Partnerships in Crime Prevention," in the M.A. degree course in crime

TABLE 23.1

Design of the Subject, JST481 Partnerships in Policing

Week	Forum and Studies	AREOL[49] Process
1	Climate setting—building trust and rapport	Entry and contracting
2	Critical assessment of partnerships in policing; identifying possible projects	
3	Working at the boundaries (Wenger 1998b)	
4	First steps: identifying goals and objectives, and contracting selected project	
5	Identifying stakeholders and boundary issues	Stakeholders and participation
6	Recognizing different perspectives and fostering participation	Achieving participation
7	Project management: milestone development with stakeholders	Achieving rigour
8	Assessing validity and reliability; background research of problem	Collecting and analyzing data: • Convergent interviewing • Focus groups
9	Finding out what people think: the Delphi technique	
10	Finding out what people think and identifying potential strategies	
11	Finding out what people think and identifying potential strategies Considering resources and applying for funding	
12, 13, 14	Evaluation as action research: the Snyder process Reflection	Evaluation as action research: the Snyder process Soft systems methodology

prevention offered by the Australian Graduate School of Policing at Charles Sturt University. Students in this course are all mature-age practitioners, some with over 20 years' experience in their field.

Several years of delivering this subject provide some examples of the unpredictability of change-oriented research, where project development is highly dependent on the resources that people enthused by a project can bring to bear on it. The design of the subject's forum combined educational, policing-specific, and action research principles, as described by Dick. The processes involved are illustrated in Table 23.1, and show how different the focus is from problem-solving methods such as SARA and PROCTOR; the focus is on people and their perspectives on the problem.

The framework for learning is structured around weekly forum entries that address the study materials in that week, and which require real-world explorations of how to use the tools provided. The students themselves are envisaged as forming a forum-based a partnership (which one student, Ken, correctly dubs a "steering committee"), exploring the potential of partnerships to address a crime problem that they have selected. The six students enrolled in the instance under discussion formed two groups, one addressing armed robberies in business premises, and the other, youths causing trouble on Friday and Saturday nights.

The three students upon whose work I will focus are Ken, a police manager in the Victoria police, in a rural area covering 4,600 square kilometres; Marissa, who works as a community safety officer in local government; and Tony, a NSW police crime prevention officer. The other three students in the subject were all police in various jurisdictions and roles, including one spending 2 years in a developing country. Their forum entries illustrate the dynamic and interactive nature of the developments which occur within the action research process. Only a few key aspects of the process are addressed here: the importance of climate setting (which was designed to take up 4 weeks) and the motivation to learn and assist others as equal partners in learning (which is evident across the sample forum entries provided below); the projects that ensued; and students' reflections on their learning.

THE IMPORTANCE OF CLIMATE SETTING, AND MOTIVATION TO LEARN AND ASSIST OTHERS AS EQUAL PARTNERS IN LEARNING

The three students' first entries, in which they were asked to provide their initial reactions to receiving the package of learning materials,[58] and what they hoped to get from their studies, included the following statements:

> When I opened the package for this subject, my response was "I hope I'm not biting off more than I can chew." ... What I would like to get from this Forum partnership is the ability to be able to communicate with others from varying work locations and backgrounds and discuss issues and problems. My contribution to the Forum partnership will be to participate and hopefully be able to have a worthwhile input. I would like to be able to think that my ideas and experiences may be able to assist someone else. [Ken]

> My first response when I opened the package was similar to many others—oh, my God, what a lot of reading! On closer examination the thought of only one essay was great and the weekly activities will force me to keep up to date (normally I'm a "get things done at the last minute" type).

> My personal goals for this subject are in two broad areas: the first is to learn the pros and cons of various types of partnerships as I am so used to the traditional government bureaucratic committee structure—in fact, it is such a committee that provides the direction for my job. I hope I will be able to implement some different and possibly improved methods of partnerships. After reading the materials in more depth I also found that the subject may help me with some particular projects I am currently working on.

> My contribution to the forum will be to share my experiences, and I think I should be able to help others in the group understand the "Council perspective," which I am sure many of you have worked with/fought against in the past. I also hope to understand more of the police perspective on these issues. [Marissa]

> I have enrolled in Areol,[59] and until it starts I have no idea what it is about or what is required of me. As far as making contact with other Areol participants, that will depend on time commitments and whether I can get involved in the discussions or not.

When I opened the package for this subject, my initial response was "Good, only one assignment." But then, I thought, that means a lot of work somewhere else. Time management will be extremely important for this subject, not only to keep up with Areol, but weekly input onto the forum is mandatory. Therefore, you cannot read ahead or fall behind and play catch up.

My personal goals for this subject are to gain further knowledge on partnerships and learn how they can assist me to work smarter.

What I would like to get from this Forum partnership is to work as a team and get other opinions on how partnerships should work and look at crime prevention from different angles and my contribution will be to hopefully call on some of my experiences to share with the group. [Tony]

They show the extent to which inquiry about personal responses and reactions acts as an important icebreaker in the on-line context, setting a positive climate for participation. Participants are able to judge where they sit in this unfamiliar context.

PROJECTS DEVELOPED IN THIS SUBJECT

As mentioned earlier, the students focused on two projects. The robbery project proved difficult to work with (because each student was focused on a slightly different type of stakeholder in their work context, and therefore the group of students did not necessarily benefit from each others' inquiries), whereas the youth project was producing significant outcomes within the fourteen-week semester. Ken introduced "his" youth project in this way:

Although this is a problem that I have encountered throughout my career it has become a growing concern since moving to the country. The last time I was a uniformed member [of police] I was dealing with this problem at a street level. I must admit I didn't give much thought on how to reduce the situation, other than charging offenders and moving people on. Now that I am in a managerial position I suppose I look at things in a different perspective. I now find myself looking for reasons why this is happening and what can be done to prevent it.

I am hoping that the partnership will mirror a sentence from Stokes-White (2000:113). A successful partnership is that it has been created from determination and will of the partner organizations themselves and has been created to tackle issues that they have identified and to which they are highly committed. If this is the case it is certainly a step in the right direction.

The organizational culture in the Victoria Police Force, although still very strong in many areas, has undergone dramatic changes over the last five years or so, particularly in the management area. We now have a totally different style of management in our hierarchy and have moved away from the autocratic method of leadership. I believe that we are now an organization that is far more conducive to the partnership style of policing. [Ken, Week 3 forum entry]

In Week 4, the students were still considering how best to go about their partnership, and negotiating roles. Marissa's lengthy entry exemplifies the extent to which students felt free to discuss ideas and challenge assumptions:

> I think S. is right and we should focus on a specific aspect of the issue, and I am happy to go with Ken's suggestion of underage and binge drinking in a particular park. I think this is a great project to involve a number of partners from outside the law enforcement area. On this issue, I mentioned recently that the friendly youth worker in the next cubicle to me at work would be great to get involved. Well, I have now actually asked him, and he is happy to provide input as we go.
>
> This one is a bit different to the previous submissions so let me explain. Both Ken and S. have objectives around the leadership/coordination of the stakeholders with different styles (committee versus coordinator). I think this is a decision best left to the stakeholders themselves after a discussion of who will commit to what (see Part 3 to this submission). I also disagree with aspects of both options. S. mentions the need to have the leadership group comprised of those with knowledge and commitment to action. Although this is most often the case, sometimes someone or some agency is left out of the equation if they don't have enough resources to commit to implementing a solution—even though they may have excellent knowledge about the problem. At this early stage you may also see the value in having a particular person involved but they may be unwilling to commit until more details are known, until they understand the issue/process better, or until you basically force them into it through some other means. As an example, I had a brief chat with our Parks and Waterways manager about this project. There was absolutely no interest at this stage; however, I can guess that at some stage we may need to involve the people who would be implementing some of our suggestions, which possibly may include a redesign/upgrade or increased maintenance of the park in question. To do this effectively they would need a good understanding of the project including the problem and the reasons for our suggested solutions. So, assuming that this is real, my next action would be to invite him to a meeting and present the issues we know now and the benefits of his involvement. Refusal at this stage could indicate I need to find someone with a similar role or decision-making ability and get them involved (e.g., the supervisor of the actual crew that cares for the park). Further apathy would result in the need for me to go over his head and seek his supervisor to direct an appropriate staff member to be involved. Although this sounds harsh (and slightly underhanded), it has often provided excellent crime prevention outcomes for two reasons: (1) the direction to be involved is often perceived as a direction to be supportive and (2) involvement often results in increased knowledge and understanding of the project and its benefits, leading to support.
>
> What I am trying to explain, really, is the need to keep it as flexible and open as possible at the start so we can start the evolution to an improved, targeted project.
>
> This means we have to be flexible about the coordinator, also. S. recommends that a police officer be the leader, and there are some good reasons for this. My bias, however would lean the other way, and I would suggest that a stakeholder with good project management and coordination skills be chosen. My additional suggestion would be that, if possible, this person not be either a police officer or a youth worker. My experience shows that the ideologies (and often the core business of their job) of these people are often in

direct conflict, and it can be difficult to be both coordinate diverse opinions and present your own opinion without actual or perceived bias. [Marissa, Week 4 forum entry]

This question of self-positioning was explicitly addressed in the learning materials, with reference to forming, storming, norming, and performing stages of group development.[28] It proved a helpful vehicle for critical self-assessment:

Although S., Marissa, and I have been agreeing on a majority of issues so far, I believe a couple of areas need to be clarified between us. (I suppose we are at the *storming* stage.)

Has any consideration been given to my idea of forming a steering committee as I suggested in Weeks 4 and 6 Activities? [Ken, Week 7 Forum Activities]

It was in Week 7 that the students first ran a session with people in their communities. Marissa worked with 3 council workers and a 16-year-old youth:

It was interesting that when I initially outlined the focus of the project every member immediately nodded, almost unconsciously understanding that we had a problem, but they disagreed totally on what the problem was. It took a fair bit of work to move the focus away from the causes and consequences of the problem (e.g., lack of attractive alternate activities and damage to the park) to the actual behavior we were looking at (misuse of alcohol in a public location). [Marissa, Week 7 Forum Entry]

In Week 8, Ken reflected on the extent of the problem in the light of the readings on collecting and analyzing the data:

I believe that our problem so far is that we may have actually underestimated the problem—not that it is an exaggeration. This is due to the fact that our statistics rely on crime being reported to the police. It is obvious by the phone calls I received after the newspaper reports and the Neighborhood Watch meeting that there was more going on than the police knew about. Hopefully, the community has become more aware of the importance of reporting crime, and with the intelligence gained from these reports our efforts can be more focused on the true problem areas. [Ken, Week 8 Forum Entry]

The use of the Delphi technique was the focus in Week 9:

I selected three people from the stakeholder group for this exercise. I anticipated that they may show more enthusiasm and come up with some constructive answers due to having a personal interest in the project topic. I endeavored to give them a question that covered their own area of expertise as well as entail a reply that may be in an area from outside their "comfort zone" that they needed to think about. I not only chose people who had an interest in the project, I tried to select ones who came from very different backgrounds. I was hoping to obtain some different points of view, initiatives, and ideas from their respective viewpoints. I predicted that I may be able to glean some potential strategies towards resolving the problem. [Ken, Week 8 Forum Entry]

The first responses from the participants were amazingly close to the most stereotypical, clichéd views from the type of person/position and the impacts they experience. ...

The final result was that while participants didn't necessarily disagree with each other, they placed varying levels of importance on particular aspects, for example, direct parental neglect versus lack of influence in choosing friends. So the end result was a general consensus on the following:

- Young people acting in an antisocial manner in public parks is not good
- Many strategies, by various agencies, need to come together to have an impact on the issue
- Some progress can be made by involving parents in some way—flexibility to individual situations being the key response.

All this, funnily enough, reflects what the research says and what we have being doing already. Does this mean the participants came to a natural agreement or that the facilitator managed to shut down opposing opinions? My opinion is that two things happened: The first is that the three people in the group are used to this method of working and are happy to rely on a partnership approach (which is sometimes an easy answer when everyone is blaming everyone else) and, also, the participants are the type of people who generally accept all viewpoints as valid and were simply trying to be accommodating. [Marissa, Week 9 Forum Entry]

There were two other participation strategies trialed by the students: focus groups and convergent interviewing. Extracts from Ken and Marissa's work follow:

I decided to try my hand at a focus group. The reason for this is twofold. Prior to transferring to my present position, like many operational police, I conducted interviews on a large range of topics on a regular basis. I would like to think that my interview techniques were fairly well "honed" by now. Since my arrival here I have taken on a different role. I am required to work much closer with the community and have found myself being continually approached regarding local issues and concerns. Although I have been a participant in numerous meetings; I would not classify them as focus groups. ...

I was able to acquire the conference room at the township's Country Fire Authority office at no cost for our meeting. The Divisional Superintendent also agreed to allow a petty cash payment for light refreshments as he felt that the project could be beneficial to the community. ...

Once the "ice had been broken" and the participants were freely sharing their ideas I narrowed the topic by steering the conversation to the specific problems at Memorial Park. A white board was then used to jot down ideas and build further discussion. ...

The forum lasted for two-and-a-half hours, with a ten-minute break in the middle. There were a few areas of disagreement, but these were talked through and a general consensus was gained. ... At the end of our forum, diaries came out to organize the next meeting! [Ken, Week 10 Forum Entry]

Marissa's use of convergent interviewing spanned two weeks, and the lengthy extract provided is from her second week's entry, showing the extent to which those outside of the immediate partnership context were prepared to contribute. Excluded are the detailed plans for each strategy.

> ... F. provided me with a detailed project plan—I thought of summarizing it, but thought it may be useful for Ken who seems to be going ahead with the project which is fantastic. ...

Proposed strategies:

- Peer-based outreach approach to 17- to 20-year-olds
- Peer-based outreach approach to 13- to 16-year-olds
- Focus groups for general youth populations

General comments:

Peer-based outreach is effective. Be mindful of the perceptions young people recruited to outreach may have of young people in the park. Is there a town "stigma" regarding these young people? Are they seen as the "no hopers"? Conversely, what would the perception of young people in the park be toward young people recruited for outreach?

Outreach is most effective when there is unconditional (no, or little [hidden] agenda—i.e., religion, "clear off," etc.) clear, open, and transparent communication. Young people need to have a level of confidence that they can relate "safely" to outreach workers. In short, is it a situation where the school prefect and Student Representative Council (SRC) chair is approaching a young person expelled and not engaged in education employment, etc.?

The context of this is within a small town/regional center—the smaller the town, the more familiar people can be (small town mentality). This links directly into recruitment for peer outreach. Obviously schools and youth committees are a source of civic-minded and motivated young people. Use them. Cater to any potential perception/values/concerns in the training provided to young people. Also consider youth centers and sports clubs.

Youth center may have an image problem, and it may be that only "young people with problems go there," which reinforces the fact that this is the case [if a youth center is chosen]. If the youth center caters to a wide/diverse range of young people, it may be a source of recruitment that may assist in the credibility of peer outreach. Young people in the park may know them already and have a more positive image of them.

Sports clubs: some, or many, of the young people in the park may have connections to football and other clubs. Similar to young people from the youth center—young people in the park may be familiar with them and have a more positive perception of them and common interests.

Strength based approach:

It is important that the whole strategy is a strength-based approach. It may be the case that young people pick up on overt or tacit scape-goating from the community, that they are seen as a problem. Outreach would be ineffective if from the start they perceive that the perception or reality is being re-enforced. An element of fun needs to be involved, and especially if it is a short term, brief intervention—interaction needs to "go somewhere." I hope this will be shown in the plan I put forward.

Media:

It may be tempting to seek some media "feel-good" coverage to promote this positive thing. Particularly in a smaller town I would suggest that no approaches be made to the media till after. There could be little control over the way the story is covered and an ill-written article about peer educators working toward cleaning up the park would undermine the project.

The plan is based on the assumptions that funding/resources are limited. I have suggested a brief intervention, with some sustainable elements so as not to leave a post-intervention void. [Marissa, Week 11 Forum Entry]

These are the developments that had occurred by Week 13:

Well, a few things have been happening down my way this last week. It appears that the news of our forum has spread around the town and I have suddenly had numerous offers of support.

The CEO of the shire [managing governmental body] has offered the services of the parks manager to our group. She has also assured me that the shire will look favorably at financing any changes to the landscape and design of Memorial Park which our focus group believes will assist with reducing our problem.

The PCCC (Police and Community Consultative Committee) and the local Rotary Club have both contacted me regarding our project and have shown a keen interest in assisting with our local youth problems. Both of these organizations have pledged financial support if our university project develops into an actual stakeholder partnership.

There is a possibility of a vacant shop opposite Memorial Park being made available for a youth club. The cost factor of this has not yet been established, but at this stage it seems to be open to favorable negotiation as it has not been occupied since before I moved to the town. There would need to be some modifications done at the shop, but with the community interest already shown I am sure some local tradesmen would volunteer their services for this.

Even though all of this is in the "embryo" stage, the local electrical store has already set aside a TV, DVD player, and computer for a donation to a new youth club. So far the community support has been astounding. It appears our little focus group has started something! [Ken, Week 13 Forum Entry]

STUDENTS' REFLECTIONS

How did the students themselves view these developments? Let's start with "Tony," who was involved in the robbery project:

We were asked to identify a crime prevention project that could be used during the studies. At the time I was a little unsure exactly what was required and how important these projects were going to be. [...] I didn't select a project I had any past dealing with, as I was happy to join a group and get involved in the discussions and learn along the way. In hindsight, I feel that we should have been involved with a project that had more angles, and would have involved more stakeholders, which is often the norm. I think robbery prevention was too narrow in its targets, and this limited our responses later on, which made our group responses into a single-minded approach and not working together in partnership. Maybe a small list of potential projects that would generate good group discussions could be added, and students asked to choose from the list a project they have had similar dealings with, which have broader responses, requiring the groups to work more as a team, like the youth group did so well. ["Tony," Week 13 Forum Entry]

I have just read over my six responses to the Week 1 Forum Activity and I feel that I would still answer them in the same way. In saying this, though, I have learned a lot and enjoyed the interaction with the rest of the participants over the last 13 or so weeks. I found the Areol exercises and the theory of action research to be very useful, and it is a theory that can be used daily. [Ken, Week 13 Forum Entry]

I just wanted to thank everyone involved in this subject. I found it very rewarding working with a wide variety of people from different backgrounds and levels of experience. I found the subject to be very engaging—I was very excited to hear from Ken that the youth project is moving forward beyond our theoretical partnership to make some real-world impacts—please keep in touch, Ken, and let me know how it goes! [Marissa, Week 13 Forum Entry]

ACTION RESEARCH AND COMMUNITIES OF PRACTICE

What is it about the educational context that allowed these developments to occur? An initial brainstorm identified the following factors:

- Students came from different occupations and areas of policing (a local government employee, general duties police, investigations) in different Australian states, as well as overseas)
- Students shared issues of interest and concern, in which they had different perspectives
- Resources (mostly people and ideas) were available to students, which broadened their understanding and allowed for different ways of interacting with key players in the problem location
- Students were clearly concerned about supporting each other in their learning.

These are all principles underpinning action research—but is there a management style that takes account of these types of factors, and how might it work in policing?

We believe that the recent work of Etienne Wenger[60–62] provides some useful notions, because he considers how participation generates, sustains, and modifies practice over time, within and across organizational boundaries. The fundamental process/entity through which this occurs is the community of practice. According to

Wenger[60,61] and Lesser and Storck,[63] the community of practice is not a new kind of organizational unit, but pervasive and informal, a different *cut* on an organization's structure, one which emphasizes the learning that occurs when people observe others' work and make links about it to their own work. A community of practice is a group of people who share a concern, a set of problems, or a passion about a topic, and who voluntarily interact and learn from and with each other in unstructured ways over a period of time, without necessarily having a particular outcome other than the work itself, or their own interest, in mind. Social, rather than individual, behavior lies at the heart of the learning thus engendered.

The origins of the concept lie in anthropological studies of a range of occupations, looking at how newcomers in apprenticeship systems move from a peripheral role to, eventually, the expert practitioner role. Through participating in work, people acquire the skills, language, behaviors, attitudes, and, indeed, identities, that are part and parcel of being a tailor, or, in this instance, a police officer or a crime prevention worker. According to Wenger,[64] a *practice* is what people develop in order to be able to do the job and have a satisfying experience at work. The concept connotes doing in a social and historical context that gives structure and meaning to what people do. It includes the explicit and implicit; what is said and what is not; what is represented and what is assumed; the language, tools, documents, images, symbols, roles, criteria, procedures, regulations, but, also, the subtle cues, rules of thumb, sensitivities, and shared world views/cultural assumptions. The latter is what people take for granted and that which fades into the background. Thus, the concept of practice does not separate knowing and doing, manual and mental, concrete from abstract, for practice engages the whole person.

In sum, then, a community of practice is a negotiated enterprise, as complex as we are, involving instrumental, personal, and interpersonal aspects of people's lives (the need to make money, be adult, efficient, have fun, do well, feel good, not be naïve, be personable, deal with boredom, think of the future, and so on).[65] It is not just *doing* the work (which is what the supervisor focuses on), but the juggling of all of these elements on a daily basis.[48] It is also an indigenous enterprise, because, although larger contexts—historical, social, cultural, or institutional—shape them, the day-to-day reality is produced by participants using the resources, and within the constraints, of their situations. The inventiveness both reflects what the organization wants and what it does not want. Thirdly, it is a regime of mutual accountability, covering what matters and what does not, what is important and why, what to do and what not to, what to pay attention to and what to ignore, what to talk about and what to leave unsaid, what to justify and what to take for granted, what to display or withhold, when actions are good enough or need work. These systems play a central role in defining circumstances under which, as community and as individuals, members feel concerned or unconcerned, and is integral to the practice. As such, it may not readily be articulated. The last characteristic of practice as a source of community coherence is the development of a shared repertoire, resources for negotiating meaning (the pile on the desk equals the work to do today, the seating representing relationships and managerial reactions to those relationships). The word *repertoire* is used to emphasize its rehearsed character and its availability. It has two characteristics that make it a resource for negotiating meaning: its reflection of a history of mutual engagement and its inherent ambiguity. This is an open-ended process, for forms of participation, perspectives and experiences of life change. Anyway, over time, in the process of sustaining a practice, we become invested in what we do, in each other, and in our shared history, and our identity anchors in each other and what we do together.

The concept of the "community of practice" is increasingly being used and seen as a valuable asset in business, particularly in terms of people who are not co-located (as was the case with this subject).[66] According to Lesser and Storck,[63] the notion of the community of practice is particularly suited to unstructured problems and sharing knowledge outside traditional boundaries. Wenger, McDermott, and Snyder,[62] interestingly enough for work focused on crime prevention, use an analogy between urban design and people's use of that space, and people's interactions in communities of practice, to suggest the seven design principles as inviting the interactions that make communities of practice come alive. These seven design principles can be related to our observations of what eventuated in our action research-based subject:

1. *Design for evolution:* Social, organizational, and physical structures (a crime prevention officer, a problem-solving meeting or electronic forum, or a community hall or park) precipitate the evolution of communities to which people bring their networks, and where new members or new problems pull the focus of the community in new directions.

2. *Open a dialogue between inside and outside perspectives:* As insiders appreciate the issues and relationships at the heart of the problem, but do not necessarily have the resources to address the problems they face in new ways, outsider perspectives are required to assist them in seeing the possibilities.

3. *Invite different levels of participation:* Good design of public space invites many forms of activity (actors and observers), and different levels and types of participation are to be expected in communities of practice. There is usually a small core group (ten to sixteen percent) at the heart of things who take on leadership roles and consistently participate; there is an active group who are selective participants (again, same percentage; three of the six students formed the first and second groups); and there are those on the periphery, whether because only one aspect interests them, they have little time, or feel they have no authority in this context (the remaining three students). These peripheral members are not like "hangers-on" in a team; their observations, actions and comments may at any time be central to the genesis of a new direction.

4. *Develop both public and private community spaces:* For public community events to work, there need to be a lot of background discussions (for example, the youth worker and the parks manager through the local government employee), which then facilitate relationship building and addressing current issues.

5. *Focus on value:* People don't actually know what the value of being in a community will be until they are part of it, and the problems and ideas emerge and get translated into ideas for action in this and other areas of life. The developments cannot be planned for, but are identifiable in hindsight.

6. *Combine familiarity and excitement:* Although familiar people, events, and patterns of communication foster candid discussions, if no problematic ideas or issues emerge naturally, the occasional injection of a challenging perspective is likely to generate valuable discussion and interesting repercussions.

7. *Create a rhythm for the community:* You need to ensure there is a balance between a breathless pace (which means people get tired and opt out) and sluggish inertia, perhaps through regular patterns of meetings (which means there are busy times and slack times), through rituals and milestones, etc.

IMPLICATIONS FOR POLICE MANAGEMENT

The patterns of interaction among the students participating in JST481 Partnerships in Crime Prevention were developed and sustained in an educational context, and it does not necessarily follow that the same patterns will be easy to set in place in the context of policing. On the other hand, developing a partnership that engenders change in an on-line environment is an unusual occurrence, so police managers who wish to increase the impact of partnerships in building safer communities may well find ideas they can build on from this example.

Communities of practice can and do develop spontaneously as people address recurring problems of practice, as described in Figure 23.1 below, whether this be within the one police organization, in cross-functional teams (such as crime management units) or across organizational boundaries, such as in Interpol, or in crime prevention partnerships.

There is a danger in adopting the view of their development proposed in Diagram 23.1, however, as it assumes that knowledgeable people coming together and talking about practice will become a community of practice, rather than the more subtle processes of acquiring knowledge in and through the work itself, which is

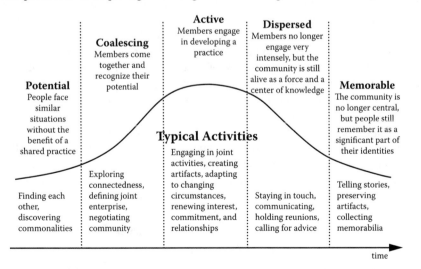

FIGURE 23.1 Stages of Development. (From Wenger, E., Communities of practice: Learning as a social system, 1998. [Published in the *Systems Thinker*, June 1998]. With permission.)

characteristic of the original studies, and the genesis of these ideas. Wenger[67] points out that people come together in organizations to earn a living, *not* to form a community of practice (although the notion of joining the "policing family" may be an exception to this rule).

It should be remembered that communities of practice differ from other kinds of organizational groups in three ways. Firstly, they define themselves as members and develop *among themselves* their own understanding of what their practice is about (it is a living process that involves whoever contributes, in whatever way, and to whatever degree, to the practice). Secondly, they are defined by their practice and come into being because participation in the practice has value to their members. Finally, they have identities as communities, and thus shape the identities of their members (this is what *we* do when faced with this type of problem). Thus, they are more than a team, a taskforce or a project group, and different from a line or staff department, even though they might form around these matters.

Although communities of practice arise naturally, this does not mean that you, as an administrator or manager, can do nothing to foster them, or, conversely, that you must intervene (running the risk of smothering their self-organizing drive). You cannot instruct people to form a community of practice, but, on the other hand, if you want what they can offer, you may be able to "seed" them, by setting appropriate processes and structures in place. Some strategies of potential value are discussed in the following sections.

Legitimizing Participation

You can support communities of practice by providing opportunities for police to talk about how their participation in communities of practice contributes to the organization as a whole, and by giving members the time to participate in the types of problem-solving activities and common work that build communities of practice. Lesser and Storck[68] see this as the structural dimension of fostering social capital. Spending time in the station, talking with colleagues by the coffee machine, telling "war stories," having access to the conference room, or regular patrol-based review mechanisms can allow a community of practice to develop and to be sustained. These are subtle processes of relationship-building, creating a friendly atmosphere and the possibility of personal exchanges, and these relational dimensions can easily be undervalued, even though they require constant work.[69–72]

Where police have areas of expertise, such as crime prevention that are not understood by others in the patrol, some attention will be needed on to how to legitimize participation both within and outside the patrol. Indeed, it may well be that the strongest links for the crime prevention officer are with other professionals in the community, based on personal networks that others will not share.

Negotiating the Strategic Context of Communities of Practice

Work involves both short-term activities that deliver tangible products (such as arrests) and sustained dense relations of mutual engagement that grow out of human sociability, which are organized around what people are there to do.[73] The value of the former is easily recognized, but the longer-term value of the latter is usually more subtle and therefore more difficult to appreciate and build in to organizational strategies. In crime prevention, because the notion of the "police family" is often foregrounded as a cultural phenomenon, it is the need for new communities of practice that incorporate communities and individuals outside of policing that must be recognized. Managers, along with crime prevention personnel, must consider what knowledge and practices a given strategy requires (and where in their communities this might be located), as well as paying attention to potential strategic directions identified by their crime-prevention focused communities of practice.

BEING ATTUNED TO HOW PEOPLE LEARN IN AND THROUGH PRACTICE

People largely learn at and through work, for example, through simply observing how others respond to the situations they face (the "buddy" system in policing) and learning how to negotiate others' preferences and idiosyncrasies. People start as different, but working together creates differences *and* similarities (they specialize, get reputations, etc.). Mutual engagement in work can create tight nodes of relationships, both of support and of conflict.[74]

This being the case, it should be possible for managers to co-locate, or to network, people working in any area or function where knowledge is unevenly distributed or where a specific problem has been recognized. You can thus foster the potential for informal learning that exists in the current policing context, while recognizing that other factors will mediate the likelihood of a community of practice developing, such as personality, judgments of competence, and style.[75]

FINE-TUNING THE ORGANIZATION

The sorts of elements that can foster or inhibit communities of practice include the level of management interest, reward systems, work processes, organizational culture, and company policies. In policing, this is likely to involve managing up as much as it involves managing down, and success may be limited—unless, we suppose, you can generate your own community of practice to address the issues.

Practice itself is a process that involves participation (which we have considered) and *reification*. Reification is the process through which aspects of human experience are captured in fixed forms (artifacts and actions such as laws, tools, or procedures) around which the negotiation of meanings becomes organized.[76] For example, all of the players in an insurance claim, and their different interests and rules, are captured in an insurance claim form. Any action or artifact can be looked at in terms of how participation and reification are distributed. An incident report can be highly reified, interpretable by a machine with no idea of its meaning, whereas a victim impact statement requires participation by the reader or listener in interpreting the meaning. Organizations too reliant on participation will have problems of coordinating activities and uncovering diverging assumptions; those relying on reification may not allow sufficient overlaps to allow for sharing experiences and interactive negotiation.[77]

Participation and reification offer two avenues for exercising influence through cultivating or promoting certain relationships or artifacts, each with distinct forms of politics. Participation involves influence, charisma, nepotism, discrimination, trust, friendship, and ambition; reification involves legislation, policies, expositions, statistics, contracts, plans, and designs. Each can be played off against the other, but control over practice usually requires a grip on both. Reviewing how participation and reification are balanced across actions and artifacts in policing can assist in fine-tuning the organization in ways that foster communities of practice.[78]

BEING ATTUNED TO BOUNDARIES

Over time, the shared histories within communities of practice create discontinuities—boundaries—between those who are and those who have not been participating (the often mentioned "us" and "them" distinctions in police culture). Many boundary markers are explicit (titles, dress, degrees, initiation rites), but subtle nuances, such as policing jargon, or social class, can be just as powerful.

Helpfully, reification and participation can cross boundaries, through boundary objects (artifacts, or places, used in different ways by several groups of people) and brokering (people introducing elements of one practice into another). Thus, in terms of *boundary objects*, an incident report or a charge sheet is not a self-contained object, but a relation between communities of practice. The design of documents, systems, and tools is the design of boundary objects, and this needs taking into account. In terms of *brokering*, this involves individuals with memberships of many communities in interpreting one community of practice for another. This often entails ambivalent relations for the individual in question, as spanning boundaries is not always comfortable: He or she belongs to both practices and to neither. Sensitivity to the complexity of balancing competing perspectives for those doing the brokering is required.[79]

BEING ATTUNED TO TRAJECTORIES

Any community of practice provides a set of potential "career" trajectories, as well as examples of actual people who have risen to prominence, and these are likely to be the most influential shapers of learning for newcomers. No matter what is said, taught, prescribed, recommended, or tested, newcomers are no fools: Once they have actual access to the practice, they soon find out what counts. What they enter is a field of possible pasts and possible futures, a history collapsed into the present where newcomers can engage with their own future as embodied by old timers—and vice versa. Different forms of engaging in practice may reflect different forms of individuality or of accountability and different responses to the same circumstances; elements of one repertoire may be inappropriate, incomprehensible, or even offensive in another community. Reconciling these diverse factors involves much more than learning the rules. This reconciliation may be *the most significant challenge faced by learners* when they move from one community to another.[80] These are processes which take time, and Sharp[81] points out that frequent reassignments and promotions can inhibit or destroy the development of communities of practice. Managers need to ensure that those allocated to roles that involve partnership work have the interest and commitment to stay in the role long enough to develop and sustain a community of practice that will survive their departure.

PROCESSES FOR CAPTURING LESSONS LEARNED

Given that the value of communities of practice only emerges over time, and the directions the learning will take are interactive, problem-centered and unpredictable, it is highly likely that any learning, and changed actions, remain part of informal rather than formal knowledge. Identifying some means of capturing and disseminating the learning is worthwhile.[82]

PROVIDING SUPPORT

Merely dedicating a position to crime prevention work, even at a significant rank, is insufficient to generate a climate that will support and extend the capacities of the role, and allow for learning. This does not mean that managers have to be *engaged* in the practice, rather it means they need to be capable of *imagining* what the work is like (which, perhaps, is what this research allows, but it also involves sharing stories and discussions), and using their power to *align* their own and others' energy and activities to contribute to this broader enterprise.[83] This alignment with the activities of those working in crime prevention involves identifying with their colleagues but, more importantly, negotiation of meanings is the other half.

> Negotiability refers to the ability, facility, and legitimacy to contribute to, take responsibility for, and shape the meanings that matter within a social configuration.[84]

There is, according to Wenger,[85] an economy of meanings (some meanings have more value than others, and some currencies cannot be used across groups). Calling the social configurations "economies of meaning" emphasizes that they involve a social system of relative values which are negotiated. Negotiating, persuading, inspiring trusting, and delegating *all* involve shared ownership of meaning, whereas literal compliance, proceduralization, violence, conformity, and submission do not involve negotiability. Thus, the way in which the police manager negotiates the value of the crime prevention enterprise, and of the contribution made to it by communities of practice, is critical to its success.

POSSIBLE PROBLEMS WITH COMMUNITIES OF PRACTICE

It must be acknowledged that the recognition of the potential contribution of communities of practice to crime prevention work does not create an unproblematic path forward. Communities of practice have different relationships with the official organization, which generate different types of challenges, as shown in Table 23.2 below.

At the present time, the likelihood is that most communities of practice connected with policing go unrecognized or are bootlegged. The question is how to recognize them without stifling them. These challenges are likely to be compounded by some of the factors that have already been identified as inhibiting change in police organizations, even though, as Ken's comments have indicated, changes are occurring. Harrison[86] points out that some American police departments have realized that to move into community policing, they need their managers to develop skills such as strategic planning, group problem solving, and dealing with group dynamics.

TABLE 23.2

Relationships to Official Organization

Relationship	Definition	Challenges Typical of the Relationship
Unrecognized	Invisible to the organization and sometimes even to members themselves	Lack of reflexivity, awareness of value and of limitation
Bootlegged	Only visible informally to a circle of people in the know	Getting resources, having an impact, keeping hidden
Legitimized	Officially sanctioned as a valuable entity	Scrutiny, over-management, new demands
Strategic	Widely recognized as central to the organization's success	Short-term pressures, blindness of success, smugness, elitism, exclusion
Transformative	Capable of redefining its environment and the direction of the organization	Relating to the rest of the organization, acceptance, managing boundaries

Source: From Wenger, E., Communities of practice: Learning as a social system, 1998. *Systems Thinker*, June 1998. With permission.

Action learning has been suggested as potentially viable and of strategic value to the Royal Canadian Mounted Police (R.C.M.P.) in their aim of developing leadership capabilities.[87] However, Geoff Mead,[88] a chief superintendent in the Hertfordshire Constabulary, not only points to the value of action research in policing (and thus, communities of practice), but notes the difficulties inherent in collaborative inquiry in a hierarchical organization and suggests it needs careful crafting to suit the particular circumstances and context. He concludes that much is possible with a little courage and a lot of determination.

CONCLUSION

Throughout this chapter we have argued that evidence-based practice is a limited approach to social research and that it requires articulation with other approaches that foreground the processes by which information is gathered, analyzed, used to implement social change policies and programs, and then to evaluate them. Problem-oriented policing and action research share some common features, but action research is a rigorous method by which social problems can be researched and addressed by stakeholders upon whom the change will have an impact. Only by using such an approach are practitioners likely to achieve the stakeholder buy-in to social change which affects them. In addition to action research's other strengths, it is, as Dick[49] says, a flexible approach, one which can absorb chance occurrences and coincidences, as emphasized by Becker,[29] even one which completely turns the project around. Action research is a democratic research method which is suitable for the development, implementation, and evaluation of local crime prevention projects.

ACKNOWLEDGMENTS

We would like to thank all of the students whose work has underpinned our observations, particularly the students in JST481: "Partnerships in Policing." Kenneth Slingsby, Marissa Racomelara, and "Tony," whose work has been extensively quoted, had, like us, no idea that their work would be used in this way. We would also like to thank David Bull for his comments on a draft of this chapter.

REFERENCES

1. Eck, J.E., Learning from experience in problem-oriented policing and situational prevention: the positive functions of weak evaluations and the negative functions of strong ones, in *Evaluation for crime prevention. Crime Prevention Studies 14*, Tilley, N., Criminal Justice Press, Monsey, New York, 2002.
2. Evidence-Based Medicine Working Group, Evidence-Based Medicine: A New Approach to Teaching the Practice of Medicine, based on the *Users' Guides to Evidence-based Medicine* and reproduced with permission from *LAMA* 268(17) American Medical Association, 1992. Retrieved from http: //www. cche.net/usersguides/ebm. asp#Abstract.
3. Kuhn, T., *The structure of scientific revolutions,* University of Chicago Press, Chicago, IL, 1962.
4. Grabosky, P., The Campbell Collaboration: what works in criminal justice, *Delivering crime prevention: making the evidence work conference,* sponsored by the Australian Institute of Criminology and Attorney General's Department of New South Wales, Carlton Crest Hotel, Sydney, 21–22 November, 2006.
5. Bushell, C., personal communication, 2006.
6. Sherman, L.W., Evidence-based policing, *Ideas in American policing,* Police Foundation, 1998.
7. Sherman, L.W., Evidence-based policing, *Ideas in American policing,* Police Foundation, 1998, p. 1.
8. Giddens, A., *The consequences of modernity,* Polity Press, Cambridge, 1991.
9. Horkheimer, M. and Adorno, T.W., *Dialectic of enlightenment*, trans. Cumming, Continuum, New York, 1969.
10. Geuss, R., *The idea of a critical theory,* Cambridge University Press, New York, 1981.
11. Harding, S., *Whose science? Whose knowledge? Thinking from Women's Lives*, Open University Press, Milton Keynes, 1991.
12. Duran, J., *Philosophies of Science/Feminist Theories*, Westview Press, Boulder, CO, 1998.
13. Dick, B., Sources of rigour in action research: addressing the issues of trustworthiness and credibility. Paper presented at the Association for Qualitative Research Conference 'Issues of rigour in qualitative research' at the Duxton Hotel, Melbourne, Victoria, 6–10 July 1999.
14. Nutley, S., The impact of research and evaluation on policy formation and delivery, Occasional Seminar, Australian Institute of Criminology, Canberra, December 2006.
15. Reiner, R., *The politics of the police* (3rd ed.), Oxford: Oxford University Press, 1998.
16. Doyal, L. and Harris, R., *Empiricism, explanation and rationality: an introduction to the philosophy of the social,* Routledge and Kegan Paul, London, 1986.
17. Burkitt, I., *Bodies of thought: embodiment, identity and modernity,* Sage, London, 1999.
18. Burkitt, I., Social selves: theories of the social formation of personality, *Current Sociology, 39*(3), 1991.
19. Mead, G.H., *Mind, self and society: from the standpoint of a social behaviourist,* University of Chicago Press, Chicago, IL, 1987.
20. Goffman, I., *Interaction ritual: essays on face to face behaviour,* Penguin, Harmondsworth, 1972.
21. Goffman, I., *The presentation of self in everyday life,* Penguin, Harmondsworth, 1976.
22. Zeichner, K.M., Reflective training and field-based experience in teacher education, *Interchange, 12*(4), 1982.

23. Schön, D.A., *How professionals think in action,* Basic Books, New York, 1983.

24. Boud, D., Keogh, R., and Walker, D., Eds., *Reflection: turning experience into learning,* Kogan Page, New York, 1986.

25. Boud, D. and Miller, N., Eds., *Working with experience: animating learning,* Routledge, London, 2001.

26. Damasio, A., *Descartes' error: emotion, reason and the human brain,* Papermac, London, 1996.

27. Layton, C., Learning selves: a case study of police students' learning in community placements, using diaries, Ph.D. thesis, University of Technology, Sydney, 2004.

28. Forsyth, D.R., *An introduction to group dynamics,* Brooks/Cole Publishing Company, Pacific Grove, CA, 1983.

29. Becker, H.S., "Foi por Acaso": Conceptualizing Coincidence, *Sociological Quarterly,* 36, 1994, pp. 183–194.

30. N.C.A.V.C., *Pathways to prevention: developmental and early intervention approaches to crime in Australia,* Commonwealth Attorney Generals Department, Canberra, 1999.

31. Lanier, M.M. and Henry, S., *Essential criminology,* Westview Press, Boulder, CO, 2004.

32. Crawford, A., *Crime prevention and community safety: politics, policies and practices,* Longman, London, 1998, p. 6.

33. Sherman, L.W., Policing for crime prevention, in *Preventing crime: what works, what doesn't, what's promising,* Sherman, L.W., Gottfredson, D.C., MacKenzie, D.L., Eck, J., Reuter, P. and Bushway, S.D., Washington, DC: National Institute of Justice, 1997, p. 3. Retrieved from http://www.ncjrs.org/works/chapter8.html.

34. Hughes, G., *Understanding crime prevention,* Open University Press, Buckingham, 1998.

35. Eck, J.E., Learning from experience in problem-oriented policing and situational prevention: the positive functions of weak evaluations and the negative functions of strong ones, in *Evaluation for crime prevention. Crime Prevention Studies 14,* Tilley, N., Criminal Justice Press, Monsey, New York, 2002, pp. 93–110.

36. Sherman, L.W. and Eck, J.E., Policing for crime prevention, in *Evidence-based crime prevention,* Sherman, L.W., Farrington, D.P., Welsh, B.C. and Layton MacKenzie, D., Eds., Routledge, London, 2002, p. 295.

37. Eck, J.E., Learning from experience in problem-oriented policing and situational prevention: the positive functions of weak evaluations and the negative functions of strong ones, in *Evaluation for crime prevention. Crime Prevention Studies 14,* Tilley, N., Criminal Justice Press, Monsey, New York, 2002, p. 111.

38. Sherman, L.W., Policing for crime prevention, in *Preventing crime: what works, what doesn't, what's promising,* Sherman, L.W., Gottfredson, D.C., MacKenzie, D.L., Eck, J., Reuter, P. and Bushway, S.D., Washington, DC: National Institute of Justice, 1997. Retrieved from http://www.ncjrs.org/works/chapter8.html.

39. Homel, R., Issues in police partnerships: U.S./Australian comparisons. Paper presented at the conference Partnerships in Crime Prevention, convened jointly by the Australian Institute of Criminology and the NCAVC, Hobart, 26–27 February1998.

40. Bright, J., The international experience, pre-conference paper for the PPP Conference, 2001. Retrieved from http://www.communitybuilders.nsw.gov.au/building_stronger/place/ppp1_3.html.

41. Arnstein, S.R., A ladder of citizen participation, *JAIP,* *36*(4), 216–224, July 1969. Retrieved from http://lithgow-schmidt.dk/sherry-arnstein/ladder-of-citizen-participation.html.

42. Bull, D. and Stratta, E., Police community consultation: an examination of its practice in England and New South Wales, *Australian and New Zealand Journal of Criminology,* *27,* 237–249, December 1994.

43. Bull, D. and Stratta, E., Police-community consultative committees: a response to paramilitary policing? *Australia and New Zealand Journal of Sociology,* *31*(3), 67–82, 1996.

44. McCallum, D., *Stakeholder identification and mobilization: draft tool for the Local-EPM Phase One Toolkit, the Philippines,* UNCHS (Habitat)/UNEP, December 2000. Retrieved from http://www.unhabitat.org/cdrom/governance/html/yellop22.htm.

45. Leigh, E., Engaging with theory, putting myself into practice. Keynote address at the *Learning and Teaching @ CSU: Bright ideas and evolving evidence* Conference, Charles Sturt University: Bathurst, September 2006.

46. Jennett, C, Elliot, G., and Robinson, P., Developing practitioner researchers for policing and related professions, in *Innovations in professional practice: influences and perspectives,* Rushbrook, P., Ed., in proceedings of the 2003 *Continuing Professional Education (CPE) Conference,* Centre for Research into Professional Practice Leaning and Education (RIPPLE), 2003.

47. Coghlan, D. and Brannick, T., *Doing Action Research in your own Organization,* Sage, London, 2001.

48. Stringer, E.T., *Action Research,* 2nd ed., Sage, Thousand Oaks, 1999.

49. Dick, B., Areol — action research and evaluation on line, 2006. Retrieved from http://www.scu.edu.au/schools/sawd/areol/areol.html.

50. Coghlan, D. and Brannick, T., *Doing Action Research in your own Organization,* Sage, London, 2001, pp. xi-xii.

51. Stringer, E.T., *Action Research,* 2nd ed., Sage, Thousand Oaks, 1999, p. 35.

52. Stringer, E.T., *Action Research,* 2nd ed., Sage, Thousand Oaks, 1999, p. 29.

53. Habermas, 1979, as cited in Stringer, E.T., *Action Research,* 2nd ed., Sage, Thousand Oaks, 1999, p. 32.

54. Stringer, E.T., *Action Research,* 2nd ed., Sage, Thousand Oaks, 1999, p. 19.

55. Coghlan, D. and Brannick, T., *Doing Action Research in your own Organization,* Sage, London, 2001, p. 16.

56. Coghlan, D. and Brannick, T., *Doing Action Research in your own Organization,* Sage, London, 2001, p. 63.

57. Coghlan, D. and Brannick, T., *Doing Action Research in your own Organization,* Sage, London, 2001, p. 64.

58. The learning resources for this subject include a Study Guide and readings (on CD-Rom) and a printed Subject Outline delineating assessment and other requirements.

59. Action Research and Evaluation on Line (Areol) is a 14 week on-line course offered as a public service by Southern Cross University and the Southern Cross Institute of Action Research.

60. Wenger, E., Communities of practice: learning as a social system, 1998. Retrieved from http://www.co-i-l.com/coil/knowledge-garden/cop/lss.shtml.

61. Wenger, E., *Communities of practice: learning, meaning and identity,* Cambridge University Press, Cambridge, 1998.

62. Wenger, E., McDermott, R., and Snyder, W.M., Seven principles for cultivating communities of practice, in *Cultivating communities of practice: a guide to managing knowledge,* Harvard Business School Press, 2001. Retrieved from http://hbswk.has.edu/item.jhtml?id=2866andt=entrepreneurship.

63. Lesser, E.L. and Storck, J., Communities of practice and organizational performance, *IBM Systems Journal,* 40(4), 2001.

64. Wenger, E., *Communities of practice: learning, meaning and identity,* Cambridge University Press, Cambridge, 1998, p. 46.

65. Wenger, E., *Communities of practice: learning, meaning and identity,* Cambridge University Press, Cambridge, 1998, pp. 78–89.

66. Lesser, E.L. and Storck, J., Communities of practice and organizational performance, *IBM Systems Journal,* 40(4), 832, 2001.

67. Wenger, E., *Communities of practice: learning, meaning and identity,* Cambridge University Press, Cambridge, 1998, pp. 45–46.

68. Lesser, E.L. and Storck, J., Communities of practice and organizational performance, *IBM Systems Journal*, 40(4), 834, 2001.

69. Stewart, T.A., The invisible key to success, *Fortune, 134*(3), 3, 1996. Retrieved from http://home.att.net/~discon/KM/invisible_key.htm.

70. Sharp, J., Communities of practice: a review of the literature, 4–5, 1997. Retrieved from http://www.tfriend.com/cop-lit.htm.

71. Wenger, E., *Communities of practice: learning, meaning and identity*, Cambridge University Press, Cambridge, 1998, pp. 74–75.

72. Lesser, E.L. and Storck, J., Communities of practice and organizational performance, *IBM Systems Journal*, 40(4), 834, 2001.

73. Wenger, E., *Communities of practice: learning, meaning and identity*, Cambridge University Press, Cambridge, 1998, p. 74.

74. Wenger, E., *Communities of practice: learning, meaning and identity*, Cambridge University Press, Cambridge, 1998, pp. 74–77.

75. Sharp, J., Communities of practice: a review of the literature, 1997. Retrieved from http://www.tfriend.com/cop-lit.htm.

76. Wenger, E., *Communities of practice: learning, meaning and identity*, Cambridge University Press, Cambridge, 1998, pp. 51–52.

77. Wenger, E., *Communities of practice: learning, meaning and identity*, Cambridge University Press, Cambridge, 1998, pp. 56–57.

78. Wenger, E., *Communities of practice: learning, meaning and identity*, Cambridge University Press, Cambridge, 1998, pp. 91–92.

79. Wenger, E., *Communities of practice: learning, meaning and identity*, Cambridge University Press, Cambridge, 1998, pp. 103–110.

80. Wenger, E., *Communities of practice: learning, meaning and identity*, Cambridge University Press, Cambridge, 1998, pp. 156–162.

81. Sharp, J., Key hypotheses in supporting communities of practice, 1997, 1. Retrieved from http://www.tfriend.com/hypothesis.html.

82. Crawford, cited in Cabanis-Brewin, J., Communities of practice in the projectized organisation, *Expert Series,* 2001, p. 3.

83. Wenger, E., *Communities of practice: learning, meaning and identity*, Cambridge University Press, Cambridge, 1998, pp. 150–181.

84. Wenger, E., *Communities of practice: learning, meaning and identity*, Cambridge University Press, Cambridge, 1998, p. 197.

85. Wenger, E., *Communities of practice: learning, meaning and identity*, Cambridge University Press, Cambridge, 1998, pp. 197–205.

86. Harrison, S.J., Police organizational culture: using ingrained values to build positive organizational improvement, The Pennsylvania State University 1998, 11. Retrieved from http://www/pamij.com/harrison.html.

87. Doherty, D., Building the next generation of leaders in the Royal Canadian Mounted Police, *The Canadian Review of Policing Research*, 5, 2004. Retrieved from http://crpr.icaap.org/issues/issue1/ddoherty.html.

88. Mead, G., Developing ourselves as police leaders: how can we inquire collaboratively in a hierarchical organization? In P. Reason (Ed.), Special Issue: The Practice of Cooperative Inquiry, *Systemic Practice and Action Research, 16*(3), 11, 2002. Retrieved from http://www.bath.ac.uk/carpp/SPAR?GeoffMead.htm.

24 Conflict of Interest and Police: An Unavoidable Problem

Stephen Coleman

CONTENTS

ABSTRACT

Conflicts of interest can arise for police in a number of different ways, such as through a relationship that a police officer has with someone involved in a police matter, through the financial interests of a police officer, or through other employment that an officer holds outside of the police service. Conflicts of interest are a problem for police as they may lead an officer into inappropriate or even illegal conduct, and they tend to create the appearance of bias in an organization that should appear to be strictly impartial in the discharge of its duties to the community. The usual method of dealing with a conflict of interest is to disclose the conflict, to remove the source of conflict, such as by officers divesting themselves of other financial interests, or to avoid the conflict, such as by officers distancing themselves from the particular matter of conflict. However, the very nature of policing is such that some officers, particularly those working in restricted circles, will be faced with conflicts of interest that cannot be dealt with by such means. These sorts of situations present an unavoidable problem for the police officers involved.

Over the last 20 years or so, conflicts of interest have come to be recognized as a significant problem in many professions. A recent book, *Conflict of Interest in the Professions*, edited by Michael Davis and Andrew Stark (2001) examined the problems that conflict of interest may cause in a wide range of professions, from law and government, through engineering, journalism, academia, the financial markets, and health care. In this chapter I wish to examine the problems that conflicts of interest may cause in what is now being recognized as an emerging profession, the profession of policing. Although conflicts of interest in this area share many of the problems of conflict of interest in other professions, I would suggest that there are features of police work that lead to conflict of interest problems that are in some ways unique, and are not amenable to resolution through use of the normal methods. It is this fact that leads me to suggest that conflict of interest is an unavoidable problem in policing.

WHAT IS A CONFLICT OF INTEREST?

In the introduction to *Conflict of Interest in the Professions*, Michael Davis provides what he terms "the standard view" of a conflict of interest.

> On the standard view, P has a conflict of interest if, and only if, (1) P is in a relationship with another requiring P to exercise judgment on the other's behalf and (2) P has a (special) interest tending to interfere with the proper exercise of judgment in that relationship ... on the standard view, an interest is any influence, loyalty, concern, emotion, or other feature of a situation tending to make P's judgment (in that situation) less reliable than it would normally be, without rendering P incompetent [2001, pp. 8–9].

That fact that a conflict of interest is a **tendency** is extremely important. Conflicts of interest do not always affect judgment, as P may be able to exercise P's judgment impartially despite the special interest. A conflict of interest is thus different from mere bias, though conflicts of interest and bias are often discussed together. As Davis notes, a known bias can (generally) be compensated for without difficulty, as it has a predictable effect. But conflict of interest is not bias, but is rather a tendency towards bias, which means that it is both more difficult to predict the effect of conflict of interest upon judgment, and more difficult to compensate for its effect.

One major difficulty in discussing conflicts of interest arises out of the term itself. The mere fact that two interests clash in some way—that is, that the interests are in conflict—does not mean that there is actually any conflict of interest in the technical sense of the term. My interest in spending time with my children may conflict with my interest in writing this chapter, but this does not constitute a conflict of interest, for I am not required to exercise judgment on another person's behalf.

In fact, in police work, most conflicts of interest involve a conflict between a role and an interest (an example of this might be a conflict between a police officer's role as an enforcer of the law and the officer's interest in maintaining a particular friendship), or between two roles (an example of this might be the conflict between an officer's role as a police officer and the officer's role, while off duty, as an investigative consultant), rather than a simple conflict between two interests.

It is important to remember that conflicts of interest arise only when a person is required to exercise judgment on behalf of another. If no judgment is required in a particular situation, then a conflict of interest will not pose a problem in that situation. Similarly, if I am required to exercise judgment, but only on my own behalf, and not on behalf of another person, organization, or institution, then conflicts of interest are not a problem in that situation, either.

A PROBLEM WITH THE STANDARD VIEW

There is a problem with the standard view, in that it seems to allow too much. Many things that we would not generally consider to be conflicts of interest seem to be conflicts of interest according to the standard view. The main difficulty here is in defining the sorts of things that might count as interests, which could conceivably come into conflict with the proper exercise of one's judgment. According to Davis' standard view, an interest is "any influence, loyalty, concern, emotion, or other feature of a situation tending to make P's judgment (in that situation) less reliable than it would normally be, without rendering P incompetent" (2001, pp. 8–9). But this list seems to be much too broad, for there are many things that may influence P's judgment, without making P incompetent, that we would not usually consider to be part of a conflict of interest.

Consider the following case, based on an example by Michael Pritchard (2002). Suppose that I am driving home from work, and stop at a red traffic light. The person in the car behind me has been momentarily distracted by the ringing of a mobile phone and doesn't notice that the light has turned red until it is too late to avoid crashing into the back of my car. I am likely to be upset, angry with the other driver, annoyed about the inconvenience that will be caused to me while I attempt to get my car repaired, and so on. A few minutes later I arrive home, and sit down to mark a pile of student's essays. Now marking essays is an exercise of judgment, and I am required to exercise that judgment on behalf of another; in this case, on behalf of the university that offered the subject for which these essays were submitted as assessment. I am likely to still be angry about the accident, and I would suggest that this will affect my judgment, in that I am likely to be more harsh than usual in marking these essays. Yet I am not rendered incompetent. This example seems to fit Davis' standard view, yet I think few people would be willing to call this a conflict of interest.

The difficulty seems to me to be the contingent nature of the conflict. There is no inherent conflict between my anger and the exercise of sound judgment in marking these essays. Although it may be a good idea for me to put off marking the essays until I am in a better mood, this seems to be more a question of being fair to the students than a question of conflict of interest. For something to qualify as a genuine conflict of interest, it would seem that there needs to be some **direct** conflict between the exercise of judgment on another's behalf, and, in the terms of Davis, a particular influence, loyalty, concern, emotion, or other feature of a situation tending to make a person's judgment less reliable than normal. As Michael Pritchard puts it, the exercise of judgment, and the interest influencing that judgment, must stand in some special relationship to each other: There must be an inherent conflict between them for this to really count as a conflict of interest (2002, pp. 8–9).

It has been suggested to me that even limiting the standard view of conflicts of interest in this way still leaves the definition too broad. Consider another example.* Suppose that we have a police officer who is receiving illicit payments from an organized crime boss. That police officer pulls over a vehicle for a traffic offense, and then discovers that the vehicle is being driven by that crime boss. Does the police

---

* This example was suggested to me by Andrew Alexandra.

officer have a conflict of interest? It is certainly tempting to say that there is no conflict of interest here, that the police officer should not have been accepting the payments in the first place, and that there is no question about what is the right thing for the police officer to do in this situation. A possible way to get around this problem with the standard view of conflicts of interest would be to limit oneself to only legitimate influences on judgment as being a part of a conflict of interest.

However, after much thought, I have realized that such a response is too hasty. I think that the police officer in this example does face a conflict of interest, albeit an illicit one, and a conflict entirely of the officer's own making. The officer is required to exercise judgment (for an officer does have discretion in how they deal with a traffic offense), the judgment is being exercised on another's behalf (in this case on behalf of the police service, or of society, or perhaps even of "the law"), and there is an influence upon that judgment that makes the exercise of judgment less reliable in that particular situation than it would normally be. To say that there is no question about what the officer ought to do is equivalent to dismissing the general problem of conflict of interest entirely. For one could say that in any case where someone faces a conflict of interest that there is no question about what they ought to do: They ought to exercise their judgment normally, and act as if there was no other influence acting upon their judgment. The problem is that this is, in practice, difficult to do (for one's judgment may be affected without one even realizing it) and even if I am able to entirely exclude the influence from the exercise of judgment, it may not appear, to an impartial observer, that this is actually the case—and when the person who is exercising the judgment is in a position of public trust, the appearance can be very important.

So in returning to our example of the police officer who is accepting payments from the organized crime boss, I would suggest that the police officer does face a conflict of interest when pulling that crime boss over for a traffic offense. Granted, it is a problem of the officer's own making. Granted, it is unlikely (!) that the officer will discuss this particular conflict of interest with a superior officer in order to determine the best way to resolve the conflict, but I believe that this still does represent a conflict of interest situation, and thus the standard view does not require further modification.

So to restate what we might call the revised standard view: P has a conflict of interest if, (1) P is in a relationship with another requiring P to exercise judgment on the other's behalf and (2) P has a (special) interest tending to interfere with the proper exercise of judgment in that relationship ... on the standard view, an interest is any influence, loyalty, concern, emotion, or other feature of a situation tending to make P's judgment (in that situation) less reliable than it would normally be, without rendering P incompetent and (3) there is an inherent, rather than a merely contingent, conflict between the exercise of judgment and the influence on that judgment.

HOW DO CONFLICTS OF INTEREST ARISE IN POLICE WORK?

Conflicts of interest can arise for police in a number of different ways. A conflict of interest may arise through a relationship that a police officer has with someone who is involved in a police matter, as either the victim of crime, or as the alleged offender, or even as a witness. A conflict of interest can arise through the financial dealings of a police officer, through other employment that a police officer holds outside of the police service, through volunteer work, through study commitments, or even through an officer's deeply held personal or religious beliefs.

Let me illustrate this with some examples:

A. Suppose a police officer is called to a domestic dispute that involves that officer's sister. Both parties involved in the dispute claim that the other has assaulted them. One aspect of the role of a police officer in such a situation is to impartially assess the claims of both parties and determine whether any charges should be laid. But there is a clear conflict of interest in this case, as the existing relationship with the officer's sister will tend to influence that officer's ability to act impartially.

B. Suppose a police officer is a financial partner in a restaurant located within that officer's patrol area. Strict parking regulations apply in the area near the restaurant, meaning that many of the restaurant's patrons park illegally. Part of the officer's role is to issue tickets to illegally parked cars, but if patrons of the restaurant are ticketed, then they are unlikely to return, which may have a severe effect on the profitability of the restaurant in the future. In this case, the officer's financial interests are the cause of the conflict of interest.

C. Suppose a police officer is engaged in secondary employment as a bartender at a pub that is well known for its generous support of community organizations and also for exceptionally good treatment of its employees. The owner is, understandably, extremely well liked and respected in the local community. This off-duty officer has noticed that the publican's under-age son, and a number of the son's friends (all also under-age), are regularly served alcohol in the main bar by the owner. In this case, the conflict of interest for the officer arises out of conflicting duties to the officer's two employers.

All of these examples illustrate different types of conflicts of interest that may arise for a police officer in the course of the officer's work, all involve the officer exercising judgment on behalf of another (at least in some sense), all involve an interest that will tend to interfere with the proper exercise of that judgment, and, in all cases, there is an inherent conflict between the exercise of judgment and the influence on that judgment.

WHAT PROBLEMS CAN CONFLICTS OF INTEREST CAUSE IN POLICE WORK?

Conflicts of interest can cause problems in policing in three main ways.

1. The exercise of good judgment is an integral part of the professional role of police, as it is for any profession. As conflicts of interest tend to affect the judgment of those involved in the conflict, they are thus a problem for police.

2. A police officer whose judgment is clouded by a conflict of interest may be led into inappropriate or illegal conduct.

3. Even when an officer acts completely impartially, conflicts of interest tend to create the appearance of bias in an organization that ought to appear to be, (and indeed ought to actually be) strictly impartial in the discharge of its duties to the community.

Problem (3) is particularly significant, as it exists not only in all cases of actual conflict of interest, and in all cases of potential conflict of interest, but also in all cases where there is a perceived conflict of interest, whether that perception is actually accurate or not. In fact, problem (3) is doubly significant, as it will apply in situations where either (1) or (2) also applies: if an officer's judgment is actually affected due to the conflict of interest, or if an officer is led into inappropriate conduct, these things will also have the effect of creating an impression of bias (which would, in these cases, be justified).

The appearance of bias is really only a significant problem for those in positions of public trust. In other situations, perception is not a significant problem. For example, suppose person A is not in a position of public trust, but is instead exercising judgment on behalf of another individual. This other individual, B, believes, incorrectly, that person A has a conflict of interest in dealing with a particular matter. If person B approaches A, and alleges that A had a conflict of interest in this matter, all that needs to be done to show that the judgment was not improperly influenced is for A to demonstrate to B that there was no conflict of interest in this matter.

On the other hand, when a person is in a position of public trust, the public perception of any situation will be extremely important. As it is virtually impossible to explain to all members of the public why in a particular situation where there was a perceived conflict of interest, there was not an actual conflict of interest, the only realistic way to deal with perceived conflicts of interest (whether the perception is accurate or not) is to treat them as if they were actual conflicts of interest. All those within the criminal justice system are bearers of the public trust. Police are a part of the criminal justice system, and the mere appearance of bias or impropriety within this system tends to undermine public confidence in the fair administration of justice. As the old adage goes, justice must not only be done, but must be seen to be done. Thus, it is important for police officers, and for all members of the criminal justice system, to learn to deal properly with conflicts of interest, whether these conflicts of interest are perceived conflicts, potential conflicts, or actual conflicts.

HOW TO DEAL WITH A CONFLICT OF INTEREST

There are three usual methods of dealing with a conflict of interest:

1. Declare the conflict of interest.
2. Remove the conflict of interest.
3. Avoid the conflict of interest.

In police work, merely declaring the conflict of interest is rarely (if ever) going to be a final solution; the usual course of affairs would involve informing a superior officer of the conflict of interest, and then working with that superior officer to ensure the conflict of interest is dealt with through either removal of the conflict or avoidance of the conflict. An example of removing the conflict of interest might be a police officer divesting him/herself of the financial interests that are the cause of the conflict. An example of avoiding a conflict of interest would be a police officer distancing him/herself from the particular matter where the conflict arises.

Thus, police officers who realize that they may have a conflict of interest due to their financial holdings in a particular enterprise in their local police district (as in example B, mentioned earlier) ought to inform a superior officer (usually an officer in a supervisory role) of this potential conflict of interest and then take steps to remove the conflict, either through divesting themselves of the financial stake in that enterprise, or through transferring to another district so as to remove themselves from the potential conflict of interest.

Similarly, police officers who are called to deal with a particular incident may realize that there is the potential for a conflict of interest, and take steps to distance themselves from the incident so as to avoid the conflict of interest. Thus, if a police officer was to be called to deal with a domestic disturbance at an address recognized as being the residence of a close friend or relative (as in example A mentioned earlier), then that police officer might inform the superior officer of the potential for a conflict of interest in that situation, and request that a different officer be dispatched to the scene of the domestic disturbance.

Dealing with a conflict of interest in either of these ways, through removal of the conflict or through avoidance of the conflict, deals with all three of the problems previously mentioned: the possibility of clouded judgment, the possibility that an officer may be led into corrupt conduct, and the perception of bias.

Many police departments around the world have recognized the problems that may be caused by conflict of interest and have introduced regulations that are designed to prevent some common conflicts of interest from arising. For example, some police departments have banned police from financial involvement in businesses within their patrol area, thus ruling out the possibility of conflicts of interest like example B above, from ever arising. Some departments have also regulated secondary employment, either through a total ban, by a ban on employment within certain industries (such as liquor, security, and the sex industry), or by requiring police to gain approval from superiors before undertaking any secondary employment. Such measures are designed to eliminate, or at least to minimize, the types of conflict of interest mentioned in example C.

I have suggested that police need to avoid, where possible, not only actual and potential conflicts of interest, but also perceived conflicts of interest as well, even where that perception is inaccurate. It should be noted that even in situations where police officers are not required to exercise any judgment, and thus a conflict of interest cannot possibly arise (as the exercise of judgment is an integral part of a conflict of interest), members of the public may still perceive a conflict of interest, due to their false beliefs about the situation. This is especially likely to be the case where the actions an officer is forced to take coincide with the actions that the officer would be likely to take if the officer was acting under the influence of some bias.

For example, consider a modified version of case A. Suppose an officer is called to a domestic dispute involving his sister, and it is absolutely clear in this particular situation that the sister has been assaulted by her spouse. Let us also suppose that in this jurisdiction, an officer is required to arrest in all domestic violence situations where there is evidence that an assault has occurred. The officer has no option but to place the sister's spouse under arrest; there is thus no exercise of judgment in this situation, and thus there is no actual conflict of interest. Yet I think it is quite clear that the sister's spouse will perceive a conflict of interest in this situation—that it will appear that the officer's judgment in the situation is biased, and thus that the public trust has been violated. Police policies regarding conflict of interest need to take situations like this into account. Such policies need to deal with actual, potential, and perceived conflicts of interest if they are to be of any real value.

Although it is possible to create regulations that prevent some types of conflicts of interest from arising, other types of conflicts, like the one illustrated in example A (in both its original and modified versions), are much more difficult to prevent through simple regulation. In these types of situations, police officers are expected to deal with conflicts of interest themselves in one of the usual ways. But what happens in situations where a conflict of interest can neither be avoided nor removed?

POLICING IN RESTRICTED CIRCLES

The very nature of policing is such that some officers, particularly those police working in restricted circles, will be faced with conflicts of interest that cannot be dealt with by such means. These sorts of situations present an unavoidable problem for the police officers involved.

D. Suppose a police officer is working alone in a small town, with a population of a few hundred people. Within a reasonably short period of time, the police officer has come to know literally everyone in town, and has formed friendships with some of the residents of the town. Now suppose one of the friends of the police officer becomes involved in an altercation in a public bar, and police attendance is required.

Such a situation fits the "revised standard view" of a conflict of interest perfectly: the police officer is required to exercise judgment in this matter, on behalf of someone else (in this case on behalf of the community), but the officer has a special interest in the situation that tends to interfere with the proper exercise of his/her judgment, and there is a direct relationship between the exercise of judgment and the influence upon that judgment. The conflict of interest cannot be removed, for the relationship between the police officer and the officer's friend already exists. The conflict of interest cannot be avoided either, as police presence is required, and our officer is the only officer in town. The police officer can certainly declare the conflict of interest, but to whom should the conflict of interest be declared? There is no realistic way of declaring the conflict of interest to a superior and requesting assistance in dealing with the matter. Declaring the conflict of interest to the parties involved in the case doesn't seem a solution to the problem either; in all likelihood those involved already know of the friendship anyway.

It appears that the only possible solution is for the police officer to deal with the situation despite a relationship with one of the parties involved in the dispute, and for the officer to try to be as impartial as possible. Yet such a solution will run headlong into the third of the major problems that conflicts of interest can cause in policing: the appearance of bias in the judgment of one who ought to be impartial.

Consider another example:

E. Let us suppose that the jurisdiction with which we are dealing is somewhat larger than in example D, and that there are a total of about twenty police officers working out of a particular station, with between five and ten officers on duty at any one time. One particular night, six officers are on duty, with two car crews of two officers each, and the remaining two officers, including the senior officer on duty, manning the police station. It is a busy night, with a reasonably large number of calls for police assistance, and the officers are kept very busy. One particular crew is called to attend a motor vehicle accident where two cars have collided at a major intersection. No one has been injured, but there is substantial property damage, with both vehicles undriveable and obstructing the intersection. Upon arrival at the scene of the accident, the senior officer in the car realizes that the driver of one of the vehicles is his mother-in-law. He immediately informs the other officers present, and the senior officer on duty, of the conflict of interest. Unfortunately, the other car crew is involved in dealing with another case, of an attempted sexual assault, and neither of the other officers on duty can leave the station.

How can a conflict of interest like this be dealt with? The other officer present at the scene of the accident can take the primary role in dealing with the incident, but this is only a partial solution at best, for both officers will have to be involved in dealing with a situation such as this. The mere presence at the accident of the officer with the conflict of interest is likely to have an effect on how the incident is handled, and if/when the driver of the other vehicle becomes aware of the relationship, the problem of apparent bias again becomes an issue.

The examples that I have given are not unrealistic; in fact, the first example is quite common in many jurisdictions around the world. The police in both of these cases are faced with a conflict of interest that can be declared, but not removed or avoided. Such cases are not uncommon in situations where police are working in restricted circles, such as in small towns or villages, in small police departments, in small specialized units (such as gaming, liquor licensing, or vice squads) or even on night shifts in major cities. When the pool of available police is small, it often becomes very difficult for a police officer to hand over to other officers jobs that involve the officer in a conflict of interest. Thus, the conflicts of interest become unavoidable. The only option in such situations is to disclose the conflict of interest, but as I shall demonstrate, this is not actually a solution for a conflict of interest in policing.

In many professions, recognizing the existence of a conflict of interest, and declaring that conflict of interest to the relevant involved parties, may be sufficient to deal with the problems that the conflict of interest raises. In other professions, however, recognizing and declaring a conflict of interest is an essential first step in dealing with the conflict, but it does not actually solve the problem. So, although it may be sufficient for a financial planner to disclose the nature and extent of any commission that the planner may receive for "selling" certain financial products, it is not sufficient for judges to simply disclose that they have a conflict of interest in a case over which they are about to preside. Why is this situation a particular problem for a judge? As I have already mentioned, it is a problem because the very nature of the justice system requires that court proceedings are conducted in a fair and impartial manner. In fact, any perception of bias within the process is generally taken to be grounds for an appeal.* Not only must the scales of justice be evenly balanced, but justice herself must be blind.

Police officers face many of the same conflict of interest problems as judges. Both police and judges are members of the criminal justice system, where, as we have seen, the mere appearance of impropriety can be a serious problem. Both the police and the judiciary are limited in the ways in which they can deal with a conflict of interest, with avoidance of conflicts of interest the most fruitful strategy for dealing with problems.

Perhaps the biggest difference between the conflict of interest problems facing judges and police officers is in their relative capacities to avoid conflicts of interest. Judges usually know what cases they will preside over and can usually see potential conflicts of interest approaching. When a conflict of interest does arise, avoidance is always a viable option, as another judge can always be found, cases can be postponed if necessary, and the courts can exercise control over the scheduling of cases to ensure that conflicts of interest are appropriately dealt with. Even in cases where there is only a single judge or magistrate in a particular town, it is still possible for this judge to avoid cases that will cause a conflict of interest, for such cases can be relocated to another town, under the jurisdiction of another judge, or they can be deferred until another judge is available to come to the town to preside over the case.

Police, on the other hand, rarely (if ever) know in advance what problems they will have to deal with, as issues requiring police attention can arise at a moment's notice. In any case, it is rare that a conflict of interest is revealed before a police officer arrives at the scene of an incident, by which time genuine avoidance of the conflict is no longer an option. Few police matters can simply be postponed until another officer is available; most matters require at least some kind of on-the-spot solution. Police are able to exercise little control over the incidents that they will have to deal with; generally speaking, police must simply go where and when they are called. Although it is true that in many cases more than one officer is present, and so an officer with a conflict of interest can distance him/herself somewhat from the incident, this falls far short of real avoidance of the conflict as the officer is still at the scene.

Consider a parallel example of this sort, well known to members of ethics committees. Imagine that a research proposal has been submitted to the ethics committee for approval, and that one of the chief investigators of the research project (who I

---

* It should also be noted that any perception of conflict of interest would be sufficient for a person being disbarred from acting as a juror on a particular case, or, if the trial has already commenced, then a juror's apparent conflict of interest would be sufficient to ensure a mistrial.

will call Professor X) is himself a member of the ethics committee. There is an obvious conflict of interest here, which can only be dealt with by Professor X removing himself from the discussion of the proposal. But is it appropriate for Professor X to be present while the proposal is being discussed? I would suggest that the mere presence of Professor X will have some influence on the committee, and thus Professor X should leave the room while the research project is being discussed. In a similar way, police officers faced with a conflict of interest ought to remove themselves from the scene of the incident. But as I have already mentioned, in many cases this is not possible, and thus even though the police officer may allow a partner to take the leading role in dealing with the incident, the mere presence of the other officer is likely to have some effect on the outcome.

Some apparently unavoidable conflicts of interest can be dealt with by shifting the exercise of judgment to another officer, even in cases where there is no other officer present at the scene. If the incident does not require an immediate discretionary decision, then it is possible for the officer at the scene, upon recognizing the conflict of interest, to defer judgment on the matter to the officer's superior, with the judgment to be made at a later point in time. For example, in case E, it may be possible for the officers at the scene to simply clear the intersection and gather information about the accident, and then pass all of this information on to a superior officer. This superior can then exercise his/her judgment, unclouded by conflict of interest, to assess whether either of the two drivers ought to be ticketed or charged.

Unfortunately, such a solution is not always feasible, for two main reasons. In many cases, an immediate discretionary decision—an exercise of judgment—will be required. For example, the officer(s) on the scene will have to make a decision as to whether or not it is necessary to make an arrest; a decision that can not usually be deferred until later. The other problem with an officer attempting to resolve a conflict of interest by passing the judgment on to a superior officer is that in many jurisdictions awareness of the problems caused by conflict of interest is low. Thus, it is quite likely that superior officers will fail to recognize the conflict of interest issues and will simply insist that junior officers, as the officers present at the scene of the incident, ought to exercise their own judgment in the matter.

When a police officer faces a conflict of interest that cannot be avoided in any of these ways, then the only option available is complete transparency, so that all can see if any bias has crept into the judgment of the officer. Although officers who are involved in cases that contain unavoidable conflict of interest cannot be blamed for their actions as they had no choice but to be involved in the matter, such cases do still cause problems, because the existence of the conflict of interest can give the impression of bias even where no bias exists. The impression of bias in such a case equates to an impression that the public trust has been violated by the officer. The officer has done no moral wrong, for the situation was forced upon the officer, but the officer still needs to be aware of the problems that may result from unavoidable involvement.

THE UNIQUENESS OF POLICE CONFLICTS OF INTEREST

So what is so important about conflicts of interest and police? What is it about conflicts of interest involving police that make them worth examining in such detail?

It is certainly not the case that all police situations involving a conflict of interest are unable to be appropriately dealt with. Many conflict of interest situations can be either avoided, or removed. There are other police situations that do not call for the exercise of any judgment or where the exercise of judgment can be deferred to another officer, and thus conflict of interest issues can be avoided. However, there will always be some situations where police will find themselves faced with a conflict of interest that cannot be avoided, and where an on-the-spot exercise of judgment is required. It is those sorts of issues that make conflict of interest in policing so difficult to deal with.

I have already suggested that police are often involved in situations where an immediate response is required. Yet there are other professions where this is also the case, such as in the medical profession. I have suggested that in police work there is the necessity not just for impartiality but also for the appearance of impartiality. Yet other professionals, such as judges, share this need for the appearance of impartiality. I have suggested that police are in a profession where there is a distinct lack of foreseeability of conflicts of interest arising, which tends to make conflicts of interest apparent only after an officer's initial involvement in an incident. But, again, this does not set policing apart, for emergency medical practitioners can also find themselves in the same position. I have suggested that there is a lack of resources available to aid police in avoiding conflicts of interest, but again this is not unique to policing.

What is unique to the profession of policing is the type of work that police officers actually do, and the means that police officers are required to use in order to carry out their duties. An extremely important part of the duty of a police officer (some, such as Bittner [1985], would even say an integral part) is the capacity to use force when required. To express this idea in different terms, it is part of the duties of a police officer for that officer to violate people's rights. A police officer violates a person's rights when the officer places that person under arrest. An officer violates a person's rights when they execute a search warrant, when they use force, when they stop and search a pedestrian on the street, when they stop a person's vehicle, and so on. All of these violations of rights will be justified and legal if the officer is carrying out their duty appropriately. In some circumstances, it will even be appropriate for a police officer to violate that most fundamental of rights—a person's right to life.

The fact that police are duty-bound to violate people's rights, up to and including the right to life, sets policing apart from any other profession. Few other professionals are faced with the duty to cause harm to others. Other professions may involve life and death matters, but these will usually only involve trying to save people's lives (as in medicine) rather than in actually causing the death of another person. Although it is true that judges may be involved in trials where death is a possible penalty for the accused, the judge will not be the one carrying out the sentence, and in fact in most jurisdictions, will not actually be the person who decides if the death penalty is to be levied against the accused, as this is usually part of the role of the jury. In fact, the only other professionals that are likely to be faced with a duty to cause physical harm to other people are members of the military and prison officers.

I would suggest that members of neither of these two professions are likely to face situations of unavoidable conflict of interest. The role of the military is to protect the nation from external threats. As the threats are external, there is little likelihood of an unavoidable conflict of interest arising for a member of the military during normal operations. Although unavoidable conflicts of interest might easily arise if the military were being used to enforce martial law, I would argue that in such a situation the military are taking on the role of the police, and thus also take on the inherent problems of that role.

Prison officers, like police, may often be placed in situations where they are required to violate the rights of other people; the very nature of a prison is, of course, to ensure that the right to liberty of the prisoners is violated. Prison officers may in some circumstances be duty-bound to use deadly force—for example to prevent the escape of a prisoner. Yet, although the role of prison officers shares these problems with police, it is unlikely that a prison officer will be faced with an unavoidable conflict of interest while they are on duty. As the prison system affords almost total control over the movements of the prisoners, it is relatively easy for conflicts of interest for prison officers to be avoided, once those conflicts come to light. For example, if a prison officer has a relative who is serving a custodial sentence, there would be a clear conflict of interest for the officer if that relative was to be imprisoned in the officer's care. But once this potential conflict of interest is declared, it is a relatively simple matter for the conflict to be avoided—for example, by sending the officer's relative to a different prison.

Thus, it can be seen that police officers are in a unique position among the professions. No other professionals whose duty includes the violation of the rights of others will face unavoidable conflicts of interest. No other professionals who face unavoidable conflicts of interest will be duty-bound to violate the rights of others.

If a person is required, as part of their duty, to violate the rights of others, then conflicts of interest that arise in that duty will be extremely important. It is a serious enough business for a police officer to have to exercise judgment, on behalf of the community, about whether or not to violate the fundamental rights of another person; having the additional complication of a conflict of interest, which will tend to influence the exercise of that judgment, is really asking too much of any person. Yet as I have shown, it is the profession of policing, where judgments of a most serious nature are likely to have to be made, where conflicts of interest are going to be, in at least some circumstances, unavoidable. It is this that makes conflicts of interest in the profession of policing so worthy of detailed examination.*

REFERENCES

Bittner, E. (1985). The capacity to use force as the core of the police role. In F. Elliston & M. Feldberg (eds.), *Moral Issues in Police Work* (pp.15–26). Totowa, NJ: Rowman & Littlefield.
Davis, M. & Stark, A. (eds.) (2001). *Conflict of Interest in the Professions.* New York: Oxford.
Davis, M. (2001). Introduction. In M. Davis & A. Stark (eds.), *Conflict of Interest in the Professions* (pp. 3–19). New York: Oxford.
Pritchard, M.S. (2002). Conflict of interest: the very idea. *Research Integrity*, 5, 6–10.

---

* I would like to thank John Kleinig, Nikki Coleman, Andrew Alexandra, and Seumas Miller for their insightful comments on earlier versions of this paper.

25 Understanding and Managing Professional Distance

Anna Corbo Crehan

CONTENTS

Also known in some professions as *professional boundaries, professional distance* refers to an obligation (or set of obligations) that derives from the nature of the professional role. More specifically, it refers to *particular* obligations that professionals have to ensure that their professional relationships with clients are not compromised. Of course, many things can compromise professional relationships: professionals putting their needs before the client's needs, a lack of impartiality on the part of the professional, and any actions on the part of professionals that compromise a client's trust in them. Professional distance is concerned with a subset of the things that can compromise professional relationships, *viz.*, a subset relating to personal relationships that exist in addition to professional relationships. That is, professional distance refers to an obligation (or set thereof) which professionals have to ensure that any additional relationship they have with a client does not compromise their professional relationship with that client.

In the policing context, there are many areas in which professional distance issues can occur. These include between police and victims, between police of different ranks, and between police trainers and police recruits. Some of these areas (e.g., when police of different ranks have both a personal and professional relationship with each other) are specific to the policing context, having no precise parallels in other professions.

In this chapter, I outline the reasons why professionals have obligations in relation to professional distance, and detail why breaches of this obligation are wrong. I then focus the rest of the chapter on various issues surrounding the management of professional distance, including what sorts of restrictions managers can justifiably impose on their staff. Throughout this discussion, issues specific to the context of police work will be identified and resolved.

EXPLAINING PROFESSIONAL DISTANCE OBLIGATIONS

I do not want to get entangled in a lengthy discussion of what constitutes a profession, so I will take as uncontroversial the three key characteristics of a profession as spelled out by Fullinwider (noting that others, e.g., Ardagh [2003], have developed far more detailed sets of characteristics). These three key characteristics are: (1) "performance for public good," (2) "special knowledge and training," and (3) the fact "that other people are rendered especially vulnerable or dependent in their relationship to the practice of the professional" (2002, p. 73). We can derive from these three characteristics a key professional obligation: to act in an objective and impartial manner so that the power imbalance between professional and client is not used to the client's detriment (e.g., by poor use of the professional's specialized knowledge and discretionary decision-making capacity, or by any other actions or omissions that are exploitative of their clients' vulnerability).

Professional distance, as used in this chapter, refers to the contours this obligation has in a situation where a professional has an additional relationship with client. Maintaining an appropriate professional distance is a way of ensuring that the integrity of a professional relationship is preserved, despite the power imbalance between professionals and their clients. Professional distance, then, is not necessarily one and the same thing in all contexts. Rather, it is whatever—in a given professional context—will ensure that the power imbalance between professional and client is regulated in a way that does not infringe on the integrity of the professional relationship.

Clearly, then, professional distance is derived from the nature of the professional role itself. Additional private or personal relationships with a client have the potential to interfere with professionals' ability to be independent and objective in their decision-making; that is, they can make a professional liable to use power for reasons relevant to a personal relationship, rather than for reasons with a sound professional basis. Moreover, such relationships could incline a professional to decisions aimed at serving some private interest rather than the public interest.

Professional distance, then, obliges a professional to keep personal and professional relationships properly separated so that the professional relationship is not undermined— that is, so that the professional can discharge the key obligation identified earlier and, indeed, be *seen* to discharge that obligation. If the professional can create a "space" between professional and personal obligations to a client, it can be ensured that those two sets of obligations are not unduly influenced by each other. So long as this "space" can be maintained, there should be no question that the professional relationship is being undertaken in the right way and for the right reasons—in particular, that it is being undertaken in a way which honours the client's trust in the professional.

Two further explanatory points:

> First, ensuring that this obligation to maintain professional distance is discharged includes ensuring that it is seen to be discharged. This requirement is two-pronged: one, the professional should not be seen to do anything that would create the perception that they were *not* discharging it. Trust will be undermined if professionals give the impression—even inadvertently—that they are not concerned to honour their clients' trust, whether or not this impression is borne out in reality. And, also, where a professional makes a decision for the purpose of maintaining professional distance, that the rationale for this decision is explained to relevant parties (e.g., if persons remove themselves from a board hearing a misconduct case against their relative, they should inform the chair of that board of the reason for their decision). Without such an explanation, although the obligation to maintain professional distance is "formally" discharged, it is not discharged in a way which makes it clear that it has been discharged.
>
> Second, so far we have not clearly differentiated the terms *additional* and *personal and private* relationships that a professional has with a client. Henceforth, it might be useful to limit ourselves to the term *additional relationship*. Generally speaking, of course, this additional relationship will be what we commonly refer to as a *personal relationship*. However, to use this latter term may be unnecessarily limiting. For example, a professional who has a brother-in-law as a client clearly has an additional relationship with the brother-in-law, just because of a sister's marriage to him, but they may not agree that they have a personal relationship due to, for instance, a falling out which has constrained nonprofessional contact between them. In the following, then, we will refer to *additional relationships*, rather than private or personal relationships, that a professional has with a client.

The brother-in-law example also brings to light an important point implied throughout the foregoing, which is that whether or not an action, behaviour, attitude, etc., breaches professional distance is not a function of the *intentions* of the professional. That is, breaches of professional distance are not limited to actions which intentionally breach such distance. They can also occur accidentally and unintentionally and probably negligently. Certainly, intentions, or lack thereof, may have a significant impact on judgments about moral culpability in relation to breaches of professional distance and determinations of what constitutes a just response to such breaches, but they do not impact on whether or not something *compromises* a professional relationship.

In sum, then, the obligation to preserve professional distance derives from the nature of the professional role, in particular from the objectivity and impartiality a professional is required to show to a client, mindful of the power imbalance between the two parties. Specifically, professional distance refers to the obligation to ensure an additional relationship with a client does not (and is not seen to) impact improperly on the professional relationship.

WHY ARE BREACHES OF PROFESSIONAL DISTANCE WRONG?

Breaches of professional distance are wrong in themselves, in that they interfere with a core obligation definitive of a professional, as explained above. Put another way, they undermine (or worse) the integrity of the professional relationship between professional and client. Such breaches also produce a number of bad consequences, which constitute additional reasons for ensuring that the appropriate professional distance is maintained. Clearly such breaches will call the professional's integrity into question, undermining their credibility with colleagues, clients and others. And this, in turn, may have a direct bearing on the extent to which they can fulfill their professional duties (e.g., a lawyer whose credibility in relation to client confidentiality was undermined would have trouble attracting clients and, thus, being able to practice at all). The profession itself may suffer as a result of an individual professional's diminished credibility (this is particularly the case in professions such as policing where the public are more likely to see police as representative members of the relevant service itself, rather than as autonomous individuals). The client may have their own credibility and integrity questioned if professional distance is not maintained (e.g., a person may be presumed to be passing a subject, or to have earned a job, only because of the patronage of the professional with whom they are in an additional relationship rather than on their own merits—which, in turn, could deleteriously affect their future study and employment opportunities). And, finally, the professional may more easily resort to wrongdoing of some sort due to the pressures caused by not maintaining the relevant professional distance (e.g., marking your nephew's work against a higher standard than others in the class to avoid any perception that he may have been marked "softly"—clearly unfair to your nephew and a form of wrongdoing).

The obligation to ensure professional distance means that there is good reason to rule out or limit the sorts of things that constitute or lead to breaches of professional distance. The key question then is what sorts of things are justified *qua* means of limiting and/or ruling out breaches of professional distance? For it is surely not true that any means at all will be justified; some will surely constitute too significant a breach of a professional's rights. The question then becomes: What can we legitimately expect of professionals in terms of ensuring professional distance in situations where they have an additional relationship with a client? Or, put another way, what can those in a position to manage, supervise, or otherwise influence a professional's behavior (e.g., professional organisations, codes of ethics and, in the policing context, the officer/supervisor role) legitimately impose on them for the sake of ensuring professional distance is kept?

Initially, the question of what constitutes a justifiable restriction on a professional vis-à-vis professional distance must turn on the issue of what a given professional can actually do to preserve professional distance. It would be morally unacceptable to expect professionals to preserve a professional distance in a way which was not achievable by them. And this draws our attention to a key distinction amongst the sorts of additional relationships that a professional may have with clients, *viz.*, the distinction between those additional relationships that the professional and client choose to form, and those additional relationships where no such choice is possible.

TWO KEY TYPES OF *ADDITIONAL* RELATIONSHIPS

What constitutes a justifiable restriction on a professional for the purposes of maintaining professional distance will differ depending on whether or not the professional has a choice about the additional relationship's existence. For ease of expression, I will refer to additional relationships that professionals do not have a choice about forming as Type N relationships, and additional relationships over which professionals can exercise a choice will be referred to as Type C relationships.

The clearest instances of Type N relationships are those involving family: We cannot choose who our parents, siblings, aunts, uncles, etc., are, nor can we choose not to be related to all these people.[1] This is also true for estranged relatives—these people will remain relatives however deep and entrenched the estrangement. In-laws "acquired" by one's own marriage also fit Type N (admittedly, we have a choice whether to marry a particular person or not—but once we make that choice, we cannot choose which people will or will not count as our in-laws).[2]

It might also appear to be the case that Type N relationships should be more broadly characterised than this. Consider: to a significant extent, the forming of relationships isn't a matter of *will* alone. That is, falling in love with someone is not simply a matter of *choosing* to be in love with them, of willing it to be the case that you *are* in love with them. Similarly, being friends with someone is not simply a matter of *choosing* to be friends with them, of *willing* it to be the case that you are friends with them. It would take me too far from the topic of this chapter to think about what the "secret ingredient" is that makes two people fall in love or that means we form friendships with some people but not with others. For my purposes here, the important point about this secret ingredient that makes some people "click" and ensures that others do not "click" at all is simply that it seems to mitigate against a person fully having a choice about which relationships they will form.

On the other hand, though, we should be careful not to overstate the extent to which this "secret ingredient" mitigates *against* choice in the forming of relationships. For it is also true that people may "click" with another but decide not to form a friendship with them, or that a person may fall in love with another but decide not to get involved in a relationship with them. Examples include situations where a person does not admit to another that they have fallen in love with them because of an imminent move overseas that would make the relationship difficult. Or where a person chooses not to let a budding friendship develop once they find out that the other person is their ex-husband's new girlfriend—because such a friendship might prove "difficult" in a number of ways.

So, while there's a level at which our choices about friends, lovers, etc., are not entirely a matter of our own will (and, to that extent, not entirely "free" choices), it is also true that there is another level at which we *can* will it to be the case whether or not a certain relationship proceeds and develops. And I believe this other level gives us sufficient reason not to classify relationships with our friends and those we are otherwise attracted to as being Type N relationships. That is, I believe it would be wrong to say that these relationships are ones which we do *not* have a choice about forming or ending—in which case, they properly belong in Type C.

In sum, then, when we look carefully at the nature of the various relationships we might have, what becomes apparent is that the number of relationships that fall *outside* the sphere of the professional's choice or will is relatively small. In general, Type N includes only family and family-derived relationships: these are the only ones of which we can say relatively unambiguously that we do *not* exercise a choice in terms of forming or ending them.

So, what about Type C relationships, those relationships that we do have a choice about forming? We've just argued that relationships with friends and those we love should be included in this category, since there is a considerable element of choice in the forming of them. So, therefore, should relationships based on sexual attraction, possibly even those of a transient nature (the proverbial "one night stand"). These are also relationships that we can make decisions about ending (unlike most family relationships): though we cannot will it to be the case that we *are* in a relationship with someone, we can will it to be the case that we are *not* in such a relationship, i.e., we can choose to take steps to end a relationship. And, indeed, this is even the case when we really want the relationship to proceed but believe it should not, despite our feelings for that person.

Also included in Type C are those relationships that we *could* form based on our relationships with others, e.g., relationships with people our daughter studies with, relationships with colleagues of our partner, a relationship with a colleague from work. These, too, are relationships over which we can exercise significant choice—to the extent of deciding not to form the relationship at all. Of course, this does not mean that we should not be civil or polite to these people; it just means that we have the opportunity to decide whether or not to have a "full-fledged" relationship with them.

POLICE OFFICERS AND ADDITIONAL RELATIONSHIPS

What sorts of additional relationships raise issues of professional distance for police officers? Clearly, there are more possible additional relationships that police officers can have than we can single out here. This section will therefore focus only on the key areas in which both additional Type C and additional Type N relationships can be problematic.

Some of the more obvious potentially problematic areas are: additional relationships police have with victims, additional relationships between police and witnesses, additional relationships with offenders and suspects, and those police have with policing students (both before the latter are sworn in as police officers—say, at the relevant police academy—and post-swearing-in, where more experienced police officers take responsibility for the further training of the junior officer in the field[3]). Bearing in mind that professional distance issues arise because of the power imbalance between professional and client (created by the professional's expertise and the client's need for that expertise and vulnerability to the professional's decisions) identifying the above as relevant additional relationships seems uncontentious.

What about relationships police have with their colleagues, with other police?[4] The hierarchical characterizes police services arguably institutionalises a number of specific power imbalances, such as the power imbalances between police of differing rank.[5] Although it might not be true that people of higher rank are necessarily experts in a particular area of policing (particularly as seniority can sometimes remove police from operational police-work), it is the case that the rank structure makes those in lower ranks vulnerable to the power and authority vested in those of higher rank. To this extent, then, the higher/lower police officer power imbalance largely mirrors the professional/client power imbalance, thus triggering similar sorts of concerns about professional distance in both cases. In sum, where colleagues are of different rank, and are engaged in an additional relationship, there is an obligation to ensure that professional distance is maintained.

Note that the preceding sentence doesn't address who exactly has responsibility for ensuring professional distance. In a typical professional–client relationship, the responsibility for ensuring professional distance falls on the professional (and not the client). In the case of policing colleagues with an additional relationship, both parties are professionals—so does this mean that both are responsible for ensuring that the obligation to maintain professional distance is discharged and, if so, are both equally responsible in this regard? As professionals, it seems reasonable to me that both parties to the relationship be responsible for ensuring the discharge of this obligation. However, if professional obligations are triggered by considerations of relative power, it also seems reasonable to say that the higher-ranked party will have more responsibility in this respect.[6]

An issue is still left unresolved by the above: if a police officer has an additional relationship with an officer of the same rank, is there a power imbalance which would trigger professional distance considerations? At first glance, the answer seems to be no. However, it is possible that power imbalances can exist even in this situation—e.g., the seniority of a constable with 6 years' experience compared to their colleague constable's 2 years' experience, would presumably lead to imbalances in power. Perhaps we need to conclude in this situation that the decision as to whether a power imbalance exists will need to be settled on a case-by-case basis that takes into account seniority as well as rank. More to the point, however, if we conclude that in a given situation where an additional relationship exists between officers of the same rank, and there is no power imbalance to trigger professional distance obligations, this does not entitle us to conclude that the issue of professional distance obligations is settled once and for all. If one party is promoted to a rank higher than that held by the other party—thus creating a power imbalance between the two—then obligations to preserve professional distance will come into play and need to be addressed.

Typically, then, police can have additional relationships with policing students (sworn and unsworn), colleagues (of same or different rank), and members of a group comprising victims, witnesses, offenders, and suspects. And all of these can be of either Type N (e.g., the officer who instructs at the academy and is an uncle to a student, the officer whose brother is also in the job, the officer whose sister-in-law is a high risk offender), or Type C.

With these clarifications in mind, we can now return to the matter of identifying what possibilities are justified as a means of limiting or ruling out breaches of professional distance.

MANAGING FOR PROFESSIONAL DISTANCE

Specifically, our question here is what sorts of responses are justified for those managing for professional distance, i.e., those responsible for identifying justifiable means of limiting and/or ruling out breaches of professional distance? It is not possible to anticipate all the situations in which a professional may face professional distance issues, much less predict the various ways open to them for resolving those issues. Therefore, the discussion in this section must necessarily be limited. At this point, I will begin focusing solely on the issue of whether banning the formation of additional Type C relationships is an ethically justifiable strategy to be imposed on a police professional. This limiting of the discussion stems not only from the need to pare down the area of discussion to something manageable but also from the fact that the policing context has some specific characteristics that other professions do not, and from the fact that banning relationships that have the potential to be problematic is a response consistent with the command and control regime of many modern police services. Pertinent, also, is the fact that banning the relevant sorts of additional relationships is simply not an option applicable to additional Type N relationships.

Is it justifiable for police supervisors and managers to make rules precluding additional Type C relationships? This would certainly bring about a radical resolution of professional distance issues; if there are no additional relationships in the first place, there can be no question of having to maintain professional distance in relation to them! But ethical issues cannot be settled merely by appeals to practical expediency.

Morally, such a restriction would constitute a serious interference with a police officer's liberty and autonomy—what we are wont these days to call their "private space." And I think we could only justify such a restriction if it were the case that the harm associated with breaches (and perceived breaches) of professional distance are so significantly damaging that they outweigh the harm caused by the restriction of a professional's liberty and autonomy.[7] I believe it is true that breaches of professional distance can result in significant harms, a number of which were noted earlier when we discussed why breaches of professional distance are wrong. Moreover, such harm can be magnified due to the fact that members of the public often see police officer as being, as it were, interchangeable with each other—i.e., rather than seeing all officers as individuals, generalising the actions of one over all others. In this way, an isolated breach of professional distance may significantly impact on all other officers, for example, by undermining the credibility of officers not involved in the matter, making all officers appear less trustworthy, or creating the suggestion that officers' actions generally stem from inappropriate motives.

Are these situations so significantly harmful that avoidance of them altogether (avoidance of even the possibility of them) outweighs the harm that the required restriction of the professional's liberty and autonomy would cause?

I believe the answer here is a firm "maybe"! Clearly, some of the possible dangers are, indeed, significantly harmful (e.g., a case being lost because of an additional relationship between a victim and police officer). But it seems possible to imagine harm that is not so harmful and which would therefore be less likely to outweigh the negatives caused by restricting an officer's liberty and autonomy (e.g., an instructor forgetting to declare that his lover is a member of the class he is teaching, but remembering to make such a declaration before any assessment occurs). Perhaps a clearer example is one from the jurisdiction of New South Wales (NSW). Here, students undertake a university course for their recruit and probationary constable training. Say a breach of professional distance occurs, and a student is required to leave their course. For nonpolice university students in NSW, this harm might not be too great: perhaps they just enrol at another university, collect the credits from work already completed, and carry on with their studies as before. But for students undertaking the course to become police officers in NSW, it is not only the specific course of study that is lost, but it is also the opportunity to join the NSW Police Force, as there is no other course which provides this opportunity. A student cannot leave the policing course and continue with their proposed (and perhaps cherished) career with the NSW Police Force—this, then, is a more significant harm than for the student who simply changes universities and carries on virtually regardless.

What all of the above indicates is that, in the absence of facts about a specific situation, we are virtually in the dark as to the consequences that might flow from a breach of professional distance and, therefore, equally in the dark as to whether those consequences would outweigh the harm caused by the restrictions necessary to ban the possibility of such breaches occurring. This would then appear to justify the conclusion that we cannot muster up an *a priori* argument that would justify employers, professional bodies or others making rules that would require professionals to avoid or discontinue certain relationships.

This does not stop us from further pursuing the general question. Note that the conclusion of the preceding paragraph is limited to employers, professional bodies, and those in related responsibilities. Is there anyone else who might logically have an interest in imposing such a restriction? The professionals themselves have such an interest. And (helpfully!) the ethical issues about restrictions on liberty and autonomy that we discussed earlier are significantly reduced if persons restrict their own autonomy or liberty so as to better access the goods they have identified as critical for their lives. If professionals restrict themselves in relation to additional Type C relationships, this lessens the importance of having to demonstrate the relative significance of the harm caused by breaches of professional distance—as we are less obliged (if at all) to demonstrate that the consequent restrictions on liberty and autonomy are justified.

Why should the professional have this interest? It seems that the following may be true: Professionals who are properly mindful of their obligations should also be properly mindful of the sorts of things that can adversely impact on those obligations—and they ought to feel obliged to avoid those things. So then, the problems caused when professional distance is breached, or is perceived to be breached, should provide professionals with compelling reasons for avoiding or discontinuing any relevant Type C relationships. Conversely, there should be no need for rules set by employers or professional bodies, because professionals themselves should be self-regulating in this respect. As individual professionals, they ought to recognise and avoid the problems that actual and perceived breaches of professional distance cause—even to the extent of ending or not forming relevant sorts of Type C relationships *which will make the avoidance of these problems difficult.*[8]

In fact, I believe we can strengthen the reasoning for why professionals ought to make such a decision. The point is difficult to explain, but I believe it is important. Type C relationships are ones that can be avoided and that have the potential to raise issues of professional distance. Of prime concern is that the decision not to avoid them may create the perception for others that the professional is prepared to risk the actualization of that potential—they are prepared to risk the sorts of harm that breaches of professional distance can cause. More strongly, I believe the prepared-ness to take this risk is characteristic of what it is for a professional to decide to be party to a relevant sort of Type C relationship. Put another way, if the professional was sufficiently mindful of the problems that professional distance raises, why risk them occurring? That they risk the occurrence of those problems suggests that they are obviously *not* sufficiently mindful of their professional obligations in terms of maintaining professional distance.

How much weight should we put on this perception? Is it actually grounds for a *reasonable suspicion* that the professional is not paying serious enough attention to the problems that breaches of professional distance may cause? I do not believe it matters whether or not the perception is reasonable. If I am right that such a percep-tion may exist, then whether or not it is reasonable is beside the point—because the mere fact of its existence (reasonable or not) will be sufficient to create the sorts of problems that occur when professional distance is not seen to be kept.

In short, then, there do seem to be very good reasons for professionals to impose on themselves a commitment to discontinuing or avoiding in the first place the sorts of additional Type C relationships that will raise issues of professional distance. Put another way, there are good reasons for professionals to decide to absent themselves from being party to an additional Type C relationship, reasons that should be clear to someone taking professional obligations seriously.

If these good reasons exist then, are we saying that professionals should act on them, that they should absent themselves from relationships as per the preceding paragraph? I believe this would be an overstatement. This can only be true if the "good reasons" we have identified for professionals acting in this way are not only "good" but unassailable. Will it definitely be the case that professionals who engage in additional Type C relationships risk being perceived as not sufficiently mindful of their professional obligations in terms of maintaining professional distance? I do not believe so, because we can envisage situations where professionals are in these sorts of additional relationship, but the relationships are managed in such a way that professional distance obligations are successfully discharged, e.g., police officers in a de facto relationship working at different police stations, and police handing over cases due to a developing personal relationship with a victim.

CONCLUSIONS

Where then does all this leave us? The following conclusions are implied by the foregoing:

- Due to the uncertainty surrounding the significance of the harms that breaches of professional distance may cause, it is not justifiable for employers, professional bodies or the like to make rules banning police officers from the forming of additional Type C relationships.[9] This leaves open the possibility that if such uncertainty could be overcome, then it may be justifiable for such rules to be made by employers, etc.[10]

- It would be justifiable for police officers to restrict themselves in this way, and indeed there is good reason for them to do so.
- These good reasons are not unassailable and so cannot be used to prescribe what a police officer should do in respect of additional Type C relationships.

This may all seem a bit wishy-washy, in that we do not seem to have identified specific yes or no answers to the key issues considered. But the importance of what we have achieved should not be understated. Clearly, one implication of the foregoing is that police services are not justified in imposing blanket restrictions on police officers' freedom to form additional Type C relationships. But this does not mean that police supervisors, managers, and the like do not have a role to play in relation to assisting police officers to meet their professional distance obligations. As is also implied in the foregoing, good decisions at management level will enable police officers to engage in additional Type C relationships in ways that ensure professional distance obligations are (and can be seen to be) discharged. For example, managers can prioritise transfer requests for officers from the same police station who form a relationship (and help with rostering decisions in the meantime), and they can reorganise classes at the academy to ensure a police instructor is not teaching or assessing his or her lover. And this is a critical point, as it leaves the rights and liberties of the professional in relation to the forming of additional Type C relationships intact, but allows for the active recognition by those in management positions that such relationships can have serious consequences for the integrity of the professional role.

In fact, not only is it the case that managers can do a number of things to help officers meet their professional distance obligations, but it seems to also be true that they should be prepared to do these things. As professionals themselves, managers have an obligation to preserve not only the integrity of their own professional role, but also—to an extent consistent with a professional's own self-regulatory responsibilities—the integrity of the professional role of those they manage. This latter will clearly call for careful judgment and perhaps even innovative decision-making in relation to subordinates with additional Type C relationships, especially in organizations where blanket bans have been indiscriminately employed as "easy" solutions to professional distance issues. But when has good management ever called for anything less?

REFERENCES

Fullinwider, R., 2002, Professional codes and moral understanding, in *Codes of Ethics and the Professions*, Coady, M. and Bloch, S., Eds., Melbourne University Press, Melbourne, Australia, chap. 4.

Ardagh, D., Professionalising a Practice: The Criteria for Consideration, Working Paper 2003/10. Centre for Applied Philosophy and Public Ethics (CAPPE), 2003. Accessed at http://www.cappe.edu.au/PDF%20Files/Ardagh2.pdf, January 29, 2005.

ENDNOTES

[1] I'm leaving aside issues such as children divorcing their parents, and variations thereof, which do not seem to yet qualify as anything approaching a standard case (or even a common non-standard case).

[2] Arguably, Type N relationships should also include at least some relationships we have because of the relationships of our family members, e.g., relationships with the in-laws of our siblings. It would seem to me that these are relationships over which we genuinely have little choice. Although I will not develop this argument here (as it does not seem necessary for establishing the standard cases to which the distinction draws our attention), I do note that it is important not to confuse "people with whom we have a relationship" with "people with whom we choose not to act on the relationship we have," e.g., it remains true that we have a relationship that we did not choose to be in with an aunt, even if we do not like that particular aunt and, in fact, never engage with her at all; and it appears true that we have a relationship with our siblings' in-laws, even if we rarely have any interaction with them.

[3] These possibilities are informed by the sorts of police training I am familiar with. There may, of course, be others (e.g., in some police training programs, students may be sworn in as officers while still training at the Academy).

[4] Clearly policing students—especially sworn ones—are really a subset of a police officer's colleagues. But given the particular professional relationship that those with responsibility for training have with these students, I think they deserve to be discussed separately.

[5] In some policing organisations, the organisational structure may be such that this claim depends on there being a direct supervisory relationship between the two. For example, given the current organisational structure of policing in NSW, it is unlikely that officers of different rank who work at different police stations (or even such officers who work at the same station but consistently on different shifts) will ever have the sort of contact that could instantiate a power imbalance. However, I think this is a contingent fact about a particular police service, rather than a feature of the rank structure *per se* so I will leave the claims above in their original form.

[6] Clearly, in other professions a professional may have any additional relationship with another professional qua client. The difference between such a case, and the case discussed here concerning two police professionals, is that in the latter both officers retain their professional role (ie., neither acts qua client).

[7] Here, I am referring to the professional's personal autonomy, not to the autonomy which is typically indicative of what it is to be a professional.

[8] The importance of the italicised words will become clearer soon, when I argue that many additional relationships of Type C can be successfully managed, i.e., managed in ways that conform with professional distance obligations.

[9] Of course, such restrictions may be justifiable in other professions, if the likely harms can be identified more readily.

[10] This possibility was not considered in any depth earlier due to considerations of space.

26 Research Literacy in Police Organizations: A Luxury That We Can Afford

Margaret Mitchell and Christine Jennett

CONTENTS

INTRODUCTION

In this chapter we will consider the place of research, and the ubiquitous "evidence based" approaches in the day-to-day work of police managers and administrators. In doing so we will examine the working culture of police organizations, and ways that research and evidence-based approaches can be incorporated. We will also describe the influences, both ideological and practical, that have emerged over the last two decades and have led to greater dependence on research in contemporary policing practice and policy.

THE PLACE OF RESEARCH IN POLICE ORGANIZATIONS

Policing organizations tend, as do other applied professions, to promote staff who are excellent, highly experienced practitioners into strategic-level management positions. Certainly, this is the case in Australia where by far the majority of senior managers in police organizations are police officers with many years of successful operational policing rather than nonuniformed employees. Senior and middle-level managers of policing may be less comfortable with strategic planning, and certainly less comfortable with planning that is based on research rather than their own intuition and experience, This may be explained by the fact that their work background in operational policing required more highly valued reactive problem-solving approaches as embodied, for example, in responding to crimes as they arise. The skills and attributes of a highly experienced practitioner may not be identical to those required for strategic management. In addition, the critical reflection on practice required to effect organizational change may not come naturally to some senior police or public servants, partly due to the hierarchical nature of the organization, which locates ultimate decision making centrally and "at the top." Although evidence-based approaches should be a significant component of strategic planning in policing organizations, a tension can exist between the desire for longer-term planning through business, corporate, and strategic plans; the need to implement change and reform; and the day-to-day requirement to respond to incidents as they arise. Research, however, has a role at each of these different levels.

Part of the social responsibility of tertiary education institutions is to contribute to considered and validated policy and practice change in public services, of which policing forms a significant sector. For this reason, in part, research on policing and police administration was regarded as the domain of academics or professional researchers with academic training, working outside of policing organizations and adopting the stance of outsiders "looking in." Often, however, the research conducted by academics outside the organization was criticized on the basis that they do not understand the culture of police nor the practical constraints of police work. There was, and in many ways still is, a deep philosophical divide between academics, that is, those who did the research, and the practitioners who did the practical work that was the focus of the research. Certainly, abstracted models that do not provide practical and applied guidance about specific problems are unlikely to appeal to stakeholders. The argument from practitioners is that rapid problem solving and practical considerations take precedence over a more considered, evidence-based approach to change implementation and evaluation. Compromise solutions have included exhorting the academics who conduct the research to be more practical in their approach and recommendations or, alternatively, creating sometimes unsteady partnerships between academics and practitioners. Overall, research has tended to be placed in the "luxury" basket rather than the "necessary" basket. We would argue, however, that it is a luxury that police managers and administrators can and must afford.

WHAT HAS LED TO A GREATER DEPENDENCE ON RESEARCH AND EVALUATION IN POLICE PRACTICE AND POLICY?

We review here the need for research literacy. Police organizations have always been numerate, in the sense that crime rates and arrest rates were measured, however the context of these crime rates, the potential cause and effect of crime in a particular area, and the relationship of different crimes to each other was not necessarily measured. Nor, typically, was individual or organizational performance measured with any degree of commitment, objectivity, or regularity. Even expensive programs may not have been properly evaluated, often because of the political or economic impetus behind the implementation of a particular program or strategy. Contemporary policing, however, demands that police activities are measured. Increasingly, statistics and objective evidence are required to understand, measure, and plan police practice, policy, and administration. Evidence, too, is the foundation of the processes of continuous improvement and change to further develop contemporary policing and police administration.

As we see it, several influences on contemporary policing have led to police managers and administrators needing to be more numerate and research-based in the way policing and police administration is understood and measured. The public sector reforms in the 1980s, and associated economic philosophies, resulted in Western police services moving, often resentfully and slowly, away from their traditional paramilitary and closed bureaucratic structures and ways of doing things, towards a more open and client-focused service to the community (Jennett, Elliot & Robinson 2003). These "new" approaches are now two decades old and were intended to replace practices seen as inefficient and ineffective, through a focus on accountability and performance measurement.

Despite the often slow implementation of such change, whether changes should have been made has not been a matter of choice on the part of those managing public sector organizations. In Australia much of this has been the result of the several large-scale inquiries or Royal Commissions into police behavior and misconduct, such as the Wood Royal Commission with New South Wales police. These, in step with other reforms in the public sector, recommended greater openness in the measurement of performance. The resultant greater visibility of the governance and management of police organizations has also stimulated an interest in the measurement of policing performance from community and stakeholders who have an interest in, among other concerns, value for money. In Australia and the United States, as elsewhere, the need to demonstrate accountability and performance measurement has also been driven by the focus on *corporate governance* in all public sector organizations.

A further pivotal influence making police organizations more numerate is the analysis of crime statistics based on computerized statistics (COMPSTAT) models, which have been adopted in one form or another throughout Western police organizations. This approach is based on highly practical questions such as how crime data, demographic data, and other intelligence can best be used to inform strategic operational planning at a local and regional level. Arguably, the COMPSTAT approach has contributed to a changed work culture in policing in which not only measurement and data but, more important, the meaning of the measurement and data has permeated organizations and into local police stations.

Furthermore, the much-used phrase "best practice" rests logically on an assumption that evidence has been used as the basis for the claim—otherwise how would we know that it is the best? As we know, however, many such claims are not grounded in evaluation. The phrase is little more than cliché or wishful thinking and has been softened more recently to "good practice." For contemporary police managers or administrators to make the claim of best practice, or even good practice, knowledge of research approaches and methods is required in order to be able to assess and compare practices. Questions about best, or good, practice have also stimulated interest in "what works." Sherman's publication, almost a decade ago in the American Police Foundation "Ideas in American Policing" series, coined the term "evidence-based policing" borrowing from its use in "evidence-based medicine" to describe the process whereby research evidence can be "pushed" into practice (Sherman 1998). This seminal article galvanized the use of the term in policing, whereas the expression "what works" has been enshrined in David Bayley's book, *What Works in Policing* (1997). Elsewhere, at the University of St. Andrews, in Scotland, Davies, Nutley, and others operate the Research Unit for Research Utilisation (RURU) the aim of which is to:

> ... facilitate the production and use of practical knowledge that will assist in enhancing the role of evidence in public policy and public services ... [and] ... develop a resource concerned with examining and improving the utilization of evidence across the key public policy and public services areas [including] criminal justice

(http://www.st-andrews.ac.uk/~ruru/role_and_rationale.htm)

Finally, questions raised in the official inquiry and by the community about what information or "intelligence" was available before September 11, 2001, that might have prevented the disaster of 9/11 raised awareness worldwide about what intelligence is, and how it can or should be used. Again this underlined the crucial importance of data collection, analysis, and interpretation in policing. In this way fundamental intelligence practices such as collecting data, analyzing it in order to see patterns in the data, and using data as the basis of prediction have moved from the sometimes rather mysterious confines of specialized policing and covert activities into regular policing. Awareness is raised among police at all levels about the meaning of data and the different analytic uses to which it can be put. The term "intelligence led policing" is now commonly used and is defined by Ratcliffe (2003) as "the application of criminal intelligence analysis as a rigorous decision-making tool to facilitate crime reduction and prevention through effective policing strategies."

BUILDING RESEARCH LITERACY INTO THE ORGANIZATION

All of these influences have pushed the use of research, evidence, and intelligence into everyday policing practice, requiring police at every level, and particularly those with management responsibilities, to become what we have called in this context *research literate*. The answer to the question police managers and administrators may ask—Why do we need to do research?—is simple: they need to demonstrate accountability and performance, and be able to systematically measure what they do or at least be sufficiently research literate to make best use of existing research. Police managers operate in a social and political environment in which facts are contested; developing plans, strategies, and initiatives can be supported by research. The need for evidence-based approaches is not to argue, however, a narrow definition of research. Included in potential sources of information useful to managers, administrators, and policy makers is "expert knowledge, existing domestic and international research; existing statistics; stakeholders consultation; evaluation of previous policies, and new research" (United Kingdom Cabinet Office 1999).

We suggest ways in which research literacy can be developed. We believe that there are better ways than engaging academics or consultants from outside the organization to conduct research. Contemporary policing needs staff who are research literate. We argue that the need for research and evidence has required a culture shift in the working context of the policing in which basic research literacy is an essential requirement. Inevitably, there will be more use of evidence-based approaches and a higher level of research literacy due to the increase of university graduates and postgraduates in police organizations. In a sense, this produces an osmotic process with research and research practices being absorbed by police organizations.

We will consider now the research skills police managers and administrators to develop skills as critical consumers of research or as active researchers themselves, and how research practice can become part of the organization.

READING RESEARCH

Useful applied work is being conducted by many police organizations on their own or in partnership with a university or consultancy company, and by research facilities dedicated to examining policing and justice, such as the Police Foundation in Washington, the Australasian Centre for Policing Research in South Australia, the Australian Institute of Criminology in Canberra, and the Home Office in London. Access to these resources provides excellent sources of research on the challenges facing police organizations, as well as the opportunity to compare different practices across the world. We suggest that police managers and administrators can make use of the burgeoning research on policing and police management but need to be sufficiently research literate to be able to draw on and critically understand the implications of this wealth of existing literature and research. Skills are required in sourcing and evaluating existing research reports and in understanding the wider significance of the research for the local area and nationally, so as to avoid reinvention of the wheel.

DOING RESEARCH

Original research is often required, particularly in order to assess local impact. Police managers need to be able to assess advice with which they are provided and to deploy resources in defensible ways, or apply programs or practices imported from another area, or even another country, and assess whether they will fit with the unique characteristics of a particular local command. The ability to understand and even to carry out quantitative and qualitative research to compare, correlate, quantify is required in order to undertake the following common projects:

- Develop programs and community projects
- Evaluate programs and projects, and use the correct research methods to devise programs to evaluate outcomes
- Identify and apply good practice from other national and international jurisdictions
- Analyze crime or performance data collected by local police offices or across jurisdictions

- Compare productivity and performance data across jurisdictions and between jurisdictions, and over time
- Survey and understand community attitudes to crime and policing
- Design policy for police practice
- Promote local or large scale organizational change
- Conduct environmental scans and audits of local crime conditions using existing information

PRACTITIONER RESEARCH AND ACTION RESEARCH

The fact is, however, that an organization's business is ongoing, so the opportunity to conduct comparison studies, or even full evaluations of programs, can place extra burdens on the organization. Those conducting research must work around the imperatives of the on-going business of the organization in encouraging research and reflection that is practical, given the constraints of the working environment. There are a number of ways in which this can be overcome, for example, by building research into day-to-day work, and a "hands on" approach can make research part of the normal routine of work. Measurement that is collected in the normal course of work, for example, can easily be used to underpin evaluation and understand the outcomes of the evaluation. However, integrating research into the cycle of change implementation and evaluation can also ensure that it is not an "extra" on top of regular work.

Through the *practitioner-research* approach, Jennett et al. (2003) present an appropriate and elegant solution, such that those doing the research are the practitioners themselves. Our working definition of the practitioner researcher, as derived from McKernan (1996), is the practitioner who inquires into work-based problems and undertakes workplace research projects. It is a form of research in which practitioners can be producers and consumers of both organizational change and the research that informs it, and the measures that evaluate its effectiveness. The model is well developed in education and nursing, but much less so among law enforcement practitioners, yet it is fitting for police officers as people learn actively while actually carrying out a task (Nutley et al. 2002), and "learning on the job" is the mode of learning preferred by police officers (Mitchell, Munro, Thomson & Jackson 1997). Moreover, modern policing organizations, which embrace team-work, flatter hierarchical structures, and a diverse workforce, cannot rely on coercive or directive-change management strategies (Dunphy & Stace 2001, pp. 65–67). It is essential that their employees "buy-in" (Perez & Shtull 2002) or feel ownership of the change process for it to be implemented effectively (Long, Wells & DeLeon-Granados 2002). Practitioner research can be seen as a means to not only to support and encourage applied research, but also as a way to build evidence-based approaches to policy and practice change into large law enforcement organizations (Nutley, Walter & Davis 2002).

In addition, the process of *action research* (Coghlan & Brannick 2001) provides a basis for a pragmatic model of research that assists in developing an articulated research program, organizational policy, and/or effecting organizational change. Action research has been defined as a "practical, technical, and critically reflective process" (McKernan 1996, p. 28) involving all those with a stake in the process, and so is an ideal way of reviewing practice, assessing the impact of a new program or policy, or incrementally introducing radical change while assessing the effect on the wider organization. It is research that can be undertaken by those within the organization, during the course of their normal duties while achieving research outcomes without disturbing too fundamentally the on-going business of the organization. McKernan (1996, p. 3) sees it as an embedded practice where "no distinction is made between the practice being researched and the process of researching it."

> The rationale for action research rests, initially, on three pillars: first, that naturalistic settings are best studied and researched by those participants experiencing the problem; second, that behaviour is highly influenced by the naturalistic surroundings in which it occurs; third, that qualitative methodologies are perhaps best suited for researching naturalistic settings. [McKernan 1996, p. 5]

We will describe it in some detail here. The action research process is a series of successive cycles, "each incorporating the possibility of providing evaluative feedback within and between cycles of action" (Ebbutt, as cited in McKernan 1996, p. 23). What makes action research particularly ecologically coherent for a police organization is that its five formalized stages match the stages that reflective managers may follow—either formally or intuitively—when they introduce organizational change (see Figure 26.1).

By following through these stages, we can see that it is an entirely reflective process of examining change while effecting the change. After formulation of the problem or the impetus for the research, successive stages of implementation, and analysis are followed. At Stage 2 the internal constraints such as features of the police organization and working culture are identified. As well, external constraints, such as the effect the views of the community, media, and politicians might have on the research or organizational change program and its outcomes are identified (McKernan 1996, p. 28). The review of the situation or needs assessment at this stage will "suggest hunches or hypotheses that will function as strategic ideas" to be tested in practice. These McKernan (1996, p. 28) has described as "intelligent" ideas rather than "correct" solutions. In policing this distinction is relevant because, as practical problem solvers, police managers may take their hunches or beliefs about as situation as correct and then go on to obtain evidence to support these beliefs. In Stage 3 the overall action plan or research design and the project management plan serves as an "operational blueprint for the project" (McKernan 1996, p. 28). At the final stage of the first cycle:

> … the researcher seeks to understand what effect [the implementation] has had and what can be learned. By such careful reflection the practitioner becomes a "self-monitoring" researcher. Data and conclusions are shared [to decide] whether further research and change are needed. If so, a second cycle of action is commenced. [McKernan 1996, p. 28]

This incremental approach to research and the resulting organizational change that interacts with the normal activities of the organization is a highly appropriate

First Action Cycle	
Stages	*Actions*
Stage 1	*Careful development of the problem statement*
Stage 2	*Conduct needs assessment*
Stage 3	*Develop "an overall plan of action" (a combined research design and project management plan)*
Stage 4	*Implement the plan and the data collection phase*
Stage 5	*Conduct evaluation of the action stages*
Second Action Cycle	
Second cycle of stages or 'action loop'	*What has been found in the first action cycle is revisited by the practitioner researcher or stakeholders to produce a revised problem statement*
Subsequent Cycles	*Subsequent repetitions of the "action loop"*

FIGURE 26.1 The action research cycles. *(Adapted from* McKernan, J. 1996. *Curriculum Action Research: A Handbook of Methods and Resources for the Reflective Practitioner.* London: Kogan.)

research framework. Monitoring the impact of external change, conducting research, and effecting organizational change in this way require what Stringer (1996) calls a reiterative process, describing it in these terms:

> The reiterative nature of action research soon becomes apparent. Where people struggle to implement activities derived from a fixed vision/version of their world, they will soon be confronted by the dynamic realities of the context. To the extent that they can construct and reconstruct their vision, taking into account the increased understanding that comes from each reiteration of the process, so they will successfully negotiate the complex web of meanings, interactions and discourses that comprise social life. [Stringer 1996:112]

UNDERSTANDING AN EVER-CHANGING LANDSCAPE

Stringer's view of action research has resonance with the realities of working within a police organization and attempting to manage it strategically. As Pawson (2006) has eloquently stated, "the real purpose of systematic review is better to understand so that policies can be properly targeted and developed to counter an ever-changing landscape of social problems." In the same way that good intelligence gathering and analysis practice involves collection of data, making sense of it and coming up with best guesses, so too managers need to do this to prepare for eventualities in response to a situation in flux. There are several examples of the radical changes that are taking place in the external environment of policing which necessarily impact on the organization and have implications for its strategic management.

Australia has been called the "Lucky Country" (Horne 1964). We have good weather, good food, and share a border with no other country. This provides us with what some have described as benign isolation. At the time of 9/11 we were described as complacent. The "Bali bombing" in 12 October 2002 brought terrorism home, if not actually to our shores, when in the resort town of Kuta on the Indonesian island of Bali, 202 people were killed—almost half of whom (88) were Australian—and a further 209 were injured. Since then, Australian police and other agencies have developed far greater responsiveness. As if to underline the necessity for vigilance, on October 1, 2005, a second terrorist attack took place in Bali in which 23 people were killed, of whom 4 were Australian; 19 Australians were injured.

As we know, a few years ago the matter of terrorism and the possibility of urban suicide bombers was the concern of only a few; now, it barely needs to be said, police organizations throughout the world, from the most strategic to the most local level, have response structures and vigilance policies in place. This issue has moved on to a concern by police as to when and where the next attack will be attempted, and deciding on and planning the appropriate police response. Police organizations are no longer in benign isolation, with the imperative being for police organizations to work cooperatively with other justice and intelligence agencies and break out of their traditional "silo" approach. Research literacy and practitioner research in order to understand the effect of these large-scale impacts on managing police organizations can underpin appropriate and measured responses to the dynamic environment of policing.

CONCLUSION

Police managers and administrators now have many reasons to familiarize themselves with the practice of research. Research literacy on the part of police managers should contribute to research-based knowledge to enable them to reflect on their practice, using the skills of the research practitioner to inform decision-making and the implementation of organizational change. This philosophical divide alluded to at the outset of this chapter has hampered the implementation of much of the research conducted. Laycock (2001), and Nutley et al. (2002) note a gap between research findings and their application by practitioners in the workplace. Despite the requirement for evidence-based policy and practice in policing, Laycock (2001) finds that the results of research do not seem consistently to find their way into in the workplace. Nutley (2003, p. 5) has said, speaking of the use of evidence in public sector organizations: "Whichever part of the public sector one is concerned with, one observation is clear: the current state of research-based knowledge is insufficient to inform many areas of policy." Nutley (2003) argues that without certain commitments being made by organizations, evidence-based policies and practices will not result. There needs to be an investment in research, and explicit mechanisms need to be devised to bring research closer together with policy and practice development. In her paper, "Narrowing the divide" (between research and public policy) Edwards (2004, p. 12) argues that to build internal capacity, encourage capacity in industry partners, and encourage understanding by industry leadership of the utility of research for policy development there needs to be a commitment to building up a "learning organization" in which research literacy is a central capacity.

There will, however, still be a time lag since research planning, initiation, and ultimate reporting and dissemination all take time (Organisation for Economic Co-operation and Development (OECD) 2004). Davies, Nutley and Walter note that the adoption of research and its subsequent impact "are not merely a function of the research findings themselves, but are likely to relate at least as strongly to the context within which those findings are delivered." (Davies, et al. 2005, p. 15). The impact of research on organizations also is not linear and may be "instrumental, influencing changes in policy, practices, and behavior, or conceptual, changing people's knowledge, understanding, and attitudes towards social issues" (Davies, et al. 2005, p. 11). Davies et al. continue:

> … many empirical studies have shown [that] only rarely will research impacts be direct, instrumental, and clearly identifiable, such as when research leads directly to specific policy choices, or when research is neatly captured and codified in tools and instruments such as guidelines, protocols, or organizational processes." (Davies et al. 2005, p. 11)

Decision making, they argue, referring to Weiss (1980, 1982) is "diffuse, and characterized by 'nondecisional processes' and the progressive establishment of new routines." In this case, research provides a "background of empirical generalizations and ideas that creep into policy deliberation" (Weiss, as cited in Davies et al. 2005, p. 11). In this sense, research can also be regarded by police as a "reality check": either the "gut feeling" can assess whether the research finding "seems right" or the research can test the gut feeling in the same way that a hypothesis is tested.

However, our purpose has not been to propose a modernist argument that a foundation of research and evidence is an assurance of "correctness"—although conclusions from research can be assessed and scrutinized in a way that intuitive decision-making and decisions based on one individual's experience cannot. Developing research literacy, critical assessment, and the approach of the practitioner researcher, however, complements the experience gained from years of policing, which still needs to be brought to bear in order to interpret findings and understand the applicability to local conditions.

REFERENCES

Bayley, D. (1997). *What Works in Policing.* USA: Oxford University Press.

Coghlan, D. & Brannick, T. (2001). *Doing Action Research in Your Own Organisation.* London: Sage.

Davies, H., Nutley, S., & Walter, I. (2005). *Assessing the impact of social science research: Conceptual methodological and practical issues.* A background discussion paper for the ESRC Symposium on Assessing Non-Academic Impact of Research, May 2005. RURU, University of St Andrews. Retrieved January 5, 2006 from http://www.st-and.ac.uk/~ruru.

Dunphy, D. & Stace, D. (2001). *Beyond the Boundaries: Leading and Re-Creating the Successful Enterprise* (2nd ed.). Sydney: McGraw-Hill Book Company.

Edwards, M. (2004). *Social Science Research and Public Policy: Narrowing the Divide.* Occasional paper. Policy Paper 2. Academy of the Social Sciences in Australia. Canberra.

Horne, D. (1964). *The Lucky Country: Australia in the Sixties.* Victoria: Penguin Books.

Jennett, C., Elliot, G., & Robinson, P. (2003). *Developing Practitioner Researchers for Policing and Related Professions.* Paper presented at Continuing Professional Education Conference, Australian National University, Canberra.

Laycock, G. (2001). *Research for police: Who needs it?* Trends and Issues in Criminal Justice, No. 211, Australian Institute of Criminology: Canberra.

Long, J., Wells, W., & DeLeon-Granados, W. (2002). Implementation issues in a community and police partnership in law enforcement space: Lessons from a case study of a community policing approach to domestic violence. *Police Practice and Research, 3,* 231–246.

Mitchell, M., Munro, A., Thomson, D., & Jackson, J. (1997). *Exposing Police Probationers to Sudden Death.* London: Home Office Police Policy Directorate.

McKernan, J. (1996). *Curriculum Action Research: A Handbook of Methods and Resources for the reflective practitioner.* London: Kogan Page.

Nutley, S. (2003). *Bridging the policy/research divide: Reflections and lessons from the UK.* Presentation to the National Institute of Governance Conference, Canberra, Australia.

Nutley, S., Walter, I., & Davies, H. (2002). *From knowing to doing: A framework for understanding the evidence-into-practice agenda,* Discussions Paper 1, Research Unit for Research Utilization, University of St. Andrews, Scotland.

Pawson, R. (2006). *Evidence Based Policy: A Realist Perspective.* London: Sage.

Perez, D.W. & Shtull, P.R. (2002). Police research and practice: An American perspective. *Police Practice and Research, 3*(3), 169–187.

Ratcliffe, J. (2003). *Intelligence-Led Policing.* Trends and Issues in Crime and Criminal Justice, No. 248, Australian Institute of Criminology, Canberra. Retrieved January 10, 2006 from http://www.aic.gov.au/publications/tandi/tandi248.html.

Sherman, L. (1998). *Evidence Based Policing.* Washington, D.C. Police Foundation.

Stringer, E. (1996). *Action Research: A Handbook for Practitioners.* California: Sage.

Weiss, C.B. (1980). Knowledge creep and decision accretion. *Knowledge, Creation, Diffusion, Utilisation, 1*(3), 381–404.

Weiss, C.B. (1982). Policy research in the context of diffuse decision making. *Journal of Higher Education, 53*(6), 619–639.

U.K. Cabinet Office. (1999). *Professional policy making for 21st century.* Reports by Strategic Policy Making Team, September. Retrieved January 5, 2006 from http://www.homeoffice.gov.uk/rds.

WORLD WIDE WEB RESOURCES

http://www.homeoffice.gov.uk/rds.
http://www.aic.gov.au.
http://www.st-andrews.ac.uk/ruru.
http://www.policefoundation.org.

Index

Note: Italicized page numbers refer to tables and illustrations.

M

U

V

W

Y